W9-BCD-735

DIPLOMACY *in the* NEAR AND MIDDLE EAST

A Documentary Record: 1914-1956

by

J. C. HUREWITZ
Associate Professor of International Relations
Near and Middle East Institute
Columbia University

VOLUME II

D. VAN NOSTRAND COMPANY, INC.
PRINCETON, NEW JERSEY
TORONTO LONDON
NEW YORK

D. VAN NOSTRAND COMPANY, INC.

120 Alexander St., Princeton, New Jersey
257 Fourth Avenue, New York 10, New York
25 Hollinger Rd., Toronto 16, Canada
Macmillan Co., Ltd., St. Martin's St., London, W.C. 2, England

All correspondence should be addressed to the principal office of the company at Princeton, N. J.

Published simultaneously in Canada by
D. VAN NOSTRAND COMPANY (Canada), LTD.

Library of Congress Catalogue Card No.: 56-9728

PRINTED IN THE UNITED STATES OF AMERICA

For Ruth Ann

PREFACE

Volume I of the present work focuses on major international issues of the period between 1535 and 1914: the evolution of the capitulatory regimes in the Ottoman Empire and Persia, the differences between the two and the political uses to which the Great Powers put them; the development of the Turkish Straits dispute from its origin in 1774; the attempts between 1639 and 1914 to establish a fixed Ottoman-Persian boundary; the formation of special administrations for Lebanon; the political and strategic effects of piercing the Suez Canal; the rise of Egypt in the nineteenth century to a status approaching sovereignty; the ambiguities attending the British occupation of Cyprus and Egypt and the creation of an Anglo-Egyptian condominium in the Sudan; the conversion of the Persian Gulf into an Anglo-Indian lake; and the European scramble for railroad and oil concessions.

The papers of volume II are intended to illuminate decisive developments in the past four decades: Entente secret schemes in World War I for dismembering the Ottoman Empire and Britain's concomitant negotiations with Arabs and Zionists; the diplomatic discord at the Turkish Straits; the Anglo-Egyptian strife over Suez and the Sudan; the intercontinental ramifications of the pervasive Palestine—and later Arab-Israel—conflict; the spectacular rise of the oil industry in the Persian Gulf zone and its complex diplomacy; the widening claim of the newly sovereign Near and Middle East states to a voice in world politics; the sapping of French influence in the region in World War II; the rapid shrinkage of British power in the succeeding decade; and the consequent competition between the United States and the USSR.

Ellipsis marks have been used only to indicate excisions in the body of documents, but not at the beginning and end to signify omission of preambles, clauses on ratification, and signatures. I have not tampered with capitalization, spelling, transliteration or obvious grammatical and punctuation errors in the original instruments. I have, however, almost always shortened "Article" to "Art.," when it is employed as a title, and in rare instances (*e.g.*, II, Doc. 28) I have replaced accompanying written numerals with Arabic numerals. Only in items for whose translation I assume responsibility and in the introductory comments have I tried to standardize the spelling and the transliteration of Near and Middle East concepts, as well as personal and place names. Redundant titles in a few instances (such as I, Doc. 36; and II, Doc. 94) have been omitted, as a space-saving device, from articles of treaties and other instruments, only after it was ascertained that the sense of the original was not in the least impaired. In cross references Roman numerals I and II, unaccompanied by any titles, refer to the respective volumes of the present work. When cross references call attention to papers in the same volume, only the document number is given.

J. C. H.

New York, N. Y.
25 April 1956

ACKNOWLEDGMENTS

This project could not have been executed without the collaboration of many institutions, colleagues, students and friends. The Council for Research in the Social Sciences, Columbia University, whose generosity made the work possible, lays me under the greatest obligation. I am especially grateful to Richard Logsdon, the director of the Columbia University libraries, and his staff for tireless services in meeting my exacting requests. I am also heavily indebted to a host of other librarians and libraries for unfailing cooperation, principally Robert F. Ogden, chief of the Near East Section, the Library of Congress; Patricia C. Armstrong, School of Advanced International Studies of the Johns Hopkins University (Washington, D. C.); Ruth Savord, Council on Foreign Relations; K. M. L. Simpson, press librarian, the Royal Institute of International Affairs (London); Stanley Cecil Sutton, India Office Library, the Commonwealth Relations Office (London); Amédée Outrey, chief of the Service des Archives of the Foreign Ministry (Paris); Lee Asch, the Carnegie Endowment for International Peace; Sylvia Landress, the Zionist Archives and library of the Palestine Foundation Fund (New York); Mason Tolman, reference librarian, New York State Library (Albany); and M. Rieunier, secretary general, the Bibliothèque Nationale (Paris).

It is indeed a pleasure to acknowledge the invaluable assistance of E. Taylor Parks, chief of the Advisory and Research Branch, Historical Division, Department of State, and his aides in tracking down available translations of basic documents and in checking the accuracy of the data accompanying many of the official instruments. I was also fortunate in receiving help from agencies of other governments, among them the Public Record Office (London), the Ministry of Foreign Affairs of Iran and of Pakistan, the Egyptian Embassy (Washington), and the Arab Information Center, the British Information Services, the Israel Office of Information and the Turkish Information Office (all in New York).

To Majid Khadduri and Roderic Davison I am most appreciative for constructive suggestions and continuing interest in the project, and to Maurice Harari, Abraham Hirsch, Ahmad Maybud and William L. Sands, for assistance with translation. I am particularly grateful to Ali Aghassi, Claude E. Boillot, Margaret Cleeve, Harold W. Glidden, Tibor Halasi-Kun, Harry N. Howard, Charles Issawi, Walter J. Levy, Bernard Lewis, Herbert J. Liebesny, Anne C. deNanteuil, V. J. Parry, Nathan A. Pelcovits, Vernon J. Puryear, Katriel P. Salmon, Muhammad Yeganeh, Anne Winslow, Sir Muhammad Zafrullah Khan and Muhammad H. al-Zayyat for various forms of counsel and cooperation. I alone, of course, bear full responsibility for the organization of the work, the selection of documents, the introductory comments and those translations not attributed to others.

I wish to thank the Controller of Her Britannic Majesty's Stationery Office, London, for permission to reproduce Docs. 4, 5(2-3), 6, 8, 10, 12(1), 15, 18, 24, 26, 29, 31-34, 36-39, 41, 43(1), 44, 46-49, 52, 55-56, 59, 61, 64-65, 69-70, 84, 89, 91, 95, 105, 107-08 and 110; the Department of State, Washington, D. C., for permission to reproduce Docs. 62, 68, 106, 111 and 114(2); *The Current Digest of the Soviet Press,* New York, for permission to reproduce Docs. 101(1-3) and 114(1); and Constable and Company, Ltd., London, for permission to reproduce Doc. 28.

To Judith Bell, Alice C. Goewey, Dorothy Harrod, Barbara Stewart and Mary V. Westerfield, who performed diverse secretarial services, I must express my gratitude. I am also indebted to Lenoir C. Wright, Edward Thomas, Oles Smolansky, R. Roland Weiser and Martin Polstein for aid at the Columbia University libraries.

I am especially grateful to the Ford Foundation for a grant to visit England and France as well as the Near and Middle East, where in the course of my travels I was able, as one of the by-products, to check many details and gather fresh material.

Beyond all others, I am beholden to my wife for her unselfish devotion in taking over many of the endless and onerous chores that inevitably attend the preparation of a work of reference.

CONTENTS

INTRODUCTION

The present work is designed to unfold European diplomacy in and on the Near and Middle East in modern times and, only secondarily, to illustrate the coincident aspects of intraregional international politics. History itself and the state of historical research have largely determined the choice. Behind a commercial façade, European influence in the Near and Middle East grew steadily in the two hundred years and more preceding the Napoleonic wars. Outward signs of imperialism did not accompany the growing European power, even in the second half of the eighteenth century when Persia was falling apart and the Ottoman Empire sinking, for the maritime states of Western Europe were distracted by competitive empire-building elsewhere, notably farther east in Asia and in the Western Hemisphere. European supremacy in the Near and Middle East started with Napoleon's occupation of Egypt in 1798 and lasted a century and a half. Intraregional diplomacy, by comparison, played a minor role throughout most of modern times. International politics among the Near and Middle East states, prior to the mid-eighteenth century, consisted chiefly in the tensions on the ill-defined and shifting Ottoman-Persian frontier. Only in the past decade, with the rapid crumbling of the established European position, have the emergent independent states in the region won increasing liberty in their dealings with one another and with the world outside.

The history of diplomacy in the Near and Middle East has remained substantially undeveloped. Nor are the reasons obscure. The Near and Middle East, which in this work embraces non-Soviet Asia from the Mediterranean to the eastern boundary of Iran plus Egypt and the Sudan in adjoining Africa, is a Western geographic concept. Among peoples of the area itself such titles as "Islamic World," or "Arab East" for the Arab belt, have a more familiar and authentic ring. But even Europeans and Americans have come to view the Near and Middle East as a geographic entity, in the main, only since World War I. Before then, the region was divided into two spheres of European diplomatic activity: (1) the Ottoman Empire; and (2) Persia (as Iran was generally known in the West before 1935), the Persian Gulf area and that substantial part of the Arabian Peninsula that either was never absorbed by the Ottoman Empire or merely came under its temporary sway.

As late as the start of the nineteenth century the Ottoman Empire still claimed, besides Arab Asia (minus most of the Arabian Peninsula) and the districts presently occupied by Israel and Turkey, a sizable segment of southeastern Europe and most of north Africa. The sultan gradually lost his outlying possessions in the century preceding World War I. The progressive disintegration of the Ottoman Empire provided openings for intervention by the Great Powers and threatened to upset the balance in Europe. What came commonly to be called the Eastern Question was thereby created. On decisions as to who was to get what, there was rarely consensus in Europe. The resulting frictions distracted the foreign ministries on the continent throughout the nineteenth century. The dynamics of the Eastern Question thus lay in Europe.

The dynamics of European political relations in Persia, the Persian Gulf area and most of the Arabian Peninsula, however, originally centered in India. The Portuguese and the Dutch withdrew as contenders in this sphere in the seventeenth century; the French, in the half century following the Seven Years' War (1757-63). With the later integration of the British position in India, the principal international problems arose from England's determination to extend its imperial possessions in the Asian subcontinent—and beyond—and safeguard them against Russia's southward expansion. From the time of Napoleon's abortive plans for the conquest of India via Egypt and later Persia (1798-1807), the Eastern Question began to fuse with the problem of the defense of India. The opening of the Suez Canal in 1869 quickened the process. But not until the peace settlement of World War I did the Near and Middle East, in its current definition, become fixed in Western thinking as a regional unit—but actually having less unity, because of the European-imposed fragmentation, than it had previously enjoyed.

Near and Middle East diplomacy, then, changed its course abruptly at the time of World War I. Before 1914 international politics in and of the region comprised fundamentally the Asian and Egyptian (-Sudanese) phases of the Eastern Question and the Arabian and Persian repercussions of the rivalry over India. Only three Near and Middle East states dealt in diplomacy with the European powers: Persia, the Ottoman Empire and—for part of the nineteenth century—quasi-independent Egypt. As the lesser principalities along the southern and eastern littorals of the Arabian Peninsula were drawn into European politics, they became British "veiled" protectorates. The Masqati shaykh, unlike his neighbors, retained to the end a measure of external sovereignty. Yet after 1891 even he surrendered much of his freedom of diplomacy to the United Kingdom.

World War I and its peace settlement altered the character of international politics in the Near and Middle East. The capitulations in most of the region were denounced or suspended (never to be restored) in the 1920's, and the principal medium of European political intervention vanished. The demise of the Ottoman Empire, in fact, "resolved" the Eastern Question. Yet while Britain and France inherited the political controls, they significantly did not annex Near and Middle East territory outright. Mandates and preferential alliances were no more than provisional arrangements; and the presence of the Western powers in various guises stimulated the growth of local nationalisms dedicated to the early realization of full sovereignty. The two or three foreign ministries that functioned before 1914 were replaced ultimately by eleven, and international politics and problems inside and outside the region were correspondingly compounded.

A massive literature has accumulated on the old Eastern Question and on the projection, into the Perso-Arabian sphere, of European international politics affecting India. Relatively little systematic research, however, has been undertaken in the Near and Middle East vernaculars, although in the last two or three decades local scholarly interest in the region's diplomatic history has begun to awaken. Still no inclusive diplomatic history of the area, as now understood, has yet appeared in Western or in Near and Middle East languages. Nor has any attempt been made to assemble the basic documentation and to disengage the material on the Near and Middle East from that relating to the Balkans and to India. Even the recent period covered by volume 2 has been comparatively neglected. The archival collections in the West beckon researchers, as do the very rich Ottoman archives in Istanbul and the more modest collections elsewhere in the region, especially those of the late Hilmi dynasty in Cairo.

The present work, which grew out of a mimeographed compilation prepared in the summer of 1951 for use by students specializing in the area, is therefore experimental. It is not, and does not pretend to be, an exhaustive collection. The Russo-Ottoman treaty of alliance of 23 December 1798/3 January 1799, the treaty of San Stefano of 1878, documentation on the French cession of Alexandretta to Turkey (1936-39) and relevant papers on the Anglo-Saʿudi dispute over the Buraymi frontier (after 1949) have been left out, as have other materials of comparable interest and value.

Documents, with few exceptions, have been reproduced practically in the whole, omitting only preambles, provisions for ratification, signatures of bilateral and multilateral instruments, and sections on geographic districts beyond the borders of the Near and Middle East. In rare instances I have pruned the instruments to the political core, as in the treaties of Sèvres (II, Doc. 31) and Lausanne (II, Doc. 41). Still, in other cases, particularly the Anglo-Ottoman treaty of the Dardanelles of 1809 (I, Doc. 32) and the American-Ottoman treaty of commerce of 1830 (I, Doc. 39), I have reproduced secret clauses that the signatories dropped before the exchange of ratifications, simply because the chosen clauses possessed an historical value of their own. The decision, in principle, to reproduce diplomatic papers at full operative length reduced the number of eligible items for the generous but finite spatial limits of a commercially feasible publication. It also complicated the problem of selectivity.

The author's broad definition of what constitutes a diplomatic document might not pass muster with foreign service officers. The reader will find in these volumes concessionary contracts, programs of nongovernmental societies, policy statements, edicts, laws, proclamations and parliamentary debates over and above such standard fare as diplomatic correspondence, treaties and analogous international acts. The choice was decided by such criteria as the dictates of space, experience in the classroom and even personal fancy, as well as availability of the papers and of monographic literature that has proved their worth. Still, the last rule was not rigidly pursued, either in recent documents whose long-range import remains to be tested, or even in those of an earlier period. Foreign Secretary Salisbury's revealing instruction of 1879 to the British Agent and Consul General in Cairo (I, Doc. 87), for example, seems to have escaped the dragnet of scholars who processed the rich Public Record Office (London) files on Egypt.

Numerous documents in these two volumes, as far as could be determined, appear in English public print for the first time. The decision to render everything into English was taken on the plea of many readers of the bilingual mimeographed edition for wholly English materials. Indeed, the alternative to a monolingual compilation is in reality a multilingual one. But, aside from the difficulties and costs of production, the reference and training utility of a multilingual collection would have been restricted in this and other English-speaking countries.

Existing translations have been used whenever possible, even though their style may be infelicitous and their accuracy open to some question. On occasion when the text proved error-laden, as in the only English version of the final French-Ottoman capitulation of 1740 that could be located, the item was omitted altogether. It should be stressed, however, that many of the English versions of foreign documents which the Department of State in Washington or the Foreign Office in London prepared, are reference or working translations and must not be construed as official translations, unless so designated.

The introductory comments to the documents are not intended to tell the story in elaborate detail. They merely sketch the significance of each document, call attention at times to related papers that were not reproduced and suggest titles to which the reader might turn for guidance. The bibliographical entries are limited to works in English and Western European languages. They include monographs and general literature and, less frequently, articles in scholarly journals. Where the practice would not produce confusion, short titles have been substituted for longer ones after the first mention or two of a study.

Diplomacy in the Near and Middle East:

A Documentary Record, 1914-1955

1. SECRET TREATY OF ALLIANCE: GERMANY AND THE OTTOMAN EMPIRE

2 August 1914

[Translated from the French text in Carl Mühlmann, *Deutschland und die Türkei, 1913–1914* (Berlin, 1929), pp. 94–95]

As the situation in Europe disintegrated rapidly after mid-July 1914, the German and Ottoman governments turned from economic to military negotiations. On 22 July, Enver Paşa, the Ottoman Minister of War, proposed to German Ambassador Baron von Wangenheim the conclusion of a secret defensive alliance against Russia. Although the instrument was signed on 2 August, the Sublime Porte, with the consent of Germany and Austria, remained neutral until the end of October. The German military mission under General Liman von Sanders, who had assumed the post of inspector-general of the Ottoman Army in January 1914, became effectively responsible for the conduct of that army. H. N. Howard, *Partition of Turkey,* pp. 83–91; K. Ziemke, *Die neue Türkei,* pp. 1–84; B. E. Schmitt, *The Coming of the War,* vol. 2, pp. 431–40; Mühlmann, *op. cit.,* pp. 1–48; L. von Sanders, *Five Years in Turkey,* chaps. 3–4; A. Emin, *Turkey in the World War,* chap. 6; Djemal Pasha, *Memories of a Turkish Statesman, 1913–1919,* chap. 3; M. Bompard, "L'Entrée en guerre de la Turquie," *La Revue de Paris,* 28 (1 July 1921), 61–85.

1. The two Contracting Powers undertake to observe strict neutrality in the present conflict between Austria-Hungary and Serbia.

2. In the event that Russia should intervene with active military measures and thus should create for Germany a *casus foederis* with respect to Austria-Hungary, this *casus foederis* would also come into force for Turkey.

3. In the event of war, Germany will leave its Military Mission at the disposal of Turkey.

[Turkey], for its part, assures the said Military Mission effective influence over the general conduct of the army, in conformity with what has been agreed upon directly by His Excellency the Minister of War and His Excellency the Chief of the Military Mission.

4. Germany obligates itself, by force of arms if need be, [to defend] [1] Ottoman territory in case it should be threatened.

5. This agreement, which has been concluded with a view to protecting the two Empires from the international complications which may result from the present conflict, enters into force at the time of its signing by the above-mentioned plenipotentiaries and shall remain valid, with any analogous mutual agreements, until 31 December 1918.

6. In the event that it shall not be denounced by one of the High Contracting Parties six months before the expiration of the maximum fixed period, this treaty shall continue in force for a further period of five years.

7. The present act shall be ratified by His Majesty the German Emperor, King of Prussia, and by His Majesty the Emperor of the Ottomans, and the ratifications shall

[1] Cipher group missing in original cabled text.—Ed.

be exchanged within one month from the date of its signing.

8. The present treaty shall remain secret and may be made public only following an agreement between the two High Contracting Parties.

2. OTTOMAN CIRCULAR ANNOUNCING THE ABROGATION OF THE CAPITULATIONS
9 September 1914

[*Foreign Relations of the United States, 1914,* pp. 1092–93]

Ever since the Crimean War, the Sublime Porte endeavored to induce the European powers to terminate the capitulatory regime. The Young Turks, after 1908, accelerated the efforts, which reached a climax in the early weeks of World War I. Despite the alliance with Germany (Doc. 1), Ottoman ministers, Enver Paşa included, took advantage of the temporary neutrality and opened negotiations with the Entente powers either for an alliance or for continued nonbelligerency. Among the Ottoman conditions was the abolition of the capitulations. But the negotiations produced no immediate result. The Sublime Porte sent the following circular to all ambassadors in Istanbul, announcing that the abrogation of the capitulations would take effect on 1 October. The ambassadors of the states already at war, in unprecedented action on 10 September, addressed identic protests to the Ottoman government. When the Ottoman Empire entered the war on the side of the Central powers on 29 October, Germany and Austria tacitly assented to the unilateral cancellation of the capitulations. The United States for its part refused to acquiesce in the Ottoman decision and, until the two countries severed diplomatic relations in April 1917, the Sublime Porte did not interfere substantially with the conduct of the American consular courts. M. Khadduri and H. J. Liebesny, eds., *Law in the Middle East,* vol. 1, chap. 13 (Liebesny); N. Sousa, *Capitulatory Regime of Turkey,* chap. 10; H. N. Howard, *Partition of Turkey,* pp. 102–06; J. A. Mazard, *Le Régime des capitulations en Turquie pendant la guerre de 1914,* pp. 20–62; A. J. Toynbee and K. P. Kirkwood, *Turkey,* chap. 9; L. E. Thayer, "The Capitulations of the Ottoman Empire and the Question of Their Abrogation as It Affects the United States," *American Journal of International Law,* 17 (1923), 207–33; E. Turlington, "Treaty Relations with Turkey," *Yale Law Journal,* 35 (1925–26), 326–43; F. Abelous, *L'Évolution de la Turquie dans ses rapports avec les étrangers,* chap. 4.

The Imperial Ottoman Government, in its sentiments of hospitality and sympathy towards the subjects of the friendly Powers, had in former times determined in a special manner the rules to which foreigners coming to the Orient to trade there should be subject, and had communicated those rules to the Powers. Subsequently those rules, which the Sublime Porte had decreed entirely of its own accord, were interpreted as privileges, corroborated and extended by certain practices, and were maintained down to our days under the name of ancient treaties (or Capitulations). Meanwhile these privileges, which on the one hand were found to be in complete opposition to the juridical rules of the century and to the principle of national sovereignty, constituted on the other hand an impediment to the progress and the development of the Ottoman Empire, just as they gave birth to certain misunderstandings in its relations with the foreign Powers; and thus they form an obstacle to the attainment of the desired degree of cordiality and sincerity in those relations.

The Ottoman Empire, surmounting all resistance, continues to march in the path of renaissance and reform which it entered upon in 1255 by the Hatti-Humayoun of Gul-Hané, and, in order to assure for itself the place which was due it in the family of the civilized peoples of Europe, it accepted the most modern juridical principles and did not deviate from the program of supporting the edifice of the State on these foundations. The establishment of the constitutional régime demonstrates with what happy success the efforts of the Ottoman Government in the way of progess were crowned.

However, as consequences deduced from the Capitulations, the intervention of foreigners in the exercise of judiciary power, which constitutes the most important basis of the sovereignty of the State; the limitation of the legislative power, by the claim put forth that many laws could not be applied to foreigners; the fact that a criminal who has committed an offense against public security is screened from the application of the laws on the sole ground of his being of foreign nationality; or again the fact that public action is compromised by the necessity of respecting in regard to the foreign delinquent all sorts of restrictions and conditions; the fact finally that, according to the nationality of the contracting parties, a difference arising from a single contract admits of a different forum and mode of procedure—all these facts and other similar restrictive privileges constitute an insurmountable barrier to all organization of tribunals begun with a view to assuring in the country the perfect working of justice.

Likewise, that consequence of the Capitulations which renders foreigners exempt and free from taxes in the Ottoman Empire renders the Sublime Porte powerless not only to procure the necessary means for providing for the carrying out of reforms, but even for satisfying current administrative needs, without having recourse to a loan. In the same order of ideas, the obstacles raised to the increase of indirect taxes result in raising the quota of direct taxes and in overburdening the Ottoman taxpayers. The fact that foreigners trading in the Ottoman Empire and enjoying there all sorts of immunities and privileges are less heavily taxed than Ottomans constitutes at the same time a manifest injustice and an infringement of the independence and dignity of the State. The Imperial Government, in spite of all these obstacles, was zealously pursuing its efforts at reform when the unforeseen outbreak of the general war brought the financial difficulties in the country to the last degree of acuteness, endangering the accomplishment of all the work which had been begun or the undertaking of which had been decided upon. Now the Sublime Porte is convinced that the only means of salvation for Turkey is to bring into being this work of reform and of development as soon as possible, and it is likewise convinced that all the steps that it takes in this direction will meet with the encouragement of all the friendly Powers.

It is on the basis of this conviction that the decision has been taken to abrogate, reckoning from October 1, 1914, the Capitulations, which up to the present have constituted a hindrance to all progress in the Empire, as well as all privileges and toleration accessory to these Capitulations or resulting from them, and to adopt as the basis of relations with all States the general principles of international law.

While having the honor of communicating the present decision, which as it is to open an era of happiness for the Ottoman Empire will for this reason, I have no doubt, be received with satisfaction by the American Government, I consider it my duty to add that the Sublime Porte, inspired exclusively in its decision by the higher interests of the Ottoman land, does not nourish, in abrogating the Capitulations, any unfriendly thought in regard to any Power and that it is quite disposed to enter upon negotiations with a view to concluding with the American Government treaties of commerce on the basis of the general principles of public international law.

3. THE UNITED KINGDOM'S RECOGNITION OF KUWAYT AS AN INDEPENDENT STATE UNDER BRITISH PROTECTION
3 November 1914

[C. U. Aitchison, comp., *A Collection of Treaties, Engagements and Sanads relating to India and Neighbouring Countries* (1933, 5th ed.), vol. 11, pp. 265–66]

Once the Young Turks joined the Central powers, Britain wasted little time in strengthening its position in the Near and Middle East. Two days before the United Kingdom formally declared war on the Sublime Porte, the British Political Resident in the Persian Gulf addressed a note to Shaykh Mubarak of Kuwayt, promising Britain's recognition of the complete severence of ties between his principality and the Ottoman Empire, in return for his cooperation in the projected Anglo-Indian campaign against lower Mesopotamia (present-day Iraq). By this action Britain removed the ambiquities of the unratified Anglo-Ottoman convention of 29 July 1913 (I, Doc. 108). P. Graves, *Life of Cox,* chap. 14; F. J. Moberly, *The Campaign in Mesopotamia, 1914–1918,* vol. 1, chaps. 2–6.

In continuation of previous letter intimating the out-break of war between the British Government and Turkey, I am ordered by the British Government to convey to Your Excellency gratitude for your loyalty and your offer of assistance, and to request you to attack Umm Qasr, Safwan and Bubiyan and to occupy them. You should endeavour, afterwards, in co-operation with Shaikh Sir Khazal Khan, Amir Abdul Aziz bin Saud and other reliable Shaikhs to liberate Basrah from Turkish possession. Should this prove to be beyond your ability, you should make arrangements, if possible, to prevent Turkish reinforcements from reaching Basrah or even Qurnah, until the arrival of the British troops whom we shall send, please God, as soon as possible. I also hope that two of our men-of-war will reach Basrah before the arrival of your troops there. And though it should be your highest aim, in this connection, to liberate Basrah and its people from Turkish rule, still we request that you should use your utmost endeavour in preventing troops and others from plundering the merchandise belonging to British merchants in Basrah and its dependencies, to protect the European residents of Basrah and to safeguard them from loss and oppression. In return for your valuable assistance in this important matter, I am ordered by the British Government to promise to Your Excellency that if we succeed therein—and we shall succeed therein, please God,—we will not return Basrah to the Turkish Government and we will not surrender it back to them at all. Furthermore I make to you, on behalf of the British Government, certain promises concerning Your Excellency personally *viz.*:—

(1) that your gardens which are now in your possession, *viz.*, the date gardens situate between Fao and Qurnah shall remain in your possession and in possession of your descendants without being subject to the payment of revenue or taxes.

(2) that if you attack Safwan, Umm Qasr and Bubiyan and occupy them the British Government will protect you from any consequences arising from that action.

4. ESTABLISHMENT OF THE BRITISH PROTECTORATE OVER EGYPT
18–19 December 1914

[*British and Foreign State Papers,* vol. 109, pp. 436–39]

As one of the first war measures in the eastern Mediterranean, Britain annexed Cyprus on 5 November 1914 (text of order-in-council in *British and Foreign State Papers,* vol. 108, pp. 165–66). Three days earlier martial law had been declared in Egypt. But more than six weeks were to elapse before Britain made up its mind on a comprehensive policy toward Egypt. The policy, once formulated, proved decisive and was disclosed to the Egyptian public in three statements of 18–19 December: the first declaring Egypt a protectorate; the second announcing the deposition of Khedive ʻAbbas Hilmi II (1892–1914), then in Istanbul, and the selection of his uncle, Husayn Kamil, as the first sultan of Egypt; and the third explaining to the sultan the meaning of the protectorate. The title of the supreme British representative in Egypt was now changed from agent and consul general to that of high commissioner. Simultaneously Britain dispensed with an Egyptian Ministry of Foreign Affairs, transferring its duties to the high commissioner. H. W. V. Temperley, *History of the Peace Conference at Paris,* vol. 6, pp. 193–97; Lord Lloyd, *Egypt since Cromer,* vol. 1, chaps. 13–14; Sir R. Storrs, *Memoirs,* chap. 7; J. Marlowe, *A History of Modern Egypt and Anglo-Egyptian Relations 1800–1953,* chap. 9; G. Young, *Egypt,* chap. 7; Sir V. Chirol, *The Egyptian Problem,* chap. 7; E. W. P. Newman, *Great Britain in Egypt,* chap. 9; M. McIlwraith, "The British Protectorate of Egypt," *The Fortnightly Review,* new ser. 107 (1 March 1920), 375–83.

1. PROCLAMATION OF PROTECTORATE, 18 DECEMBER 1914

His Britannic Majesty's Secretary of State for Foreign Affairs gives notice that, in view of the state of war arising out of the action of Turkey, Egypt is placed under the protection of His Majesty and will henceforth constitute a British Protectorate.

The suzerainty of Turkey over Egypt is thus terminated, and His Majesty's Government will adopt all measures necessary for the defence of Egypt, and protect its inhabitants and interests.

2. DEPOSITION OF KHEDIVE ʻABBAS HILMI II, 19 DECEMBER 1914

His Britannic Majesty's Secretary of State for Foreign Affairs gives notice that, in view of the action of His Highness Abbas Hilmi Pasha, lately Khedive of Egypt, who has adhered to the King's enemies, His Majesty's Government have seen fit to depose him from the Khediviate, and that high dignity has been offered, with the title of Sultan of Egypt, to His Highness Prince Hussein Kamel Pasha, eldest living Prince of the family of Mohammed Ali, and has been accepted by him.

3. NOTE ON THE PROTECTORATE BY ACTING HIGH COMMISSIONER MILNE CHEETHAM TO SULTAN HUSAYN KAMIL, 19 DECEMBER 1914

I AM instructed by His Majesty's Principal Secretary of State for Foreign Affairs to bring to the notice of your Highness the circumstances preceding the outbreak of war between His Britannic Majesty and the Sultan of Turkey and the changes which the war entails in the status of Egypt.

In the Ottoman Cabinet there were two parties. On the one side was a moderate party, mindful of the sympathy extended by Great Britain to every effort towards reform in Turkey, who recognized that in the war in which His Majesty was already engaged no Turkish interests were concerned, and welcomed the assurance of His Majesty and his Allies that neither in Egypt nor elsewhere would the war be used as a pretext for any action injurious to Ottoman interests. On the other side a band of unscrupulous military adventurers looked to find in a war of aggression, waged in concert with His Majesty's enemies, the means of retrieving the disasters, military, financial, and economic, into which they had already plunged their country. Hoping to the last that wiser counsels might prevail, His Majesty and his Allies, in spite of repeated violations of their rights, abstained from retaliatory action until compelled thereto by the crossing of the Egyptian frontier by armed bands and by unprovoked attacks on Russian open ports by the Turkish naval forces under German officers.

His Majesty's Government are in possession of ample evidence that ever since the outbreak of war with Germany His Highness Abbas Hilmi Pasha, late Khedive of

Egypt, has definitely thrown in his lot with His Majesty's enemies.

From the facts above set out, it results that the rights over Egypt, whether of the Sultan, or of the late Khedive, are forfeit to His Majesty.

His Majesty's Government have already, through the General Officer Commanding His Majesty's Forces in Egypt, accepted exclusive responsibility for the defence of Egypt in the present war. It remains to lay down the form of the future Government of the country, freed, as I have stated, from all rights of suzerainty or other rights heretofore claimed by the Ottoman Government.

Of the rights thus accruing to His Majesty, no less than of those exercised in Egypt during the last thirty years of reform, His Majesty's Government regard themselves as trustees for the inhabitants of Egypt. And His Majesty's Government have decided that Great Britain can best fulfil the responsibilities she has incurred toward Egypt by the formal declaration of a British Protectorate, and by the government of the country under such Protectorate by a Prince of the Khedivial family.

In these circumstances I am instructed by His Majesty's Government to inform your Highness that, by reason of your age and experience, you have been chosen as the Prince of the family of Mehemet Ali most worthy to occupy the Khedivial position, with the title and style of the Sultan of Egypt; and, in inviting your Highness to accept the responsibilities of your high office, I am to give you the formal assurance that Great Britain accepts the fullest responsibility for the defence of the territories under your Highness against all aggression whencesoever coming; and His Majesty's Government authorize me to declare that after the establishment of the British Protectorate now announced all Egyptian subjects wherever they may be will be entitled to receive the protection of His Majesty's Government.

With the Ottoman suzerainty there will disappear the restrictions heretofore placed by the Ottoman firmans upon the numbers and organisation of your Highness's army and upon the grant by your Highness of honorific distinctions.

As regards foreign relations, His Majesty's Government deem it most consistent with the new responsibilities assumed by Great Britain that the relations between your Highness's Government and the representatives of foreign Powers should henceforth be conducted through His Majesty's representative in Cairo.

His Majesty's Government have repeatedly placed on record that the system of treaties, known as the Capitulations, by which your Highness's Government is bound, are no longer in harmony with the development of the country; but, in the opinion of His Majesty's Government, the revision of those treaties may most conveniently be postponed until the end of the present war.

In the field of internal administration, I am to remind your Highness that, in consonance with the traditions of British policy, it has been the aim of His Majesty's Government, while working through and in the closest association with the constituted Egyptian authorities, to secure individual liberty, to promote the spread of education, to further the development of the natural resources of the country, and, in such measure as the degree of enlightenment of public opinion may permit, to associate the governed in the task of government. Not only is it the intention of His Majesty's Government to remain faithful to such policy, but they are convinced that the clearer definition of Great Britain's position in the country will accelerate progress towards self-government.

The religious convictions of Egyptian subjects will be scrupulously respected as are those of His Majesty's own subjects, whatever their creed. Nor need I affirm to your Highness that, in declaring Egypt free from any duty of obedience to those who have usurped political power at Constantinople, His Majesty's Government are animated by no hostility towards the Caliphate. The past history of Egypt shows, indeed, that the loyalty of Egyptian Mahommedans towards the Caliphate is independent of any political bonds between Egypt and Constantinople.

The strengthening and progress of Mahommedan institutions in Egypt is naturally a matter in which His Majesty's Government take a deep interest and with which your Highness will be specially concerned, and in carrying out such reforms as may be considered necessary, your Highness may count upon the sympathetic support of His Majesty's Government.

I am to add that His Majesty's Government rely with confidence upon the loyalty, the good sense, and self-restraint of Egyptian subjects to facilitate the task of the General Officer Commanding His Majesty's Forces, who is entrusted with the maintenance of internal order, and with the prevention of the rendering of aid to the enemy.

5. THE CONSTANTINOPLE AGREEMENT
4 March–10 April 1915

The wartime secret arrangements among the Entente powers for the partition of the Ottoman Empire comprised essentially four sets of undertakings: the Constantinople agreement, the London agreement (26 April 1915), the Sykes-Picot agreement (April-October 1916) and the Saint-Jean de Maurienne agreement (April-August 1917). The so-called Constantinople agreement was not drawn up as a single instrument. It consisted, instead, of diplomatic exchanges between Russia, Britain, and France over a period of five weeks. The Russian Foreign Minister, Sergei Dmitriyevich Sazonov, initiated the formal exchanges with the ambassadors at St. Petersburg of the two allied governments on 19 February/4 March 1915, by stating Russia's desire to annex Istanbul and the straits in the event of an Entente victory. The British and French governments, in recognizing Russia's claims, put forward their counterclaims, which in the case of Britain embraced Persia and the Arabian Peninsula as well as the Ottoman Empire. While not all of the documents concerned have been reproduced below, those selected present the essential elements of the tripartite undertaking. H. N. Howard, *Partition of Turkey,* chap. 4; M. T. Florinsky, *Russia,* vol. 2, pp. 1347–50; W. L. Langer, "Russia, the Straits Question, and the European Powers, 1904–8," *English Historical Review,* 44 (1929), 59–85; R. J. Kerner, "Russia, the Straits, and Constantinople, 1914–1915," *Journal of Modern History,* I (1929), 400–15; M. Paléologue, *An Ambassador's Memoirs,* vol. 1, chaps. 9–10; J. T. Shotwell and F. Deák, *Turkey at the Straits,* chap. 10.

1. *Aide-Mémoire* FROM RUSSIAN FOREIGN MINISTER TO BRITISH AND FRENCH AMBASSADORS AT PETROGRAD, 19 FEBRUARY/4 MARCH 1915[1]

The course of recent events leads His Majesty Emperor Nicholas to think that the question of Constantinople and of the Straits must be definitively solved, according to the time-honored aspirations of Russia.

Every solution will be inadequate and precarious if the city of Constantinople, the western bank of the Bosphorus, of the Sea of Marmara and of the Dardanelles, as well as southern Thrace to the Enez-Midye line, should henceforth not be incorporated into the Russian Empire.

Similarly, and by strategic necessity, that part of the Asiatic shore that lies between the Bosphorus, the Sakarya River and a point to be determined on the Gulf of Izmit, and the islands of the Sea of Marmara, the Imbros Islands and the Tenedos Islands must be incorporated into the [Russian] Empire.

The special interests of France and of Great Britain in the above region will be scrupulously respected.

The Imperial Government entertains the hope that the above considerations will be

---

[1] Translated from the French text in E. L. Woodward and R. Butler, eds., *Documents on British Foreign Policy 1919–1939* (London, 1952), 1st ser., vol. 4, pp. 635–36.

sympathetically received by the two Allied Governments. The said Allied Governments are assured similar understanding on the part of the Imperial Government for the realization of plans which they may frame with reference to other regions of the Ottoman Empire or elsewhere.

2. BRITISH *Aide-Mémoire* TO THE RUSSIAN GOVERNMENT, 27 FEBRUARY/12 MARCH 1915 [2]

Subject to the war being carried on and brought to a successful conclusion, and to the desiderata of Great Britain and France in the Ottoman Empire and elsewhere being realised, as indicated in the Russian communication herein referred to, His Majesty's Government will agree to the Russian Government's *aide-mémoire* relative to Constantinople and the Straits, the text of which was communicated to His Britannic Majesty's Ambassador by his Excellency M. Sazonof on February 19th/March 4th instant.

3. BRITISH MEMORANDUM TO THE RUSSIAN GOVERNMENT, 27 FEBRUARY/12 MARCH 1915 [3]

His Majesty's Ambassador has been instructed to make the following observations with reference to the *aide-mémoire* which this Embassy had the honour of addressing to the Imperial Government on February 27/March 12, 1915.

The claim made by the Imperial Government in their *aide-mémoire* of February 19/March 4, 1915, considerably exceeds the desiderata which were foreshadowed by M. Sazonof as probable a few weeks ago. Before His Majesty's Government have had time to take into consideration what their own desiderata elsewhere would be in the final terms of peace, Russia is asking for a definite promise that her wishes shall be satisfied with regard to what is in fact the richest prize of the entire war. Sir Edward Grey accordingly hopes that M. Sazonof will realise that it is not in the power of His Majesty's Government to give a greater proof of friendship than that which is afforded by the terms of the above-mentioned *aide-mémoire*. That document involves a complete reversal of the traditional policy of His Majesty's Government, and is in direct opposition to the opinions and sentiments at one time universally held in England and which have still by no means died out. Sir Edward Grey therefore trusts that the Imperial Government will recognise that the recent general assurances given to M. Sazonof have been most loyally and amply fulfilled. In presenting the *aide-mémoire* now, His Majesty's Government believe and hope that a lasting friendship between Russia and Great Britain will be assured as soon as the proposed settlement is realised.

From the British *aide-mémoire* it follows that the desiderata of His Majesty's Government, however important they may be to British interests in other parts of the world, will contain no condition which could impair Russia's control over the territories described in the Russian *aide-mémoire* of February 19/March 4, 1915.

In view of the fact that Constantinople will always remain a trade *entrepôt* for South-Eastern Europe and Asia Minor, His Majesty's Government will ask that Russia shall, when she comes into possession of it, arrange for a free port for goods in transit to and from non-Russian territory. His Majesty's Government will also ask that there shall be commercial freedom for merchant-ships passing through the Straits, as M. Sazonof has already promised.

Except in so far as the naval and military operations on which His Majesty's Government are now engaged in the Dardanelles may contribute to the common cause of the Allies, it is now clear that these operations, however successful, cannot be of any advantage to His Majesty's Government in the final terms of peace. Russia alone will, if the war is successful, gather the direct fruits of these operations. Russia should therefore, in the opinion of His Majesty's Government, not now put difficulties in the way of any Power which may, on reasonable terms, offer to co-op-

---

[2] Woodward and Butler, *op. cit.*, p. 636.

[3] *Ibid.*, pp. 636–38.

erate with the Allies. The only Power likely to participate in the operations in the Straits is Greece. Admiral Carden has asked the Admiralty to send him more destroyers, but they have none to spare. The assistance of a Greek flotilla, if it could have been secured, would thus have been of inestimable value to His Majesty's Government.

To induce the neutral Balkan States to join the Allies was one of the main objects which His Majesty's Government had in view when they undertook the operations in the Dardanelles. His Majesty's Government hope that Russia will spare no pains to calm the apprehensions of Bulgaria and Roumania as to Russia's possession of the Straits and Constantinople being to their disadvantage. His Majesty's Government also hope that Russia will do everything in her power to render the co-operation of these two States an attractive prospect to them.

Sir E. Grey points out that it will obviously be necessary to take into consideration the whole question of the future interests of France and Great Britain in what is now Asiatic Turkey; and, in formulating the desiderata of His Majesty's Government with regard to the Ottoman Empire, he must consult the French as well as the Russian Government. As soon, however, as it becomes known that Russia is to have Constantinople at the conclusion of the war, Sir E. Grey will wish to state that throughout the negotiations, His Majesty's Government have stipulated that the Mussulman Holy Places and Arabia shall under all circumstances remain under independent Mussulman dominion.

Sir E. Grey is as yet unable to make any definite proposal on any point of the British desiderata; but one of the points of the latter will be the revision of the Persian portion of the Anglo-Russian Agreement of 1907 so as to recognise the present neutral sphere as a British sphere.

Until the Allies are in a position to give to the Balkan States, and especially to Bulgaria and Roumania, some satisfactory assurance as to their prospects and general position with regard to the territories contiguous to their frontiers to the possession of which they are known to aspire; and until a more advanced stage of the agreement as to the French and British desiderata in the final peace terms is reached, Sir E. Grey points out that it is most desirable that the understanding now arrived at between the Russian, French, and British Governments should remain secret.

4. FRENCH AMBASSADOR IN PETROGRAD TO RUSSIAN FOREIGN MINISTER, 1/14 MARCH 1915 [4]

I should be grateful to Your Excellency for informing His Imperial Majesty that the Government of the French Republic, having studied the conditions of the peace to be imposed on Turkey, would like to annex Syria together with the region of the Gulf of Alexandretta and Cilicia up to the Taurus [mountain] range. I should be happy to inform my government, without delay, of the Imperial Government's consent.

5. RUSSIAN ASSISTANT MINISTER OF FOREIGN AFFAIRS TO RUSSIAN FOREIGN MINISTER, 2/15 MARCH 1915 [5]

The French ambassador has told me that it is his impression that Syria "includes Palestine." I deemed it useful to remind him that there is in Jerusalem an independent governor.

6. RUSSIAN FOREIGN MINISTER TO RUSSIAN AMBASSADOR IN PARIS, 3/16 MARCH 1915 [6]

After arrival at General Headquarters, the French Ambassador informed me of the contents of Delcassé's telegram which asks for consent by Russia to the annexation of Syria and Cilicia by France. Paléologue explains that in his opinion the French Government refers also to Palestine

---

[4] Translated from the French text in J. Polonsky, trans., *Documents diplomatiques secrets russes 1914–1917 d'après les archives du ministère des affairs étrangères à Pétrograd* (Paris, 1928), p. 288.

[5] Translated from French text in Polonsky, *op. cit.*, p. 290.

[6] Translated from French text in Polonsky, *op. cit.*, p. 290.

when speaking of Syria. However, since in this telegram there is no question of Palestine, it would be desirable to elucidate whether the explanation of the Ambassador really corresponds to the view of the French Government. This question appears important to us; for, if the Imperial Government should be prepared largely to satisfy France's desires concerning Syria and Cilicia proper, it is indispensable to study the question with closer attention, if the Holy Places are involved.

7. RUSSIAN FOREIGN MINISTER TO RUSSIAN AMBASSADOR IN PARIS, 5/18 MARCH 1915 [7]

On 23 February [8 March 1915] the Ambassador of France declared to me, in the name of his Government, that France was prepared to consider in the most benevolent manner the realization of our desires relative to Constantinople and the Straits, which I explained to you in my telegram No. 937 and for which I charged you to express my gratitude to M. Delcassé. In these earlier conversations with you Delcassé had assured us several times that we could count on the sympathy of France and had simply pleaded the necessity of elucidating the attitude of England, from whom he feared objections, before he could himself give more formal assurances in the sense already indicated.

Now, today, the British Government has expressed to us in writing its full accord in the matter of the annexation by Russia of the Straits and Constantinople within the boundaries fixed by us; it has simply formulated one reservation concerning the safeguard of its economic interests and an equally benevolent attitude on our part toward the political aspirations of England in other areas.

Insofar as it concerns me personally, the assurance received from Delcassé is amply sufficient, because of the complete confidence that he inspires in me; but the Imperial Government would desire the French Government to issue more precise declarations like [those of the] British Government regarding its assent to the complete realization of our desires.

[7] Translated from the French text in E. A. Adamov, comp., *Constantinople et les détroits* (Paris, 1930), vol. 1, pp. 215–16.

8. RUSSIAN FOREIGN MINISTER TO RUSSIAN AMBASSADOR IN LONDON, 7/20 MARCH 1915 [8]

Referring to the memorandum of the British Embassy here of 12 March, will you please express to Grey the profound gratitude of the Imperial Government for the complete and definitive approval of Great Britain to a solution of the question of the Straits and Constantinople that satisfies Russia's desires. The Imperial Government appreciates fully the sentiments of the British Government and is convinced that the sincere recognition of their respective interests will guarantee in perpetuity firm friendship between Russia and Great Britain. Having already given assurances respecting the commercial regime in the Straits and Constantinople, the Imperial Government sees no objection to confirming its assent to the establishment (1) of free transit through Constantinople for all goods not deriving from or destined for Russia and (2) free passage through the Straits for merchant vessels.

With a view to facilitating the capture of the Dardanelles undertaken by the Allies, the Imperial Government will endeavor to obtain the intervention on reasonable terms of those states whose help is considered useful by Great Britain and France.

The Imperial Government completely shares the view of the British Government on the maintenance of the Muslim Holy Places under an independent Muslim government. It is necessary to elucidate at once whether [those places] will remain under the suzerainty of Turkey, the Sultan retaining the title of Caliph, or it is contemplated to create new independent states, in order to permit the Imperial Government to formulate its views in full knowledge of the case. For its part the Imperial Government desires that the Caliphate should be separated from Turkey. In any case, the freedom of pilgrimage must be completely secured.

[8] Translated from the French text in Adamov, *op. cit.*, vol. 1, pp. 217–219.

The Imperial Government confirms its assent to the inclusion of the neutral zone of Persia in the English sphere of influence. At the same time, however, [the Imperial Government] regards it as equitable to stipulate that the districts adjoining the cities of Isfahan and Yazd, forming with them an inseparable whole, should be reserved for Russia in view of the interests that Russia possesses there; a part of the neutral zone which now forms a wedge between the Russian and Afghan frontiers and touches Russia's frontier at Zulfiqar, must also be included in the Russian sphere of influence.

Railway construction in the neutral zone constitutes for the Imperial Government a question of capital significance that will require further amicable discussion.

The Imperial Government expects that in the future its full liberty of action will be recognized in the sphere of influence thus delimited and that in particular it will enjoy the right preferentially [to develop] its financial and economic policy.

Finally, the Imperial Government considers it desirable simultaneously to solve the question of northern Afghanistan adjoining Russia in conformity with the wishes expressed on the subject by [the Imperial Government] in the course of negotiations last year.

9. *Note Verbale*, FROM FRENCH AMBASSADOR AT PETROGRAD TO RUSSIAN FOREIGN MINISTER, 28 MARCH/10 APRIL 1915 [9]

The Government of the [French] Republic will give its agreement to the Russian *aide-mémoire* addressed by M. Isvolsky to M. Delcassé on 6 March last [Doc. 1, above], relating to Constantinople and the Straits, on condition that war shall be prosecuted until victory and that France and Great Britain realise their plans in the Orient as elsewhere, as it is stated in the Russian *aide-mémoire*.

6. SECRET (LONDON) AGREEMENT: THE ENTENTE POWERS AND ITALY
26 April 1915

[Great Britain, *Parliamentary Papers, 1920,* Misc. No. 7, Cmd. 671]

The Entente powers, in an effort to bring Italy into the war on their side, expressed willingness to recognize certain Italian claims against the Ottoman Empire. To this end the following agreement, which became effective upon signature, was concluded in London. Only the articles pertaining to the Near and Middle East have been reproduced. Italy declared war against Austria on 23 May 1915. H. N. Howard, *Partition of Turkey,* pp. 143–48; R. W. Seton-Watson, "Italian Intervention and the Secret Treaty of London," *The Slavonic Review,* 5 (1926–27), 271–97.

ART. 8. Italy shall receive entire sovereignty over the Dodecanese Islands which she is at present occupying.

ART. 9. Generally speaking, France, Great Britain and Russia recognise that Italy is interested in the maintenance of the balance of power in the Mediterranean and that, in the event of the total or partial partition of Turkey in Asia, she ought to obtain a just share of the Mediterranean region adjacent to the province of Adalia, where Italy has already acquired rights and interests which formed the subject of an Italo-British convention. The zone which shall eventually be allotted to Italy shall be delimited, at the proper time, due account being taken of the existing interests of France and Great Britain.

The interests of Italy shall also be taken into consideration in the event of the territorial integrity of the Turkish Empire being maintained and of alterations being made in the zones of interest of the Powers.

If France, Great Britain and Russia occupy any territories in Turkey in Asia during the course of the war, the Mediter-

[9] Translated from the French text in Woodward and Butler, *op. cit.*, p. 638.

ranean region bordering on the Province of Adalia within the limits indicated above shall be reserved to Italy, who shall be entitled to occupy it.

ART. 10. All rights and privileges in Libya at present belonging to the Sultan by virtue of the Treaty of Lausanne are transferred to Italy. . . .

ART. 12. Italy declares that she associates herself in the declaration made by France, Great Britain and Russia to the effect that Arabia and the Moslem Holy Places in Arabia shall be left under the authority of an independent Moslem Power.

ART. 13. In the event of France and Great Britain increasing their colonial territories in Africa at the expense of Germany, those two Powers agree in principle that Italy may claim some equitable compensation, particularly as regards the settlement in her favour of the questions relative to the frontiers of the Italian colonies of Eritrea, Somaliland and Libya and the neighbouring colonies belonging to France and Great Britain. . . .

7. BRITISH TREATY WITH THE IDRISI SAYYID OF SABYA 30 April 1915

(Ratified by the Viceroy of Indian, Delhi, 6 November 1915)

[C. U. Aitchison, comp., *Collection of Treaties* (1933, 5th ed.), vol. 11, p. 177]

Among the principalities along the western littoral of the Arabian Peninsula only Yemen under Iman Yahya remained loyal to the Sublime Porte in World War I. The sharif of Mecca had already intimated to Britain his desire to revolt against the sultan but did not enter into any formal arrangements until a few months later (Doc. 8). As a precautionary measure against possible trouble from Imam Yahya, the British political resident in Aden concluded the treaty appearing below with the shaykh of the tribal district of Sabya, geographically part of a larger territory north of Yemen called 'Asir. In a second agreement of 22 January 1917 (text in Aitchison, *op. cit.*, pp. 178–79), Britain recognized "that the Farsan Islands have been captured by the Idrisi Saiyid from the hands of the Turks and have become part and parcel of the Idrisi's domains, in all of which his independence is assured." The Idrisi principality was more of an allied than a protected territory, for its ruler did not surrender his sovereignty, external or internal, apart from a nonalienation clause in the 1917 instrument that applied to the Farsan islands and "the places situate on his sea-board" (article 3). It should also be noted that the government of India, as a relic from the period before the Suez Canal, still managed British affairs in southwest Arabia. Aitchison, *op. cit.*, pp. 40–41; Great Britain, Admiralty, *A Handbook of Arabia,* (1916), vol. 1, pp. 139–42; H. F. Jacob, *Kings of Arabia,* chap. 9.

This Treaty of Friendship and Goodwill is signed by Major-General D. G. L. Shaw, the Political Resident, Aden, on behalf of the British Government, and by Sayed Mustafa bin Sayed Abdul Ali on the part of His Eminence Saiyid Muhammad bin Ali bin Muhammad bin Ahmed bin Idris, the Idrisi Saiyid and Amir of Sabia and its environments.

2. Its main objects are to war against the Turks and to consolidate a pact of friendship between the British Government and the Idrisi Saiyid, abovementioned and his Tribesmen.

3. The Idrisi Saiyid agrees to attack and to endeavour to drive the Turks from their stations in the Yemen and to the best of his power to harass the Turkish troops in the direction of the Yemen, and to extend his territories at the expense of the Turks.

4. The Saiyid's prime objective will be against the Turks only, and he will abstain from any hostile or provocative action against Imam Yahya so long as the latter does not join hands with the Turks.

5. The British Government undertakes to safeguard the Idrisi Saiyid's territories from all attack on the seaboard from any enemy who may molest him; to guarantee his independence in his own domain and

at the conclusion of the war to use every diplomatic means in its power to adjudicate between the rival claims of the Idrisi Saiyid and the Imam Yahya or any other rival.

6. The British Government has no desire to enlarge its borders in Western Arabia, but wishes solely to see the various Arab Rulers living peacefully and amicably together each in his own sphere, and all in friendship with the British Government.

7. As a mark of its appreciation of the work to be performed by the Idrisi Saiyid, the British Government has aided him with both funds and munitions and will continue to assist him in the prosecution of the war so long as it lasts in accordance with the measures of the Idrisi's activities.

8. Finally, while maintaining a strict blockade on all Turkish ports in the Red Sea, the British Government has for some months past been giving the Idrisi Saiyid full and free scope to trade and traffic between his ports and Aden, and this concession the British Government in token of the friendship existing will continue uninterruptedly to maintain.

9. This Treaty will be held to be valid after its ratification by the Government of India.

8. THE HUSAYN-McMAHON CORRESPONDENCE
14 July 1915–10 March 1916

[Great Britain, *Parliamentary Papers, 1939,* Misc. No. 3, Cmd. 5957]

Amir 'Abdallah, the second son of Sharif Husayn of Mecca, conferred at Cairo in February 1914 with Lord Kitchener, British Agent and Consul General in Egypt, hinting that his father with outside encouragement might stage an insurrection against the Sultan. The United Kingdom was then striving with the Sublime Porte and Germany for a general settlement of the issues between them, so that Kitchener dampened 'Abdallah's enthusiasm. The situation changed, once the Ottoman Empire became involved in the war. Kitchener, then Secretary of State for War in London, sought an agreement with Sharif Husayn. Formal views were exchanged in correspondence conducted over an eight-month period by Husayn and Sir Henry McMahon, the first British High Commissioner for Egypt. The negotiations culminated in a mutually acceptable military alliance but in an ambiguous political understanding that was not clarified at the time, so as not to delay the arrangements for the Arab revolt. Indeed, the political understanding was destined never to be clarified, and the ambiguous interpretations of the imperfect instruments caused boundless troubles in later years, particularly in relation to the Palestine problem. The Husayn-McMahon exchanges comprised altogether ten letters, of which four (numbers 1, 4, 7, 8) have been selected for this compilation. The sharif, in letter number 5, observed that "the two *vilayets* [Ottoman provinces] of Aleppo and Beirut and their sea coasts are purely Arab *vilayets,* and there is no difference between a Moslem and a Christian Arab; they are both descendants of one forefather." To this the high commissioner replied in letter number 6 that "With regard to the *vilayets* of Aleppo and Beirut, the Government of Great Britain have fully understood and taken careful note of your observations, but, as the interests of our ally, France, are involved in them both the question will require careful consideration and a further communication on the subject will be addressed to you in due course." G. Antonius, *Arab Awakening,* chaps. 7–12; P. L. Hanna, *British Policy in Palestine,* chap. 2; Esco Foundation, *Palestine,* vol. 1, pp. 63–70; Sir R. Storrs, *Memoirs,* chap. 8; "Report of a Committee set up to consider certain Correspondence between Sir Henry McMahon and the Sharif of Mecca in 1915 and 1916," *Parliamentary Papers, 1939,* Cmd. 5974; T. E. Lawrence, *Seven Pillars of Wisdom.*

1. FROM SHARIF HUSAYN, 14 JULY 1915

Whereas the whole of the Arab nation without any exception have decided in these last years to live, and to accomplish their freedom, and grasp the reins of their administration both in theory and practice; and whereas they have found and felt that it is to the interest of the Government of Great Britain to support them and aid them to the attainment of their firm and lawful intentions (which are based upon the maintenance of the honour and dignity of their life) without any ulterior motives whatsoever unconnected with this object;

And whereas it is to their (the Arabs') interest also to prefer the assistance of the Government of Great Britain in consideration of their geographical position and economic interests, and also of the attitude of the above-mentioned Government, which is known to both nations and therefore need not be emphasized;

For these reasons the Arab nation see fit to limit themselves, as time is short, to asking the Government of Great Britain, if it should think fit, for the approval, through her deputy or representative, of the following fundamental propositions, leaving out all things considered secondary in comparison with these, so that it may prepare all means necessary for attaining this noble purpose, until such time as it finds occasion for making the actual negotiations:—

Firstly.—England to acknowledge the independence of the Arab countries, bounded on the north by Mersina and Adana up to the 37° of latitude, on which degree fall Birijik, Urfa, Mardin, Midiat, Jezirat (Ibn 'Umar), Amadia, up to the border of Persia; on the east by the borders of Persia up to the Gulf of Basra; on the south by the Indian Ocean, with the exception of the position of Aden to remain as it is; on the west by the Red Sea, the Mediterranean Sea up to Mersina. England to approve of the proclamation of an Arab Khalifate of Islam.

Secondly.—The Arab Government of the Sherif to acknowledge that England shall have the preference in all economic enterprises in the Arab countries whenever conditions of enterprises are otherwise equal.

Thirdly.—For the security of this Arab independence and the certainty of such preference of economic enterprises, both high contracting parties to offer mutual assistance, to the best ability of their military and naval forces, to face any foreign Power which may attack either party. Peace not to be decided without agreement of both parties.

Fourthly.—If one of the parties enters upon an aggressive conflict, the other party to assume a neutral attitude, and in case of such party wishing the other to join forces, both to meet and discuss the conditions.

Fifthly.—England to acknowledge the abolition of foreign privileges in the Arab countries, and to assist the Government of the Sherif in an International Convention for confirming such abolition.

Sixthly.—Articles 3 and 4 of this treaty to remain in vigour for fifteen years, and, if either wishes it to be renewed, one year's notice before lapse of treaty to be given.

Consequently, and as the whole of the Arab nation have (praise be to God) agreed and united for the attainment, at all costs and finally, of this noble object, they beg the Government of Great Britain to answer them positively or negatively in a period of thirty days after receiving this intimation; and if this period should lapse before they receive an answer, they reserve to themselves complete freedom of action. Moreover, we (the Sherif's family) will consider ourselves free in word and deed from the bonds of our previous declaration which we made through Ali Effendi.

2. FROM SIR HENRY MCMAHON, 24 OCTOBER 1915

I have received your letter of the 29th Shawal, 1333, with much pleasure and your expressions of friendliness and sincerity have given me the greatest satisfaction.

I regret that you should have received from my last letter the impression that I regarded the question of the limits and boundaries with coldness and hesitation; such was not the case, but it appeared to me that the time had not yet come when that question could be discussed in a conclusive manner.

I have realised, however, from your last letter that you regard this question as one of vital and urgent importance. I have, therefore, lost no time in informing the Government of Great Britain of the contents of your letter, and it is with great pleasure that I communicate to you on their behalf the following statement, which

I am confident you will receive with satisfaction:—

The two districts of Mersina and Alexandretta and portions of Syria lying to the west of the districts of Damascus, Homs, Hama and Aleppo cannot be said to be purely Arab, and should be excluded from the limits demanded.

With the above modification, and without prejudice of our existing treaties with Arab chiefs, we accept those limits.

As for those regions lying within those frontiers wherein Great Britain is free to act without detriment to the interests of her ally, France, I am empowered in the name of the Government of Great Britain to give the following assurances and make the following reply to your letter:—

(1) Subject to the above modifications, Great Britain is prepared to recognize and support the independence of the Arabs in all the regions within the limits demanded by the Sherif of Mecca.

(2) Great Britain will guarantee the Holy Places against all external aggression and will recognise their inviolability.

(3) When the situation admits, Great Britain will give to the Arabs her advice and will assist them to establish what may appear to be the most suitable forms of government in those various territories.

(4) On the other hand, it is understood that the Arabs have decided to seek the advice and guidance of Great Britain only, and that such European advisers and officials as may be required for the formation of a sound form of administration will be British.

(5) With regard to the *vilayets* of Bagdad and Basra, the Arabs will recognise that the established position and interests of Great Britain necessitate special administrative arrangements in order to secure these territories from foreign aggression, to promote the welfare of the local populations and to safeguard our mutual economic interests.

I am convinced that this declaration will assure you beyond all possible doubt of the sympathy of Great Britain towards the aspirations of her friends the Arabs and will result in a firm and lasting alliance, the immediate results of which will be the expulsion of the Turks from the Arab countries and the freeing of the Arab peoples from the Turkish yoke, which for so many years has pressed heavily upon them.

I have confined myself in this letter to the more vital and important questions, and if there are any other matters dealt with in your letters which I have omitted to mention, we may discuss them at some convenient date in the future.

It was with very great relief and satisfaction that I heard of the safe arrival of the Holy Carpet and the accompanying offerings which, thanks to the clearness of your directions and the excellence of your arrangements, were landed without trouble or mishap in spite of the dangers and difficulties occasioned by the present sad war. May God soon bring a lasting peace and freedom to all peoples!

I am sending this letter by the hand of your trusted and excellent messenger, Sheikh Mohammed Ibn Arif Ibn Uraifan, and he will inform you of the various matters of interest, but of less vital importance, which I have not mentioned in this letter.

3. FROM SHARIF HUSAYN, 1 JANUARY 1916

We received from the bearer your letter, dated the 9th Safar (the 14th December, 1915), with great respect and honour, and I have understood its contents, which caused me the greatest pleasure and satisfaction, as it removed that which had made me uneasy.

Your honour will have realised, after the arrival of Mohammed (Faroki) Sherif and his interview with you, that all our procedure up to the present was of no personal inclination or the like, which would have been wholly unintelligible, but that everything was the result of the decisions and desires of our peoples, and that we are but transmitters and executants of such decisions and desires in the position they (our people) have pressed upon us.

These truths are, in my opinion, very important and deserve your honour's special attention and consideration.

With regard to what had been stated in

your honoured communication concerning El Iraq as to the matter of compensation for the period of occupation, we, in order to strengthen the confidence of Great Britain in our attitude and in our words and actions, really and veritably, and in order to give her evidence of our certainty and assurance in trusting her glorious Government, leave the determination of the amount to the perception of her wisdom and justice.

As regards the northern parts and their coasts, we have already stated in our previous letter what were the utmost possible modifications, and all this was only done so to fulfil those aspirations whose attainment is desired by the will of the Blessed and Supreme God. It is this same feeling and desire which impelled us to avoid what may possibly injure the alliance of Great Britain and France and the agreement made between them during the present wars and calamities; yet we find it our duty that the eminent minister should be sure that, at the first opportunity after this war is finished, we shall ask you (what we avert our eyes from to-day) for what we now leave to France in Beirut and its coasts.

I do not find it necessary to draw your attention to the fact that our plan is of greater security to the interests and protection of the rights of Great Britain than it is to us, and will necessarily be so whatever may happen, so that Great Britain may finally see her friends in that contentment and advancement which she is endeavouring to establish for them now, especially as her Allies being neighbours to us will be the germ of difficulties and discussion with which there will be no peaceful conditions. In addition to which the citizens of Beirut will decidedly never accept such dismemberment, and they may oblige us to undertake new measures which may exercise Great Britain, certainly not less than her present troubles, because of our belief and certainty in the reciprocity and indeed the identity of our interests, which is the only cause that caused us never to care to negotiate with any other Power but you. Consequently, it is impossible to allow any derogation that gives France, or any other Power, a span of land in those regions.

I declare this, and I have a strong belief, which the living will inherit from the dead, in the declarations which you gave in the conclusion of your honoured letter. Therefore, the honourable and eminent Minister should believe and be sure, together with Great Britain, that we still remain firm to our resolution which Storrs learnt from us two years ago, for which we await the opportunity suitable to our situation, especially in view of that action the time of which has now come near and which destiny drives towards us with great haste and clearness, so that we and those who are of our opinion may have reasons for such action against any criticisms or responsibilities imposed upon us in future.

Your expression "we do not want to push you to any hasty action which might jeopardise the success of your aim" does not need any more explanation except what we may ask for, when necessary, such as arms, ammunition, &c.

I deem this sufficient, as I have occupied much of your Honour's time. I beg to offer you my great veneration and respect.

4. FROM SIR HENRY MCMAHON, 25 JANUARY 1916

We have received with great pleasure and satisfaction your letter of the 25th Safar (the 1st January) at the hands of your trusty messenger, who has also transmitted to us your verbal messages.

We fully realise and entirely appreciate the motives which guide you in this important question, and we know well that you are acting entirely in the interests of the Arab peoples and with no thought beyond their welfare.

We take note of your remarks concerning the *vilayet* of Bagdad, and will take the question into careful consideration when the enemy has been defeated and the time for peaceful settlement arrives.

As regards the northern parts, we note with satisfaction your desire to avoid anything which might possibly injure the alliance of Great Britain and France. It is, as you know, our fixed determination that nothing shall be permitted to interfere in the slightest degree with our united prosecution of this war to a victorious conclusion. Moreover, when the victory has been won, the friendship of Great Britain and France will become yet more firm and enduring, cemented by the blood of Englishmen and Frenchmen who have died side by side fighting for the cause of right and liberty.

In this great cause Arabia is now associated, and God grant that the result of our mutual efforts and co-operation will bind us in a lasting friendship to the mutual welfare and happiness of us all.

We are greatly pleased to hear of the action you are taking to win all the Arabs over to our joint cause, and to dissuade them from giving any assistance to our enemies, and we leave it to your discretion to seize the most favourable moment for further and more decided measures.

You will doubtless inform us by the bearer of this letter of any manner in which we can assist you and your requests will always receive our immediate consideration.

You will have heard how El Sayed Ahmed el Sherif el Senussi has been beguiled by evil advice into hostile action, and it will be a great grief to you to know that he has been so far forgetful of the interests of the Arabs as to throw in his lot with our enemies. Misfortune has now overtaken him, and we trust that this will show him his error and lead him to peace for the sake of his poor misguided followers.

We are sending this letter by the hand of your good messenger, who will also bring to you all our news.

9. BRITISH TREATY WITH IBN SA'UD
26 December 1915

(Ratified by the Viceroy of India, Simla, 18 July 1916)

[C. U. Aitchison, comp., *Collection of Treaties* (1933, 5th ed.), vol. 11, pp. 206–08]

The House of Sa'ud fell on evil days in the early eighteen eighties and lost its patrimony—the district of al-Najd—to a quondam ally, the House of Rashid, whose original bailiwick embraced the Jabal Shammar in north central Arabia. 'Abd-al-'Aziz b. 'Abd-al-Rahman al-Faysal al-Sa'ud (1881–1953) reoccupied Riyad, the Sa'udi capital of the Najd, on 15 January 1902. By May 1913 'Abd-al-'Aziz not only recovered the Najd in its entirety but conquered the district of al-Hasa from the Ottomans, thus converting the Sa'udi shaykhdom into a Persian Gulf principality. The Anglo-Ottoman draft convention of 29 July 1913 recognized the Sa'udi amirate as part of the Ottoman Empire (article 11, I, Doc. 108). After the outbreak of war the India government desired to broaden Britain's special treaty system in the Persian Gulf Zone to encompass all the shaykhdoms along the eastern coast of Arabia. Since the Jabal Shammar fell into the Ottoman sphere, the Anglo-Sa'udi treaty aimed militarily at encouraging Sa'udi warfare against the Rashidi shaykhdom. But ibn Sa'ud also took a hostile view of Sharif Husayn, who was at the time in the midst of his negotiations with the British Foreign Office. Thus two ministries in London were in effect subsidizing antagonistic Arabian chieftains. "Indeed, the officials of the India Office, had they been driven into a corner by infuriated British tax-payers," later observed Arnold J. Toynbee (*Survey of International Affairs, 1925,* vol. 1, p. 283), "might have represented with some plausibility that in purchasing Ibn Sa'ūd's benevolent neutrality at £5,000 sterling a month they had made a better bargain than their colleagues at the Foreign Office who had contracted to pay £200,000 a month of the tax-payers' money for Husayn's military co-operation." In the 1915 treaty, it should be noted, ibn Sa'ud assented to the same status—a British veiled protectorate—as that of the Persian Gulf shaykhdoms near-by. H. St. J. Philby, *Sa'udi Arabia,* chaps. 9–10; P. Graves, *Life of Cox,* chaps. 14–16; *Survey of International Affairs, 1925,* vol. 1, pp. 271–88.

I. The British Government do acknowledge and admit that Najd, Al Hassa, Qatif and Jubail, and their dependencies and territories, which will be discussed and determined hereafter, and their ports on the shores of the Persian Gulf are the countries of Bin Sa'ud and of his fathers before him, and do hereby recognise the said Bin Sa'ud as the Independent Ruler thereof and absolute Chief of their tribes, and after him his sons and descendants by inheritance; but the selection of the individual shall be in accordance with the nomination (*i.e.*, by the living Ruler) of his successor; but with the proviso that he shall not be a person antagonistic to the British Government in any respect; such as, for example, in regard to the terms mentioned in this Treaty.

II. In the event of aggression by any Foreign Power on the territories of the countries of the said Bin Sa'ud and his descendants without reference to the British Government and without giving her an opportunity of communicating with Bin Sa'ud and composing the matter, the British Government will aid Bin Sa'ud to such extent and in such a manner as the British Government after consulting Bin Sa'ud may consider most effective for protecting his interests and countries.

III. Bin Sa'ud hereby agrees and promises to refrain from entering into any correspondence, agreement, or treaty, with any Foreign Nation or Power, and further to give immediate notice to the Political authorities of the British Government of any attempt on the part of any other Power to interfere with the above territories.

IV. Bin Sa'ud hereby undertakes that he will absolutely not cede, sell, mortgage lease, or otherwise dispose of the above territories or any part of them, or grant concessions within those territories to any Foreign Power, or to the subjects of any Foreign Power, without the consent of the British Government.

And that he will follow her advice unreservedly provided that it be not damaging to his own interests.

V. Bin Sa'ud hereby undertakes to keep open within his territories, the roads leading to the Holy Places, and to protect pilgrims on their passage to and from the Holy Places.

VI. Bin Sa'ud undertakes, as his father did before him, to refrain from all aggression on, or interference with the territories of Kuwait, Bahrain, and of the Shaikhs of Qatar and the Oman Coast, who are under the protection of the British Government, and who have treaty relations with the said Government; and the limits of their territories shall be hereafter determined.

VII. The British Government and Bin Sa'ud agree to conclude a further detailed treaty in regard to matters concerning the two parties.

10. TRIPARTITE (SYKES-PICOT) AGREEMENT FOR THE PARTITION OF THE OTTOMAN EMPIRE: BRITAIN, FRANCE AND RUSSIA
26 April–23 October 1916

[E. L. Woodward and R. Butler, eds., *Documents on British Foreign Policy, 1919–1939,* 1st ser., vol. 4, pp. 241–51]

British Foreign Minister Sir Edward Grey on 21 October 1915 apprized the French Ambassador in London, Paul Cambon, of the Husayn-McMahon exchanges then in process and proposed that the two governments might discuss their respective interests in Ottoman Asia. The details of the Anglo-French negotiations were entrusted to Sir Mark Sykes and Charles François Georges-Picot, who contrived by February 1916 a provisional formula for the division of the Arab provinces. Sykes and Georges-Picot in March proceeded to Russia to confer with Sazonov. The Russian Foreign Minister declared his government's willingness to endorse the Anglo-French suggestions in return for Anglo-French approval of Russian territorial claims in northeastern Anatolia. To these claims the two western allies—France on 13/26 April and England on 10/23 May 1916—gave their sanction, although final clarification did not take place until 10/23 October 1916. The Entente governments formalized the tripartite understanding—commonly labeled the Sykes-Picot agreement—in an exchange of eleven letters, of which the four that are reprinted here present all the essential data. P. L. Hanna, *British Policy in Palestine,* chap. 2; H. N. Howard, *Partition of Turkey,* pp. 181–86; S. Leslie, *Mark Sykes, His Life and Letters,* pp. 249–58; G. Antonius, *Arab Awakening,* chap. 13; D. Lloyd George, *The Truth about the Peace Treaties,* vol. 2, pp. 1022–26, 1082–1100 and map on p. 1024; R. de Gontaut-Biron, *Comment la France s'est installée en Syrie* (1918–1919), chaps. 1–2; H. F. Frischwasser-Ra'anan, *Frontiers of a Nation,* chap. 3.

1. SIR EDWARD GREY TO PAUL CAMBON, 15 MAY 1916 [1]

I shall have the honour to reply fully in a further note to your Excellency's note of the 9th instant, relative to the creation of an Arab State, but I should meanwhile be grateful if your Excellency could assure me that in those regions which, under the conditions recorded in that communication, become entirely French, or in which French interests are recognised as predominant, any existing British concessions, rights of navigation or development, and the rights and privileges of any British religious, scholastic, or medical institutions will be maintained.

His Majesty's Government are, of course, ready to give a reciprocal assurance in regard to the British area.

2. GREY TO CAMBON, 16 MAY 1916 [2]

I have the honour to acknowledge the receipt of your Excellency's note of the 9th instant, stating that the French Government accept the limits of a future Arab State, or Confederation of States, and of those parts of Syria where French interests predominate, together with certain conditions attached thereto, such as they result from recent discussions in London and Petrograd on the subject.

I have the honour to inform your Excellency in reply that the acceptance of the whole project, as it now stands, will involve the abdication of considerable British interests, but, since His Majesty's Government recognise the advantage to the general cause of the Allies entailed in producing a more favourable internal political situation in Turkey, they are ready to accept the arrangement now arrived at, provided that the co-operation of the Arabs is secured, and that the Arabs fulfil the conditions and obtain the towns of Homs, Hama, Damascus, and Aleppo.

It is accordingly understood between the French and British Governments—

1. That France and Great Britain are prepared to recognize and protect [3] an independent Arab States or a Confederation of Arab States in the areas (A) and (B) marked on the annexed map, under the suzerainty of an Arab chief. That in area (A) France, and in area (B) Great Britain, shall have priority of right of enterprise and local loans. That in area (A) France, and in area (B) Great Britain, shall alone supply advisers or foreign functionaries at the request of the Arab State or Confederation of Arab States.

2. That in the blue area France, and in the red area Great Britain, shall be allowed to establish such direct or indirect administration or control as they desire and as they may think fit to arrange with the Arab State or Confederation of Arab States.

3. That in the brown area there shall be established an international administration, the form of which is to be decided upon after consultation with Russia, and subsequently in consultation with the other Allies, and the representatives of the Shereef of Mecca.

4. That Great Britain be accorded (1) the ports of Haifa and Acre, (2) guarantee of a given supply of water from the Tigris and Euphrates in area (A) for area (B). His Majesty's Government, on their part, undertake that they will at no time enter into negotiations for the cession of Cyprus to any third Power without the previous consent of the French Government.

5. That Alexandretta shall be a free port as regards the trade of the British Empire,

---

[1] Equivalent to Cambon's reply of same date.

[2] Conforms to Cambon's letter of 9 May 1916.

[3] "Protect" changed to "uphold" in accordance with Cambon-Crewe exchange of 25 and 30 August 1916.

and that there shall be no discrimination in port charges or facilities as regards British shipping and British goods; that there shall be freedom of transit for British goods through Alexandretta and by railway through the blue area, whether those goods are intended for or originate in the red area, or (B) area, or area (A); and there shall be no discrimination, direct or indirect, against British goods on any railway or against British goods or ships at any port serving the areas mentioned.

That Haifa shall be a free port as regards the trade of France, her dominions and protectorates, and there shall be no discrimination in port charges or facilities as regards French shipping and French goods. There shall be freedom of transit for French goods through Haifa and by the British railway through the brown area, whether those goods are intended for or originate in the blue area, area (A), or area (B), and there shall be no discrimination, direct or indirect, against French goods on any railway, or against French goods or ships at any port serving the areas mentioned.

6. That in area (A) the Bagdad Railway shall not be extended southwards beyond Mosul, and in area (B) northwards beyond Samarra, until a railway connecting Bagdad with Aleppo via the Euphrates Valley has been completed, and then only with the concurrence of the two Governments.

7. That Great Britain has the right to build, administer, and be sole owner of a railway connecting Haifa with area (B), and shall have a perpetual right to transport troops along such a line at all times.

It is to be understood by both Governments that this railway is to facilitate the connexion of Bagdad with Haifa by rail, and it is further understood that, if the engineering difficulties and expense entailed by keeping this connecting line in the brown area only make the project unfeasible, that the French Government shall be prepared to consider that the line in question may also traverse the polygon Banias-Keis Marib-Salkhad Tell Otsda-Mesmie before reaching area (B).

8. For a period of twenty years the existing Turkish customs tariff shall remain in force throughout the whole of the blue and red areas, as well as in areas (A) and (B), and no increase in the rates of duty or conversion from *ad valorem* to specific rates shall be made except by agreement between the two powers.

There shall be no interior customs barriers between any of the above-mentioned areas. The customs duties leviable on goods destined for the interior shall be collected at the port of entry and handed over to the administration of the area of destination.

9. It shall be agreed that the French Government will at no time enter into any negotiations for the cession of their rights and will not cede such rights in the blue area to any third Power, except the Arab State or Confederation of Arab States, without the previous agreement of His Majesty's Government, who, on their part, will give a similar undertaking to the French Government regarding the red area.

10. The British and French Governments, as the protectors of the Arab State,[4] shall agree that they will not themselves acquire and will not consent to a third Power acquiring territorial possessions in the Arabian peninsula, nor consent to a third Power installing a naval base either on the east coast, or on the islands, of the Red Sea. This, however, shall not prevent such adjustment of the Aden frontier as may be necessary in consequence of recent Turkish aggression.

11. The negotiations with the Arabs as to the boundaries of the Arab State or Confederation of Arab States shall be continued through the same channel as heretofore on behalf of the two Powers.

12. It is agreed that measures to control the importation of arms into the Arab territories will be considered by the two Governments.

I have further the honour to state that, in order to make the agreement complete, His Majesty's Government are proposing to the Russian Government to exchange

[4] The phrase "as the protectors of the Arab State" was deleted in August 1916 at the request of France.

notes analogous to those exchanged by the latter and your Excellency's Government on the 26th April last. Copies of these notes will be communicated to your Excellency as soon as exchanged.

I would also venture to remind your Excellency that the conclusion of the present agreement raises, for practical consideration, the question of the claims of Italy to a share in any partition or rearrangement of Turkey in Asia, as formulated in article 9 of the agreement of the 26th April, 1915, between Italy and the Allies.

His Majesty's Government further consider that the Japanese Government should be informed of the arrangements now concluded.

3. SIR EDWARD GREY TO COUNT BENCKENDORFF, RUSSIAN AMBASSADOR IN LONDON, 10/23 MAY 1916[5]

I have received from the French Ambassador in London copies of the notes exchanged between the Russian and French Governments on the 26th ultimo, by which your Excellency's Government recognise, subject to certain conditions, the arrangement made between Great Britain and France, relative to the constitution of an Arab State or a Confederation of Arab States, and to the partition of the territories of Syria, Cilicia, and Mesopotamia, provided that the co-operation of the Arabs is secured.

His Majesty's Government take act with satisfaction that your Excellency's Government concur in the limits set forth in that arrangement, and I have now the honour to inform your Excellency that His Majesty's Government, on their part, in order to make the arrangement complete, are also prepared to recognise the conditions formulated by the Russian Government and accepted by the French Government in the notes exchanged at Petrograd on the 26th ultimo.

In so far, then, as these arrangements directly affect the relations of Russia and Great Britain, I have the honour to invite the acquiescence of your Excellency's Government in an agreement on the following terms:—

1. That Russia shall annex the regions of Erzeroum, Trebizond, Van, and Bitlis, up to a point subsequently to be determined on the littoral of the Black Sea to the west of Trebizond.

2. That the region of Kurdistan to the south of Van and of Bitlis between Mush, Sert, the course of the Tigris, Jezireh-ben-Omar, the crest-line of the mountains which dominate Amadia, and the region of Merga Var, shall be ceded to Russia; and that starting from the region of Merga Var, the frontier of the Arab State shall follow the crest-line of the mountains which at present divide the Ottoman and Persian Dominions. These boundaries are indicated in a general manner and are subject to modifications of detail to be proposed later by the Delimitation Commission which shall meet on the spot.

3. That the Russian Government undertake that, in all parts of the Ottoman territories thus ceded to Russia, any concessions accorded to British subjects by the Ottoman Government shall be maintained. If the Russian Government express the desire that such concessions should later be modified in order to bring them into harmony with the laws of the Russian Empire, this modification shall only take place in agreement with the British Government.

4. That in all parts of the Ottoman territories thus ceded to Russia, existing British rights of navigation and development, and the rights and privileges of any British religious, scholastic, or medical institutions shall be maintained. His Majesty's Government, on their part, undertake that similar Russian rights and privileges shall be maintained in those regions which, under the conditions of this agreement, become entirely British, or in which British interests are recognised as predominant.

5. The two Governments admit in principle that every State which annexes any part of the Ottoman Empire is called upon to participate in the service of the Ottoman Debt.

[5] Corresponds to Sazonov-Paléologue exchange of 13/26 April and Count Benckendorff to Viscount Grey of 19 August/1 September 1916.

4. GREY TO BENCKENDORFF, 10/23 OCTOBER 1916

In reply to Your Excellency's note of the 1st ultimo, regarding the arrangement between Great Britain, Russia, and France, relative to the creation of an Arab State, or of a Confederation of Arab States, and to the partition of the territories of Syria, Cilicia, and Mesopotamia, provided that the cooperation of the Arabs is secured, I have the honour to state that His Majesty's Government take note of the reservation formulated by the Imperial Russian Government at the end of article 4 of the arrangement respecting the rights of the Imperial Government to *grand cabotage* in the Black Sea, and of the desire manifested by that Government that this question should be submitted later to a friendly examination by the Governments of the parties interested.

11. BRITISH TREATY WITH THE SHAYKH OF QATAR
3 November 1916

(Ratified by the Viceroy of India, Delhi, 23 March 1918)

[C. U. Aitchison, comp., *Collection of Treaties* (1933, 5th ed.), vol. 11, pp. 258–60]

Lord Curzon, during his viceroyship of India (1899–1905), recommended the inclusion of the Qatar principality in Britain's special treaty system for the Persian Gulf shaykhdoms. But Whitehall rejected the proposal because the British ambassador at Istanbul "argued that were this attempted it would be good-bye to any hope of getting the Turks out of Bubiyan Island in the territory of the Sheikh of Kuweit" (P. Graves, *Life of Cox,* p. 100). In article 11 of the unratified Anglo-Ottoman convention of 29 July 1913 (I, Doc. 108) the Sublime Porte finally abandoned its claims to Qatar. The peninsula, however, was not converted into a British veiled protectorate until 1916. The agreement with the shaykh of Qatar affirmed the usual obligations in which the Trucial Shaykhs acquiesced—suppression of the slave trade, preservation of the maritime peace, nonalienation of territory and surrender to the United Kingdom of external sovereignty—and accorded to British nationals broad economic privileges. Graves, *op. cit.*, chap. 9; Great Britain, Admiralty, *A Handbook of Arabia,* (1916), vol. 1, chap. 8; H. J. Liebesny, "International Relations of Arabia, the Dependent Areas," *Middle East Journal,* I (1947), 148–68.

I. I, Shaikh 'Abdullah bin Jasim bin Thani, undertake that I will, as do the friendly Arab Shaikhs of Abu Dhabi, Dibai, Shargah, Ajman, Ras-ul-Khaima and Umm-al-Qawain, co-operate with the High British Government in the suppression of the slave trade and piracy and generally in the maintenance of the Maritime Peace.

To this end, Lieutenant-Colonel Sir Percy Cox, Political Resident in the Persian Gulf, has favoured me with the Treaties and Engagements, entered into between the Shaikhs abovementioned and the High British Government, and I hereby declare that I will abide by the spirit and obligations of the aforesaid Treaties and Engagements.

II. On the other hand, the British Government undertakes that I and my subjects and my and their vessels shall receive all the immunities, privileges and advantages that are conferred on the friendly Shaikhs, their subjects and their vessels. In token whereof, Sir Percy Cox has affixed his signature with the date thereof to each and every one of the aforesaid Treaties and Engagements in the copy granted to me and I have also affixed my signature and seal with the date thereof to each and every one of the aforesaid Treaties and Engagements, in two other printed copies of the same Treaties and Engagements, that it may not be hidden.

III. And in particular, I, Shaikh Abdullah, have further published a proclamation forbidding the import and sale of arms into my territories and port of Qatar; and in consideration of the undertaking into which I now enter, the British Government on its part agrees to grant me facilities to purchase and import, from the Muscat Arms Warehouse or such other place as the British Government may approve, for my personal use, and for the arming of my dependents, such arms and ammunition as I may reasonably need and apply for in such fashion as may be arranged hereafter through the Political Agent, Bahrein. I undertake absolutely that arms and ammunition thus supplied to me shall under no circumstances be re-exported from my territories or sold to the public, but shall be reserved solely for supplying the needs of my tribesmen and dependents whom I have to arm for the maintenance of order in my territories and the protection of my Frontiers. In my opinion the amount of my yearly requirements will be up to five hundred weapons.

IV. I, Shaikh 'Abdullah, further undertake that I will not have relations nor correspond with, nor receive the agent of, any other Power without the consent of the High British Government; neither will I, without such consent, cede to any other Power or its subjects, land either on lease, sale, transfer, gift, or in any other way whatsoever.

V. I also declare that, without the consent of the High British Government, I will not grant pearl-fishery concessions, or any other monopolies, concessions, or cable landing rights, to anyone whomsoever.

VI. The Customs dues on the goods of British merchants imported to Qatar shall not exceed those levied from my own subjects on their goods and shall in no case exceed five per cent. *ad valorem.* British goods shall be liable to the payment of no other dues or taxes of any other kind whatsoever, beyond that already specified.

VII. I, Shaikh 'Abdullah, further, in particular, undertake to allow British subjects to reside in Qatar for trade and to protect their lives and property.

VIII. I also undertake to receive, should the British Government deem it advisable, an Agent from the British Government, who shall remain at Al Bidaa for the transaction of such business as the British Government may have with me and to watch over the interests of British traders residing at my ports or visiting them upon their lawful occasions.

IX. Further, I undertake to allow the establishment of a British Post Office and a Telegraph installation anywhere in my territory whenever the British Government should hereafter desire them. I also undertake to protect them when established.

X. On their part, the High British Government, in consideration of these Treaties and Engagements that I have entered into with them, undertake to protect me and my subjects and territory from all aggression by sea and to do their utmost to exact reparation for all injuries that I, or my subjects, may suffer when proceeding to sea upon our lawful occasions.

XI. They also undertake to grant me good offices, should I or my subjects be assailed by land within the territories of Qatar. It is, however, thoroughly understood that this obligation rests upon the British Government only in the event of such aggression whether by land or sea, being unprovoked by any act or aggression on the part of myself or my subjects against others.

12. TRIPARTITE (SAINT-JEAN DE MAURIENNE) AGREEMENT FOR THE PARTITION OF THE OTTOMAN EMPIRE: BRITAIN, FRANCE AND ITALY

19 April–26 September 1917

[Decisions taken at Saint-Jean de Maurienne, E. F. Woodward and R. Butler, *British Documents, 1919–1939,* 1st ser., vol. 4, pp. 638–39; agreement of 18 August, translated from French text, *ibid.,* pp. 640–41]

When the Sykes-Picot agreement (Doc. 10) became known in Rome, the Quirinal began to press for a clarification of the agreement of London of April 1915 (Doc. 6), so that Italy might be assured its desired share of Ottoman territory. The Marquis Imperiali, Italian Ambassador to St. James, presented a memorandum to the British Foreign Office in

November 1916 elaborating upon Italian claims, which apparently overlapped with certain districts in Anatolia already assigned to France under the Sykes-Picot formula. To dissolve the differences before they hardened, the four Entente powers commenced exploratory talks on Italian interests in the eastern Mediterranean at the British Foreign Office on 29 January 1917. For the second quadripartite meeting of 12 February, Foreign Secretary Arthur Balfour had a map drafted "marking out for purposes of discussion an Italian sphere of influence in South-West Anatolia, which should be equal in importance to the French sphere, but should not interfere with it." But Imperiali emphatically refused even to discuss a plan that diverged "so widely" from the Italian suggestions of November (E. L. Woodward and R. Butler, 1st ser., vol. 4, pp. 24–25). By the time the matter could be examined for decision by the prime ministers, who met on 19 April 1917 in a railway car at Saint-Jean de Maurienne, a small mountain village on the Franco-Italian frontier, the tsarist regime had given way to the provisional government and Russia was not represented. Present at the conference were David Lloyd George, Alexandre Félix Joseph Ribot and Paolo Bozelli together with the Italian Foreign Minister, Baron Sonnino. On the basis of the principles that the premiers approved, a formal agreement was later framed, incorporating Italian claims in a broadened Sykes-Picot formula. The three governments endorsed the draft, subject to Russian assent, in an exchange of notes (18 August-26 September 1917). The internal situation in Russia, however, had so far disintegrated that its approval was never procured. For the Bolshevik regime, as one of its first acts after coming to power on 7 November 1917, repudiated all tsarist international commitments. E. F. Woodward and R. Butler, *British Documents, 1919–1939,* 1st ser., vol. 4, pp. 24–25, 638–39, 642, 848–51; D. Lloyd George, *Truth about Peace Treaties,* vol. 2, pp. 772–83; D. H. Miller, *My Diary at the Conference of Paris,* vol. 20, pp. 335–38; H. N. Howard, *Partition of Turkey,* pp. 186–87.

1. PRELIMINARY DECISIONS TAKEN AT SAINT-JEAN DE MAURIENNE, 19 APRIL 1917

. . . . *Asia Minor.*

M. Ribot made objections regarding assignment of Mersina and Adana to Italy, but admitted facilities should be granted to commerce of the Interior in the direction of Mersina as in the case of Alexandretta and Haifa. The Italian zone will commence at a point to be determined west of Mersina.

Baron Sonnino asked for the inclusion in Italian zone of occupation of everything which so figures on Mr. Balfour's map. He asked, besides, that the northern part of the vilayet of Smyrna be also included. Mr. Lloyd George and M. Ribot undertake to submit this claim to their Governments.

It was agreed that the interests of the other Powers already established in the different zones shall be scrupulously respected, but that the Powers concerned in these interests shall not make use of them as a means of political action.

An exchange of views took place as to the situation which might result for the Allied Powers at the moment of peace with respect to the Ottoman Empire. After the discussion, Mr. Lloyd George made the following proposal, which was accepted:—

It is agreed that if, at the time when peace is made, the total or partial possession of territories contemplated in the agreements concluded between France, Great Britain, Italy and Russia, as regards attribution to them of a part of the Ottoman Empire, could not be granted entirely to one or several of the Powers in question, then the interests of those Powers would be taken afresh into equitable consideration. . . .

In a general way, the Ministers undertook to recommend the above decisions to their Governments.

2. AGREEMENT APPROVED IN LONDON, 18 AUGUST 1915

Subject to Russia's assent.

1. The Italian Government adheres to the stipulations contained in articles 1 and 2 of the Franco-British [Sykes-Picot] agreements of 9 and 16 May 1916. For their part, the governments of France and of Great Britain cede to Italy, under the same conditions of administration and of interests, the green and "C" zones as marked on the attached map [omitted here].

2. Italy undertakes to make Smyrna a free port for the commerce of France, its colonies and its protectorates, and for the commerce of the British Empire and its dependencies. Italy shall enjoy the rights and privileges that France and Great Britain have reciprocally granted themselves in the ports of Alexandretta, of Haifa, and of St. Jean d'Acre, in accordance with article 5 of the said agreements. Mersina shall be a free port for the commerce of Italy, its colonies and its protectorates, and there shall be neither difference of treatment nor advantages in port rights which may be refused to the navy or the merchandise of Italy. There shall be free transit through Mersina, and by railroad across the vilayet of Adana, for Italian merchandise bound to and from the Italian zone. There shall be no difference of treatment, direct or indirect, at the expense of Italian merchandise or ships in any port along the coast of Cilicia serving the Italian zone.

3. The form of international administration in the yellow zone [same as Sykes-Picot brown zone] mentioned in article 3 of the said agreements of 9 and 16 May shall be decided together with Italy.

4. Italy, insofar as she is concerned, approves the provisions on the ports of Haifa and of Acre contained in article 4 of the same agreements.

5. Italy adheres, in that which relates to the green zone and zone "C", to the two paragraphs of article 8 of the Franco-British agreements concerning the customs regime that shall be maintained in the blue and red zones, and in zones "A" and "B".

6. It is understood that the interests that each Power possesses in the zones controlled by the other Powers shall be scrupulously respected, but that the Powers concerned with these interests shall not use them as means for political action.

7. The provisions contained in articles 10, 11 and 12 of the Franco-English agreements, concerning the Arabian Peninsula and the Red Sea, shall be considered as fully binding on Italy as if that Power were named in the articles with France and Great Britain as a contracting party.

8. It is understood that if, at the conclusion of peace, the advantages embodied in the agreements contracted among the allied Powers regarding the allocation to each of a part of the Ottoman Empire cannot be entirely assured to one or more of the said Powers, then in whatever alteration or arrangement of provinces of the Ottoman Empire resulting from the war the maintenance of equilibrium in the Mediterranean shall be given equitable consideration, in conformity with article 9 of the London agreement of 26 April 1915.

9. It has been agreed that the present memorandum shall be communicated to the Russian Government, in order to permit it to make its views known.

13. THE BRITISH (BALFOUR) DECLARATIONS OF SYMPATHY WITH ZIONIST ASPIRATIONS
4 June–2 November 1917

[Cambon letter from N. Sokolow, *History of Zionism,* vol. 2, p. 53; official Zionist formula from World Zionist Organization, Executive, *Political Report to the XIIth Congress,* pp. 71–72; the Balfour Declaration from *The Times* (London), 9 November 1917]

Wartime negotiations between the World Zionist Organization and the British government started tardily and proceeded at a snail's pace. Zionist spokesmen in Britain, led by Chaim Weizmann, a Russian-born chemistry professor at the University of Manchester, and Nahum Sokolow, a Russian-born journalist and member of the Zionist Executive who had come to England late in 1914, concentrated on winning the interest of individual members of the British Cabinet. The government assigned Sir Mark Sykes in February 1917 the task of treating with the Zionist leaders. Sokolow visited (March-June 1917) the continent to seek the official endorsement of the Zionist program by France and Italy and returned with an encouraging letter from French Foreign Minister, Jules Cambon. Baron Lionel Walter Rothschild on 18 July 1917 submitted to the British Foreign Office for cabinet consideration the Zionist draft of a declaration of British sympathy for Zionism. In the interval of more than three months before the government took a decision, intermittent—and at times spirited—discussion of the subject took place within the cabinet, and at least one official British effort was made to obtain in advance the blessing of President Wilson. Foreign Minister Arthur James Balfour sent the revised government version of the statement—since known as the Balfour Declaration—in the form of a letter to Lord Rothschild. The Balfour Declaration was not intended as a secret document and appeared in the press shortly after its issuance. P. L. Hanna, *British Policy in Palestine,* pp. 30–38; D. Lloyd George, *Truth about Peace Treaties,* vol. 2, chap. 23; B. E. C. Dugdale, *Arthur James Balfour,* vol. 2, chap. 11; C. Weizmann, *Trial and Error,* chaps. 14–18; Esco Foundation, *Palestine,* vol. 1, pp. 74–118; S. Adler, "The Palestine Question in the Wilson Era," *Jewish Social Studies,* 10 (1948), 303–34; S. Sykes, *Two Studies in Virtue* (Eng. ed.), pp. 107–235; see also references to I, Doc. 98.

1. CAMBON LETTER TO SOKOLOW, 4 JUNE 1919

You were good enough to present the project to which you are devoting your efforts, which has for its object the development of Jewish colonization in Palestine. You consider that, circumstances permitting, and the independence of the Holy Places being safeguarded on the other hand, it would be a deed of justice and of reparation to assist, by the protection of the Allied Powers, in the renaissance of the Jewish nationality in that Land from which the people of *Israel* were exiled so many centuries ago.

The French Government, which entered this present war to defend a people wrongfully attacked, and which continues the struggle to assure the victory of right over might, can but feel sympathy for your cause, the triumph of which is bound up with that of the Allies.

I am happy to give you herewith such assurance.

2. OFFICIAL ZIONIST FORMULA, 18 JULY 1917

H.M. Government, after considering the aims of the Zionist Organisation, accepts the principle of recognising Palestine as the National Home of the Jewish people and the right of the Jewish people to build up its National life in Palestine under a protection to be established at the conclusion of Peace, following upon the successful issue of the war.

H.M. Government regards as essential for the realisation of this principle the grant of internal autonomy to the Jewish nationality in Palestine, freedom of immigration for Jews, and the establishment of a Jewish National Colonising Corporation for the re-settlement and economic development of the country.

The conditions and forms of the internal autonomy and a charter for the Jewish National Colonising Corporation should, in the view of H.M. Government, be elaborated in detail and determined with the representatives of the Zionist Organisation.

3. THE BALFOUR DECLARATION, 2 NOVEMBER 1917

I have much pleasure in conveying to you, on behalf of his Majesty's Government, the following declaration of sympathy with Jewish Zionist aspirations which has been submitted to and approved by the Cabinet:—

His Majesty's Government view with favour the establishment in Palestine of a national home for the Jewish people, and will use their best endeavours to facilitate the achievement of this object, it being clearly understood that nothing shall be done which may prejudice the civil and religious rights of existing non-Jewish communities in Palestine, or the rights and political status enjoyed by Jews in any other country.

I should be grateful if you would bring this declaration to the knowledge of the Zionist Federation.

14. SOVIET APPEAL TO MUSLIM WORKERS IN RUSSIA AND THE EAST
3 December 1917

[*The Soviet Union and Peace* (New York, n.d., ca. 1930), pp. 28–30]

The "All-Russian Congress of Soviets of Workers, Soldiers and Peasants' Deputies" unanimously adopted a decree on 8 November 1917, the day after the Bolsheviks took over the reins of government. The decree, in part, declared that the new "Government annuls, immediately and unconditionally, the secret treaties [concluded by the tsarist regime with other powers], in so far as they have for their object . . . to give benefits and privileges to the Russian landowners and capitalists, to maintain or to increase annexation by the Great Russians" [text in F. A. Golder, comp., *Documents of Russian History, 1914–1917* (New York, 1927), pp. 620–23]. In line with this decision the Soviet government began to make public the texts of the Allied secret agreements, those on the partition of the Ottoman Empire included. At the end of November the Council of the People's Commissars appealed to "the People of the Belligerent Counties" to join the Russian Socialist Federal Soviet Republic in negotiating an armistice and "a people's peace" and announced that "We have published the secret agreements of the Tsar and the bourgeoisie with the allies and have declared them not binding for the Russian people" (text in *The Soviet Union and Peace,* pp. 26–28). The following declaration, the first addressed exclusively to the Muslim world, formed part of a Bolshevik campaign to arouse Russia's southern neighbors to revolt against European imperialism. H. N. Howard, *Partition of Turkey,* pp. 198–200; H. Temperley, *History of Paris Peace Conference,* vol. 6, chap. 1, part 1; L. Fischer, *The Soviets in World Affairs,* vol. 1, chap. 1; F. Kazemzadeh, *The Struggle for Transcaucasia (1917–1921);* O. Caroe, *Soviet Empire,* chaps. 6–7; E. H. Carr, *The Bolshevik Revolution 1917–1923,* pp. 329–50.

Comrades! Brothers!

Great events are occurring in Russia! An end is drawing near to the murderous war, which arose out of the bargainings of foreign powers. The rule of the plunderers, exploiting the peoples of the world, is trembling. The ancient citadel of slavery and serfdom is cracking under the blows of the Russian Revolution. The world of violence and oppression is approaching its last days. A new world is arising, a world of the toilers and the liberated. At the head of this revolution is the Workers' and Peasants' Government in Russia, the Council of People's Commissars.

Revolutionary councils of workers', soldiers' and peasants' deputies are scattered over the whole of Russia. The power in the country is in the hands of the people. The toiling masses of Russia burn with the single desire to achieve an honest peace and help the oppressed people of the world to win their freedom.

Russia is not alone in this sacred cause. The mighty summons to freedom emitted by the Russian Revolution, has aroused all the toilers in the East and West. The people of Europe, exhausted by war, are already stretching out their hands to us, in our work for peace. The workers and soldiers of the West are already rallying around the banner of socialism, storming the strongholds of imperialism. Even far-off India, that land which has been oppressed by the European "torchbearers of civilisation" for so many centuries, has raised the standard of revolt, organising its councils of deputies, throwing the hated yoke of slavery from its shoulders, and summoning the people of the East to the struggle for freedom.

The sway of capitalist plunder and violence is being undermined. The ground is slipping from under the feet of the imperialist pillagers.

In the face of these great events, we appeal to you, toiling and dispossessed Mohammedan workers, in Russia and the East.

Mohammedans of Russia, Volga and Crimean Tartars, Kirghisi and Sarti in Siberia and Turkestan, Turcos and Tartars in the Trans-Caucasus, Chechenzi and mountain Cossacks! All you, whose mosques and shrines have been destroyed, whose faith and customs have been violated by the Tsars and oppressors of Russia! Henceforward your faith and customs, your national and cultural departments, are declared free and inviolable! Organise your national life freely and unimpeded. It is your right. Know that your rights, like those of all the peoples of Russia, will be guarded by the might of the revolution and its organs, the Councils of Workers', Soldiers' and Peasants' Deputies!

Support this revolution and its representative Government!

Mohammedans of the East! Persians, Turks, Arabs and Indians! All you whose bodies and property, freedom and native land have been for centuries exploited by the European beasts of prey! All you whose countries the plunderers who began the war now desire to share among themselves! We declare that the secret treaties of the deposed Tsar as to the annexation of Constantinople, confirmed by the late Kerensky Government—are now null and void. The Russian Republic, and its Government, the Council of People's Commissars, are opposed to the annexation of foreign lands: Constantinople must remain in the hands of the Mohammedans.

We declare that the treaty for the division of Persia is null and void. Immediately after the cessation of military activities troops will be withdrawn from Persia and the Persians will be guaranteed the right of free self-determination.

We declare that the treaty for the division of Turkey and the subduction from it of Armenia, is null and void. Immediately after the cessation of military activities, the Armenians will be guaranteed the right of free self-determination of their political fate.

It is not from Russia and its revolutionary Government that you have to fear enslavement, but from the robbers of European imperialism, from those who have laid your native lands waste and converted them into their colonies.

Overthrow these robbers and enslavers of your lands! Now, when war and ruin are breaking down the pillars of the old world, when the whole world is burning with indignation against the imperialist brigands, when the least spark of indignation bursts out in a mighty flame of revolution, when even the Indian Mohammedans, oppressed and tormented by the foreign yoke, are rising in revolt against their slave-drivers—now it is impossible to keep silent. Lose no time in throwing off the yoke of the ancient oppressors of your land! Let them no longer violate your hearths! You must yourselves be masters in your own land! You yourselves must arrange your life as you yourselves see fit! You have the right to do this, for your fate is in your own hands!

Comrades! Brothers!

Advance firmly and resolutely towards an honest, democratic peace!

We bear the liberation of the oppressed peoples of the world on our banners!

Mohammedans in Russia!

Mohammedans in the East!

We look to you for sympathy and support in the work of renewing of the world!

15. BRITISH AND ANGLO-FRENCH STATEMENTS TO THE ARABS
January–November 1918

[Great Britain, *Parliamentary Papers, 1939,* Cmd. 5974, pp. 48–51]

Early in 1918 the Constantinople and Sykes-Picot agreements (Docs. 5, 10) became common property in Arab Asia, thanks to the generosity of the Soviet government which released them and to German and Ottoman officials who exploited the opportunities for useful propaganda. Thrown into the potpourri was the Balfour Declaration (Doc. 13), which was a public instrument from the start. Arab nationalists began to raise their eyebrows, and British officials to issue statements of reassurance. The British government on 4 January 1918 instructed Commander D. G. Hogarth of the (British) Arab Bureau in Cairo to deliver to King Husayn of the Hijaz, formerly sharif of Mecca, a message stressing that the Balfour Declaration did not conflict with earlier promises to the Arabs (see also Cmd. 5964, pp. 4–5). The high commissioner for Egypt, Sir Reginald Wingate, was authorized to explain, in response to a formal inquiry by seven Arab spokesmen from Ottoman Asia then resident in Cairo, British war aims in the Arabian Peninsula and the Arab provinces to the north. The extract from a report to London by Sir Edmund Allenby, commanding general of the Egyptian Expeditionary Force which wrested from Ottoman control the Syria-Lebanon-Palestine area, disclosed the conditions under which Amir Faysal, King Husayn's third son, was permitted to set up a provisional Arab government at Damascus. The Anglo-French declaration was distributed throughout the future mandated zone a week after the signature of the Ottoman armistice. To these statements tireless reference was later made, especially in the mandated territories; and through all, it will be seen, the principle of self-determination permeated. G. Antonius, *Arab Awakening,* chap. 13; P. L. Hanna, *British Policy in Palestine,* chaps. 2–3; P. W. Ireland, *'Iraq,* chaps. 7–9; A. H. Hourani, *Syria and Lebanon,* chap. 2.

1. THE HOGARTH MESSAGE, JANUARY 1918

(1) The Entente Powers are determined that the Arab race shall be given full opportunity of once again forming a nation in the world. This can only be achieved by the Arabs themselves uniting, and Great Britain and her Allies will pursue a policy with this ultimate unity in view.

(2) So far as Palestine is concerned we are determined that no people shall be subject to another, but

(*a*) in view of the fact that there are in Palestine shrines, Wakfs and Holy places, sacred in some cases to Moslems alone, to Jews alone, to Christians alone, and in others to two or all three, and inasmuch as these places are of interest to vast masses of people outside Palestine and Arabia, there must be a special régime to deal with these places approved of by the world.

(*b*) As regards the Mosque of Omar it shall be considered as a Moslem concern alone and shall not be subjected directly or indirectly to any non-Moslem authority.

(3) Since the Jewish opinion of the world is in favour of a return of Jews to Palestine and inasmuch as this opinion must remain a constant factor, and further as His Majesty's Government view with favour the realisation of this aspiration, His Majesty's Government are determined that in so far as is compatible with the freedom of the existing population both economic and political, no obstacle should be put in the way of the realisation of this ideal.

In this connexion the friendship of world Jewry to the Arab cause is equivalent to support in all states where Jews have a political influence. The leaders of the movement are determined to bring about the success of Zionism by friendship and cooperation with the Arabs, and such an offer is not one to be lightly thrown aside.

2. THE DECLARATION TO THE SEVEN, CA. 16 JUNE 1918

His Majesty's Government have considered the memorial of the seven with the greatest care. His Majesty's Government fully appreciate the reasons why the memorialists desire to retain their anonymity, and the fact that the memorial is anonymous has not in any way detracted from the importance which His Majesty's Government attribute to the document.

The areas mentioned in the memorandum fall into four categories:—

1. Areas in Arabia which were free and independent before the outbreak of war;

2. Areas emancipated from Turkish control by the action of the Arabs themselves during the present war;

3. Areas formerly under Ottoman dominion, occupied by the Allied forces during the present war;

4. Areas still under Turkish control.

In regard to the first two categories, His Majesty's Government recognise the complete and sovereign independence of the Arab inhabiting these areas and support them in their struggle for freedom.

In regard to the areas occupied by Allied forces, His Majesty's Government draw the attention of the memorialists to the texts of the proclamations issued respectively by the General Officers Commanding in Chief on the taking of Bagdad and Jerusalem. These proclamations embody the policy of His Majesty's Government towards the inhabitants of those regions. It is the wish and desire of His Majesty's Government that the future government of these regions should be based upon the principle of the consent of the governed and this policy has and will continue to have the support of His Majesty's Government.

In regard to the areas mentioned in the fourth category, it is the wish and desire of His Majesty's Government that the oppressed peoples of these areas should obtain their freedom and independence and towards the achievement of this object His Majesty's Government continue to labour.

His Majesty's Government are fully aware of, and take into consideration, the difficulties and dangers which beset those who work for the regeneration of the populations of the areas specified.

In spite, however, of these obstacles His Majesty's Government trust and believe that they can and will be overcome, and wish to give all support to those who desire to overcome them. They are prepared to consider any scheme of co-operation which is compatible with existing military operations and consistent with the political principles of His Majesty's Government and the Allies.

3. ALLENBY'S CONDITIONS TO FAYSAL'S PROVISIONAL ARAB REGIME AT DAMASCUS, 17 OCTOBER 1918

I gave the Amir Faisal an official assurance that whatever measures might be taken during the period of military administration they were purely provisional and could not be allowed to prejudice the final settlement by the peace conference, at which no doubt the Arabs would have a representative. I added that the instructions to the military governors would preclude their mixing in political affairs, and that I should remove them if I found any of them contravening these orders. I reminded the Amir Faisal that the Allies were in honour bound to endeavour to reach a settlement in accordance with the wishes of the peoples concerned and urged him to place his trust wholeheartedly in their good faith.

4. ANGLO-FRENCH DECLARATION, 7 NOVEMBER 1918

The object aimed at by France and Great Britain in prosecuting in the East the War let loose by the ambition of Germany is the complete and definite emancipation of the peoples so long oppressed by the Turks and the establishment of national governments and administrations deriving their authority from the initiative and free choice of the indigenous populations.

In order to carry out these intentions France and Great Britain are at one in encouraging and assisting the establishment of indigenous Governments and administrations in Syria and Mesopotamia, now liberated by the Allies, and in the territories the liberation of which they are engaged in securing and recognising these as soon as they are actually established.

Far from wishing to impose on the populations of these regions any particular institutions they are only concerned to ensure by their support and by adequate assistance the regular working of Governments and administrations freely chosen by the populations themselves. To secure impartial and equal justice for all, to facilitate the economic development of the country by inspiring and encouraging local initiative, to favour the diffusion of education, to put an end to dissensions that have too long been taken advantage of by Turkish policy, such is the policy which the two Allied Governments uphold in the liberated territories.

16. LEGAL AND POLITICAL (BREST-LITOVSK) TREATY: RUSSIA AND THE OTTOMAN EMPIRE
3 March 1918

(Ratifications exchanged, Berlin, 12 July 1918)

[U.S., Department of State, *Texts of the Russian "Peace"* (Washington, 1918), pp. 167–71]

The Soviet government concluded a separate armistice on 5 December 1917 and acceded four months later to the rigorous conditions of peace laid down by Germany and its allies. The following instrument was appended to the general peace treaty, signed on the same day at Brest-Litovsk by Russia and the Central powers. In the treaty with the Sublime Porte Russia restored the districts of Kars and Ardahan, annexed from the sultan's realm in 1878, and surrendered its claim to capitulatory privileges in the Ottoman Empire. A. L. P. Dennis, *Foreign Policies of Soviet Russia,* chap. 9; E. H. Carr, *Bolshevik Revolution 1917–1923,* pp. 339–50.

Art. I. The following provisions have been made to regulate the details of execution and the delivery of occupied territory dealt with in Paragraph 2 of Article 4 of the joint treaty of peace.

1. To that end the Russian Republic undertakes to withdraw to the other side of the boundary line as it was before the war all its forces now in the said provinces as well as all its officers, both civil and military, in a period of from six to eight weeks from the signature of the present treaty.

2. The commanders in chief of the Russian and Turkish armies operating on the Asiatic front shall determine in accordance with the provisions of paragraph 1 the modus of evacuation and withdrawal of the Russian troops beyond the frontier, as also the means apt to ensure its safety.

3. At the time of the evacuation of the occupied territory, Russia will insure safety therein until it is again occupied by Ottoman troops. It shall take appropriate measures to prevent acts of vengeance, plunder, crimes, or other trespasses from being committed; to conserve intact and preserve from destruction the structures and buildings in the said territory, inclusive of military establishments, as well as all furniture and equipment. The army commanders of the contracting parties will settle those important points on the spot.

It is understood that the portable and other railroads laid in the said territory, as also the rolling stock and bridges, shall be allowed to stand as they are so as to make the revictualing of the population easier. The same will apply to military establishments.

4. The Russian Republic will use one division to guard the frontier along a distance of about five hundred kilometers or more, will demobilize all the remainder of the army and carry it to the interior of the country.

5. The Russian Republic undertakes to demobilize and dissolve the Armenian bands whether of Russian or Turkish nationality now in the Russian and Ottoman occupied provinces and entirely to disband them.

6. The two contracting parties will conclude an agreement for the settlement of the revictualing of the inhabitants of the said provinces until normal conditions are restored.

7. The Russian Republic shall not concentrate troops along the border or in Caucasia exceeding one division, not even for drills, until general peace is established.

If it should become necessary to resort to such a concentration for reasons of public safety in the interior, a previous notice must be given to the powers of the Quadruple Alliance.

On the other hand, Turkey is compelled by the necessity of carrying on the war against its other adversaries to keep its army on a war footing.

Art. II. Within three months after the ratification of the present treaty two Turkish-Russian Joint Commissioners shall be appointed by the contracting parties; one of these will be charged with the duty of reestablishing the dividing line between Turkish and Russian territory from the point where the three boundaries, Turkish, Russian, and Persian, meet to the point where the line strikes the boundary of the three Sandjaks of Kars, Erdehan, and Batum. Along that stretch the boundary line as it was before the war will be followed; the monuments that may have been destroyed in the course of the war operations shall be rebuilt and repaired in accordance with the maps and protocols of the boundary commission of 1880.

The second commission will mark the boundary between Russia and the three Sandjaks to be evacuated in accordance with Paragraph 3 of Article IV of the joint treaty of peace. The frontier shall be restored there as it existed before the Turkish-Russian war of 1877 and 1878.

ART. III. The inhabitants and communes in the territory of either contracting party, holding property and usufruct rights on real property lying on the other side of the border will enjoy, operate, or lease, manage or convey such property by themselves or by proxy.

The said inhabitants or representatives of the said communes will be allowed freely to cross the boundary line upon presentation of passes issued to them by the proper authorities of their domicile and authenticated by those of the other party.

Facilities in crossing the line free of duty will be granted to local agricultural products, farming implements, food stuffs, fertilizers, seed, building material, and cattle for farm work, carried by the said inhabitants or representatives of communes.

The contracting parties reserve for a future special arrangement the settlement of the details of the provisions set forth in the foregoing two paragraphs.

ART. IV. The contracting parties undertake to grant on and after the ratification of the present treaty, exequaturs to the Consuls General and vice consuls of career of either party in all ports, cities, or other places in the territory of the others, except those where objection may be seen to recognizing such officers, provided the same exception applies to all foreign powers.

With regard to the privileges, powers, and duties of the said officers during the transitory period referred to in Article VI, the same rules shall, on condition of reciprocity, apply to them as apply to like officers of the most favored nation.

ART. V. Each contracting party undertakes to pay an indemnity for all the damages and losses caused during the war within the territories by its agents or people to the consular buildings and furniture as well as to the consular officers and employees of the other party.

ART. VI. All the treaties, conventions, undertakings, or other instruments and agreements previously existing between the contracting parties having been made null and void, *pro facto,* by the very occurrence of the war, the Imperial Ottoman Government and the Government of the Russian Republic undertake to conclude a consular convention and such other instruments as they may deem necessary for the adjustment of their juridical relations. These instruments shall be perfected within the time set by Appendix V to the joint treaty of peace for the conclusion of a treaty of commerce and navigation. The transitory period in which to apply the provisions in the last paragraph of Article IV as also the right of denouncement granted to the parties will be the same as those stated in the said appendix.

ART. VII. The post and telegraph relations between the Ottoman Empire and Russia will be re-established immediately upon the ratification of the present treaty in accordance with the postal and telegraphic conventions, arrangements, and regulations of the international union.

ART. VIII. In pursuance of the principle laid down in Article VII of the joint treaty of peace the two contracting parties declare that they consider to be null and void all previous international instruments intended to create spheres of influence and exclusive interests in Persia. The two Governments will withdraw their troops from the Persian territory. To that end they shall communicate with the Government of that country about the details of the evacuation and the measures apt also to insure for the political independence and territorial integrity of that country the respect of the several states.

ART. IX. All laws, regulations, and ordinances enforced in the territory of one of the contracting parties against the citizens or subjects of the other party by reason of the state of war existing in their country and intended to change these personal rights in any way (war laws) become inoperative after the ratification of the joint treaty of peace.

The juristic persons and corporations recognized by the local laws of one of the parties as belonging to the nationality of the other party shall be considered in this respect as citizens or subjects of the said other party.

ART. X. All debts due to private or juristic persons or corporations, citizens, or subjects of one of the parties within the territory of the other party are restored to their ante bellum status.

The contracting parties agree to apply to the debts due to their respective citizens or subjects the provisions found in Sections 2 and 3 of Article 2 of the Russo-German Supplementary Treaty signed at Brest-Litovsk on 3 March, 1918. (Chapter 3).

The citizens or subjects of either party shall in addition enjoy the greater facilities which each of the parties may see fit to adopt in behalf of its own nationals who may have been unable on account of the war events, to secure in good time the safeguard of their rights.

ART. XI. Russian subjects of the Moslem faith will be allowed to emigrate to Turkey after disposing of their property and to carry their patrimony with them.

ART. XII. Persons whose rights have been invaded under the war laws mentioned in Article VIII, will, as far as possible, be reinstated in the said rights. After ratification of the present treaty both sides shall simultaneously return the property seized under the said laws. In addition each party undertakes simultaneously to pay indemnity for the damage caused to the subjects of the other party in their lives or health as a result of the measures taken against them and in their property as a result of liquidation, seizure, requisition, or forcible disposition of their real and personal estates. The mode of appraising the losses sustained by reason of the circumstances above enumerated and all matters connected therewith, as also the procedure to be followed in the premises shall be settled by the contracting parties under the same conditions as those determined by Articles 2, 3, and 4 (Chapter 4) of the supplementary German-Russian treaty of 3 March, 1918.

ART. XIII. Prisoners of war who are invalid or unfit for military service shall be immediately sent home. The other prisoners of war and all other persons arrested as a measure of military or public order shall be exchanged as soon as possible after the signature of the present treaty; the exchange will be effected through special commissioners appointed by both parties.

The transportation of prisoners of war to a port of departure or to the frontier will be at the expense of the captor state. Civilian prisoners will be immediately released. The contracting party which arrested or interned them shall bear the cost of transportation from the place where they are held or interned to the residence from which they were taken.

ART. XIV. Each contracting party will apply to the prisoners of war and interned civilians in its territory, and also to the citizens or subjects of the other party, the amnesty clauses inserted in Article 1 (Chapter 7) of the supplementary German-Russian treaty signed at Brest-Litovsk on 3 March, 1918.

ART. XV. The present supplementary treaty shall go into effect, in so far as it is not otherwise provided, at the same time as the joint treaty of peace signed at Brest-Litovsk on 3 March, 1918.

17. DENUNCIATION OF TSARIST RUSSIAN PRIVILEGES IN PERSIA BY THE SOVIET AND PERSIAN GOVERNMENTS
26 June–27 July 1918

[J. Rives Childs, comp., *Perso-Russian Treaties and Notes of 1828–1931* (Library of Congress typescript), pp. 70–75]

Faced with civil war and the massive problem of consolidating its authority over the territory of Russia, the Soviet regime in the first few months sought to placate its smaller neighbors in Asia, among them Persia. The Soviet Commissar of Foreign Affairs, Leon Trotsky, as one of the earliest gestures of friendship toward Persia, denounced on 14 January 1918 the Anglo-Russian convention of 1907 (I, Doc. 105) and "the preceding as well as the subsequent [tsarist] treaties which, in whatever form, limit and restrict the right of the Persian people to a free and independent existence" (text in Childs typescript, pp. 64–65). On 26 June Foreign Commissar Georgi Vasilyevich Chicherin addressed a more explicit note to the Persian government, announcing the voluntary nullification by Moscow of all Russian concessions and special privileges (among them, the capitulations) in Persia and all Persian debts to Tsarist Russia. The Persian Cabinet responded a month later with a complementary decision, abrogating all the earlier Russian instruments. Yet the matter was not formally settled until the Perso-Soviet treaty of 26 February 1921 (Doc. 33) went into effect. G. Lenczowski, *Russia and the West in Iran, 1918-1948,* chap. 3; M. Beloff, *The Foreign Policy of Soviet Russia,* vol. 2, chap. 9; A. L. P. Dennis, *Foreign Policies of Soviet Russia,* chap. 10.

1. CHICHERIN NOTE TO PERSIAN GOVERNMENT, 26 JUNE 1918

In our note of January 14, 1918, No. 137, published afterwards in No. 11 of the Bulletin of the All-Russian Central Executive Committee of the Soviet of Workmen's, Soldiers' and Peasants' Deputies, of the same year, the former People's Commissar for Foreign Affairs informed the Persian people of the main foundations of Soviet Russian policy in its relations with Persia.

In the development of the principles mentioned in this note, annulling once and for all those treaties and conventions which were violently extorted from Persia by the Russian Tsarist Government, or contradicted the principle of the integrity and inviolability of Persia, or limited and impeded the liberty of development and realization of the will of the Persian People on the territories occupied by them and the adjacent Seas, the People's Commissariat for Foreign Affairs of the R.S.F.S.R. from now on expresses its full readiness to enter into negotiations with the Persian Government for the conclusion of new treaties, consular conventions, and other conventions, on the principle of free accords and mutual respect of peoples.

Taking into consideration the ruin of northern Persia by the armies of the old Russian Government, together with the Turkish and English Armies of Occupation, responsibility for the disastrous consequences of which falls entirely on the capitalistic governments of England, Turkey and Tsarist Russia, the Russian Soviet Government, animated by friendly-disposed sentiments towards Persia, downtrodden by the united imperialists, wishes to afford just conpensation for those damages caused by Russian troops, assuming that the Persian Government, leaning on the help of the Persian People, will find means of obtaining compensation for the corresponding damages caused by the Imperialistic Government of England.

In its efforts to compensate the Persian People, the Soviet Government proclaims that:

1) All payments of Persia, according to Tsarist obligations, are annulled.

2) Russia, once and forever, renounces any claim on the revenue from customs, telegraphs, posts and so forth.

3) The Caspian Sea, after the evacuation of the piratical vessels of English Imperialism, will be declared freely open to the navigation of vessels bearing the Persian flag.

4) The boundary of Soviet Russia with Persia will be established in accordance with the free will of the population living on the frontiers of the territory.

5) All former Russian governmental and private concessions are no longer in force.

6) The Russian Bank d'Escompte of Persia, with all its lands and buildings and with all its branches existing in Persia, are declared the property of the free Persian people.

7) The telegraph line, Meshed-Seistan; the telegraphs of the Astrabed district; the telegraph of the highway Enzeli-Teheran; all the highways built by the Russian armies during their occupation of Persia during the war period 1914–1918, with all their appurtenances; all the appurtenances of the port of Enzeli, with all its property such as the electric station, moles, buildings, inventory and so forth; the Julfa-Tabriz railroad with its branch to Safian, with all the railway property, inventory, buildings and so forth; and also all the Russian postal institutions, telephones, and telegraph lines in Persia are given over to the use and disposition of the free independent Persian people who will have to recompense the employers and workmen of the above-mentioned institutions.

8) The former consular jurisdiction is entirely transformed.

9) The ecclesiastical mission of Urumiah is entirely abolished.

10) Russian citizens residing in Persia are obliged to pay all kinds of taxes (contributions and collections) equally with the local population, if these collections are imposed legally and in conformity with the public need.

11) The Russian Government is prepared, together with the Persian Government, to examine the question of the landed possessions of Russian citizens in Persia, the means of renting, the payment of taxes and so forth, and to decide such matters in the interest of the Persian and Russian people.

12) The Russo-Persian boundary is open to free circulation and transport of merchandise. To Persia is allowed the right of transit through Russia of merchandise of any origin and character.

13) The Russian Soviet Government is willing, together with the Persian Government, to draw up railway, steamship and other tariff schedules governing the conveyance, through Russian means of transport, of Persian goods.

14) Russia renounces all participation in the organization of military units on Persian territory.

15) The Russian Government consents to the abolition of the institution of the "kargusarists."

16) To Persia is given the right to nominate its consuls in all cities and places of Soviet Russia and also in Turkestan and the Trans-Caspian Provinces and in Bokhara and Khiva, allied to us.

Proclaiming and proposing the above-mentioned, the People's Commissar for Foreign Affairs cherishes the firm conviction that the present steps of the Russian Soviet Government open a new era in the history of mutual relations between Russia and Persia, to whom the Russian people of the Revolution are sending their brotherly greetings and sincere wishes for the throwing off of the exhausted shoulders of the Persian People the weight of the English and Allied Imperialists, who are bent on definitely crushing Persia, chained hands and feet.

The Russian people believe that the fifteen million people of Iran cannot die, that possessing such a glorious and heroic past, and having on the pages of its history and culture a name enjoying the just admiration of all the civilized world, they will throw off, with a powerful impulse, its century-old lethargy and will cast off the weight of the abominable robbers and range themselves in the fraternal ranks of free and cultured people in a new serene triumph for the good of all mankind.

2. DECREE BY PERSIAN COUNCIL OF MINISTERS, 27 JULY 1918

Whereas the treaties, agreements, and concessions taken from Persia during the last hundred years by the despotic Russian Government and its people had been secured from Persia either by duress and force or through illegitimate means, such as threats and bribes, and are against the interests of Persia;

Whereas the Great Powers of the world have, since the beginning of the present war, in various ways announced to the people of the world the protection, integrity, and economic and political independence of the weak nations;

Whereas the new Government of Russia has announced as its goal the liberty and integrity of the nations, and has particularly, repeatedly, officially and unofficially announced the abrogation of all concessions and treaties which had been taken from Persia by the Russians;

Whereas the above-mentioned concessions, in addition to having been forcibly taken from Persia—against the interests of the country—together with those secured from Persia after the establishment of the Persian Constitutional Government—against the provisions of the Constitution—have either not been put into force, or have been very badly executed, or their provisions have not been complied with; not only the defined rights of the Government have not been respected, but in many cases these concessions by transfer or abuse of their provisions, have been the source of political and economic difficulties and pretexts, injuring the integrity of the country and the interests of the people;

Whereas the Government and people of Persia have the same right as all other nations and governments to be benefitted by their resources and their natural liberty;

Therefore, the Council of Ministers, at their meeting of July 27, 1918, have resolved the abrogation of all above-mentioned treaties, agreements and concessions. The Ministry of Foreign Affairs is hereby instructed to announce the text of this decision to all the officials and representatives of foreign governments at the court of Persia, and to all Persian Ministers at the courts of foreign governments. The Ministry of Public Works, Commerce and Agriculture is to inform the public of the same through its proper means.

The original of this decision is kept in the files of the President of the Council of Ministers.

18. ARMISTICE (MUDROS): THE OTTOMAN EMPIRE AND THE ALLIED POWERS
30 October 1918

[Great Britain, *Parliamentary Papers, 1919,* Cmd. 53, pp. 25–27]

The Sublime Porte capitulated to the allied powers nearly a fortnight before the German surrender. With Russia eliminated, Britain remained the only Entente power with fighting forces in the Near and Middle East. The United Kingdom accordingly drew up in the name of the allies the terms of the Ottoman armistice. The negotiations, which lasted a week, took place on board His Britannic Majesty's Ship *Agamemnon,* at the port of Mudros on the island of Lemnos. Sir F. Maurice, *The Armistices of 1918,* chap. 2; H. N. Howard, *Partition of Turkey,* pp. 208–13; Sir C. V. F. Townsend, *My Campaign in Mesopotamia,* chap. 20; H. H. Cumming, *Franco-British Rivalry in the Post-War Near East,* chap. 6.

1. Opening of Dardanelles and Bosphorus and secure access to the Black Sea. Allied occupation of Dardanelles and Bosphorus forts.

2. Positions of all minefields, torpedo tubes, and other obstructions in Turkish waters to be indicated, and assistance given to sweep or remove them as may be required.

3. All available information as to mines in the Black Sea to be communicated.

4. All Allied prisoners of war and Armenian interned persons and prisoners to be collected in Constantinople and handed over unconditionally to the Allies.

5. Immediate demobilization of the Turkish Army except for such troops as are required for surveillance of frontiers and for the maintenance of internal order. (Num-

ber of effectives and their dispositions to be determined later by the Allies after consultation with the Turkish Government.)

6. Surrender of all war vessels in Turkish waters or in waters occupied by Turkey; these ships to be interned at such Turkish port or ports as may be directed, except such small vessels as are required for police or similar purposes in Turkish territorial waters.

7. The Allies to have the right to occupy any strategic points in the event of a situation arising which threatens the security of the Allies.

8. Free use by Allied ships of all ports and anchorages now in Turkish occupation and denial of their use by the enemy. Similar conditions to apply to Turkish mercantile shipping in Turkish waters for purposes of trade and the demobilization of the army.

9. Use of all ship repair facilities at all Turkish ports and arsenals.

10. Allied occupation of the Taurus tunnel system.

11. Immediate withdrawal of Turkish troops from North-West Persia to behind the pre-war frontier has already been ordered and will be carried out.

Part of Trans-Caucasia has already been ordered to be evacuated by Turkish troops, the remainder to be evacuated if required by the Allies after they have studied the situation there.

12. Wireless telegraphy and cable stations to be controlled by the Allies, Turkish Government messages excepted.

13. Prohibition to destroy any naval, military, or commercial material.

14. Facilities to be given for the purchase of coal and oil fuel and naval material from Turkish sources after the requirements of the country have been met.

None of the above material to be exported.

15. Allied control officers to be placed on all railways, including such portions of Trans-Caucasian railways now under Turkish control, which must be placed at the free and complete disposal of the Allied authorities, due consideration being given to the needs of the population.

This clause to include Allied occupation of Batum. Turkey will raise no objection to the occupation of Baku by the Allies.

16. Surrender of all garrisons in Hejaz, Assir, Yemen, Syria, and Mesopotamia to the nearest Allied commander; and the withdrawal of troops from Cilicia, except those necessary to maintain order, as will be determined under Clause 5.

17. Surrender of all Turkish officers in Tripolitania and Cyrenaica to the nearest Italian garrison. Turkey guarantees to stop supplies and communications with those officers if they do not obey the order to surrender.

18. Surrender of all ports occupied in Tripolitania and Cyrenaica, including Misurata, to the nearest Allied garrison.

19. All Germans and Austrians, naval, military and civilian, to be evacuated within one month from Turkish dominions, those in remote districts as soon after as may be possible.

20. Compliance with such orders as may be conveyed for the disposal of the equipment, arms and ammunition, including transport, of that portion of the Turkish Army which is demobilized under Clause 5.

21. An Allied representative to be attached to the Turkish Ministry of Supplies in order to safeguard Allied interests. This representative to be furnished with all information necessary for this purpose.

22. Turkish prisoners to be kept at the disposal of the Allied Powers. The release of Turkish civilian prisoners and prisoners over military age to be considered.

23. Obligation on the part of Turkey to cease all relations with the Central Powers.

24. In case of disorder in the six Armenian vilayets the Allies reserve to themselves the right to occupy any part of them.

25. Hostilities between the Allies and Turkey shall cease from noon, local time, on Thursday, 31st October, 1918.

19. AMIR FAYSAL'S MEMORANDUM TO THE SUPREME COUNCIL AT THE PARIS PEACE CONFERENCE
1 January 1919

[David Hunter Miller, *My Diary at the Conference of Paris* (New York, 1924), vol. 4, pp. 297–99]

The British Commander, General Sir Edmund (later Field Marshal Viscount) Allenby, at the time of the Anglo-Arab occupation of Syria in October 1918 permitted Amir Faysal, the third son of King Husayn of the Hijaz, to set up a provisional Arab government with its capital at Damascus (Doc. 15). Pending the decision of the peacemakers at Paris, the area of the provisional Arab state was labeled Occupied Enemy Territory East, which comprised essentially the A and B zones of the Sykes-Picot agreement (Doc. 10) minus the corridor to Persia. At Paris Faysal formally headed the delegation of the Hijaz, which claimed to speak for all Arab Asia, a claim that did not go unchallenged in the Arabian Peninsula. The brief for Arab Asia, developed in the following memorandum, was amplified by Faysal on 6 February 1919 when he appeared before the Supreme Council accompanied by T. E. Lawrence and three members of the Hijazi delegation. G. Antonius, *Arab Awakening,* chap. 14; H. W. V. Temperley, *History of the Paris Peace Conference,* vol. 6, pp. 134–45; P. L. Hanna, *British Policy in Palestine,* chap. 3; A. H. Hourani, *Syria and Lebanon,* chap. 2; D. Lloyd George, *Truth about the Peace Treaties,* vol. 2, chaps. 22, 23; R. Lansing, *The Big Four,* pp. 161–77.

The country from a line Alexandretta—Persia southward to the Indian Ocean is inhabited by "Arabs"—by which we mean people of closely related Semitic stocks, all speaking the one language, Arabic. The non-Arabic-speaking elements in this area do not, I believe, exceed one per cent. of the whole.

The aim of the Arab nationalist movements (of which my father became the leader in war after combined appeals from the Syrian and Mesopotamian branches) is to unite the Arabs eventually into one nation. As an old member of the Syrian Committee I commanded the Syrian revolt, and had under me Syrians, Mesopotamians, and Arabians.

We believe that our ideal of Arab unity in Asia is justified beyond need of argument. If argument is required, we would point to the general principles accepted by the Allies when the United States joined them, to our splendid past, to the tenacity with which our race has for 600 years resisted Turkish attempts to absorb us, and, in a lesser degree, to what we tried our best to do in this war as one of the Allies.

My father has a privileged place among Arabs, as their successful leader, and as the head of their greatest family, and as Sherif of Mecca. He is convinced of the ultimate triumph of the ideal of unity, if no attempt is made now to force it, by imposing an artificial political unity on the whole, or to hinder it, by dividing the area as spoils of war among great Powers.

The unity of the Arabs in Asia has been made more easy of late years, since the development of railways, telegraphs, and air-roads. In old days the area was too huge, and in parts necessarily too thinly peopled, to communicate common ideas readily.

The various provinces of Arab Asia—Syria, Irak, Jezireh, Hedjaz, Nejd, Yemen—are very different economically and socially, and it is impossible to constrain them into one frame of government.

We believe that Syria, an agricultural and industrial area thickly peopled with sedentary classes, is sufficiently advanced politically to manage her own internal affairs. We feel also that foreign technical advice and help will be a most valuable factor in our national growth. We are willing to pay for this help in cash; we cannot sacrifice for it any part of the freedom we have just won for ourselves by force of arms.

Jezireh and Irak are two huge provinces, made up of three civilised towns, divided by large wastes thinly peopled by semi-nomadic tribes. The world wishes to exploit Mesopotamia rapidly, and we therefore believe that the system of government there will have to be buttressed by the men and material resources of a great foreign Power. We ask, however, that the Government be Arab, in principle and spirit, the selective rather than the elective principle being necessarily followed in the neglected districts, until time makes the broader basis possible. The main duty of the Arab Government there would be to oversee the educational processes which are to advance the tribes to the moral level of the towns.

The Hedjaz is mainly a tribal area, and the government will remain, as in the past, suited to patriarchal conditions. We appreciate these better than Europe, and propose therefore to retain our complete independence there.

The Yemen and Nejd are not likely to submit their cases to the Peace Conference. They look after themselves, and adjust their own relations with the Hedjaz and elsewhere.

In Palestine the enormous majority of the people are Arabs. The Jews are very close to the Arabs in blood, and there is no conflict of character between the two races. In principles we are absolutely at one. Nevertheless, the Arabs cannot risk assuming the responsibility of holding level the scales in the clash of races and religions that have, in this one province, so often involved the world in difficulties. They would wish for the effective super-position of a great trustee, so long as a representative local administration commended itself by actively promoting the material prosperity of the country.

In discussing our provinces in detail I do not lay claim to superior competence. The powers will, I hope, find better means to give fuller effect to the aims of our national movement. I came to Europe, on behalf of my father and the Arabs of Asia, to say that they are expecting the Powers at the Conference not to attach undue importance to superficial differences of condition, and not to consider them only from the low ground of existing European material interests and supposed spheres. They expect the powers to think of them as one potential people, jealous of their language and liberty, and ask that no step be taken inconsistent with the prospect of an eventual union of these areas under one sovereign government.

In laying stress on the difference in the social condition of our provinces, I do not wish to give the impression that there exists any real conflict of ideals, material interests, creeds, or character rendering our union impossible. The greatest obstacle we have to overcome is local ignorance, for which the Turkish Government is largely responsible.

In our opinion, if our independence be conceded and our local competence established, the natural influences of race, language, and interest will soon draw us together into one people; but for this the Great Powers will have to ensure us open internal frontiers, common railways and telegraphs, and uniform systems of education. To achieve this they must lay aside the thought of individual profits, and of their old jealousies. In a word, we ask you not to force your whole civilisation upon us, but to help us to pick out what serves us from your experience. In return we can offer you little but gratitude.

20. TENTATIVE RECOMMENDATIONS FOR PRESIDENT WILSON BY THE INTELLIGENCE SECTION OF THE AMERICAN DELEGATION TO THE PEACE CONFERENCE

21 January 1919

[David Hunter Miller, *My Diary at the Conference of Paris,* (New York, 1924), vol. 4, pp. 254–67]

A pervasive, although hardly definitive, British influence is manifest on the policy recommendations of the United States for the Near and Middle East prepared by the intelligence section of the American delegation at Paris for the guidance of President Wilson. Nor is it surprising, since the interests of Britain in that region at the time were pervasive while those of the United States fell largely under the heading of cultural relations. Only the territorial section of the report relating to the Near and Middle East is reproduced below. H. N. Howard, *Partition of Turkey,* chap. 7; C. Seymour and E. M. House, eds., *What Really Happened at Paris,* chap. 8.

21. CONSTANTINOPLE AND THE STRAITS

1) It is recommended that there be established in the Constantinople region an internationalized state.

An internationalized state will, it is thought, be most likely to do impartial justice to the various interests of the many states concerned in the commerce that will pass the Straits, and to diminish the keen historic jealousies that have obstructed the flow of trade. We understand that such a proposal is generally accepted.

2) It is recommended that the new state be given such a governmental organization by the appointment of a Power as a mandatory of the League of Nations or otherwise, as may seem most expedient to the peace conference.

The state about Constantinople is instituted for special purposes and in order to serve the needs and interests, often conflicting, of many nations, strong and weak, varying greatly in location and necessities.

This state should bear a special relation to the nations which are to associate themselves in a world League, and it should be made the business of some organ of such a League to see that the purposes for which the state is instituted are fulfilled.

Whether this can best be accomplished by the selection of a governor or of a single power to act as the mandatory of the League, or otherwise, can be better determined after the main features of the League have been decided upon, and in accordance with the greater experience of that time.

3a) It is recommended that the boundaries of the proposed state include the entire littoral of the Straits and of the Sea of Marmora.

We are informed by the technical advisors in international law that the assignment of any portion of the littoral of the Sea of Marmora or of the Straits to an independent sovereign power would result in many embarrassments, raising questions of commerce, of territorial waters, of possible naval rights, etc., etc., and would render more difficult the prime object in this region as set forth in Recommendation 2).

Adjacent states would of course enjoy adequate rights of access to the waters of the internationalized area.

It is recommended that the boundaries of the proposed state:

3b) On the European side follow the general direction of the Enos-Midia line, adapted to the physical and economic features of the country.

3c) On the Asiatic side follow in part the line of the Sakaria river, include within the new state the towns of Brussa and Panderma, and emerge on the Aegean at a point north of Ineh, as shown on map 19 [omitted].

The new state should include the land that may be needed to serve such immediate material wants of the capital as garden and dairy products, water supply, etc., but it should be sufficiently restricted in area to reduce to the lowest terms the task of administration.

3b The Enos-Midia line offers the best frontier on the European side if Recommendation 3a) is accepted, since it rests upon the best historic, topographic, and ethnic basis.

3c The line on the Asiatic side is drawn so as not to separate the valley floors and the hill pastures, and follows the stream courses and watersheds as on the European side.

Brussa, a former Turkish capital with a population of 75,000, located about 16 miles from the Sea of Marmora, is included in the new state in order to prevent the Turks from making it their capital. As such it might easily become the center of international intrigues, disturbing the large Turkish population in and about Constantinople and, therefore, the stability and smooth administration of the new international state.

4) It is recommended that the Bosphorus, Sea of Marmora, and Dardanelles be permanently opened as a free passageway to the ships and commerce of all nations, under international guarantees.

This declaration is in such full harmony with the spirit of the new world order, and is so nearly axiomatic from the standpoint of international justice, as to require no elucidation.

22. TURKEY

1) It is recommended that there be established a Turkish Anatolian state, with boundaries as indicated on map 20 [omitted].

An outstanding feature is the presence, in Asia Minor, west of the Anti-Taurus Mountains, of a solid block of Turkish Moslems. They constitute a sound Anatolian peasantry whose chance of independent development deserves every consideration. The fact is patent, and with fresh opportunities of development the proposed state may in time have both stability and power. Not the least of its assets would be freedom from the burden of governing alien peoples of different faith, whose oppression by the Turk has reacted upon him morally and politically, with well-known evil effects.

The new state is delimited on the west by a line roughly parallel to the Bosphorus-Dardanelles thoroughfare and would form the frontier between the Turkish state and the internationalized Constantinople region. The line has been drawn so as to separate Brussa from Turkey, because it is the ancient capital from which, if it were left in the possession of Turkey, there might be launched successive projects of international intrigue that would defeat the purposes for which the Constantinople state is established. It would be far better, from an international standpoint and also from the standpoint of the physical development of the Turkish folk, if their capital were established well within their new borders, say at Konia, at which center both ethnic and historic sentiment. It was once the capital of the Moslems.

Although an alternative Greek area is shown in the Smyrna region, it is not part of this recommendation that it be assigned to Greece. The arguments for such assignment have been scrutinized with great care, and it is felt to be unsafe from every standpoint, commercial, strategic, and political, to give Greece a foothold upon the mainland of Asia Minor. The possession of the Dodecanese puts Greek people, Greek ships and Greek merchants, at the very doors of the new state. To give her a foothold upon the mainland would be to invite immediate trouble. Greece would press her claims for more territory; Turkey would feel that her new boundaries were run so as to give her a great handicap at the very start. The harbor of Smyrna has been for centuries an outlet for the products of the central Anatolian valleys and upland.

The recommended state of Turkey would be one-sixth larger than Italy, and would have a population of about 5,700,000.

23. ARMENIA

1) It is recommended that there be established an Armenian state as delimited on map 20 [omitted].

The Armenian problem is a singularly difficult one from the standpoint of the establishment of new states, because, except for a small area north of Lake Van and in Kars and Erivan, the Armenians are everywhere in the minority. They constitute not more than thirty or thirty-five per cent. of the population.

It is held that the principle of majorities should not apply in this case, because of the conditions under which the Armenian people have lived in the past. They have suffered from every handicap of nature and man; they have been massacred and deported by hundreds of thousands; they have been the subject of international political intrigue; and at this moment, helpless and weak as they are, they are being pressed for the unfavorable settlement of their affairs by big Powers seeking to define spheres of future political and commercial interests. It would be a departure from the principle of fair dealing if at this time their every claim were not heard with patience, and their new state established under conditions that would in some manner right historic wrongs.

As for the non-Armenian elements included within the proposed state, they could be adequately protected by international guarantees, according to the principle invoked in so many other cases of mixed nationalities in highly disputed and critical zones.

The singular configuration of the new state, as defined on the map, is fixed by nature. The Anti-Taurus and Taurus mountains are topographical features of the first rank. They are natural barriers. The boundaries would run for the most part through thinly populated regions. Although remote from the main currents of the world's trade, Armenia's two outlets on the Black Sea and the Mediterranean would ensure that vitalizing contact needed for economic security. Topographically and commercially the Cilician region of Adana belongs to the Armenian highlands, and not to Turkish Anatolia or Syria on either side.

The inclusion of the former Russian provinces of Kars and Erivan, with the sub-districts of Akhalkalki and Akhaltsikh, is determined by the fact that they contain the largest block of Armenian peoples. The delimitation on the map is both ethnographic and topograhic in character, and is based upon the expressed desire of the leaders of the present Armenian Republic in the Caucasus.

To Armenia has been assigned a good harbor at Trebizond, which has the additional advantage of uniting with the Armenians about one-half of the strong minority of Greeks in this area.

2) It is recommended that the Armenian state be placed under the supervision of a mandatory of the League of Nations.

This recommendation is all but axiomatic, because of the inexperience and defects of the population, its mixed character, and its weakness.

24. MESOPOTAMIA

1) It is recommended that there be established a Mesopotamian state.

The Mesopotamian area, as defined on map 20, is a racial unit. There is Arab linguistic unity south of a line drawn from Alexandretta to the Persian border. Above this line live Arabs, Armenians, Turks, Kurds and Assyrians, each group speaking a distinct language. Below this line there is comparatively a much higher degree of unity. It is essential to the development of the great irrigation projects below Baghdad that the headwaters of the Tigris River, and as much of the Euphrates as possible, should be under a single administration. The welfare of the foothills of Kurdistan and of the great steppe region of Mesopotamia is bound up with the irrigable lowlands of the Tigris and Euphrates basin.

To separate the headwater area of the Tigris and Euphrates drainage basins from the irrigated valley floors and lowlands further down-stream would be to create sources of dispute and render doubly difficult the task of establishing a suitable government.

The southern border of the area lies at the edge of the Arabian desert, where new relationships come in and different political treatment.

2) It is recommended that there be applied to the Mesopotamian state the mandatory principle, but no recommendation is

made as to the Power to be selected to carry out this principle.

3) It is recommended that no solution be adopted which would preclude the incorporation of this state in an Arab confederation, if a desire for such incorporation should take actual form in Mesopotamia.

Nothing should be done to preclude the possibility of the future development of an Arab confederation, including Mesopotamia, as an alternate solution which would be desirable.

25. SYRIA

1) It is recommended that there be established a Syrian state.

While Syria belongs to the Arab-speaking world, it has an unusually large European population, close commercial and cultural relations with Europe, a strong Christian element and a sedentary mode of life. It should therefore be separated at the outset from the nomad Arab area.

Its eastern boundary has been drawn with these considerations in mind, and runs just beyond the border of the sown land, so as to include all of the grain-growing regions, of which the Hauran, below Damascus, is the richest. The northern boundary of Syria is quite artificial, and indeed this boundary could not be drawn on racial lines.

The new state would have a population of about 400,000, and would about equal in area the state of Bulgaria.

2) It is recommended that there be applied to the Syrian state the mandatory principle, but no recommendation is made as to the Power to be selected to carry out this principle.

3) It is recommended that no obstacle be interposed against the final incorporation of the Syrian state in an Arab confederation, if the tendency toward this solution should develop in the country.

There is a possibility of the future development of an Arab confederation which will include all of the Arab-speaking portions of the former Turkish Empire. The present strength of this Arab movement is hard to gauge. It would be the best solution from the standpoint of the welfare and development of the Arab states.

26. PALESTINE

1) It is recommended that there be established a separate state of Palestine.

The separation of the Palestinian area from Syria finds justification in the religious experience of mankind. The Jewish and Christian churches were born in Palestine, and Jerusalem was for long years, at different periods, the capital of each. And while the relation of the Mohammedans to Palestine is not so intimate, from the beginnnig they have regarded Jerusalem as a holy place. Only by establishing Palestine as a separate state can justice be done to these great facts.

As drawn upon the map, the new state would control its own source of water power and irrigation, on Mount Hermon in the east to the Jordan; a feature of great importance since the success of the new state would depend upon the possibilities of agricultural development.

2) It is recommended that this state be placed under Great Britain as a mandatory of the League of Nations.

Palestine would obviously need wise and firm guidance. Its population is without political experience, is racially composite, and could easily become distracted by fanaticism and bitter religious differences.

The success of Great Britain in dealing with similar situations, her relation to Egypt, and her administrative achievements since General Allenby freed Palestine from the Turk, all indicate her as the logical mandatory.

3) It is recommended that the Jews be invited to return to Palestine and settle there, being assured by the Conference of all proper assistance in so doing that may be consistent with the protection of the personal (especially the religious) and the property rights of the non-Jewish population, and being further assured that it will be the policy of the League of Nations to recognize Palestine as a Jewish state as soon as it is a Jewish state in fact.

It is right that Palestine should become a Jewish state, if the Jews, being given the full opportunity, make it such. It was the cradle and home of their vital race, which has made large spiritual contributions to mankind, and is the only land in which they can hope to find a home of their own; they being in this last respect unique among significant peoples.

At present, however, the Jews form barely a sixth of the total population of 700,000 in Palestine, and whether they are to form a majority, or even a plurality, of the population in the future state remains uncertain. Palestine, in short, is far from being a Jewish country now. England, as mandatory, can be relied on to give the Jews the privileged position they should have without sacrificing the rights of non-Jews.

4) It is recommended that the holy places and religious rights of all creeds in Palestine be placed under the protection of the League of Nations and its mandatory.

The basis for this recommendation is self-evident.

27. ARABIA

1) It is recommended that the desert portion of the Arabian peninsula, exclusive of the agricultural areas of Syria and of the Euphrates and Tigris valleys, be treated as a separate block.

In regard to this large desert area of Arabia, it is unwise to take decisive action at present. The Kingdom of Hedjaz under the Cherif of Mecca is at the present time the strongest in the group of Arabian tribal states; nevertheless it is not so powerful that a successful single Arab confederation can be built around it. It is only this week that the Hedjaz forces have been able to recapture their own city of Medina.

2) It is recommended that in regard to the present tribal states, numbering over twenty, which exist in the peninsula, no definite action be taken.

The chieftains of the inner desert tribes, especially Ibn Saud, are absolutely opposed to extension on the part of the king of Hedjaz. The sheikhs of Asir and Yemen would look with equal hostility on the consolidation of his power.

3) It is recommended that the area with regard to which no definite action shall be taken be that bounded on the north by the Euphrates River from the bend where it turns southeast to a point just below the town of Hit, and from that point onward by a line which stretches out into the desert, ending at the Persian Gulf below Koweit; and on the west by the Red Sea, the eastern boundary of Palestine, and a line through the desert delimiting the agricultural portions of Syria.

The boundaries of this Arab block, in which no definite action can be taken, are so drawn as to distinguish the desert tribal civilization from the civilization of the sedentary Arabs of the irrigable lands of the Tigris and Euphrates valleys, below Baghdad, and of the fertile and very productive lands of the Syrian Arabs, from Aleppo down to a point below Damascus. In the north the desert tribes must be given access to the Euphrates river from Hit to the northward bend of the river, for the purpose of watering their flocks.

4) It is recommended that the policing of the Red Sea, Indian Ocean, and Persian Gulf Coasts of Arabia, and the border lands behind these, be left to the British Empire.

The Power which understands best how to handle the Arabs is the British Empire. By controlling the coastal areas and the markets along the edge of the desert at which the desert tribes must trade, the British Indian Office has been able to exercise some influence over the inland tribes.

5) It is recommended that in spite of the political prominence of the King of the Hedjaz, he be not aided to establish an artificial and unwelcomed dominion over tribes unwilling to accept his rule.

The King of the Hedjaz and his sons should not receive support in an attempt to establish an artificial domination over tribes of about similar strength. If, however, it can be shown that the movement for Arab unity is natural and real, and that such unity can be developed without the use of force, the movement should be given encouragement and support.

The proposal of the delegates of the King of the Hedjaz that a mixed commission be sent to Syria to learn the actual desires of the Syrians and report to the peace conference, is entirely fair and should receive support.

21. THE ZIONIST ORGANIZATION'S MEMORANDUM TO THE SUPREME COUNCIL AT THE PEACE CONFERENCE
3 February 1919

[David Hunter Miller, *My Diary at the Conference of Paris,* (New York, 1924), vol. 5, pp. 15–29]

The Supreme Council heard the Zionist case on 27 February 1919. In connection therewith the Zionist delegation to the Paris Peace Conference—speaking for the World Zionist organization and its branches in the United States and Russia and for the Jewish community in Palestine—framed a memorandum in the form of draft resolutions, to which were attached explanatory statements and proposals to the "Mandatary" power. Many of the suggestions of the memorandum found their way, after revision, into a draft mandate for Palestine formulated by the Zionist Organization and circulated at the end of March 1919 (text in Miller, *op. cit.*, vol. 7, pp. 369–75) and, after further revision, into the mandatory instrument approved by the Council of the League of Nations (Doc. 38). P. L. Hanna, *British Policy in Palestine,* chap. 3; Esco Foundation, *Palestine,* vol. 1, chap. 3; C. Weizmann, *Trial and Error,* chap. 22; F. E. Manuel, *The Realities of American-Palestine Relations,* chap. 6; J. Cohn, *England und Palästina,* chap. 6; H. F. Frischwasser-Ra'anan, *Frontiers of a Nation,* chap. 5.

The Zionist Organisation respectfully submits the following draft resolutions for the consideration of the Peace Conference:

1. The High Contracting Parties recognise the historic title of the Jewish people to Palestine and the right of the Jews to reconstitute in Palestine their National Home.

2. The boundaries of Palestine shall be as declared in the Schedule annexed hereto.

3. The sovereign possession of Palestine shall be vested in the League of Nations and the Government entrusted to Great Britain as mandatary of the League.

4. (Provision to be inserted relating to the application in Palestine of such of the general conditions attached to mandates as are suitable to the case.)

5. The mandate shall be subject also to the following special conditions:

(I) Palestine shall be placed under such political, administrative and economic conditions as will secure the establishment there of the Jewish National Home and ultimately render possible the creation of an autonomous Commonwealth, it being clearly understood that nothing shall be done which may prejudice the civil and religious rights of existing non-Jewish communities in Palestine or the rights and political status enjoyed by Jews in any other country.

(II) To this end the Mandatary Power shall *inter alia*

(a) Promote Jewish immigration and close settlement on the land, the established rights of the present non-Jewish population being equitably safeguarded.

(b) Accept the co-operation in such measures of a Council representative of the Jews of Palestine and of the world that may be established for the development of the Jewish National Home in Palestine and entrust the organisation of Jewish education to such Council.

(c) On being satisfied that the constitution of such Council precludes the making of private profit, offer to the Council in priority any concession for public works or for the development of natural resources which it may be found desirable to grant.

(III) The Mandatary Power shall encourage the widest measure of self-government for localities practicable in the conditions of the country.

(IV) There shall be for ever the fullest freedom of religious worship for all creeds in Palestine. There shall be no discrimination among the inhabitants with regard to citizenship and civil rights, on the grounds of religion or of race.

(V) (Provision to be inserted relating to the control of the Holy Places).

THE BOUNDARIES OF PALESTINE

SCHEDULE

The boundaries of Palestine shall follow the general lines set out below:

Starting on the North at a point on the Mediterranean Sea in the vicinity of Sidon and following the watersheds of the foothills of the Lebanon as far as JISR EL KARAON, thence to EL BIRE, following the dividing line between the two basins of the WADI EL KORN and the WADI ET TEIM thence in a southerly direction following the dividing line between the Eastern and Western slopes of the HERMON, to the vicinity West of BEIT JENN, thence Eastward following the northern watersheds of the Nahr Mughaniye close to and west of the Hedjaz Railway.

In the East a line close to and West of the Hedjaz Railway terminating in the Gulf of Akaba.

In the South a frontier to be agreed upon with the Egyptian Government.

In the West the Mediterranean Sea.

The details of the delimitations, or any necessary adjustments of detail, shall be settled by a Special Commission on which there shall be Jewish representation.

STATEMENT

The Historic Title

The claims of the Jews with regard to Palestine rest upon the following main considerations:

(1) The land is the historic home of the Jews; there they achieved their greatest development, from that centre, through their agency, there emanated spiritual and moral influences of supreme value to mankind. By violence they were driven from Palestine, and through the ages they have never ceased to cherish the longing and the hope of a return.

(2) In some parts of the world, and particularly in Eastern Europe, the conditions of life of millions of Jews are deplorable. Forming often a congested population, denied the opportunities which would make a healthy development possible, the need of fresh outlets is urgent, both for their own sake and in the interest of the population of other races, among whom they dwell. Palestine would offer one such outlet. To the Jewish masses it is the country above all others in which they would most wish to cast their lot. By the methods of economic development to which we shall refer later, Palestine can be made now as it was in ancient times, the home of a prosperous population many times as numerous as that which now inhabits it.

(3) But Palestine is not large enough to contain more than a proportion of the Jews of the world. The greater part of the fourteen millions or more scattered through all countries must remain in their present localities, and it will doubtless be one of the cares of the Peace Conference to ensure for them, wherever they have been oppressed, as for all peoples, equal rights and humane conditions. A Jewish National Home in Palestine will, however, be of high value to them also. Its influence will permeate the Jewries of the world: it will inspire these millions, hitherto often despairing, with a new hope; it will hold out before their eyes a higher standard; it will help to make them even more useful citizens in the lands in which they dwell.

(4) Such a Palestine would be of value also to the world at large, whose real wealth consists in the healthy diversities of its civilisations.

(5) Lastly the land itself needs redemption. Much of it is left desolate. Its present condition is a standing reproach. Two things are necessary for that redemption—

a stable and enlightened Government, and an addition to the present population which shall be energetic, intelligent, devoted to the country, and backed by the large financial resources that are indispensable for development. Such a population the Jews alone can supply.

Inspired by these ideas, Jewish activities particularly during the last thirty years have been directed to Palestine within the measure that the Turkish administrative system allowed. Some millions of pounds sterling have been spent in the country particularly in the foundation of Jewish agricultural settlements. Those settlements have been for the most part highly successful.

With enterprise and skill the Jews have adopted modern scientific methods and have shown themselves to be capable agriculturalists. Hebrew has been revived as a living language, it is the medium of instruction in the schools and the tongue is in daily use among the rising generation. The foundations of a Jewish University have been laid at Jerusalem and considerable funds have been contributed for the creation of its building and for its endowment. Since the British occupation, the Zionist Organisation has expended in Palestine approximately £50,000 a month upon relief, education and sanitation. To promote the future development of the country great sums will be needed for drainage, irrigation, roads, railways, harbours and public works of all kinds, as well as for land settlement and house building. Assuming a political settlement under which the establishment of a Jewish National Home in Palestine is assured the Jews of the world will make every effort to provide the vast sums of money that will be needed. . . .

[Here follow a recital of the Balfour Declaration and of its endorsement by the French Foreign Minister and reference to support of Zionism and the Balfour Declaration by other allied governments.]

GREAT BRITAIN AS MANDATARY OF THE LEAGUE OF NATIONS

We ask that Great Britain shall act as Mandatary of the League of Nations for Palestine. The selection of Great Britain as Mandatary is urged on the ground that this is the wish of the Jews of the world and the League of Nations in selecting a Mandatary will follow as far as possible, the popular wish of the people concerned.

The preference on the part of the Jews for a British Trusteeship is unquestionably the result of the peculiar relationship of England to the Jewish Palestinian problem. The return of the Jews to Zion has not only been a remarkable feature in English literature, but in the domain of statecraft it has played its part, beginning with the readmission of the Jews under Cromwell. It manifested itself particularly in the 19th century in the instructions given to British Consular representatives in the Orient after the Damascus Incident; in the various Jewish Palestinian projects suggested by English non-Jews prior to 1881; in the letters of endorsement and support given by members of the Royal Family and Officers of the Government to Lawrence Oliphant and finally, in the three consecutive acts which definitely associated Great Britain with Zionism in the minds of the Jews viz.—the El Arish offer in 1901; the East African offer in 1903, and lastly the British Declaration in favour of a Jewish National Home in Palestine in 1917. Moreover, the Jews who have gained political experience in many lands under a great variety of governmental systems, whole-heartedly appreciate the advanced and liberal policies adopted by Great Britain in her modern colonial administration. . . .

[Here follows a recital of the selection of Great Britain as mandatory power by the American Jewish Congress and a conference of Palestine Jews at Jaffa.]

BOUNDARIES

The boundaries above outlined are what we consider essential for the necessary economic foundation of the country. Palestine must have its natural outlets to the seas and the control of its rivers and their headwaters. The boundaries are sketched with the general economic needs and historic traditions of the country in mind, factors which necessarily must also be considered by the Special Commission in fixing the definite boundary lines. This Commission will bear in mind that it is highly desirable, in the interests of economical administration that the geographical area of Palestine should be as large as possible so that it may eventually contain a large and thriving population which could more easily bear the burdens of modern civilised government than a small country with a necessary limitation of inhabitants.

The economic life of Palestine, like that of every other semi-arid country depends on the available water supply. It is, therefore, of vital importance not only to secure all water resources already feeding the country, but also to be able to conserve and control them at their sources.

The Hermon is Palestine's real "Father of Waters" and cannot be severed from it without striking at the very root of its economic life. The Hermon not only needs reafforestation but also other works before it can again adequately serve as the water reservoir of the country. It must therefore be wholly under the control of those who will most willingly as well as most adequately restore it to its maximum utility. Some international arrangement must be made whereby the riparian rights of the people dwelling south of the Litani River may be fully protected. Properly cared for these head waters can be made to serve in the development of the Lebanon as well as of Palestine.

The fertile plains east of the Jordan, since the earliest Biblical times, have been linked economically and politically with the land west of the Jordan. The country which is now very sparsely populated, in Roman times supported a great population. It could now serve admirably for colonisation on a large scale. A just regard for the economic needs of Palestine and Arabia demands that free access to the Hedjaz Railway throughout its length be accorded both Governments.

An intensive development of the agriculture and other opportunities of Transjordania make it imperative that Palestine shall have access to the Red Sea and an opportunity of developing good harbours on the Gulf of Akaba. Akaba, it will be recalled, was the terminus of an important trade route of Palestine from the days of Solomon onwards. The ports developed in the Gulf of Akaba should be free ports through which the commerce of the Hinterland may pass on the same principle which guides us in suggesting that free access be given to the Hedjaz Railway.

PROPOSALS TO THE MANDATARY POWER

In connection with the Government to be set up by the Mandatary of the League of Nations until such time as the people of Palestine shall be prepared to undertake the establishment of representative and responsible Government proposals will be made in due course to the Mandatary Power to the following effect:

1. In any instrument establishing the constitution of Palestine the Declarations of the Peace Conference shall be recited as forming an integral part of that constitution.

2. The Jewish people shall be entitled to fair representation in the executive and legislative bodies and in the selection of public and civil servants. In giving such representation the Mandatary Power shall consult the Jewish Council hereinafter mentioned.

Neither law nor custom shall preclude the appointment of a citizen of Palestine as chief of the executive.

3. That in encouraging the self government of localities the Mandatary Power shall secure the maintenance by local communities of proper standards of administration in matters of education, communal, or regional activities. In granting or enlarging local autonomy regard shall be had to the readiness and ability of the community to attain such standards. Local autonomous communities shall be empowered and encouraged to combine and cooperate for common purposes.

4. Education without distinction of race shall be assisted from public funds.

5. Hebrew shall be one of the official languages of Palestine and shall be employed in all documents, decrees and an-

nouncements and on all stamps, coins, and notes issued by the Government.

6. The Jewish Sabbath and Holy Days shall be recognised as legal days of rest.

7. All inhabitants continuing to reside in Palestine who on the day of , 19 , have their domicile in Palestine, except those who elect in writing within six months from such date to retain their foreign citizenship, shall become citizens of Palestine, and they and all persons in Palestine or naturalised under the laws of Palestine after the day of , 19 , shall be citizens thereof and entitled to the protection of the Mandatary Power on behalf of the Government of Palestine.

LAND COMMISSION

Recognising that the general progress of Palestine must begin with the reform of the conditions governing land tenure and settlement, the Mandatary Power shall appoint a Commission (upon which the Jewish Council shall have representation) with power:

(a) To make survey of the land and to schedule all lands that may be made available for close settlement, intensive cultivation and public use.

(b) To propose measures for determining and registering titles of ownership of land.

(c) To propose measures for supervising transactions in land with a view of preventing land speculation.

(d) To propose measures for the close settlement, intensive cultivation and public use of land, where necessary by compulsory purchase at a fair pre-war price and further by making available all waste lands unoccupied and inadequately cultivated lands or lands without legal owners, and state lands.

(e) To propose measures for the taxation and the tenure of land and in general any progressive measures in harmony with the policy of making the land available for close settlement and intensive cultivation.

(f) To propose measures whereby the Jewish Council may take over all lands available for close settlement and intensive cultivation.

(g) In all such measures the established rights of the present population shall be equitably safeguarded.

THE JEWISH COUNCIL FOR PALESTINE

1. A Jewish Council for Palestine shall be elected by a Jewish Congress representative of the Jews of Palestine and of the entire world, which shall be convoked in Jerusalem on or before the First day of January, 1920, or as soon thereafter as possible, by the Provisional Jewish Council hereinafter mentioned.

The Jewish Congress shall determine its functions as well as the constitution and functions of the Jewish Council in conformity with the purpose and spirit of the Declarations of the Peace Conference and of the powers conferred by the mandatary power upon the Jewish Council.

2. The Jewish Council shall be recognised as a legal entity and shall have power:

(a) To co-operate and consult with and to assist the Government of Palestine in any and all matters affecting the Jewish people in Palestine and in all such cases to be and to act as the representative of the Jewish people.

(b) To participate in the development and administration of immigration, close land settlement, credit facilities, public works, services, and enterprises, and every other form of activity conducive to the development of the country. The organisation of Jewish education to be entrusted to such Council.

(c) To acquire and hold Real Estate.

(d) To acquire and exercise concessions for public works and the development of natural resources.

(e) With the consent of the Jewish inhabitants concerned or their accredited representatives, to assess such inhabitants for the purpose of stimulating and maintaining education, communal, charitable and other public institutions (including the Jewish Council) and other activities primarily concerned with the welfare of the Jewish people in Palestine.

(f) With the approval of the Mandatary Power and upon such terms and conditions as the Mandatary Power may prescribe, to administer the immigration laws of Palestine in so far as they affect Jewish immigration.
(g) With the approval of the Mandatary Power, to issue bonds, debentures, or other obligations, the proceeds of any or all of which to be expended by the Jewish Council for the benefit of the Jewish people or for the development of Palestine.
(h) The Jewish Council shall hold all of its property and income in trust for the benefit of the Jewish people.

3. A provisional Jewish Council of representatives of the Zionist Organisation, of the Jewish population in Palestine, and of such other approved Jewish organisations as are willing to cooperate in the development of a Jewish Palestine shall be formed forthwith by the Zionist Organisation. Such Provisional Jewish Council shall exercise all of the powers and perform all of the duties of the Jewish Council until such time as the Jewish Council shall be formally constituted by the Jewish Congress.

4. Finally when in the opinion of the Mandatary Power, the inhabitants of Palestine shall be able to undertake the establishment of Representative and Responsible Government, such steps shall be taken as will permit the establishment of such government through the exercise of a democratic franchise, without regard to race or faith; and the inhabitants of Palestine under such government, shall continue to enjoy equal civil and political rights as citizens irrespective of race or faith. . . .

[Here follows a description of the Zionist Organization.]

22. SUMMARY RECORD OF A SECRET MEETING OF THE SUPREME COUNCIL AT PARIS TO CONSIDER THE SYKES-PICOT AGREEMENT
20 March 1919

[*Foreign Relations of the United States: The Paris Peace Conference, 1919,* vol. 5 (Washington, 1944), pp. 1–14]

Until the collapse of the tsarist regime in mid-March 1917, the allied war effort in the Near and Middle East was an Anglo-Russian effort, with the United Kingdom assuming the lion's share of the burden. Thereafter allied military responsibilities in the region devolved wholly upon the British Empire. This is merely one way of saying that Britain's stake in the Near and Middle East substantially overtopped that of all its allies combined. Further supporting evidence, if it were needed, could be found in the fact that the United Kingdom formed the lowest common denominator in all the major wartime agreements and engagements on the area either among the allied powers or with the Arabs and the Zionists. Even as the victorious allies assembled in Paris to conclude an enduring peace, Britain and France had begun to clash over Near and Middle East objectives. Britain's elastic attitude toward the Sykes-Picot agreement (Doc. 10) sprang primarily from the need in London to reconcile the differences not only between England and France but within the British government between the Foreign and India Offices. Besides, Britain's separate engagements with Arabs and Jews were already being interpreted as contradictory. But France, as the basis for its claims in Ottoman Asia, adopted a rigid attitude toward the Sykes-Picot formula, except where subsequently modified by Anglo-French accord, as in the transfer of the Mosul district to the British sphere and acquiescence in a British administration for Palestine. In this connection France was determined to establish a direct administration in Zone A (Syria) as well as the Blue Zone (Lebanon, Syrian coast and Cilicia). The British resisted the French demand, and the consequent Anglo-French dispute came to a head at a secret meeting of the Big Four on 20 March 1919. The summary record of the meeting throws into clear light the respective positions of Britain, France and the United States. The French case was presented by the Foreign Minister, Stephen Jean Marie Pichon. H. N. Howard, *Partition of Turkey,* chap. 7; R. S. Baker, *Woodrow Wilson and World Settlement,* vol. 1, chap. 4, vol. 2, chap. 33; D. Lloyd George, *Truth about the Peace Treaties,* vol. 2, chap. 22; H. H.

Cumming, *Franco-British Rivalry in the Post-War Near East,* chap. 8.

M. Clemenceau suggested that M. Pichon should open the discussion.

M. Pichon began by explaining that the origin of this question was the agreement of May 1916 (Sykes-Picot) concluded between Great Britain and France in regard to Mesopotamia, Syria, and the adjoining regions. This agreement had two objects. First, to detach the Arabs from the Turks; second, to decide the claims of Great Britain and France. He then proceeded to explain the principles of the dispositions made on a map. The agreement fixed a zone coloured blue within which France would exercise direct administration, and a zone coloured red in which England would exercise direct administration. In addition, there was a zone coloured white enclosed by a blue line within which France should exercise indirect administration, known as zone A. and a corresponding zone enclosed in a red line within which Great Britain would exercise indirect administration (Zone B). At this stage it was unnecessary to say anything of the subsequent agreement with Italy. Within the A. and B. zones it was intended to favour the creation of an independent Arab State or Confederation of Arab States. In area A. France, and [in] area B. Great Britain should alone supply advisers or foreign functionaries at the request of the Arab State or Confederation of Arab States. In addition Great Britain was to be accorded the ports of Haifa and Acre. Haifa was to be a free port as regards the trade of France, and there was to be freedom of transit for French goods through Haifa by the British railway, for which facilities were to be given. Alexandretta, which fell in the blue area, was to be a free port as regards the trade of the British Empire, and there was to be freedom of traffic for British goods through Alexandretta by railway through the blue area. In addition, there were certain customs and political stipulations. Such were the general dispositions of 1916 which he emphasised were designed:—

(1) To favour the establishment of an Arab State or Confederation of States and to detach the Arabs from Turkey:

and

(2) To decide between the claims of Great Britain and France.

The above agreement confirmed, by an exchange of Notes between M. Paul Cambon and Sir Edward Grey (Lord Grey), declarations which had been made by Great Britain as early as 1912, in which Great Britain had disinterested herself and recognised the rights of France in Syria, subject only to Great Britain's insistence on keeping untouched her economic rights. In short, Great Britain had declared she had no political claims, but that her economic rights must remain intact in Syria.

Since the conclusion of the Agreement of 1916 there had been a long further correspondence and an exchange of many Notes between France and Great Britain concerning particularly various local interests. This brought us to the most recent period in which the French made, he would not say a protest against, but a series of observations in regard to, the British attitude in Syria. The whole series of these had recently been handed by the President of the Council to Lord Milner.

The incidents referred to in this correspondence were chiefly due to the disproportion in the relative contingents furnished by Great Britain and France to the campaign in Syria. It had only been possible for France to send a very small number of troops to Syria in consequence of the large demands made on her for the protection of French soil and to the prominent part played by her armies in Salonica. Great Britain, however, had interested herself far more in the Turkish campaigns, and had sent many troops which had been led by General Allenby. From that disproportion there resulted a great many incidents. Eventually, the President of the Council had thought it right to bring them before the British Government with a view to putting an end to the faction and the friction which now existed.

From all the declarations made by the British and French Governments he only wanted to quote one, namely, that of

November 9, 1918. This was particularly important as showing the disinterested attitude of both Governments towards the Arabs. This declaration had been communicated shortly after its issue by the French Ambassador in Washington to President Wilson.

Mr. Lloyd George interpolated at this point that this announcement, which was the latest expression of policy by the two Governments, was more important than all the old agreements.

M. Pichon then read the declaration of November 9, 1918 [Doc. 15(4)]. . . .

As the difficulties between the two Governments continued, and as the French Government particularly did not wish them to reach a point where ultimate agreement would be compromised, the President of the Council, on his visit to London in December 1918, had asked Mr. Lloyd George to confirm the agreement between the two countries. Mr. Lloyd George had replied that he saw no difficulty about the rights of France in Syria and Cilicia, but he made demands for certain places which he thought should be included in the British zone, and which, under the 1916 agreement, were in the French zone of influence, namely, Mosul. He also asked for Palestine. M. Clemenceau had, on his return to Paris, been desirous that this suggestion should be examined in the most favourable spirit. In consequence, he had ordered a scheme of agreement to be prepared, with the inclusion of Mosul in the British zone of influence, and this had been handed to the British Government on the 15th February, 1919. The letter which accompanied this proposal had asked for a recognition of the historic and traditional case for including the regions claimed in the French zone. It had pointed out that there was no Government in the world which had such a position as France in the regions claimed. It had given an exposition of the historic rights of France dating from the time of Louis XIV. M. Pichon continued by pointing out that French intervention in Syria had been frequent, the last instance being the case of the expedition organised in Syria and Lebanon in 1860, which had resulted in the establishment of the status of the Lebanon. France, he pointed out, had a great number of hospitals in Syria. There were a great number of schools in many villages, and some 50,000 children were educated in French primary schools. There were also a number of secondary schools and one great university in Beyrout. Moreover, the railway system of Syria was French, and included the Beyrout to Damascus line, and the Tripoli-Homs line, which latter it was proposed to prolong to the Euphrates and to unite with the Bagdad system. Altogether it was contemplated to have a system of 1,233 kilometres, of which 683 kilometres had already been constructed. Beyrout was entirely a French port. The gas and electricity works were French, and the same applied to the lighting along the coast. This was not the limit of French enterprise, for France had perfected the agriculture and the viticulture of Syria and had established many factories. No other country had anything like so complete a development in these regions. Hence, France could not abandon her rights. Moreover, France strongly protested against any idea of dividing Syria. Syria had geographical and historic unity. The French Government frankly avowed that they did not want the responsibility of administering Palestine, though they would prefer to see it under an international administration. What they asked was:—

(1) That the whole Syrian region should be treated as a unit:

and

(2) That France should become the mandatory of the League of Nations of this region.

On January 30 of this year Mr. Lloyd George had urged the Conference to reconsider the distribution of troops in Turkey and the Caucasus with the object of lightening the heavy burden which fell on Great Britain. As a result, the Military Representatives had been asked to prepare a plan. The scheme of the Military Representatives provided for:—

The occupation by France of Syria and Cilicia, with 2 divisions and 1 cavalry brigade:

The occupation by Great Britain of Mesopotamia, including Mosul, by 2 divisions and 1 cavalry brigade:

The occupation by Italy of the Caucasus and Konia.

The economy which Great Britain would achieve by this plan would have amounted to 10 divisions of infantry and 4 divisions of cavalry. The plan of the Military Representatives had been placed on the Agenda Paper of the Conference, but at Lord Milner's request the subject had been adjourned and had never been discussed.

About this time a conversaton had taken place between M. Clemenceau and M. Pichon and Mr. Lloyd George and Mr. Balfour, as a result of which Sir Maurice Hankey had handed M. Pichon a map containing a British counter proposal to the French proposal of February 15. This scheme provided for a great limitation of the territory to come under French influence, both on the east and on the south as regards the Jebel Druse. The French Government was quite unable to take this project into consideration. Recently Lord Milner had left a map with M. Clemenceau containing yet another project, which M. Pichon proceeded to explain, and which, he added, greatly circumscribed the French area. It was evident that the French Government could not look at this scheme either, even though they had the greatest desire to reach an agreement. No one felt more deeply than he what Great Britain and France owed to each other, and no one had a greater desire to reach an agreement. It was, however, quite impossible to accept a proposal such as that put forward by Lord Milner. It would be absolutely indefensible in the Chamber. It was enough for the Chamber to know that the Government were in negotiation with Great Britain for the handing over of Mosul to create a movement that had resulted in a proposal in the Budget Committee for a diminution of credits for Syria. This had not been a mere budget trick, but represented a real movement of public opinion. French opinion would not admit that France could be even partly excluded after the sacrifices she had made in the War, even if she had not been able to play a great part in the Syrian campaign. In consequence, the minimum that France could accept was what had been put forward in the French Government's Note to Mr. Lloyd George, the object of which had been to give satisfaction to his desire for the inclusion of Mosul in the British zone.

Mr. Lloyd George said that M. Pichon had opened as though the question of the mandate for Syria was one between Great Britain and France. There was, in fact, no such question so far as Great Britain was concerned. He wished to say at once that just as we had disinterested ourselves in 1912, so we now disinterested ourselves in 1919. If the Conference asked us to take Syria, we should reply in the negative. The British Government had definitely decided this because otherwise it would be said afterwards in France that they had created disturbances in order to keep the French out. Hence, the British Government definitely intended to have nothing to do with Syria. The question of the extent to which Great Britain and France were concerned was cleared up in the interview he had had with M. Clemenceau in London, and at which he had said that he wanted Mosul with the adjacent regions and Palestine.

As there was no question between France and Great Britain in regard to Syria, we could examine the question in as disinterested a spirit as we could a Carpathian boundary to be decided in accordance with the general principles accepted by the Conference. He wished to make this clear before General Allenby said what he had to say. In regard to Mosul, he wished to acknowledge the cordial spirit in which M. Pichon had met our desires.

But if there was a French public opinion there was also a British public opinion, and it must be remembered that the whole burden of the Syrian campaign had fallen upon Great Britain. The number of French troops taking part in the campaign had been so small as to make no difference. Sometimes they had been helpful, but not on all occasions. The British Empire and India had maintained from 900,000 to 1,000,000 troops in Turkey and the Caucasus. Their casualties had amounted to 125,000, the campaign had cost hundreds of millions of pounds. He himself had done his best to induce M. Clemenceau's predecessors to take part in the campaign. He had also pressed Marshal Foch on the subject, and to this day he had in his possession a rough plan drawn up by Marshal Foch during an air raid at Boulogne. He had begged the French Government to cooperate, and had pointed out to them that it would enable them to occupy Syria, although, at the time, the British troops had not yet occupied Gaza. This had occurred in 1917 and 1918, at a time when the heaviest casualties in France also were being incurred by British troops. From that time onwards most of the heavy and continuous fighting in France had been done by British troops, although Marshal Pétain had made a number of valuable smaller attacks. This was one of the reasons why he had felt justified in asking Marshal Foch for troops. He had referred to this in order to show that the reason we had fought so hard in Palestine was not because we had not been fighting in France. M. Pichon seemed to think that we were departing from the 1916 agreement in other respects, as well as in respect to Mosul and Palestine. In fact, we were not. M. Pichon had omitted in his lucid statement to explain that the blue area in which France was "allowed to establish such direct or indirect administration or control as they may desire and as they may think fit to arrange with the Arab State or Confederation of Arab States" did not include Damascus, Homs, Hama, or Aleppo. In area A. France was "prepared to recognise and uphold an independent Arab State or Confederation of Arab States . . . under the suzerainty of an Arab Chief." Also in area A. France would "have priority of right of enterprise and local loans . . . and . . . "shall alone supply advisers or foreign functionaries at the request of the Arab State or Confederation of Arab States." Was France prepared to accept that? This, however, was not a question between Great Britain and France. It was a question between France and an agreement which we had signed with King Hussein.

(At this point M. Orlando and General Diaz entered).

M. Pichon said he wished to say one word. In the new arrangements which were contemplated no direct administration whatsoever was claimed by France. Since the Agreement of 1916, the whole mandatory system had been adopted. If a mandate were granted by the League of Nations over these territories, all that he asked was that France should have that part put aside for her.

Mr. Lloyd George said that we could not do that. The League of Nations could not be used for putting aside our bargain with King Hussein. He asked if M. Pichon intended to occupy Damascus with French troops? If he did, it would clearly be a violation of the Treaty with the Arabs.

M. Pichon said that France had no convention with King Hussein.

Mr. Lloyd George said that the whole of the agreement of 1916 (Sykes-Picot), was based on a letter from Sir Henry McMahon to King Hussein from which he quoted [Doc. 8(2)]. . . .

M. Pichon said that this undertaking had been made by Great Britain (*Angleterre*) alone. France had never seen it until a few weeks before when Sir Maurice Hankey had handed him a copy.

Mr. Lloyd George said the agreement might have been made by England (*Angleterre*) alone, but it was England (*Angleterre*) who had organised the whole of the Syrian campaign. There would have been no question of Syria but for England (*Angleterre*). Great Britain had put from 900,000 to 1,000,000 men in the field against Turkey, but Arab help had been essential; that was a point on which General Allenby could speak.

General Allenby said it had been invaluable.

Mr. Lloyd George, continuing, said that it was on the basis of the above quoted letter that King Hussein had put all his resources into the field which had helped us most materially to win the victory. France had for practical purposes accepted our undertaking to King Hussein in signing the 1916 agreement. This had not been M.

Pichon, but his predecessors. He was bound to say that if the British Government now agreed that Damascus, Homs, Hama, and Aleppo should be included in the sphere of direct French influence, they would be breaking faith with the Arabs, and they could not face this. He was particularly anxious for M. Clemenceau to follow this. The agreement of 1916 had been signed subsequent to the letter to King Hussein. In the following extract from the agreement of 1916 France recognised Arab independence:—

"It is accordingly understood between the French and British Governments:—

(1) That France and Great Britain are prepared to recognise and uphold an independent Arab State or Confederation of Arab States in the areas A. and B. marked on the annexed map under the suzerainty of an Arab Chief."

Hence, France, by this act, practically recognised our agreement with King Hussein by excluding Damascus, Homs, Hama, and Aleppo from the blue zone of direct administration, for the map attached to the agreement showed that Damascus, Homs, Hama, and Aleppo were included, not in the zone of direct administration, but in the independent Arab State.

M. Pichon said that this had never been contested, but how could France be bound by an agreement the very existence of which was unknown to her at the time when the 1916 agreement was signed? In the 1916 agreement France had not in any way recognised the Hedjaz. She had undertaken to uphold "an independent Arab State or Confederation of Arab States," but not the King of the Hedjaz. If France was promised a mandate for Syria, she would undertake to do nothing except in agreement with the Arab State or Confederation of States. This is the role which France demanded in Syria. If Great Britain would only promise her good offices, he believed that France could reach an understanding with Feisal.

President Wilson said that he would now seek to establish his place in the Conference. Up to the present he had had none. He could only be here, like his colleague M. Orlando, as one of the representatives assembled to establish the peace of the world. This was his only interest, although, of course, he was a friend of both parties to the controversy. He was not indifferent to the understanding which had been reached between the British and French Governments, and was interested to know about the undertakings to King Hussein and the 1916 agreement, but it was not permissible for him to express an opinion thereon. (He would, however, like to point out that one of the parties to the 1916 agreement had been Russia, and Russia had now disappeared. Hence, the partnership of interest had been dissolved, since one of the parties had gone out. This seemed to him to alter the basis of the agreement. (The point of view of the United States of America was, however, indifferent to the claims both of Great Britain and France over peoples unless those peoples wanted them.) One of the fundamental principles to which the United States of America adhered was the consent of the governed. This was ingrained in the United States of America thought. Hence, the only idea from the United States of America point of view was as to whether France would be agreeable to the Syrians. The same applied as to whether Great Britain would be agreeable to the inhabitants of Mesopotamia. (It might not be his business, but if the question was made his business, owing to the fact that it was brought before the Conference, the only way to deal with it was to discover the desires of the population of these regions.) He recalled that, in the Council of Ten, Resolutions had been adopted in regard to mandatories, and they contained a very carefully thought out graduation of different stages of mandate according to the civilisation of the peoples concerned. One of the elements in those mandates was the desire of the people over whom the mandate was to be exercised. The present controversy broadened out into very important questions. Cilicia, for example, from its geographical position, cut Armenia off from the Mediterranean. If there was one mandatory in the south, and another in the north of Armenia, there would be a great danger of friction, since the troublesome population lived in the south. Hence, the controversy broadened into a case affecting the peace of the whole world in this region. He hoped, therefore, that the question would be discussed from this point of view. If this were agreed to, he hoped that he might ask General Allenby certain questions. If the participation of M. Orlando and himself were recognised as a matter of right and not of courtesy, the question he wanted to know was whether the undertaking to King Hussein, and the 1916 agreement, provided an arrangement which would work. If not, and you asked his opinion, he would reply that we ought to ask what is the opinion of the people in the part of the world concerned. He was told that, if France insisted on occupying Damascus and Aleppo, there would be instant war. Feisal had said that he could not say how many men he had had in the field at one time, as it had been a fluctuating figure, but from first to last he had probably had 100,000 men.

General Allenby said that he had never had so many at one time.

President Wilson said that, nevertheless, from first to last France would have to count on having 100,000 troops against her. This would mean that France must send a large number of troops. He was greatly concerned in a fight between friends, since he was the friend of France and the friend of Feisal. He was very concerned to know if a "scrap" was developing. Hence, he asked that it might be taken for granted that this question was on the Council table, since it was one of interest to the peace of the world, and that it was not merely a question of agreement between France and Great Britain. The Turkish Empire at the present time was as much in solution as though it were made of quicksilver. Austria, at any rate, had been broken into pieces, and the pieces remained, but the Turkish Empire was in complete solution. The Councils of the world would have to take care of it. For his part, he was quite disinterested, since the United States of America did not want anything in Turkey. They would be only too delighted if France and Great Britain would undertake the responsibility. Lately, however, it had been put to him that he must approach his own people on this matter, and he intended to try, although it would mean some very good talking on his part. He admitted that the United States of America must take the responsibilities, as well as the benefits, of the League of Nations. Nevertheless, there was great antipathy in the United States of America to the assumption of these responsibilities. Even the Philippines were regarded as something hot in the hand that they would like to drop. If we said to the French Government "Occupy this region," What would happen? He had a method to propose of finding out, which he would develop later.

Mr. Lloyd George suggested that General Allenby should be questioned at this point.

President Wilson asked the following question:—

If before we arrive at a permanent settlement under the League of Nations we invite France to occupy the region of Syria, even as narrowly defined, what would the result be?

General Allenby said there would be the strongest possible opposition by the whole of the Moslems, and especially by the Arabs. Shortly after the capture of Damascus, Feisal had been allowed to occupy and administer the city. He had said that he would like to be helped in the administration. A little later, after the setting up of the military administration in these regions, General Allenby had put French administrators in the blue area. When they arrived Amir Feisal had said that he could not retain the command of the Arab Army if France occupied the ports. He had said that it meant that he was occupying a house without a door, and it would be said that he had broken faith with the Arab nation. Feisal had originally asked if he could occupy Beyrout and the ports. General Allenby had replied in the affirmative, but had told him that he must withdraw when the Allied Armies came along, and he had done so. To Feisal's protests against the occupation by the French of places in the blue zone, General Allenby had replied that he himself was in charge of the administration, as Commander-in-Chief; and that the French officers appointed as administrators must be regarded not as French officers, but as Allied military officers. Feisal had then said that he would admit it for the present, but would it last for ever? General Allenby had replied that the League of Nations intended to give the small nations the right of self-determination. Feisal had insisted that "if put under French control" he would oppose to the uttermost. General Allenby had replied that at present there was no French control, but only the control of the Allies, and that eventually Feisal's rights would be considered. Soon afterwards he had visited Beyrout, and there and in other places deputations had come to protest against the French administration. These had included various Christians, Orthodox and Protestants, as well as Mussulmans. General Allenby had again replied that it was not a French administration, but merely officers put in by himself as Allied Commander-in-Chief. Every time he had been in that country he had found the greatest opposition to French administration. He had done his utmost to make a *rapprochement* among the Arabs and the French, but without success. The French liaison officers did not get on well with the Arabs. M. Picot had been with him to Damascus and Aleppo and was perfectly conversant with the situation. M. Picot would say that General Allenby had done his best to create good feeling. Lately, Sir Mark Sykes had been to Beyrout, Aleppo, and Damascus with M. Picot and had done his best. Nevertheless, the misunderstanding continued. If the French were given a mandate in Syria, there would be serious trouble and probably war. If Feisal undertook the direction of operations there might be a huge war covering the whole area, and the Arabs of the Hedjaz would join. This would necessitate the employment of a very large force. This would probably involve Great Britain also if they were in Palestine. It might even involve them in Egypt, and the consequences would be incalculable.

He had gone with M. Picot to Damascus and had seen there Ali Riza el Rikaby Pasha, the Governor of the territory to the east of Damascus. The administration had not been doing well. There was practically no Budget, and it had been necessary to give him advisers. General Allenby had given him two British advisers, Majors Cornwallis and Stirling. M. Picot had subsequently sent a very good man named Captain Cousse, to replace a liaison officer (Captain Mercier) who had been there before who had not got on with the Arabs because he had stood too much on his dignity. Even Captain Cousse, however, had not been able to get on well. Afterwards, General Allenby had sent a British financial expert, and had invited M. Picot to send a French financial expert. The British adviser, Colonel Graves, had cooperated with M. Moulin, the French adviser. They reported very badly on the finance. There had practically been no Budget. Then General Allenby had withdrawn Colonel Graves. M. Moulin was still there, but was meeting great difficulties owing to Ali Riza el Rikaby's dislike of the French administration. General Allenby had visited Damascus with M. Picot and had there interviewed Riza el Rikaby Pasha. General Allenby produced at the Conference a document containing the gist of the communication made by him to Riza el Rikaby Pasha. A copy of this document in Arabic and English had been left with Riza el Rikaby Pasha.

In reply to Mr. Lloyd George he said that at Damascus there was a brigade of infantry and two regiments of cavalry. The Sherifian troops were only used for police purposes, since the Sherifian Army was still in process of formation.

(At this point there was an adjournment).

President Wilson suggested that the fittest men that could be obtained should be selected to form an Inter-Allied Commission to go to Syria, extending their inquiries, if they led them, beyond the confines of Syria. Their object should be to elucidate the state of opinion and the soil to be worked on by any mandatory. They should be asked to come back and tell the Conference what they found with regard to these matters. He made this suggestion, not because he lacked confidence in the experts whose views he had heard, such as Dr. Howard Bliss and General Allenby. These, however, had been involved in some way with the population, with special objects either educational or military. If we were to send a Commission of men with no previous contact with Syria, it would, at any rate, convince the world that the Conference had tried to do all it could to find the most scientific basis possible for a settlement. The Commission should be composed of an equal number of French, British, Italian and American representatives. He would send it with carte blanche to tell the facts as they found them.

M. Clemenceau said he adhered in principle to an inquiry, but it was necessary to have certain guarantees. The inquiry must not confine itself to Syria. Mandates were required for Palestine, Mesopotamia, and Armenia, and other parts of the Turkish Empire as well as Syria. The peoples of these districts were not isolated. They were all connected by historical and religious and other links, including mutual feuds and old quarrels existed between all of them. Without contesting what General Allenby had said, he wished it to be recorded, if there were a procès-verbal, that many Syrians were not Arab, and that if the Syrians were put under the Arabs they would revolt. He knew quite well the great share taken by Feisal in the Syrian campaign, and he thought that the British were also a little afraid of it. The whole inquiry would be an extremely delicate one. Orientals were very timid and afraid to say what was at the back of their minds. It was very difficult to get the real feelings of the people. It was very important, therefore, that the inquiry should not be merely superficial. Hence, he would ask for twenty-four hours of reflection before setting up the Commission. He might like to send some French Arabs there, as Feisal only represented one side of the Arab race. Moreover, Feisal was practically a soldier of England. That was a fact that all the world knew. He said he would revolt if the French were at Damascus, but, as a matter of fact, French artillery had recently been sent there and had been received quite well. He had made every effort to bring himself to agree with the principles propounded by President Wilson, but something must be said for the historical claims and for the efforts that nations had made in different regions. For example, insistence on an Arab outlet to the sea would destroy the claim of one nation in that part of the world. The Members of the Commission must be very carefully selected, and they must inquire into every Turkish mandate. Subject to these provisions he was prepared to accept President Wilson's proposal in principle.

Mr. Lloyd George said he had no objection to an inquiry into Palestine and Mesopotamia, which were the regions in which the British Empire were principally concerned. Neither would he object to an inquiry into Armenia, in which they were not so closely concerned.

President Wilson said he saw advantages in a unified inquiry into Turkish mandates.

Mr. Lloyd George said if this extension was to be given to the Commission it was essential it should get to work at once, as the burden of military forces in Turkey fell mainly on the British.

Mr. Balfour said that he felt these proposals might postpone the making of peace.

President Wilson said this was not so. For the purposes of peace all that was necessary to tell Turkey was that she would have nothing.

Mr. Lloyd George said that Turkey was entitled to know who would be the mandatory for Turkish territory.

President Wilson said it was rather that they ought to know how much was to remain Turkish.

Mr. Lloyd George said that the question of who was to be mandatory of Anatolia would make all the difference for the arrangements for Turkey.

President Wilson said that Turkey was entitled to know if she was to have territory of her own, and that other parts of Turkey were to be placed under the League of Nations. Subsequently she would be informed who would be her next-door neighbour.

Mr. Lloyd George said he supposed that

if the evidence were so overwhelming that, for example, the British Empire was ruled out of Mesopotamia they would be free to consider whether they could take a mandate elsewhere in Turkey?

President Wilson said this was an administrative matter and not one of sovereignty. Turkey was entitled to knowledge on all questions affecting the sovereignty.

M. Pichon suggested that, in order to avoid delay, the Commission might divide into Sub-Commissions working in different sections.

Mr. Balfour asked whether it would be wise to include Western Anatolia in the purview of the Commission. Constantinople was mainly a military question—(President Wilson said a strategic question)—but south of the region which went with Constantinople came regions to which the Greeks laid claim.

Mr. Lloyd George said there was no suggestion that the Commission was to travel beyond Armenia.

At Mr. Lloyd George's request:—

> President Wilson undertook to draft a Terms of Reference to the Commission.

23. OTTOMAN MEMORANDUM TO THE SUPREME COUNCIL OF THE PARIS PEACE CONFERENCE 23 June 1919

[David Hunter Miller, *My Diary at the Conference of Paris* (New York, 1924), vol. XVI, pp. 479–84]

When the Supreme Council at Paris granted a hearing to an Ottoman delegation in mid-June 1919, the Sublime Porte could probably speak for no one but the few individuals actually in the service of the state. The Arab provinces in Asia were wholly detached, the Fertile Cressent (later mandate zone) by British military occupation and the Arabian Peninsula by the severence of all formal ties. Anatolia itself was dismembered into French (from 19 January 1919) and Italian (29 April) zones of occupation in accordance with the secret wartime arrangements; and Greek troops landed (14 May) with allied blessings at Izmir (Smyrna) ostensibly for police action, but unabashedly intent on conquest. The Big Four in Paris were seriously discussing the establishment in the west of a Constantinopolitan state and in the east of an Armenian state. An interallied fleet lay at anchor (since 13 November 1918) at Istanbul harbor. The Ottoman memorandum appealing to the Supreme Council to preserve the territorial integrity of the Ottoman Empire must be viewed in this context. H. N. Howard, *Partition of Turkey,* chap. 7; K. Ziemke, *Die neue Türkei,* pp. 101–23.

The Ottoman Delegation, in accordance with the desire expressed by Their Excellencies, the Allied plenipotentiaries, at the interview which it had the honour to have with them on the 17th June, begs leave to set forth as follows the views of the Imperial Ottoman Government as regards the new organisation of the Empire.

Although the political and economic situation of Turkey and her time-honoured relations of friendship with the Western Powers, made it incumbent on her to observe towards them an attitude of friendly neutrality, she was, owing to unfortunate circumstances and in spite of the manifest opposition of the national will, dragged into a fatal war.

It would be idle to dwell at length on the misdeeds committed during these last four years, which brought sufferings upon the Mussulman population quite as much as upon the Christians.

Turkey has a glorious history and a glorious past. She has given proof of power not only on the field of battle but also in manifestations of an intellectual order, and the mere organisation of an Empire which was one of the most vast in the world, proves, above all, a very pronounced political sense. The Ottoman Empire was never, in spite of affirmations of certain peoples interested in her downfall, a curse or a cyclone, such as were the Empires of Genghis and of Tamerlane. Its political organisation was at one moment able to assure a peaceful existence for some hundred millions of subjects established on different continents and of distinct races and religions. The Patriarchates, Communities and Sects had, in matters of faith, broad religious autonomy thanks to a wise and tolerant administration.

On the day that the Turks recognised the advantages of European civilisation, they did not hesitate to adopt a series of reforms; they were helped with much interest in this assimilation of modern civilisation, which worked so well, that in less than a quarter of a century Turkey was received into the European concert. The Turks, who still remember the brilliant position which they thereby attained, only desire to begin again their forward march towards improvement with the help of the Great Powers of the West.

Having set forth what occurred in the past, Ottoman Delegation comes to questions affecting the present and declares, in the first instance, that although the question which concerns Turkey presents three different points, it is in regard to its solution indivisible.

These points are the following:

(a) Thrace in Europe.

(b) The Turkish parts of Asia.

(c) Arabia.

The Ottoman Delegation has therefore the honour to submit to the Peace Conference the following considerations:

1. *Thrace.* In order to ensure a durable peace in this part of Europe, it is desirable to lay down a frontier line which will prevent the town of Adrianople, on which depends the security of the capital, from being easily attacked. The districts situated to the north and west of the vilayet of Adrianople, including Western Thrace, where the Turks are in great majority, should, by virtue of President Wilson's principles, as well as for economic reasons, come within the limits of that vilayet. This problem was examined at length in 1878 at Berlin by the Delegates of Great Britain and Russia, who found no other solution than that of adopting a frontier line beginning at Zoitun-Brunu, on the Black Sea, running into the interior by way of Demir-Halny to Mustafa-Pasha, and from there to Kara-Balkan. From Keucheva the frontier should follow the River Kara-Su, which flows into the Ægean Sea to the east of Kavalla, exactly opposite the Island of Thases.

2. *Asia Minor.* In Asia the Turkish lands are bounded on the north by the Black Sea, on the East by the Turco-Russian and Turco-Persian frontiers as they were before the war, including on the south the vilayets of Mosul and Diabekir, as well as a part of the province of Aleppo as far as the Mediterranean.

3. *The islands near the coast,* which belong to Asia Minor from an historical and economic point of view, should remain under Ottoman sovereignty with a great measure of autonomy, in order that it may be possible to prevent smuggling and ensure the safety of the coast.

4. *Armenia.* If the Armenian republic established at Erivan is recognised by the Powers of the Entente, the Ottoman Delegation will consent to discuss *ad referendum* the frontier line which is to separate the new republic from the Ottoman State. The Imperial Government would grant to the Armenians who wish to expatriate themselves in order to establish themselves in the new republic, all facilities in its power. As regards those who might wish to remain in Turkey and who are scattered in Thrace, the Caucasus and elsewhere, they would enjoy, like the other minorities, free cultural, moral and economic developments.

5. *Arabia.* The Arab provinces lying to the south of the Turkish countries, and including Syria, Palestine, the Hedjaz, the Asyr, the Yemen, Irak, and all the other regions which were recognised as forming an integral part of the Ottoman Empire before the war, would have a large measure of administrative autonomy, under the sovereignty of His Imperial Majesty the Sultan. Representatives of His Imperial Majesty the Sultan would be appointed at the Holy Places (Mecca, Medina and Jerusalem), and will have a guard of honour of limited numbers.

The hallowed custom of sending every year the sacred caravan (surre) to the Holy Places shall be maintained with its usual ceremonies and in its usual form, as the despatch of this caravan is one of the ancient prerogatives of the Khalifate.

The distribution of the revenues of the pious foundations (vakfs) shall continue without hindrance as in the past. These *vakfs* were founded partly by the Ottoman Sultan and partly by private individuals, and have always been administered by the Khalifate. This system shall be maintained in its entirety.

The Governor of each autonomous province shall be appointed by His Imperial Majesty the Sultan, except in the Hedjaz, to which may be granted a special organisation in agreement with the Power most directly interested in it. In all the Arab countries the Ottoman flag shall fly on the territory of the *smaret* (principality) or autonomous province. Justice shall be done in the name of His Imperial Majesty, the Sultan, and the coinage shall bear his name Tughra.

6. *Egypt and Cyprus.* The Ottoman Government is quite willing to enter into negotiations at the proper moment with the Government of His Britannic Majesty with a view to define clearly the political status of Egypt and of the Island of Cyprus.

The Ottoman Government, having stated above its opinion as regards the new organisation of the Empire, reserves the right also of communicating subsequently to the Peace Conference its point of view regarding financial, economic and juridical questions.

It is understood that as soon as this organisation is settled, the Interallied forces of occupation shall be withdrawn from Ottoman territory in a short time which shall be settled by agreement unless their provisional retention is necessary in some parts of Arabia.

Nobody in Turkey is unaware of the gravity of the moment. The ideas of the Ottoman people are however well defined:

It will not accept the dismemberment of the Empire or its division under different mandates. No government may oppose the will of the people, among whom are counted populations from beyond the Taurus and even Nomads of the Desert, who will not separate themselves from that Ottoman unity which has been established and hallowed for so many centuries.

From the manifestations of a great number of patriotic Committees formed in the provinces, and from the great meetings held in Constantinople (in which hundreds of thousands of citizens took part on every occasion) and from the language of the telegrams which the Government daily receives from all classes of the population, there emanates but one constant thought: unity and independence.

Trusting in the sentiments of justice of the Peace Conference the Ottoman people does not despair of reaching a solution in conformity with its legitimate aspirations and one fitted to ensure in the East that durable peace which is so greatly needed.

24. ARTICLE 22 OF THE COVENANT OF THE LEAGUE OF NATIONS
28 June 1919

[Great Britain, *Parliamentary Papers, 1920,* Treaty Series No. 11, Cmd. 964, pp. 11–12]

The Covenant of the League of Nations, approved by the Paris Peace Conference on 28 April 1919, was incorporated into the Treaty of Versailles, signed precisely two months later. Article 22 of the Covenant provided for the mandates system under the League's general supervision. Paragraph 4 of article 22 pertained to the Asian provinces of the Ottoman Empire and formed with the Husayn-McMahon correspondence (Doc. 8) the principal basis of later Arab claims to independence in the mandated territories. D. H. Miller, *The Drafting of the Covenant,* vol. 1, chap. 9; H. D. Hall, *Mandates, Dependencies and Trusteeship,* chaps. 2–10; N. Bentwich, *The Mandates System,* chaps. 1–3; Q. Wright, *Mandates under the League of Nations,* chaps. 1–3; H. N. Howard, *Partition of Turkey,* chap. 10; P. L. Hanna, *British Policy in Palestine,* chaps. 3–8; P. W. Ireland, *'Iraq,* chaps. 13–16;

A. H. Hourani, *Syria and Lebanon*, chaps. 9–13; W. F. Boustany, *The Palestine Mandate, Invalid and Impracticable;* W. E. Hocking, *The Spirit of World Politics*, chaps. 16–22.

ART. 22. To those colonies and territories which as a consequence of the late war have ceased to be under the sovereignty of the States which formerly governed them and which are inhabited by peoples not yet able to stand by themselves under the strenuous conditions of the modern world, there should be applied the principle that the well-being and development of such peoples form a sacred trust of civilisation and that securities for the performance of this trust should be embodied in this Covenant.

The best method of giving practical effect to this principle is that the tutelage of such peoples should be entrusted to advanced nations who by reason of their resources, their experience or their geographical position can best undertake this responsibility, and who are willing to accept it, and that this tutelage should be exercised by them as Mandatories on behalf of the League.

The character of the mandate must differ according to the stage of the development of the people, the geographical situation of the territory, its economic conditions and other similar circumstances.

Certain communities formerly belonging to the Turkish Empire have reached a stage of development where their existence as independent nations can be provisionally recognised subject to the rendering of administrative advice and assistance by a Mandatory until such time as they are able to stand alone. The wishes of these communities must be a principal consideration in the selection of the Mandatory.

Other peoples, especially those of Central Africa, are at such a stage that the Mandatory must be responsible for the administration of the territory under conditions which will guarantee freedom of conscience and religion, subject only to the maintenance of public order and morals, the prohibition of abuses such as the slave trade, the arms traffic and the liquor traffic, and the prevention of the establishment of fortifications or military and naval bases and of military training of the natives for other than police purposes and the defence of territory, and will also secure equal opportunities for the trade and commerce of other Members of the League.

There are territories, such as South-West Africa and certain of the South Pacific Islands, which, owing to the sparseness of their population, or their small size, or their remoteness from the centres of civilisation, or their geographical contiguity to the territory of the Mandatory, and other circumstances, can be best administered under the laws of the Mandatory as integral portions of its territory, subject to the safeguards above mentioned in the interests of the indigenous population.

In every case of Mandate, the Mandatory shall render to the Council an annual report in reference to the territory committed to its charge.

The degree of authority, control or administration to be exercised by the Mandatory shall, if not previously agreed upon by the Members of the League, be explicitly defined in each case by the Council.

A permanent Commission shall be constituted to receive and examine the annual reports of the Mandatories and to advise the Council on all matters relating to the observance of the mandates.

25. RESOLUTION OF THE GENERAL SYRIAN CONGRESS AT DAMASCUS
2 July 1919

[From the King-Crane Commission Report in *Foreign Relations of the United States: Paris Peace Conference, 1919*, vol. 12, pp. 780–81]

The arrival of the King-Crane Commission (Doc. 27) in Damascus on 25 June 1919 encouraged Arab nationalists in Occupied Enemy Territory East (the provisional Arab state under Amir Faysal) to convene a General Syrian Congress at the capital with delegates from Lebanon and Palestine for the purpose of framing a statement of their position. The resolution, adopted on 2 July and presented to the American investigative body, left no doubt of the nationalist dislike of the projected French mandate over Syria and of the proposed establishment in Palestine of a Jewish National Home. The so-called Greater Syria Scheme, as a modern political concept, may be said to have originated at the first General Syrian Congress. P. David, *Un Gouvernement arabe à Damas, le congrès syrien;* G. Antonius, *Arab Awakening,* chap. 14; A. H. Hourani, *Syria and Lebanon,* chap. 2; R. de Gontaut-Biron, *Comment la France s'est installée en Syrie,* chap. 13.

We the undersigned members of the General Syrian Congress, meeting in Damascus on Wednesday, July 2nd, 1919, made up of representatives from the three Zones, viz., the Southern, Eastern, and Western, provided with credentials and authorizations by the inhabitants of our various districts, Moslems, Christians, and Jews, have agreed upon the following statement of the desires of the people of the country who have elected us to present them to the American Section of the International Commission; the fifth article was passed by a very large majority; all the other articles were accepted unanimously.

1. We ask absolutely complete political independence for Syria within these boundaries. The Taurus System on the North; Rafah and a line running from Al Jauf to the south of the Syrian and the Hejazian line to Akaba on the south; the Euphates and Khabur Rivers and a line extending east of Abu Kamal to the east of Al Jauf on the east; and the Mediterranean on the west.

2. We ask that the Government of this Syrian country should be a democratic civil constitutional Monarchy on broad decentralization principles, safeguarding the rights of minorities, and that the King be the Emir Feisal, who carried on a glorious struggle in the cause of our liberation and merited our full confidence and entire reliance.

3. Considering the fact that the Arabs inhabiting the Syrian area are not naturally less gifted than other more advanced races and that they are by no means less developed than the Bulgarians, Serbians, Greeks, and Roumanians at the beginning of their independence, we protest against Article 22 of the Covenant of the League of Nations, placing us among the nations in their middle stage of development which stand in need of a mandatory power.

4. In the event of the rejection by the Peace Conference of this just protest for certain considerations that we may not understand, we, relying on the declarations of President Wilson that his object in waging war was to put an end to the ambition of conquest and colonization, can only regard the mandate mentioned in the Covenant of the League of Nations as equivalent to the rendering of economical and technical assistance that does not prejudice our complete independence. And desiring that our country should not fall a prey to colonization and believing that the American Nation is farthest from any thought of colonization and has no political ambition in our country, we will seek the technical and economical assistance from the United States of America, provided that such assistance does not exceed 20 years.

5. In the event of America not finding herself in a position to accept our desire for assistance, we will seek this assistance from Great Britain, also provided that such assistance does not infringe the complete independence and unity of our country and that the duration of such assistance does not exceed that mentioned in the previous article.

6. We do not acknowledge any right claimed by the French Government in any part whatever of our Syrian country and refuse that she should assist us or have a hand in our country under any circumstances and in any place.

7. We oppose the pretentions of the Zionists to create a Jewish commonwealth in the southern part of Syria, known as Palestine, and oppose Zionist migration to any part of our country; for we do not acknowledge their title but consider them a grave peril to our people from the na-

tional, economical, and political points of view. Our Jewish compatriots shall enjoy our common rights and assume the common responsibilities.

8. We ask that there should be no separation of the southern part of Syria, known as Palestine, nor of the littoral western zone, which includes Lebanon, from the Syrian country. We desire that the unity of the country should be guaranteed against partition under whatever circumstances.

9. We ask complete independence for emancipated Mesopotamia and that there should be no economical barriers between the two countries.

10. The fundamental principles laid down by President Wilson in condemnation of secret treaties impel us to protest most emphatically against any treaty that stipulates the partition of our Syrian country and against any private engagement aiming at the establishment of Zionism in the southern part of Syria; therefore we ask the complete annulment of these conventions and agreements.

The noble principles enunciated by President Wilson strengthen our confidence that our desires emanating from the depths of our hearts, shall be the decisive factor in determining our future; and that President Wilson and the free American people will be our supporters for the realization of our hopes, thereby proving their sincerity and noble sympathy with the aspiration of the weaker nations in general and our Arab people in particular.

We also have the fullest confidence that the Peace Conference will realize that we would not have risen against the Turks, with whom we had participated in all civil, political, and representative privileges, but for their violation of our national rights, and so will grant us our desires in full in order that our political rights may not be less after the war than they were before, since we have shed so much blood in the cause of our liberty and independence.

We request to be allowed to send a delegation to represent us at the Peace Conference to defend our rights and secure the realization of our aspirations.

26. AGREEMENTS: GREAT BRITAIN AND PERSIA
9 August 1919

[Great Britain, *Parliamentary Papers, 1919,* Persia No. 1, Cmd. 300]

The Russian withdrawal from northern Persia, after Tsar Nicholas II abdicated in mid-March 1917, produced a power vacuum that Anglo-Indian forces tried to fill. Once the war was over, however, the British Government favored a prompt liquidation of British military commitments in the Near and Middle East, Persia included. But Lord Curzon, as acting Foreign Secretary, was defining policy on Persia. He had always "dreamt of creating a chain of vassal states stretching from the Mediterranean to the Pamirs and protecting, not the Indian frontiers merely, but our communications with our further Empire. . . . In this chain of buffer states . . . Persia was to him at once the weakest and the most vital link" [H. Nicolson, *Curzon, the Last Phase* (London, 1934), pp. 121–22]. The opportunity had come to reinforce this link by placing Persia in preferential treaty relations with the United Kingdom. Curzon's program could scarcely have failed in the preliminary phase, for Whitehall continued only on a slightly reduced scale its generous wartime grants to the Persian government, reputedly approximating £225,000 sterling per month. But the terms of the agreements, signed at Tehran on 9 August 1919, were cast so manifestly in Britain's interest that opposition in Persia grew progressively more vocal. The instruments were never ratified by the Persian *Majlis* (legislature) and, in the spring of 1921 soon after a *coup d'état,* were repudiated by the new government of Sayyid Ziya-al-Din Tabatabai and Riza Khan. Nicolson, *op. cit.,* chap. 5; P. Graves, *Life of Cox,* chap. 19; G. Lenczowski, *Russia and the West in Iran,* chap. 2; J. M. Balfour, *Recent Happenings in Persia;* E. Lesueur, *Les Anglais en Perse,* part 1, chaps. 1–3.

1. THE POLITICAL AND MILITARY AGREEMENT

Preamble: In virtue of the close ties of friendship which have existed between the two Governments in the past, and in the conviction that it is in the essential and mutual interests of both in future that these ties should be cemented, and that the progress and prosperity of Persia should be promoted to the utmost, it is hereby agreed between the Persian Government on the one hand, and His Britannic Majesty's Minister, acting on behalf of his Government, on the other, as follows:—

1. The British Government reiterate, in the most categorical manner, the undertakings which they have repeatedly given in the past to respect absolutely the independence and integrity of Persia.

2. The British Government will supply, at the cost of the Persian Government, the services of whatever expert advisers may, after consultation between the two Governments, be considered necessary for the several departments of the Persian Administration. These advisers shall be engaged on contracts and endowed with adequate powers, the nature of which shall be the matter of agreement between the Persian Government and the advisers.

3. The British Government will supply, at the cost of the Persian Government, such officers and such munitions and equipment of modern type as may be adjudged necessary by a joint commission of military experts, British and Persian, which shall assemble forthwith for the purpose of estimating the needs of Persia in respect of the formation of a uniform force which the Persian Government proposes to create for the establishment and preservation of order in the country and on its frontiers.

4. For the purpose of financing the reforms indicated in clauses 2 and 3 of this agreement, the British Government offer to provide or arrange a substantial loan for the Persian Government, for which adequate security shall be sought by the two Governments in consultation in the revenues of the customs or other sources of income at the disposal of the Persian Government. Pending the completion of negotiations for such a loan the British Government will supply on account of it such funds as may be necessary for initiating the said reforms.

5. The British Government fully recognizing the urgent need which exists for the improvement of communications in Persia, with a view both to the extension of trade and the prevention of famine, are prepared to co-operate with the Persian Government for the encouragement of Anglo-Persian enterprise in this direction, both by means of railway construction and other forms of transport; subject always to the examination of the problems by experts and to agreement between the two Governments as to the particular projects which may be most necessary, practicable, and profitable.

6. The two Governments agree to the appointment forthwith of a joint Committee of experts for the examination and revision of the existing Customs Tariff with a view to its reconstruction on a basis calculated to accord with the legitimate interests of the country and to promote its prosperity.

2. THE LOAN AGREEMENT

ART. 1. The British Government grant a loan of £2,000,000 sterling to the Persian Government, to be paid to the Persian Government as required in such instalments and at such dates as may be indicated by the Persian Government after the British Financial Adviser shall have taken up the duties of his office at Tehran, as provided for in the aforesaid agreement.

ART. 2. The Persian Government undertakes to pay interest monthly at the rate of 7 per cent. per annum upon sums advanced in accordance with article 1 up to 20th March, 1921, and thereafter to pay monthly such amount as will suffice to liquidate the principal sum and interest thereon at 7 per cent. per annum in twenty years.

ART. 3. All the revenues and Customs receipts assigned in virtue of the contract of the 8th May, 1911, for the repayment of the loan of £1,250,000 are assigned for the repayment of the present loan with continuity of all conditions stipulated in the said contract, and with priority over all debts other than the 1911 loan and subsequent advances made by the British Government. In case of insufficiency of the receipts indicated above the Persian Government undertakes to make good the necessary sums from other resources, and for this purpose the Persian Government hereby assigns to the service of the present loan, and of the other advances above mentioned, in priority and with continuity of conditions stipulated in the aforesaid contract, the Customs receipts of all other regions, in so far as these receipts are or shall be at its disposal.

ART. 4. The Persian Government will have the right of repayment of the present loan at any date out of the proceeds of any British loan which it may contract for.

27. RECOMMENDATIONS OF THE KING-CRANE COMMISSION ON SYRIA AND PALESTINE
28 August 1919

[*Foreign Relations of the United States: Paris Peace Conference, 1919,* vol. 12, pp. 787–99]

At the meeting of the Big Four on 20 March 1919 (Doc. 22) President Wilson proposed that an Inter-Allied Commission visit Syria "to elucidate the state of opinion and the soil to be worked on by any mandatory" and to report their findings to the peace conference. Such "a Commission of men with no previous contact with Syria," argued the President, would "convince the world that the Conference had tried to do all it could to find the most scientific basis possible for a settlement." The Supreme Council adopted Wilson's suggestion. But the French refused to appoint representatives, and, although the British had already named theirs, Whitehall also withdrew. As a result only the two American members, Henry C. King and Charles R. Crane, proceeded to the area with their staff. They arrived at Jaffa on 10 June and filed their report and recommendations with the American delegation at Paris less than forty days later. "Whether or not the methods were adequate or the time spent sufficient," one keen observer has noted, "the report remains the first instance of American concern, at the top level, with basic information about the area independently obtained" (E. A. Speiser, *The United States and the Near East,* p. 70). The King-Crane inquiry, however, proved to have no more than academic interest. Neither the European powers nor the United States gave it serious consideration. Reprinted here is only one segment of the long report. H. N. Howard, "An American Experiment in Peace-Making, the King-Crane Commission," *The Moslem World,* 32 (April 1942), 122–46; D. H. Miller, *My Diary,* vol. 7, pp. 169–70, vol. 15, pp. 505–08; R. de Gontaut-Biron, *Comment la France s'est installée en Syrie,* chap. 13; M. Paillarès, *Le Kémalisme devant les alliés,* pp. 1–31; G. Antonius, *Arab Awakening,* chap. 14; Esco Foundation, *Palestine,* vol. 1, pp. 213–22; R. S. Baker, *Woodrow Wilson and World Settlement,* vol. 2, chap. 34.

The Commissioners make to the Peace Conference the following recommendations for the treatment of Syria:

1. We recommend, as most important of all, and in strict harmony with our instructions, that whatever foreign administration (whether of one or more powers) is brought into Syria, should come in, not at all as a colonizing Power in the old sense of that term, but as a Mandatary under the League of Nations, with the clear consciousness that "the well-being and development" of the Syrian people form for it a "sacred trust."

(1) To this end the mandate should have a limited term, the time of expiration to be determined by the League of Nations, in the light of all the facts as brought out from year to year, in the annual reports of the Mandatory to the League or in other ways.

(2) The Mandatary Administration should have, however, a period and power sufficient to ensure the success of the new State; and especially to make possible carrying through important educational and economic undertakings, essential to secure founding of the State.

(3) The Mandatory Administration should be characterized from the beginning by a strong and vital educational emphasis, in clear recognition of the imperative necessity of education for the citizens of

a democratic state, and the development of a sound national spirit. This systematic cultivation of national spirit is particularly required in a country like Syria, which has only recently come to self-consciousness.

(4) The Mandatory should definitely seek, from the beginning of its trusteeship, to train the Syrian people to independent self-government as rapidly as conditions allow, by setting up all the institutions of a democratic state, and by sharing with them increasingly the work of administration, and so forming gradually an intelligent citizenship, interested unselfishly in the progress of the country, and forming at the same time a large group of disciplined civil servants.

(5) The period of "tutelage" should not be unduly prolonged, but independent self-government should be granted as soon as it can safely be done; remembering that the primary business of government is not the accomplishment of certain things, but the development of citizens.

(6) It is peculiarly the duty of the Mandatary in a country like Syria, and in this modern age, to see that complete religious liberty is ensured, both in the constitution and in the practice of the state, and that a jealous care is exercised for the rights of all minorities. Nothing is more vital than this for the enduring success of the new Arab State.

(7) In the economic development of Syria, a dangerous amount of indebtedness on the part of the new State should be avoided, as well as any entanglements financially with the affairs of the Mandatory Power. On the other hand the legitimate established privileges of foreigners such as rights to maintain schools, commercial concessions, etc., should be preserved, but subject to review and modification under the authority of the League of Nations in the interest of Syria. The Mandatory Power should not take advantage of its position to force a monopolistic control at any point to the detriment either of Syria or of other nations; but it should seek to bring the new State as rapidly as possible to economic independence as well as to political independence.

Whatever is done concerning the further recommendations of the Commission, the fulfillment of at least the conditions now named should be assured, if the Peace Conference and the League of Nations are true to the policy of mandatories already embodied in "The Covenant of the League of Nations." This should effectively guard the most essential interests of Syria, however the machinery of administration is finally organized. The Damascus Congress betrayed in many ways their intense fear that their country would become, though under some other name, simply a colonial possession of some other Power. That fear must be completely allayed.

2. We recommend, in the second place that the unity of Syria be preserved, in accordance with the earnest petition of the great majority of the people of Syria.

(1) The territory concerned is too limited, the population too small, and the economic, geographic, racial and language unity too manifest, to make the setting up of independent states within its boundaries desirable, if such division can possibly be avoided. The country is very largely Arab in language, culture, traditions, and customs.

(2) This recommendation is in line with important "general considerations" already urged, and with the principles of the League of Nations, as well as in answer to the desires of the majority of the population concerned.

(3) The precise boundaries of Syria should be determined by a special commission on boundaries, after the Syrian territory has been in general allotted. The Commissioners believe, however, that the claim of the Damascus Conference to include Cilicia in Syria is not justified, either historically or by commercial or language relations. The line between the Arabic-speaking and the Turkish-speaking populations would quite certainly class Cilicia with Asia Minor, rather than with Syria. Syria, too, has no such need of further sea coast as the large interior sections of Asia Minor.

(4) In standing thus for the recognition of the unity of Syria, the natural desires

of regions like the Lebanon, which have already had a measure of independence, should not be forgotten. It will make for real unity, undoubtedly, to give a large measure of local autonomy, and especially in the case of strongly unified groups. Even the "Damascus Program" which presses so earnestly the unity of Syria, itself urges a government "on broad decentralization principles."

Lebanon has achieved a considerable degree of prosperity and autonomy within the Turkish Empire. She certainly should not find her legitimate aspirations less possible within a Syrian national State. On the contrary, it may be confidently expected that both her economic and political relations with the rest of Syria would be better if she were a constituent member of the State, rather than entirely independent of it.

As a predominantly Christian country, too, Lebanon naturally fears Moslem domination in a unified Syria. But against such domination she would have a four-fold safeguard: her own large autonomy; the presence of a strong Mandatary for the considerable period in which the constitution and practice of the new State would be forming; the oversight of the League of Nations, with its insistence upon religious liberty and the rights of minorities; and the certainty that the Arab Government would feel the necessity of such a state, if it were to commend itself to the League of Nations. Moreover, there would be less danger of a reactionary Moslem attitude, if Christians were present in the state in considerable numbers, rather than largely segregated outside the state, as experience of the relations of different religious faiths in India suggests.

As a predominantly Christian country, it is also to be noted that Lebanon would be in a position to exert a stronger and more helpful influence if she were within the Syrian State, feeling its problems and needs, and sharing all its life, instead of outside it, absorbed simply in her own narrow concerns. For the sake of the larger interests, both of Lebanon and of Syria, then, the unity of Syria is to be urged. It is certain that many of the more thoughtful Lebanese themselves hold this view. A similar statement might be made for Palestine; though, as "the holy Land" for Jews and Christians and Moslems alike, its situation is unique, and might more readily justify unique treatment, if such treatment were justified anywhere. This will be discussed more particularly in connection with the recommendation concerning Zionism.

3. We recommend, in the third place, that Syria be placed under on[e] Mandatory Power, as the natural way to secure real and efficient unity.

(1) To divide the administration of the provinces of Syria among several mandataries, even if existing national unity were recognized; or to attempt a joint mandatory of the whole on the commission plan: —neither of these courses would be naturally suggested as the best way to secure and promote the unity of the new State, or even the general unity of the whole people. It is conceivable that circumstances might drive the Peace Conference to some such form of divided mandate; but it is not a solution to be voluntarily chosen, from the point of view of the larger interests of the people, as considerations already urged indicate.

(2) It is not to be forgotten, either, that, however they are handled politically, the people of Syria are there, forced to get on together in some fashion. They are obliged to live with one another—the Arabs of the East and the people of the Coast, the Moslems and the Christians. Will they be helped or hindered, in establishing tolerable and finally cordial relations, by a single mandatary? No doubt the quick mechanical solution of the problem of difficult relations is to split the people up into little independent fragments. And sometimes, undoubtedly, as in the case of the Turks and Armenians, the relations are so intolerable as to make some division imperative and inevitable. But in general, to attempt complete separation only accentuates the differences and increases the antagonism. The whole lesson of the modern social consciousness points to the necessity of understanding "the other half," as it can be un-

derstood only by close and living relations. Granting reasonable local autonomy to reduce friction among groups, a single mandatary ought to form a constant and increasingly effective help to unity of feeling throughout the state, and ought to steadily improve group relations.

The people of Syria, in our hearings, have themselves often insisted that, so far as unpleasant relations have hitherto prevailed among various groups, it has been very largely due to the direct instigation of the Turkish Government. When justice is done impartially to all; when it becomes plain that the aim of the common government is the service of all classes alike, not their exploitation, decent human relations are pretty certain to prevail, and a permanent foundation for such relations to be secured—a foundation which could not be obtained by dividing men off from one another in antagonistic groups.

The Commissioners urge, therefore, for the largest future good of all groups and regions alike, the placing of the whole of Syria under a single mandate.

4. We recommend, in the fourth place, that Emir Feisal be made the head of the new united Syrian State.

(1) This is expressly and unanimously asked for by the representative Damascus Congress in the name of the Syrian people, and there seems to be no reason to doubt that the great majority of the population of Syria sincerely desire to have Emir Feisal as ruler.

(2) A constitutional monarchy along democratic lines, seems naturally adapted to the Arabs, with their long training under tribal conditions, and with their traditional respect for their chiefs. They seem to need, more than most people, a King as the personal symbol of the power of the State.

(3) Emir Feisal has come, too, naturally into his present place of power, and there is no one else who could well replace him. He had the great advantage of being the son of the Sherif of Mecca, and as such honored throughout the Moslem world. He was one of the prominent Arab leaders who assumed responsibility for the Arab uprising against the Turks, and so shared in the complete deliverance of the Arab-speaking portions of the Turkish Empire. He was consequently hailed by the "Damascus Congress" as having "merited their full confidence and entire reliance." He was taken up and supported by the British as the most promising candidate for the headship of the new Arab State—an Arab of the Arabs, but with a position of wide appeal through his Sherifian connection, and through his broad sympathies with the best in the Occident. His relations with the Arabs to the east of Syria are friendly, and his kingdom would not be threatened from that side. He undoubtedly does not make so strong an appeal to the Christians of the West Coast, as to the Arabs of the East; but no man can be named who would have a stronger general appeal. He is tolerant and wise, skillful in dealing with men, winning in manner, a man of sincerity, insight, and power. Whether he has the full strength needed for his difficult task it is too early to say; but certainly no other Arab leader combines so many elements of power as he, and he will have invaluable help throughout the mandatory period.

The Peace Conference may take genuine satisfaction in the fact that an Arab of such qualities is available for the headship of this new state in the Near East.

5. We recommend, in the fifth place, serious modification of the extreme Zionist Program for Palestine of unlimited immigration of Jews, looking finally to making Palestine distinctly a Jewish State.

(1) The Commissioners began their study of Zionism with minds predisposed in its favor, but the actual facts in Palestine, coupled with the force of the general principles proclaimed by the Allies and accepted by the Syrians have driven them to the recommendation here made.

(2) The Commission was abundantly supplied with literature on the Zionist program by the Zionist Commission to Palestine; heard in conferences much concerning the Zionist colonies and their claims· and personally saw something of what had been accomplished. They found much to approve in the aspirations and plans of the Zionists, and had warm appreciation for

the devotion of many of the colonists, and for their success, by modern methods, in overcoming great natural obstacles.

(3) The Commission recognized also that definite encouragement had been given to the Zionists by the Allies in Mr. Balfour's often quoted statement, in its approval by other representatives of the Allies. If, however, the strict terms of the Balfour Statement are adhered to—favoring "the establishment in Palestine of a national home for the Jewish people," "it being clearly understood that nothing shall be done which may prejudice the civil and religious rights of existing non-Jewish communities in Palestine"—it can hardly be doubted that the extreme Zionist Program must be greatly modified. For "a national home for the Jewish people" is not equivalent to making Palestine into a Jewish State; nor can the erection of such a Jewish State be accomplished without the gravest trespass upon the "civil and religious rights of existing non-Jewish communities in Palestine." The fact came out repeatedly in the Commission's conference with Jewish representatives, that the Zionists looked forward to a practically complete dispossession of the present non-Jewish inhabitants of Palestine, by various forms of purchase.

In his address of July 4, 1918, President Wilson laid down the following principle as one of the four great "ends for which the associated peoples of the world were fighting": "The settlement of every question, whether of territory, of sovereignty, of economic arrangement, or of political relationship upon the basis of the free acceptance of that settlement by the people immediately concerned, and not upon the basis of the material interest or advantage of any other nation or people which may desire a different settlement for the sake of its own exterior influence or mastery." If that principle is to rule, and so the wishes of Palestine's population are to be decisive as to what is to be done with Palestine, then it is to be remembered that the non-Jewish population of Palestine—nearly nine-tenths of the whole—are emphatically against the entire Zionist program. The tables show that there was no one thing upon which the population of Palestine were more agreed than upon this. To subject a people so minded to unlimited Jewish immigration, and to steady financial and social pressure to surrender the land, would be a gross violation of the principle just quoted, and of the peoples' rights, though it kept within the forms of law.

It is to be noted also that the feeling against the Zionist program is not confined to Palestine, but shared very generally by the people throughout Syria, as our conferences clearly showed. More than 72 per cent—1350 in all—of all the petitions in the whole of Syria were directed against the Zionist program. Only two requests—those for a united Syria and for independence—had a larger support. This general feeling was only voiced by the "General Syrian Congress," in the seventh, eighth and tenth resolutions of their statement [paras. 7, 8, 10, Doc. 25]. . . .

The Peace Conference should not shut its eyes to the fact that the anti-Zionist feeling in Palestine and Syria is intense and not lightly to be flouted. No British officer, consulted by the Commissioners, believed that the Zionist program could be carried out except by force of arms. The officers generally thought that a force of not less than fifty thousand soldiers would be required even to initiate the program. That of itself is evidence of a strong sense of the injustice of the Zionist program, on the part of the non-Jewish populations of Palestine and Syria. Decisions, requiring armies to carry out, are sometimes necessary, but they are surely not gratuitously to be taken in the interests of a serious injustice. For the initial claim, often submitted by Zionist representatives, that they have a "right" to Palestine, based on an occupation of two thousand years ago, can hardly be seriously considered.

There is a further consideration that cannot justly be ignored, if the world is to look foward to Palestine becoming a definitely Jewish state, however gradually that may take place. That consideration grows out of the fact that Palestine is "the Holy

Land" for Jews, Christians, and Moslems alike. Millions of Christians and Moslems all over the world are quite as much concerned as the Jews with conditions in Palestine, especially with those conditions which touch upon religious feeling and rights. The relations in these matters in Palestine are most delicate and difficult. With the best possible intentions, it may be doubted whether the Jews could possibly seem to either Christians or Moslems proper guardians of the holy places, or custodians of the Holy Land as a whole. The reason is this: the places which are most sacred to Christians—those having to do with Jesus—and which are also sacred to Moslems, are not only not sacred to Jews, but abhorrent to them. It is simply impossible, under those circumstances, for Moslems and Christians to feel satisfied to have these places in Jewish hands, or under the custody of Jews. There are still other places about which Moslems must have the same feeling. In fact, from this point of view, the Moslems, just because the sacred places of all three religions are sacred to them, have made very naturally much more satisfactory custodians of the holy places than the Jews could be. It must be believed that the precise meaning, in this respect, of the complete Jewish occupation of Palestine has not been fully sensed by those who urge the extreme Zionist program. For it would intensify, with a certainty like fate, the anti-Jewish feeling both in Palestine and in all other portions of the world which look to Palestine as "the Holy Land."

In view of all these considerations, and with a deep sense of sympathy for the Jewish cause, the Commissioners feel bound to recommend that only a greatly reduced Zionist program be attempted by the Peace Conference, and even that, only very gradually initiated. This would have to mean that Jewish immigration should be definitely limited, and that the project for making Palestine distinctly a Jewish commonwealth should be given up.

There would then be no reason why Palestine could not be included in a united Syrian State, just as other portions of the country, the holy places being cared for by an International and Inter-religious Commission, somewhat as at present, under the oversight and approval of the Mandatary and of the League of Nations. The Jews, of course, would have representation upon this Commission.

6. The Recommendations now made lead naturally to the necessity of recommending what Power shall undertake the single Mandate for all Syria.

(1) The considerations already dealt with suggest the qualifications, ideally to be desired in this Mandatory Power: First of all it should be freely desired by the people. It should be willing to enter heartily into the spirit of the mandatory system, and its possible gift to the world, and so be willing to withdraw after a reasonable period, and not seek selfishly to exploit the country. It should have a passion for democracy, for the education of the common people and for the development of national spirit. It needs unlimited sympathy and patience in what is practically certain to be a rather thankless task; for no Power can go in, honestly to face actual conditions (like landownership, for example) and seek to correct these conditions, without making many enemies. It should have experience in dealing with less developed peoples, and abundant resources in men and money.

(2) Probably no Power combines all these qualifications, certainly not in equal degree. But there is hardly one of these qualifications that has not been more or less definitely indicated in our conferences with the Syrian people and they certainly suggest a new stage in the development of the self-sacrificing spirit in the relations of peoples to one another. The Power that undertakes the single mandate for all Syria, in the spirit of these qualifications, will have the possibility of greatly serving not only Syria but the world, and of exalting at the same time its own national life. For it would be working in direct line with the high aims of the Allies in the war, and give proof that those high aims had not been abandoned. And that would mean very much just now, in enabling the nations to

keep their faith in one another and in their own highest ideals.

(3) The Resolutions of the Peace Conference of January 30, 1919, quoted in our Instructions, expressly state for regions to be "completely severed from the Turkish Empire," that "the wishes of these communities must be a principal consideration in the selection of the Mandatary Power." Our survey left no room for doubt of the choice of the majority of the Syrian people. Although it was not known whether America would take a mandate at all; and although the Commission could not only give no assurances upon that point, but had rather to discourage expectation; nevertheless, upon the face of the returns, America was the first choice of 1152 of the petitions presented—more than 60 per cent—while no other Power had as much as 15 per cent for first choice.

And the conferences showed that the people knew the grounds upon which they registered their choice for America. They declared that their choice was due to knowledge of America's record: the unselfish aims with which she had come into the war; the faith in her felt by multitudes of Syrians who had been in America; the spirit revealed in American educational institutions in Syria, especially the College in Beirut, with its well known and constant encouragement of Syrian national sentiment; their belief that America had no territorial or colonial ambitions, and would willingly withdraw when the Syrian state was well established as her treatment both of Cuba and the Philippines seemed to them to illustrate; her genuinely democratic spirit; and her ample resources.

From the point of view of the desires of the "people concerned," the Mandate should clearly go to America.

(4) From the point of view of qualifications, too, already stated as needed in the Mandatory for Syria, America, as first choice of the people, probably need not fear careful testing, point by point, by the standard involved in our discussion of qualifications; though she has much less experience in such work than Great Britain, and is likely to show less patience; and though her definite connections with Syria have been less numerous and close than those of France. She would have at least the great qualification of fervent belief in the new mandatary system of the League of Nations, as indicating the proper relations which a strong nation should take toward a weaker one. And, though she would undertake the mandate with reluctance, she could probably be brought to see, how logically the taking of such responsibility follows from the purposes with which she entered the war, and from her advocacy of the League of Nations.

(5) There is the further consideration, that America could probably come into the Syrian situation, in the beginning at least, with less friction than any other Power. The great majority of Syrian people, as has been seen, favor her coming, rather than that of any other power. Both the British and the French would find it easier to yield their respective claims to America than to each other. She would have no rival imperial interests to press. She would have abundant resources for the development of the sound prosperity of Syria; and this would inevitably benefit in a secondary way the nations which have had closest connection with Syria, and so help to keep relations among the Allies cordial. No other Power probably would be more welcome, as a neighbor, to the British, with their large interests in Egypt, Arabia, and Mesopotamia; or to the Arabs and Syrians in these regions; or to the French with their long-established and many-sided interests in Beirut and the Lebanon.

(6) The objections to simply recommending at once a single American Mandate for all Syria are: first of all, that it is not certain that the American people would be willing to take the Mandate; that it is not certain that the British or French would be willing to withdraw, and would cordially welcome America's coming—a situation which might prove steadily harassing to an American administration; that the vague but large encouragement given to the Zionist aims might prove particularly embarrassing to America, on account of her large and influential Jewish population; and that,

if America were to take any mandate at all, and were to take but one mandate, it is probable that an Asia Minor Mandate would be more natural and important. For there is a task there of such peculiar and world-wide significance as to appeal to the best in America, and demand the utmost from her, and as certainly to justify her in breaking with her established policy concerning mixing in the affairs of the Eastern Hemisphere. The Commissioners believe, moreover, that no other Power could come into Asia Minor, with hands so free to give impartial justice to all the peoples concerned.

To these objections as a whole, it is to be said, that they are all of such a kind that they may resolve themselves; and that they only form the sort of obstacles that must be expected, in so large and significant an undertaking. In any case they do not relieve the Commissioners from the duty of recommending the course which, in their honest judgment, is the best course, and the one for which the whole situation calls.

The Commissioners, therefore, recommend, as involved in the logic of the facts, that the United States of America be asked to undertake the single Mandate for all Syria.

If for any reason the mandate for Syria is not given to America, then the Commissioners recommend, in harmony with the express request of the majority of the Syrian people, that the mandate be given to Great Britain. The tables show that there were 1073 petitions in all Syria for Great Britain as Mandatory, if America did not take the mandate. This is very greatly in excess of any similar expression for the French. On the contrary—for whatever reason—more than 60 percent of all the petitions, presented to the Commission, directly and strongly protested against any French Mandate. Without going into a discussion of the reasons for this situation, the Commissioners are reluctantly compelled to believe that this situation itself makes it impossible to recommend a single French mandate for all Syria. The feeling of the Arabs of the East is particularly strong against the French. And there is grave reason to believe that the attempt to enforce a French Mandate would precipitate war between the Arabs and the French, and force upon Great Britain a dangerous alternative. The Commissioners may perhaps be allowed to say that this conclusion is contrary to their own earlier hope, that—because of France's long and intimate relations with Syria, because of her unprecedented sacrifices in the war, and because the British Empire seemed certain to receive far greater accessions of territory from the war—it might seem possible to recommend that France be given the entire mandate for Syria. But the longer the Commission remained in Syria, the more clear it became that that course could not be taken.

The Commissioners recommend, therefore, that if America cannot take the mandate for all Syria, that it be given to Great Britain; because of the choice of the people concerned; because she is already on the ground and with much of the necessary work in hand; because of her trained administrators; because of her long and generally successful experience in dealing with less developed peoples; and because she has so many of the qualifications needed in a Mandatory Power, as we have already considered them.

We should hardly be doing justice, however, to our sense of responsibility to the Syrian people, if we did not frankly add some at least of the reasons and misgivings, variously expressed and implied in our conferences, which led to the preference for an American mandate over a British mandate. The people repeatedly showed honest fear that in British hands the mandatory power would become simply a colonizing power of the old kind; that Great Britain would find it difficult to give up the colonial theory, especially in case of a people thought inferior; that she would favor a civil service and pension budget too expensive for a poor people; that the interests of Syria would be subordinated to the supposed needs of the Empire; that there would be, after all, too much exploitation of the country for Britain's benefit; that she would never be ready to withdraw and give the country real independence; that she did not really believe in universal education, and would not provide adequately for it; and that she already had more territory in her possession—in spite of her fine colonial record—than was good either for herself or for the world. These misgivings of the Syrian people unquestionably largely explain their demand for "absolute independence," for a period of "assistance" of only twenty years, their protest against Article 22 of the Covenant of the League of Nations, etc. They all mean that whatever Power the Peace Conference shall send into Syria, should go in as a true mandatory under the League of Nations, and for a limited term. Anything else would be a betrayal of the Syrian people. It needs to be emphasized, too, that under a true mandatory for Syria, all the legitimate interests of all the nations in Syria would be safeguarded. In particular, there is no reason why any tie that France has had with Syria in the past should be severed or even weakened under the control of another mandatory power, or in an independent Syria.

There remains only to be added, that if France feels so intensely concerning her present claims in Syria, as to threaten all cordial relations among the Allies, it is of course possible to give her a mandate over the Lebanon (not enlarged), separated from the rest of Syria, as is desired by considerable groups in that region. For reasons already given, the Commissioners cannot recommend this course, but it is a possible arrangement.

28. THE TURKISH NATIONAL PACT
28 January 1920

[Arnold J. Toynbee, *The Western Question in Greece and Turkey* (London, Constable, 1922), pp. 209–10]

Resistance to the partition of Anatolia, the heartland of the Ottoman Turks, took organized shape in the north central highlands, the one area neither occupied by foreign troops nor inhabited by a substantial non-Turkish population in revolt. A permanent nationalist association led by General Mustafa Kemal Paşa (1881–1938) came into being by midsummer 1919, realistic enough to accept the loss of the Ottoman non-Turkish provinces but dedicated to the defense of the sovereignty and territorial integrity of Anatolia and eastern Thrace. The Turkish nationalists defined and refined the principles of their organization at its constituent congress in Erzurum (23 July–7 August 1919) and at a second congress in Sivas (4–11 September). An index of the popularity of the nationalist movement was the adoption by the newly elected lower chamber of the Ottoman legislature as early as 28 January 1920 of the National Pact, embodying the platform of what had come to be known as *Anadolu ve Rumeli Müdafaa-i Hukuk Cemiyeti* (the Association for the Defense of the Rights of Anatolia and Rumelia). R. H. Davison, "Turkish Diplomacy from Mudros to Lausanne," *The Diplomats 1919–1939,* ed. by G. A. Craig and F. Gilbert, chap. 6; and R. H. Davison, "Middle East Nationalism, Lausanne, Thirty Years Later," *Middle East Journal,* 7 (1953), 324–48; Mustafa Kemal (Atatürk), *A Speech Delivered by Ghazi Mustapha Kemal . . . October 1927;* A. Emin, *Turkey in the World War,* chaps. 25–27; A. J. Toynbee and K. P. Kirkwood, *Turkey,* chap. 5; L. V. Thomas and R. N. Frye, *The United States and Turkey and Iran,* part 1, chap. 4; K. Ziemke, *Die neue Türkei,* pp. 124–38; D. Webster, *Turkey of Atatürk,* chap. 7; E. G. Mears, ed., *Modern Turkey,* chap. 25; H. N. Howard, *Partition of Turkey,* chap. 8; C. Price, *The Rebirth of Turkey,* chaps. 14–18.

The Members of the Ottoman Chamber of Deputies recognise and affirm that the independence of the State and the future of the Nation can be assured by complete respect for the following principles, which represent the maximum of sacrifice which can be undertaken in order to achieve a just and lasting peace, and that the continued existence of a stable Ottoman Sultanate and society is impossible outside of the said principles:

ART. 1. Inasmuch as it is necessary that the destinies of the portions of the Turkish

Empire which are populated exclusively by an Arab majority, and which on the conclusion of the armistice of the 30th October 1918 were in the occupation of enemy forces, should be determined in accordance with the votes which shall be freely given by the inhabitants, the whole of those parts whether within or outside the said armistice line which are inhabited by an Ottoman Moslem majority, united in religion, in race and in aim, imbued with sentiments of mutual respect for each other and of sacrifice, and wholly respectful of each other's racial and social rights and surrounding conditions, form a whole which does not admit of division for any reason in truth or in ordinance.

ART. 2. We accept that, in the case of the three [Kurdish] Sandjaks which united themselves by a general vote to the mother country when they first were free, recourse should again be had, if necessary, to a free popular vote.

ART. 3. The determination of the juridical status of Western Thrace also, which has been made dependent on the Turkish peace, must be effected in accordance with the votes which shall be given by the inhabitants in complete freedom.

ART. 4. The security of the city of Constantinople, which is the seat of the Caliphate of Islam, the capital of the Sultanate, and the headquarters of the Ottoman Government, and of the Sea of Marmora must be protected from every danger. Provided this principle is maintained, whatever decision may be arrived at jointly by us and all other Governments concerned, regarding the opening of the Bosphorus to the commerce and traffic of the world, is valid.

ART. 5. The rights of minorities as defined in the treaties concluded between the Entente Powers and their enemies and certain of their associates shall be confirmed and assured by us—in reliance on the belief that the Moslem minorities in neighbouring countries also will have the benefit of the same rights.

ART. 6. It is a fundamental condition of our life and continued existence that we, like every country, should enjoy complete independence and liberty in the matter of assuring the means of our development, in order that our national and economic development should be rendered possible and that it should be possible to conduct affairs in the form of a more up-to-date regular administration.

For this reason we are opposed to restrictions inimical to our development in political, judicial, financial, and other matters.

The conditions of settlement of our proved debts shall likewise not be contrary to these principles.

29. OIL AGREEMENT: GREAT BRITAIN AND FRANCE
24 April 1920

[Great Britain, *Parliamentary Papers, 1920,* Misc. No. 11, Cmd. 675]

Owing to the insistence of France, the Sykes-Picot agreement (Doc. 10) formed the basis of Anglo-French postwar negotiations for a Near and Middle East settlement. The Mosul *vilâyet* (province), it will be recalled, originally fell into the projected French zone of influence. In return for French postwar acquiescence in reassigning the district to the proposed zone of direct British administration, France sought a 25 per cent interest in any concession that might exploit Mosul's oil resources. Britain was willing to conclude such an engagement with France. Indeed, instruments were initialed in 8 April and 21 December 1919 (texts in E. L. Woodward and R. Butler, *Documents on British Foreign Policy,* 1st ser., vol. 4, pp. 1089–92, 1114–16), but France refused to confirm either one until its further demand for a single French mandate over Syria as well as Lebanon was granted. This demand encountered a British stone wall, for it conflicted with McMahon's commitments to Husayn and with England's early postwar policy of supporting Faysal's provisional Arab government at Damascus. Anglo-French discord allowed political affairs in the former Ottoman provinces to drift along aimlessly until the Arab nationalists precipitated a crisis. On 8 March 1920 a second General Syrian Congress convened at Damascus (Doc.

25), proclaiming the independence of Syria (including Lebanon, Palestine and what later came to be known as Transjordan), and named Faysal king. This action (repudiated on 15 March by France and Britain) and the consequent Arab attacks on Jews in Jerusalem (4–6 April) drove home to the British government the urgency of an early settlement. When the Supreme Council reassembled in San Remo on 19 April, the British finally acceded to the French request for an enlarged Syrian mandate, thus making possible the conclusion of the following oil agreement, confirmed on 25 April by the French and British prime ministers. Articles 4–6, relating to Rumania and Russia, have been omitted. Woodward and Butler, *op. cit.,* pp. 1089–1119 (documents); H. N. Howard, *Partition of Turkey,* pp. 242–43; P. L. Hanna, *British Policy in Palestine,* chap. 3; S. H. Longrigg, *Oil in the Middle East,* chap. 3; A. Apostol and A. Michelson, *La Lutte pour le pétrole,* pp. 53–63; K. Hoffmann, *Ölpolitik,* chap. 5; B. Shwadran, *The Middle East, Oil and the Great Powers,* chap. 7; E. H. Davenport and S. R. Cooke, *Cil Trusts and Anglo-American Relations,* chap. 6; F. Delaisi, *Oil, Its Influence on Politics,* pp. 54–83; A. Mohr, *The Oil War,* chap. 11.

By order of the two Governments of France and Great Britain, the undersigned representatives have resumed, by mutual consent, the consideration of an agreement regarding petroleum.

2. This agreement is based on the principles of cordial co-operation and reciprocity in those countries where the oil interests of the two nations can be usefully united. This memorandum relates to the following States or countries:—

Roumania, Asai Minor, territories of the old Russian Empire, Galicia, French Colonies and British Crown Colonies.

3. The agreement may be extended to other countries by mutual consent. .

7. *Mesopotamia.*—The British Government undertake to grant to the French Government or its nominee 25 per cent. of the net output of crude oil at current market rates which His Majesty's Government may secure from the Mesopotamian oilfields, in the event of their being developed by Government action; or in the event of a private petroleum company being used to develop the Mesopotamian oilfields, the British Government will place at the disposal of the French Government a share of 25 per cent. in such company. The price to be paid for such participation to be no more than that paid by any of the other participants to the said petroleum company. It is also understood that the said petroleum company shall be under permanent British control.

8. It is agreed that, should the private petroleum company be constituted as aforesaid, the native Government or other native interests shall be allowed, if they so desire, to participate up to a maximum of 20 per cent. of the share capital of the said company. The French shall contribute one-half of the first 10 per cent. of such native participation and the additional participation shall be provided by each participant in proportion to his holdings.

9. The British Government agree to support arrangements by which the French Government may procure from the Anglo-Persian Company supplies of oil, which may be piped from Persia to the Mediterranean through any pipe-line which may have been constructed within the French mandated territory and in regard to which France has given special facilities, up to the extent of 25 per cent. of the oil so piped, on such terms and conditions as may be mutually agreed between the French Government and the Anglo-Persian Company.

10. In consideration of the above-mentioned arrangements, the French Government shall agree, if it is desired and as soon as application is made, to the construction of two separate pipe-lines and railways necessary for their construction and maintenance and for the transport of oil from Mesopotamia and Persia through French spheres of influence to a port or ports on the Eastern Mediterranean. The port or ports shall be chosen in agreement between the two Governments.

11. Should such pipe-line and railways cross territory within a French sphere of influence, France undertakes to give every facility for the rights of crossing without any royalty or wayleaves on the oil transported. Nevertheless, compensation shall be

payable to the landowners for the surface occupied.

12. In the same way France will give facilities at the terminal port for the acquisition of the land necessary for the erection of depots, railways, refineries, loading wharfs, &c. Oil thus exported shall be exempt from export and transit dues. The material necessary for the construction of the pipe-lines, railways, refineries and other equipment shall also be free from import duties and wayleaves.

13. Should the said petroleum company desire to lay a pipe-line and a railway to the Persian Gulf, the British Government will use its good offices to secure similar facilities for that purpose.

14. *North Africa and other Colonies.*—The French Government will give facilities to any Franco-British group or groups of good standing, which furnish the necessary guarantees and comply with French laws, for the acquisition of oil concessions in the French colonies, protectorates and zones of influence, including Algeria, Tunis and Morocco. It should be noted that the French Parliament has resolved that groups so formed must contain at least 67 per cent. French interests.

15. The French Government will facilitate the granting of any concessions in Algeria which are now under consideration as soon as the applicants have complied with all the requirements of the French laws.

16. *British Crown Colonies.*—In so far as existing regulations allow, the British Government will give to French subjects who may wish to prospect and exploit petroliferous lands in the Crown Colonies similar advantages to those which France is granting to British subjects in the French colonies.

17. Nothing in this agreement shall apply to concessions which may be the subject of negotiations initiated by French or British interests.

30. UNITED STATES INTERWAR OIL POLICY IN THE NEAR AND MIDDLE EAST
12 May 1920–8 November 1923

[Davis letter from *Foreign Relations of the United States, 1920,* vol. 2, pp. 651–55; Hughes letter, *ibid., 1923,* vol. 2, 717–18]

The United States insisted in the interwar years on the application of the "open door" principle not in the mandated territories alone but throughout the Near and Middle East. The policy, as it bore upon American interest in oil, was elaborated less than three weeks after the signature of the Anglo-French petroleum agreement at San Remo (Doc. 29) by the Department of State in a protest that Ambassador John W. Davis presented to Foreign Secretary Lord Curzon (first entry below). United States diplomatic persistence in this matter later enabled American firms to take an active part in the development of the region's oil resources (Docs. 44, 54). The United States also adduced the further principle of assisting without partiality all American companies that requested such diplomatic aid. Secretary of State Charles Evans Hughes formulated the government's position most succinctly in a letter to President Coolidge (second entry below). B. Gerig, *The Open Door and the Mandates System,* particularly chap. 6; *International Petroleum Cartel,* chaps. 3–4; S. H. Longrigg, *Oil in the Middle East,* chap. 3; H. L. Hoskins, *The Middle East, Problem Area in World Politics,* chap. 10; K. Hoffman, *Ölpolitik,* chaps. 6–8; B. Shwadran, *The Middle East, Oil and the Great Powers,* chap. 7.

1. U.S. AMBASSADOR DAVIS TO FOREIGN SECRETARY CURZON, 12 MAY 1920

Pursuant to the instructions of my Government, I have the honour to inform Your Lordship that the Government of the United States has been officially [*unofficially*] [1] informed that the Mandates for Mesopotamia and Palestine have been assigned to Great Britain; the Mandate for

[1] The correction was authorized by a telegram from the Department, dated July 12, 1920, 4 p.m. (file no. 800.6363/148a).

Mesopotamia being given subject to friendly arrangement with the Italian Government regarding economic rights.

The Government of the United States desires to point out that during the Peace negotiations at Paris leading up to the Treaty of Versailles, it consistently took the position that the future Peace of the world required that as a general principle any Alien territory which should be acquired pursuant to the Treaties of Peace with the Central Powers must be held and governed in such a way as to assure equal treatment in law and in fact to the commerce of all nations. It was on account of and subject to this understanding that the United States felt itself able and willing to agree that the acquisition of certain enemy territory by the victorious powers would be consistent with the best interests of the world. The representatives of the principal Allied Powers in the discussion of the Mandate principles expressed in no indefinite manner their recognition of the justice and far-sightedness of such a principle and agreed to its application to the Mandates over Turkish territory.

The Administration of Palestine and Mesopotamia during the interim period of military occupation has given rise to several communications between the United States Government and that of Great Britain relative to matters that had created the unfortunate impression in the minds of the American public that the Authorities of His Majesty's Government in the occupied region had given advantage to British oil interests which were not accorded to American Companies and further that Great Britain had been preparing quietly for exclusive control of the oil resources in this region. The impression referred to has, it is believed, been due in large part to reports of authoritative statements regarding the general Oil Policy of Great Britain and of actual work such as the construction of pipe lines, railways and refineries, the operations of certain oil wells, the acquisitions of dockyards, cotton investigations and permitted researches by certain individuals whose activities, though stated to be solely in behalf of the civil Administration, were attended by circumstances which created the impression that some benefit at least would accrue to British oil interests.

Certain of the occurrences above referred to have been explained by his Majesty's Government as due to military necessity, and certain others as due to laxity on the part of local authorities. It must be realized, however, that it his been difficult for the American people to reconcile all of these reports with the assurance of His Majesty's Government that "the provisional character of the military occupation does not warrant the taking of decisions by the occupying power in matters concerning the future economic development of the country," and that the invitation [*initiation*] of new undertakings and the exercise of rights under concessions would be prohibited. The United States Government has confidence in the good faith of His Majesty's Government in attempting to carry out the assurances given by His Majesty's Foreign Office, but desires to point out that the considerations above referred to indicate the difficulty in insuring the local execution of such undertakings and the necessity for careful measures to guarantee the practical fulfillment of the principles expressed and agreed to during the peace negotiations at Paris.

With this thought in mind, the Government of the United States ventures to suggest the following propositions, which embody or illustrate the principles which the United States Government would be pleased to see applied in the occupied or mandated regions and which are submitted as furnishing a reasonable basis for discussions. In the event of such discussions it would be assumed that the legal situation as regards economic resources in the occupied or mandated regions would remain *in statu quo* pending an agreement:

(1) That the Mandatory Power strictly adhere and conform to the principles expressed and agreed to during the peace negotiations at Paris and to the principles embodied in Mandate "A" prepared in London for adoption by the League of Nations by the Commission on Mandatories.

(2) That there be guaranteed to the na-

tionals or subjects of all nations treatment equal in law and in fact to that accorded nationals or subjects of the Mandatory Power with respect to taxation or other matters affecting residence, business, profession, concessions, freedom of transit for persons and goods, freedom of communication, trade, navigation, commerce, industrial property, and other economic rights or commercial activities.

(3) That no exclusive economic concessions covering the whole of any Mandated region or sufficiently large to be virtually exclusive shall be granted and that no monopolistic concessions relating to any commodity or to any economic privilege subsidiary and essential to the production, development, or exploitation of such commodity shall be granted.

(4) That reasonable provision shall be made for publicity of applications for concessions and of Governmental Acts or Regulations relating to the economic resources of the Mandated territories; and that in general regulations or legislation regarding the granting of concessions relating to exploring or exploiting economic resources or regarding other privileges in connection with these shall not have the effect of placing American citizens or companies or those of other nations or companies controlled by American citizens or nationals of other countries at a disadvantage compared with the nationals or companies of the Mandate nation or companies controlled by nationals of the Mandate nation or others.

The fact that certain concessions were granted in the mandated regions by the Turkish Government is, of course, an important factor which must be given practical consideration. The United States Government believes that it is entitled to participate in any discussions relating to the status of such concessions not only because of existing vested rights of American citizens, but also because the equitable treatment of such concessions is essential to the initiation and application of the general principles in which the United States Government is interested.

No direct mention has been made herein of the question of establishment of monopolies directly or indirectly by or in behalf of the Mandatory Government. It is believed, however, that the establishment of monopolies by or in behalf of the Mandatory Government would not be consistent with the principles of trusteeship inherent in the Mandatory idea. His Majesty's Government has stated its conception of the necessity for the control of oil production in these territories in time of national emergency. The Government of the United States does not intend at present to suggest arrangements that shall extend to any consideration not included in an enlightened interpretation of what constitutes its legitimate commercial interests. The question of control in times of national emergencies of supplies which may be deemed essential by Great Britain is a subject which the United States Government deems a matter for separate discussion.

The Government of the United States realizes the heavy financial obligations which will arise in connection with the administration of the Mandatory. It believes, however, that any attempt toward reimbursement by the adoption of a policy of monopolization or of exclusive concessions and special favours to its own nationals, besides being a repudiation of the principles already agreed to would prove to be unwise even from the point of view of expediency both on economic and political grounds. It also believes that the interests of the world as well as that of the two respective countries can best be served by a friendly co-operation or a friendly and equal competition between the citizens of the two countries and citizens of other nationalities.

The Government of the United States would be glad to receive an early expression of the views of His Majesty's Government, especially in order to reassure public opinion in the United States.

I have the honour further to acquaint Your Lordship that this Note is not designed by way of reply to the Allied Note from San Remo, which will be answered separately.

2. SECRETARY HUGHES TO PRESIDENT COOLIDGE, 8 NOVEMBER 1923

It has recently been brought to my attention that the Sinclair Oil Company has felt a certain dissatisfaction at what they consider their failure to receive proper support from this Department, particularly in connection with their effort to secure an oil concession in North Persia. In a letter I wrote to Mr. Harding under date of October 28, 1922, of which I attach a copy,[2] I gave some of the details of the competition which had arisen in North Persia between the Sinclair and Standard Oil Companies, a matter which Mr. Archibald Roosevelt, of the former company, had laid before the President. In order that you may be fully advised I should be glad if you could find it possible to glance through that letter.

This Department's attitude of impartiality as between the competing American companies, which I emphasized in that letter, has been scrupulously followed and I am now informing the Sinclair Oil Company that while I have no reason to believe that the Persian Government is in doubt on this point I am quite prepared to re-emphasize this position through our Legation at Teheran and also to indicate that it is the Government's policy to give appropriate diplomatic support to American interests abroad.

This general question raises a point which I feel to be of sufficient importance to bring to your attention; namely, the proper attitude of this Government toward American commercial enterprise abroad. From time to time there has been some dissatisfaction expressed in business circles because this Department's attitude toward American business interests in the foreign field differs somewhat from the attitude in similar matters of the British, French and other European governments. The latter are not loath to interfere politically in support of the business interests of their nationals to a degree which is not followed by this Department. Our position is that we are always ready to give appropriate support to our nationals in seeking opportunities for business enterprise abroad, but we do not undertake to make the government a party to the business negotiations or use political pressure for the benefit of private interests in order to obtain particular concessions, or intervene in favor of one American interest as against another. We are persistent in our efforts to maintain the open door policy, or equality of commercial opportunity, but we do not attempt to assume obligations for the government, expressed or implied, which under our system we could not undertake to discharge.

American companies which might prefer a policy of more direct interference on their behalf by the government are inclined, in my opinion, to overlook the fact that American prestige and reputation for fairness has been enhanced, and consequently business opportunities of our nationals have been increased, by the correct policy which this government has followed. I find that in many parts of the world American business is welcomed largely because foreign countries realize that they can deal with American interests on a business basis without fearing political complications.

It is hardly necessary to point out that the other course desired by some business men, intent on their own immediate interests, would not only be contrary to our traditions and foreign policy, but if persistently followed would involve us in political intrigues and in difficulties which other governments with different exigencies and aims find it impossible to escape and from which we have happily been free.

While I do not feel that the question presented by the informal representations on the part of the Sinclair Company calls for any other action than I have indicated above, I desire briefly to summarize our attitude should the matter otherwise be brought to your attention.

[2] Not printed.

31. POLITICAL CLAUSES OF THE TREATY OF SÈVRES
10 August 1920

[Great Britain, *Parliamentary Papers, 1920,* Treaty Series No. 11, Cmd. 964, pp. 16–32]

Once Britain and France settled their differences over the projected mandates (Doc. 29), the Supreme Council at San Remo was able by 26 April 1920 to agree on the clauses of the Ottoman treaty. The Ottoman government, under the instrument, surrendered all the non-Turkish provinces and much of Anatolia. Control over the straits was vested in an international commission, the capitulatory regime was re-established (article 261, not reproduced; see part 9 for economic clauses) and traditional minority rights were reimposed on a nonreciprocal basis (part 4, not reproduced). The Ottoman delegation received the instrument in Paris on 11 May and reluctantly signed it in Sèvres three months later. But the treaty imposed on the Ottoman government was never ratified. By the summer of 1920 the nationalist regime under Mustafa Kemal at Ankara, which was bearing the brunt of the struggle against the Greeks, would have no part of the proposed settlement, and as time wore on the imperial government at Istanbul progressively lost authority to the nationalists. Ultimately the allies were forced to negotiate a fresh settlement at Lausanne (Doc. 41). E. L. Woodward and R. Butler, *British Documents on Foreign Policy,* 1st ser., vol. 4, chaps. 2–4 (documents); D. Lloyd George, *Truth about the Peace Treaties,* vol. 2, chaps. 19–26; G. A. Craig and F. Gilbert, eds., *The Diplomats 1919–1939,* chap. 6 (R. H. Davison); H. N. Howard, *Partition of Turkey,* chap. 7; K. Ziemke, *Die neue Türkei,* pp. 101–38; P. L. Hanna, *British Policy in Palestine,* chap. 3.

PART III. POLITICAL CLAUSES

SECTION I. CONSTANTINOPLE

ART. 36. Subject to the provisions of the present Treaty, the High Contracting Parties agree that the rights and title of the Turkish Government over Constantinople shall not be affected, and that the said Government and His Majesty the Sultan shall be entitled to reside there and to maintain there the capital of the Turkish State.

Nevertheless, in the event of Turkey failing to observe faithfully the provisions of the present Treaty, or of any treaties or conventions supplementary thereto, particularly as regards the protection of the rights of racial, religious or linguistic minorities, the Allied Powers expressly reserve the right to modify the above provisions, and Turkey hereby agrees to accept any dispositions which may be taken in this connection.

SECTION II. STRAITS

ART. 37. The navigation of the Straits, including the Dardanelles, the Sea of Marmora and the Bosphorus, shall in future be open, both in peace and war, to every vessel of commerce or of war and to military and commercial aircraft, without distinction of flag.

These waters shall not be subject to blockade, nor shall any belligerent right be exercised nor any act of hostility be committed within them, unless in pursuance of a decision of the Council of the League of Nations.

ART. 38. The Turkish Government recognizes that it is necessary to take further measures to ensure the freedom of navigation provided for in Article 37, and accordingly delegates, so far as it is concerned, to a Commission to be called the "Commission of the Straits," and hereinafter referred to as "the Commission," the control of the waters specified in Article 39.

The Greek Government, so far as it is concerned, delegates to the Commission the same powers and undertakes to give it in all respects the same facilities.

Such control shall be exercised in the name of the Turkish and Greek Governments respectively, and in the manner provided in this Section.

ART. 39. The authority of the Commission will extend to all the waters between the Mediterranean mouth of the Dardanelles and the Black Sea mouth of the Bosphorus, and to the waters within three miles of each of these mouths.

This authority may be exercised on shore to such extent as may be necessary for the execution of the provisions of this Section.

ART. 40. The Commission shall be composed of representatives appointed respectively by the United States of America (if and when that Government is willing to participate), the British Empire, France, Italy, Japan, Russia (if and when Russia becomes a member of the League of Nations), Greece, Roumania, and Bulgaria and Turkey (if and when the two latter States become members of the League of Nations). Each Power shall appoint one representative. The representatives of the United States of America, the British Empire, France, Italy, Japan and Russia shall each have two votes. The representatives of Greece, Roumania, and Bulgaria and Turkey shall each have one vote. Each Commissioner shall be removable only by the Government which appointed him. . . .

SECTION III. KURDISTAN

ART. 62. A Commission sitting at Constantinople and composed of three members appointed by the British, French and Italian Governments respectively shall draft within six months from the coming into force of the present Treaty a scheme of local autonomy for the predominantly Kurdish areas lying east of the Euphrates, south of the southern boundary of Armenia as it may be hereafter determined, and north of the frontier of Turkey with Syria and Mesopotamia, as defined in Article 27, II. (2) and (3). If unanimity cannot be secured on any question, it will be referred by the members of the Commission to their respective Governments. The scheme shall contain full safeguards for the protection of the Assyro-Chaldeans and other racial or religious minorities within these areas, and with this object a Commission composed of British, French, Italian, Persian and Kurdish representatives shall visit the spot to examine and decide what rectifications, if any, should be made in the Turkish frontier, where, under the provisions of the present Treaty, that frontier coincides with that of Persia.

ART. 63. The Turkish Government hereby agrees to accept and execute the decisions of both the Commissions mentioned in Article 62 within three months from their communication to the said Government.

ART. 64. If within one year from the coming into force of the present Treaty the Kurdish peoples within the areas defined in Article 62 shall address themselves to the Council of the League of Nations in such a manner as to show that a majority of the population of these areas desires independence from Turkey, and if the Council then considers that these peoples are capable of such independence and recommends that it should be granted to them, Turkey hereby agrees to execute such a recommendation, and to renounce all rights and title over these areas.

The detailed provisions for such renunciation will form the subject of a separate agreement between the Principal Allied Powers and Turkey.

If and when such renunciation takes place, no objection will be raised by the Principal Allied Powers to the voluntary adhesion to such an independent Kurdish State of the Kurds inhabiting that part of Kurdistan which has hitherto been included in the Mosul Vilayet.

SECTION IV. SMYRNA

ART. 65. The provisions of this Section will apply to the city of Smyrna and the adjacent territory defined in Article 66, until the determination of their final status in accordance with Article 83. . . .

ART. 67. A Commission shall be constituted within fifteen days from the coming into force of the present Treaty to trace on the spot the boundaries of the territories described in Article 66. This Commission shall be composed of three members nominated by the British, French and Italian Governments respectively, one member nominated by the Greek Government, and one nominated by the Turkish Government.

ART. 68. Subject to the provisions of this Section, the city of Smyrna and the territory defined in Article 66 will be assimilated, in the application of the present Treaty, to territory detached from Turkey.

ART. 69. The city of Smyrna and the territory defined in Article 66 remain under Turkish sovereignty. Turkey however transfers to the Greek Government the exercise of her rights of sovereignty over the city of Smyrna and the said territory. In witness of such sovereignty the Turkish flag shall remain permanently hoisted over an outer fort in the town of Smyrna. The fort will be designated by the Principal Allied Powers.

ART. 70. The Greek Government will be responsible for the administration of the city of Smyrna and the territory defined in Article 66, and will effect this administration by means of a body of officials which it will appoint specially for the purpose.

ART. 71. The Greek Government shall be entitled to maintain in the city of Smyrna and the territory defined in Article 66 the military forces required for the maintenance of order and public security.

ART. 72. A local parliament shall be set up with an electoral system calculated to ensure proportional representation of all sections of the population, including racial, linguistic and religious minorities. Within six months from the coming into force of the present Treaty the Greek Government shall submit to the Council of the League of Nations a scheme for an electoral system complying with the above requirements; this scheme shall not come into force until approved by a majority of the Council.

The Greek Government shall be entitled to postpone the elections for so long as may be required for the return of the inhabitants who have been banished or deported by the Turkish authorities, but such postponement shall not exceed a period of one year from the coming into force of the present Treaty.

ART. 73. The relations between the Greek administration and the local parliament shall be determined by the said administration in accordance with the principles of the Greek Constitution. . . .

ART. 83. When a period of five years shall have elapsed after the coming into force of the present Treaty the local parliament referred to in Article 72 may, by a majority of votes, ask the Council of the League of Nations for the definitive incorporation in the Kingdom of Greece of the city of Smyrna and the territory defined in Article 66. The Council may require, as a preliminary, a plebiscite under conditions which it will lay down.

In the event of such incorporation as a result of the application of the foregoing paragraph, the Turkish sovereignty referred to in Article 69 shall cease. Turkey hereby renounces in that event in favour of Greece all rights and title over the city of Smyrna and the territory defined in Article 66. . . .

SECTION VI. ARMENIA

ART. 88. Turkey, in accordance with the action already taken by the Allied Powers, hereby recognises Armenia as a free and independent State.

ART. 89. Turkey and Armenia as well as the other High Contracting Parties agree to submit to the arbitration of the President of the United States of America the question of the frontier to be fixed between Turkey and Armenia in the Vilayets of Erzerum, Trebizond, Van and Bitlis, and to accept his decision thereupon, as well as any stipulations he may prescribe as to access for Armenia to the sea, and as to the demilitarisation of any portion of Turkish territory adjacent to the said frontier.

ART. 90. In the event of the determination of the frontier under Article 89 involving the transfer of the whole or any part of the territory of the said Vilayets to Armenia, Turkey hereby renounces as from the date of such decision all rights and title over the territory so transferred. The provisions of the present Treaty applicable to territory detached from Turkey shall thereupon become applicable to the said territory.

The proportion and nature of the financial obligations of Turkey which Armenia will have to assume, or of the rights which will pass to her, on account of the transfer of the said territory will be determined in accordance with Articles 241 to 244, Part

VIII (Financial Clauses) of the present Treaty.

Subsequent agreements will, if necessary, decide all questions which are not decided by the present Treaty and which may arise in consequence of the transfer of the said territory.

ART. 91. In the event of any portion of the territory referred to in Article 89 being transferred to Armenia, a Boundary Commission, whose composition will be determined subsequently, will be constituted within three months from the delivery of the decision referred to in the said Article to trace on the spot the frontier between Armenia and Turkey as established by such decision.

ART. 92. The frontiers between Armenia and Azerbaijan and Georgia respectively will be determined by direct agreement between the States concerned.

If in either case the States concerned have failed to determine the frontier by agreement at the date of the decision referred to in Article 89, the frontier line in question will be determined by the Principal Allied Powers, who will also provide for its being traced on the spot.

ART. 93. Armenia accepts and agrees to embody in a Treaty with the Principal Allied Powers such provisions as may be deemed necessary by these Powers to protect the interests of inhabitants of that State who differ from the majority of the population in race, language, or religion.

Armenia further accepts and agrees to embody in a Treaty with the Principal Allied Powers such provisions as these Powers may deem necessary to protect freedom of transit and equitable treatment for the commerce of other nations.

SECTION VII. SYRIA, MESOPOTAMIA, PALESTINE

ART. 94. The High Contracting Parties agree that Syria and Mesopotamia shall, in accordance with the fourth paragraph of Article 22, Part I (Covenant of the League of Nations), be provisionally recognised as independent States subject to the rendering of administrative advice and assistance by a Mandatory until such time as they are able to stand alone.

A Commission shall be constituted within fifteen days from the coming into force of the present Treaty to trace on the spot the frontier line described in Article 27, II (2) and (3). This Commission will be composed of three members nominated by France, Great Britain and Italy respectively, and one member nominated by Turkey; it will be assisted by a representative of Syria for the Syrian frontier, and by a representative of Mesopotamia for the Mesopotamian frontier.

The determination of the other frontiers of the said States, and the selection of the Mandatories, will be made by the Principal Allied Powers.

ART. 95. The High Contracting Parties agree to entrust, by application of the provisions of Article 22, the administration of Palestine, within such boundaries as may be determined by the Principal Allied Powers, to a Mandatory to be selected by the said Powers. The Mandatory will be responsible for putting into effect the declaration originally made on November 2, 1917, by the British Government, and adopted by the other Allied Powers, in favour of the establishment in Palestine of a national home for the Jewish people, it being clearly understood that nothing shall be done which may prejudice the civil and religious rights of existing non-Jewish communities in Palestine, or the rights and political status enjoyed by Jews in any other country.

The Mandatory undertakes to appoint as soon as possible a special Commission to study and regulate all questions and claims relating to the different religious communities. In the composition of this Commission the religious interests concerned will be taken into account. The Chairman of the Commission will be appointed by the Council of the League of Nations.

ART. 96. The terms of the mandates in respect of the above territories will be formulated by the Principal Allied Powers and submitted to the Council of the League of Nations for approval.

ART. 97. Turkey hereby undertakes, in

accordance with the provisions of Article 132, to accept any decisions which may be taken in relation to the questions dealt with in this Section.

SECTION VIII. HEDJAZ

ART. 98. Turkey, in accordance with the action already taken by the Allied Powers, hereby recognises the Hedjaz as a free and independent State, and renounces in favour of the Hedjaz all rights and titles over the territories of the former Turkish Empire situated outside the frontiers of Turkey as laid down by the present Treaty, and comprised within the boundaries which may ultimately be fixed.

ART. 99. In view of the sacred character attributed by Moslems of all countries to the cities and the Holy Places of Mecca and Medina, His Majesty the King of Hedjaz undertakes to assure free and easy access thereto to Moslems of every country who desire to go there on pilgrimage or for any other religious object, and to respect and ensure respect for the pious foundations which are or may be established there by Moslems of any countries in accordance with the precepts of the law of the Koran.

ART. 100. His Majesty the King of the Hedjaz undertakes that in commercial matters the most complete equality of treatment shall be assured in the territory of the Hedjaz to the persons, ships and goods of nationals of any of the Allied Powers, or of any of the new States set up in the territories of the former Turkish Empire, as well as to the persons, ships and goods of nationals of States, Members of the League of Nations.

SECTION IX. EGYPT, SOUDAN, CYPRUS

1.—EGYPT

ART. 101. Turkey renounces all rights and title in or over Egypt. This renunciation shall take effect as from November 5, 1914. Turkey declares that in conformity with the action taken by the Allied Powers she recognizes the Protectorate proclaimed over Egypt by Great Britain on December 18, 1914.

ART. 102. Turkish subjects habitually resident in Egypt on December 18, 1914, will acquire Egyptian nationality *ipso facto* and will lose their Turkish nationality, except that if at that date such persons were temporarily absent from, and have not since returned to, Egypt they will not acquire Egyptian nationality without a special authorisation from the Egyptian Government.

ART. 103. Turkish subjects who became resident in Egypt after December 18, 1914, and are habitually resident there at the date of the coming into force of the present Treaty may, subject to the conditions prescribed in Article 105 for the right of option, claim Egyptian nationality, but such claim may in individual cases be refused by the competent Egyptian authority.

ART. 104. For all purposes connected with the present Treaty, Egypt and Egyptian nationals, their goods and vessels, shall be treated on the same footing, as from August 1, 1914, as the Allied Powers, their nationals, goods and vessels, and provisions in respect of territory under Turkish sovereignty, or of territory detached from Turkey in accordance with the present Treaty, shall not apply to Egypt.

ART. 105. Within a period of one year after the coming into force of the present Treaty persons over eighteen years of age acquiring Egyptian nationality under the provisions of Article 102 will be entitled to opt for Turkish nationality. In case such persons, or those who under Article 103 are entitled to claim Egyptian nationality, differ in race from the majority of the population of Egypt, they will within the same period be entitled to opt for the nationality of any State in favour of which territory is detached from Turkey, if the majority of the population of that State is of the same race as the person exercising the right to opt.

Option by a husband covers a wife and option by parents covers their children under eighteen years of age.

Persons who have exercised the above right to opt must, except where authorised to continue to reside in Egypt, transfer within the ensuing twelve months their place of residence to the State for which they have opted. They will be entitled to retain their immovable property in Egypt, and may carry with them their movable property of every description. No export or import duties or charges may be imposed upon them in connection with the removal of such property.

ART. 106. The Egyptian Government shall have complete liberty of action in regulating the status of Turkish subjects in Egypt and the conditions under which they may establish themselves in the territory.

ART. 107. Egyptian nationals shall be entitled, when abroad, to British diplomatic and consular protection.

ART. 108. Egyptian goods entering Turkey shall enjoy the treatment accorded to British goods.

ART. 109. Turkey renounces in favour of Great Britain the powers conferred upon His Imperial Majesty the Sultan by the Convention signed at Constantinople on October 29, 1888, relating to the free navigation of the Suez Canal.

ART. 110. All property and possessions in Egypt belonging to the Turkish Government pass to the Egyptian Government without payment.

ART. 111. All movable and immovable property in Egypt belonging to Turkish nationals (who do not acquire Egyptian nationality) shall be dealt with in accordance with the provisions of Part IX (Economic Clauses) of the present Treaty.

ART. 112. Turkey renounces all claim to the tribute formerly paid by Egypt.

Great Britain undertakes to relieve Turkey of all liability in respect of the Turkish loans secured on the Egyptian tribute.

These loans are:

The guaranteed loan of 1855;

The loan of 1894 representing the converted loans of 1854 and 1871;

The loan of 1891 representing the converted loan of 1877.

The sums which the Khedives of Egypt have from time to time undertaken to pay over to the houses by which these loans were issued will be applied as heretofore to the interest and the sinking funds of the loans of 1894 and 1891 until the final extinction of those loans. The Government of Egypt will also continue to apply the sum hitherto paid towards the interest on the guaranteed loan of 1855.

Upon the extinction of these loans of 1894, 1891 and 1855, all liability on the part of the Egyptian Government arising out of the tribute formerly paid by Egypt to Turkey will cease.

2.—SOUDAN

ART. 113. The High Contracting Parties declare and place on record that they have taken note of the Convention between the British Government and the Egyptian Government defining the status and regulating the administration of the Soudan, signed on January 19, 1899, as amended by the supplementary Convention relating to the town of Suakin signed on July 10, 1899.

ART. 114. Soudanese shall be entitled when in foreign countries to British diplomatic and consular protection.

3.—CYPRUS

ART. 115. The High Contracting Parties recognise the annexation of Cyprus proclaimed by the British Government on November 5, 1914.

ART. 116. Turkey renounces all rights and title over or relating to Cyprus, including the right to the tribute formerly paid by that island to the Sultan.

ART. 117. Turkish nationals born or habitually resident in Cyprus will acquire British nationality and lose their Turkish nationality, subject to the conditions laid down in the local law.

SECTION X. MOROCCO, TUNIS

ART. 118. Turkey recognises the French Protectorate in Morocco, and accepts all the consequences thereof. This recognition shall take effect as from March 30, 1912.

ART. 119. Moroccan goods entering Turkey shall be subject to the same treatment as French goods.

ART. 120. Turkey recognises the French Protectorate over Tunis and accepts all the consequences thereof. This recognition shall take effect as from May 12, 1881.

Tunisian goods entering Turkey shall be

subject to the same treatment as French goods.

SECTION XI. LIBYA, AEGEAN ISLANDS

ART. 121. Turkey definitely renounces all rights and privileges which under the Treaty of Lausanne of October 18, 1912, were left to the Sultan in Libya.

ART. 122. Turkey renounces in favour of Italy all rights and title over the following islands of the Aegean Sea; Stampalia (Astropalia), Rhodes (Rhodos), Calki (Kharki), Scarpanto, Casos (Casso), Pscopis (Tilos), Misiros (Nisyros), Calymnos (Kalymnos), Leros, Patmos, Lipsos (Lipso), Sini (Symi), and Cos (Kos), which are now occupied by Italy, and the islets dependent thereon, and also over the island of Castellorizzo. . .

SECTION XIII. GENERAL PROVISIONS

ART. 132. Outside her frontiers as fixed by the present Treaty Turkey hereby renounces in favour of the Principal Allied Powers all rights and title which she could claim on any ground over or concerning any territories outside Europe which are not otherwise disposed of by the present Treaty.

Turkey undertakes to recognize and conform to the measures which may be taken now or in the future by the Principal Allied Powers, in agreement where necessary with third Powers, in order to carry the above stipulation into effect. . . .

ART. 139. Turkey renounces formally all rights of suzerainty or jurisdiction of any kind over Moslems who are subject to the sovereignty or protectorate of any other State.

No power shall be exercised directly or indirectly by any Turkish authority whatever in any territory detached from Turkey or of which the existing status under the present Treaty is recognised by Turkey.

32. TRIPARTITE (SÈVRES) AGREEMENT ON ANATOLIA: THE BRITISH EMPIRE, FRANCE AND ITALY
10 August 1920

[Great Britain, *Parliamentary Papers, 1920,* Treaty Series No. 12, Cmd. 963]

The three European powers, at the time of the signature of the Ottoman peace treaty, concluded the following agreement, recognizing southwestern Anatolia as the area of Italian and Cilicia as the area of French special interests. But the tripartite agreement did not go into effect, for it rested on the Ottoman peace treaty which was never ratified. For references, see Doc. 31.

The British, French and Italian Governments, respectively represented by the undersigned Plenipotentiaries,

Being anxious to help Turkey, to develop her resources, and to avoid the international rivalries which have obstructed these objects in the past,

Being desirous to meet the request of the Turkish Government that it should receive the necessary assistance in the reorganisation of the administration of justice, the finances, the gendarmerie and the police, in the protection of religious, racial and linguistic minorities and in the economic development of the country,

Considering that the autonomy or eventual independence of Kurdistan has been recognised by them, and that it is desirable, with a view to facilitating the development of that country and the provision of any assistance which may be required in its administration, to avoid international rivalries in such matters,

Recognising the respective special interests of Italy in Southern Anatolia and of France in Cilicia and the western part of Kurdistan bordering on Syria, up to Jezireh ibn Omar, as these areas are hereafter defined,

Have agreed upon the following provisions:

ART. 1. There shall be perfect equality in Turkey between the Contracting Powers in the composition of all international commissions, whether existing or to be established (including the different services dependent thereon) charged with the reorganisation and supervision in a manner consistent with the independence of the country of the different public services (judicial and financial administrations, gendarmerie and police) and of ensuring the protection of racial, religious and linguistic minorities.

However, in the event of the Turkish Government, or the Government of Kurdistan, being desirous of obtaining external assistance in the local administration or police of the areas in which the special interests of France and Italy are respectively recognised, the Contracting Powers undertake not to dispute the preferential claim of the Power whose special interests in such areas are recognised to supply such assistance. This assistance shall be specially directed towards enhancing the protection afforded to racial, religious or linguistic minorities in the said areas.

ART. 2. In accordance with the provisions of the Treaty of Peace with Turkey, the nationals of the Contracting Powers, their ships and aircraft, and products and manufactured articles coming from or going to the territories, Dominions, Colonies or Protectorates of the said Powers, shall enjoy in the said areas perfect equality in all matters relating to commerce and navigation, and particularly as regards transit, customs and similar matters.

Nevertheless, the Contracting Powers undertake not to apply, nor to make or support applications on behalf of their nationals, for industrial or commercial concessions in an area in which the special interests of one of the said Powers are recognised, except in cases where such Power declines or is unable to take advantage of its special position.

ART. 3. The Contracting Powers undertake to render diplomatic support to each other in maintaining their respective positions in the areas in which their special interests are recognised.

ART. 4. The Anatolian railway, the Mersina-Tarsus-Adana railway and that part of the Bagdad railway which lies in Turkish territory as defined by the Treaty of Peace with Turkey shall be worked by a company whose capital will be subscribed by British, French and Italian financial groups. Part of the capital will be allotted to British, French and Italian groups in return for the interests that such groups may respectively have held in the Bagdad line as a whole on August 1, 1914; the rest of the capital will be divided equally between the British, French and Italian groups.

Nevertheless, in exchange for the whole or part of the interests owned by French nationals on August 1, 1914, in the Bagdad railway line, the French Government reserves the right to have conceded to it and to work the whole or part of the railway lines (including the Mersina-Tarsus-Adana line) which lie in the area in which its interests are specially recognised. In such event the share of French nationals in the company provided for in the preceding paragraph will be reduced by a proportion corresponding to the value of the lines which are thus conceded to the French Government. This right of the French Government must be exercised within twelve months from the coming into force of the Treaty of Peace with Turkey.

In the operations of the company constituted as provided by the first paragraph of this Article account will be taken of the particular rights and interests of the respective Governments which are recognised in the areas defined by the present agreement, but in such a way as not to injure the good working of the railways.

The Contracting Powers agree to support the unification in the near future of the entire railway system in the territory which remains Turkish by the establishment of a joint company for working the lines. The division of the capital of this new company will be settled by agreement between the groups concerned.

The company constituted as provided by the first paragraph of this Article, as well as any company which may be formed for the purpose indicated in the fourth paragraph, will alike be bound to comply with the provisions of Part XI (Ports, Waterways and Railways) of the Treaty of Peace with Turkey, and in particular to accord absolute equality of treatment in respect of railway rates and facilities to goods and passengers of whatever nationality, destination or origin. The French Government undertakes, in the event of its exercising the right provided for in the second paragraph of this Article, to comply with the same provisions in respect of any railway line so conceded to it. . . .

[Article 5 defines the boundaries of the French and Italian zones of special interest.]

ART. 6. In relation to the territories detached from the former Turkish Empire and placed under mandate by the Treaty of Peace with Turkey, the Mandatory Power will enjoy *vis-à-vis* of the other Contracting Powers the same rights and privileges as the Powers whose special interests are respectively recognised in the areas defined in Article 5 enjoy in the said areas.

ART. 7. All concessions for exploiting the coal basin of Heraclea, as well as the means of transport and loading connected with these concessions, are reserved for the Italian Government, without prejudice to all rights of the same nature (concessions granted or applied for) acquired by Allied or neutral nationals up to October 30, 1918. As regards rights of exploitation belonging to Turkish subjects, their indemnification will take place in agreement with the Turkish Government, but at the cost of the Italian Government.

Nevertheless, on the date on which the Italian Government or the Italian companies shall have brought their annual production of coal up to an amount equal to that produced as on January 1, 1930, by companies belonging on October 30, 1918, to Allied or neutral nationals, the Italian Government agrees in a spirit of equity to reserve for the Société ottomane d'Eraclée, constituted with French capital (in the event of the latter not having previously expressed the wish to be brought out or to abandon the renewal of its concession), a quarter share in the interest which may be formed, once Italy or the Italian companies shall have reached a production of coal equal in amount to that of the said Allied and neutral nationals as on January 1, 1930.

The two Governments will give each other mutual diplomatic support with a view to securing from the Turkish Government the issue of fresh ordinances, ensuring the exploitation of the mining rights conceded, the establishment of means of transport, such as mining railways and every facility for loading, as well as the eventual employment of other than Turkish labour, and corresponding to the demands of modern methods of exploitation. It is hereby agreed that all concessions, whether granted after or before the issue of the above ordinances, will be equally entitled to all benefits and advantages resulting from their coming into force.

ART. 8. The French and Italian Governments will withdraw their troops from the respective areas where their special interests are recognised when the Contracting Powers are agreed in considering that the said Treaty of Peace is being executed and that the measures accepted by Turkey for the protection of Christian minorities have been put into force and their execution effectively guaranteed.

ART. 9. Each of the Contracting Powers whose special interests are recognised in any area in Turkish territory shall accept therewith the responsibility for supervising the execution of the Treaty of Peace with Turkey with regard to the protection of minorities in such area.

ART. 10. Nothing in this agreement shall prejudice the right of nationals of third States to free access for commercial and economic purposes to any of the areas defined in Article 5, subject to the reservations which are contained in the Treaty of Peace with Turkey, or which have been voluntarily accepted for themselves in the present agreement by the Contracting Powers.

33. TREATY OF FRIENDSHIP: PERSIA AND RUSSIA
26 February–12 December 1921

(Ratifications exchanged, Tehran, 26 February 1922)
[*British and Foreign State Papers,* vol. 114, pp. 901–09]

Armenia, Azarbayjan and Georgia declared their independence during the civil war in Russia (1918–20), and the communist regime had to reconquer the territory. Because of restiveness in Transcaucasia, the Soviet government found it prudent to court neighboring Turkey and Persia. Moscow could trade in Persia on the deepening anti-British feeling to which the unratified Anglo-Persian agreements of 9 August 1919 (Doc. 26) gave rise. Yet negotiations dragged for a formal bilateral instrument which would embody, among other clauses, the Soviet unilateral cancellation of tsarist privileges in Persia (Doc. 17). Signatures were not appended to the Russo-Persian treaty of friendship until five days after the *coup de'état* staged by Colonel Riza Khan of the Persian Cossack Brigade in collaboration with a group of politicians headed by Sayyid Ziya-al-Din Tabatabai. At this point the new regime in Persia sought international recognition, so that the two governments found mutual advantage in reaching a formal understanding. Nevertheless Persia deferred ratifications until after Moscow evacuated Red Army units in the fall of 1921 from Gilan, which they had occupied after crushing the White Russian forces in Azarbayjan in May 1920, and the Soviet diplomatic representative at Tehran gave the Persian government satisfactory written clarification of the meaning of articles 3, 5, 6, 13 and 20 of the draft treaty. G. Lenczowski, *Russia and the West in Iran,* chap. 3; M. Beloff, *The Foreign Policy of Soviet Russia,* vol. 2, chap. 9; A. L. P. Dennis, *Foreign Policies of Soviet Russia,* chap. 10; L. Fischer, *Soviets in World Affairs,* vol. 1, chap. 13; G. Ducroq, "La politique du gouvernement des Soviets en Perse," *Revue du monde musulman,* 52 (December 1922), 84–180; A. Palmieri, *La Politica asiatica dei bolscevichi,* chap. 4; É. Lesueur, *Les Anglais en Perse,* pp. 25–49, 137–71.

ART. I. In order to confirm its declarations regarding Russian policy towards the Persian nation, which formed the subject of correspondence on the 14th January, 1918, and the 26th June, 1919, the R.S.F.S.R. formally affirms once again that it definitely renounces the tyrannical policy carried out by the colonising Governments of Russia which have been overthrown by the will of the workers and peasants of Russia.

Inspired by this principle, and desiring that the Persian people should be happy and independent and should be able to dispose freely of its patrimony, the Russian Republic declares the whole body of treaties and conventions concluded with Persia by the Tsarist Government, which crushed the rights of the Persian people, to be null and void.

II. The R.S.F.S.R. expresses its reprobation of the policy of the Tsarist Governments of Russia, which, on the pretext of ensuring the independence of the peoples of Asia, concluded, without the consent of the latter, treaties with European Powers, the sole object of which was to subjugate those peoples.

This criminal policy, which infringed upon the independence of the countries of Asia and which made the living nations of the East a prey to the cupidity and the tyranny of European robbers, is abandoned unconditionally by Federal Russia.

Federal Russia, therefore, in accordance with the principles laid down in Articles I and IV of this Treaty, declares its refusal to participate in any action which might destroy or weaken Persian sovereignty. It regards as null and void the whole body of treaties and conventions concluded by the former Russian Government with third parties in respect of Persia or to the detriment of that country.

III. The two Contracting Powers agree to accept and respect the Russo-Persian frontiers, as drawn by the Frontier Commission in 1881.

At the same time, in view of the repugnance which the Russian Federal Government feels to enjoying the fruit of the policy of usurpation of the Tsarist Government, it renounces all claim to the Achouradeh Islands and to the other islands on the Astrabad Littoral, and restores to Persia the village of Firouzeh and the adjacent land ceded to Russia in virtue of the Convention of the 28th May, 1893.

The Persian Government agrees for its part that the Russian Sarakhs, or "old" Sarakhs, and the land adjacent to the Sarakhs River, shall be retained by Russia.

The two High Contracting Parties shall have equal rights of usage over the Atrak River and the other frontier rivers and waterways. In order finally to solve the question of the waterways and all disputes concerning frontiers or territories, a Commission, composed of Russian and Persian representatives, shall be appointed.

IV. In consideration of the fact that each nation has the right to determine freely its political destiny, each of the two Contracting Parties formally expresses its desire to abstain from any intervention in the internal affairs of the other.

V. The two High Contracting Parties undertake—

1. To prohibit the formation or presence within their respective territories of any organisations or groups of persons, irrespective of the name by which they are known, whose object is to engage in acts of hostility against Persia or Russia, or against the allies of Russia.

They will likewise prohibit the formation of troops or armies within their respective territories with the aforementioned object.

2. Not to allow a third party or any organisation, whatever it be called, which is hostile to the other Contracting Party, to import or to convey in transit across their countries material which can be used against the other Party.

3. To prevent by all means in their power the presence within their territories or within the territories of their allies of all armies or forces of a third party in cases in which the presence of such forces would be regarded as a menace to the frontiers, interests or safety of the other Contracting Party.

VI. If a third party should attempt to carry out a policy of usurpation by means of armed intervention in Persia, or if such power should desire to use Persian territory as a base of operations against Russia, or if a foreign Power should threaten the frontiers of Federal Russia or those of its allies, and if the Persian Government should not be able to put a stop to such menace after having been once called upon to do so by Russia, Russia shall have the right to advance her troops into the Persian interior for the purpose of carrying out the military operations necessary for its defence. Russia undertakes, however, to withdraw her troops from Persian territory as soon as the danger has been removed.

VII. The considerations set forth in Article VI have equal weight in the matter of the security of the Caspian Sea. The two High Contracting Parties therefore have agreed that Federal Russia shall have the right to require the Persian Government to send away foreign subjects, in the event of their taking advantage of their engagement in the Persian navy to undertake hostile action against Russia.

VIII. Federal Russia finally renounces the economic policy pursued in the East by the Tsarist Government, which consisted in lending money to the Persian Government, not with a view to the economic development of the country, but rather for purposes of political subjugation.

Federal Russia accordingly renounces its rights in respect of the loans granted to Persia by the Tsarist Governments. It regards the debts due to it as void, and will not require their repayment. Russia likewise renounces its claims to the resources of Persia which were specified as security for the loans in question.

IX. In view of the declaration by which it has repudiated the colonial and capitalist policy which occasioned so many misfortunes and was the cause of so much bloodshed, Federal Russia abandons the continuation of the economic undertakings of the Tsarist Government, the object of which was the economic subjugation of Persia. Federal Russia therefore cedes to the Persian Government the full ownership of all funds and of all real and other property which the Russian Discount Bank possesses on Persian territory, and likewise transfers to it all the assets and liabilities of that bank. The Persian Government nevertheless agrees that in the towns where it has been decided that the Russian Socialist Republic may establish consulates, and where buildings exist belonging to the Discount Bank, one of these buildings, to be chosen by the Russian Government, shall be placed at the disposal of the Russian Consulate, free of charge.

X. The Russian Federal Government, having abandoned the colonial policy, which consisted in the construction of roads and telegraph lines more in order to obtain military influence in other countries than for the purpose of developing their civilisations, and being desirous of providing the Persian people with those means of communication indispensable for the independence and development of any nation, and also in order to compensate the Persian people as far as possible for the losses incurred by the sojourn in its territory of the Tsarist armies, cedes free of charge to the Persian Government the following Russian installations:—

(*a.*) The high-roads from Enzeli to Tehran, and from Kazvin to Hamadan, and all land and installations in connection with these roads.

(*b.*) The railroad Djoulfa-Tauris-Sofian-Urmia, with all installations, rolling-stock and accessories.

(*c.*) The landing-stages, warehouses, steamships, canals, and all means of transport of the lake of Urmia.

(*d.*) All telegraph and telephone lines established in Persia by the Tsarist Governments, with all movable and immovable installations and dependencies.

(*e.*) The port of Enzeli and the warehouses, with the electrical installation, and other buildings.

XI. In view of the fact that the Treaty of Turkomantchai, concluded on the 10th February, 1828 [old style], between Persia and Russia, which forbids Persia, under the terms of Article 8, to have vessels in the waters of the Caspian Sea, is abrogated in accordance with the principles set forth in Article I of the present Treaty, the two High Contracting Parties shall enjoy equal rights of free navigation on that sea, under their own flags, as from the date of the signing of the present Treaty.

XII. The Russian Federal Government, having officially renounced all economic interests obtained by military preponderance, further declares that, apart from the concessions which form the subject of Articles IX and X, the other concessions obtained by force by the Tsarist Government and its subjects shall also be regarded as null and void.

In conformity with which the Russian Federal Government restores, as from the date of the signing of the present Treaty, to the Persian Government, as representing the Persian people, all the concessions in question, whether already being worked or not, together with all land taken over in virtue of those concessions.

Of the lands and properties situated in Persia and belonging to the former Tsarist Government, only the premises of the Russian Legation at Tehran and at Zerguendeh with all movable and immovable appurtenances, as well as all real and other property of the Consulates and Vice-Consulates, shall be retained by Russia. Russia abandons, however, her right to administer the village of Zerguendeh, which was arrogated to itself by the former Tsarist Government.

XIII. The Persian Government, for its part, promises not to cede to a third Power, or to its subjects, the concessions and property restored to Persia by virtue of the present Treaty, and to maintain those rights for the Persian nation.

XIV. The Persian Government, recognising the importance of the Caspian fisheries for the food supply of Russia, promises to conclude with the Food Service of the Russian Socialist Federal Soviet Republic immediately upon the expiry of the legal period of these existing engagements, a contract relating to the fisheries, containing appropriate clauses. Furthermore, the Persian Government promises to examine, in agreement with the Government of the Russian Socialist Federal Soviet Republic, the means of at once conveying the produce of the fisheries to the Food Service of Soviet Russia pending the conclusion of the above contract.

XV. In accordance with the principle of liberty of conscience proclaimed by Soviet Russia, and with a desire to put an end, in Moslem countries, to religious propaganda, the real object of which was to exercise political influence over the masses and thus to satisfy the rapacity of the Tsarist Government, the Government of Soviet Russia declares that the religious settlements established in Persia by the former Tsarist Governments are abolished. Soviet Russia will take steps to prevent such missions from being sent to Persia in the future.

Soviet Russia cedes unconditionally to the nation represented by the Persian Government the lands, property and buildings belonging to the Orthodox Mission situated at Urmia, together with the other similar establishments. The Persian Government shall use these properties for the construction of schools and other institutions intended for educational purposes.

XVI. By virtue of the communication from Soviet Russia dated the 25th June, 1919, with reference to the abolition of consular jurisdictions, it is decided that Russian subjects in Persia and Persian subjects in Russia shall, as from the date of the present Treaty, be placed upon the same footing as the inhabitants of the towns in which they reside; they shall be subject to the laws of their country of residence, and shall submit their complaints to the local Courts.

XVII. Persian subjects in Russia and Russian subjects in Persia shall be exempt from military service and from all military taxation.

XVIII. Persian subjects in Russia and Russian subjects in Persia shall, as regards travel within the respective countries, enjoy the rights granted to the most favoured nations other than countries allied to them.

XIX. Within a short period after the signature of the present Treaty, the two High Contracting Parties shall resume commercial relations. The methods to be adopted for the organisation of the import and export of goods, methods of payment, and the customs duties to be levied by the Persian Government on goods originating in Russia, shall be determined, under a commercial Convention, by a special Commission consisting of representatives of the two High Contracting Parties.

XX. Each of the two High Contracting Parties grants to the other the right of transit for the transport of goods passing through Persia or Russia and consigned to a third country.

The dues exacted in such cases shall not be higher than those levied on the goods of the most favoured nations other than countries allied to the Russian Socialist Federal Soviet Republic.

XXI. The two High Contracting Parties shall open telegraphic and postal relations between Russia and Persia within the shortest possible period after the signature of the present Treaty.

The conditions of these relations shall be fixed by a postal and telegraphic Convention.

XXII. In order to consolidate the good relations between the two neighbouring Powers and to facilitate the realisation of the friendly intentions of each country towards the other, each of the High Contracting Parties shall, immediately after the signature of the present Treaty, be represented in the capital of the other by a Plenipotentiary Representative, who shall enjoy the rights of extra-territoriality and other privileges to which diplomatic representatives are entitled by international law and usage and by the regulations and customs of the two countries.

XXIII. In order to develop their mutual relations, the two High Contracting Parties shall establish Consulates in places to be determined by common agreement.

The rights and duties of the Consuls shall be fixed by a special Agreement to be concluded without delay after the signature of the present Treaty. This Agreement shall conform to the provisions in force in the two countries with regard to consular establishments. . . .

XXV. The present Treaty is drawn up in Russian and Persian. Both texts shall be regarded as originals and both shall be authentic.

XXVI. The present Treaty shall come into force immediately upon signature. . . .

EXCHANGE OF NOTES, 12 DECEMBER 1921

1. *From the Persian Foreign Minister*

The Persian Government and the Mejlis have observed that Articles V and VI of the Treaty concluded between our two countries are worded vaguely; the Mejlis, moreover, desires that the retrocession of Russian concessions to the Persian Government should be made without reserve or condition, and that Article XX should be so worded as to allow the Persian Government full powers for the transit of imports and exports. Conversations have taken place with you on these questions, and you have given explanations with regard to Articles V and VI and promises concerning Articles XIII and XX, to the effect that if the Treaty were passed by the Mejlis you would give all the assistance in your power to ensure that the two Articles in question should be revised on the lines desired by the Mejlis and the Persian Government. The Persian Government and the Mejlis are most desirous that friendly relations should be re-established between our two Governments, and that the Treaty, which is based upon the most amicable sentiments, should be concluded as soon as possible.

I have, therefore, the honour to request you to give in writing your explanations with regard to the interpretation of Articles V and VI, and to repeat the promises of support which you have already given as regards the revision of Articles XIII and XX, in order that the Persian Government may be enabled to secure the passing of the Treaty by the Mejlis.

I also wish to ask you to take the necessary steps to repair the error which has been made in Article III, in which the word "Commission" was written instead of "Treaty," as the only Treaty which was concluded in 1881 was a frontier delimitation Treaty, and this is the Treaty referred to in Article III.

2. *From the Russian Diplomatic Representative, Tehran*

In reply to your letter dated the 20th day of Ghows, I have the honour to inform you that Articles V and VI are intended to apply only to cases in which preparations have been made for a considerable armed attack upon Russia or the Soviet Republics allied to her, by the partisans of the régime which has been overthrown or by its supporters among those foreign Powers which are in a position to assist the enemies of the Workers' and Peasants' Republics and at the same time to possess themselves, by force or by underhand methods, of part of the Persian territory, thereby establishing a base of operations for any attacks—made either directly or through the counter-revolutionary forces—which they might meditate against Russia or the Soviet Republics allied to her. The Articles referred to are therefore in no sense intended to apply to verbal or written attacks directed against the Soviet Government by the various Persian groups, or even by any Russian *émigrés* in Persia, in so far as such attacks are generally tolerated as between neighbouring Powers animated by sentiments of mutual friendship.

With regard to Articles XIII and XX, and the small error to which you draw attention in Article III with reference to the Convention of 1881, I am in a position to state categorically, as I have always stated, that my Government, whose attitude towards the Persian nation is entirely friendly, has never sought to place any restriction upon the progress and prosperity of Persia. I myself fully share this attitude, and would be prepared, should friendly relations be maintained between the two countries, to promote negotiations with a view to a total or partial revision of these Articles on the lines desired by the Persian Government, as far as the interests of Russia permit.

In view of the preceding statements, I trust that, as you promised me in your letter, your Government and the Mejlis will ratify the Treaty in question as soon as possible.

34. TREATY OF FRIENDSHIP: TURKEY AND RUSSIA
16 March 1921

(Ratifications exchanged, Kars, 13 September 1921)

[*British and Foreign State Papers,* vol. 118, pp. 990–96]

Early in 1921 the provisional nationalist government in Turkey under Mustafa Kemal, like the new regime in next-door Persia, was looking for friends. Because of British support for the Greek invasion and the continued occupation of large segments of Anatolia by French and Italian forces, Soviet Russia could exploit strong popular sentiments against the victorious allies. Moscow and Ankara agreed to establish diplomatic relations as early as 24 August 1920, and the first diplomat representing nationalist Turkey in Soviet Russia reached his post on 8 November. The treaty with the Ankara regime was concluded in Moscow and, though similar to that with Persia (Doc. 33), was formulated in less blatantly propagandist phraseology. A. L. P. Dennis, *Foreign Policies of Soviet Russia,* chaps. 9, 10; L. Fischer, *Soviets in World Affairs,* vol. 1, chap. 12; *Survey of International Affairs, 1920–1923,* pp. 361–76; K. Ziemke, *Die neue Türkei,* pp. 177–80; W., "Les Relations russo-turques depuis l'avenement du Bolchevisme," *Revue du monde musulman,* 52 (December 1922), 181–206.

The Government of the Russian Socialist Federal Soviet Republic and the Government of the Grand National Assembly of Turkey, sharing as they do the principles of the liberty of nations, and the right of each nation to determine its own fate, and taking into consideration, moreover, the common struggle undertaken against imperialism, foreseeing that the difficulties arising for the one would render worse the position of the other, and inspired by the desire to bring about lasting good relations and uninterrupted sincere friendship between themselves, based on mutual interests, have decided to sign an agreement to assure amicable and fraternal relations between the two countries. . . .

ART. I. Each of the contracting parties agrees not to recognise any peace treaty or other international agreement imposed upon the other against its will. The Government of the R.S.F.S.R. agrees not to recognise any international agreement relating to Turkey which is not recognised by the National Government of Turkey, at present represented by the Grand National Assembly.

The expression "Turkey" in the present treaty is understood to mean the territories included in the Turkish National Pact on the 28th January, 1920, elaborated and proclaimed by the Ottoman Chamber of Deputies in Constantinople, and communicated to the press and to all foreign Governments.

The north-east frontier of Turkey is fixed as follows: A line which begins at the village of Sari, situated on the coast of the Black Sea, goes over the mountain Khedis Mga, then by the line of watershed of the mountains Shavshet Dagh and Kapni Dagh, after which it follows the northern border of the sanjaks of Ardahan and Kars, then the thalweg of the Rivers Arpa-Chai and Araxes to the mouth of the Lower Kara Su. (A detailed description of the frontier and connected matters is given in Annex I (A) and (B) and on the attached map signed by both contracting parties.)[1]

II. Turkey agrees to cede to Georgia the right of suzerainty over the town and the port of Batum, and the territory situated to the north of the frontier mentioned in Article I, which formed a part of the district of Batum, on the following conditions:—

(*a.*) The population of the localities specified in the present Article shall enjoy a generous measure of autonomy, assuring to each community its cultural and religious rights, and allowing them to enact agrarian laws in accordance with the wishes of the population of the said districts.

(*b.*) Turkey will be granted free transit for all Turkish imports and exports through

[1] Not reproduced.

the port of Batum, without payment of taxes and customs duties and without delays. The right of making use of the port of Batum without special expenses is assured to Turkey.

III. Both contracting parties agree that the Nakhichevan district, with the boundaries shown in Annex 1 (C) to the present treaty, shall form an autonomous territory under the protection of Azerbaijan, on condition that the latter cannot transfer this protectorate to any third State. In the Nakhichevan region, which forms a triangle enclosed within the Araxes Valley and the line of the mountains Daghna (3,829), Veli Dagh (4,121), Bagarsik (6,587), Kemurlu Dagh (6,930), the boundary of the above-mentioned district beginning at the Kemurlu Dagh (6,930), passing over Serai Bulak Dagh (8,071) and the station of Ararat, and finishing at the junction of the Kara Su and the Araxes, will be determined by a commission composed of delegates of Turkey, Azerbaijan and Armenia.

IV. The contracting parties, establishing contact between the national movement for the liberation of the Eastern peoples and the struggle of the workers of Russia for a new social order, solemnly recognise the right of these nations to freedom and independence, also their right to choose a form of government according to their own wishes.

V. In order to assure the opening of the Straits to the commerce of all nations, the contracting parties agree to entrust the final elaboration of an international agreement concerning the Black Sea to a conference composed of delegates of the littoral States, on condition that the decisions of the above-mentioned conference shall not be of such a nature as to diminish the full sovereignty of Turkey or the security of Constantinople, her capital.

VI. The contracting parties agree that the treaties concluded heretofore between the two countries do not correspond with their mutual interests, and therefore agree that the said treaties shall be considered as annulled and abrogated.

The Government of the R.S.F.S.R. declares that it considers Turkey to be liberated from all financial and other liabilities based on agreements concluded between Turkey and the Tsarist Government.

VII. The Government of the R.S.F.S.R., holding that the Capitulations régime is incompatible with the full exercise of sovereign rights and the national development of any country, declares this régime and any rights connected therewith to be null and void.

VIII. The contracting parties undertake not to tolerate in their respective territories the formation and stay of organisations or associations claiming to be the Government of the other country or of a part of its territory and organisations whose aim is to wage warfare against the other State.

Russia and Turkey mutually accept the same obligation with regard to the Soviet Republic of the Caucasus.

"Turkish territory," within the meaning of this Article, is understood to be territory under the direct civil and military administration of the Government of the Grand National Assembly of Turkey.

IX. To secure uninterrupted communication between the two countries, both contracting parties undertake to carry out urgently, and in agreement one with the other, all necessary measures for the security and development of the railway lines, telegraph and other means of communication, and to assure free movement of persons and goods between the two countries. It is agreed that the regulations in force in each country shall be applied as regards the movement, entry and exit of travellers and goods.

X. The nationals of both of the contracting parties residing on the territory of the other shall be treated in accordance with the laws in force in the country of their residence, with the exception of those connected with national defence, from which they are exempt. The nationals of the contracting parties will be exempt from the provisions of the present Article as regards family rights, rights of succession and juridical capacity. These latter rights shall be settled by a special agreement.

XI. The contracting parties agree to treat the nationals of one of the parties residing in the territory of the other in accordance with the most-favoured-nation principles.

This Article will not be applied to citizens of the Soviet Republics allied with Russia, nor to nationals of Mussulman States allied with Turkey.

XII. Any inhabitant of the territories forming part of Russia prior to 1918, and over which Turkish sovereignty has been acknowledged by the Government of the R.S.F.S.R., in the present treaty, shall be free to leave Turkey and to take with him all his goods and possessions or the proceeds of their sale. The population of the territory of Batum, sovereignty over which has been granted to Georgia by Turkey, shall enjoy the same right.

XIII. Russia undertakes to return, at her own expense within three months, to the north-east frontier of Turkey all Turkish prisoners of war and interned civilians in the Caucasus and in European Russia, and those in Asiatic Russia within six months, dating from the signature of the present treaty. The details concerning the repatriation of these prisoners will be fixed by a special agreement, which will be concluded immediately after the signature of the present treaty.

XIV. The contracting parties agree to conclude in as short a time as possible a consular agreement and other arrangements regulating all economic, financial and other questions which are necessary for the establishment of friendly relations between the two countries, as set forth in the preamble to the present treaty.

XV. Russia undertakes to take the necessary steps with the Transcaucasian Republics with a view to securing the recognition by the latter, in their agreement with Turkey, of the provisions of the present treaty which directly concern them.

XVI. The present treaty shall be subject to the formality of ratification. Ratifications shall be exchanged as soon as possible at Kars. With the exception of Article XIII, the present treaty shall come into force at the moment of the exchange of ratifications.

35. AGREEMENT (ANKARA) FOR THE PROMOTION OF PEACE: FRANCE AND THE PROVISIONAL (NATIONALIST) GOVERNMENT OF TURKEY
20 October 1921

(Approved by the French Government and entered into force, 28 October 1921)
[League of Nations, *Treaty Series,* No. 1284, vol. 54 (1926–27), pp. 178–93]

Italian and French designs on southern Anatolia collapsed as Turkish nationalists compelled the European powers to fight for the territory. Italy, the first to retire, ended its occupation of the Antalya zone on 5 July 1921. French forces for their part suffered serious losses in Cilicia. The evacuation of Maraş in February 1920 was followed two months later, when nationalist guerrillas captured an entire French unit, by withdrawal from Urfa. Franco-Turkish hostilities did not cease after the provisional armistice of 30 May 1920, so that Turkish irregulars were able to oust French troops from Antep (present-day Gaziantep) by 8 February 1921. The French government finally decided to leave Cilicia altogether and concentrate its efforts on Syria and Lebanon. To this end an agreement—the first between the provisional Turkish nationalist government and a Western European power—was concluded at Ankara on 20 October 1921 by Henri Franklin-Bouillon and Yusuf Kemal Bey, the Turkish nationalist Foreign Minister. The Angora (Ankara) or Franklin-Bouillon accord, as it is commonly known, brought into the open the grave differences between France and Britain over the Turkish settlement. Anglo-French friction shored up immeasurably the nationalist position, as did France's *de facto* recognition of the provisional regime (despite the Quai d'Orsay's vigorous denial at the time), France's deliberate abandonment of substantial war matériel in Cilicia, and the release of nationalist troops from the former Italian and French fronts for operations against the Greeks on the sole remaining front in the west. Omitted below are the notes which the plenipotentiaries exchanged. Mustafa

Kemal (Atatürk), *A Speech Delivered . . . October 1927,* pp. 523–27; G. A. Craig and F. Gilbert, eds., *The Diplomats 1919–1939,* chap. 6 (by R. H. Davison); H. W. V. Temperley, *History of the Paris Peace Conference,* vol. 6, pp. 33–35; H. H. Cumming, *Franco-British Rivalry in the Post-war Near East,* chap. 12; E. R. Vere-Hodge, *Turkish Foreign Policy, 1918–1948,* pp. 33–37; K. Ziemke, *Die neue Türkei,* pp. 153–63.

1. THE FRANCO-TURKISH AGREEMENT

ART. I. The High Contracting Parties declare that from the date of the signature of the present Agreement the state of war between them shall cease; the armies, the civil authorities and the people shall be immeately informed thereof.

ART. II. As soon as the present Agreement has been signed, the respective prisoners of war and also all French and Turkish persons detained or imprisoned shall be set at liberty and conducted, at the cost of the party which detained them, to the nearest town which shall be designated for this purpose. The benefit of this Article tends to all detained persons and prisoners of both Parties irrespective of the date and place of detention, of imprisonment or of capture.

ART. III. Within a maximum period of two months from the date of the signature of the present Agreement, the Turkish troops shall withdraw to the north and the French troops to the south of the line specified in Article VIII.

ART. IV. The evacuation and the occupation which shall take place within the period provided in Article III shall be carried out to a form to be decided upon by mutual agreement by a mixed commission appointed by the military commanders of the two Parties.

ART. V. A complete amnesty shall be granted by the two Contracting Parties in the regions evacuated as soon as they are re-occupied.

ART. VI. The Government of the Grand National Assembly of Turkey declares that the rights of minorities solemnly recognised in the National Covenant will be confirmed by it on the same basis as that established by the conventions on this subject between the *Entente* Powers, their enemies and certain of their Allies.

ART. VII. A special administrative *régime* shall be established for the district of Alexandretta. The Turkish inhabitants of this district shall enjoy every facility for their cultural development. The Turkish language shall have official recognition.

ART. VIII. The line mentioned in Article III is fixed and determined as follows:

The frontier line shall start at a point to be selected on the Gulf of Alexandretta immediately to the south of the locality of Payas and will proceed generally towards Meidan-Ekbes (leaving the railway station and the locality to Syria);

thence it will bend towards the south-east so as to leave the locality of Marsova to Syria and that of Karnaba as well as the town of Killis to Turkey; thence it will join the railway at the station of Choban-bey. Then it will follow the Baghdad Railway, of which the track as far as Nisibin will remain on Turkish territory; thence it will follow the old road between Nisibin and Jeziret-ibn-Omar where it will join the Tigris. The localities of Nisibin and Jeziret-ibn-Omar as well as the road will remain Turkish; but the two countries shall have the same rights to the use of this road.

The stations and sidings of the section between Choban-bey and Nisibin shall belong to Turkey as forming parts of the track of the railway.

A commission comprising delegates of the two Parties will be constituted, within a period of one month from the signature of the present Agreement, to determine the above-mentioned line. This commission shall begin its labours within the same period.

ART. IX. The tomb of Suleiman Shah, the grandfather of the Sultan Osman, founder of the Ottoman dynasty (the tomb known under the name of Turk Mézari), situated at Jaber-Kalesi, shall remain, with its appurtenances, the property of Turkey, who may appoint guardians for it and may hoist the Turkish flag there.

ART. X. The Government of the Grand National Assembly of Turkey agrees to the transfer of the concession of the section of the Baghdad Railway between Bozanti and Nisibin as well as of the several branches constructed in the vilayet of Adana to a French group nominated by the French Government, with all the rights, privileges and advantages attached to the concessions, particularly as regards working and traffic.

Turkey shall have the right to transport troops by railway from Meidan-Ekbes to Choban-bey in Syrian territory and Syria shall have the right to transport troops by railway from Choban-bey to Nisibin in Turkish territory.

In principle no differential tariff shall be levied over this section and these branches. However, should a case arise, the two Governments reserve the right to examine by mutual agreement any departure from this rule which may become necessary.

Failing agreement, each Party will resume its liberty of action.

ART. XI. A mixed commission shall be constituted after the ratification of the present Agreement with a view to the conclusion of a Customs Convention between Turkey and Syria. The terms and also the duration of this Convention shall be fixed by this commission. Until the conclusion of the above-mentioned Convention the two countries will preserve their liberty of action.

ART. XII. The waters of Kuveik shall be shared between the city of Aleppo and the district to the north remaining Turkish, in such a way as to give equitable satisfaction to the two Parties.

The city of Aleppo may also organise, at its own expense, a water supply from the Euphrates in Turkish territory in order to meet the requirements of the district.

ART. XIII. The inhabitants, whether settled or semi-nomadic, who enjoy rights of pasturage or who own property on one or other side of the line fixed in Article VIII shall continue to exercise their rights as in the past. They shall be able, for this purpose, freely and without payment of any duty of Customs or of pasturage or any other tax, to transport from one side to the other of the line their cattle with their young, their implements, their tools, their seeds and their agricultural produce, it being well understood that they are liable for the payment of the imposts and taxes due to the country where they are domiciled.

2. TURKISH OBSERVATIONS

On proceeding to sign the Agreement concluded this day between the Government of the Grand National Assembly of Turkey and the Government of the French Republic, Youssouf Kémal Bey, the Turkish Plenipotentiary, made the following observations, of which M. Franklin-Bouillon, French Plenipotentiary, took note:

The Turkish Plenipotentiary desires to make express reservations in respect of the settlement of questions concerning the participation of Syria in the Ottoman Debt, concerning property belonging to the State, the Crown and the Evkaf, and concerning all other points arising out of the change in the legal position of that country, questions which will have to be settled on the conclusion of the general Treaty of Peace.

As regards the Alexandretta and Antioch Districts, Youssouf Kémal Bey declares that it is necessary to grant the inhabitants the right to adopt a special flag containing the Turkish flag. The French Plenipotentiary agreed that it was desirable to accord such a right to the inhabitants of these districts and promised to approach his Government for the purpose.

In regard to the complete amnesty mentioned in Article V, which is to be granted by the two Contracting Parties, the French Plenipotentiary declares that he will recommend his Government to take the necessary steps to allow the inhabitants of the Alexandretta and Antioch districts to benefit by the said amnesty.

In respect of Article X, the Turkish Plenipotentiary makes the following declarations:

Firstly, the kilometric guarantee was established under the deeds of concession of the Baghdad Railway on the basis of the total receipts for the whole line. It is absolutely necessary that the kilometric guarantee for the Turkish Bozanti-Nisibin section should, as in the past, be fixed on the basis of the total receipts of the whole Baghdad line.

The French Plenipotentiary undertakes to draw the attention of his Government to the justice of this claim.

Secondly, the Plenipotentiaries of the two Parties agree that the fixing of the rates for Turkish military traffic to be carried by rail in Turkish territory shall be reserved for further examination. They also agree that both States should give due notice, whenever they desire to avail themselves of the right referred to in Article X, second paragraph, of the Franco-Turkish Agreement.

The Turkish Plenipotentiary makes the following request which the French Plenipotentiary agrees to support when it is considered by his Government:

In the port of Alexandretta, Turkish nations, Turkish property and the Turkish flag shall have entire freedom to the use of the port. In this and in every other respect they shall be treated on terms of complete equality with the inhabitants, property and shipping of the country.

In this port an area should be leased to Turkey to be used for direct transit of goods coming from or consigned to that country. Every facility should be given to Turkey for linking up this area with the railway connecting Alexandretta with Turkish territory and also in regard to the installation, the leasing and the working of the said area.

No duty or charge other than such tonnage, wharfage, pilotage, lighthouse and quarantine dues as are also levied on the inhabitants, the property and the flag of the country shall be imposed on Turkish nationals, Turkish property or the Turkish flag when goods coming from or consigned to Turkey pass through this port in transit.

36. TERMINATION OF THE BRITISH PROTECTORATE IN EGYPT
28 February–15 March 1922

[Communication to the Sultan and declaration to Egypt from Great Britain, *Parliamentary Papers, 1922,* Egypt No. 1, Cmd. 1592; Foreign Office circular from Egypt No. 2, Cmd. 1617]

In the three years immediately following the end of World War I, Anglo-Egyptian relations went from bad to worse. The Milner Mission, after investigation in Egypt (December 1919–March 1920) and negotiation with Sa'd Pasha Zaghlul and other Egyptian nationalist leaders in London (July–August 1920), failed to produce an Anglo-Egyptian understanding. The mission, in its report of December 1920 (*Parliamentary Papers, 1921,* Egypt No. 1, Cmd. 1131), recommended the replacement of the protectorate by an "independent" Egypt in treaty alliance with the United Kingdom, which would enjoy "such rights as are necessary to safeguard her special interests," including the maintenance of a military force on Egyptian soil and the appointment of British financial and judicial advisers to the Egyptian government. A year of negotiation on the basis of the Milner formula produced no rapproachement. The situation instead seemed to be getting out of hand. Field Marshall Viscount Allenby, the High Commissioner, warned Foreign Secretary Curzon on 12 January 1922 that "if the hopes of Egypt are once more disappointed . . . I despair of any future for the country, which will relapse into a state of alternating outbreaks and repressions. . . ." (Cmd. 1592, p. 20). As a result of Allenby's warning and his consequent threat to resign, the British government substantially adopted the Milner formula for a unilateral declaration of policy. The High Commissioner was authorized to notify Sultan Fuad that the Egyptians might proceed to set up autonomous institutions and to declare to the public Britain's recognition of Egypt "as an independent sovereign State." A fortnight later the Foreign Office addressed a circular to British diplomatic missions everywhere for communication to the government to which each was accredited, announcing the termination of the protectorate and the preservation of the *status quo* in "certain matters in which the interests and obligations of the British Empire are specially involved," pending the conclusion of an Anglo-Egyptian agreement. H. W. V. Temperley, *History of the Paris Peace Conference,* vol. 6, pp. 193–205; H. Nicolson, *Curzon, the Last Phase,* chap. 6; Sir V. Chirol, *The Egyp-*

tian Problem, chaps. 7, 10–11, 14; *Survey of International Affairs, 1925,* vol. 1, pp. 189–201; Lord Lloyd, *Egypt since Cromer,* vol. 1, chap. 20, vol. 2, chaps. 2–4; A. P. Wavell, *Allenby in Egypt,* chaps. 1–4; J. Marlowe, *History of Modern Egypt,* chaps. 9–10; C. Issawi, *Egypt at Mid-Century,* pp. 47–50; Royal Institute of International Affairs, *Great Britain and Egypt, 1914–1951,* chap. 1; M. McIlwraith, "The British Protectorate of Egypt," *The Fortnightly Review,* new ser. 107 (March 1920), 375–83.

1. ALLENBY'S COMMUNICATION TO SULTAN FUAD, 28 FEBRUARY 1922

I have the honour to bring to your Highness's notice that certain passages of the explanatory note which I addressed to you on the 3rd December, 1921, were interpreted, to my great disappointment, in a manner not in accordance with the intention and policy of His Majesty's Government.

2. Judging by many comments which have been published on the subject of this note, it would appear that many Egyptians were under the impression that Great Britain was about to abandon her liberal and favourable attitude towards Egyptian aspirations and to make use of her special position in Egypt in order to maintain a political and administrative régime incompatible with the freedom she had offered.

3. Such an interpretation of the intentions of His Majesty's Government was quite mistaken. On the contrary, the explanatory note emphasised the dominating principle that the guarantees claimed by Great Britain are not designed to involve the continuance of an actual or virtual protectorate. Great Britain, as it is stated therein, sincerely desires to see "an Egypt enjoying the national prerogatives and the international position of a sovereign State."

4. If Egyptians have regarded these guarantees as being out of keeping with the position of a free country they have, on the other hand, lost sight of the fact that Great Britain has been obliged to claim them out of consideration for her own security in face of a situation which demands great prudence on her part, particularly in the matter of the disposition of her troops. Present world conditions, however, and the state of effervescence which has prevailed in Egypt since the armistice are not permanent factors, and it is to be hoped that while, on the one hand, the former will eventually improve, on the other hand, the time will come when, in the language of that note, Egypt's record will give confidence in her own guarantees.

5. As to any desire to interfere in the internal administration of Egypt, His Majesty's Government have sufficiently stated, and repeat, that their most ardent desire is to place in Egyptian hands the conduct of their own affairs. The draft agreement proposed by Great Britain did not depart from this idea, and in making provision for the presence of two British officials in the Ministries of Finance and Justice, it was not her intention to use these two officials for the purpose of intervening in Egyptian affairs, but solely in order to preserve the contact requisite for protecting foreign interests.

6. Such is the sole bearing of the guarantees that were demanded by Great Britain. They were claimed without any desire to impede Egyptians enjoying the full rights of a national Government.

7. Animated as she is by these intentions, it will be understood that it is repugnant to Great Britain on the one hand to see Egyptians delay by their own acts the realisation of an ideal aimed at by both parties, and on the other to be compelled herself to intervene to re-establish order when it is threatened in such a way as to arouse the fears of foreigners and to involve the interests of foreign Powers. It would be much to be regretted if Egyptians should see in the exceptional measures which have recently been taken any prejudice to the ideal to which they aspire or an intention on the part of His Majesty's Government to alter the policy I have indicated. In taking these measures, the sole desire of His Majesty's Government has been to put an end to a harmful agitation which, by arousing popular passions, might have such consequences as to jeopardise the whole result of the efforts of the Egyptian nation. These measures were taken

primarily in the interest of the Egyptian cause, which has everything to gain by being studied in an atmosphere of calm and friendly discussion.

8. Now that tranquillity seems to be re-establishing itself, thanks to the wise spirit which is the root of the Egyptian character and asserts itself in times of crisis, I am happy to be able to announce to your Highness and His Majesty's Government are prepared to recommend the accompanying declaration for the approval of Parliament. This will, I am confident, establish a régime of mutual confidence and lay the foundation for a satisfactory and final solution of the Egyptian problem.

9. There is no obstacle to the re-establishment forthwith of an Egyptian Ministry for Foreign Affairs which will prepare the way for the creation of the diplomatic and consular representation of Egypt.

10. The creation of a Parliament with a right to control the policy and administration of a constitutionally responsible Government is a matter for your Highness and the Egyptian people to determine. Should circumstances arise to delay the coming into force of the Act of Idemnity with application to all inhabitants of Egypt mentioned in the declaration accompanying this note, I desire to inform your Highness that I shall be prepared, pending the repeal of the proclamation of the 2nd November, 1914, to suspend the application of martial law in respect of all matters affecting the free exercise of the political rights of Egyptians.

11. It is now for Egypt to respond, and it is to be hoped she will justly appreciate the good intentions of Great Britain, and that reflection and not passion will guide her attitude.

2. ALLENBY'S DECLARATION TO EGYPT, 28 FEBRUARY 1922

Whereas His Majesty's Government, in accordance with their declared intentions, desire forthwith to recognise Egypt as an independent sovereign State; and

Whereas the relations between His Majesty's Government and Egypt are of vital interest to the British Empire;

The following principles are hereby declared:—

1. The British Protectorate over Egypt is terminated, and Egypt is declared to be an independent sovereign State.

2. So soon as the Government of his Highness shall pass an Act of Indemnity with application to all inhabitants of Egypt, martial law as proclaimed on the 2nd November, 1914, shall be withdrawn.

3. The following matters are absolutely reserved to the discretion of His Majesty's Government until such time as it may be possible by free discussion and friendly accommodation on both sides to conclude agreements in regard thereto between His Majesty's Government and the Government of Egypt:—

(*a.*) The security of the communications of the British Empire in Egypt;
(*b.*) The defence of Egypt against all foreign aggression or interference, direct or indirect;
(*c.*) The protection of foreign interests in Egypt and the protection of minorities;
(*d.*) The Soudan.

Pending the conclusion of such agreements, the *status quo* in all these matters shall remain intact.

3. FOREIGN OFFICE CIRCULAR TO BRITISH DIPLOMATIC MISSIONS, 15 MARCH 1922

His Majesty's Government, with the approval of Parliament, have decided to terminate the protectorate declared over Egypt on the 18th December, 1914, and to recognise her as an independent sovereign State. In informing the Government to which you are accredited of this decision you should communicate the following notification:—

When the peace and prosperity of Egypt were menaced in December 1914 by the intervention of Turkey in the Great War in alliance with the Central Powers, His Majesty's Government terminated the suzerainty of Turkey over Egypt, took the country under their protection and declared it to be a British protectorate.

The situation is now changed. Egypt has

emerged from the war prosperous and unscathed, and His Majesty's Government, after grave consideration and in accordance with their traditional policy, have decided to terminate the protectorate by a declaration in which they recognise Egypt as an independent sovereign State, while preserving for future agreements between Egypt and themselves certain matters in which the interests and obligations of the British Empire are specially involved. Pending such agreements, the *status quo* as regards these matters will remain unchanged.

The Egyptian Government will be at liberty to re-establish a Ministry for Foreign Affairs and thus to prepare the way for the diplomatic and consular representation of Egypt abroad.

Great Britain will not in future accord protection to Egyptians in foreign countries, except in so far as may be desired by the Egyptian Government and pending the representation of Egypt in the country concerned.

The termination of the British protectorate over Egypt involves, however, no change in the *status quo* as regards the position of other Powers in Egypt itself.

The welfare and integrity of Egypt are necessary to the peace and safety of the British Empire, which will therefore always maintain as an essential British interest the special relations between itself and Egypt long recognised by other Governments. These special relations are defined in the declaration recognising Egypt as an independent sovereign State. His Majesty's Government have laid them down as matters in which the rights and interests of the British Empire are vitally involved, and will not admit them to be questioned or discussed by any other Power. In pursuance of this principle, they will regard as an unfriendly act any attempt at interference in the affairs of Egypt by another Power, and they will consider any aggression against the territory of Egypt as an act to be repelled with all the means at their command.

37. STATEMENT OF BRITISH POLICY (CHURCHILL MEMORANDUM) ON PALESTINE
1 July 1922

[Great Britain, *Parliamentary Papers, 1922,* Cmd. 1700, pp. 17–21]

British troops occupied Palestine in 1917–18. The country, whose boundaries were yet to be determined, continued under military administration until 30 June 1920, without clear policy guidance from London. The civil administration, launched on . July, was responsible to the Foreign Office until February 1921, when the Colonial Office assumed jurisdiction over the class A mandates. The terms of the mandate for Palestine (Doc. 38) were first framed in December 1920. But owing to developments in Syria and Transjordan, the draft was basically altered in August 1921 and further modified on the eve of its provisional approval by the Council of the League of Nations in July 1922. In these early years Britain exercised only *de facto* authority in Palestine. For the Ottoman Empire, having failed to ratify the treaty of Sèvres (Doc. 31), had not yet formally relinquished its sovereignty. The League Council, accordingly, could do nothing about final confirmation of the provisions of the projected mandate. In the circumstances, the British government came under pressure from the Arab nationalists to repudiate Zionism and from the Zionists to reaffirm England's adherence to the Jewish National Home policy. Colonial Secretary Winston Churchill, in the face of the conflicting pressures, made public on 1 July 1922, a statement of policy on Palestine that survived, in its major aspects, until July 1937. P. L. Hanna, *British Policy in Palestine;* Great Britain, *Parliamentary Papers, 1937,* Cmd. 5479, *Palestine Royal Commission Report;* F. F. Andrews, *The Holy Land under Mandate,* 2 vols.; Sir R. Storrs, *Memoirs,* chaps. 13–17; G. Antonius, *Arab Awakening,* chaps. 14, 16; Esco Foundation, *Palestine,* vol. 1, chaps. 5–8, vol. 2, chaps. 9–11.

The Secretary of State for the Colonies has given renewed consideration to the existing political situation in Palestine, with a very earnest desire to arrive at a settlement of the outstanding questions which have given rise to uncertainty and unrest among certain sections of the population. After consultation with the High Commissioner for Palestine the following statement has been drawn up. It summarises the essential parts of the correspondence that has already taken place between the Secretary of State and a Delegation from the Moslem Christian Society of Palestine, which has been for some time in England, and it states the further conclusions which have since been reached.

The tension which has prevailed from time to time in Palestine is mainly due to apprehensions, which are entertained both by sections of the Arab and by sections of the Jewish population. These apprehensions, so far as the Arabs are concerned, are partly based upon exaggerated interpretations of the meaning of the Declaration favouring the establishment of a Jewish National Home in Palestine, made on behalf of His Majesty's Government on 2nd November, 1917. Unauthorised statements have been made to the effect that the purpose in view is to create a wholly Jewish Palestine. Phrases have been used such as that Palestine is to become "as Jewish as England is English." His Majesty's Government regard any such expectation as impracticable and have no such aim in view. Nor have they at any time contemplated, as appears to be feared by the Arab Delegation, the disappearance or the subordination of the Arabic population, language or culture in Palestine. They would draw attention to the fact that the terms of the Declaration referred to do not contemplate that Palestine as a whole should be converted into a Jewish National Home, but that such a Home should be founded *in Palestine*. In this connection it has been observed with satisfaction that at the meeting of the Zionist Congress, the supreme governing body of the Zionist Organisation, held at Carlsbad in September, 1921, a resolution was passed expressing as the official statement of Zionist aims "the determination of the Jewish people to live with the Arab people on terms of unity and mutual respect, and together with them to make the common home into a flourishing community, the upbuilding of which may assure to each of its peoples an undisturbed national development."

It is also necessary to point out that the Zionist Commission in Palestine, now termed the Palestine Zionist Executive, has not desired to possess, and does not possess, any share in the general administration of the country. Nor does the special position assigned to the Zionist Organisation in Article IV of the Draft Mandate for Palestine imply any such functions. That special position relates to the measures to be taken in Palestine affecting the Jewish population, and contemplates that the Organisation may assist in the general development of the country, but does not entitle it to share in any degree in its Government.

Further, it is contemplated that the status of all citizens of Palestine in the eyes of the law shall be Palestinian, and it has never been intended that they, or any section of them, should possess any other juridical status.

So far as the Jewish population of Palestine are concerned, it appears that some among them are apprehensive that His Majesty's Government may depart from the policy embodied in the Declaration of 1917. It is necessary, therefore, once more to affirm that these fears are unfounded, and that that Declaration, re-affirmed by the Conference of the Principal Allied Powers at San Remo and again in the Treaty of Sèvres, is not susceptible of change.

During the last two or three generations the Jews have recreated in Palestine a community, now numbering 80,000, of whom about one-fourth are farmers or workers upon the land. This community has its own political organs; an elected assembly for the direction of its domestic concerns; elected councils in the towns; and an organisation for the control of its schools. It has its elected Chief Rabbinate and Rabbinical Council for the direction of its religious affairs. Its business is conducted in Hebrew as a vernacular language, and a Hebrew press serves its needs. It has its distinctive intellectual life and displays considerable economic activity. This community, then, with its town and country population, its political, religious and social organisations, its own language, its own customs, its own life, has in fact "national" characteristics. When it is asked what is meant by the development of the Jewish National Home in Palestine, it may be answered that it is not the imposition of a Jewish nationality upon the inhabitants of Palestine as a whole, but the further development of the existing Jewish community, with the assistance of Jews in other parts of the world, in order that it may become a centre in which the Jewish people as a whole may take, on grounds of religion and race, an interest and a pride. But in order that this community should have the best prospect of free development and provide a full opportunity for the Jewish people to display its capacities, it is essential that it should know that it is in Palestine as of right and not on sufferance. That is the reason why it is necessary that the existence of a Jewish National Home in Palestine should be internationally guaranteed, and that it should be formally recognised to rest upon ancient historic connection.

This, then, is the interpretation which His Majesty's Government place upon the Declaration of 1917, and, so understood, the Secretary of State is of opinion that it does not contain or imply anything which need cause either alarm to the Arab population of Palestine or disappointment to the Jews.

For the fulfilment of this policy it is necessary that the Jewish community in Palestine should be able to increase its numbers by immigration. This immigration cannot be so great in volume as to exceed whatever may be the economic capacity of the country at the time to absorb new arrivals. It is essential to ensure that the immigrants should not be a burden upon the people of Palestine as a whole, and that they should not deprive any section of the present population of their employment. Hitherto the immigration has fulfilled these conditions. The number of immigrants since the British occupation has been about 25,000.

It is necessary also to ensure that persons who are politically undesirable are excluded from Palestine, and every precaution has been and will be taken by the Administration to that end.

It is intended that a special committee should be established in Palestine, consisting entirely of members of the new Legislative Council elected by the people, to confer with the Administration upon matters relating to the regulation of immigration. Should any difference of opinion arise between this committee and the Administration, the matter will be referred to His Majesty's Government, who will give it special consideration. In addition, under Article 81 of the draft Palestine Order in Council, any religious community or considerable section of the population of Palestine will have a general right to appeal, through the High Commissioner and the Secretary of State, to the League of Nations on any matter on which they may consider that the terms of the Mandate are not being fulfilled by the Government of Palestine.

With reference to the Constitution which it is now intended to establish in Palestine, the draft of which has already been published, it is desirable to make certain points clear. In the first place, it is not the case, as has been represented by the Arab Delegation, that during the war His Majesty's Government gave an undertaking that an independent national government should be at once established in Palestine. This representation mainly rests upon a letter dated the 24th October, 1915, from Sir Henry McMahon, then His Majesty's High Commissioner in Egypt, to the Sherif of Mecca, now King Hussein of the Kingdom of the Hejaz. That letter is quoted as conveying the promise to the Sherif of Mecca to recognise and support the independence of the Arabs within the territories proposed by him. But this promise was given subject to a reservation made in the same letter, which excluded from its scope, among other territories, the portions of Syria lying to the west of the district of Damascus. This reservation has always been regarded by His Majesty's Government as covering the vilayet of Beirut and the independent Sanjak of Jerusalem. The whole of Palestine west of the Jordan was thus excluded from Sir H. McMahon's pledge.

Nevertheless, it is the intention of His Majesty's Government to foster the establishment of a full measure of self-government in Palestine. But they are of opinion that, in the special circumstances of that country, this should be accomplished by gradual stages and not suddenly. The first step was taken when, on the institution of a civil Administration, the nominated Advisory Council, which now exists, was established. It was stated at the time by the High Commissioner that this was the first step in the development of self-governing institutions, and it is now proposed to take a second step by the establishment of a Legislative Council containing a large proportion of members elected on a wide franchise. It was proposed in the published draft that three of the members of this Council should be non-official persons nominated by the High Commissioner, but representations having been made in opposition to this provision, based on cogent considerations, the Secretary of State is prepared to omit it. The Legislative Council would then consist of the High Commissioner as President and twelve elected and ten official members. The Secretary of State is of opinion that before a further measure of self-government is extended to Palestine and the Assembly placed in control over the Executive, it would be wise to allow some time to elapse. During this period the institutions of the country will have become well established; its financial credit will be based on firm foundations, and the Palestinian officials will have been enabled to gain experience of sound methods of government. After a few years the situation will be again reviewed, and if the experience of the working of the constitution now to be established so warranted, a larger share of authority would then be extended to the elected representatives of the people.

The Secretary of State would point out that already the present Administration has transferred to a Supreme Council elected by the Moslem community of Palestine the entire control of Moslem religious endowments (Wakfs), and of the Moslem religious Courts. To this Council the Administration has also voluntarily restored considerable revenues derived from ancient endowments which had been sequestrated by the Turkish Government. The Education Department is also advised by a committee representative of all sections of the population, and the Department of Commerce and Industry has the benefit of the co-operation of the Chambers of Commerce which have been established in the principal centres. It is the intention of the Administration to associate in an increased degree similar representative committees with the various Departments of the Government.

The Secretary of State believes that a policy upon these lines, coupled with the maintenance of the fullest religious liberty in Palestine and with scrupulous regard for the rights of each community with reference to its Holy Places, cannot but commend itself to the various sections of the population, and that upon this basis may be built up that spirit of co-operation upon which the future progress and prosperity of the Holy Land must largely depend.

38. THE MANDATE FOR PALESTINE
24 July 1922

[Great Britain, *Parliamentary Papers, 1922,* Cmd. 1785]

The mandatory instruments for Syria (and Lebanon), Mesopotamia [Iraq] and Palestine (and Transjordan) paralleled one another in regard to defense, foreign relations, the suspension of capitulations, extradition, religious freedom, assurances of equal treatment to nationals of states members of the League of Nations, provision for a law of antiquities, mandatory responsibility to the Council of the League of Nations and recourse to the Permanent Court of International Justice in the event of a dispute between the mandatory and another members of the League. The mandate for Palestine, however, differed from the others in certain fundamental respects. Under article 1 of the Syrian and Iraqi mandates, the mandatory was required to frame an organic law within three years of the coming into force of the mandate and was "to facilitate the progressive development" of these countries "as independent states." Comparable clauses were lacking in the Palestine instrument, which vested in the mandatory "full powers of legislation and of administration, save as they may be limited by the terms of this mandate." The Palestine Mandate, which provided only for "the development of self-governing institutions" (article 2), was formulated palpably in the Zionist interest, as attested by articles 2, 4, 6, 11, 22 and 23. Article 25—inserted in August 1921—stipulated that the mandatory was entitled, with the League Council's consent, "to postpone or withhold application" of the Jewish National Home provisions from "the territories lying between the Jordan and the eastern boundary of Palestine as ultimately determined." The United Kingdom, in fact, exercised the right and called into being the amirate of Transjordan (Doc. 52). As far as the League Council was concerned, the mandated territories in former Ottoman Asia did not go into effect until 29 September 1923. P. L. Hanna, *British Policy in Palestine,* chap. 3; J. C. Hurewitz, *The Struggle for Palestine,* chap. 1; A. H. Hourani, *Syria and Lebanon,* chap. 9; P. W. Ireland, *'Iraq,* chap. 19; N. Bentwich, *Mandates System,* chap. 2.

The Council of the League of Nations:

Whereas the Principal Allied Powers have agreed, for the purpose of giving effect to the provisions of Article 22 of the Covenant of the League of Nations, to entrust to a Mandatory selected by the said Powers the administration of the territory of Palestine, which formerly belonged to the Turkish Empire, within such boundaries as may be fixed by them; and

Whereas the Principal Allied Powers have also agreed that the Mandatory should be responsible for putting into effect the declaration originally made on November 2nd, 1917, by the Government of His Britannic Majesty, and adopted by the said Powers, in favour of the establishment in Palestine of a national home for the Jewish people, it being clearly understood that nothing should be done which might prejudice the civil and religious rights of existing non-Jewish communities in Palestine, or the rights and political status enjoyed by Jews in any other country; and

Whereas recognition has thereby been given to the historical connection of the Jewish people with Palestine and to the grounds for reconstituting their national home in that country; and

Whereas the Principal Allied Powers have selected His Britannic Majesty as the Mandatory for Palestine; and

Whereas the mandate in respect of Palestine has been formulated in the following terms and submitted to the Council of the League for approval; and

Whereas His Britannic Majesty has accepted the mandate in respect of Palestine and undertaken to exercise it on behalf of the League of Nations in conformity with the following provisions; and

Whereas by the afore-mentioned Article 22 (paragraph 8), it is provided that the degree of authority, control or administration to be exercised by the Mandatory, not having been previously agreed upon by the Members of the League, shall be explicitly defined by the Council of the League of Nations;

Confirming the said mandate, defines its terms as follows:

ART. 1. The Mandatory shall have full powers of legislation and of administration, save as they may be limited by the terms of this mandate.

ART. 2. The Mandatory shall be responsible for placing the country under such political, administrative and economic conditions as will secure the establishment of the Jewish national home, as laid down in the preamble, and the development of self-governing institutions, and also for safeguarding the civil and religious rights of all the inhabitants of Palestine, irrespective of race and religion.

ART. 3. The Mandatory shall, so far as circumstances permit, encourage local autonomy.

ART. 4. An appropriate Jewish agency

shall be recognised as a public body for the purpose of advising and co-operating with the Administration of Palestine in such economic, social and other matters as may affect the establishment of the Jewish national home and the interests of the Jewish population in Palestine, and, subject always to the control of the Administration, to assist and take part in the development of the country.

The Zionist organisation, so long as its organisation and constitution are in the opinion of the Mandatory appropriate, shall be recognised as such agency. It shall take steps in consultation with His Britannic Majesty's Government to secure the co-operation of all Jews who are willing to assist in the establishment of the Jewish national home.

ART. 5. The Mandatory shall be responsible for seeing that no Palestine territory shall be ceded or leased to, or in any way placed under the control of, the Government of any foreign Power.

ART. 6. The Administration of Palestine, while ensuring that the rights and position of other sections of the population are not prejudiced, shall facilitate Jewish immigration under suitable conditions and shall encourage, in co-operation with the Jewish agency referred to in Article 4, close settlement by Jews on the land, including State lands and waste lands not required for public purposes.

ART. 7. The Administration of Palestine shall be responsible for enacting a nationality law. There shall be included in this law provisions framed so as to facilitate the acquisition of Palestinian citizenship by Jews who take up their permanent residence in Palestine.

ART. 8. The privileges and immunities of foreigners, including the benefits of consular jurisdiction and protection as formerly enjoyed by Capitulation or usage in the Ottoman Empire, shall not be applicable in Palestine.

Unless the Powers whose nationals enjoyed the afore-mentioned privileges and immunities on August 1st, 1914, shall have previously renounced the right to their re-establishment, or shall have agreed to their non-application for a specified period, these privileges and immunities shall, at the expiration of the mandate, be immediately re-established in their entirety or with such modifications as may have been agreed upon between the Powers concerned.

ART. 9. The Mandatory shall be responsible for seeing that the judicial system established in Palestine shall assure to foreigners, as well as to natives, a complete guarantee of their rights.

Respect for the personal status of the various peoples and communities and for their religious interests shall be fully guaranteed. In particular, the control and administration of Wakfs shall be exercised in accordance with religious law and the dispositions of the founders.

ART. 10. Pending the making of special extradition agreements relating to Palestine, the extradition treaties in force between the Mandatory and other foreign Powers shall apply to Palestine.

ART. 11. The Administration of Palestine shall take all necessary measures to safeguard the interests of the community in connection with the development of the country, and, subject to any international obligations accepted by the Mandatory, shall have full power to provide for public ownership or control of any of the natural resources of the country or of the public works, services and utilities established or to be established therein. It shall introduce a land system appropriate to the needs of the country, having regard, among other things, to the desirability of promoting the close settlement and intensive cultivation of the land.

The Administration may arrange with the Jewish agency mentioned in Article 4 to construct or operate, upon fair and equitable terms, any public works, services and utilities, and to develop any of the natural resources of the country, in so far as these matters are not directly undertaken by the Administration. Any such arrangements shall provide that no profits distributed by such agency, directly or indirectly, shall exceed a reasonable rate of interest on the capital, and any further profits shall be utilised by it for the benefit of the country in a manner approved by the Administration.

ART. 12. The Mandatory shall be entrusted with the control of the foreign relations of Palestine and the right to issue exequaturs to consuls appointed by foreign Powers. He shall also be entitled to afford diplomatic and consular protection to citizens of Palestine when outside its territorial limits.

ART. 13. All responsibility in connection with the Holy Places and religious buildings or sites in Palestine, including that of preserving existing rights and of securing free access to the Holy Places, religious buildings and sites and the free exercise of worship, while ensuring the requirements of public order and decorum, is assumed by the Mandatory, who shall be responsible solely to the League of Nations in all matters connected herewith, provided that nothing in this article shall prevent the Mandatory from entering into such arrangements as he may deem reasonable with the Administration for the purpose of carrying the provisions of this article into effect; and provided also that nothing in this mandate shall be construed as conferring upon the Mandatory authority to interfere with the fabric or the management of purely Moslem sacred shrines, the immunities of which are guaranteed.

ART. 14. A special Commission shall be appointed by the Mandatory to study, define and determine the rights and claims in connection with the Holy Places and the rights and claims relating to the different religious communities in Palestine. The method of nomination, the composition and the functions of this Commission shall be submitted to the Council of the League for its approval, and the Commission shall not be appointed or enter upon its functions without the approval of the Council.

ART. 15. The Mandatory shall see that complete freedom of conscience and the free exercise of all forms of worship, subject only to the maintenance of public order and morals, are ensured to all. No discrimination of any kind shall be made between the inhabitants of Palestine on the ground of race, religion or language. No person shall be excluded from Palestine on the sole ground of his religious belief.

The right of each community to maintain its own schools for the education of its own members in its own language, while conforming to such educational requirements of a general nature as the Administration may impose, shall not be denied or impaired.

ART. 16. The Mandatory shall be responsible for exercising such supervision over religious or eleemosynary bodies of all faiths in Palestine as may be required for the maintenance of public order and good government. Subject to such supervision, no measures shall be taken in Palestine to obstruct or interfere with the enterprise of such bodies or to discriminate against any representative or member of them on the ground of his religion or nationality.

ART. 17. The Administration of Palestine may organise on a voluntary basis the forces necessary for the preservation of peace and order, and also for the defence of the country, subject, however, to the supervision of the Mandatory, but shall not use them for purposes other than those above specified save with the consent of the Mandatory. Except for such purposes, no military, naval or air forces shall be raised or maintained by the Administration of Palestine.

Nothing in this article shall preclude the Administration of Palestine from contributing to the cost of the maintenance of the forces of the Mandatory in Palestine.

The Mandatory shall be entitled at all times to use the roads, railways and ports of Palestine for the movement of armed forces and the carriage of fuel and supplies.

ART. 18. The Mandatory shall see that there is no discrimination in Palestine against the nationals of any State Member of the League of Nations (including companies incorporated under its laws) as compared with those of the Mandatory or of any foreign State in matters concerning taxation, commerce or navigation, the exercise of industries or professions, or in the treatment of merchant vessels or civil aircraft.

Similarly, there shall be no discrimination in Palestine against goods originating in or destined for any of the said States, and there shall be freedom of transit under equitable conditions across the mandated area.

Subject as aforesaid and to the other provisions of this mandate, the Administration of Palestine may, on the advice of the Mandatory, impose such taxes and customs duties as it may consider necessary, and take such steps as it may think best to promote the development of the natural resources of the country and to safeguard the interests of the population. It may also, on the advice of the Mandatory, conclude a special customs agreement with any State the territory of which in 1914 was wholly included in Asiatic Turkey or Arabia.

ART. 19. The Mandatory shall adhere on behalf of the Administration of Palestine to any general international conventions already existing, or which may be concluded hereafter with the approval of the League of Nations, respecting the slave traffic, the traffic in arms and ammunition, or the traffic in drugs, or relating to commercial equality, freedom of transit and navigation, aerial navigation and postal, telegraphic and wireless communication or literary, artistic or industrial property.

ART. 20. The Mandatory shall co-operate on behalf of the Administration of Palestine, so far as religious, social and other conditions may permit, in the execution of any common policy adopted by the League of Nations for preventing and combating disease, including diseases of plants and animals.

ART. 21. The Mandatory shall secure the enactment within twelve months from this date, and shall ensure the execution of a Law of Antiquities based on the following rules. This law shall ensure equality of treatment in the matter of excavations and archæological research to the nations of all States Members of the League of Nations.

(1) "Antiquity" means any construction or any product of human activity earlier than the year A.D. 1700.

(2) The law for the protection of antiquities shall proceed by encouragement rather than by threat.

Any person who, having discovered an antiquity without being furnished with the authorisation referred to in paragraph 5, reports the same to an official of the competent Department, shall be rewarded according to the value of the discovery.

(3) No antiquity may be disposed of except to the competent Department, unless this Department renounces the acquisition of any such antiquity.

No antiquity may leave the country without an export licence from the said Department.

(4) Any person who maliciously or negligently destroys or damages an antiquity shall be liable to a penalty to be fixed.

(5) No clearing of ground or digging with the object of finding antiquities shall be permitted, under penalty of fine, except to persons authorised by the competent Department.

(6) Equitable terms shall be fixed for expropriation, temporary or permanent, of lands which might be of historical or archæological interest.

(7) Authorisation to excavate shall only be granted to persons who show sufficient guarantees of archæological experience. The Administration of Palestine shall not, in granting these authorisations, act in such a way as to exclude scholars of any nation without good grounds.

(8) The proceeds of excavations may be divided between the excavator and the competent Department in a proportion fixed by that Department. If division seems impossible for scientific reasons, the excavator shall receive a fair indemnity in lieu of a part of the find.

ART. 22. English, Arabic and Hebrew shall be the official languages of Palestine. Any statement or inscription in Arabic on stamps or money in Palestine shall be repeated in Hebrew, and any statement or inscription in Hebrew shall be repeated in Arabic.

ART. 23. The Administration of Palestine shall recognise the holy days of the respective communities in Palestine as legal days of rest for the members of such communities.

ART. 24. The Mandatory shall make to the Council of the League of Nations an annual report to the satisfaction of the Council as to the measures taken during the year to carry out the provisions of the mandate. Copies of all laws and regulations promulgated or issued during the year shall be communicated with the report.

ART. 25. In the territories lying between the Jordan and the eastern boundary of Palestine as ultimately determined, the Mandatory shall be entitled, with the consent of the Council of the League of Nations, to postpone or withhold application of such provisions of this mandate as he may consider inapplicable to the existing local conditions, and to make such provision for the administration of the territories as he may consider suitable to those conditions, provided that no action shall be taken which is inconsistent with the provisions of Articles 15, 16 and 18.

ART. 26. The Mandatory agrees that, if any dispute whatever should arise between the Mandatory and another Member of the League of Nations relating to the interpretation or the application of the provisions of the mandate, such dispute, if it cannot be settled by negotiation, shall be submitted to the Permanent Court of International Justice provided for by Article 14 of the Covenant of the League of Nations.

ART. 27. The consent of the Council of the League of Nations is required for any modification of the terms of this mandate.

ART. 28. In the event of the termination of the mandate hereby conferred upon the Mandatory, the Council of the League of Nations shall make such arrangements as may be deemed necessary for safeguarding in perpetuity, under guarantee of the League, the rights secured by Articles 13 and 14, and shall use its influence for securing, under the guarantee of the League, that the Government of Palestine will fully honour the financial obligations legitimately incurred by the Administration of Palestine during the period of the mandate, including the rights of public servants to pensions or gratuities.

39. TREATY OF ALLIANCE: GREAT BRITAIN AND IRAQ
10 October 1922

(Ratifications exchanged, Baghdad, 19 December 1924)

[Great Britain, *Parliamentary Papers, 1925,* Treaty Series No. 17, Cmd. 2370]

In the insurrection of 1920 (June–September) the nationalists of Mesopotamia (Iraq) gave dramatic emphasis to their demands for full independence. But the territory by then had been awarded to the United Kingdom as a class A mandate. The treaty of 1922 constituted little more than a nominal compromise between the Iraqi nationalist and British positions. The Iraqis, it was true, were vested with limited control over foreign affairs and with a larger measure of autonomy in domestic affairs. But the mandatory instrument in effect was not basically modified, and Britain was empowered under the treaty and its subsidiary agreements (not reproduced) to discharge its mandatory obligations. The nationalists remained discontent even after the signature of the protocol of 30 April 1923 (not reproduced) which reduced the duration of the 1922 treaty from twenty years to "not later than four years from the ratification of peace with Turkey." P. W. Ireland, *'Iraq,* chaps. 19–20; M. Khadduri, *Independent Iraq, a Study in Iraqi Politics since 1932,* chaps. 1–2; S. H. Longrigg, *'Iraq 1900 to 1950,* chap. 5.

ART. I. At the request of His Majesty the King of Iraq, His Britannic Majesty undertakes subject to the provisions of this Treaty to provide the State of Iraq with such advice and assistance as may be required during the period of the present Treaty, without prejudice to her national sovereignty. His Britannic Majesty shall be represented in Iraq by a High Commissioner and Consul-General assisted by the necessary staff.

ART. II. His Majesty the King of Iraq

undertakes that for the period of the present Treaty no gazetted official of other than Iraq nationality shall be appointed in Iraq without the concurrence of His Britannic Majesty. A separate agreement shall regulate the numbers and conditions of employment of British officials so appointed in the Iraq Government.

ART. III. His Majesty the King of Iraq agrees to frame an Organic Law for presentation to the Constituent Assembly of Iraq and to give effect to the said law, which shall contain nothing contrary to the provisions of the present Treaty and shall take account of the rights, wishes and interests of all populations inhabiting Iraq. This Organic Law shall ensure to all complete freedom of conscience and the free exercise of all forms of worship, subject only to the maintenance of public order and morals. It shall provide that no discrimination of any kind shall be made between the inhabitants of Iraq on the ground of race, religion or language, and shall secure that the right of each community to maintain its own schools for the education of its own members in its own language, while conforming to such educational requirements of a general nature as the Government of Iraq may impose, shall not be denied or impaired. It shall prescribe the constitutional procedure, whether legislative or executive, by which decisions will be taken on all matters of importance, including those involving questions of fiscal, financial and military policy.

ART. IV. Without prejudice to the provisions of Articles XVII and XVIII of this Treaty, His Majesty the King of Iraq agrees to be guided by the advice of His Britannic Majesty tendered through the High Commissioner on all important matters affecting the international and financial obligations and interests of His Britannic Majesty for the whole period of this Treaty. His Majesty the King of Iraq will fully consult the High Commissioner on what is conducive to a sound financial and fiscal policy and will ensure the stability and good organisation of the finances of the Iraq Government so long as that Government is under financial obligations to the Government of His Britannic Majesty.

ART. V. His Majesty the King of Iraq shall have the right of representation in London and in such other capitals and places as may be agreed upon by the High Contracting Parties. Where His Majesty the King of Iraq is not represented he agrees to entrust the protection of Iraq nationals to His Britannic Majesty. His Majesty the King of Iraq shall himself issue exequaturs to representatives of Foreign Powers in Iraq after His Britannic Majesty has agreed to their appointment.

ART. VI. His Britannic Majesty undertakes to use his good offices to secure the admission of Iraq to membership of the League of Nations as soon as possible.

ART. VII. His Britannic Majesty undertakes to provide such support and assistance to the armed forces of His Majesty the King of Iraq as may from time to time be agreed by the High Contracting Parties. A separate agreement regulating the extent and conditions of such support and assistance shall be concluded between the High Contracting Parties and communicated to the Council of the League of Nations.

ART. VIII. No territory in Iraq shall be ceded or leased or in any way placed under the control of any Foreign Power; this shall not prevent His Majesty the King of Iraq from making such arrangements as may be necessary for the accommodation of foreign representatives and for the fulfilment of the provisions of the preceding Article.

ART. IX. His Majesty the King of Iraq undertakes that he will accept and give effect to such reasonable provisions as His Britannic Majesty may consider necessary in judicial matters to safeguard the interests of foreigners in consequence of the non-application of the immunities and privileges enjoyed by them under capitulation or usage. These provisions shall be embodied in a separate agreement, which shall be communicated to the Council of the League of Nations.

ART. X. The High Contracting Parties agree to conclude separate agreements to secure the execution of any treaties, agreements or undertakings which His Britannic

Majesty is under obligation to see carried out in respect of Iraq. His Majesty the King of Iraq undertakes to bring in any legislation necessary to ensure the execution of these agreements. Such agreements shall be communicated to the Council of the League of Nations.

ART. XI. There shall be no discrimination in Iraq against the nationals of any State, member of the League of Nations, or of any State to which His Britannic Majesty has agreed by treaty that the same rights should be ensured as it would enjoy if it were a member of the said League (including companies incorporated under the laws of such State), as compared with British nationals or those of any foreign State in matters concerning taxation, commerce or navigation, the exercise of industries or professions, or in the treatment of merchant vessels or civil aircraft. Nor shall there be any discrimination in Iraq against goods originating in or destined for any of the said States. There shall be freedom of transit under equitable conditions across Iraq territory.

ART. XII. No measure shall be taken in Iraq to obstruct or interfere with missionary enterprise or to discriminate against any missionary on the ground of his religious belief or nationality, provided that such enterprise is not prejudicial to public order and good government.

ART. XIII. His Majesty the King of Iraq undertakes to co-operate, in so far as social, religious and other conditions may permit, in the execution of any common policy adopted by the League of Nations for preventing and combating disease, including diseases of plants and animals.

ART. XIV. His Majesty the King of Iraq undertakes to secure the enactment, within twelve months of the coming into force of this Treaty, and to ensure the execution of a Law of Antiquities based on the rules annexed to Article 421 of the Treaty of Peace signed at Sèvres on the 10th August, 1920. This Law shall replace the former Ottoman Law of Antiquities, and shall ensure equality of treatment in the matter of archæological research to the nationals of all States members of the League of Nations, and of any State to which His Britannic Majesty has agreed by treaty that the same rights should be ensured as it would enjoy if it were a member of the said League.

ART. XV. A separate agreement shall regulate the financial relations between the High Contracting Parties. It shall provide, on the one hand, for the transfer by His Britannic Majesty's Government to the Government of Iraq of such works of public utility as may be agreed upon and for the rendering by His Britannic Majesty's Government of such financial assistance as may from time to time be considered necessary for Iraq, and, on the other hand, for the progressive liquidation by the Government of Iraq of all liabilities thus incurred. Such agreement shall be communicated to the Council of the League of Nations.

ART. XVI. So far as is consistent with his international obligations His Britannic Majesty undertakes to place no obstacle in the way of the association of the State of Iraq for customs or other purposes with such neighbouring Arab States as may desire it.

ART. XVII. Any difference that may arise between the High Contracting Parties as to the interpretation of the provisions of this Treaty shall be referred to the Permanent Court of International Justice provided for by Article 14 of the Covenant of the League of Nations. In such case, should there be any discrepancy between the English and Arabic texts of this Treaty, the English shall be taken as the authoritative version.

ART. XVIII. This Treaty shall come into force as soon as it has been ratified by the High Contracting Parties after its acceptance by the Constituent Assembly, and shall remain in force for twenty years, at the end of which period the situation shall be examined, and if the High Contracting Parties are of opinion that the Treaty is no longer required it shall be terminated. Termination shall be subject to confirmation by the League of Nations unless before that date Article VI of this Treaty has come into effect, in which case notice of termination shall be communicated to the Council of the League of Nations. Nothing shall prevent the High Contracting Parties from reviewing from time to time the provisions of this Treaty, and those of the separate Agreements arising out of Articles VII, X and XV, with a view to any revision which may seem desirable in the circumstances then existing, and any modification which may be agreed upon by the High Contracting Parties shall be communicated to the Council of the League of Nations.

40. UNITED STATES INTERESTS AND CONDITIONS OF PARTICIPATION IN THE LAUSANNE CONFERENCE
30 October–10 November 1922

[*Foreign Relations of the United States, 1923,* vol. 2, pp. 884–88, 893–97]

When plans were announced for the Lausanne conference on a settlement with Turkey (Doc. 41), the United States informed the sponsoring governments—Britain, France and Italy—of its desire to take part as observer in the deliberations. In an *aide-mémoire* presented to the three European governments on 30 October 1922, the United States stipulated the terms of American participation and outlined the American interests that it wished to safeguard. Secretary of State Charles Evans Hughes, in a separate confidential instruction of the same date, elaborated upon the subject for the guidance of the ambassadors involved. The General Board of the Navy on 10 November drew up a memorandum, advocating that "the United States should have representation on the [projected] international commission of control [over the Turkish Straits] and in all positions subordinate to that commission, equal to that of any other foreign power." This proposal, however, did not receive cabinet approval. Yet the attitude of the Navy's General Board in 1922, in the light of developments a quarter of a century later, has more than academic interest. J. C. Grew, *Turbulent Era,* vol. 1, chaps. 18–20, and "The Peace Conference of Lausanne, 1922–23," *The Department of State Bulletin,* 33 (26 September 1955), 497–506; R. W. Child, *A Diplomat Looks at Europe,* chap. 4; R. H. Davison, "Middle East Nationalism: Lausanne Thirty Years Later," *Middle East Journal,* 7 (1953), 324–48.

1. U.S. *Aide-Mémoire* TO BRITAIN, FRANCE AND ITALY, 30 OCTOBER 1922

The Conference proposed for the purpose of drawing up a treaty of peace with Turkey will have primarily to deal with the problems resulting from the state of belligerency between the Allied Powers, Turkey, and Greece. The United States was neither at war with Turkey nor a party to the Armistice of 1918 and does not desire to participate in the final peace negotiations or to assume responsibility for the political and territorial adjustments which may be effected.

While maintaining this reserve in regard to certain phases of the Near East settlement the Government of the United States does not desire to leave the impression that it regards its interests as less entitled to consideration than those of any other Power, or that it is disposed to relinquish rights enjoyed in common with other powers, or proper commercial opportunity, or that it is unconcerned with the humanitarian interests involved.

For the purpose of clarity certain subjects of particular American concern may be briefly summarized.

(1) The maintenance of capitulations which may be essential to the appropriate safeguarding of non-Moslem interests.

(2) The protection, under proper guarantees, of philanthropic, educational and religious institutions.

(3) Appropriate undertakings in regard to the freedom of opportunity, without discrimination or special privilege, for commercial enterprise.

(4) Indemnity for losses suffered by Americans in Turkey as a result of arbitrary and illegal acts.

(5) Suitable provisions for the protection of minorities.

(6) Assurances touching the freedom of the Straits.

(7) Reasonable opportunity for archeological research and study.

This brief summary, while not exhaustive, may serve to indicate the general nature of American interests. To safeguard such interests and to facilitate the exchange of views the Government of the United States is prepared to send observers to the proposed conference if this action is agreeable to the Powers concerned. Without participating in the negotiations of the treaty of peace, these observers would be able to indicate this Government's position in greater detail than is possible in this *Aide Memoire* and they could also inform the American Government of the attitude of other Powers in matters where there are mutual interests.

As the object in view in submitting this suggestion is the elimination of any possible cause of misunderstanding, it is considered appropriate to call attention to the attitude of the United States in respect to secret treaties and agreements. It is not felt that arrangements previously made with respect to Turkish territory, which provide for the establishment of zones of special commercial and economic influence, such, for example, as the Tripartite Agreement of 1920, are consonant with the principle of the equality of economic opportunity. It is assumed that the Allied Powers will not now desire, and do not now intend, to carry into effect previous arrangements of this nature.

The United States has no desire to take any action which might embarrass the Allied Powers in the proper effort to secure peace. It desires nothing which need conflict with the interests of other countries, if the principle of commercial opportunity for all nations is recognized at the outset. The United States has no intention of seeking for itself or its nationals a position of special privilege but it desires to protect its rights and to assure the Open Door. Finally it wishes to afford protection to its citizens who wish to continue the humanitarian work which has been carried on for generations in the Near East and is rendered more essential than ever by the present conditions.

2. SECRETARY HUGHES' INSTRUCTIONS TO U.S. AMBASSADORS AT LONDON, PARIS AND ROME, 30 OCTOBER 1922

(A) As the United States is not at war with Turkey it will not be a signatory of the treaty of peace concluded to put an end to this war or a party to the conference for the purpose of negotiating such a treaty. It is appreciated, however, that it will be practically impossible for the Allies to conduct negotiations without dealing with matters in which this Government is interested.

(B) To permit the Allies to conclude their negotiations without any attempt to present Department's views or to obtain assurances for protection of American interests would leave this Government with a *fait accompli* so far as the relations between the Allies and the Turks were concerned. It would be difficult for us to obtain better terms than the Allies had arranged while we would probably not be in a position to share some of the advantages which the Allies might have obtained for such concessions as they might have felt called upon to make.

(C) The following course of action has therefore been determined upon:

(1) A memorandum giving a statement of the nature and scope of American interests in the Near East will be communicated to the British, French and Italian Governments and later to other Governments if this appears to be desirable. This would serve as a caveat and a basis upon which we could take the part of a candid friend with interests to be protected.

(2) American observers will be present during the course of the negotiations, ready at any opportune or critical moment to interpose the necessary word for our protection. If it appeared that there was a common interest to be served as, for example, with respect to capitulations, protection of educational institutions, et cetera, we would be advised by our observers and in a position immediately to express our point of view.

(3) We shall be prepared to avail ourselves of the first appropriate opportunity to make a treaty with Turkey to protect

American interests. Whenever suitable assurances can be received from Turkey which would permit the negotiation of such a treaty full powers could be sent.

The interests which the Department would desire to protect can briefly be summarized as follows:

OUTLINE OF AMERICAN INTERESTS

(1) *Capitulations.*—The Department appreciates that the Turks will in all probability strongly oppose the retention of the capitulations and that the Allies may take divergent views, certain Powers perhaps consenting to barter particular rights under the capitulations for concessions without value for us. It will be difficult, if not impossible, for the United States to maintain the capitulations intact, as would be desirable. It is felt, however, that we should insist upon the retention of the capitulations which are essential to the protection of American citizens. As regards economic capitulations which refer to measures of taxation, customs dues, et cetera, certain concessions might be made provided satisfactory guarantees of another nature to protect American business enterprise could be obtained.

(2) *Protection of American Educational Philanthropic and Religious Institutions.*—The list of institutions recognized by the Sublime Porte in 1907 should be brought up to date and Turkey should recognize them collectively and individually, grant rights to hold property in the corporate name of the institution, permit reopening of institutions closed since 1914, the establishment of new schools, the use of the English language, and the enjoyment of privileges of Ottoman institutions as regards taxation and customs exemption.

(3) *Protection of American Commercial Interests.*—We should oppose the policy of spheres of influence, exemplified by Tripartite agreement signed at Sèvres August 1920 and maintain the principle of the "Open Door" and equality of opportunity. Assurances should be secured that discriminatory taxation will not be levied and if capitulatory right of consent to any change in tariff be abandoned satisfactory guarantees for trade and commerce should be obtained.

(4) *Claims for Damages.*—Any new arrangement we may make with Turkey should include provision for indemnities for requisitions, loss of life or property resulting from illegal action of Turkish authorities since 1914.

(5) *Protection of Minorities.*—American sentiment demands that this Government exert its full influence to protect minorities. As a result, however, of deportations since 1915 it is believed that a relatively small number of Christians remain in Anatolia and it will be difficult to formulate any effective plan for insuring protection of the scattered remnants of the Christian population in Asia Minor. The most feasible solution of the problem might possibly be an exchange of Christian and Moslem minorities in Asia Minor and Greece. The question of the Christian minorities in Europe, particularly in Constantinople, is one of special interest to this Government and we shall exert appropriate influence for their protection.

The question of the homeland of the Armenians may be raised. It is possible that upon the return of more settled conditions in Russia, the Russian Caucasus may offer the best refuge for Armenians from Turkey.

(6) *Freedom of the Straits.*—Of the two phases of this question relating to the time of peace and the time of war, the Department is not disposed to become involved in commitments concerning the latter, particularly when Turkey or the Great Powers of Europe may be the belligerents. It is of distinct interest to this Government, however, to obtain effective assurances that the Straits would be open in time of peace for both merchant ships and ships of war to proceed to Constantinople and through the Black Sea. This Sea is a highway of commerce and should not be under the exclusive control of Turkey and of Russia.

(7) *International Financial Control.*—The Commission controlling the Ottoman Public Debt, some 60 per cent of which are held in France, 22 per cent in Germany, 14 per cent in England and Holland, composed

before 1914 of French, British, Italian, German, Austrian and Turkish members, administers six important sources of Ottoman revenue and largely influences trade and commerce. If Turkey should apply to us for a loan, the possibility of its consolidation with existing foreign debt would place us in an advantageous position respecting the administration and liquidation of the latter. Both financial and commercial questions in general should receive careful consideration.

(*8*) *Archeological Research.*—American institutions are particularly interested in securing adequate provision to permit archeological research and study in Turkish territory.

(*9*) *General Observations.*—This Government may further desire to conclude with Turkey naturalization and parcel post conventions.

To summarize: While it is neither natural nor desirable that we should participate in the peace conference or become involved in the negotiations regarding policies and aims in which we have no share it is essential that the Department should be constantly in command of adequate information, keen for the protection of American interests, ready to throw the full weight of our influence to obtain assurances for the freedom of the Straits and the protection of minorities, candid as to our views and in a position at any suitable time to make the separate agreement which at some time must be made with the Turkish Government recognized by the Powers. No point of advantage should be forfeited, no just influence lost, no injurious commitments made. We should maintain the integrity of our position as an independent power which has not been concerned with the rivalries of other nations which have so often made the Near East the theater of war.

3. POLICY RECOMMENDATIONS ON THE TURKISH STRAITS BY THE GENERAL BOARD OF THE U.S. NAVY, 10 NOVEMBER 1922

The General Board has considered the following question . . . [:]

"Having in view the present and prospective Near East situation and the present and prospective interests of the United States in the Near East, what should be the American policy regarding the control and navigation of the Dardanelles?["]

2. The vicinity of the Dardanelles has always been one of international tension incident to the centering of ethnological conflicts and of highly important international trade routes—both land and sea. American interest in the Near East, as elsewhere, is closely allied with any arrangements that will promote world-peace. That solution of the Dardanelles question which will give the greatest prospect of lasting peace in the Near East is likely to accord best with American interests.

3. Certain features of the Dardanelles question change but little from decade to decade. The permanency of these features indicate them as the basis of arrangements concerning the Dardanelles. These features will be discussed briefly.

4. The Dardanelles is a great public highway provided by nature leading to a sea that washes the shores of Turkey, Russia, Roumania, Bulgaria, and some lesser states, and that receives the waters of five great navigable rivers. This sea in consequence does not belong to a single power as it once did, but belongs to all the world as a part of the highway of trade. Any and every attempt to block or impede the access of seaborne commerce to this sea,—the Black Sea,—is subversive of world organization and contrary to world interests, as it will set up international pressures and tensions that will lead inevitably to renewed wars.

5. Russia, potentially one of the greatest of world powers, exports in normal times one-half of all her products via the Black Sea. Russia has no other sea outlet comparable in importance with that through the Dardanelles. The importance to Russia of this outlet will increase greatly with the growth of Russian population, and, especially, with the improvement of Russia's means of internal transportation. No solution that imposes an artificial barrier between so great a power and the sea can contain within it the elements of permanency,—of stability.

6. A large part of the commerce of Austria, Czecho-Slovakia, Hungary, Jugo-Slavia, Roumania and Bulgaria finds its way to the high seas via the Danube and the Dardanelles. This commerce too requires freedom of exit. The necessity for equal freedom of transit in both directions needs no argument.

7. The considerations briefly outlined above have led to a general acceptance by the powers and by Turkey of the principle of freedom of passage through the straits for the merchant vessels of all nations. Experience in many places throughout the world has shown that the acceptance of a principle is not always sufficient to secure its impartial execution. The administration of affairs that follows, and is supposedly based upon, the acceptance of the principle is fully as important as the acceptance of the principle itself in determining the course of events. Until conditions in the Near East are stabilized equality of opportunity is best secured by equal participation in administration by the interested parties.

8. The granting of freedom of passage through the Dardanelles is not in itself sufficient to secure for American ships the same opportunities as may be enjoyed by the merchant ships of other powers. We must secure by agreement equality of rights and the same privileges as other foreign powers in all that relates to commercial and naval operations. With no attempt at enumeration we may mention the dependence of successful maritime commerce on radio, cable, fuel, wharfage, lighterage, pilotage, anchorage, towage, and inspection facilities. The insidious effect of discriminatory treatment in these respects may handicap our ships so badly as to drive them out of business.

9. Attention is particularly invited to the fact that, due to the present political and economic condition of all territories tributary to the Black Sea, the general situation is that of a new and as yet unorganized market of prodigious size offering the greatest opportunity to trade enterprise; and that steps taken and arrangements made now may influence profoundly our commercial life in the future. We can not claim special rights, but we can with full justice insist on equal rights.

10. The question of freedom of navigation of the Dardanelles for vessels of war is more complex and less capable of permanent settlement than the questions relating to merchant vessels. Whatever rights of navigation of the Straits are granted to other than Black Sea powers must of necessity be granted to the Black Sea powers themselves. When there are no naval powers bordering on the Black Sea that maintain fleets of importance in that sea it is to the interest of other powers, and especially to those powers that have political or economic ambitions in the Black Sea to have the navigation of the Dardanelles open to their vessels of war. They are thus able to use at least the show of force to further their interests. When there is a fleet of importance based within the Black Sea the interest of other powers regarding freedom of navigation of the Straits for vessels of war is reversed and they then desire that no force may issue from the Black Sea to interfere with or to be in a position to threaten their interests elsewhere. They are then willing to forego the advantages of access for themselves to gain the security that comes from a virtual internment of Black Sea fleets. The destruction of the Russian Black Sea fleet entirely changed the policy of Great Britain in relation to the Dardanelles. The General Board believes that the natural solution of the question, as well as the one most favorable to American interest and influence in world affairs is complete freedom of navigation of the Straits for all vessels of war.

11. There is no parallel between the necessary status of the Dardanelles and that of the Panama Canal. In the Dardanelles the history of instability, of conflicting interests, of discriminatory treatment, of sole access of powers to the sea and so forth, in addition to the fact that nature provided the Dardanelles while America provided the Panama Canal should separate very effectively the two questions in all their aspects.

12. The Straits are natural water ways that in equity belong not to one power but

to all. Furthermore, every solution of their control so far attempted that has been based on the rights of one power as against other powers has been a provocative solution. The question has never been settled because all solutions have been partial to the power at the time dominant.

13. Regardless of the principles that may be adopted nothing but superiority of force, either on the spot or available, will be adequate to maintain, against the vital interest of a great power or against the vital interest of Turkey, freedom of navigation of the Straits in time of war. If the fortifications are razed, the potential control of the Straits in war will be shifted to the British fleet. The demilitarization of Mitylene, Lemnos, Imbros and Samothraki, if proposed, would be distinctly in line with the future control of the Straits by naval forces instead of by fixed fortifications. This would mean British control because at present the British fleet with its outlying bases is strongest of all fleets.

14. No law nor treaty is likely to prevent blockade in time of war if the blockading nation is sufficiently powerful on the sea.

15. Experience has shown that control of the Straits by Turkey has been neither impartial nor stable, and that Turkey is unavoidably susceptible to outside pressure. This fact indicates that, under present conditions, international control of the Straits is less open to objection than control by Turkey. No single foreign power could be expected to do otherwise than favor unduly its own commerce were it placed in control of the navigation of the Straits.

SUMMARY

16. The General Board is of the opinion that American interests demand:

(*a*) That if an international commission of control of the Straits is set up, the United States have representation on the international commission of control and in all positions subordinate to that commission, equal to that of any other foreign power.

(*b*) That the Straits, including the Dardanelles, the Sea of Marmora, and the Bosphorus, be open to the free navigation of the merchant ships of all flags without distinction or preference.

(*c*) That the United States and its nationals have the same rights and privileges within and adjacent to the waters above mentioned as are possessed or may be granted to any other foreign power or to its nationals. These privileges to include all such matters as the erection and operation of radio stations, the establishment and operation of fuel depots and storehouses, the use of cables, pilotage, lighterage, wharfage, towage, inspection, clearance, etc., and the use without discrimination of public commercial facilities.

(*d*) That the Straits including the Dardanelles, the Sea of Marmora, and the Bosphorus, be open to the free navigation of the vessels of war of all flags.

(*e*) That no belligerent right be exercised and no hostile act committed within the Straits including the Dardanelles, the Sea of Marmora, and the Bosphorus.

(*f*) That all fortifications commanding these waters be razed and that no new fortifications be erected.

41. THE (LAUSANNE) TREATY OF PEACE WITH TURKEY AND THE ACCOMPANYING STRAITS CONVENTION
24 July 1923

(The instruments went into force on 6 August 1924, with the deposit in Paris of the requisite number of ratifications)

[Great Britain, *Parliametary Papers, 1923,* Treaty Series No. 16, Cmd. 1929]

With the decisive defeat of the Greeks and the conclusion of an armistice on 11 October 1922, the Turkish nationalists cleared the last of the foreign troops from Anatolian soil. Only the inter-allied fleet at Istanbul reminded the nationalists of the occupation. Recognizing the inevitability of a fresh peace to replace the unratified treaty of Sèvres (Doc. 31), the allies on 27 October issued invitations to the imperial government at Istanbul and the provisional nationalist government at Ankara to attend a peace conference in Lausanne. The nationalist regime, however, demonstrated that it alone represented Turkey. The Grand National Assembly at Ankara abolished the Sultanate on 1 November and three days later declared the Ottoman government no longer in existence. The conditions that the nationalist delegation brought with it to the Lausanne Conference (20 November 1922–4 February 1923, 23 April–24 July 1923) had been substantially defined in the National Pact (Doc. 28), adopted nearly three years earlier. While prepared to accept the separation of the Arab provinces, the nationalists were nevertheless dedicated to maintaining the integrity of Anatolia proper and the security of Istanbul and to assuring Turkish participation in any regime for the straits and the abolition of the capitulations. These principles all found their way into the instruments—the only negotiated peace of World War I—signed by the British Empire, France, Italy, Japan, Greece, Bulgaria, Rumania and Turkey at Lausanne on 24 July 1923. The convention on the Straits (one of the Lausanne instruments), which provided for an international supervisory commission under the permanent presidency of Turkey, established a regime that represented, from the European viewpoint, "a compromise between the interests of the Black Sea Powers—particularly those of Russia—seeking preferential treatment, and the ambition of the Allies—particularly of Great Britain—seeking complete freedom" (J. T. Shotwell and F. Deák, *Turkey at the Straits,* p. 117). Russia signed the straits convention on 14 August 1923 but later failed to ratify it. Reproduced below are only selected articles from the political section of the peace treaty and from the straits conventions. Great Britain, *Parliamentary Papers, 1923,* Turkey No. 1, Cmd. 1814, "Lausanne Conference on Near Eastern Affairs, 1922-23" (proceedings); J. C. Grew, *Turbulent Era,* vol. 1, chaps. 18–20; G. A. Craig and F. Gilbert, eds., *The Diplomats,* chap. 6, (by R. H. Davison); R. H. Davison, "Middle East Nationalism, Lausanne Thirty Years later," *Middle East Journal,* 7 (1953), 324–48; H. N. Howard, *Partition of Turkey,* chap. 9; L. Fischer, *Soviets in World Affairs,* vol. 1, chap. 12; A. L. P. Dennis, *Foreign Policies of Soviet Russia,* chap. 9; Shotwell and Deák, *op. cit.,* chaps. 11–12; B. Georges-Gaulis, *La Nouvelle Turquie,* chaps. 5, 7.

1. THE TREATY OF PEACE WITH TURKEY

ART. 1. From the coming into force of the present Treaty, the state of peace will be definitely re-established between the British Empire, France, Italy, Japan, Greece, Roumania and the Serb-Croat-Slovene State of the one part, and Turkey of the other part, as well as between their respective nationals.

Official relations will be resumed on both sides and, in the respective territories, diplomatic and consular representatives will receive, without prejudice to such agreements as may be concluded in the future, treatment in accordance with the general principles of international law. . . .

ART. 15. Turkey renounces in favour of Italy all rights and title over the following islands: Stampalia (Astrapalia), Rhodes (Rhodos), Calki (Kharki), Scarpanto, Casos (Casso), Piscopis (Tilos), Misiros (Nisyros), Calimnos (Kalymnos), Leros, Patmos, Lipsos (Lipso), Simi (Symi), and Cos (Kos), which are now occupied by Italy, and the islets dependent thereon, and also over the island of Castellorizzo.

ART. 16. Turkey hereby renounces all rights and title whatsoever over or respecting the territories situated outside the frontiers laid down in the present Treaty and the islands other than those over which her sovereignty is recognised by the said Treaty, the future of these territories and islands being settled or to be settled by the parties concerned.

The provisions of the present Article do not prejudice any special arrangements arising from neighbourly relations which have been or may be concluded between Turkey and any limitrophe countries.

ART. 17. The renunciation by Turkey of all rights and titles over Egypt and over the Soudan will take effect as from the 5th November, 1914.

ART. 18. Turkey is released from all undertakings and obligations in regard to the Ottoman loans guaranteed on the Egyptian tribute, that is to say, the loans of 1855, 1891 and 1894. The annual payments made by Egypt for the service of these loans now forming part of the service of the

Egyptian Public Debt, Egypt is freed from all other obligations relating to the Ottoman Public Debt.

ART. 19. Any questions arising from the recognition of the State of Egypt shall be settled by agreements to be negotiated subsequently in a manner to be determined later between the Powers concerned. The provisions of the present Treaty relating to territories detached from Turkey under the said Treaty will not apply to Egypt.

ART. 20. Turkey hereby recognises the annexation of Cyprus proclaimed by the British Government on the 5th November, 1914.

ART. 21. Turkish nationals ordinarily resident in Cyprus on the 5th November, 1914, will acquire British nationality subject to the conditions laid down in the local law, and will thereupon lose their Turkish nationality. They will, however, have the right to opt for Turkish nationality within two years from the coming into force of the present Treaty, provided that they leave Cyprus within twelve months after having so opted.

Turkish nationals ordinarily resident in Cyprus on the coming into force of the present Treaty who, at that date, have acquired or are in process of acquiring British nationality, in consequence of a request made in accordance with the local law, will also thereupon lose their Turkish nationality.

It is understood that the Government of Cyprus will be entitled to refuse British nationality to inhabitants of the island who, being Turkish nationals, had formerly acquired another nationality without the consent of the Turkish Government.

ART. 22. Without prejudice to the general stipulations of Article 27, Turkey hereby recognises the definite abolition of all rights and privileges whatsoever which she enjoyed in Libya under the Treaty of Lausanne of the 18th October, 1912, and the instruments connected therewith. . . .

ART. 27. No power or jurisdiction in political, legislative or administrative matters shall be exercised outside Turkish territory by the Turkish Government or authorities, for any reason whatsoever, over the nationals of a territory placed under the sovereignty or protectorate of the other Powers signatory of the present Treaty, or over the nationals of a territory detached from Turkey.

It is understood that the spiritual attributions of the Moslem religious authorities are in no way infringed.

ART. 28. Each of the High Contracting Parties hereby accepts, in so far as it is concerned, the complete abolition of the Capitulations in Turkey in every respect.

ART. 29. Moroccans, who are French nationals ("ressortissants") and Tunisians shall enjoy in Turkey the same treatment in all respects as other French nationals ("ressortissants").

Natives ("ressortissants") of Libya shall enjoy in Turkey the same treatment in all respects as other Italian nationals ("ressortissants").

The stipulations of the present Article in no way prejudge the nationality of persons of Tunisian, Libyan and Moroccan origin established in Turkey.

Reciprocally, in the territories the inhabitants of which benefit by the stipulations of the first and second paragraphs of this Article, Turkish nationals shall benefit by the same treatment as in France and in Italy respectively.

The treatment to which merchandise originating in or destined for the territories, the inhabitants of which benefit from the stipulations of the first paragraph of this Article, shall be subject in Turkey, and, reciprocally, the treatment to which merchandise originating in or destined for Turkey shall be subject in the said territories shall be settled by agreement between the French and Turkish Governments.

ART. 30. Turkish subjects habitually resident in territory which in accordance with the provisions of the present Treaty is detached from Turkey will become *ipso facto*, in the conditions laid down by the local law, nationals of the State to which such territory is transferred.

ART. 31. Persons over eighteen years of age, losing their Turkish nationality and obtaining *ipso facto* a new nationality under Article 30, shall be entitled within a period of two years from the coming into force of the present Treaty to opt for Turkish nationality.

ART. 32. Persons over eighteen years of age, habitually resident in territory detached from Turkey in accordance with the present Treaty, and differing in race from the majority of the population of such territory shall, within two years from the coming into force of the present Treaty, be entitled to opt for the nationality of one of the States in which the majority of the population is of the same race as the person exercising the right to opt, subject to the consent of that State.

ART. 33. Persons who have exercised the right to opt in accordance with the provisions of Articles 31 and 32 must, within the succeeding twelve months, transfer their place of residence to the State for which they have opted.

They will be entitled to retain their immovable property in the territory of the other State where they had their place of residence before exercising their right to opt.

They may carry with them their movable property of every description. No export or import duties may be imposed upon them in connection with the removal of such property.

ART. 34. Subject to any agreements which it may be necessary to conclude between the Governments exercising authority in the countries detached from Turkey and the Governments of the countries where the persons concerned are resident, Turkish nationals of over eighteen years of age who are natives of a territory detached from Turkey under the present Treaty, and who on its coming into force are habitually resident abroad, may opt for the nationality of the territory of which they are natives, if they belong by race to the majority of the population of that territory, and subject to the consent of the Government exercising authority therein. This right of option must be exercised within two years from the coming into force of the present Treaty. . . .

ART. 37. Turkey undertakes that the stipulations contained in Articles 38 to 44 shall be recognised as fundamental laws, and that no law, no regulation, nor official action shall conflict or interfere with these stipulations, nor shall any law, regulation, nor official action prevail over them.

ART. 38. The Turkish Government undertakes to assure full and complete protection of life and liberty to all inhabitants of Turkey without distinction of birth, nationality, language, race or religion.

All inhabitants of Turkey shall be entitled to free exercise, whether in public or private, of any creed, religion or belief, the observance of which shall not be incompatible with public order and good morals.

Non-Moslem minorities will enjoy full freedom of movement and of emigration, subject to the measures applied, on the whole or on part of the territory, to all Turkish nationals, and which may be taken by the Turkish Government for national defence, or for the maintenance of public order.

ART. 39. Turkish nationals belonging to non-Moslem minorities will enjoy the same civil and political rights as Moslems.

All the inhabitants of Turkey, without distinction of religion, shall be equal before the law.

Differences of religion, creed or confession shall not prejudice any Turkish national in matters relating to the enjoyment of civil or political rights, as, for instance, admission to public employments, functions and honours, or the exercise of professions and industries.

No restrictions shall be imposed on the free use by any Turkish national of any language in private intercourse, in commerce, religion, in the press, or in publications of any kind or at public meetings.

Notwithstanding the existence of the official language, adequate facilities shall be given to Turkish nationals of non-Turkish speech for the oral use of their own language before the Courts.

ART. 40. Turkish nationals belonging to non-Moslem minorities shall enjoy the same treatment and security in law and in fact as other Turkish nationals. In particular, they shall have an equal right to establish, manage and control at their own expense, any charitable, religious and social institutions, any schools and other establishments for instruction and education, with the right to use their own language and to exercise their own religion freely therein.

ART. 41. As regards public instruction, the Turkish Government will grant in those towns and districts, where a considerable proportion of non-Moslem nationals are resident, adequate facilities for ensuring that in the primary schools the instruction shall be given to the children of such Turkish nationals through the medium of their own language. This provision will not prevent the Turkish Government from making the teaching of the Turkish language obligatory in the said schools.

In towns and districts where there is a considerable proportion of Turkish nationals belonging to non-Moslem minorities, these minorities shall be assured an equitable share in the enjoyment and application of the sums which may be provided out of public funds under the State, municipal or other budgets for educational, religious, or charitable purposes.

The sums in question shall be paid to the qualified representatives of the establishments and institutions concerned.

ART. 42. The Turkish Government undertakes to take, as regards non-Moslem minorities, in so far as concerns their family law or personal status, measures permitting the settlement of these questions in accordance with the customs of those minorities.

These measures will be elaborated by special Commissions composed of representatives of the Turkish Government and of representatives of each of the minorities concerned in equal number. In case of divergence, the Turkish Government and the Council of the League of Nations will appoint in agreement an umpire chosen from amongst European lawyers.

The Turkish Government undertakes to grant full protection to the churches, synagogues, cemeteries, and other religious establishments of the above-mentioned minorities. All facilities and authorisation will be granted to the pious foundations, and to the religious and charitable institutions of the said minorities at present existing in Turkey, and the Turkish Government will not refuse, for the formation of new religious and charitable institutions, any of the necessary facilities which are granted to other private institutions of that nature.

ART. 43. Turkish nationals belonging to non-Moslem minorities shall not be compelled to perform any act which constitutes a violation of their faith or religious observances, and shall not be placed under any disability by reason of their refusal to attend Courts of Law or to perform any legal business on their weekly day of rest.

This provision, however, shall not exempt such Turkish nationals from such obligations as shall be imposed upon all other Turkish nationals for the preservation of public order.

ART. 44. Turkey agrees that, in so far as the preceding Articles of this Section affect non-Moslem nationals of Turkey, these provisions constitute obligations of international concern and shall be placed under the guarantee of the League of Nations. They shall not be modified without the assent of the majority of the Council of the League of Nations. The British Empire, France, Italy and Japan hereby agree not to withhold their assent to any modification in these Articles which is in due form assented to by a majority of the Council of the League of Nations.

Turkey agrees that any Member of the Council of the League of Nations shall have the right to bring to the attention of the Council any infraction or danger of infraction of any of these obligations, and that the Council may thereupon take such action and give such directions as it may deem proper and effective in the circumstances.

Turkey further agrees that any difference of opinion as to questions of law or of fact arising out of these Articles between the Turkish Government and any one of the other Signatory Powers or any other Power, a member of the Council of the League of Nations, shall be held to be a dispute of an international character under Article 14 of the Covenant of the League of Nations. The Turkish Government hereby consents that any such dispute shall, if the other party thereto demands, be referred to the

Permanent Court of International Justice. The decision of the Permanent Court shall be final and shall have the same force and effect as an award under Article 13 of the Covenant. . . .

2. CONVENTION ON THE REGIME OF THE STRAITS

ART. 1. The High Contracting Parties agree to recognise and declare the principle of freedom of transit and of navigation by sea and by air in the Strait of the Dardanelles, the Sea of Marmora and the Bosphorus, hereinafter comprised under the general term of the "Straits."

ART. 2. The transit and navigation of commercial vessels and aircraft, and of war vessels and aircraft in the Straits in time of peace and in time of war shall henceforth be regulated by the provisions of the attached Annex.

ANNEX. RULES FOR THE PASSAGE OF COMMERCIAL VESSELS AND AIRCRAFT, AND OF WAR VESSELS AND AIRCRAFT THROUGH THE STRAITS

1. *Merchant Vessels, including Hospital Ships, Yachts and Fishing Vessels and non-Military Aircraft*

(a.) *In Time of Peace.* Complete freedom of navigation and passage by day and by night under any flag and with any kind of cargo, without any formalities, or tax, or charge whatever (subject, however, to international sanitary provisions) unless for services directly rendered, such as pilotage, light, towage or other similar charges, and without prejudice to the rights exercised in this respect by the services and undertakings now operating under concessions granted by the Turkish Government. . . .

(b.) *In Time of War, Turkey being Neutral.* Complete freedom of navigation and passage by day and by night under the same conditions as above. The duties and rights of Turkey as a neutral Power cannot authorise her to take any measures liable to interfere with navigation through the Straits, the waters of which, and the air above which, must remain entirely free in time of war, Turkey being neutral just as in time of peace. . . .

(c.) *In Time of War, Turkey being a Belligerent.* Freedom of navigation for neutral vessels and neutral non-military aircraft, if the vessel or aircraft in question does not assist the enemy, particularly by carrying contraband, troops or enemy nationals. Turkey will have the right to visit and search such vessels and aircraft, and for this purpose aircraft are to alight on the ground or on the sea in such areas as are specified and prepared for this purpose by Turkey. The rights of Turkey to apply to enemy vessels the measures allowed by international law are not affected.

Turkey will have full power to take such measures as she may consider necessary to prevent enemy vessels from using the Straits. These measures, however, are not to be of such a nature as to prevent the free passage of neutral vessels, and Turkey agrees to provide such vessels with either the necessary instructions or pilots for the above purpose.

2. *Warships, including Fleet Auxiliaries, Troopships, Aircraft Carriers and Military Aircraft*

(a) *In Time of Peace.* Complete freedom of passage by day and by night under any flag, without any formalities, or tax, or charge whatever, but subject to the following restrictions as to the total force:—

> The maximum force which any one Power may send through the Straits into the Black Sea is not to be greater than that of the most powerful fleet of the littoral Powers of the Black Sea existing in that sea at the time of passage; but with the proviso that the Powers reserve to themselves the right to send into the Black Sea, at all times and under all circumstances, a force of not more than three ships, of which no individual ship shall exceed 10,000 tons.

Turkey has no responsibility in regard to the number of war vessels which pass through the Straits. . . .

(b) *In Time of War, Turkey being Neutral.* Complete freedom of passage by day and by night under any flag, without any formalities, or tax, or charge whatever, under the same limitations as in paragraph 2 (*a*).

However, these limitations will not be applicable to any belligerent Power to the prejudice of its belligerent rights in the Black Sea.

The rights and duties of Turkey as a neutral Power cannot authorise her to take any measures liable to interfere with navigation through the Straits, the waters of which, and the air above which, must remain entirely free in time of war, Turkey being neutral, just as in time of peace.

Warships and military aircraft of belligerents will be forbidden to make any capture, to exercise the right of visit and search, or to carry out any other hostile act in the Straits. . . .

(c) *In Time of War, Turkey being Belligerent.* Complete freedom of passage for neutral warships, without any formalities, or tax, or charge whatever, but under the same limitations as in paragraph 2 (*a*).

The measures taken by Turkey to prevent enemy ships and aircraft from using the Straits are not to be of such a nature as to prevent the free passage of neutral ships and aircraft, and Turkey agrees to provide the said ships and aircraft with either the necessary instructions or pilots for the above purpose.

Neutral military aircraft will make the passage of the Straits at their own risk and peril, and will submit to investigation as to their character. For this purpose aircraft are to alight on the ground or on the sea in such areas as are specified and prepared for this purpose by Turkey.

3.

(*a.*) The passage of the Straits by submarines of Powers at peace with Turkey must be made on the surface.

(*b.*) The officer in command of a foreign naval force, whether coming from the Mediterranean or the Black Sea, will communicate, without being compelled to stop, to a signal station at the entrance to the Dardanelles or the Bosphorus, the number and the names of vessels under his orders which are entering the Straits.

These signal stations shall be notified from time to time by Turkey; until such signal stations are notified, the freedom of passage for foreign war vessels in the Straits shall not thereby be prejudiced, nor shall their entry into the Straits be for this reason delayed.

(*c*) The right of military and non-military aircraft to fly over the Straits, under the conditions laid down in the present rules, necessitates for aircraft—

(i) Freedom to fly over a strip of territory of five kilometres wide on each side of the narrow parts of the Straits;

(ii) Liberty, in the event of a forced landing, to alight on the coast or on the sea in the territorial waters of Turkey.

4. Limitations of Time of Transit for Warships

In no event shall warships in transit through the Straits, except in the event of damage or peril of the sea, remain therein beyond the time which is necessary for them to effect their passage, including the time of anchorage during the night if necessary for safety of navigation.

5. Stay in the Ports of the Straits and of the Black Sea

(*a*) Paragraphs 1, 2 and 3 of this Annex apply to the passage of vessels, warships and aircraft through and over the Straits and do not affect the right of Turkey to make such regulations as she may consider necessary regarding the number of men-of-war and military aircraft of any one Power which may visit Turkish ports or aerodromes at one time, and the duration of their stay.

(*b*) Littoral Powers of the Black Sea will also have a similar right as regards their ports and aerodromes. . . .

ART. 6. Subject to the provisions of Article 8 concerning Constantinople, there shall exist, in the demilitarised zones and islands [defined in article 4], no fortifications, no permanent artillery organisation, no submarine engines of war other than submarine vessels, no military aerial organisation, and no naval base.

No armed forces shall be stationed in the demilitarised zones and islands except the police and gendarmerie forces necessary for the maintenance of order; the armament of such forces will be composed only of revolvers, swords, rifles and four Lewis guns per hundred men, and will exclude any artillery.

In the territorial waters of the demilitarised zones and islands, there shall exist no submarine engines of war other than submarine vessels.

Notwithstanding the preceding paragraphs Turkey will retain the right to transport her armed forces through the demilitarised zones and islands of Turkish territory, as well as through their territorial waters, where the Turkish fleet will have the right to anchor.

Moreover, in so far as the Straits are concerned, the Turkish Government shall have the right to observe by means of aeroplanes or balloons both the surface and the bottom of the sea. Turkish aeroplanes will always be able to fly over the waters of the Straits and the demilitarised zones of Turkish territory, and will have full freedom to alight therein, either on land or on sea.

In the demilitarised zones and islands and in their territorial waters, Turkey and Greece shall similarly be entitled to effect such movements of personnel as are rendered necessary for the instruction outside these zones and islands of the men recruited therein.

Turkey and Greece shall have the right to organise in the said zones and islands in their respective territories any system of observation and communication, both telegraphic, telephonic and visual. Greece shall be entitled to send her fleet into the territorial waters of the demilitarised Greek islands, but may not use these waters as a base of operations against Turkey nor for any military or naval concentration for this purpose. . . .

ART. 10. There shall be constituted at Constantinople an International Commission composed in accordance with Article 12 and called the "Straits Commission". .

ART. 12. The Commission shall be composed of a representative of Turkey, who shall be President, and representatives of France, Great Britain, Italy, Japan, Bulgaria, Greece, Roumania, Russia, and the Serb-Croat-Slovene State, in so far as these Powers are signatories of the present Convention, each of these Powers being entitled to representation as from its ratification of the said Convention.

The United States of America, in the event of their acceding to the present Convention, will also be entitled to have one representative on the Commission.

Under the same conditions any independent littoral States of the Black Sea which are not mentioned in the first paragraph of the present Article will possess the same right. . . .

ART. 15. The Straits Commission will carry out its functions under the auspices of the League of Nations, and will address to the League an annual report giving an account of its activities, and furnishing all information which may be useful in the interests of commerce and navigation; with this object in view the Commission will place itself in touch with the departments of the Turkish Government dealing with navigation through the Straits. . . .

ART. 18. The High Contracting Parties, desiring to secure that the demilitarisation of the Straits and of the contiguous zones shall not constitute an unjustifiable danger to the military security of Turkey, and that no act of war should imperil the freedom of the Straits or the safety of the demilitarised zones, agree as follows:—

Should the freedom of navigation of the Straits or the security of the demilitarised zones be imperilled by a violation of the provisions relating to freedom of passage, or by a surprise attack or some act of war or threat of war, the High Contracting Parties, and in any case France, Great Britain, Italy and Japan, acting in conjunction, will meet such violation, attack, or other act of war or threat of war, by all the means that the Council of the League of Nations may decide for this purpose.

So soon as the circumstance which may have necessitated the action provided for in the preceding paragraph shall have ended, the régime of the Straits as laid down by the terms of the present Convention shall again be strictly applied.

The present provision, which forms an integral part of those relating to the demilitarisation and to the freedom of the Straits, does not prejudice the rights and obligations of the High Contracting Parties under the Covenant of the League of Nations.

42. CONVENTION ON AMERICAN RIGHTS IN SYRIA AND LEBANON: THE UNITED STATES AND FRANCE
4 April 1924

[*U.S. Treaty Series,* No. 695]

Although the United States did not join the League of Nations, the American government maintained that its nationals were entitled in the mandated countries to rights and privileges identical to those conferred on citizens of states members of the League. The United States sought primarily to persuade Britain and France to acquiesce in the "open door" economic policy in the Near and Middle East (Doc. 30) and secondarily to protect the interests of American religious missions. United States negotiations with France and England for conventions on American rights in Syria (and Lebanon) and Palestine respectively lasted more than four years. The two conventions concluded in 1924 were alike in structure and content, each reciting in the preamble the full text of the pertinent mandatory instrument. The conventions differed in one respect only. That on Palestine (signed on 3 December 1924, *U.S. Treaty Series,* No. 728) included a provision that made all valid extradition treaties and conventions between the United States and Britain applicable to the mandated land. No comparable clause appears in the convention with France on Syria and Lebanon. A third convention between the United States, Britain and Iraq (*U.S. Treaty Series,* No. 835), falling into the same class, was not signed until 9 January 1930. B. Gerig, *The Open Door and the Mandates System;* E. A. Speiser, *The United States and the Near East,* chap. 10; J. C. Hurewitz, *Middle East Dilemmas,* chap. 4; C. J. Friedrich, *American Policy toward Palestine.*

ART. 1. Subject to the provisions of the present convention the United States consents to the administration by the French Republic, pursuant to the aforesaid mandate, of Syria and the Lebanon.

ART. 2. The United States and its nationals shall have and enjoy all the rights and benefits secured under the terms of the mandate to members of the League of Nations and their nationals, notwithstanding the fact that the United States is not a member of the League of Nations.

ART. 3. Vested American property rights in the mandated territories shall be respected and in no way impaired.

ART. 4. A duplicate of the annual report to be made by the mandatory under Article 17 of the mandate shall be furnished to the United States.

ART. 5. Subject to the provisions of any local laws for the maintenance of public order and public morals, the nationals of the United States will be permitted freely to establish and maintain educational, philanthropic and religious institutions in the mandated territory, to receive voluntary applicants and to teach in the English language.

ART. 6. Nothing contained in the present convention shall be affected by any modification which may be made in the terms of the mandate as recited above unless such modification shall have been assented to by the United States.

43. BRITISH POLICY IN EGYPT
7 October–22 November 1924

[The MacDonald statement to Allenby from *Parliamentary Papers, 1924,* Egypt No. 1, Cmd. 2269; Allenby's communications from *The Times* (London), 24 November 1924]

Sultan Fuad assumed the title of King a fortnight after Britain's unilateral termination on 28 February 1922 of its protectorate over Egypt (Doc. 36). A new constitution, drafted by a special commission, was promulgated on 21 April 1923. Sa'd Pasha Zaghlul became prime minister, for his Wafdist Party won a crushing victory in the first general election (January 1924) under the new constitution—as it was to do in every subsequent unfettered election under the monarchy. James Ramsay MacDonald, who served as Prime Minister and Foreign Minister in Britain's first Labor government, prodded the Egyptians to open treaty negotiations in London in September 1924. But the talks deadlocked early in October, before the diplomatic opponents could establish any common ground. MacDonald on 7 October addressed a policy statement to High Commissioner Allenby, emphasizing, among other points, that the British were, and intended to remain, masters of the administration in the Sudan. Meanwhile, the unabating postwar acts of political terrorism, directed chiefly against Britain, reached a climax on 19–20 November 1924 in the assassination of Sir Lee Stack, the Governor-General and *Sirdar* (Commander-in-Chief) of the Egyptian Army. British response, prompt and repressive, was designed to undermine Egypt's position in the Sudan. But the threat in Allenby's first communication—which like the second was read aloud in English to Zaghlul Pasha at the Egyptian Premier's office by the Field Marshal while a British cavalry regiment waited outside and blocked the approach to the Egyptian Parliament building—merely drove the Egyptian *fallahin* (peasants) into the arms of the nationalists and compounded the already complex question of the Sudan's political future. Austen Chamberlain, Foreign Secretary in the new Conservative government, reversed London's position on the question in mid-December 1924, too tardily however to repair the damage. *Survey of International Affairs, 1925,* vol. 1, pp. 189–230; A. P. Wavell, *Allenby in Egypt,* chap. 7; Lord Lloyd, *Egypt since Cromer,* vol. 2, chaps. 5–6; M. Abbas, *Sudan Question,* chaps. 5–6.

1. MACDONALD'S DESPATCH TO ALLENBY, 7 OCTOBER 1924

In the course of my conversations with the Egyptian Prime Minister his Excellency explained to me the modifications in the *status quo* in Egypt on which he felt bound to insist. If I have correctly understood him they were as follows:—

(*a.*) The withdrawal of all British forces from Egyptian territory.

(*b.*) The withdrawal of the financial and judicial advisers.

(*c.*) The disappearance of all British control over the Egyptian Government, notably in connection with foreign relations, which Zaghlul Pasha claimed were hampered by the notification of His Majesty's Government to foreign Powers on the 15th March, 1922, that they would regard as an unfriendly act any attempt at interference in the affairs of Egypt by another Power.

(*d.*) The abandonment by His Majesty's Government of their claim to protect foreigners and minorities in Egypt.

(*e.*) The abandonment by His Majesty's Government of their claim to share in any way in protecting the Suez Canal.

As regards the Sudan, I drew attention to certain statements which his Excellency had made as President of the Council of Ministers before the Egyptian Parliament during the course of the summer. On the 17th May, according to my information, Zaghlul Pasha stated that the fact that a foreign officer was Commander-in-Chief of the Egyptian army and the retention in that army of British officers were inconsistent with the dignity of independent Egypt. The expression of such sentiments in an official pronouncement by the responsible head of the Egyptian Government has obviously placed not only Sir Lee Stack as Sirdar, but all British officers attached to the Egyptian army, in a difficult position. I also had in mind that, in June, Zaghlul Pasha was reported to have claimed for Egypt complete rights of ownership over the Sudan and characterized the British Government as usurpers.

His Excellency observed that in making the above statements he was merely voicing the opinion not only of the Egyptian Parliament, but of the Egyptian nation, and I gathered that he still adhered to that position. Such statements, however, must inevitably have affected the minds of Egyptians employed in the Sudan, and of the Sudanese personnel of the Egyptian army. They have indeed made it appear that loyalty to the Egyptian Government is something different from and inconsistent with loyalty to the existing administration of the Sudan. As a result, not only has there been an entire change in the spirit of Anglo-Egyptian co-operation which has in the past prevailed in the Sudan, but also Egyptian subjects serving under the Sudan Government have been encouraged to regard themselves as propagandists of the Egyptian Government's views, with results that if persisted in, in the absence of any agreement, would render their presence in the Sudan under the existing régime a source of danger to public order.

I promised in the course of our first conversation to be perfectly frank with his Excellency. Then and subsequently I left him under no illusion as to the position which His Majesty's Government are compelled to take up in regard to Egypt and the Sudan. Your Lordship will recall that when His Majesty's Government withdrew the British protectorate over Egypt in 1922, they reserved certain matters for eventual settlement by agreement. Though I have by no means abandoned hope that on further consideration, the basis of an agreement acceptable to both countries can be found, the attitude adopted by Zaghlul Pasha has rendered such agreement impossible for the present. I raised the question of the Canal straight away because its security is of vital interest to us both in peace and in war. It is no less true to-day than in 1922 that the security of the communications of the British Empire in Egypt remain a vital British interest and that absolute certainty that the Suez Canal will remain open in peace as well as in war for the free passage of British ships is the foundation on which the entire defensive strategy of the British Empire rests. The 1888 Convention for the free navigation of the Canal was an instrument devised to secure that object. Its ineffectiveness for this purpose was demonstrated in 1914, when Great Britain herself had to take steps to ensure that the Canal would remain open. No British Government in the light of that experience can divest itself wholly, even in favour of an ally, of its interest in guarding such a vital link in British communications. Such a security must be a feature of any agreement come to between our two Governments, and I see no reason why accommodation is impossible, given good will.

The effective co-operation of Great Britain and Egypt in protecting those communications might in my view have been ensured by the conclusion of a treaty of close alliance. The presence of a British force in Egypt provided for by such a treaty freely entered into by both parties on an equal footing would in no way be incompatible with Egyptian independence, whilst it would be an indication of the specially close and intimate relations between the two countries and their determination to co-operate in a matter of vital concern to both. It is not the wish of His Majesty's Government that this force should in any way interfere with the functions of the Egyptian Government or encroach upon Egyptian sovereignty and I emphatically said so. It is not the intention of His Majesty's Government to assume any responsibility for the actions or conduct of the Egyptian Government or to attempt to control or direct the policy which that Government may see fit to adopt.

So far as my conversations with Zaghlul Pasha turned on the question of the Sudan, they have only served to show his persistence in the attitude disclosed in his previous public utterances. I must adhere to the statements I made on the subject in the House of Commons. About that neither in Egypt nor in the Sudan should there be any doubt. If there is, it will only lead to trouble.

In the meantime the duty of preserving order in the Sudan rests in fact upon His Majesty's Government and they will take every step necessary for this purpose. Since going there, they have contracted heavy moral obligations by the creation of a good system of administration; they cannot allow that to be destroyed; they regard their responsibilities as a trust for the Sudan people; there can be no question of their abandoning the Sudan until their work is done.

His Majesty's Government have no desire to disturb existing arrangements, but they must point out how intolerable is a *status quo* which enables both military and civil officers and officials to conspire against civil order, and unless the *status quo* is accepted and loyally worked until such time as a new arrangement may be reached, the Sudan Government would fail in its duty were it to allow such conditions to continue.

His Majesty's Government have never failed to recognise that Egypt has certain material interests in the Sudan which must be guaranteed and safeguarded—these being chiefly concerned with her share of the Nile water and the satisfaction of any financial claims which she may have against the Sudan Government. His Majesty's Government have always been prepared to secure these interests in a way satisfactory to Egypt.

I have in the preceding paragraphs defined the position which His Majesty's Government are compelled to take up in regard to Egypt and the Sudan and which I conceive it to be my duty to conserve unimpaired.

2. ALLENBY'S FIRST COMMUNICATION, 22 NOVEMBER 1924

On behalf of His Britannic Majesty's Government I make the following communication to Your Excellency:—

The Governor-General of the Sudan and Sirdar of the Egyptian Army, who was also a distinguished officer of the British Army, has been brutally murdered in Cairo.

His Majesty's Government consider that this murder, which holds up Egypt as at present governed to the contempt of civilized peoples, is the natural outcome of a campaign of hostility to British rights and British subjects in Egypt and Sudan, founded upon a heedless ingratitude for benefits conferred by Great Britain, not discouraged by Your Excellency's Government, and fomented by organizations in close contact with that Government.

Your Excellency was warned by His Majesty's Government little more than a month ago of the consequences of failing to stop this campaign, more particularly as concerned the Sudan. It has not been stopped. The Egyptian Government have now allowed the Governor-General of Sudan to be murdered and have proved that they are incapable or unwilling to protect foreign lives.

His Majesty's Government therefore require that the Egyptian Government shall:

(1) Present ample apology for the crime.

(2) Prosecute an inquiry into the authorship of the crime with the utmost energy and without respect of persons and bring the criminals, whoever they are and whatever their age, to condign punishment.

(3) Henceforth forbid and vigorously suppress all popular political demonstrations.

(4) Pay forthwith to His Majesty's Government a fine of £500,000.

(5) Order within twenty-four hours the withdrawal from the Sudan of all Egyptian officers and the purely Egyptian units of Egyptian army with such resulting changes as shall be hereafter specified.

(6) Notify the competent department that the Sudan Government will increase the area to be irrigated at Gezira from 300,000 feddans to an unlimited figure as need may arise.

(7) Withdraw all opposition in the respects hereafter specified to the wishes of His Majesty's Government concerning the protection of foreign interests in Egypt.

Failing immediate compliance with these demands, His Majesty's Government will at once take appropriate action to safeguard their interests in Egypt and the Sudan.

I take this opportunity to renew to Your Excellency the assurance of my high consideration.

3. ALLENBY'S SECOND COMMUNICATION, 22 NOVEMBER 1924

With reference to my preceding communication, I have the honour to inform Your Excellency, on behalf of His Britannic Majesty's Government, that their specific requirements respecting the Army in the Sudan and the protection of foreign interests in Egypt are as follows:—

(1) The Egyptian officers and purely Egyptian units of the Egyptian Army having been withdrawn, Sudanese units of the Egyptian Army shall be converted into a Sudan defence force, owing allegiance to the Sudan Government alone and under the supreme command of the Governor-General, in whose name all commissions will be given.

(2) Rules and conditions governing the service, discipline, and retirement of foreign officials still employed by the Egyptian Government, and financial conditions governing pensions of foreign officials who have left service, shall be revised in accordance with the wishes of His Majesty's Government.

(3) Pending the conclusion of an agreement between the two Governments regarding the protection of foreign interests in Egypt, the Egyptian Government shall maintain the posts of financial and judicial advisers and preserve their powers and privileges as contemplated on the abolition of the Protectorate and shall respect the status and present attributions of the European Department of the Ministry of Interior as already laid down by Ministerial Order, and give due weight to such recommendations as the Director-General may make upon matters falling within his sphere.

44. TURKISH PETROLEUM COMPANY CONCESSION IN IRAQ
14 March 1925

[Great Britain, Colonial Office, *Special Report by His Majesty's Government . . . to the Council of the League of Nations on the Progress of 'Iraq during the period 1920–1931,* Colonial No. 58 (1931), pp. 303–15]

The San Remo oil agreement of 1920 (Doc. 29) preserved the Turkish Petroleum Company (TPC) formula of 1914 (I, Doc. 111), with French interests merely replacing the original German. No sooner was the ink dry on the Anglo-French arrangement than United States companies, with the support of their government, began to demand the right of equal opportunity to bid for concessions in the mandated territories (Doc. 30), a demand which TPC resisted with the determined backing of the British Foreign Office. To add to the difficulties, TPC's claim to exclusive rights rested not on a formal concession but merely on the Grand Vezir's promise of a concession in the Mosul *vilâyet* (province) a few weeks before the outbreak of World War I (I, Doc. 114). But the Mosul *vilâyet* was located in the projected mandated territory of Mesopotamia (Iraq), over which the successor British-controlled government exercised only *de facto* sovereignty pending the consummation of an operant peace with Turkey. The dispute with the Americans, though not yet resolved, shrank in dimension, once TPC agreed in principle to admit American participation. Negotiations —which endured for six years—with this end in view were launched in July 1922. The conclusion of the peace with Turkey, a year later (Doc. 41), cleared the ground—despite Turkey's surviving claim to the Mosul *vilâyet* (Doc. 46)—for the negotiations between TPC and the Iraqi government, which commenced late in 1923 and lasted well over a year. Supplemental agreements of 24 March 1931 (texts in *Special Report on the Progress of 'Iraq, 1920–31,* pp. 316–26), among other modifications of the original act of concession, restricted the concessionary area of the Iraq Petroleum Company (as TPC became known after 8 June 1929) to 32,000 square miles east of the Tigris in the *vilâyets* of Mosul and

Baghdad and required the company to construct by 1935 a pipeline to the Mediterranean. In the area west of the Tigris the British Oil Development Company (BOD)—a consortium comprising British (46 per cent), Italian (30 per cent) and French-Swiss and German-Dutch (12 per cent each) interests, although the relative ownership later altered in favor of the Italian and German investors—acquired a concession on 25 May 1932. The operating company, called Mosul Oilfields, was purchased in 1936 by IPC, which five years later had BOD reassign the 1932 concession to the Mosul Petroleum Company, an IPC subsidiary. *International Petroleum Cartel,* chap. 4; S. H. Longrigg, *Oil in the Middle East,* chaps. 3, 5; J. A. Loftus, "Middle East Oil, the Pattern of Control," *Middle East Journal,* 2 (1948), 17–32; K. Hoffman, *Ölpolitik,* chap. 15; B. Shwadran, *The Middle East, Oil and the Great Powers,* chap. 8.

ART. 1. The Government hereby grant to the Company, on the terms hereinafter mentioned, the exclusive right (subject to Article 6 hereof) to explore, prospect, drill for, extract and render suitable for trade petroleum, naphtha, natural gases, ozokerite, and the right to carry away and sell the same and the derivatives thereof.

ART. 2. The period of this Convention shall be 75 years from the date hereof. At the expiration of the said period the rights given to the Company by Article 1 hereof shall determine and all the Company's land, buildings, wells, wharves, roads, pipe and railway lines, machinery, plant and fixtures of every sort in 'Iraq, used for the Company's operations hereunder, shall become the property of the Government free of charge.

ART. 3. The area to which this Convention relates (hereinafter called "the defined area") shall, where not otherwise stated, be 'Iraq except the Transferred Territories and the region formerly the wilayat of Basrah, provided that as soon as the territorial limits of 'Iraq have been determined a supplementary convention expressly delimiting the defined area shall be executed between the Government and the Company, and provided also that within cemeteries, buildings used for religious worship, and Antiquities as defined in the Antiquities Law, 1924, neither the Company nor any other person shall have the right to carry on any of the operations named in Article 1 hereof.

ART. 4. The Company shall, within eight months after the date of this Convention, commence a detailed geological survey in at least three different districts of the defined area, and in the event of this provision not being complied with this Convention shall become entirely null and void on the expiration of the said period. For the purpose of the said survey the Company's servants and agents shall have power to enter upon any part of the defined area free of charge.

ART. 5. Within 32 months after the date of this Convention the Company shall select 24 rectangular plots, each of an area of eight square miles, and within three years after the date of this Convention the Company shall start drilling operations therein, working continuously with a minimum of six rigs, and in the event of this provision not being complied with this Convention shall become entirely null and void.

During the 36 months subsequent to such three years the Company shall drill not less than 36,000 feet, and thereafter, in each year of the period before it orders a pipeline to a port for export shipment, the Company shall drill at least 12,000 feet, provided that no drilling shall be required when the whole of such plots shall have been fully tested, and provided also that any drilling during the aforesaid three years, and any excess drilling over the amounts named herein, shall be credited to the amount required subsequently to such drilling. In the event of any breach of this obligation the Government may give the Company written notice to remedy the same, and in the event of the Company not doing so within six months of such notice the Government shall have the right to cancel this Convention, without prejudice to any claim which the Government may have for damages. All drilling shall be efficient and workmanlike.

The Company shall order the said pipeline as soon as it shall be commercially justifiable, and shall complete the construction of the same as soon as practicable. If the Company shall not have placed an order for the said pipeline before the expiration of four years after declaring the whole of the said plots to be fully tested, it shall thereupon abandon all rights under this Convention, provided that the Government shall acquire from the Company, at a price equal to their commercial value (which shall be agreed or, failing agreement, settled under Article 40 hereof), any wells (excluding the oil therein), pipelines, refineries or other works which are in use or under construction for the supply of 'Iraq's requirements under Article 14 hereof.

ART. 6. The Government shall, not later than four years after the date of this Convention, and annually thereafter, select not less than 24 rectangular plots, each of an area of eight square miles, and the Government shall offer the same for competition, by sealed tender, between all responsible corporations, firms and individuals, without distinction of nationality, who desire leases. Both the Company and any such prospective lessee may indicate any plots (other than those selected under Article 5 hereof) to be offered among such 24, and the same shall be offered accordingly by the Government. The Company shall give all such prospective lessees such geological information as it possesses with respect to the plots to be offered for competition. For the purpose of this Article the Company shall act as the Government's agent and shall advertise the said plots in the leading newspapers of 'Iraq and the leading petroleum newspapers of the world, and the tenders shall be opened and adjudicated upon by the Company in its head office in 'Iraq in the presence of a duly authorised representative of the Government. The sale proceeds of such competition shall be handed by the Government to the Company. The Government shall grant to the highest bidder for each plot, unless he shall be disapproved by the Government on reasonable grounds to be given within 60 days, a lease thereof for the remaining period of this Convention, conferring all the rights and imposing all the obligations stated in Articles 1, 2 (except the first sentence), 3, 7 to 14, 17 to 31, 33, 34, 37, 39, 40 and 42 hereof, and binding the lessee (1) to drill, in an efficient and workmanlike manner, not less than 1,500 feet during the three years subsequent to the execution of the lease, and thereafter in each year not less than 500 feet, until the plot shall have been fully tested, provided that any drilling in excess of the said amounts shall be credited to the amount required subsequently to such drilling; (2) to submit to Government inspection in accordance with Article 16 hereof, and to pay the Government £55 per annum; (3) to accept the conditions stated in Article 38 hereof, except that the words "not later than twenty years after the execution of the lease" shall be substituted for the words "not later than 30 years after the date of this Convention." Each lessee shall deposit with the Government the sum of £2,000, and in the event of any breach of his obligations under clause (1) of the preceding sentence the said sum shall be liable to forfeiture to the Government.

Thirty per cent. of the capacity of the Company's pipeline aforesaid shall be available for the transportation of oil won by such lessees, at a cost to them not exceeding one-twelfth of one anna per barrel per mile.

Any plot which has been offered for competition without being disposed of may be dealt with by the Company in the same manner as if it had been selected under Article 5 hereof, provided that if the Company fails to carry out the obligation numbered (1) above such plot will again be subject to competition.

In the event of termination of this Convention by the Government under Article 13 hereof the Government shall take the place of the Company in relation to the lessees aforesaid.

ART. 7. Subject to the due fulfilment of Article 30 hereof, the Company shall maintain in good working order all borings, so long as they are economically productive, and shall limit the damage done to the surface of the lands in or upon which the said borings are situate to that which is necessary for the purposes of its operations.

ART. 8. The Company shall cause to be made, and kept at its office or offices in 'Iraq, correct and intelligible plans of all borings, workings and operations, and shall at its own cost furnish to the Government

(*a*) within six months after the end of each year, a report on its operations;

(*b*) within 30 days after the end of each month, a statement of the depth drilled in each well;

(*c*) within 30 days of their completion, copies not exceeding six in number of all geological reports and geological maps made by the Company's staff;

(*d*) within 30 days of receipt of a written request from the Government, copies not exceeding six in number of such other maps and plans, made by the Company's staff, as may be required by the Government, and of such other reports by the Company's staff as may be reasonably required by the Government; and the duly authorized representative of the Government shall have access at all reasonable times to all geological maps which are not printed.

Such maps, plans, reports and statements shall be treated as confidential by the Government.

ART. 9. The Company shall take all practical measures to prevent the injurious access of water to the oil-bearing formations, and of noxious waste products into the waters of 'Iraq, and if any well be abandoned shall plug it immediately upon the casing being withdrawn.

ART. 10. In consideration of the privileges herein conceded, the Company shall pay to the Government a royalty per ton of the substances (other than natural gas) comprised in Article 1 hereof and saved in field storage tanks or reservoirs by the Company, but for the purpose of this provision the Company shall be entitled to deduct from the gross quantity so won and saved:—

(*a*) all water and foreign substances;

(*b*) all petroleum distributed under Article 17 hereof;

(*c*) all substances used within 'Iraq by the Company for its operations hereunder. The royalty shall be fixed in manner following:—

(1) Until a date twenty years after the completion of a pipeline to a port for export shipment the rate of royalty shall be four shillings (gold).

(2) For each period of ten years after the said date the rate of four shillings (gold) shall be increased or reduced by the percentage by which the profit or loss shall be greater or less during the five years immediately preceding such period than during the first fifteen of the aforesaid twenty years, provided that (*a*) "profit or loss" shall mean the difference between the average market price per ton of the aforesaid substances and the average cost per ton of producing, transporting, refining and distributing the same; (*b*) "average market price per ton" shall mean the total prices (ascertained as closely as possible) obtained for the products of the said substances, divided by the total tonnage (ascertained as closely as possible) of such products, and "average cost per ton" shall mean the estimated total cost of producing, transporting, refining and distributing the said substances divided by the said tonnage; (*c*) the minimum rate shall be two shillings (gold) and the maximum rate six shillings (gold).

Example

	£	*s.*	*d.*
Average market price per ton during the 15 years ...	10	0	0
Average cost per ton during the same period	9	0	0
Profit	£1	0	0
Average market price per ton during the 5 years ...	9	10	0
Average cost per ton during the same period	8	5	0
Profit	£1	5	0

Profit has increased by 25 per cent. Therefore royalty is increased by 25 per cent., i.e., from 4s. to 5s.

The accounts submitted to the Government for the purposes of this subsection shall be treated as confidential by the Government.

The Company shall also pay a royalty of two pence per thousand cubic feet of all natural gas it sells, calculated at an absolute pressure of one atmosphere and at a temperature of 60 degrees Fahrenheit.

The royalties due up to the end of each calendar year shall be paid within three months thereafter. If notice of abandonment be given under Article 38 hereof, the royalties due up to the date of such notice shall be paid before its expiration.

ART. 11. The Company shall measure, in a method approved from time to time by the Government (which approval shall not be unreasonably withheld), all substances comprised in Article 1 hereof and won and saved, and the duly authorised representatives of the Government shall have the right (1) to examine such measuring; (2) to examine and test the appliances used for such measuring. If, upon such examination or testing, any such appliance shall be found to be out of order, the Government may require that the same be put in order by, and at the expense of, the Company, and if such requisition be not complied with in a reasonable time the Government may cause the said appliance to be put in order, and may recover the expense of so doing from the Company, and if upon such examination as aforesaid any error shall be discovered in any such appliance, such error shall, if the Government so decide after hearing the Company's explanation, be considered to have existed for three calendar months previous to the discovery thereof, or from the last occasion of examining the same in case such occasion shall be within such period of three calendar months, and the royalty shall be adjusted accordingly. If the Company desire to alter any measuring appliance it shall give reasonable notice to the Government, to enable a representative of the Government to be present during such alteration.

ART. 12. The Company shall keep full and correct accounts of all substances measured as aforesaid, and of all quantities exempted from royalty under Article 10 hereof, and the duly authorised representative of the Government shall have access at all reasonable times to the books of the Company containing such accounts, and shall be at liberty to make extracts therefrom, and the Company shall, at its own expense, within three calendar months after the end of each calendar year, deliver to the Government an abstract of such accounts for such year and a statement of the amount of royalty due to the Government for such year. Such accounts shall be treated as confidential by the Government, with the exception of such figures therein as they think it necessary to publish.

ART. 13. If the royalties or any part thereof shown by such accounts to be due, or awarded by arbitration, for any year shall be unpaid for the space of three calendar months after the end of such year, or after the award of the arbitrator, whichever be later, the Government shall have the right to prohibit all export of petroleum and other products until the sum in question be paid. And if payment be not made within three months after the expiration of the aforesaid three months the Government shall have the right to terminate this Convention and to take without payment all the property of the Company within 'Iraq, including the oil collected in the storage tanks and elsewhere.

ART. 14. Subject to Article 5 hereof the Company, if so required by the Government, (*a*) shall produce as soon as possible 40,000 tons of petroleum in each of two consecutive years; (*b*) shall afterwards, as soon as possible, refine therefrom, adjacently to a railway, such petrol, kerosene and fuel oil as may be required from time to time for local consumption (hereinafter called 'Iraq's requirements); (*c*) when such refining has begun, shall not export petroleum until 'Iraq's requirements have been met, provided that if any person, other than the Company and lessees under Article 6 hereof, shall hereafter be granted the right to extract petroleum from any region of 'Iraq the Company shall no longer be obliged to supply 'Iraq's requirements in that portion of 'Iraq which is outside the defined area, to the extent to which they can be met from the petroleum produced by such other person; (*d*) shall keep in stock and reserve for the Government, in such position or positions as the Government may require, and at the expense of the Government if any extra expense is directly incurred for this purpose, not less than twice the Government's average monthly consumption of such refined products.

ART. 15. The price at which any of 'Iraq's requirements shall be sold at any 'Iraq refinery (*a*) before the completion of a pipeline to a port for export shipment, shall be at least 35 per cent. less, during any calendar month, than the wholesale price, during the previous calendar month but one, of the nearest similar product at Swansea (excluding sales to any subsidiary of the Anglo-Persian Oil Company); (*b*) after such completion, shall not exceed, during any calendar month, the said wholesale price, less the difference between the cost of transportating crude petroleum from the Company's well-head to Swansea and the cost of transporting it to the 'Iraq refinery. Requirements of petrol and lowest-grade kerosene under clause (*b*) of Article 14 shall be sold in bulk to the public at a depôt in Baghdad at a price not exceeding the total of (1) the price fixed under this Article, (2) the railway charges from the refinery, and (3) one anna per gallon for petrol and nine pies per gallon for kerosene, provided that if the cost of selling in Baghdad differs, by more than 33⅓ per cent., from such cost at the date of this Convention, item no. (3) shall be increased or reduced by the percentage of the difference.

At any time after the export of petroleum through the pipeline aforesaid has begun, the Government shall have the right (1) to acquire, at a price to be agreed, or fixed under Article 40 hereof, the buildings, machinery and plant used exclusively for refining and marketing 'Iraq's requirements; (2) to buy from the Company, at any such refinery, the crude petroleum necessary, from time to time, for producing 'Iraq's requirements, at the lowest price at which the Company is then selling crude petroleum, less the difference between the cost of transporting crude petroleum from well-head to the point of such sale and the cost of transporting it to the refinery. On the Government taking over the said buildings, machinery and plant, the Company's obligations under clauses (*b*) and (*d*) of Article 14 shall determine.

The taking out of 'Iraq for trading purposes, or in the bunkers of vessels not owned by the Government, of products or crude petroleum sold at prices fixed under this Article, or of the products of such crude petroleum, shall not be permitted by the Government.

The term "cost" in this Article shall include management, office, accounting, insurance and protection expenses, and depreciation and interest at such rates as may be agreed, or fixed under Article 40 hereof.

ART. 16. Any duly authorized representative of the Government shall have the right, to any reasonable extent and at all reasonable times, to inspect all operations carried on by the Company within 'Iraq. The Company shall, on request, place at the disposal of such representative a proper person to explain such operations, and to afford such information as such representative may reasonably require. From 1st November, 1925, the Company shall pay the Government, quarterly in advance, the sum of £1,400 per annum on account of the expenses of such inspection.

ART. 17. If the Company, by virtue of the exclusive right given to it under Article 1 hereof, forbids or obstructs the taking of petroleum by any inhabitant of the defined area from a locality from which such inhabitant has been accustomed to take petroleum free of cost, or free except for Government tax, it shall monthly or quarterly furnish to him from its tanks, free of cost, for local consumption, an amount of petroleum equivalent to the average monthly or quarterly amount he has been accustomed so to take previous to such forbidding or obstructing. Any dispute as to such amount shall be settled by agreement between the Government and the Company.

ART. 18. On the occasion of a state of emergency (of which the Government shall be the sole judge), the Company shall use its utmost endeavours to increase the supply of petroleum and products thereof for the Government's own consumption, to the extent the Government shall require, and the Government shall afford to the Company all reasonable assistance.

ART. 19. Subject to Article 22 hereof the Company may erect and use telegraphic and telephonic apparatus within 'Iraq for the purposes of this Convention, but except as hereinafter mentioned no such apparatus shall be erected without the previous licence of the Government, which shall not be withheld if they decline to provide the facilities required by the Company, nor shall their decision be unreasonably delayed. The Government shall have the right at any time, if the interests of the public so require, to purchase at a price to be agreed, or, failing agreement, fixed under Article 40 hereof, any apparatus erected by the Company under the provisions of this Article. The charges, if any, imposed upon the Company by the Government for a licence to erect such apparatus, or to use the same, or for any telegraphic, telephonic or radio facilities provided by the Government within 'Iraq, shall not be unreasonable or higher than those ordinarily imposed upon other industrial undertakings. Telegraphic and telephonic apparatus may be erected without licence for internal service within the Company's premises, provided that no such apparatus shall be carried without licence across a public right of way. In the erection and use of any apparatus erected or used under the provisions of this Article the Company will observe the general requirements of the Government in accordance with the Telegraph Proclamation, 1920, or other laws for the time being in force governing telegraphic, telephonic and radio communications.

ART. 20. The Company may construct and operate:—

(*a*) within plots selected under Article 5 or Article 6 hereof, and the Company's refineries, power houses, workshops, tank depôts, export depôts and stores in 'Iraq, such railways as may be necessary for its operations hereunder;

(*b*) elsewhere within the defined area, such railways, of a gauge not exceeding two feet six inches, as may be necessary for the Company's operations hereunder, and such other railways (except for the purpose of a pipeline to a Mediterranean port) as may be necessary for the purpose of other pipelines, or for connecting such plots and premises with another railway or transportation system, or with sources of supply of materials produced in 'Iraq, unless suitable railway facilities for such purposes are already provided by the Government or by a person holding a concession from the Government;

(*c*) elsewhere within the region formerly the wilayat of Basrah, such railways as may be necessary for the purpose of the Company's pipeline, or for connecting the premises aforesaid with another railway or transportation system;

provided that plans of any such railway, other than those to be constructed within such plots and premises, shall be submitted to the Government for their approval, which shall not be unreasonably withheld, nor shall their decision be delayed more than 60 days, and provided also that the Company shall construct no such railway of a gauge exceeding two feet six inches, otherwise than within such plots and premises, unless the Government, or a person holding a concession from the Government in that behalf, do not within three months after receipt of a written request from the Company to construct the same agree to do so, or do not within six months after such receipt proceed with such construction, or do not complete the same within a reasonable time.

The Company may construct and operate such railways as may be necessary for the purpose of a pipeline to a Mediterranean port, provided that plans of the same shall be submitted to the Government for their approval, which shall not be unreasonably withheld or delayed, and provided also that without the permission of the Government, which shall not be unreasonably withheld or delayed, no such railway shall be constructed of a gauge exceeding two feet six inches.

The Government shall have the right at any time, if the interests of the public so require, to purchase at a price to be agreed, or, failing agreement, fixed under Article 40 hereof, any railway of a gauge exceeding two feet six inches constructed by the Company, otherwise than within the plots and premises aforesaid, but on any railway so purchased the Government shall provide at reasonable rates all reasonable traffic requirements of the Company. The Company's rail vehicles shall not be sent over Government railways without the approval of the Government, and Government rail vehicles shall not be sent over the Company's railways without the approval of the Company, but such approval in either case shall not be unreasonably withheld, nor shall the decision be delayed more than 30 days.

The Company may, within 'Iraq, dig, sink, drive, build, construct, erect, lay and operate such pits, shafts, wells, trenches, excavations, dams, drains, watercourses, factories, plants, tanks, reservoirs, refineries, pipelines (subject to Article 22 hereof), pumping stations, offices, houses, buildings, wharves, and other terminal facilities, vessels, conveyances, ferries, bridges and other works, whether of the nature hereinbefore mentioned or not, as may be necessary for its operations hereunder, provided that before constructing any dam, drain, reservoir, watercourse, ferry, bridge or wharf, otherwise than within its own premises, the Company shall submit plans of the same to the Government for their approval, which shall not be unreasonably withheld, nor shall their decision be unreasonably delayed, or, in the case of a ferry or bridge, delayed more than 30 days. In granting their approval for the construction of any ferry or bridge which is suitable for public use, the Government may require that the same shall be available for public use, subject to payment of fair compensation to the Company. Before erecting any refinery or factory outside plots selected under Articles 5 and 6 hereof, the Company shall obtain the Government's approval, which shall not be unreasonably withheld, of the site thereof.

The Company shall have the right to place contracts for drilling, pipelaying, building and other works, within 'Iraq.

ART. 21. The Company may occupy such lands within 'Iraq as may be necessary for the purposes of its business, upon the following terms:—

(*a*) Non-cultivable lands belonging to the Government will be leased to the Company for the period of this Convention at a rent of two annas per hectare per annum. The Company may relinquish any such land at any time, and the Government may require the relinquishment of any such land, other than plots selected under Articles 5 and 6 hereof, which is not used within a reasonable time. Lands so relinquished which subsequently become necessary for the Company's business will again be leased to the Company subject to the conditions aforesaid.

(*b*) Subject to the approval of the Government, which shall not be unreasonably withheld or delayed, cultivable lands belonging to the Government will be leased to the Company for the period of this Convention at a fair rent on the basis of the surface value of the lands, which rent shall be agreed between the Government and the Company or, failing agreement, fixed under Article 40 hereof. The Company may relinquish any such land at any time, and the Government may require the relinquishment of any such land, other than plots selected under Articles 5 and 6 hereof, which is not used within a reasonable time, provided that the Company shall pay fair compensation if any land so relinquished has been rendered by the Company unfit for cultivation. Lands so relinquished which subsequently become necessary for the Company's business will again be leased to the Company subject to the conditions aforesaid.

(*c*) Lands not belonging to the Government shall be acquired by agreement between the Company and the person concerned, or failing agreement the Government will regard such lands as being required for a work of public utility and will acquire them according to the law for the time being in force, and at the expense in all things of the Company, provided that in fixing the value of such lands no regard shall be had to the purpose for which they may be used by the Company, and provided also that lands so acquired by the Government shall be registered in the name of the Government but placed free of charge at the disposal of the Company during the period of this Convention.

(*d*) Whenever it has been decided that lands are to be leased or acquired under subsection (*b*) or (*c*) of this Article, the Company may, if it thinks fit, occupy all or part thereof before the rent or price to be paid has been fixed. Before, however, so occupying such lands the Company shall obtain the Government's approval, but the Government's decision shall not be unreasonably delayed, and their approval shall not be unreasonably withheld though it may be given subject to reasonable notice by the Company to the person concerned and subject to payment by the Company of a fair deposit.

ART. 22. The Company shall be entitled, within 'Iraq, to place and maintain, over, under and along land belonging to the Government, free of any charge for such land, any pipelines required for its operations hereunder, and any telegraphic or telephonic apparatus erected with the licence of the Government under the provisions of Article 19 hereof, but it shall repair or pay compensation for any damage done by such pipelines or apparatus or by their placing or maintenance. The Government also undertake to empower the Company to place and maintain such telegraphic and telephonic apparatus within 'Iraq, over, under and along land not belonging to the Government, free of any charge for such land, on condition that it does as little damage as possible and shall be liable to pay compensation for damage done by such apparatus or by its placing or maintenance.

ART. 23. Nothing in this Convention shall limit the right of the Government to make or maintain, upon, under, along or in the vicinity of land in the possession of the Company within 'Iraq, such roads, railways, canals, protective bunds, flood protection works, police posts, military works, pipe, telegraph and telephone lines, as shall be expedient, and to pass at all times over and along such works; provided always that such right shall be exercised in such manner as not to endanger the operations or interfere with the rights of the Company under this Convention, and provided also that the Company shall receive fair compensation for the occupation by such works of any non-Government land in its possession, and that any rent payable to the Government for Government land in the Company's possession occupied by such works, other than pipe, telegraph and telephone lines, shall be remitted.

ART. 24. Nothing in this Convention shall limit the right of the Government, or of any person authorised by them in that behalf, to search for and get any substances, other than those comprised in Article 1 hereof, in, upon or under the lands within the defined area, except lands occupied by wells of the Company, provided always that such right shall be exercised in such manner as not to endanger the operations or interfere with the rights of the Company under Article 1 hereof (including the right to drill through such substances), and provided also that fair compensation shall be paid by the Government or by the person authorised, as the case may be, for all damage which the Company may sustain through the exercise of the said reserved rights. In any concession which they grant for such reserved rights the Government shall bind the concessionnaire to pay such compensation to the Company.

ART. 25. The Company may take away, subject to the usual regulations and upon payment of the usual charges, if any, such surface soil, timber, clay, ballast, lime, gypsum, stone and similar substances, belonging to the Government and within 'Iraq, as may be necessary for the Company's operations hereunder. The Company may also, upon payment of the usual charges, if any, and subject to the approval of the Government, which shall not be unreasonably withheld or delayed, take away or use any water, belonging to the Government and within 'Iraq, that may be necessary for the Company's operations hereunder, but so as not to prejudice irrigation or existing navigation, or to deprive any lands, houses or watering places for cattle of a reasonable supply of water from time to time.

ART. 26. The Company shall be entitled to use, for its operations hereunder, any railway, tramway, road, canal, river, waterway or port in 'Iraq, on payment of the charges, if any, ordinarily imposed upon other industrial undertakings for the like use of such railway, tramway, road, canal, river, waterway or port.

ART. 27. No other or higher taxes, impositions, duties, fees or charges, whether Government or municipal or port, shall be imposed upon the Company, or upon its property or privileges or employees within 'Iraq, than those ordinarily imposed from time to time upon other industrial undertakings, or upon their property or privileges or employees. No taxes, impositions, duties, fees or charges, whether Government or municipal, shall be imposed upon the borings of the Company, or upon the substances comprised in Article 1 hereof before their removal from the ground, or upon substances comprised in Article 1 hereof and used by the Company for the purposes of its operations hereunder.

ART. 28. The Company shall be entitled to import into 'Iraq free of customs duties (1) all materials, machinery, plant and stores which are necessary for the finding, winning, refining, storing and transporting of the substances comprised in Article 1 hereof, and for the storing and transporting of the said materials, machinery, plant and stores, or of materials produced in 'Iraq; (2) all materials, including electric fittings, for the construction of offices and houses (*a*) in any plot selected under Article 5 or Article 6 hereof, imported within ten years after the commencement of drilling therein, (*b*) adjacent to and required for any refinery or pipeline within 'Iraq, imported within ten years after the commencement of its construction. Goods imported free of duty shall not be sold by the Company for use in 'Iraq, otherwise than to lessees under Article 6 hereof, unless they are damaged or depreciated, in which case they shall incur import duty on their assessed value at the time of sale.

The Company shall be entitled to export free of customs duties (*a*) all substances comprised in Article 1 hereof, (*b*) goods imported free of duty, provided they go out by the route by which they came in.

The ordinary duties shall be leviable on goods not herein exempted from duty.

ART. 29. The employees of the Company within 'Iraq shall, so far as possible, be subjects of the Government, but managers, engineers, chemists, drillers, foremen, mechanics, other skilled workmen and clerks may be brought from outside 'Iraq if qualified persons of these descriptions cannot be found in 'Iraq, and provided that the Company will, as far as reasonably practicable, and as early as possible, train 'Iraqis in these capacities. The entry of all foreign personnel into 'Iraq shall be subject to the immigration laws for the time being in force, provided that such laws shall not prejudice the rights of the Company above mentioned.

ART. 30. The Company shall take all reasonable measures to carry out the objects of this Convention, and shall make and pay reasonable satisfaction and compensation for all injury which it or its employees or agents, in exercise of the liberties and powers granted hereunder, may do to the property or rights of other parties, and shall at all times save harmless and keep indemnified the Government from and against all actions, suits, claims and demands by such parties in respect of such injury. The Government shall likewise take all reasonable measures to facilitate the carrying out of the objects of this Convention, and to protect the property of the Company and its employees and agents within 'Iraq, provided that the Company shall not be entitled to claim any damages from the Government for any failure to comply with this obligation. When entering into, granting or confirming any agreement, licence or concession, other than this Convention, the Government shall protect the rights of the Company hereunder. Nothing in this Convention shall prevent the Government from exercising the right to prohibit, in the interests of public security, the entry into, or remaining in, any area of any person or persons employed by the Company.

ART. 31. While at war with another nation the Government shall have the right to use the Company's railways, other means of transport, bridges, wharves, telegraphs and telephones, within 'Iraq, on payment of fair compensation.

ART. 32. The Company shall be and remain a British Company registered in Great Britain, and having its principal place of business within His Britannic Majesty's dominions, and the Chairman shall at all times be a British subject. The Memorandum and Articles of Association of the Company shall be deposited with the Government and revised to embdoy such provisions of this Convention as the Government may require.

ART. 33. The Company shall be at liberty to form one or more subsidiary companies, under its own control, for the working of this Convention, should it consider this to be necessary. Any such subsidiary company, shall, in respect of the area in which it operates, enjoy all the rights and privileges granted to the Company hereunder and assume all the engagements and responsibilities herein expressed, except the engagement expressed in the first sentence of Article 32 hereof.

ART. 34. Whenever an issue of shares is offered by the Company to the general public, subscription lists shall be opened in 'Iraq simultaneously with lists opened elsewhere, and 'Iraqis in 'Iraq shall be given a preference to the extent of at least twenty per cent. of such issue.

ART. 35. The Government shall have the right to appoint a Director to the Board of the Company, who shall enjoy the same rights and privileges, and receive the same emoluments from the Company, as the other Directors.

ART. 36. Not later than four months from the date of this Convention the Company shall deposit with the Government British Government securities, payable to bearer, of the value of £35,000, which shall be returned to the Company when it has spent £70,000 upon operations hereunder carried on within 'Iraq, but shall be forfeited to the Government upon cancellation of this Convention under Article 4 or Article 5 thereof. Previous to such return or forfeiture, the interest upon such securities shall be payable to the Company. If the Company shall fail to make the deposit within the period aforesaid the Government may cancel this Convention.

ART. 37. Except as otherwise provided in Articles 4, 5, 13 and 36 hereof, the penalty for any breach of this Convention shall be damages, which shall be fixed by agreement or under Article 40 hereof.

ART. 38. The Company shall have the right to abandon permanently to the Government all rights hereunder, upon giving three months' notice in writing of its intention so to do, and this Convention shall absolutely determine on the date fixed for such determination in such notice, and if such notice be given not later than 30 years after the date of this Convention the Company shall be entitled, on such determination, to remove, free of all taxes and duties, all plant, buildings, stores, material and property of every sort, provided that for a period of three months from the receipt of such notice the Government may purchase the same at a price equal to the replacement value at that date, less depreciation, which price shall be agreed or, failing agreement, settled under Article 40 hereof.

ART. 39. No failure or omission on the part of the Company to carry out or perform any of the stipulations, covenants or conditions of this Convention shall give the Government any claim against the Company, or be deemed a breach of this Convention, in so far as the same arises from *force majeure,* and if through *force majeure* the fulfilment by the Company of any of the conditions of this Convention be delayed, the period of such delay, together with such period as may be necessary for the restoration of any damage done during such delay, shall be added to the periods fixed by this Convention, provided always that no addition shall be made to the period fixed in Article 2 hereof unless the production or export of petroleum by the Company shall be totally suspended, for not less than 60 consecutive days, through *force majeure* occurring within 'Iraq.

ART. 40. If at any time during or after the currency of this Convention any doubt, difference, or dispute shall arise between the Government and the Company concerning the interpretation or execution hereof, or anything herein contained, or in connection herewith, or the rights and liabilities of either party hereunder, the same shall, failing any agreement to settle it in another way, be referred to two arbitrators, one of whom shall be chosen by each party, and a referee who shall be chosen by the arbitrators before proceeding to arbitration. Each party shall nominate its arbitrator within 30 days of being requested in writing by the other party to do so. In the event of the arbitrators failing to agree upon a referee, the Government and the Company shall, in agreement, appoint a referee, and in the event of their failing to agree they shall request the President of the Permanent Court of International Justice to appoint a referee. The decision of the arbitrators, or in the case of a difference of opinion between them the decision of the referee, shall be final. The place of arbitration shall be such as may be agreed by the parties, and in default of agreement shall be Baghdad.

ART. 41. The Company shall, within eight months after the date of this Convention, open an office in 'Iraq, in charge of a person empowered to transact business with the Government. All plans, notices and other communications required hereunder to be sent to the Government shall be sent to such Minister or other person as the Council of Ministers may from time to time nominate in that behalf, and all communications required hereunder to be sent to the Company shall be sent to the head office of the Company in 'Iraq. Any such plan, notice or communication shall be deemed to be delivered if the sender obtains from the addressee a receipt for the same, or if it is delivered through a notary public.

ART. 42. Any action to be taken hereunder by the Government shall be taken by such Minister or other person as the Council of Ministers may from time to time nominate for the purpose of such action.

ART. 43. In the event of any discrepancy between the meanings of the English and Arabic versions hereof, the English version shall prevail.

45. TREATY OF FRIENDSHIP AND NEUTRALITY: TURKEY AND THE USSR
17 December 1925

(Ratifications exchanged, Istanbul, 29 June 1926; broadened, 17 December 1929 and 7 March 1931; prolonged for five years, 30 October 1931, and for ten years, 7 November 1935; denounced by the USSR, 19 March 1945)

[League of Nations, *Treaty Series,* No. 3610, vol. 157 (1935), pp. 353–69]

Moscow's suspicions of the European treaties signed at Locarno on 1 December 1925 matched Ankara's dislike of the decision, taken by the Council of the League of Nations fifteen days later, awarding the *vilâyet* of Mosul to Iraq (Doc. 46). The coincidence of grievances brought Turkey and the USSR together in the following instrument, the first in a series of bilateral arrangements that Russia concluded with next-door neighbors in eastern Europe and southwestern Asia in the years immediately following. To the principle of nonintervention, enshrined in the 1921 Soviet-Turkish treaty (Doc. 34), were added the principles of nonaggression and neutrality in the 1925 compact. In prolonging the treaty for two years on 17 December 1929, each signatory declared that no incompatible, secret agreement "exists between itself and other States in the immediate neighbourhood by land or sea of the other Party" and undertook "not to institute, without referring to the other Party, any negotiations for the conclusion of [secret] political agreements with

States in the immediate neighbourhood by land or sea of the said Party, and only to conclude such agreements with the consent of the latter. . . ." A further protocol of 7 March 1931 stipulated that "Neither of the High Contracting Parties shall proceed to lay down any naval fighting unit whatsoever for the purpose of strengthening its fleet in the Black Sea or in neighbouring seas, or to place orders for any such unit in foreign shipyards, or to take any other measure the effect of which would be to increase the present strength of its war fleet in the above-mentioned seas, without having notified the second Contracting Party six months previously." Only the original treaty of 1925 and its accompanying protocols appear below. *Survey of International Affairs, 1928,* pp. 358–74; M. Beloff, *The Foreign Policy of Soviet Russia,* vol. 2, chap. 3; M. W. Graham, Jr., "The Soviet Security System," *International Conciliation,* September 1929, pp. 343–425; K. Ziemke, *Die neue Türkei,* pp. 359–73.

ART. 1. In the case of military action being taken against either Contracting Party by one or more other Powers, the other Contracting Party undertakes to maintain neutrality as towards the first Contracting Party.

Note: The expression "military action" shall not be held to include military manœuvres, since they do not cause any prejudice to the other Party.

ART. 2. Each Contracting Party undertakes to abstain from any aggression against the other; it likewise undertakes not to participate in any alliance or agreement of a political character with one or more other Powers directed against the other Contracting Party, or in any alliance or agreement with one or more other Powers directed against the military or naval security of the other Contracting Party. Furthermore, each of the two Contracting Parties undertakes not to participate in any hostile act by one or more other Powers directed against the other Contracting Party.

ART. 3. The present Treaty shall come into force as soon as it is ratified and shall remain in force for three years. After that period the Treaty shall be regarded as extended automatically for a period of one year, unless one of the Contracting Parties notifies its desire to terminate the Treaty six months before its expiry.

PROTOCOL I. It is in any case understood that each Contracting Party retains full freedom of action as regards its relations of all kinds with other Powers outside the limits of the undertakings the conditions of which are laid down in the present Treaty.

PROTOCOL II. The two Contracting Parties agree that the expression "of a political character" as used in Article 2 of the Treaty of to-day's date should include all such financial or economic agreements between Powers as are directed against the other Contracting Party.

PROTOCOL III. The two Contracting Parties also undertake to enter into negotiations to determine the methods of settling disputes which may arise between them and which it may not be possible to settle through the ordinary diplomatic channels.

46. FRONTIER TREATY: THE UNITED KINGDOM AND IRAQ AND TURKEY

5 June 1926

(Ratifications exchanged, Ankara, 18 July 1926)

[Great Britain, *Parliamentary Papers, 1930,* Treaty Series No. 7, Cmd. 3488]

At the Lausanne Conference in 1922–23 Turkey claimed the Mosul *vilâyet* (province), which was already incorporated *de facto* into the territory of the projected mandate for Iraq. Since the Turkish delegation did not withdraw its claims, the peace treaty (Doc. 41) left open the delimitation of the frontier with Iraq. Article 3(2) laid down that, if Britain and Turkey failed to conclude an amicable arrangement within nine months, the dispute should be referred to the Council of the League of Nations. This was in fact the course pursued in September 1924, after direct talks in the preceding May had proved sterile. The League Council appointed an investigate commission whose recommendation that Iraq should retain Mosul the Council endorsed on 16 December 1925. The Ankara regime reluctantly assented to the decision in the following treaty, which included article 14 as a sop to wounded nationalist sensitivities in Turkey. K. Zeimke, *Die neue Türkei,* pp. 296–330; H. N. Howard, *Partition of Turkey,* 336–40; S. H. Longrigg, *'Iraq 1900 to 1950,* chap. 5; J. C. Hurewitz, *Middle East Dilemmas,* chap. 5; *Survey of International Affairs, 1925,* vol. 1, pp. 471–528; H. C. Luke, *Mosul and Its Minorities;* A. J. Toynbee and K. P. Kirkwood, *Turkey,* chap. 17.

1. THE TREATY

Chapter I. Frontier between Turkey and Iraq

ART. 1. The frontier line between Turkey and Iraq is definitely laid down following the line adopted by the Council of the League of Nations at its session on the 29th October, 1924, and set forth hereunder:[1]

Nevertheless the above-mentioned line is modified to the south of Alamun and Ashuta so as to include in Turkish territory that part of the road which connects these two places and which crosses Iraq territory.

ART. 2. Subject to the last paragraph of article 1, the frontier line described in the above-mentioned article constitutes the frontier between Turkey and Iraq, and is traced on the map (Scale $\frac{1}{250000}$) annexed to the present Treaty.[2] In case of divergence between the text and the map the text will prevail.

ART. 3. A boundary commission shall be appointed to trace on the ground the frontier defined in article 1. This commission shall be composed of two representatives appointed by the Turkish Government, two representatives appointed jointly by His Majesty's Government and the Government of Iraq, and a president, who shall be a Swiss national, to be nominated by the President of the Swiss Confederation, if he is willing to do so.

The commission shall meet as soon as possible, and in any case within six months from the coming into force of the present Treaty.

The decisions of the commission shall be taken by a majority and shall be binding on all the High Contracting Parties.

The boundary commission shall endeavour in all cases to follow as nearly as may be possible the definitions given in the present Treaty.

The expenses of the commission shall be divided equally between Turkey and Iraq.

The States concerned undertake to give assistance to the boundary commission, either directly or through local authorities, in everything that concerns the accommodation, labour, materials (sign posts, boundary marks) necessary for the accomplishment of its task.

They undertake further to safeguard the trigonometrical points, signs, posts or frontier marks erected by the commission.

The boundary marks shall be placed so as to be visible from each other. They shall be numbered, and their position and their number shall be noted on a cartographic document.

The definitive record of the boundary laid down, and the maps and documents attached thereto shall be made out in triplicate, of which two copies shall be forwarded to the Governments of the two interested States, and the third to the Government of the French Republic, in order that authentic copies may be delivered to the Powers signatory of the Treaty of Lausanne.

ART. 4. The nationality of the inhabitants of the territories ceded to Iraq in virtue of the provisions of article 1 is regulated by articles 30–36 of the Treaty of Lausanne. The High Contracting Parties agree that the right of option provided for in articles 31, 32 and 34 of the said Treaty may be exercised during a period of twelve months from the coming into force of the present Treaty.

Turkey reserves nevertheless her liberty of action in so far as concerns the recognition of the option of such of the above-mentioned inhabitants as may opt for Turkish nationality.

ART. 5. Each of the High Contracting

[1] Annex, describing Brussels line, omitted.

[2] Map not reproduced.

Parties accepts as definitive and inviolable the frontier line fixed by article 1 and undertakes to make no attempt to alter it.

Chapter II. Neighbourly Relations

ART. 6. The High Contracting Parties undertake reciprocally to oppose by all means in their power any preparations made by one or more armed individuals with the object of committing acts of pillage or brigandage in the neighbouring frontier zone and to prevent them from crossing the frontier.

ART. 7. Whenever the competent authorities designated in article 11 learn that preparations are being made by one or more armed individuals with the object of committing acts of pillage or brigandage in the neighbouring frontier zone they shall reciprocally inform each other without delay.

ART. 8. The competent authorities designated in article 11 shall reciprocally inform each other as quickly as possible of any act of pillage or brigandage which may have been perpetrated on their territory. The authorities of the party receiving the notice shall make every effort in their power to prevent the authors of such acts from crossing the frontier.

ART. 9. In the event of one or more armed individuals, guilty of a crime or misdemeanour in the neighbouring frontier zone, succeeding in taking refuge in the other frontier zone, the authorities of the latter zone are bound to arrest such individuals in order to deliver them, in conformity with the law, to the authorities of the other party whose nationals they are, together with their booty and their arms.

ART. 10. The frontier zone to which this chapter of the present Treaty shall apply is the whole of the frontier which separates Turkey from Iraq and a zone 75 kilometres in width on each side of that frontier.

ART. 11. The competent authorities to whom the execution of this chapter of the Treaty is entrusted are the following:—

For the organisation of general co-operation and responsibility for the measures to be taken:—

On the Turkish side: the military commandant of the frontier;

On the Iraq side: the mutessarifs of Mosul and of Arbil.

For the exchange of local information and urgent communications:—

On the Turkish side: the authorities appointed with the consent of the Valis;

On the Iraq side: the kaimakams of Zakho, Amadia, Zibar and Rowanduz.

The Turkish and Irak Governments may, for administrative reasons, modify the list of their competent authorities, giving notice of such modification either through the permanent frontier commission provided for in article 13 or through the diplomatic channel.

ART. 12. The Turkish and Iraq authorities shall refrain from all correspondence of an official or political nature with the chiefs, sheikhs, or other members of tribes which are nationals of the other State and which are actually in the territory of that State.

They shall not permit in the frontier zone any organisation for propaganda or meeting directed against either State.

ART. 13. In order to facilitate the execution of the provisions of the present chapter of this Treaty, and, in general, the maintenance of good neighbourly relations on the frontier, there shall be set up a permanent Frontier Commission composed of an equal number of officials appointed from time to time for this purpose by the Turkish and Iraq Governments respectively. This commission shall meet at least once every six months, or oftener if circumstances require it.

It shall be the duty of this commission, which shall meet alternately in Turkey and in Iraq, to endeavour to settle amicably all questions concerning the execution of the provisions of this chapter of the Treaty, and any other frontier question on which an agreement shall not have been reached between the local frontier officials concerned.

The commission shall meet for the first time at Zakho within two months from the coming into force of the present Treaty.

Chapter III. General Provisions

ART. 14. With the object of enlarging the field of common interests between the two countries, the Iraq Government shall pay to the Turkish Government for a period of twenty-five years from the coming into force of the present Treaty 10 per cent. on all royalties which it shall receive:—

(*a.*) from the Turkish Petroleum Company under article 10 of its concession of the 14th March, 1925;

(*b.*) from such companies or persons as may exploit oil under the provisions of article 6 of the above-mentioned concession;

(*c.*) from such subsidiary companies as may be constituted under the provisions of article 33 of the above-mentioned concession.

ART. 15. The Turkish and Irak Governments agree to enter into negotiations as soon as possible for the purpose of concluding an extradition treaty in accordance with the usages prevailing among friendly States.

ART. 16. The Irak Government undertakes not to disturb or molest any persons established on its territory on account of their political opinions or conduct in favour of Turkey up to the time of the signature of the present Treaty, and to grant them full and complete amnesty.

All sentences pronounced under the above heading shall be annulled, and all proceedings already instituted shall be stayed.

ART. 17. The present Treaty shall come into force on the date of exchange of ratifications.

Chapter II of the present Treaty shall remain in force for a period of ten years from the date of the coming into force of the present Treaty.

After the termination of a period of two years from the coming into force of the present Treaty each of the Contracting Parties shall have the right to denounce this chapter in so far as it provisions concern that party, the denunciation taking effect one year after the date on which notice thereof shall have been given.

2. SPECIAL ARRANGEMENT AFFIRMED BY EXCHANGE OF NOTES

With reference to article 14 of the Treaty signed by us to-day, we have the honour to declare that if, within twelve months from the coming into force of this Treaty, the Turkish Government desires to capitalise its share of the royalties mentioned in the said article, it shall notify the Iraq Government of its desire, and the latter, within thirty days after the receipt of this notice, shall pay to the Turkish Government in full satisfaction on account of this article the sum of £500,000 sterling.

On the other hand, it is understood that the Turkish Government undertakes not to divest itself of its interests in the said royalties without previously giving the Iraq Government the opportunity of acquiring those interests at a price not higher than that which any third party may be ready to pay.

It is agreed that the present exchange of notes constitutes an integral part of the Treaty signed to-day.

47. TREATY OF AMITY AND COMMERCE (SAN'A): ITALY AND YEMEN
2 September 1926

(Ratifications exchanged, San'a, 22 December 1926)

[*British and Foreign State Papers,* vol. 124, pp. 1011–13]

The Ottoman Empire conquered Yemen in the sixteenth century, only to lose it in the seventeenth and reoccupy it in the nineteenth (1849–72). Imam Yahya (1904–48), religious leader of the Zaydi Shi'ah sect in the Yemeni highlands, concluded an agreement with the Sublime Porte in 1911 (confirmed in 1913). The Imam was vested with limited religious and legal autonomy but remained in tributary relationship with the Sultan, whose suzerainty he recognized. Loyal to the Ottomans in World War I, Yahya asserted his independence immediately after the Mudros armistice (Doc. 18). He occupied in 1919 certain districts in the Aden hinterland belonging to shaykhs in protectorate relations with Britain and later refused to surrender the districts, claiming that historically they formed part of his patrimony. Anglo-Yemeni talks in 1925 bore no fruit. Primarily to annoy London, the Imam began to court the Italians in Eritrea on the Red Sea coast opposite Yemen. The Italians required little prompting, as the Eritrean Governor, Cavaliere Jacopo Gasparini, attested in signing the following treaty of amity and commerce with his Arabian neighbor. Italy thus became the first European country to recognize Yemen's independence. A supplemental secret agreement of 1 June 1927 (text in *Documents on International Affairs, 1928,* pp. 222–24) promised Italians limited capitulatory rights, but its preambular reference to an alliance stated an Italian objective rather than an accomplishment. Still, Italy remained the only European power with some measure of political influence at San'a through the early years of World War II. *Survey of International Affairs, 1925,* vol. 1, pp. 320–24; H. Scott, *In the High Yemen,* passim; H. F. Jacob, "The Kingdom of Yemen, its Place in the Comity of Nations" (Grotius Society, London), *Problems of War and Peace,* 18 (1933), 131–53.

ART. 1. The Government of His Majesty the King of Italy recognise the full and absolute independence of the Yemen and of its Sovereign, His Majesty the Imam Jahia.

The Italian Government will abstain from all interference in the Kingdom of His Majesty the King of Yemen that might be incompatible with the provisions of the first paragraph of the present article.

2. The two Governments undertake to facilitate commercial relations between their respective countries.

3. The Government of His Majesty the King of Yemen declare that it is their desire to import from Italy the supplies, *i.e.*, the technical means and material which can advantageously be employed for the economic development of the Yemen, as also the technical staff.

The Italian Government declare their readiness to do all that is possible in order that the technical means and material and the staff shall be despatched under the most favourable conditions as regards quality, price and salaries.

4. The provisions of articles 2 and 3 do not limit the liberty of the two parties with regard to commerce and supplies.

5. No merchant of either of the two States may import or carry on trade in articles prohibited by the two Governments in their respective countries.

Both Governments shall have power to confiscate articles imported into their respective countries contrary to a prohibition to import or deal in them when such prohibition has been made known.

6. The present treaty shall not come into force until the ratification of His Majesty the King of Italy has reached His Majesty the Imam Jahia, King of the Yemen.

7. The present treaty shall have a duration of 10 years from the date of the ratification mentioned in article 6, and 6 months before its expiration the two parties shall come to an understanding in case they desire to replace it or to prolong it.

8. In witness whereof His Majesty the Imam Jahia, King of the Yemen, and his Excellency Cavaliere Jacopo Gasparini, in the name of His Majesty the King of Italy, have signed the present treaty drawn up in two exactly identical copies, in the Arabic and in the Italian languages.

Since, however, there is nobody attached to His Majesty the King of Yemen who knows perfectly the Italian language, as the negotiations in respect of the present treaty of friendship and commerce were carried on by both parties in Arabic, and as his Excellency Cavaliere Jacopo Gasparini has assured himself that the Arabic text is exactly equivalent to the Italian, the two parties agree to be bound, in case of doubt or of divergent interpretations of the two texts, by the Arabic text interpreted according to the classical language.

48. PROTECTORATE (MECCA) AGREEMENT: 'ASIR AND HIJAZ, NAJD AND DEPENDENCIES
21 October 1926

(Pomulgated, 7 January 1927)

[*British and Foreign State Papers,* vol. 135, pp. 379–80]

Ottoman forces, under the terms of the Mudros armistice (Doc. 18), surrendered the Yemeni *tihamah* or coastal plain to the British, who in turn handed over Luhayyah in 1919 and Hudaydah two years later to the Idrisi Sayyid Muhammad bin 'Ali (Doc. 7). After the death of Sayyid Muhammad on 20 March 1923, a struggle broke out among the Idrisi contenders for the princely throne. Internal strife weakened the defenses of 'Asir, as the Idrisi shaykhadom came to be known, and enabled Imam Yahya of Yemen to reconquer Luhayyah and Hudaydah in 1924–25 and to attempt the annexation of 'Asir itself in the next year. To forestall Yemeni designs, Sayyid Hasan bin 'Ali in the following instrument surrendered his external sovereignty to ibn Sa'ud, then styled King of the Hijaz and Sultan of Najd and its Dependencies. On 20 November 1930 the Idrisi province lost its internal sovereignty as well and became fully a part of the Sa'udi domain (Italian translations of pertinent texts may be found in *Oriente Moderno,* vol. 10, pp. 640–42. *Survey of International Affairs, 1925,* vol. 1, pp. 320–24, *1928,* pp. 319–20, *1934,* pp. 310–21.

Praise be to God alone!

Between the King of the Hejaz, Sultan of Nejd and its dependencies; and the Imam Sayed al-Hassan ibn Ali al-Idrisi. Desiring a complete understanding and with a view to the preservation of the existence of the Arab countries, and to the strengthening of ties between the Princes of the Arab peninsula, the following agreement has been reached between His Majesty the King of the Hejaz, Sultan of Nejd and its dependencies, Abdul-Aziz ibn Abdul-Rahman Al Faisal Al Saud and His Lordship the Imam of Asir, the Sayyid al-Hassan ibn Ali al-Idrisi:—

ART. 1. His Lordship the Imam Sayyid al-Hassan ibn Ali al-Idrisi acknowledges the ancient marches described in the treaty of the 10th Safar, 1339,[1] made between the Sultan of Nejd and the Imam Sayyid Mohammad ibn Ali al-Idrisi, and which were at that date subject to the House of Idrisi, as being in virtue of this agreement under the suzerainty of His Majesty the King of Hejaz, Sultan of Nejd and its dependencies.

2. The Imam of Asir may not enter into political negotiations with any Government or grant any economic concession to any person except with the sanction of His Majesty the King of Hejaz, Sultan of Nejd and its dependencies.

3. The Imam of Asir may not declare war or make peace except with the sanction of His Majesty the King of the Hejaz, Sultan of Nejd and its dependencies.

4. The Imam of Asir may not cede any part of the territories of Asir described in article 1.

5. The King of the Hejaz, Sultan of Nejd and its dependencies, recognises the rulership of the present Imam of Asir, during his lifetime, of the territories defined in article 1, and thereafter (extends the same recognition) to whomsoever the House of Idrisi and the competent authorities of the Imamate may agree upon.

6. The King of the Hejaz, Sultan of Nejd and its dependencies, agrees that the internal administration of Asir, the supervision of its tribal affairs, appointments and dismissals, for example, pertain to the rights of the Imam of Asir, provided such administration is in harmony with Sharia law and justice according to the practice of both governments.

7. The King of the Hejaz, Sultan of Nejd and its dependencies, undertakes to repel all internal and external aggression which may befall the territories of Asir as defined in article 1 and this by agreement between

[1] English translation of this treaty may be found in *British and Foreign State Papers,* vol. 135, pp. 377–78.

the two contracting parties according to the circumstances and exigencies of interest.

8. Both parties agree to adhere to this agreement and to carry out its obligations.

9. This agreement will be effective after confirmation by the two high contracting parties.

10. This agreement has been drawn up in Arabic in two copies, of which one will be preserved by each of the two contracting parties.

11. This agreement will be known as "the Mecca Agreement."

49. TREATY (JIDDAH): THE UNITED KINGDOM AND KING IBN SA'UD OF THE HIJAZ AND OF NAJD AND ITS DEPENDENCIES 20 May 1927

(Ratifications exchanged, Jiddah, 17 September 1927)

[Great Britain, *Parliamentary Papers, 1927,* Treaty Series No. 25, Cmd. 2951]

The Anglo-Najdi treaty of 26 December 1915 (Doc. 9) placed the then Amir ibn Sa'ud's principality in the same category of veiled protectorate status as that of the lesser Persian Gulf shaykhdoms. But the 1915 treaty became, in the words of Toynbee, "an anachronism in the course of ten years during which Ibn Sa'ūd, by his successive conquests of Jabal Shammar and Hijāz, had built up his Wahhābi principality into a state stretching from the Persian Gulf to the Red Sea and embracing the Holy Cities of Islam" (*Survey of International Affairs, 1928,* p. 285). Formal relations between the two countries were accordingly readjusted under the following instrument, which recognized "the complete and absolute independence of the dominions" of King ibn Sa'ud. The frontier question, to which reference is made in an accompanying exchange of notes (not reproduced), still remains open (cf. *Parliamentary Papers, 1925,* Cmd. 2566). The treaty of Jiddah was renewed on 3 October 1936 and 3 October 1943; at the second date article 8 was amended automatically to prolong the agreement "for successive periods of seven solar years unless either of the two High Contracting Parties shall have given notice to the other six months before the expiration of any of the said periods. . . ." (Treaty Series No. 10 (1937), Cmd. 5380, and Treaty Series No. 13 (1947), Cmd. 7064). H. St. J. Philby, *Sa'udi Arabia,* chaps. 10–11; C. A. Nallino, *L'Arabia Sa'udiana; Survey of International Affairs, 1925,* vol. 1, pp. 271–324, and *1928,* pp. 284–307; R. Sanger, *The Arabian Peninsula,* chap. 3.

ART. 1. His Britannic Majesty recognises the complete and absolute independence of the dominions of His Majesty the King of the Hejaz and of Nejd and its Dependencies.

ART. 2. There shall be peace and friendship between His Britannic Majesty and His Majesty the King of the Hejaz and of Nejd and its Dependencies. Each of the high contracting parties undertakes to maintain good relations with the other and to endeavour by all the means at its disposal to prevent his territories being used as a base for unlawful activities directed against peace and tranquillity in the territories of the other party.

ART. 3. His Majesty the King of the Hejaz and of Nejd and its Dependencies undertakes that the performance of the pilgrimage will be facilitated to British subjects and British-protected persons of the Moslem faith to the same extent as to other pilgrims, and announces that they will be safe as regards their property and their person during their stay in the Hejaz.

ART. 4. His Majesty the King of the Hejaz and of Nejd and its Dependencies undertakes that the property of the aforesaid pilgrims who may die within the territories of His Majesty and who have no lawful trustee in those territories shall be handed over to the British Agent in Jeddah or to such authority as he may appoint for the purpose, to be forwarded by him to the rightful heirs of the deceased pilgrims; provided that the property shall not be handed over to the British representative until the formalities of the competent tribunals have been compiled with and the dues prescribed under Hejazi or Nejdi laws have been duly collected.

ART. 5. His Britannic Majesty recognises the national (Hejazi or Nejdi) status of all subjects of His Majesty the King of the Hejaz and of Nejd and its Dependencies who may at any time be within the territories of His Britannic Majesty or territories under the protection of His Britannic Majesty.

Similarly, His Majesty the King of the Hejaz and of Nejd and its Dependencies recognises the national (British) status of all subjects of His Britannic Majesty and of all persons enjoying the protection of His Britannic Majesty who may at any time be within the territories of His Majesty the King of the Hejaz and of Nejd and its Dependencies; it being understood that the principles of international law in force between independent Governments shall be respected.

ART. 6. His Majesty the King of the Hejaz and of Nejd and its Dependencies undertakes to maintain friendly and peaceful relations with the territories of Kuwait and Bahrain, and with the Sheikhs of Qatar and the Oman Coast, who are in special treaty relations with His Britannic Majesty's Government.

ART. 7. His Majesty the King of the Hejaz and of Nejd and its Dependencies undertakes to co-operate by all the means at his disposal with His Britannic Majesty in the suppression of the slave trade.

ART. 8. The present treaty shall be ratified by each of the high contracting parties and the ratifications exchanged as soon as possible. It shall come into force on the day of the exchange of ratifications and shall be binding during seven years from that date. In case neither of the high contracting parties shall have given notice to the other six months before the expiration of the said period of seven years of his intention to terminate the treaty it shall remain in force and shall not be held to have terminated until the expiration of six months from the date on which either of the parties shall have given notice of the termination to other party.

ART. 9. The treaty concluded between His Britannic Majesty and His Majesty the King of the Hejaz and of Nejd and its Dependencies (then Ruler of Nejd and its then Dependencies) on the 26th December, 1915, shall cease to have effect as from the date on which the present treaty is ratified.

ART. 10. The present treaty has been drawn up in English and Arabic. Both texts shall be of equal validity; but in case of divergence in the interpretation of any part of the treaty the English text shall prevail.

ART. 11. The present treaty shall be known as the Treaty of Jeddah.

50. SOVIET CASPIAN SEA FISHERIES CONCESSION IN PERSIA
1 October 1927

(Ratifications exchanged, Tehran, 31 January 1928; expired, 30 January 1953)
[League of Nations, *Treaty Series,* No. 2621, vol. 112 (1931), pp. 350–60]

The Soviet-Persian treaty of 1921 (Doc. 33), which in part provided for the cancellation of Tsarist Russian concessions in Persia, made one significant exception. Persia undertook (article 14) to reissue the Caspian Sea fisheries concession to the Food Service of the RSFRS "immediately upon the expiry of the legal period of these existing engagements." Soviet attempts to conduct the fisheries enterprise without a formal concession created difficulties, which were multiplied when a Persian arbitration commission decided on 8 November 1922 that the existing concession, owned by a White Russian family named Lianozov, should be extended for fifteen years longer. But on 10 August 1923 Martin Georgiyevich Lianozov, under conditions that were not fully disclosed, ceded the fisheries installations and properties in Persia to the State Fisheries of the Soviet Supply Commissariat. Soviet-Persian negotiations however continued to move slowly. The American adviser to the Persian Ministry of Finance (1922–27), Arthur Millspaugh, resisted Soviet demands and pressures for the implementation of the disputed article 14. Soon after Millspaugh's departure the requested instrument was signed in Moscow. Exclusive rights to exploit the Caspian fisheries were assigned to a joint Soviet-Persian company under a Persian chairman. But owing to the absence of precise stipulations in the concessionary contract and the failure of Persians to obtain representation in the marketing agencies, the sales of the fishing industry became a Soviet monopoly and most of the profits found their way to Moscow. The twenty-five-year contract expired at the height of the Anglo-Iranian oil crisis of the early nineteen fifties and was not renewed. The protocols and notes accompanying the act of concession are not reproduced below. V. Conolly, *Soviet Economic Policy in the East,* chap. 3; A. C. Millspaugh, *The American Task in Persia,* pp. 294–302; E. Groseclose, *Introduction to Iran,* pp. 74–75, 134–39, 186.

ART. I. By the present Agreement the Persian Government grants on the following conditions, to a special mixed commercial and industrial Company organised by the Persian Government and the Government of the Union of Soviet Socialist Republics, a concession to catch and prepare fish along the Persian South-Caspian coast within the boundaries defined in Article II of the present Agreement.

In the present Agreement, the abovementioned mixed Company shall be termed "the Company."

ART. II. The boundaries of the fisheries for which the Company is granted a concession shall coincide with the boundaries of the concession formerly granted by the Persian Government to Lianozov Brothers. The rivers running into the sea within the boundaries of the concession shall be excluded therefrom. The line where they flow into the sea shall be the boundary between these rivers and the waters of the concession.

The mouths of the following rivers shall form an exception:

(a) Safid-Rud, the two arms of which (Safid-Rud and Mussa-Chay), being shallow, prevent fishing at the mouth. For this reason the Company shall be entitled to fish in these arms as far as the limits where the former fisheries of Lianozov Brothers are at present situated at the mouth.

(b) Babol, in the district of Meshed-i-Sar, in view of the shallow water at the mouth. The Company shall also be entitled to fish at this place within the limits of the former fisheries of Lianozov Brothers.

(c) The river Gorgan with its arms Kara-Su, up to the boundary of the former fisheries of Lianozov Brothers.

If the mouths of rivers within the limits of the concession change their course with the lapse of time, or the rivers form new arms, the fishing rights granted to the Company shall be applicable to the new courses and arms.

Note: With regard to the fishing-places within the limits mentioned in this Agreement, the Company is not restricted except by the provisions of the present Agreement.

ART. III. In order to regulate the fishing work of the Company, the following provisions are adopted:

(a) All scaleless fish (Haram) within the limits of the concession belong to the Company, and the Company's fishermen or private fishermen must sell them to the Company at prices which the Company shall from time to time fix in advance.

(b) All scaled fish (Halal) may be caught by private fishermen as well as by the Company's fishermen; they belong to the fishermen, who may sell them to anyone they choose, including the Company.

(c) In order that the Company and private fishermen of Persian nationality may not hinder each other's work, fishing areas shall be allotted to private fishermen for three-year periods by agreement between the Persian Government and the Management of the Company. The Company, for its part, undertakes to lay down and publish every three years the rules and conditions governing the admission of private fishermen to the waters where fishing is carried on directly by the Company.

ART. IV. The duration of the concession granted to the Company shall be 25 years from the date when the present Agreement comes into force. On the expiry of this period of 25 years, the obligations of the Persian Government arising out of Article

14 of the Treaty of February 26, 1921, shall be considered terminated. If the Persian Government does not wish to renew the Company's concession to the above-mentioned fisheries, the Company shall be considered dissolved, and its property shall be divided equally between the two parties, with the exception of the plots of land assigned free of charge to the Company by the Persian Government under Article 17 of the present Agreement. These plots shall revert to the Persian Government. The Persian Government undertakes, if the Company's concession is not renewed, not to grant a concession in respect of these fisheries to any third Power and its nationals for a period of 25 years thereafter. It undertakes to exploit them exclusively through the appropriate agencies of the Persian Government, and not to engage any specialists other than Persian subjects for the exploitation of these fisheries.

ART. V. The Persian and Soviet Governments shall have equal shares of 50% in the Company.

ART. VI. In order to improve the organisation of the fisheries, to purchase the necessary fishing gear and appliances, and to defray the costs of exploiting the fisheries, the Company shall form a total capital which must not exceed three million tomans. Should this capital be found to be too high, the Parties shall create a total capital commensurate with actual requirements, one half being paid by the Persian Government and the other half by the Government of the Union of Soviet Socialist Republics. Both Parties shall pay in their shares at dates agreed upon between them, as required for the development of the undertaking. The payment due for the catch of previous years, which, according to Article XIII of the present Agreement, must be made to the Persian Government, shall be placed to the account of the Persian Government's share in the total capital required for exploitation. If the Persian Government does not pay its share in cash, the procedure established by Article VII of the present Agreement shall be followed. In that case, the following sums, which should have been paid to the Persian Government, shall be paid to the Soviet Government to be offset against the amounts due to that Government by the Persian Government:

(a) Payment for the grant of the concession, in accordance with Article VIII.

(b) 50% of the net profits, in accordance with Article IX.

The Persian Government shall, however, be entitled, at any time it thinks fit, to effect and complete, in cash, the payment of its outstanding contributions. In that case, the sums mentioned in points *(a)* and *(b)* of this Article shall be paid to the Persian Treasury. After the Persian Government has paid its share of the total capital required for exploitation, the sums mentioned in points *a)* and *b)* of this Article shall be paid direct to the Persian Government.

ART. VII. If the sums mentioned in Article VI are insufficient to cover the Persian Government's share of the capital which is found to be actually necessary in accordance with Article VI, and if the Persian Government does not pay the remainder of its share, this part of the Persian Government's share shall be paid by the Soviet Government after a notification *ad hoc* has been made by the Persian Government to the Government of the Union of Soviet Socialist Republics. After the Persian Government has been informed by the Soviet Government that the payment has been made, it shall pay 8% interest per annum on the amount advanced by the Soviet Government from the date of payment until the Persian Government's contributions to the above-mentioned capital has been made in full. With regard to the apportionment of the Company's profits, the Soviet Government shall not be entitled, even in cases provided for in the present Article, to receive a higher proportion of the Company's net profits than that specified in Article IX of the present agreement, *i.e.*, 50%.

It is understood that the payment by the Persian Government of the above-mentioned 8% shall not be taken into account in the apportionment of the profits in accordance with Article IX of the present Agreement.

ART. VIII. The annual payment made by the Company to the Persian Government for the grant of the concession in accordance with the present Agreement shall be effected as follows:

(1) 80,000 tomans per annum from the gross receipts of the Company as a payment for the concession rights;

(2) 15% of the remaining gross profit, which, after deduction of administrative and working expenses, shall be regarded as the Company's net profit.

The above-mentioned sums are not reckoned in the profit to which the Persian Government, as a shareholder in the Company, is entitled in accordance with Article IX of the present Agreement.

ART. IX. The whole of the net profit obtained from the Company's operations shall be divided equally—*i.e.*, 50% to each Party—between the Persian and Soviet Governments, share-holders in the Company.

Note: The Company undertakes to dispose of the products of the fisheries at the most favourable price on the Soviet, Persian or foreign markets, selecting the market where the prices are most remunerative.

ART. X. The Board of Management of the Company, directing all its business and having its head office in Teheran, shall consist of six members appointed for one year. Three members shall be appointed by the Persian Government and three by the Soviet Government. The rulings and decisions of the Board of Management shall be given by a majority of votes.

The members of the Board of Management shall be appointed by both Parties not later than one month after the date when the present Agreement comes into force. The Chairman of the Board shall be one of its Persian members and shall be appointed by the Persian Government.

If, within thirty days after the expiry of the above-mentioned period of one month, either Party has not appointed any or all of the members of the Board, the Board shall, until those members are appointed, be regarded as competent to decide all questions with the members already appointed.

ART. XI. Both Parties agree that, in addition to Soviet specialists, Persian specialists who are Persian nationals shall be widely used at the fisheries, for which purpose the Company undertakes to organise suitable training for Persian specialists in its work. As specialists of Persian nationality become available, they shall be engaged by the company and shall take the place of Soviet specialists. The remaining employees, labourers and fishery workmen, not requiring special knowledge, must be Persian nationals.

All employees of the Company must act and work in accordance with the instructions approved by the Board of the Company. At the same time, the Parties agree that the Company shall not have the right to engage other persons than Persian nationals and Soviet citizens.

ART. XII. The Company shall be subject to all laws, decrees and regulations by the Persian Council of Ministers for Persian companies, that are, or may hereafter be, in force in Persia. The Persian Government has the right, within the limits of these laws, decrees and regulations, to supervise the operations of the Company.

ART. XIII. From the year 1923, *i.e.*, after the year 1922, for which accounts have already been settled by a payment of 50,000 tomans, until the present Agreement comes into force, the Government of the Union of Soviet Socialist Republics shall pay to the Persian Government 50,000 tomans per annum for the exploitation of the fisheries.

In return for this the Persian Government shall waive payments of the outstanding Customs duties and other taxes on the fishery products exported and the fishing gear imported during those years.

ART. XIV. The Company's working year shall begin on October 1st, that month corresponding to the Persian month of Mehr. The Company shall settle its accounts with the Persian and Soviet Governments for each year not later than the beginning of the following month of April, which corresponds to the Persian month of Farvardine.

ART. XV. In order to avoid loss of time, the Company may start exploiting the fisheries immediately the capital necessary for beginning its work is paid up and the Company has notified the Persian Government that it is starting its work. The Parties shall pay the shares of the capital due from them at dates decided by the Board of the Company. If the Persian Government does not pay its share at the date fixed by the Board of Management of the Company, the Soviet Government shall pay this share in the manner specified in Article VII of the present Agreement.

ART. XVI. The Governments of Persia and of the Union of Soviet Socialist Republics shall grant complete exemption from Customs duties and other taxes levied on imports and exports, and also the right of free transit and coasting trade, for appliances, gear, products and other supplies required by the Company for operating the fisheries, and for all kinds of fish products obtained from the fisheries. In all cases, however, the above-mentioned articles shall not be exempt from Customs inspection. The Customs Administrations of both Parties, whilst carrying out the laws, regulations and provisions relating to Customs inspection, shall render every assistance to the Company in order to facilitate the above-mentioned importation and exportation.

ART. XVII. The Persian Government agrees to place at the disposal of the Company, free of cost, in the Concession area, such plots of land as are required for the fishery buildings and auxiliary plant. The Company undertakes to effect a settlement to the private owners of plots of land required for the above-mentioned buildings and plant.

ART. XVIII. The Governments of Persia and of the Union of Soviet Socialist Republics shall, each within its own spheres, render such assistance as may be necessary, for the work of the Company.

In particular, the Persian Government shall assist the Company both in preventing any illicit fishing in the waters leased by the latter and in ensuring that the Haram fish are really delivered to the Company.

ART. XIX. As the maintenance of order in the concession area is in the hands of the Persian Government, it agrees to render the Company such assistance as may be needed to carry into effect the provisions of the present Agreement, and to guard the warehouses and other fishery buildings.

ART. XX. The present Agreement shall be ratified by both Parties in accordance with the provisions of their laws. Ratification must take place in both countries as early as possible.

The Agreement shall come into force on the date of the exchange of ratifications, which shall take place at Teheran.

ART. XXI. The present Agreement has been drawn up and signed in the Persian, Russian and French languages, and each of the signatory Parties receives one copy in each language; all three copies shall be regarded as authentic for the interpretation of the Agreement. In case of a dispute as to the interpretation of the Agreement, the French text shall be followed.

51. TREATY OF GUARANTEE AND NEUTRALITY: PERSIA AND THE USSR
1 October 1927

(Ratifications exchanged, Tehran, 31 January 1928)
[League of Nations, *Treaty Series,* No. 2620, vol. 112 (1931), pp. 292–95]

Simultaneously with the signature of the Caspian Seas fisheries concession (Doc. 50), the USSR and Persia concluded the following treaty. By this act Persia was brought into Soviet defense arrangements along the European and Near and Middle East periphery of Russia. Accompanying the treaty were two protocols, not reproduced, in which the signatories declared that they had "no international obligations whatsoever contrary to the said Treaty and will not undertake such obligations during the whole duration of that Treaty" and stated that article 6 of the 1921 Perso-Russian treaty (Doc. 33) continued in full vigor. Also omitted below is an exchange of notes reaffirming Persia's fidelity to its obligations as a member of the League of Nations. M. Beloff, *The Foreign Policy of Soviet Russia,* vol. 2, chap. 9; *Survey of International Affairs, 1928,* pp. 358–74; M. W. Graham, Jr., "The Soviet Security System," *International Conciliation,* September 1929, pp. 343–425.

ART. 1. The mutual relations between Persia and the Union of Soviet Socialist Republics shall continue to be governed by the Treaty of February 26, 1921, of which all the articles and provisions shall remain in force, and which shall be applicable throughout the territory of the Union of Soviet Socialist Republics.

ART. 2. Each of the High Contracting Parties undertakes to refrain from any aggression and from any hostile acts directed against the other Party, and not to introduce its military forces into the territory of the other Party.

Should either of the Contracting Parties become the victim of aggression on the part of one or more third Powers, the other Contracting Party agrees to observe neutrality throughout the duration of the conflict, while the Party which is the victim of the aggression shall not violate that neutrality, notwithstanding any strategical, tactical or political considerations or any advantages it might thereby obtain.

ART. 3. Each of the Contracting Parties agrees to take no part, whether *de facto* or *de jure,* in political alliances or agreements directed against the safety of the territory or territorial waters of the other Contracting Party or against its integrity, independence or sovereignty.

Each of the Contracting Parties likewise agrees to take no part in any economic boycotts or blockades organised by third Powers against one of the Contracting Parties.

ART. 4. In view of the obligations laid down in Articles 4 and 5 of the Treaty of February 26, 1921, each of the Contracting Parties, being determined to abstain from any intervention in the internal affairs of the other Party and from any propaganda or campaign against the Government of the other Party, shall strictly forbid its officials to commit such acts in the territory of the other Party.

Should the citizens of either of the Contracting Parties in the territory of the other Party engage in any propaganda or campaign prohibited by the authorities of this latter Party, the Government of that territory shall have the right to put a stop to the activities of such citizens and to impose the statutory penalties.

The two Parties likewise undertake, in virtue of the above-mentioned Articles, not to encourage or to allow in their respective territories the formation or activities of: (1) organisations or groups of any description whatever, whose object is to overthrow the Government of the other Contracting Party by means of violence, insurrection or outrage; (2) organisations or groups usurping the office of the Government of the other country or part of its territory, also having as their object the subversion of the Government of the other Contracting Party by the above-mentioned means, a breach of its peace and security, or an infringement of its territorial integrity.

In accordance with the foregoing principles, the two Contracting Parties likewise undertake to prohibit military enrolment and the introduction into their territory of armed forces, arms, ammunition, and all other war material, intended for the organisations mentioned above.

ART. 5. The two Contracting Parties undertake to settle by a pacific procedure appropriate to the circumstances all disputes of any description which may arise between them and which it has not been possible to settle through the ordinary diplomatic channels.

ART. 6. Apart from the obligations undertaken by the two Contracting Parties in virtue of the present Treaty, the two Parties shall retain full freedom of action in their international relations.

ART. 7. The present Treaty is concluded for a period of three years and shall be approved and ratified within the shortest possible time by the legislative organs of the two Parties, after which it shall come into force.

The exchange of the instruments of ratification shall take place at Teheran one month after ratification.

After the expiry of the original period of validity, the Treaty shall be regarded as automatically prolonged for successive periods of one year until one of the Contracting Parties notifies the other of its desire to denounce the Treaty. In that case the present Treaty shall remain in force for six months from the date of the notification of its denunciation by one of the Parties.

ART. 8. The present Treaty is drawn up in the Persian, Russian, and French languages, in three authentic copies for each of the Contracting Parties.

For the purpose of interpretation, all three texts shall be regarded as authentic. In the case of any divergencies with regard to interpretation, the French text shall prevail.

52. AGREEMENT: THE UNITED KINGDOM AND TRANSJORDAN
20 February 1928

(Ratifications exchanged, 'Amman, 31 October 1929; amended 2 June 1934 and 19 July 1941; superseded, 17 June 1946 by a preferential alliance)

[Great Britain, *Parliamentary Papers, 1930,* Treaty Series No. 7, Cmd. 3488]

The amirate of Transjordan owed its birth to an accident of history. The desert tract east of the Jordan became lost in the postwar shuffle of boundaries and sovereignty rights. When the United Kingdom on 27 March 1921 recognized Amir 'Abdallah as provisional ruler of the district, it did so chiefly to dissuade King Husayn's impetuous son from executing his threat to take military action against the French in Syria, an attempt which London feared might provide an excuse for French forces to move into the British-claimed zone. The installation of 'Abdallah in 'Amman demanded the revision in August 1921 of the draft Palestine mandate (Doc. 38). For trans-Jordan had already been assigned to the area of the projected Palestine mandate by the Franco-British convention of 23 December 1920 (*Parliamentary Papers, 1921,* Misc. No. 4, Cmd. 1195), and the first draft of the mandatory instrument (*ibid.,* Misc. No. 3, Cmd. 1176), completed earlier that month, placed no territorial restrictions on the Jewish National Home within the mandated land. Whitehall transformed the provisional arrangement for 'Abdallah into a permanent one on 25 May 1923, subject to the establishment of a constitutional regime and the conclusion of an agreement that would enable the United Kingdom "to fulfil its international obligations in respect of the territory" (text in *Survey of International Affairs, 1925,* vol. 1, p. 362). But nearly five years elapsed before the agreement was framed. It left Transjordan within the Palestine mandate, providing however for a separate government which was vested, under close mandatory supervision, with a substantial measure of domestic autonomy but which enjoyed no external autonomy. The Amir's dependence from the outset on the mandatory's grants-in-aid to balance the Transjordan budget reinforced British controls. Article 1 of the Anglo-Transjordan agreement was modified in June 1934 (*Parliamentary Papers, 1934,* Cmd. 4999), among other purposes, authorizing the Amir to appoint consuls to near-by Arab states. P. L. Hanna, *British Policy in Palestine,* pp. 74–78; *Survey of International Affairs, 1925,* vol. 1, pp. 361–63, and *1928,* pp. 321–28; P. Graves, *Memoirs of King Abdullah of Transjordan;* C. S. Jarvis, *Arab Command,* chaps. 5–14; B. Toukan, *A Short History of Trans-Jordan,* chaps. 44–49.

ART. 1. His Highness the Amir agrees that His Britannic Majesty shall be represented in Trans-Jordan by a British Resident acting on behalf of the High Commissioner for Trans-Jordan, and that communications between His Britannic Majesty and all other Powers on the one hand and the Trans-Jordan Government on the other shall be made through the British Resident and the High Commissioner aforesaid.

His Highness the Amir agrees that the ordinary expenses of civil government and administration and the salaries and expenses of the British Resident and his staff will be borne entirely by Trans-Jordan. His Highness the Amir will provide quarters for the accommodation of British members of the staff of the British Resident.

ART. 2. The powers of legislation and of administration entrusted to His Britannic Majesty as Mandatory for Palestine shall be exercised in that part of the area under Mandate known as Trans-Jordan by His Highness the Amir through such constitutional government as is defined and determined in the Organic Law of Trans-Jordan and any amendment thereof made with the approval of His Britannic Majesty.

Throughout the remaining clauses of this Agreement the word "Palestine," unless otherwise defined, shall mean that portion of the area under Mandate which lies to the west of a line drawn from a point two miles west of the town of Akaba on the Gulf of that name up the centre of the Wady Araba, Dead Sea and River Jordan to its junction with the River Yarmuk; thence up the centre of that river to the Syrian frontier.

ART. 3. His Highness the Amir agrees that for the period of the present Agreement no official of other than Trans-Jordan nationality shall be appointed in Trans-Jordan without the concurrence of His Britannic Majesty. The numbers and conditions of employment of British officials so appointed in the Trans-Jordan Government shall be regulated by a separate Agreement.

ART. 4. His Highness the Amir agrees that all such laws, orders or regulations as may be required for the full discharge of the international responsibilities and obligations of His Britannic Majesty in respect of the territory of Trans-Jordan shall be adopted and made, and that no laws, orders or regulations shall be adopted or made in Trans-Jordan which may hinder the full discharge of such international responsibilities and obligations.

ART. 5. His Highness the Amir agrees to be guided by the advice of His Britannic Majesty tendered through the High Commissioner for Trans-Jordan in all matters concerning foreign relations of Trans-Jordan, as well as in all important matters affecting the international and financial obligations and interests of His Britannic Majesty in respect of Trans-Jordan. His Highness the Amir undertakes to follow an administrative, financial and fiscal policy in Trans-Jordan such as will ensure the stability and good organisation of his Government and its finances. He agrees to keep His Britannic Majesty informed of the measures proposed and adopted to give due effect to this undertaking, and further agrees not to alter the system of control of the public finances of Trans-Jordan without the consent of His Britannic Majesty.

ART. 6. His Highness the Amir agrees that he will refer for the advice of His Britannic Majesty the annual Budget law and any law which concerns matters covered by the provisions of this Agreement, and any law of any of the following classes, namely:—

(1.) Any law affecting the currency of Trans-Jordan or relating to the issue of bank-notes.

(2.) Any law imposing differential duties.

(3.) Any law whereby persons who are nationals of any States Members of the League of Nations or of any State to which His Britannic Majesty has agreed by treaty that the same rights should be ensured as it would enjoy if it were a member of the said League, may be subjected or made liable to any disabilities to which persons who are British subjects or nationals of any foreign State are not also subjected or made liable.

(4.) Any special law providing for succession to the Amir's throne, or for the establishment of a Council of Regency.

(5.) Any law whereby the grant of land or money or other donation or gratuity may be made to himself.

(6.) Any law under which the Amir may assume sovereignty over territory outside Trans-Jordan.

(7.) Any law concerning the jurisdiction

of the Civil Courts over foreigners.

(8.) Any law altering, amending or adding to the details of the provisions of the Organic Law.

ART. 7. Except by agreement between the two countries there shall be no customs barrier between Palestine and Trans-Jordan, and the Customs tariff in Trans-Jordan shall be approved by His Britannic Majesty.

The Government of Palestine shall pay to the Trans-Jordan Government the estimated amount of customs duties levied on the part of the goods entering Palestine from territory other than Trans-Jordan which subsequently enters Trans-Jordan for local consumption, but shall be entitled to withhold from the sums to be paid on this account the estimated amount of customs duties levied by Trans-Jordan on that part of the goods entering Trans-Jordan from other than Palestine territory, which subsequently enters Palestine for local consumption. The trade and commerce of Trans-Jordan shall receive at Palestinian Ports equal facilities with the trade and commerce of Palestine.

ART. 8. So far as is consistent with the international obligations of His Britannic Majesty no obstacle shall be placed in the way of the association of Trans-Jordan for customs or other purposes with such neighbouring Arab States as may desire it.

ART. 9. His Highness the Amir undertakes that he will accept and give effect to such reasonable provisions as His Britannic Majesty may consider necessary in judicial matters to safeguard the interests of foreigners.

These provisions shall be embodied in a separate Agreement, which shall be communicated to the Council of the League of Nations, and, pending the conclusion of such Agreement, no foreigner shall be brought before a Trans-Jordan Court without the concurrence of His Britannic Majesty.

His Highness the Amir undertakes that he will accept and give effect to such reasonable provisions as His Britannic Majesty may consider necessary in judicial matters to safeguard the law and jurisdiction with regard to questions arising out of the religious beliefs of the different religious communities.

ART. 10. His Britannic Majesty may maintain armed forces in Trans-Jordan, and may raise, organise and control in Trans-Jordan such armed forces as may in his opinion be necessary for the defence of the country and to assist His Highness the Amir in the preservation of peace and order.

His Highness the Amir agrees that he will not raise or maintain in Trans-Jordan or allow to be raised or maintained any military forces without the consent of His Britannic Majesty.

ART. 11. His Highness the Amir recognises the principle that the cost of the forces required for the defence of Trans-Jordan is a charge on the revenues of that territory. At the coming into force of this Agreement, Trans-Jordan will continue to bear one-sixth of the cost of the Trans-Jordan Frontier Force, and will also bear, as soon as the financial resources of the country permit, the excess of the cost of the British forces stationed in Trans-Jordan, so far as such forces may be deemed by His Britannic Majesty to be employed in respect of Trans-Jordan, over the cost of such forces if stationed in Great Britain, and the whole cost of any forces raised for Trans-Jordan alone.

ART. 12. So long as the revenues of Trans-Jordan are insufficient to meet such ordinary expenses of administration (including any expenditure on local forces for which Trans-Jordan is liable under Article 11) as may be incurred with the approval of His Britannic Majesty, arrangements will be made for a contribution from the British Treasury by way of grant or loan in aid of the revenues of Trans-Jordan. His Britannic Majesty will also arrange for the payment of the excess of the cost of the British forces stationed in Trans-Jordan and deemed by His Britannic Majesty to be employed in respect of Trans-Jordan, insofar and for such time as the revenues of

Trans-Jordan are insufficient to bear such excess.

ART. 13. His Highness the Amir agrees that all such laws, orders or regulations as may from time to time be required by His Britannic Majesty for the purposes of Article 10 shall be adopted and made, and that no laws, orders or regulations shall be adopted or made in Trans-Jordan which may, in the opinion of His Britannic Majesty, interfere with the purposes of that Article.

ART. 14. His Highness the Amir agrees to follow the advice of His Britannic Majesty with regard to the proclamation of Martial Law in all or any part of Trans-Jordan and to entrust the administration of such part or parts of Trans-Jordan as may be placed under Martial Law to such officer or officers of His Britannic Majesty's forces as His Britannic Majesty may nominate. His Highness the Amir further agrees that on the re-establishment of civil government a special law shall be adopted to indemnify the armed forces maintained by His Britannic Majesty for all acts done or omissions or defaults made under Martial Law.

ART. 15. His Britannic Majesty may exercise jurisdiction over all members of the armed forces maintained or controlled by His Britannic Majesty in Trans-Jordan.

For the purposes of this and the five preceding Articles, the term "armed forces" shall be deemed to include civilians attached to or employed with the armed forces.

ART. 16. His Highness the Amir undertakes that every facility shall be provided at all times for the movement of His Britannic Majesty's forces (including the use of wireless and land-line telegraphic and telephonic services and the right to lay land-lines), and for the carriage and storage of fuel, ordnance, ammunition and supplies on the roads, railways and waterways and in the ports of Trans-Jordan.

ART. 17. His Highness the Amir agrees to be guided by the advice of His Britannic Majesty in all matters concerning the granting of concessions, the exploitation of natural resources, the construction and operation of railways, and the raising of loans.

ART. 18. No territory in Trans-Jordan shall be ceded or leased or in any way placed under the control of any foreign Power; this shall not prevent His Highness the Amir from making such arrangements as may be necessary for the accommodation of foreign representatives and for the fulfilment of the provisions of the preceding Articles.

ART. 19. His Highness the Amir agrees that, pending the making of special extradition agreements relating to Trans-Jordan, the Extradition Treaties in force between His Britannic Majesty and foreign Powers shall apply to Trans-Jordan.

ART. 20. This Agreement shall come into force so soon as it shall have been ratified by the High Contracting Parties after its acceptance by the constitutional Government to be set up under Article 2. The constitutional Government shall be deemed to be provisional until the Agreement shall have been so approved. Nothing shall prevent the High Contracting Parties from reviewing from time to time the provisions of this Agreement with a view to any revision which may seem desirable in the circumstances then existing.

ART. 21. The present Agreement has been drawn up in two languages, English and Arabic, and the Plenipotentiaries of each of the High Contracting parties shall sign two English copies and two Arabic copies. Both texts shall have the same validity, but in case of divergence between the two in the interpretation of one or other of the Articles of the present Agreement, the English text shall prevail.

53. PROVISIONAL COMMERCIAL AGREEMENT: THE UNITED STATES AND PERSIA
14 May 1928

[*U.S. Executive Agreement Series,* No. 19]

The American-Persian treaty of 1856 (I, Doc. 69) expired on 10 May 1928 in accordance with Riza Shah's unilateral abrogation of the capitulations (text of circular to foreign legations in Tehran, 10 May 1927, giving one year's notice of intention in *Documents on International Affairs, 1928,* p. 200). The two governments on 14 May 1928 concluded by an exchange of notes between the American Minister in Tehran and the Acting Foreign Minister of Persia a provisional agreement to regulate diplomatic and commercial relations and the treatment of their respective nationals. Only the Persian note appears here, for the two with the necessary changes are substantially identical. The Acting Foreign Minister, in a separate note of the same date (not reproduced), declared that American missionaries "will be authorized to carry on their charitable and educational work on the condition that it contravenes neither the public order nor the laws and regulations of Persia." But later Persian legislation sharply curtailed missionary programs. A further note of 11 July 1928 (*U.S. Executive Agreement Series,* No. 20) stated that, pending a definitive convention, non-Muslim American citizens in Persia "shall be subject to their national laws" in the matter of personal status. But the two governments did not sign any definitive instrument until 1943, when they concluded a reciprocal trade agreement (*U.S. Executive Agreement Series,* No. 410). *Survey of International Affairs, 1928,* pp. 347–58; A. Matine-Daftary, *La Suppression des capitulations en Perse,* chaps. 6–10; E. Groseclose, *Introduction to Iran,* pp. 109–15, 140.

I have the honor to advise you that my Government, animated by the sincere desire to terminate as soon as possible the negotiations now in progress with the Government of the United States relative to the conclusion of a treaty of friendship, as well as establishment, consular, customs, and commercial conventions, has directed me to communicate to you, in its name, the following provisional stipulations:

1. On and after May 10, 1928, the diplomatic representation of the United States of America in Persian territory shall enjoy, on condition of complete reciprocity, the privileges and immunities sanctioned by generally recognized international law.

The consular representatives of the United States of America in Persian territory, duly provided with an exequatur, shall be permitted, on condition of complete reciprocity, to reside there in the localities to which they were admitted up to that time.

They shall enjoy, on the condition of complete reciprocity, the honorary privileges and personal immunities in regard to jurisdiction and fiscal matters sanctioned by generally recognized international law.

2. On and after May 10, 1928, the nationals of the United States in Persia shall on the basis of complete reciprocity be admitted and treated in accordance with the rules and practices of generally recognized international law.

In respect of their persons and property, rights and interests, they shall enjoy there the fullest protection of the laws and the territorial authorities of the country, and they shall not be treated in regard to the above-mentioned matters in a manner less favorable than the nationals of other foreign countries.

They shall enjoy, in every respect, the same general treatment as the nationals of the country, without being entitled, however, to the treatment reserved to nationals alone, to the exclusion of all other foreigners.

Matters of personal status and family law shall be treated in special notes to be drawn up and exchanged as soon as possible.

3. On and after May 10, 1928, and as long as the present provisions shall remain in force, and on condition of complete reciprocity, merchandise produced or manu-

factured in the United States, its territories and possessions, on their entry into Persia, shall enjoy the tariff accorded to the most favored nation, so that the treatment accorded to the United States for its merchandise shall not be less favorable than the legal treatment accorded to a third country.

In respect to the régime applicable to the commerce of the United States of America, in the matter of import and export and other duties and charges relating to commerce, as well as to transit, warehousing, and the facilities accorded to commercial travelers' samples, and as to facilities, tariffs, and quantities in connection with the licensing and prohibition of imports and exports, Persia shall accord to the United States, its territories, and possessions, on condition of complete reciprocity, a treatment not less favorable than that accorded to the commerce of any other foreign country.

It is understood that other or higher duties shall not be applied to the importation into or the sale in Persia of any articles, produced or manufactured in the United States, its territories and possessions, than those which would be payable on like articles produced or manufactured by any other foreign country.

Similarly and on condition of complete reciprocity, no other or higher duties shall be imposed in Persia on the exportation of any articles to the United States, its territories or possessions, than those which would be payable on the exportation of like articles to any other foreign country.

On condition of complete reciprocity, any lowering of duties of any kind that may be granted by Persia in favor of the products of any other country shall be immediately applicable, without request and without compensation, to the commerce of the United States, its territories and possessions, with Persia.

It is understood that these provisions do not refer to the prohibitions and restrictions authorized by the laws and regulations in force in Persia for protection of the food supply, sanitary administration in regard to human, animal, or vegetable life, the interests of public safety and fiscal interests.

The stipulations of the present note shall go into effect to-day and they shall remain respectively in force until the entry into effect of the corresponding treaty and conventions referred to in the first paragraph of this note or until the expiration of a period of thirty days from the notice which may be given to the Government of the United States by my Government of its intention to terminate them, but in case my Government should be prevented from fulfilling its engagements by the effect of a legislative measure, these stipulations shall lapse.

I would be glad to have confirmation of our understanding on these points.

54. THE GROUP (RED LINE) AGREEMENT OF THE TURKISH (IRAQ) PETROLEUM COMPANY
31 July 1928

[U.S., 84th Cong., House of Representatives, Committee on the Judiciary, *Hearings before Antitrust Subcommittee* (Subcommittee No. 5), part 2, pp. 1004–33]

The invitation of 1922 to American oil companies to take part in the Turkish Petroleum (TPC) stirred a hornet's nest. The American "open door" plan (Doc. 30) conflicted with "the self-denying ordinance" (article 10) in TPC's 1914 reorganization arrangement (I, Doc. 111), and TPC's owners—particularly the Compagnie Française des Pétroles (Doc. 57) and Calouste Sarkis Gulbenkian, the beneficiary "five percenter"—were determined not to abandon the restrictive clause. The American proposal that TPC become a nonprofit-making crude oil distributing agency aroused the fury of Gulbenkian, who represented not an operating oil company but his own self-identifying "Participations and Investments, Ltd.," and who was interested therefore not in crude oil but in monetary returns. The American firms—comprising at the start the Atlantic Refining, the Gulf Refining, Mexican

Petroleum, Sinclair Consolidated Oil, Standard Oil of New York, Standard Oil of New Jersey and the Texas companies—created the Near East Development Corporation (NEDC) to represent them as a unit in the TPC transaction. NEDC insisted on a full partnership together with the Anglo-Persian Oil Company (APOC), the Royal Dutch-Shell and Cie. Française des Pétroles, a request that dictated the reallocation of shares. Various schemes were advanced but rejected, since they entailed reducing the shares of the minority owners. In the end APOC was selected, for it boasted a 47.5 per cent interest, the largest single holding. APOC's attitude, however, was precisely the reverse of Gulbenkian's: the British enterprise was interested in crude oil and not monetary payments. But APOC's demand for an overriding royalty—a bonus in the form of a stated percentage of the crude oil produced by TPC—in return for surrendering part of its shares encountered stiff resistance from the remaining corporate owners. Little wonder that the group agreement took six years to consummate, with the foreign offices in Britain, France and the United States at times almost as deeply entangled in the negotiations as the oil companies. Indeed, the negotiations might well have consumed an even longer period, had it not been for the discovery of oil in prodigious quantities on 15 October 1927 at Baba Gurgur just north of Kirkuk in Mosul province, a discovery that immediately shifted the problems from the realm of theory to that of fact. In the same month the French company produced a map of the Near and Middle East marked with a red line around the late Ottoman Empire within its 1914 frontiers, including the entire Arabian Peninsula, its offshore islands, and Cyprus, but excluding Kuwayt and Egypt. The zone enclosed by the red line became "the defined area" within which the self-denying provisions were to operate. The Texas and Sinclair companies withdrew from NEDC and Pan-American Petroleum and Transport replaced Mexican before the discovery of the Baba Gurgur gusher. About 1930 the Standards of New York and New Jersey bought the interests in NEDC of Pan-American Petroleum and Atlantic Refining and in 1934 that of Gulf Refining. Meanwhile, in 1931 Standard of New York merged with Vacuum Oil Company to form what came to be known as the Socony-Vacuum Oil Company. The Red Line Agreement remained formally in effect until November 1948. *International Petroleum Cartel,* chap. 4 (map of Red Line Agreement opposite p. 60); S. H. Longrigg, *Oil in the Middle East,* chap. 5; B. Shwadran, *The Middle East, Oil and the Great Powers,* chap. 9.

An agreement made the Thirty-first day of July 1928 BETWEEN D'ARCY EXPLORATION COMPANY LIMITED a Company incorporated under the Companies Acts 1908 to 1917 whose registered office is situate at Britannic House Finsbury Circus in the City of London (hereinafter called "the D'Arcy Company") of the first part THF ANGLO-SAXON PETROLEUM COMPANY LIMITED a Company incorporated under the Companies Acts 1862 to 1900 whose registered office is situate at St Helens Court Leadenhall Street in the City of London (hereinafter called "the Anglo-Saxon Company") of the second part COMPAGNIE FRANCAISE DES PÉTROLES a Société Anonyme incorporated under the laws of France whose siège social is situate at No. 63 Avenue Victor Emmanuel III Paris in the Republic of France (hereinafter called "the French Company") of the third part NEAR EAST DEVELOPMENT CORPORATION a Company incorporated under the laws of the State of Delaware U.S.A. whose principal office is situate at 26 Broadway New York U.S.A. (hereinafter called "the American Company") of the fourth part PARTICIPATIONS AND INVESTMENTS LIMITED a Company incorporated under the laws of the Dominion of Canada whose principal office is situate at Dominion Bank Building, King Street, Toronto (hereinafter called "the Participations Company") of the fifth part and TURKISH PETROLEUM COMPANY LIMITED a Company incorporated under the Companies (Consolidation) Act 1908 whose registered office is situate at No. 97 Gresham Street in the City of London (hereinafter called "the Turkish Company") of the sixth part

Whereas the Turkish Company was incorporated on the 31st day of January 1911 under the Companies (Consolidation) Act 1908.

And whereas the capital of the Turkish Company is now £2,000,000 divided into

2,000,000 shares of £1 each the whole of which are issued.

And whereas immediately prior to the execution hereof the shares of the Turkish Company were held as follows:

away and sell the same and the derivatives thereof within the areas upon the terms and subject to the provisions and conditions in the Iraq Concession described or contained.

Name of Shareholder.	Serial Number of Shares held.	Total Number of Shares held.
The Anglo-Saxon Petroleum Co. Ltd.	20,001 — 56,000 601,001 — 790,000 1,300,001 — 1,525,000	450,000
Calouste Sarkis Gulbenkian	59,001 — 60,000 595,751 — 601,000 1,250,001 — 1,256,250	12,500
D'Arcy Exploration Co. Ltd.	80,004 — 156,000 160,001 — 558,985 1,525,001 — 1,999,982	949,964
Lloyds Bank City Office Nominees Ltd.	56,001 — 59,000 156,001 — 160,000 559,001 — 580,000 580,001 — 595,750 1,256,251 — 1,281,250 1,281,251 — 1,300,000	87,500
Sir John Buck Lloyd	80,002 558,991 — 558,995 1,999,983 — 1,999,988	12
Compagnie Francaise des Pétroles	1 — 20,000 60,000 — 80,000 790,001 — 1,000,000 1,000,001 — 1,250,000	500,000
Sir John Cadman	80,003 558,996 — 559,000 1,999,989 — 1,999,994	12
Arthur Charles Hearn	80,001 558,986 — 558,990 1,999,995 — 2,000,000	12
		2,000,000

And whereas on the 14th day of March 1925 a Convention (hereinafter called the "Iraq Concession" which expression shall include any extension or modification thereof) was entered into between the Government of Iraq of the one part and the Turkish Company of the other part, whereby the said Government granted to the Turkish Company the exclusive right to explore prospect drill for extract and render suitable for trade petroleum naphtha natural gases and ozokerite and the right to carry

And whereas it has been agreed that the American Company and the Participations Company shall respectively become shareholders in the Turkish Company in manner hereafter appearing.

And whereas from time to time the questions have arisen between the parties hereto or some of them in connection with or arising out of the Turkish Company or its undertaking or business or the engagements or rights of the parties in connection therewith.

And whereas with a view to settling such questions and to codifying for the future their rights and obligations the parties hereto have agreed to enter into these presents.

Now in consideration of the premises it is hereby agreed and declared as follows:—

PRELIMINARY

1. (i) Each of the parties hereto of the first five parts hereby contracts with each of the other of such parties and with the Turkish Company that they will observe and will procure their respective Associated Companies (as hereinafter defined) to observe the provisions of this Agreement and each of the said parties shall be responsible for any breach or non-observance of this Agreement committed by any Associated Company of such party in the same manner and to the same extent as if such breach or non-observance had been committed by such party itself.

(ii) The provisions of this Agreement other than clauses 5 (i) and 26 hereof shall apply only to the area (hereinafter called "the defined area") bordered in red on the map attached hereto as explained by the notes and descriptions set out on such map.

(iii) In this Agreement the expression "Associated Company" as regards each of the parties hereto of the first five parts means and includes:—

(a) Any Company over which such party either alone or in conjunction with any other party or parties hereto and/or in conjunction with one or more Associated Companies of any party hereto can now or hereafter exercise control either directly or indirectly and whether such control be exercisable by means of the possession of a majority of votes or of the right of appointing directors or by contract or in any manner whatsoever whether similar to the above or not.

(b) As regards the American Company each of the Companies specified in Schedule A hereto.

(c) Any Company over which any Associated Company of such party either alone or in conjunction with any one or more Associated Companies of any party hereto can now or hereafter exercise control either directly or indirectly and whether such control be exercisable by means of the possession of a majority of votes or of the right of appointing directors or by contract or in any manner whatsoever whether similar to the above or not.

(iv) The Turkish Company hereby contracts with each of the other parties hereto that it will observe and will procure any General Operating Company formed as hereafter mentioned and any company over which it can now or hereafter exercise control either directly or indirectly and whether such control be exercisable by means of the possession of a majority of votes or of the right of appointing directors or by contract or in any manner whatsoever whether similar to the above or not (all of which Companies are intended to be included in the expression "Associated Company" as applied to the Turkish Company) to observe the provisions of this Agreement, and the Turkish Company shall be responsible for any breach or non-observance of the provisions of this Agreement committed by any Associated Company of the Turkish Company in the same manner and to the same extent as if such breach or non-observance had been committed by the Turkish Company.

A Company shall cease to be an Associated Company of any party hereto within the meaning of these presents if and when and so long as it shall cease to fulfil the conditions contained in this clause and as regards the American Company the Companies specified in Schedule A hereto as Associated Companies of that Company shall cease to be such if and so long as they are not directly or indirectly interested in the American Company.

Provided always that no party hereto shall be held responsible for any breach or non-observance of this Agreement by an Associated Company of such party if such party can shew that it has used its utmost endeavours to prevent such breach or non-observance.

DISTRIBUTION OF CAPITAL OF THE TURKISH COMPANY

2. The share capital of the Turkish Company as at the date hereof shall be redistributed among the parties of the first five parts in the proportions following that is to say:—

	% of Such Capital
The D'Arcy Company (hereinafter called Group A)	23.75
The Anglo-Saxon Company (hereinafter called Group B)	23.75
The French Company (hereinafter called Group C)	23.75
The American Company (hereinafter called Group D)	23.75
The Participations Company (hereinafter called Group E)	5.00
	100.00

Groups A, B, C, D, and E are hereinafter collectively called the "Groups."

3. (i) For the purpose of the last preceding clause immediately upon the execution of this Agreement:—

(a) The D'Arcy Company shall deliver or procure to be delivered to the American Company duly executed and certified transfers of 474,964 shares of the Turkish Company now registered in the name of the D'Arcy Company and 36 like shares now registered as to 12 in the name of the said Sir John Cadman, as to 12 in the name of the said Sir John B. Lloyd and as to 12 in the name of the said A. C. Hearn, against payment by the American Company of the sum of £490.265 5s. 9d. on the First day of August 1928 and will execute and do or procure to be executed and done all documents deeds acts and things necessary for effectually vesting the said shares in the American Company.

(b) The French Company shall deliver to the Anglo-Saxon Company a duly executed and certified transfer of 25,000 shares of the Turkish Company against payment by the Anglo Saxon Company of the sum of £25,948 1s. 3d. on the First day of August 1928 and will execute and do or procure to be executed and done all documents deeds acts and things necessary for effectually vesting the said shares in the Anglo-Saxon Company.

(c) The Participations Company shall procure to be delivered to itself duly executed and certified transfers of 87,500 shares of the Turkish Company now registered in the name of Lloyds Bank City Office Nominees Limited and of 12,500 like shares now registered in the name of Calouste Sarkis Gulbenkian against payment to him of the sum of £103,210 3s. 11d. on the First day of August 1928 and will execute and do and procure to be executed and done all documents deeds acts and things necessary for effectually vesting the said shares in the Participations Company.

BOARD OF DIRECTORS AND GENERAL MEETINGS OF THE TURKISH COMPANY

4. (i) Groups A, B, C and D (each herein termed a "Major Group") shall each be entitled to appoint two Directors on the Board of the Turkish Company and Group E (herein termed "a Minor Group") shall be entitled to appoint one Director.

Provided always that as and when by reason of transfer of shares or by new issues of share capital or otherwise the basic proportion (as hereinafter defined) for the time being of any Major Group falls below 11.875 per cent. the right of representation of such Major Group shall be reduced from two Directors to one Director.

Provided further that should the basic proportion for the time being of any Major Group fall below 5.9375 per cent. such Major Group shall cease to have the rights attaching to a Major Group and shall thereafter only be entitled to such rights as attach to a Minor Group and shall be treated as a Minor Group for all purposes of this Agreement and of the Articles of Association of the Turkish Company.

(ii) In the event of the basic proportion for the time being of any Group falling below 2.5 per cent. such Group shall lose the right of representation by any Director on the Board of the Turkish Company.

(iii) The phrase the "basic proportion" or the "basic proportions," shall wherever used in this Agreement mean the proportion which from time to time the aggregate nominal value of all Ordinary Shares in the Turkish Company and all General Operating Companies (as hereinafter defined) held by each Group bears to the total nominal value of all such Ordinary Shares held by all the Groups. For the purposes of this Agreement a share shall be deemed to be an Ordinary Share if it entitles the holder to dividends at an unlimited rate and Shares which any Group is entitled to subscribe and has subscribed (even if not then allotted) shall be treated for the purposes of this clause as held by such Group. Shares having no nominal value shall be deemed to be of a nominal value equal to the price at which they were first issued by the Company of whose capital they form part.

(iv) Any appointment or removal of Directors by any Group shall be made in writing left at the registered office of the Turkish Company signed by or on behalf of the Group.

(v) In addition to the Directors to be appointed by the Groups one Director may be appointed by the Government of Iraq and the Board may elect not exceeding two persons one to be Chairman of the Board and/or one to be a Managing Director of the Turkish Company.

(vi) All the Directors shall enjoy the same rights and privileges and the Chairman shall not have a casting vote.

(vii) The Articles of Association of the Turkish Company shall forthwith be altered so as to provide that Resolutions at Board Meetings can only be carried if the Directors or one of the Directors appointed by at least three of the Major Groups vote in favour thereof and that no Resolution at a General Meeting of Shareholders shall be carried unless the votes attaching to the Shares then held by at least three of the Major Groups be cast in favour of it.

OPERATING COMPANIES UNDER THE TURKISH COMPANY

5. (i) The Turkish Company except as herein otherwise expressly provided shall not be concerned engaged or interested directly or indirectly in acquiring exploring testing and proving oilfields and operations incidental thereto except within the defined area and a separate Company or Companies shall be constituted to work any field or fields within such area which it shall in accordance with this Agreement be decided to develop or to provide pipe lines storage or other facilities in connection therewith and any such Company is hereinafter referred to as an Operating Company. Neither the Turkish Company nor any Operating Company shall except as herein expressly provided be engaged or interested in the refining or marketing of oil either within or outside the defined area.

(ii) The Turkish Company in exercising its right under the Iraq Concession to select plots shall select plots the area of each of which shall not exceed 8 square miles, and each of which shall if geologically advisable be such that the length thereof shall not exceed twice the breadth.

6. (i) Such Operating Companies shall be of two kinds—General and Special—and shall only be formed with the approval of the Turkish Company and shall immediately after incorporation be made by the Turkish Company to execute under seal a covenant with the Turkish Company and each Group undertaking to be bound by this Agreement so far as applicable to such Company and in particular (in the case of a General Operating Company) to deliver free of cost to the D'Arcy Company any oil produced by such Operating Company the delivery of which to the D'Arcy Company as royalty oil fails to be procured by the parties hereto under Clause 12 hereof and no Company which has not entered into such covenant shall be entitled to be treated as an Operating Company or be eligible for any of the purposes of this Agreement as an Operating Company.

(ii) Prior to the formation of any such Operating Company the Turkish Company shall determine the amount and character of the payment or other form of interest which it shall receive from such Operating Company in consideration of the cession to it by the Turkish Company of its rights properties or concessions or any part thereof provided that the Turkish Company shall make provision for the delivery of the Royalty Oil (if any) due to the D'Arcy Company in respect of selected plots under Clause 12 hereof and provided further that in respect of any plots under Article 6 of the Iraq Concession no other consideration for such cession shall be receivable by the Turkish Company than the amount of the bid by tender paid over to the Turkish Company by the Government of Iraq under the provisions of that Article.

(iii) General Operating Companies shall be so constituted that the voting control at General Meetings thereof shall be vested in the Turkish Company and the Turkish Company shall not in any circumstances part with such control. Special Operating Companies shall as far as legally possible be so constituted that the power to appoint the Directors thereof shall be vested in the Turkish Company.

(iv) The right to subscribe to the first issue of ordinary share capital of Operating Companies shall be offered to the Groups in the basic proportions and shares refused by any of the Groups shall be re-offered among the other Groups in those proportions and according to their desire to take up such shares and so on until all the Groups have been satisfied. Subsequent issues of such ordinary share capital shall be made in accordance with the provisions of clause 9 (i) hereof.

7. (i) A "General Operating Company" shall be

(a) Any Operating Company formed for the purposes of the exploitation of any of the first 24 plots to be selected under Article 5 of the Iraq Concession; (b) Any Operating Company formed for the exploitation of plots under Article 6 of the Iraq Concession or of other concessions in cases in which all the Groups are associated; (c) any Operating Company formed for the construction of pipe lines of storage facilities of port works of refineries or other purposes common to the Turkish Company and all the Groups.

(ii) A "Special Operating Company" shall be one formed in cases in which all the groups may not wish to participate for the exploitation of plots under Article 6 of the Iraq Concession or of other concessions or for other purposes not common to all the Groups.

8. (i) In the election of Directors of every General Operating Company the Turkish Company shall always appoint such persons as to secure that the Board of Directors of that Company shall include persons nominated by the Major and Minor Groups respectively equal in number to their respective nominees on the Board of the Turkish Company if such Groups wish to exercise this right and in the election of Directors of every Special Operating Company the Turkish Company shall if such Groups wish to exercise this right always appoint such persons as to secure that the Board of Directors of that Company shall consist of persons nominated by the Group or Groups participating in the Special Operating Company substantially in proportion to their participation but so that on the Board of Directors of every Special Operating Company there shall always be at least one Director nominated by each Group participating therein on condition that such Group's shareholding interest is not less than 2.5 per cent. of the issued capital of such Special Operating Company.

(ii) The provisions above referred to in clause 4 (vi) and (vii) with regard to method of voting at Board Meetings shall so far as is legally possible equally apply to any General Operating Company as well as to the Turkish Company.

ISSUES OF CAPITAL AND TRANSFERS

9. (i) The provisions in the new Articles of Association of the Turkish Company set out in Schedule C hereto with regard to the offer of shares on any increase of capital to existing shareholders shall so far as legally possible be incorporated in the

constitution of every Operating Company.

(ii) Subject to the making of the transfers of shares referred to in clause 3 hereof the provisions in the said new Articles of Association containing restrictions on transfers of shares shall be maintained and provisions in similar terms containing restrictions on transfers of shares shall so far as legally possible be incorporated in the constitution of every Operating Company.

(iii) No person or Company shall be permitted to become a shareholder in the Turkish Company or any Operating Company except on the basis that such person or Company acknowledges that the Turkish Company or such Operating Company is bound by this Agreement.

CONCESSIONS AND PRODUCTION

10. (i) All the parties hereto agree that the Turkish Company or a nominee of the Turkish Company shall except as hereinafter mentioned have the sole right to seek for or obtain oil concessions within the defined area and each of the Groups hereby covenants and agrees with the Turkish Company and with the other Groups that excepting only as herein provided or authorized such Group will not nor will any of its Associated Companies either personally or through the intermediary of any person firm company or corporation seek for or obtain or be interested directly or indirectly in any such oil concession or be interested directly or indirectly in the production of oil within the defined area or in the purchase of any such oil otherwise than through the Turkish Company or an Operating Company under the Turkish Company. PROVIDED always that as regards any plot offered for completion under Article 6 of the Iraq Concession if the Groups are unanimous in determining to tender for a lease of such plot then a tender for such plot shall be made by a nominee on behalf of the said Groups and if such tender is successful the lease of such plot when acquired shall be transferred forthwith to a General Operating Company in which each Group shall be entitled to be offered its participation in accordance with clause 6 hereof and such General Operating Company shall be entitled to own and operate the said plot free from the restrictions in this sub-clause. If the Groups are not unanimous in determining to tender for a lease of any such plot then if any one or more Groups is in favour of so tendering a nominee of such Group or Groups shall be at liberty to tender for a lease of such plot and if successful in obtaining such a lease such Group or Groups shall procure such nominee forthwith to transfer the same to an Operating Company in which each Group shall be entitled to be offered its participation in accordance with clause 6 hereof.

Provided further that as regards any area other than plots under Article 6 of the Iraq Concession if the Turkish Company does not determine to apply for any oil concession then if any two Groups are in favour of so applying the Turkish Company shall be bound forthwith to grant permission to a nominee of those Groups to seek for and obtain such concession on the terms that if successful such Groups shall forthwith transfer the same to an Operating Company in which each Group shall be entitled to be offered its participation in accordance with clause 6 hereof.

(ii) Without prejudice to any other remedy any lease concession or other interest that may be obtained by any Group in breach of the provisions of this Agreement and all the interest of any person or company or corporation intended to be bound by this Agreement in any such lease concession or interest shall be held in trust for a Special Operating Company in which the Groups (other than the Group committing the breach) shall be entitled to participate in accordance with clause 6 hereof.

11. The American Company and any of its Associated Companies shall as regards any plot offered for competition under Article 6 of the Iraq Concession be entitled to apply for and obtain a lease thereof and if successful it shall, notwithstanding anything contained in clause 10 hereof, not be bound to transfer such plot to an Operating Company but shall be entitled to retain and develop or dispose of the same for its own account. But the American Com-

pany or any of its Associated Companies before so acting shall thirty days before the date fixed for the closing of the tenders give notice in writing to the Turkish Company that it intends to avail itself of the provisions of this clause and shall then within ten days thereafter be entitled to receive similar notice from such of the other Groups as propose to put in tenders pursuant to clause 10 hereof. If the American Company or any of its Associated Companies avails itself of its rights under this clause then it shall notwithstanding anything in this Agreement contained forfeit any right it otherwise might have had to the offer of a participation in any such plot which shall be transferred to a separate Special Operating Company to be formed to operate this particular plot alone.

ROYALTY OIL

12. (i) The parties hereto agree (but as regards the Groups only so far as their powers as shareholders of the Turkish Company and any General Operating Company or through the right to nominate Directors permit) to procure the delivery free of cost to the D'Arcy Company but subject to the provisions hereinafter contained of ten per cent. (hereinafter called royalty oil) of all crude oil produced by any General Operating Company from 24 plots in Iraq each identical with a plot of such General Operating Company such plots to be selected by the D'Arcy Company at its option either within one month after the ultimate date at which the Turkish Company itself shall make its final selection of 24 plots under Article 5 of the Iraq Concession or within one month after the order is given by the Turkish Company through a General Operating Company for the construction of a pipeline to the Mediterranean and up to either of those dates the D'Arcy Company may relinquish any plot previously selected and may select in place thereof any other plot worked or taken up by any General Operating Company. Provided that if the D'Arcy Company shall relinquish any plot previously selected and select in place thereof any other plot, the D'Arcy Company shall be debited with any royalty oil it may have received from the plot first selected against any royalty oil it would have been entitled to from the plot so substituted if it had originally selected such plot.

(ii) Delivery of royalty oil shall be made in respect of each selected plot at the gathering station or stations for such plot and not at the wells' mouth it being the intention of the parties hereto that the royalty oil shall be drawn from each selected plot in proportion to the oil produced therefrom and that the cost of producing such oil and transporting the same to the nearest available gathering station shall be borne by the Turkish Company or any one or more General Operating Companies as the case may be but that the cost of transporting such oil from the gathering station to any other destination shall be borne by the D'Arcy Company.

(iii) In calculating the royalty oil to be delivered to the D'Arcy Company there shall be deducted from the total oil produced from each selected plot:—

(a) All water and foreign substances provided that neither the Turkish Company nor any General Operating Company shall be under any obligation to separate such water and foreign substances or any of them from such oil and

(b) All oil lost up to the point of delivery to the D'Arcy Company including all oil which the Turkish Company or any General Operating Company working the plot from which it is produced may be bound to supply free in compensation for damage to native wells caused by operations on such plot.

(c) All oil produced by any General Operating Company in Iraq and used in connection with the operations on any such plot up to the point of delivery to the D'Arcy Company.

(iv) Royalty oil shall rank proportionately with all other oil produced by General Operating Companies in respect of rights to and cost of transport or other facilities provided by the Turkish Company or by any General Operating Company.

WORKING AGREEMENT

13. (i) The Turkish Company hereby agrees with each of the Groups that it will offer or procure the Operating Company producing or purchasing the same to offer all crude oil whether purchased by the Turkish Company or produced or purchased by any Operating Company which is available for sale (exclusive of the royalty oil deliverable to the D'Arcy Company under the provisions hereinbefore contained) to the Groups for purchase by them upon the terms and conditions following that is to say:—

(a) The Turkish Company shall be responsible for the division of all such oil amongst the Groups and shall in this connection supervise the relations between the Groups and conduct all correspondence and keep all accounts and for so doing shall receive the sums referred to in sub-clauses (iii) (b) (4) (iv) (b) and (v) hereof.

(b) Such oil shall be offered to the Groups in the basic proportions as existing when the offer is made but oil from any Special Operating Company shall be offered to those Groups which have contributed to the subscribed ordinary share capital of such Special Operating Company in the proportion in which such Groups are interested in such Special Operating Company.

(c) Delivery shall (subject to pipe-line facilities being available and subject to the provisions of this Agreement) be made in cargo lots if so desired at each Group's option either on board a vessel or vessels or into such Group's own storage tanks either at the Mediterranean terminal of the pipe-line or in case the Turkish Company through a General Operating Company shall provide a pipe-line to any other terminal or terminals then at such terminal or terminals or partly at one and partly at the other as nearly as possible in proportion to the quantities available at such terminals. Provided always that if the pipeline capacity is available and subject to the rights of other users delivery may be effected at each Group's option wholly at any available terminal or in such proportions at different terminals subject as aforesaid as each Group may desire.

(d) On or before the first day of each quarter of the year the Turkish Company shall notify each of the Groups of the estimated quantity of crude oil and/or refined products (if any) and of the source from which the oil will be derived in each case which the Group notified will be entitled to purchase during (a) the quarter beginning three calendar months after the due date for giving such notice and (b) each of the three succeeding quarters.

(e) Not later than fifteen days after the first day of each quarter or the receipt of such notice whichever shall be the later each Group shall notify the Turkish Company of the quantity (not exceeding the amount so offered) and particulars of the source of production of the oil which such Group will purchase during the next succeeding quarter notifying at the same time the approximate dates places and methods of delivery desired which quantity shall be as nearly as possible equally spread over the quarter. Any Group which fails to notify the Turkish Company in accordance with this sub-paragraph of the quantity which it elects to purchase shall be deemed to have declined such quantity. Provided always that so far as the Participations Company is concerned the period within which such Group shall notify the Turkish Company as aforesaid shall be 18 days instead of 15 days and in the event of the four Major Groups declining the whole of the oil offered to them the Turkish Company shall forthwith notify the Participations Company.

(f) Payment for all quantities delivered during any calendar month shall be due and payable on the last day of the following calendar month to the Turkish Company in London or other place agreed by the Turkish Company in sterling or other currency agreed by the Turkish Company. The Turkish Company will effect the distribution of the payments to the Operating Companies concerned. Any payment in arrear shall carry interest at the rate of £10 per centum per annum.

(g) Any Group which at any time is in

arrear in its payments under this clause or otherwise in default under this agreement (including in particular default under clause 12) shall without prejudice to any other remedies lose its right to receive oil under this clause so long as it is in arrear or in default and also during the remainder of the quarter during which such default occurred and during the whole of the quarter in which such arrears are paid off or default made good and shall forfeit all quantities it would have been entitled to purchase or receive during such period which quantities shall be offered to the other Groups not in arrear or default.

(h) Any Group which has failed during any quarter to take delivery of the quantity which it notified the Turkish Company it would take shall automatically forfeit the right to receive any balance of which it has not taken delivery and shall be debited with any loss sustained by the Turkish Company or any Operating Company as a result of its failure to take delivery.

(i) The Turkish Company shall as soon as reasonably possible offer or procure to be offered to the Groups which have accepted their full quotas any quantities not accepted in accordance with sub-paragraph (e) or forfeited in accordance with sub-paragraphs (g) and (h) of this sub-clause or any oil in excess of the estimate under sub-paragraph (d) of this sub-clause and each Group shall notify the Turkish Company within ten days after receipt of such offer of the maximum quantity of such additional oil that it is willing to purchase during the following quarter and so on until all the Groups shall have been satisfied and the provisions of the foregoing sub-paragraphs shall apply as nearly as possible to any offer or acceptance of any quantities under this sub-paragraph.

(ii) In case there shall remain for delivery during the next succeeding quarter after complying with the provisions of sub-paragraphs (e) to (i) inclusive of sub-clause (i) of this clause any surplus oil which none of the Groups is willing to purchase then and in that case only the Turkish Company shall be at liberty to dispose of such surplus to any other person or persons and in case the Turkish Company shall find it impossible to sell such surplus at a price arrived at in accordance with the provisions of sub-clause (iii) hereof then such surplus shall before being sold to any other person or persons at any lower price first be offered at such lower price to the Groups in the basic proportions and the provisions of sub-clause (i) shall apply to such subsequent offer as nearly as may be.

(iii) The price at which the crude oil produced by each General Operating Company and available for division among all the Groups shall be offered under sub-clause (i) of this clause in the first instance to the Groups shall be determined half-yearly in the following manner:—

(a) For the first two quarters in each calendar year the cost f.o.b. seaboard terminal for the first half of the previous year shall be the basis and for the last two quarters of each calendar year the cost f.o.b. seaboard terminal for the second half of the previous year shall be the basis. Provided that until the above scale can be applied the basis shall be a figure to be estimated by the Board of the Turkish Company and calculated as nearly as possible to be the cost f.o.b. seaboard terminal for the quarter in question. The price shall in each case be calculated for each General Operating Company separately.

(b) The cost f.o.b. at the seaboard terminal referred to in paragraph (a) above shall include:—

(1) The cost of production to each General Operating Company of the oil at the gathering station on the field including royalties and the cost of production of royalty oil (where applicable) and overhead expenses.

(2) The cost of services rendered by General Operating Companies such as transport by the main pipe-lines—storage facilities at the gathering stations and at the terminal—anchorage for steamers—pumpage and port works—dehydrating plant—common refinery and similar facilities which for the purpose of this Agreement it may be agreed to provide for ends common to the

Turkish Company and all the Groups such cost to be determined in the manner set out below.

(3) Charges for services if any rendered by Special Operating Companies or third parties.

(4) An additional sum to be fixed by the Board of the Turkish Company not exceeding 5/-per ton.

In determining for the purposes of this clause the cost of production at a gathering station and the cost of the services above mentioned allowance shall be made for reasonable depreciation and repayment of capital having regard to the probable life of the fields, plant and other installations together with interest at £6 per centum per annum on the amount shown in the capital account year by year.

The accounts of the Turkish Company and its General Operating Companies shall be audited annually by the same Auditors who shall be Chartered Accountants and who in addition to the usual audit shall determine and certify the cost f.o.b. at the seaboard terminal as above mentioned and their certificate shall be final.

(iv) (a). The rights of user of the Groups of the available capacity of any particular common facility such as is contemplated in sub-clause (iii) (b) (2) above.

(i) When the Groups are associated in any General Operating Company shall be in the proportions in which they are from time to time in fact taking the oil.

(ii) When any of the Groups are associated in any Special Operating Company shall be a right attaching to such Special Operating Company which right shall extend only to the balance of any such available capacity after the requirements (as determined under sub-clause (i) above) of all the Groups when associated in any General Operating Company have been met and shall for each such Special Operating Company be in the proportion which the oil production of that Special Operating Company bears to the aggregate oil production of all Special Operating Companies who can make commercial use of any such particular common facility and within any such Special Operating Company its facilities shall be available to the participants therein in the proportion in which they are from time to time in fact taking such oil.

(b) The basis of charge to any Special Operating Company for the use of the above common facilities and the additional sum as in sub-clause (iii) (b) (4) above shall be determined by the Turkish Company prior to the formation of each Special Operating Company provided that for all Special Operating Companies operating in Iraq the additional sum shall be identical and for all Special Operating Companies there shall be an identical basis of charge for the use of identical common facilities.

(v). The Turkish Company or a General Operating Company shall alone have the right to purchase on any field any crude oil available for purchase. The price at which crude oil purchased by the Turkish Company or any General Operating Company shall be offered to the Groups shall be the cost to the Turkish Company or such Operating Company at the place of delivery plus cost of delivery therefrom to f.o.b. vessel or terminal storage tanks as referred to in sub-clause (i) (c) plus an additional sum not exceeding 2/6 per ton. such cost to be certified by the Auditors of the Turkish Company, whose certificate shall be final.

PIPE-LINE

14. (i) As soon as sufficient oil production has been secured to justify in the opinion of the Board of the Turkish Company the construction of a trunk pipe-line the Turkish Company shall proceed through one or more of its General Operating Companies with the construction of a pipe-line to a Mediterranean port including the necessary gathering lines.

(ii) In the event of the pipe-line facilities reserved for the transportation of oil by lessees pursuant to Article 6 of the Iraq Concession falling materially short of the production obtained by lessees and requiring transportation through the said pipeline system and if there should be no General Operating Company willing or able to find the capital required to build additional pipe-line facilities then any Special Operating Company or any Group who may desire that the additional pipe-line facilities shall be provided may require the Turkish Company through a General Operating Company to proceed as rapidly as reasonably possible with the construction of such additional facilities provided that any such Special Operating Company or Group provides the whole of the capital required on a basis which will not subject the Turkish Company or its General Operating Company as the case may be to any liability in connection therewith in excess of the net profits to arise from the use of such additional pipe-line facilities the whole of which net profits shall be applied in payment of interest on and repayment of the said capital. Such additional pipe-line facilities shall when provided be reserved by the Turkish Company or its General Operating Company exclusively when required for the transportation of oil belonging to the Special Operating Company or Group which shall have supplied the capital until such capital with interest and a premium of twenty-five per centum shall have been repaid in full. The additional pipe-line facilities shall be the property of the said General Operating Company but the capital advanced with the said premium thereon shall if required by the Special Operating Company or Group providing the same or by the Turkish Company be secured by a first charge thereon until repaid by the General Operating Company out of the net profits as aforesaid.

15. (i) The location of the Mediterranean terminal of the trunk pipe-line shall be selected by the Turkish Company at a place where sufficient land can be acquired by a General Operating Company upon which to construct its own seaboard terminal and upon which land each of the Groups for itself or for one or more of its Associated Companies may if desired and according to the basic proportions of such Group but adequately for normal commercial requirements in each case take leases of land for their respective refineries or storage plants. The ownership of all such land shall at all times be retained by the Turkish Company or a General Operating Company.

(ii) The Turkish Company shall through a General Operating Company provide at the Mediterranean terminal of its pipe-line reasonable and adequate facilities having regard to the production including storage tanks suitable loading facilities anchorage for steamers awaiting loading and pipe-line facilities connecting the individual plants (if any) of the Groups with the pipe-line terminal and with the terminal wharves and loading berths of the Operating Companies.

(iii) The provisions of this clause shall apply *mutatis mutandis* to any other terminal of a trunk pipe-line which may be constructed by the Turkish Company through a General Operating Company.

REFINING

16. (i) Within the area in which the Turkish Company is under an obligation to refine or supply oil for local markets under the Iraq Concession the Turkish Company or a General Operating Company shall alone have the right to refine oil in such area but the Turkish Company or a General Operating Company shall not refine in excess of the consumption of such area and none of the Groups nor any of their Associated Companies shall be at liberty to refine oil in such area and each of the Groups agrees with the other parties hereto and each of them that (excepting only as herein expressly provided) such Group will not nor will any of its Associated Companies directly or indirectly be engaged or interested (except through the Turkish Company or an Operating Company) in the refining of oil in such area but nothing herein contained shall preclude any of the Groups or any of their Associated Companies from owning or operating refineries at the terminus of any main pipe-line at a point accessible to Tank ships.

(ii) With the consent in writing of all the Major Groups for the time being the Turkish Company may through a General Operating Company erect and operate refineries at any point accessible to Tank ships

(a) for the refining of such oil as may be offered to the Groups under the provisions of clause 13 hereof and as may not be from time to time purchased by them or any of them and/or

(b) for the refining of oil on account of any or all the Groups but so that all Groups shall have the same rights in the basic proportions to have oil refined for their account.

(iii) All products refined under the preceding sub-clause (ii) (a) shall in the first instance be offered on equal terms to the Groups in the basic proportions.

Except as above authorized or in fulfillment of any obligation under any concession to be granted to it, neither the Turkish Company nor any Operating Company shall be concerned engaged or interested directly or indirectly in the refining of oil.

MARKETING

17. Within the area in which the Turkish Company is under an obligation to supply oil for local markets under the Iraq Concession the Turkish Company or a General Operating Company shall alone have the right to market in such area the oil or the products of the oil obtained under the Iraq Concession and none of the Groups nor any of their Associated Companies shall be at liberty to market any such oil or any product thereof in such area and each of the Groups agrees with the other parties and each of them that neither it nor any of its Associated Companies will directly or indirectly except through the Turkish Company or a General Operating Company be engaged or interested in the marketing of such oil and products in such area.

Except as above authorized or in fulfilment of any obligation under any concession to be granted to it neither the Turkish Company nor any Operating Company shall be concerned engaged or interested directly or indirectly in the marketing of oil.

ASSIGNMENT OF INTEREST

18. (i) None of the Groups shall be entitled to assign its interest under this Agreement, unless

(a) such assignment shall relate to the whole of the interest hereunder of the Group (hereinafter called "the Assignor Group") assigning its interest.

(b) such assignment shall be to a Company (hereinafter called the "Assignee Company") the shareholders in which are at the date of assignment identical with the shareholders for the time being in the Assignor Group, and

(c) the Assignee Company shall contemporaneously with such assignment enter into a contract with all the parties hereto other than the Assignor Group and with each of them agreeing to be bound by all the provisions of this Agreement in the same way as if it had been a party hereto in the place of the Assignor Group, and

(d) the Assignor Group shall contemporaneously with such assignment as aforesaid transfer to the Assignee Company all shares, debentures or other securities or interests whatsoever of the Assignor Group of and in the Turkish Company and every Operating Company

and the parties hereto may refuse to recognise the title of any assignee in respect of any assignment unless all the provisions of this sub-clause shall have been complied with. Provided always that in the event of any Group desiring to assign its whole interest under this Agreement on terms which comply with the foregoing conditions the other Groups shall waive any right they may have under the Articles of Association of the Turkish Company or any Operating Company in connection with such assignment to purchase the share of the Assignor Group in the Turkish Company or any Operating Company and Provided further that nothing in this Agreement contained shall be deemed in any way to restrict the right of any holder of shares in any Company a party hereto to transfer such shares.

(ii) In case the Turkish Company shall assign any part of its concession rights it shall obtain from the assignee a formal undertaking entered into with the parties hereto and with each of them to accede to and become bound by the provisions of this Agreement.

MISCELLANEOUS PROVISIONS

19. (i) The Turkish Company and all General Operating Companies shall on request furnish to each of the Groups all such geological reports and information as may come into its or their possession relating to the subject matter of this Agreement and shall not communicate to any Group information of any kind without on request giving the like information to each and every one of them and like duties shall rest upon all Special Operating Companies with regard to such Groups as participate therein.

(ii) It is hereby agreed that so far as arrangements can properly be made without prejudicing the rights of the Turkish Company or any of its Operating Companies or any of the parties hereto the business of the Turkish Company and its Operating Companies shall so far as reasonably possible be so conducted as to avoid multiple taxation.

FORCE MAJEURE

20. (i) If any party hereto by reason of any cause whatsoever beyond the control of such party commits any breach of this Agreement such party and any party or parties hereto liable jointly with such party shall to the extent to which breach is due to such cause be relieved from liability therefor.

(ii) No cause shall be deemed beyond the control of any party if it was within the control of such party's Associated Companies or in the case of the Turkish Company of the Turkish Company's General Operating Companies.

ARTICLES OF ASSOCIATION

21. The Groups shall use all their voting power and influence and rights for the purpose of procuring

(a) The adoption of the new Article of Association of the Turkish Company set out in Schedule C hereto

(b) The incorporation in the constitution of every General Operating Company of the Turkish Company of provisions of a like character so far as legally possible to those contained in Articles 3, 4, 8, 9, 11, 12, 13, 34, 35, 36, 56, 62, 74, 88, 89, 97, 98, 99 and 100 of the Articles of Association of the Turkish Company and such as shall enable this Agreement to be carried into effect.

(c) The incorporation in the constitution of every Special Operating Company of the Turkish Company of provisions of a like character so far as legally possible to those contained in articles 11, 12, 13, 35 and 36 of the Articles of Association of the Turkish Company and such as shall enable this Agreement to be carried into effect.

(d) That at no time without the consent of all the Groups shall Articles 3, 4, 8, 9, 11, 12, 13, 34, 35, 36, 56, 62, 69, 70, 71, 74, 88, 89, 97, 98, 99 and 100 of the Articles of Association of the Turkish Company or the corresponding Articles of any General Operating Company of the Turkish Company be modified or amended.

DURATION

22. This Agreement shall remain in force so long as the Turkish Company shall continue in existence and/or so long as any concessions granted or hereafter to be granted to the Turkish Company or any of its Operating Companies continue to remain in force and shall be deemed to be a separate contract in respect of the obligations imposed on the parties hereto in reference to each separate year.

JURISDICTION AND INTERPRETATION

23. (i) The parties hereto are for the purposes of this Agreement to be deemed to be domiciled in the City of London at the addresses following:—

The D'Arcy Company at Britannic House, Finsbury Circus, London E.C.2.

The Anglo-Saxon Company at St. Helen's Court, Leadenhall Street, London, E.C.3.

The French Company at the office of Messrs. Denton, Hall & Burgin, Solicitors, or of their successors in business.

The American Company at the office of

Messrs. Piesse & Sons, Solicitors, or of their successors in business.

The Participations Company at the office of Messrs. Freshfield, Leese & Munns, Solicitors, or of their successors in business.

The Turkish Company at 97 Gresham Street, London, E.C. 2. and the parties hereto hereby submit to the jurisdiction of the English Courts and agree that any summons writ or other process and any notice requiring to be served on them respectively may be served at the said respective addresses and that the persons named are respectively authorised to accept service and that such service shall be deemed to be good service on them respectively.

(ii) Provided always that any party hereto may at any time and from time to time during the currency of this Agreement by notice in writing to the Turkish Company change the name and address of the party above-mentioned as authorised to accept service on its behalf by substituting therefor the name of some other party at an address within the City or County of London in England and after any such notice has been served this Agreement shall be read as if the name of such party and address had been substituted for that above-mentioned as regards the party giving the said notice.

(iii) Any summons writ or other process or any notice requiring to be served on any party may be served by delivering the same or by posting the same in London in a prepaid registered letter addressed to the said party at the aforesaid address and the same shall be deemed to have been served on the day after that on which it was so posted.

24. This Agreement shall be construed according to and be governed by English Law.

ARBITRATION

25. If any question or dispute shall arise between the parties hereto or between any one or more of them or between any one or more of them on the one hand and other or others of them on the other hand in anyway arising out of or in connection with this Agreement or as to the true meaning or construction thereof or as to the rights or liabilities of any of the parties hereto and if it shall be decided by the parties at variance to resolve their difference by arbitration then such question or dispute shall be referred to the decision of a sole arbitrator to be agreed upon or failing agreement to be nominated by a judge of the High Court of Justice in England and the decision of such arbitrator shall be final and binding upon all parties to the arbitration. The provisions of the Arbitration Act 1889 and of any statutory modification thereof in force shall apply to any such arbitration.

WAIVER OF CLAIMS

26. As from the date hereof this Agreement shall be deemed to contain all the existing contractual rights of any party hereto against any other party or other parties hereto in connection with the defined area and/or in connection with the Turkish Company and each party hereto waives as against every other party hereto any claim whatsoever which it or he may have or claim to have arising out of or in connection with any pre-existing contract or arrangement or alleged contract or arrangement in connection with such area and/or the Turkish Company.

In Witness whereof the parties hereto have respectively executed these presents the day and year first above written.

55. TREATY OF FRIENDSHIP AND COMMERCE: THE USSR AND YEMEN
1 November 1928

(Ratifications exchanged, San'a, 24 June 1929; renewed in 1939 and on 31 October 1955)

[*British and Foreign State Papers,* vol. 129, pp. 949–51]

Even in tsarist days Russia never developed extensive relations with, or special interests in, the Arabian Peninsula. In an obvious effort to embarrass Britain, the USSR granted *de jure* recognition to ibn Sa'ud as king of the Hijaz on 11 February 1926, just one month after he had acquired the title, and three years later elevated its consul general at Jiddah to the rank of minister. In each instance the United Kingdom and other European powers followed suit. The treaty with Yemen, reproduced below, served a similar purpose of annoying the United Kingdom in an area which it regarded as a British sphere of influence. After a full decade of halting trade relations, the USSR in 1938 abruptly withdrew its diplomatic and financial missions from the two independent kingdoms of the Arabian Peninsula. V. Conolly, *Soviet Trade from the Pacific to the Levant,* chaps. 7–8; H. St. J. Philby, *Sa'udi Arabia,* chap. 11, passim; G. Kirk, *The Middle East in the War,* pp. 487–89.

In conformity with the goodwill and wishes of the Government of the Union of Soviet Socialist Republics on the one part and of His Majesty the King of the Yemen, the Imam Yahia, the son of the Imam Mohammed Hamideddin, and his Government, on the other, and the efforts of both parties to establish normal official relations, and also to lay the foundations of economic intercourse between the two countries, and to promote the development of such intercourse; and based also on the grounds of sincerity in the establishment of friendly relations between the two Governments and their peoples, and on the recognition of the mutual equality of the parties in everything that concerns the rights and general circumstances that exist between the countries and peoples;

The above-mentioned parties have agreed to conclude this treaty of friendship and commerce, and to regard it as a preliminary step towards those negotiations for the conclusion of the requisite agreements that future circumstances may make necessary consequent on the measure of the development and expansion of the economic connexions between the two countries, such as those concerning commerce or others on which both parties shall have agreed. At the present time they have agreed to the following:—

1. The Government of the U.S.S.R. recognise the complete and absolute independence of the Government of the Yemen region and its King, His Majesty the Imam Yahia, the son of the Imam Mohammed Hamideddin, and his sovereignty. His Majesty the King of the Yemen and his Government value the sincere disposition and noble sentiments which the Government of the U.S.S.R. cherish towards the Yemen State and its people, and also towards the other nations of the East. And therefore between the contracting parties there have been established official relations in harmony with the preamble stated above.

2. The contracting parties undertake to facilitate commercial intercourse between the two States. In accordance with this undertaking the nationals of both parties shall have the right, after receiving permission for that purpose, to enter into the territory of the other State, and in accordance with its laws to stay there, occupying themselves with commerce and carrying out all necessary activities on condition that all cases which may arise between the nationals of the two parties shall be decided by the local courts of the State in which they are, and in accordance with its legislation.

Trade in goods that are prohibited by the laws of one of the parties may be forbidden, and the goods confiscated by either of the Governments should such be found within its territory.

The contracting parties undertake to assist in granting every facility compatible with local legislation in respect of the taxes and customs duties on the goods belonging to the nationals of the two States.

3. This treaty shall enter into force and be applied by both Governments after it has been signed and ratified by the Government of the U.S.S.R. in the customary official manner, with effect from the day when His Majesty the King of Yemen, the Imam Yahia, receives an official intimation from the above-mentioned Government.

4. This treaty of friendship and commerce shall continue in force and be applied for a period of 10 years, reckoning from the date specified in article 3. On the expiration of that period, the continuance of the treaty or its replacement by another shall depend on the wish of both contracting parties, and on whatsoever agreement they may arrive at in the future.

5. This treaty of friendship and commerce is called "the Treaty of Sanaa."

It consists of a preamble, the conclusion that follows below, and 5 articles, including the present one. It is drawn up in the Arabic language in two copies, which have to be exchanged between the two contracting parties.

56. TREATY OF PREFERENTIAL ALLIANCE: THE UNITED KINGDOM AND IRAQ
30 June 1930

(Ratifications exchanged, Baghdad, 26 January 1931; superseded, 5 April 1955, by United Kingdom's accession to Turco-Iraqi Pact)

[Great Britain, *Parliamentary Papers, 1931,* Treaty Series No. 15, Cmd. 3797]

The significance of the Anglo-Iraqi treaty of 1930 stemmed from the fact that it provided for the termination of a mandate—the first such example, followed in the Near and Middle East only in Transjordan sixteen years later—and established a new pattern of Anglo-Arab relations. If Britain was prepared to surrender its mandate by 1930, it arrived at this position reluctantly, only after the painful experience of persistent agitation among nationalists in the trust territory and a wide segment of the public in England. The instrument itself—based in its main principles on the draft of an Anglo-Egyptian treaty of 7–8 May 1930 (text in *Parliamentary Papers, 1930,* Egypt No. 1, Cmd. 3575, pp. 35–38) that Egypt rejected because of disagreement over the projected clause on the Sudan—assured the United Kingdom a preferential status in Iraq. For the duration of the alliance Britain was allowed to retain two air bases (at al-Shu'aybah in the vicinity of Basrah and at al-Habbaniyah near Baghdad) and to make use of all Iraqi facilities for the transit of British armed forces (land, naval and air). Under accompanying notes (not reproduced) British ambassadors in Baghdad were to enjoy "precedence in relation to the [diplomatic] representatives of other Powers," and the Iraq government undertook to request a British advisory military mission and normally to engage, in consultation with Whitehall, "British subjects when in need of the services of foreign officials." The twenty-five year treaty, which became operative on Iraq's admission to membership in the League of Nations on 3 October 1932, proved vital to the United Kingdom in the Near and Middle East campaigns of World War II. P. W. Ireland, *'Iraq,* chaps. 22–23; S. H. Longrigg, *'Iraq 1900 to 1950,* chaps. 6–7; M. Khadduri, *Independent Iraq,* chap. 11; *Survey of International Affairs, 1934,* pp. 109–216.

ART. 1. There shall be perpetual peace and friendship between His Britannic Majesty and His Majesty the King of 'Iraq.

There shall be established between the High Contracting Parties a close alliance in consecration of their friendship, their cordial understanding and their good relations, and there shall be full and frank consultation between them in all matters of foreign policy which may affect their common interests.

Each of the High Contracting Parties undertakes not to adopt in foreign countries an attitude which is inconsistent with the alliance or might create difficulties for the other party thereto.

ART. 2. Each High Contracting Party will be represented at the Court of the other High Contracting Party by a diplomatic representative duly accredited.

ART. 3. Should any dispute between 'Iraq and a third State produce a situation which involves the risk of a rupture with that State, the High Contracting Parties will concert together with a view to the settlement of the said dispute by peaceful means in accordance with the provisions of the Covenant of the League of Nations and of any other international obligations which may be applicable to the case.

ART. 4. Should, notwithstanding the provisions of Article 3 above, either of the High Contracting Parties become engaged in war, the other High Contracting Party will, subject always to the provisions of Article 9 below, immediately come to his aid in the capacity of an ally. In the event of an imminent menace of war the High Contracting Parties will immediately concert together the necessary measures of defence. The aid of His Majesty the King of 'Iraq in the event of war or the imminent menace of war will consist in furnishing to His Britannic Majesty on 'Iraq territory all facilities and assistance in his power including the use of railways, rivers, ports, aerodromes and means of communication.

ART. 5. It is understood between the High Contracting Parties that responsibility for the maintenance of internal order in 'Iraq and, subject to the provisions of Article 4 above, for the defence of 'Iraq from external aggression rests with His Majesty the King of 'Iraq. Nevertheless His Majesty the King of 'Iraq recognises that the permanent maintenance and protection in all circumstances of the essential communications of His Britannic Majesty is in the common interest of the High Contracting Parties. For this purpose and in order to facilitate the discharge of the obligations of His Britannic Majesty under Article 4 above His Majesty the King of 'Iraq undertakes to grant to His Britannic Majesty for the duration of the Alliance sites for air bases to be selected by His Britannic Majesty at or in the vicinity of Basra and for an air base to be selected by His Britannic Majesty to the west of the Euphrates. His Majesty the King of 'Iraq further authorises His Britannic Majesty to maintain forces upon 'Iraq territory at the above localities in accordance with the provisions of the Annexure of this Treaty on the understanding that the presence of those forces shall not constitute in any manner an occupation and will in no way prejudice the sovereign rights of 'Iraq.

ART. 6. The Annexure hereto shall be regarded as an integral part of the present Treaty.

ART. 7. This Treaty shall replace the Treaties of Alliance signed at Baghdad on the tenth day of October, One thousand nine hundred and twenty-two of the Christian Era, corresponding to the nineteenth day of Safar, One thousand three hundred and forty-one, Hijrah, and on the thirteenth day of January, One thousand nine hundred and twenty-six, of the Christian Era, corresponding to the twenty-eighth day of Jamadi-al-Ukhra, One thousand three hundred and forty-four, Hijrah, and the subsidiary agreements thereto, which shall cease to have effect upon the entry into force of this Treaty. It shall be executed in duplicate, in the English and Arabic languages, of which the former shall be regarded as the authoritative version.

ART. 8. The High Contracting Parties recognise that, upon the entry into force of this Treaty, all responsibilities devolving under the Treaties and Agreements referred to in Article 7 hereof upon His Britannic Majesty in respect of 'Iraq will, in so far as His Britannic Majesty is concerned, then automatically and completely come to an end, and that such responsibilities, in so far as they continue at all, will devolve upon His Majesty the King of 'Iraq alone.

It is also recognised that all responsibilities devolving upon His Britannic Majesty in respect of 'Iraq under any other international instrument, in so far as they continue at all, should similarly devolve upon His Majesty the King of 'Iraq alone, and the High Contracting Parties shall immediately take such steps as may be necessary to secure the transference to His Majesty the King of 'Iraq of these responsibilities.

ART. 9. Nothing in the present Treaty is intended to or shall in any way prejudice the rights and obligations which devolve, or may devolve, upon either of the High Contracting Parties under the Covenant of the League of Nations or the Treaty for the Renunciation of War signed at Paris on the twenty-seventh day of August, One thousand nine hundred and twenty-eight.

ART. 10. Should any difference arise relative to the application or the interpretation of this Treaty and should the High Contracting Parties fail to settle such difference by direct negotiation, then it shall be dealt with in accordance with the provisions of the Covenant of the League of Nations.

ART. 11. This Treaty shall be ratified and ratifications shall be exchanged as soon as possible. Thereafter it shall come into force as soon as 'Iraq has been admitted to membership of the League of Nations.

The present Treaty shall remain in force for a period of twenty-five years from the date of its coming into force. At any time after twenty years from the date of the coming into force of this Treaty, the High Contracting Parties will, at the request of either of them, conclude a new Treaty which shall provide for the continued maintenance and protection in all circumstances of the essential communications of His Britannic Majesty. In case of disagreement in this matter the difference will be submitted to the Council of the League of Nations. . . .

ANNEXURE TO TREATY OF ALLIANCE

1. The strength of the forces maintained in 'Iraq by His Britannic Majesty in accordance with the terms of Article 5 of this Treaty shall be determined by His Britannic Majesty from time to time after consultation with His Majesty the King of 'Iraq.

His Britannic Majesty shall maintain forces at Hinaidi for a period of five years after the entry into force of this Treaty in order to enable His Majesty the King of 'Iraq to organise the necessary forces to replace them. By the expiration of that period the said forces of His Britannic Majesty shall have been withdrawn from Hinaidi. It shall be also open to His Britannic Majesty to maintain forces at Mosul for a maximum period of five years from the entry into force of this Treaty. Thereafter it shall be open to His Britannic Majesty to station his forces in the localities mentioned in Article 5 of this Treaty, and His Majesty the King of 'Iraq will grant to His Britannic Majesty for the duration of the Alliance leases of the necessary sites for the accommodation of the forces of His Britannic Majesty in those localities.

2. Subject to any modifications which the two High Contracting Parties may agree to introduce in the future, the immunities and privileges in jurisdictional and fiscal matters, including freedom from taxation, enjoyed by the British forces in 'Iraq will continue to extend to the forces referred to in Clause 1 above and to such of His Britannic Majesty's forces of all arms as may be in 'Iraq in pursuance of the present Treaty and its annexure or otherwise by agreement between the High Contracting Parties, and the existing provisions of any local legislation affecting the armed forces of His Britannic Majesty in 'Iraq shall also continue. The 'Iraq Government will take the necessary steps to ensure that the altered conditions will not render the position of the British forces as regards immunities and privileges in any way less favourable than that enjoyed by them at the date of the entry into force of this Treaty.

3. His Majesty the King of 'Iraq agrees to provide all possible facilities for the movement, training and maintenance of the forces referred to in Clause 1 above and to accord to those forces the same facilities for the use of wireless telegraphy as those enjoyed by them at the date of the entry into force of the present Treaty.

4. His Majesty the King of 'Iraq undertakes to provide at the request and at the expense of His Britannic Majesty and upon such conditions as may be agreed between the High Contracting Parties special guards from his own forces for the protection of such air bases as may, in accordance with the provisions of this Treaty, be occupied by the forces of His Britannic Majesty,

and to secure the enactment of such legislation as may be necessary for the fulfilment of the conditions referred to above.

5. His Britannic Majesty undertakes to grant whenever they may be required by His Majesty the King of 'Iraq all possible facilities in the following matters, the cost of which will be met by His Majesty the King of 'Iraq.

1. Naval, military and aeronautical instruction of 'Iraqi officers in the United Kingdom.

2. The provision of arms, ammunition, equipment, ships and aeroplanes of the latest available pattern for the forces of His Majesty the King of 'Iraq.

3. The provision of British naval, military and air force officers to serve in an advisory capacity with the forces of His Majesty the King of 'Iraq.

6. In view of the desirability of identity in training and methods between the 'Iraq and British armies, His Majesty the King of 'Iraq undertakes that, should he deem it necessary to have recourse to foreign military instructors, these shall be chosen from amongst British subjects.

He further undertakes that any personnel of his forces that may be sent abroad for military training will be sent to military schools, colleges and training centres in the territories of His Britannic Majesty, provided that this shall not prevent him from sending to any other country such personnel as cannot be received in the said institutions and training centres.

He further undertakes that the armament and essential equipment of his forces shall not differ in type from those of the forces of His Britannic Majesty.

7. His Majesty the King of 'Iraq agrees to afford, when requested to do so by His Britannic Majesty, all possible facilities for the movement of the forces of His Britannic Majesty of all arms in transit across 'Iraq and for the transport and storage of all supplies and equipment that may be required by these forces during their passage across 'Iraq. These facilities shall cover the use of the roads, railways, waterways, ports and aerodromes of 'Iraq, and His Britannic Majesty's ships shall have general permission to visit the Shatt-al-Arab on the understanding that His Majesty the King of 'Iraq is given prior notification of visits to 'Iraq ports.

57. LAW RATIFYING THE CONVENTION BETWEEN FRANCE AND THE COMPAGNIE FRANÇAISE DES PÉTROLES
25 July 1931

[Translated from the French in *Journal officiel de la république française,* 30 July 1931, pp. 8354–56]

The French interest in the TPC under the 1920 San Remo oil agreement (Doc. 29) was assigned in 1923 to a French corporation expressly formed for the purpose, the Compagnie Française des Pétroles (CFP). Obviously influenced by the example of the United Kingdom's participation in the Anglo-Persian Oil Company (I, Doc. 112), the French government eventually obtained 35 per cent of the stock and 40 per cent of the voting rights in CFP, after eight years of tangled negotiations. CFP became the staunchest corporate guardian of the Red Line agreement (Doc. 54). Despite efforts of the French government to preserve the national purity of CFP, French subsidiaries of New Jersey Standard procured a 9 per cent interest in the company. For references, see Docs. 44, 54.

ART. 1. The Government is authorized to execute the convention of 17 May 1924 between the Ministries of Finance, Commerce and Industry, on one part, and the Compagnie Française des Pétroles [CFP], on the other.

2. The Government is authorized to execute the convention of 25 June 1930 between the Ministries of Finance, Commerce and Industry, on one part and the CFP, on the other, subject to the amendment of 4 March 1931, under the conditions stipulated by the law of 30 March 1928, and: 1) with the reservation of the possible revision, after a period of twenty years, of article 12 of the said convention; 2) with

the reservation that the refund mentioned in the amendment of 4 March 1931 shall be calculated at 2 percent of the price of each delivered product, but this refund may not be lower than an average of 8 francs per ton.

However, the State reserves for itself the right to raise from 25 percent to 35 percent, or to an intermediate percentage, the subscription envisaged in articles 1, 2 and 3 of the convention, the voting advantage of 5 percent of the total votes envisaged in article 4 being maintained under the same conditions. The State shall have a period of two months, after the promulgation of the present law, to notify the company of the percentage of subscription that it will select.

3. The provisions of article 6 of the law of 26 April 1930, relating to the issuance of special stock with privileged rights of voting, are voided in favor of the State or of the institutions or public services that it may substitute for itself in the execution of these conventions. . . .

CONVENTION OF 17 MAY 1924

1. It is first of all recalled that the CFP, having been designated for this purpose by the French Government, is authorized to acquire the 40,000 shares, hitherto German, that constitute French participation in the capital of the Turkish Petroleum Company, Ltd. [TPC], in conformity with article 7 of the San Remo agreement of 24 April 1920 [Doc. 29];

2. The CFP shall make this acquisition at its own expense, risk, and danger, and may not request the French Government for guarantee of interest on the funds which [the Company may] devote to that purpose. Moreover, the Company shall in the future exercise all rights and sustain all costs connected with the said shares under the conditions of a normal, independent stockholder, except as otherwise provided in the present convention and subject to the intervention of the Government Commissioners in accordance with article 30 of [the Company] statutes as recalled below.

3. *Termination of participation:*—The CFP may neither withdraw from the TPC, nor surrender part of its stock, except with the written consent of the French Government.

4. *Statutes:*—The CFP, prior to its designation by the Government, has given the latter a series of essential guarantees by inserting into its statutes articles 2, 18, 21, 24, and 30, which provide for the State's agreement to the administration and management of the Company and accept regular supervision by the Government's Commissioners.

5. *Commercial contracts:*—From the moment that the TPC begins production, the French State shall enjoy a right of priority to a tonnage which may reach a maximum of 80 percent of the portion of products to which the CFP may be entitled as a participant. This priority shall be met at uniform prices and shall depend on the demands of the French Government. However, if the French State should fail to exercise its option by a mutually agreed date, and if the Company should have concluded contracts with third parties for the delivery of quantities thus made available, the prevailing rights of option of the French State shall not hinder the execution of these contracts.

6. *Special account and particular reserve account:*—a) The CFP shall enter in its books an account which will be established as stipulated below and which will be designed to permit the calculation of the State's allotment in the Company's excess profits resulting from its participation in the TPC; this account will be labeled hereafter, for the sake of simplicity, the "special account."

b) The following sums shall be credited to the special account:

(1) Interest from preferred obligations or shares of the Turkish Petroleum Company, Ltd. and dividends from the various grades of shares subscribed to by the CFP; deductions will be made for all taxes and charges levied by foreign governments (Iraq, Turkey, Great Britain, etc.) so that only the sums actually accruing to the CFP will be counted.

(2) The equivalent value, at current world market prices, of all crude oil and of

all refined products that may be offered at option by the TPC to the CFP in its capacity as stockholder of the TCP; [this clause becomes operative], it is understood, only insofar as the CFP actually profits from such an option.

These prices shall be set at the point of delivery by the TPC, account being taken of the difference in transportation and other costs of these oils and products [from comparable costs of] products of the same quality which may serve as the basis for comparison.

c) The following shall be charged against the account:

(1) Sums actually paid to the TPC by the CFP for the said quantities of crude and refined products.

(2) All expenses of the CFP which may result, directly or indirectly, from its participation in the TPC, such as: costs of travel, of missions and of inspection, unloading costs, storage costs, etc.

(3) A percentage of the general costs of the central administration of the CFP, calculated on the basis of the capital immobilized by the CFP in the TPC, and in the installations and establishments referred to in paragraph (e) (2) of the present article, compared with the capital invested by the CFP in other enterprises in which it may participate.

(4) Prior deductions set aside for the legal reserve, various reserves for depreciation and amortization according to practices of intelligent management, insofar as the prior deductions relate to the investments made by the CFP, either in the TPC, or in installations involving the participation of the State.

A particular account shall be opened comprising all the above reserves. No withdrawal may be made from this account for any objective alien to its own purpose; every withdrawal must receive the prior approval of the Government's Commissioners, so that the rights of the State to the total sums placed in reserve may be maintained.

d) The favorable balance, if any, of the special account will constitute the profit.

e) Of this profit, the CFP shall have, firstly, the right to a first dividend calculated on the base of a cumulative interest of 10 percent of the total of invested capital, as defined below:

(1) The total of the payments made by the CFP in redemption of the shares and obligations of the TPC to which it subscribed and which were not amortized.

(2) The total of all the sums immobilized by the CFP to exercise the rights flowing from its shares in the TPC, and particularly the sums necessary for the creation of pumping stations, reservoirs, embarkation ports, warehouses, etc., insofar as these installations and establishments are required for the exercise of the said rights.

Of the above sums, the following will be deducted:

I. The total of the sums listed under the heading: general amortization reserve.

II. The total of the sums listed under the headings: depreciation reserves [*réserves de prévoyance*] or emergency reserves [*réserves pour éventualités diverses*].

The following shall not be deducted: sums listed in the balance sheet under legal reserve, reserve against loss from fire, and, in general, reserves set aside for a special purpose, on condition however that the total of non-deducted reserves shall not exceed five percent of the total invested capital.

f) Whenever for any operation the profits defined above should exceed ten percent of the invested capital, the surplus of the profits shall be applied, first of all, to the completion, if need be, of the normal annual interest of ten percent for all preceding operations, without penalty for delay [*sans intérêts de retard*].[1]

If there remains any balance after these deductions, this balance shall constitute the excess profit.

The State's allotment of the excess profit shall be determined in accordance with the following table:

[1] This paragraph was amended by article 8 of the convention of 25 June 1930; see below p. 186 [Ed. note]

10% of excess profit [amounting to] less than 2% of capital
15% of excess profit [ranging] between 2 and 4% of capital
20% of excess profit [ranging] between 4 and 6% of capital
25% of excess profit [ranging] between 6 and 10% of capital
30% of excess profit [ranging] between 10 and 20% of capital
35% of excess profit [ranging] between 20 and 30% of capital
40% of excess profit [ranging] between 30 and 40% of capital
45% of excess profit [ranging] between 40 and 50% of capital
50% of excess profit [ranging] between 50 and 60% of capital
55% of excess profit [ranging] between 60 and 70% of capital
60% of excess profit [ranging] between 70 and 80% of capital
65% of excess profit [ranging] between 80 and 90% of capital
70% of excess profit [ranging] between 90 and 100% of capital
75% of excess profit larger than 100% of capital.

7. *Term:*—The present convention shall remain in force for the entire period of the Mesopotamia oil concession to the TPC.

If for any reason whatsoever the TPC should renounce [its rights to] the exploitation of the [oil] deposits prior to the lapse of the present concession, this convention shall be deemed null and void.

8. *Liquidation:*—At the expiration of the present convention, or if the CFP, duly authorized, cedes to a third party the totality or a part of its stock in the TPC, which form the object of the present agreement, the special account and the particular reserve account which form the object of paragraph 4 of article 6 (c) shall be liquidated as follows:

a. By the payment to the CFP of the sums that may be necessary for the partial or total payment of the 10 percent cumulative annual interest, as indicated in article 6 (e) above.

b. If available funds permit, by payment to the CFP of all sums required for the full or partial payment of all non-amortized balances of capital invested in the TPC and in the installations exploited for the joint benefit of the State and of the CFP.

If the total of credit balances in the special account and in the particular reserve account permit the two said payments in full, the French State shall become *ipso facto* the owner of the stock of the TPC referred to in this agreement and not ceded to a third party, and of the ancillary installations exploited for common profit.

Furthermore, the balance, if such exists, shall be divided between the State and the CFP as if it were an excess profit and, therefore, according to the table which is part of article 6 (f) above. The amount of base capital to which this excess profit will be related shall be the amount of capital immobilized by the CFP before the initiation of liquidation procedures.

If the total of credit balance in the special account fund and in the particular reserve account should be inadequate, the French State will have the right to provide the difference, thus assuring for itself ownership of the stock and of the installations.

If the State should not exercise this right, two possibilities may be envisaged:

I. The total of credit balances in the special account and the particular reserve account is inadequate for the full payment of the sums anticipated in paragraph (a) of the present article:

In this case, the State has no right to the TPC stock; the CFP has no appeal against the State, and the two parties are liberated from all reciprocal obligations.

II. The total of the credit balances in the special account and in the particular reserve account is adequate to assure the full payment of the sums anticipated in paragraph (a) of the present article.

In this case, the balance of the two accounts, after full payment of the said two sums, shall serve to compensate the CFP for a part of the TPC stock that it owns, and the State shall become the owner of the stock thus repaid.

9. *Disagreements:*—Disagreements that may arise between the French Government

and the CFP concerning the interpretation and execution of the clauses of the present convention shall be settled according to the procedure anticipated in article 30 of the statutes of the Company.

10. The costs of stamps and of registration for the present convention shall be borne by the CFP. . . .

CONVENTION OF 25 JUNE 1930

It has been agreed that the provisions of the convention of 19 March 1929 [not reproduced in the law—Ed.] are replaced by the following:

1. The Board of Directors of the CFP undertakes to engage in the necessary deliberations and to fulfill all legal and statutory formalities so that, within a period of two months after the promulgation of the law ratifying the present convention, the capitalization of the CFP, such as it may be at that time, will be increased by one third under the conditions stipulated in articles 2, 4, and 5 of the present convention, by means of the creation of new "A" and "B" shares, the subscription of which will be reserved for the State, in such a manner that when the increase of capitalization will have taken place, the State shall be in possession of twenty-five percent of the capitalization.

2. The shares issued according to article 1 above shall be upon their release like the existing shares. They shall be issued at par of 500 francs payable in full upon issuance. The State payments shall not be subject to registration fees, the other expenses connected with the operation being borne by the Company.

3. The CFP undertakes to reserve for the State, whenever [the Company's] capital may henceforth be increased, a preferential right of subscription to such shares as will assure [the State] at all times the ownership of one quarter of the outstanding capital, it being understood that the State shall not enjoy this preferential right to 25 percent unless it maintains its interest in the Company and exercises its subscription rights in full, subject to the provisions stipulated in article 5 of the present convention.

Otherwise the preferential right of the State shall be reduced to equality with the percentage of stock that it owns.

4. As long as the State shall own 25 percent of the capital of the CFP, by virtue of articles 1 and 3 above, the number of "A" shares held by the State and the number of votes to which it shall be entitled because of these shares shall be such that the State by statute shall have 30 percent of the total number of votes corresponding to the shares of all categories.

If the State should cease to hold 25 percent of the capital as determined above, the number of shares of category "A" in the State's possession and the number of votes attached to these shares will be such as to equal the percentage of the capital to which the State has subscribed.

5. The State will have the right to cause the National Office of Liquid Fuels to underwrite the stock reserved for the State in accordance with articles 1, 2, and 3 above. In this case, the rights accruing to the State by articles 3 and 4 above will benefit the National Office of Liquid Fuels.

The State will have the right to grant the shares that it holds, by virtue of its participation in the capital, together with the rights appertaining to these shares, to public institutions or services having civil personality. In this case, with respect to the application of subscription and voting rights reserved for the State under articles 3 and 4 above, the shares held by the State, by the National Office of Liquid Fuels, and other public institutions and services will be grouped together.

The cession of subscription rights to third parties other than public institutions or services having civil personality shall be subject to the agreement of the Board of Directors of the CFP. If the Board should disapprove of the assignee proposed by the State, the Board will be bound to have the right or rights of subscription, the cession of which will have been requested, bought by someone of its own choice, within the period provided by the subscription. This operation shall be concluded at the rate quoted at the Exchange [*Bourse*] for "B" shares on the day of the cession.

The cession to third parties, even with the agreement of the Board of Directors of the CFP, under the conditions provided in the preceding section, shall take place subject to the application of the provisions of the last section of article 3 and of the last section of article 4.

6. If the Board of Directors should, faced with a request for transfer of "A" shares, as specified by article 11 of the statutes, deem it unwise, in agreement with the Government Commissioners, to accept the demand, and if it should thereafter propose as beneficiaries of the transfer of the said stock persons of its own choice, 30 percent of these shares shall be reserved for the State.

7. Article 30 of the statutes shall be amended to harmonize with the following provisions:

The State's supervision of the Company will be assured by two representatives, who, besides the normal powers of directors, shall exercise the powers reserved by the statutes for the Commissioners of the Government.

If the intervention of the Government's Commissioners should lead to the suspension of a decision by the Board of Directors on an authorization for the transfer of "A" stock, and if, after a second deliberation, the Board of Directors should maintain its position, [the matter] shall be resolved by a decision of the Minister of Finance and the Minister of Commerce and Industry, in consultation with the Council of Ministers [Cabinet].

For all questions mentioned in the eighth paragraph of article 30 of the statutes—all questions bearing on the general policy of the Government—such as:

a) Every act of the Company on questions of foreign, naval or military policy;

b) Every act tending to modify the structure of the Company by merger, absorption or any other manner,

and for these questions only, if the Commissioners of the Government should formulate such a demand, any proposal whatever placed on the agenda of an ordinary or extraordinary general assembly must receive for adoption three quarters of the votes of the stockholders present or represented. The Commissioners shall inform the Board of their decision at the Board's second meeting, convoked under the provisions of the seventh paragraph of article 30 of the statutes [expressly] to discuss the agenda to which the observations of the Commissioners will have given rise.

8. The table inserted in article 6 of the convention of 17 May 1924 shall remain unchanged.

Paragraph (f) of the same article 6 is voided and replaced by the following:

"Whenever for any operation the profits defined by the convention should exceed 10 percent of the invested capital, the surplus of these profits shall be applied, first of all, to the completion, if need be, of the annual 6 percent interest on capital for all the preceding operations for which the profits defined by the Convention will not have reached 10 percent, without penalty for delay [*sans intérêt de retard*]."

9. The CFP, which has formed, as agreed, an affiliated company called Compagnie Française de Raffinage [CFR], whose principal object will be to construct in France rational manufacturing equipment for the distillation and refining of petroleum products and has underwritten for its own account 55 percent of the stock issued by the said Company, undertakes that it will cede its shares of the CFR, up to 49 percent of the capital, only to the State or to a person acceptable to the State.

The Company further agrees to participate, in the full measure of its rights, in such future increases of capital as may be decided upon.

The Company undertakes, in the name of the CFR, to have articles 10, 11, and 12 of the present convention ratified by the said Company.

10. Over and above the preceding shares, the CFP, which has also underwritten a tenth of the capital of the CFR, agrees to hand over to the State the corresponding shares, at their purchase price without any maturation, upon the promulgation of the law ratifying the present convention. The State shall have the right to participate in the same 10 percent proportion in such

future increases of capital of the CFR, as may be decided upon.

The State will have the right to have the National Office of Liquid Fuels take over [*reprendre*] or underwrite the stock of the CFR. The said stock and the rights of subscription appertaining thereto may be ceded only to a public institution or service having civil personality and designated by the Government.

11. The State's supervision of the Board of Directors of the CFR shall be exercised by two Commissioners appointed by the Government; their power will be those vested in the Directors by the statutes. They shall furthermore enjoy the same prerogatives and [rights of] communication as accounting commissioners [*commissaires aux comptes*].

12. [Amendment of 4 March 1931.] In view of the participation of the CFP in the CFR, the State shall take the necessary measures to permit the CFR to process, by integral refining, a tonnage of crude oil, of its derivatives and residues equal to 25 percent of the total of declared annual products finished for consumption.

The CFR shall therefore be licensed to deliver its products for domestic consumption either directly on its own account or through any other parties holding general or special import licenses.

The above license is independent of those that may be granted, in conformity with common law, to the CFR, for the account of the distributors affiliated with that Company.

13. The present convention shall be null and void in case the CFP should fail, within the specified period, to obtain from the stockholders the necessary authorizations which the Board of Directors of that Company agrees to seek.

It shall similarly be null and void, if the present convention should fail to receive the sanction of Parliament before 1 August 1930.

The date when the present convention will enter into force shall be fixed by decree of the Council of Ministers [Cabinet], after it has obtained from Parliament the necessary authorizations. . . .

ADDITION TO CONVENTION OF 25 JUNE 1930 BY AMENDMENT OF 4 MARCH 1931

Article 5 of the convention of 17 May 1924 provides that the State shall enjoy a right of priority to a tonnage which may reach a maximum of 80 percent of the portion of products to which the CFP may be entitled as a participant in the IPC [Iraq Petroleum Company]. It is understood that this maximum shall relate to the total tonnage of the various products to which it exercises the right of priority and that, in consequence, the 80 percent limit may be exceeded for certain products, if it is not reached for others, in a manner to establish, in the aggregate, a compensation in tonnage.

If the refining of crude oil, to which the CFP may be entitled by reason of its participation in the IPC, is effected by an affiliated Company (such as the CFR), the CFP undertakes on behalf of this affiliate to guarantee to the State the free exercise of its right of priority to the finished products extracted by that affiliated Company from the said crude oil.

This having been explained insofar as concerns deliveries to the State under its right of priority, at prices fixed as provided by article 5 of the convention of 17 May 1924, the CFP will accord to the State a refund uniformly set at 8 francs per ton of delivered product, whatever the nature of the product may be.

58. REVISED AGREEMENT: PERSIA AND THE ANGLO-PERSIAN OIL COMPANY
29 April 1933

(Ratified by the Persian *Majlis*, 28 May 1933; promulgated by Riza Shah, 29 May 1933; denounced by Iran (Persia) 1 May 1951)

[League of Nations, *Official Journal*, 13 (December 1932) 1653–60]

"The Anglo-Persian Oil Company has been repeatedly informed by the Persian Government that the D'Arcy Concession of 1901 does not protect the interests of the Persian Government and that it is necessary to place relations between [the two] . . . on a new basis which will provide for the real interests of Persia," read a note that the Persian Finance Minister handed to the company's resident director in Tehran on 27 November 1932. The finance minister went on to apprise the resident director that "the only way to safeguard . . . [his government's] rights is by a cancellation of the D'Arcy concession, and this Ministry, in accordance with the decision of the Persian Government, has to notify you that, as from this date, it has cancelled the D'Arcy concession and will consider it void" (text in League of Nations, *Official Journal,* (13 December 1932) 2301). The *Majlis* (legislature) ratified the act of abrogation on 20 December 1932. Persian grievances at the time were basically economic. The extreme fluctuations in the marketing of oil meant that the Persian government could not depend on a stable annual revenue from the company. Thus the company's latest payment to the government for 1931 amounted to £306,872, as contrasted with payments four and nearly five times as high in the two preceding years. Besides, Iraq had concluded a new agreement with the Iraq Petroleum Company in March 1931 (Doc. 44), assuring the Iraqi government a substantial—for the period—annual minimum revenue. The United Kingdom, not in its capacity as principal stockholder but for the purpose of protecting the interests of its nationals, threatened to refer the dispute to the Permanent Court of International Justice. Iran, however, denied the competence of the Court in the matter. Britain finally submitted the question to the Council of the League of Nations on 14 December 1932, and through the good offices of its rapporteur, Dr. Eduard Beneš, the dispute was amicably settled with the conclusion in Tehran of a fresh agreement. *Survey of International Affairs, 1934,* pp. 224–47; S. H. Longrigg, *Oil in the Middle East,* chap. 4; B. Shwadran, *The Middle East, Oil and the Great Powers;* M. Nakhai, *Le Pétrole en Iran,* pp. 49–71; Z. Azami, *Le Pétrole en Perse,* pp. 111–28.

DEFINITIONS

The following definitions of certain terms used in the present Agreement are applicable for the purposes hereof, without regard to any different meaning which may or might be attributed to those terms for other purposes:

"The Government" means the Imperial Government of Persia;

"The Company" means the Anglo-Persian Oil Company Limited and all its subordinate companies;

"The Anglo-Persian Oil Company Limited" means the Anglo-Persian Oil Company Limited or any other body corporate to which, with the consent of the Government (Article 26), this Concession might be transferred;

"Subordinate Company" means any company for which the Company has the right to nominate directly or indirectly more than one-half of the directors, or in which the Company hold, directly or indirectly, a number of shares sufficient to assure it more than 50 per cent of all voting rights at the general meetings of such a company.

"Petroleum" means crude oil, natural gases, asphalt, ozokerite, as well as all products obtained either from these substances or by mixing these substances with other substances.

"Operations of the Company in Persia" means all industrial, commercial and technical operations carried on by the Company exclusively for the purposes of this Concession.

ART. 1. The Government grants to the Company, on the terms of this concession, the exclusive right, within the territory of the Concession, to search for and extract petroleum as well as to refine or treat in any other manner and render suitable for commerce the petroleum obtained by it.

The Government also grants to the Company, throughout Persia, the non-exclusive right to transport petroleum, to refine or treat it in any other manner and to render it suitable for commerce, as well as to sell it in Persia and to export it.

ART. 2. A. The territory of the Concession, until December 31st, 1938, shall be the territory to the south of the violet line drawn on the map [1] signed by both parties and annexed to the present Agreement.

B. The Company is bound, at latest by December 31st, 1938, to select on the territory above-mentioned one or several areas of such shape and such size and so situated as the Company may deem suitable. The total area of the area or areas selected must not exceed one hundred thousand English square miles (100,000 square miles), each linear mile being equivalent to 1,609 metres.

The Company shall notify to the Government in writing on December 31st, 1938, or before that date, the area or areas which it shall have selected as above provided. The maps and data necessary to identify and define the area or areas which the Company shall have selected shall be attached to each notification.

C. After December 31st, 1938, the Company shall no longer have the right to search for and extract petroleum except on the area or areas selected by it under paragraph B above, and the territory of the Concession, after that date, shall mean only the area or areas so selected and the selection of which shall have been notified to the Government as above provided.

ART. 3. The Company shall have the non-exclusive right to construct and to own pipe-lines. The Company may determine the position of its pipe-lines and operate them.

ART. 4. A. Any unutilised lands belonging to the Government, which the Company shall deem necessary for its operations in Persia and which the Government shall not require for purposes of public utility, shall be handed over gratuitously to the Company.

The manner of acquiring such lands shall be the following: Whenever any land becomes necessary to the Company, it is bound to send to the Ministry of Finance a map or maps on which the land which the Company needs shall be shown in colour. The Government undertakes, if it has no objection to make, to give its approval within a period of three months after receipt of the Company's request.

B. Lands belonging to the Government, of which use is being made, and which the Company shall need, shall be requested of the Government in the manner prescribed in the preceding paragraph, and the Government, in case it should not itself need these lands and should have no objection to make, shall give, within a period of three months, its approval to the sale asked for by the Company.

The price of these lands shall be paid by the Company; such price must be reasonable and not exceed the current price of lands of the same kind and utilised in the same manner in the district.

C. In the absence of a reply from the Government to requests under paragraphs A and B above, after the expiry of two months from the date of receipt of the said requests, a reminder shall be sent by the Company to the Government; should the Government fail to reply to such reminder within a period of one month, its silence shall be regarded as approval.

D. Lands which do not belong to the Government and which are necessary to the Company shall be acquired by the Company, by agreement with the parties interested, and through the medium of the Government.

In case agreement should not be reached as to the prices, the Government shall not allow the owners of such lands to demand a price higher than the prices commonly current for neighbouring lands of the same nature. In valuing such lands, no regard shall

[1] The map annexed to the original document is not reproduced.

be paid to the use to which the Company may wish to put them.

E. Holy places and historical monuments, as well as all places and sites of historical interest, are excluded from the foregoing provisions, as well as their immediate surroundings for a distance of at least 200 metres.

F. The Company has the non-exclusive right to take within the territory of the Concession, but not elsewhere, on any unutilised land belonging to the State, and to utilise gratuitously for all the operations of the Company, any kinds of soil, sand, lime, gypsum, stone and other building materials. It is understood that if the utilisation of the said materials were prejudicial to any rights whatever of third parties, the Company should indemnify those whose rights were infringed.

ART. 5. The operations of the Company in Persia shall be restricted in the following manner:

(1) The construction of any new railway line and of any new port shall be subject to a previous agreement between the Government and the Company;

(2) If the Company wishes to increase its existing service of telephones, telegraphs, wireless and aviation in Persia, it shall only be able so to do with the previous consent of the Government.

If the Government requires to utilise the means of transport and communication of the Company for national defence or in other critical circumstances, it undertakes to impede as little as possible the operations of the Company, and to pay it fair compensation for all damages caused by the utilisation above mentioned.

ART. 6. A. The Company is authorised to effect, without special licence, all imports necessary for the exclusive needs of its employees on payment of the Custom duties and other duties and taxes in force at the time of importation.

The Company shall take the necessary measures to prevent the sale or the handing over of products imported to persons not employed by the Company.

B. The Company shall have the right to import, without special licence, the equipment, material, medical and surgical instruments and pharmaceutical products, necessary for its dispensaries and hospitals in Persia, and shall be exempt in respect thereof from any Custom duties and other duties and taxes in force at the time of importation, or payments of any nature whatever to the Persian State or to local authorities.

C. The Company shall have the right to import, without any licence and exempt from any Custom duties and from any taxes or payments of any nature whatever to the Persian State or to local authorities, anything necessary exclusively for the operations of the Company in Persia.

D. The exports of petroleum shall enjoy Customs immunity and shall be exempt from any taxes or payments of any nature whatever to the Persian State or to local authorities.

ART. 7. A. The Company and its employees shall enjoy the legal protection of the Government.

B. The Government shall give, within the limits of the laws and regulations of the country, all possible facilities for the operations of the Company in Persia.

C. If the Government grants concessions to third parties for the purpose of exploiting other mines within the territory of the Concession, it must cause the necessary precautions to be taken in order that these exploitations do not cause any damage to the installations and works of the Company.

D. The Company shall be responsible for the determination of dangerous zones for the construction of habitations, shops and other buildings, in order that the Government may prevent the inhabitants from settling there.

ART. 8. The Company shall not be bound to convert into Persian currency any part whatsoever of its funds, in particular any proceeds of the sale of its exports from Persia.

ART. 9. The Company shall immediately make its arrangements to proceed with its operations in the province of Kermanshah through a subsidiary company with a view to producing and refining petroleum there.

ART. 10. I. The sums to be paid to the

Government by the Company in accordance with this Agreement (besides those provided in other articles) are fixed as follows:

(*a*) An annual royalty, beginning on January 1st, 1933, of four shillings per ton petroleum sold for consumption in Persia or exported from Persia;

(*b*) Payment of a sum equal to twenty per cent (20%) of the distribution to the ordinary stockholders of the Anglo-Persian Oil Company Limited, in excess of the sum of six hundred and seventy-one thousand two hundred and fifty pounds sterling (£671,250), whether that distribution be made as dividends for any one year or whether it relates to the reserves of that company, exceeding the reserves which, according to its books, existed on December 31st, 1932;

(*c*) The total amount to be paid by the Company for each calendar (Christian) year under sub-clauses (*a*) and (*b*) shall never be less than seven hundred and fifty thousand pounds sterling (£750,000).

II. Payments by the Company under this Article shall be made as follows:

(*a*) On March 31st, June 30th, September 30th and December 31st of each year, on each occasion one hundred and eighty-seven thousand five hundred pounds sterling (£187,500) (the payment relating to March 31st, 1933, shall be made immediately after the ratification of the present Agreement);

(*b*) On February 28th, 1934, and thereafter on the same date in each year, the amount of the tonnage royalty for the previous year provided for in sub-clause I (*a*) less the sum of seven hundred and fifty thousand pounds sterling (£750,000), already paid under sub-clause II (*a*);

(*c*) Any sums due to the Government under sub-clause I (*b*) of this article shall be paid simultaneously with any distributions to the ordinary stockholders.

III. On the expiration of this Concession, as well as in the case of surrender by the Company under Article 25, the Company shall pay to the Government a sum equal to twenty per cent (20%) of:

(*a*) The surplus difference between the amount of the reserves (General Reserve) of the Anglo-Persian Oil Company Limited, at the date of the expiration of the Concession or of its surrender, and the amount of the same reserves at December 31st, 1932;

(*b*) The surplus difference between the balance carried forward by the Anglo-Persian Oil Company Limited at the date of the expiration of the Concession or of its surrender and the balance carried forward by that Company at December 31st, 1932.

Any payment due to the Government under this clause shall be made within a period of one month from the date of the general meeting of the Company following the expiration or the surrender of the Concession.

IV. The Government shall have the right to check the returns relating to sub-clause I (a) which shall be made to it at latest on February 28th for the preceding year.

V. To secure the Government against any loss which might result from fluctuations in the value of English currency, the parties have agreed as follows:

(*a*) If, at any time, the price of gold in London exceeds six pounds sterling per ounce (ounce troy), the payments to be made by the Company in accordance with the present Agreement (with the exception of sums due to the Government under sub-clause I (*b*) and clause III (*a*) and (*b*) of this article and sub-clause I (*a*) of Article 23) shall be increased by one thousand four hundred and fortieth part $\frac{1}{1440}$ for each penny of increase of the price of gold above six pounds sterling (£6) per ounce (ounce troy) on the due date of the payments;

(*b*) If, at any time, the Government considers that gold has ceased to be the general basis of values and that the payments above mentioned no longer give it the security which is intended by the parties, the parties shall come to an agreement as to a modification of the nature of the security above mentioned or, in default of such an arrangement, shall submit the question to the Arbitration Court (Article 22) which shall decide whether the security provided in sub-clause (*a*) above ought to be altered and if so, shall settle the provisions to be substituted therefor and shall fix the period to which such provisions shall apply.

VI. In case of a delay, beyond the dates fixed in the present Agreement, which might be made by the Company in the payment of sums due by it to the Government, interest at five per cent (5%) per annum shall be paid for the period of delay.

ART. 11. I. The Company shall be completely exempt, for its operations in Persia, for the first thirty years, from any taxation present or future of the State and of local authorities; in consideration therefor the following payments shall be made to the Government:

(*a*) During the first fifteen years of this Concession, on February 28th of each year and, for the first time, on February 28th, 1934, nine pence for each of the first six million (6,000,000) tons of petroleum, on which the royalty provided for in Article 10, I (*a*), is payable for the preceding calendar (Christian) year, and six pence for each ton in excess of the figure of six million (6,000,000) tons above defined;

(*b*) The Company guarantees that the amount paid under the preceding sub-clause shall never be less than two hundred and twenty-five thousand pounds sterling (£225,000);

(*c*) During the fifteen years following, one shilling for each of the first six million (6,000,000) tons of petroleum, on which the royalty provided for in Article 10, I (*a*), is payable for the preceding calendar year, and nine pence for each ton in excess of the figure of 6,000,000 tons above defined.

(*d*) The Company guarantees that the amount paid under the preceding sub-clause (*c*) shall never be less than three hundred thousand pounds sterling (£300,000).

II. Before the year 1963, the parties shall come to an agreement as to the amounts of the annual payments to be made, in consideration of the complete exemption of the Company for its operations in Persia from any taxation of the State and of local authorities, during the second period of thirty years extending until December 31st, 1993.

ART. 12. A. The Company, for its operations in Persia in accordance with the present Agreement, shall employ all means customary and proper to ensure economy in and good returns from its operations, to preserve the deposits of petroleum and to exploit its Concession by methods in accordance with the latest scientific progress.

B. If, within the territory of the Concession, there exist other mineral substances than petroleum or woods and forests belonging to the Government, the Company may not exploit them in accordance with the present Concession, nor object to their exploitation by other persons (subject to the due compliance with the terms of clause C or Article 7); but the Company shall have the right to utilise the said substances or the woods and forests above mentioned if they are necessary for the exploration or the extraction of petroleum.

C. All boreholes which, not having resulted in the discovery of petroleum, produce water or precious substances, shall be reserved for the Government which shall immediately be informed of these discoveries by the Company, and the Government shall inform the Company as soon as possible if it wishes to take possession of them. If it wishes to take possession, it shall watch that the operations of the Company be not impeded.

ART. 13. The Company undertakes to send, at its own expense and within a reasonable time, to the Ministry of Finance, whenever the representative of the Government shall request it, accurate copies of all plans, maps, sections and any other data whether topographical, geological or of drilling relating to the territory of the Concession, which are in its possession.

Furthermore, the Company shall communicate to the Government throughout the duration of the Concession all important scientific and technical data resulting from its work in Persia.

All these documents shall be considered by the Government as confidential.

ART. 14. A. The Government shall have the right to cause to be inspected at its wish, at any reasonable time, the technical activity of the Company in Persia, and to nominate for this purpose technical specialist experts.

B. The Company shall place at the disposal of the specialist experts nominated to this end by the Government, the whole of its records relative to scientific and technical data, as well as all measuring apparatus and means of measurement, and these specialist experts shall, further, have the right to ask for any information in all the offices of the Company and on all the territories in Persia.

ART. 15. The Government shall have the right to appoint a representative who shall be designated "Delegate of the Imperial Government." This representative shall have the right:

(1) To obtain from the Company all the information to which the stockholders of the Company are entitled;

(2) To be present at all the meetings of the Board of Directors, of its committees and at all the meetings of stockholders, which have been convened to consider any question arising out of the relations between the Government and the Company:

(3) To preside *ex officio,* with a casting vote, over the Committee to be set up by the Company for the purpose of distributing the grant for and supervising the professional education in Great Britain of Persian nationals referred to in Article 16.

(4) To request that special meetings of the Board of Directors be convened at any time, to consider any proposal that the Government shall submit to it. These meetings shall be convened within fifteen days from the date of the receipt by the Secretary of the Company of a request in writing to that end.

The Company shall pay to the Government to cover the expenses to be borne by it in respect of the salary and expenses of the above-mentioned delegate a year by sum of two thousand pounds sterling (£2,000). The Government shall notify the Company in writing of the appointment of this delegate and of any changes in such appointment.

ART. 16. I. Both parties recognise and accept as the principle governing the performance of this Agreement the supreme necessity, in their mutual interest, of maintaining the highest degree of efficiency and of economy in the administration and the operations of the Company in Persia.

II. It is, however, understood that the Company shall recruit its artisans as well as its technical and commercial staff from among Persian nationals to the extent that it shall find in Persia persons who possess the requisite competence and experience. It is likewise understood that the unskilled staff shall be composed exclusively of Persian nationals.

III. The parties declare themselves in agreement to study and prepare a general plan of yearly and progressive reduction of the non-Persian employees with a view to replacing them in the shortest possible time and progressively by Persian nationals.

IV. The Company shall make a yearly grant of ten thousand pounds sterling in order to give in Great Britain, to Persian nationals, the professional education necessary for the oil industry.

The said grant shall be expended by a Committee which shall be constituted as provided in Article 15.

ART. 17. The Company shall be responsible for organising and shall pay the cost of the provision, control and upkeep of sanitary and public health services, according to the requirements of the most modern hygiene practised in Persia, on all the lands of the Company and in all buildings, and dwellings, destined by the Company for the use of its employees, including the workmen employed within the territory of the Concession.

ART. 18. Whenever the Company shall make issues of shares to the public, the subscription lists shall be opened at Teheran at the same time as elsewhere.

ART. 19. The Company shall sell for internal consumption in Persia, including the needs of the Government, motor spirit, kerosene and fuel oil, produced from Persian petroleum, on the following basis:

(*a*) On the first of June in each year, the Company shall ascertain the average Roumanian f.o.b. prices for motor spirit, kerosene and fuel oil and the average Gulf of Mexico f.o.b. prices for each of these products during the preceding period of twelve months ending on April 30th. The lowest of these average prices shall be selected. Such prices shall be the "basic prices" for a period of one year, beginning on June 1st. The "basic prices" shall be regarded as being the prices at the refinery.

(*b*) The Company shall sell (1) to the Government for its own needs, and not for resale, motor spirit, kerosene and fuel oil at the basic prices, provided in sub-clause (*a*) above, with a deduction of twenty-five per cent (25%); (2) to other consumers at the basic prices with a deduction of ten per cent (10%).

(*c*) The Company shall be entitled to add to the basic prices mentioned in sub-clause (*a*), all actual costs of transport and of distribution and of sale, as well as any imposts and taxes on the said products.

(*d*) The Government shall forbid the export of the petroleum products sold by the Company under the provisions of this article.

ART. 20. I. (*a*) During the last ten years of the Concession, or during the two years from the notice preceding the surrender of the Concession provided in Article 25, the Company shall not sell or otherwise alienate, except to subordinate companies, any of its immovable properties in Persia. During the same period, the Company shall not alienate or export any of its movable property whatever except such as has become unutilisable.

(*b*) During the whole of the period preceding the last ten years of the Concession, the Company shall not alienate any land obtained by it gratuitously from the Government; it shall not export from Persia any movable property, except in the case when such property shall have become unutilisable or shall be no longer necessary for the operations of the Company in Persia.

II. At the end of the Concession, whether by expiration of time or otherwise, all the property of the Company in Persia shall become the property of the Government in proper working order and free of any expenses and of any encumbrances.

III. The expression "all the property" comprises all the lands, buildings and workshops, constructions, wells, jetties, roads, pipe-lines, bridges, drainage and water-supply systems, engines, installations and equipments (including tools) of any sort, all means of transport and communication in Persia (including, for example, automobiles, carriages, aeroplanes), any stocks and any other objects in Persia which the Company is utilising in any manner whatsoever for the objects of the Concession.

ART. 21. The contracting parties declare that they base the performance of the present Agreement on principles of mutual goodwill and good faith as well as on a reasonable interpretation of this Agreement.

The Company formally undertakes to have regard at all times and in all places to the rights, privileges and interests of the Government and shall abstain from any action or omission which might be prejudicial to them.

This Concession shall not be annulled by the Government and the terms therein contained shall not be altered either by general or special legislation in the future, or by administrative measures or any other acts whatever of the executive authorities.

ART. 22. A. Any differences between the parties of any nature whatever and in particular any differences arising out of the interpretation of this Agreement and of the rights and obligations therein contained as well as any differences of opinion which may arise relative to questions for the settlement of which, by the terms of this Agreement, the agreement of both parties is necessary, shall be settled by arbitration.

B. The party which requests arbitration shall so notify the other party in writing. Each of the parties shall appoint an arbitrator, and the two arbitrators, before proceeding to arbitration, shall appoint an umpire. If the two arbitrators cannot, within two months, agree on the person of the umpire, the latter shall be nominated, at the request of either of the parties, by the President of the Permanent Court of International Justice. If the President of the Permanent Court of International Justice belongs to a nationality or a country which, in accordance with clause C, is not qualified to furnish the umpire, the nomination shall be made by the Vice-President of the said Court.

C. The umpire shall be of a nationality other than Persian or British; furthermore, he shall not be closely connected with Persia or with Great Britain as belonging to a dominion, a protectorate, a colony, a mandated country or other country administered or occupied by one of the two countries above mentioned or as being or having been in the service of one of these countries.

D. If one of the parties does not appoint its arbitrator or does not advise the other party of its appointment, within sixty days of having received notification of the request for arbitration, the other party shall have the right to request the President of the Permanent Court of International Justice (or the Vice-President in the case provided at the end of clause B) to nominate a sole arbitrator, to be chosen from among persons qualified as above mentioned, and, in this case, the difference shall be settled by this sole arbitrator.

E. The procedure of arbitration shall be that followed, at the time of arbitration, by the Permanent Court of International Justice. The place and time of arbitration shall be fixed by the umpire or by the sole arbitrator provided for in clause D, as the case may be.

F. The award shall be based on the juridical principles contained in Article 38 of the Statutes of the Permanent Court of International Justice. There shall be no appeal against the award.

G. The expenses of arbitration shall be borne in the manner determined by the award.

ART. 23. I. In full settlement of all the claims of the Government of any nature in respect of the past until the date of coming into force of this Agreement (except in regard to Persian taxation), the company: (*a*) shall pay within a period of thirty days from the said date the sum of one million pounds sterling (£1,000,000) and, besides, (*b*) shall settle the payments due to the Government for the financial years 1931 and 1932 on the basis of Article 10 of this Agreement and not on that of the former D'Arcy Concession, after deduction of two hundred thousand pounds sterling (£200,-000) paid in 1932 to the Government as an advance against the royalties and £113,403 3*s* 10*d*. placed on deposit at the disposal of the Government.

II. Within the same period, the Company shall pay to the Government in full settlement of all its claims in respect of taxation for the period from March 21st, 1930, to December 31st, 1932, a sum calculated on the basis of sub-clause (*a*) of clause I of Article 11, but without the guarantee provided in sub-clause (*b*) of the same clause.

ART. 24. If, by reason of the annulment of the D'Arcy Concession, litigation should arise between the Company and private persons on the subject of the duration of leases made in Persia before December 1st, 1932, within the limits allowed by the D'Arcy Concession, the litigation shall be decided according to the rules of interpretation following:

(*a*) If the lease is to determine, according to its terms, at the end of the D'Arcy Concession, it shall retain its validity until May 28th, 1961, notwithstanding the annulment of the said Concession;

(*b*) If it has been provided in the lease that it shall be valid for the duration of the D'Arcy Concession and, in the event of its renewal, for the duration of the renewed Concession, the lease shall retain its validity until December 31st, 1993.

ART. 25. The Company shall have the right to surrender this Concession at the end of any Christian calendar year, on giving to the Government notice in writing two years previously.

On the expiry of the period above provided, the whole of the property of the Company in Persia (defined in Article 20, III) shall become free of cost and without encumbrances the property of the Government in proper working order and the Company shall be released from any engagement for the future. In case there should be disputes between the parties concerning their engagements before the expiry of the period above provided, the differences shall be settled by arbitration as provided in Article 22.

ART. 26. This Concession is granted to the Company for the period beginning on the date of its coming into force and ending on December 31st, 1993.

Before the date of December 31st, 1993, this Concession can only come to an end in the case that the Company should surrender the Concession (Article 25) or in the case that the Arbitration Court should declare the Concession annulled as a consequence of default of the Company in the performance of the present Agreement.

The following cases only shall be regarded as default in that sense:

(*a*) If any sum awarded to Persia by the Arbitration Court has not been paid within one month of the date of the award;

(*b*) If the voluntary or compulsory liquidation of the Company be decided upon.

In any other cases of breach of the present Agreement by one party or the other, the Arbitration Court shall establish the responsibilities and determine their consequences.

Any transfer of the Concession shall be subject to confirmation by the Government.

59. TREATY OF FRIENDSHIP AND MUTUAL COOPERATION: BRITAIN AND YEMEN
11 February 1934

(Ratifications exchanged, San'a, 4 September 1934)

[Great Britain, *Parliamentary Papers, 1934,* Treaty Series No. 34, Cmd. 4752]

Treaty negotiations between the United Kingdom and Yemen, which commenced in 1919, endured with protracted suspensions for a decade and a half. In the interval, Italy (Doc. 47), the USSR (Doc. 55) and the Netherlands [on 12 March 1933, text in League of Nations, *Treaty Series,* No. 3384, vol. 146, pp. 359–67] concluded agreements with Imam Yahya. The continued Yemeni occupation of territory claimed by the Aden Protectorate kept Anglo-Yemeni relations strained, and in 1928 the R.A.F. drove the Imam's forces across the Yemeni border. Yahya retaliated by seizing some forty hostages from Aden. Their release became one of the conditions on which the British insisted, when parleys were resumed in October 1931, and the Imam's failure to satisfy the British demand contributed to the long delay in the signature of the treaty. The forty-year instrument left the boundary dispute unsettled. The recurrence of frontier incidents in 1949 led to the reopening of negotiations which culminated on 20 January 1951 in fresh arrangements including the establishment of diplomatic relations (Great Britain, *Parliamentary Papers, 1952,* Treaty Series No. 42, Cmd. 8590). *Survey of International Affairs, 1925,* vol. 1, pp. 320–24, *1928,* pp. 307–19, *1934,* pp. 308–10; also references to Doc. 47.

ART. 1. His Majesty the King of Great Britain, Ireland and the British Dominions beyond the Seas, Emperor of India, acknowledges the complete and absolute independence of His Majesty the King of the Yemen, the Imam, and his kingdom in all affairs of whatsoever kind.

ART. 2. There shall always be peace and friendship between the high contracting parties, who undertake to maintain good relations with each other in every respect.

ART. 3. The settlement of the question of the southern frontier of the Yemen is deferred pending the conclusion, in whatever way may be agreed upon by both high contracting parties in a spirit of friendship and complete concord, free from any dispute or difference, of the negotiations which shall take place between them before the expiry of the period of the present treaty.

Pending the conclusion of the negotiations referred to in the preceding paragraph, the high contracting parties agree to maintain the situation existing in regard to the frontier on the date of the signature of this treaty, and both high contracting parties undertake that they will prevent, by all means at their disposal, any violation by their forces of the above-mentioned frontier, and any interference by their subjects, or from their side of that frontier, with the affairs of the people inhabiting the other side of the said frontier.

ART. 4. After the coming into force of the present treaty, the high contracting parties shall, by mutual agreement and concord, enter into such agreements as shall be necessary for the regulation of commercial and economic affairs, based on the principles of general international practice.

ART. 5. (1) The subjects of each of the high contracting parties who wish to trade in the territories of the other shall be amenable to the local laws and decrees, and shall receive equal treatment to that enjoyed by the subjects of the most favoured Power.

(2) Similarly, the vessels of each of the high contracting parties and their cargoes shall receive, in the ports of the territories of the other, treatment equal to that accorded to the vessels and their cargoes of the most favoured Power, and the passengers in such vessels shall be treated in the ports of the territories of the other party in the same manner as those in the vessels of the most favoured Power therein.

(3) For the purposes of this article in relation to His Majesty the King of Great Britain, Ireland and the British Dominions beyond the Seas, Emperor of India:—

(*a*) The word "territories" shall be deemed to mean the United Kingdom of Great Britain and Northern Ireland, India and all His Majesty's Colonies, protectorates and all mandated territories in respect of which the mandate is exercised by His Majesty's Government in the United Kingdom.

(*b*) The word "subjects" shall be deemed to mean all subjects of His Majesty wherever domiciled, all the inhabitants of countries under His Majesty's protection, and, similarly, all companies incorporated in any of His Majesty's territories shall be deemed to be subjects of His Majesty.

(*c*) The word "vessels" shall be deemed to mean all merchant vessels registered in any part of the British Commonwealth of Nations.

ART. 6. This treaty shall be the basis of all subsequent agreements that may be concluded between the high contracting parties now and in the future for the purposes of friendship and amity. The high contracting parties undertake not to assist nor to connive at any action directed against the friendship and concord now sincerely existing between them.

ART. 7. The present treaty shall be ratified as soon as possible after signature, and the instruments of ratification shall be exchanged at San'a. It shall come into force on the date of the exchange of ratifications, and shall thereafter remain in force for a period of forty years.

60. CONVENTION (MONTREUX) ON THE TURKISH STATES REGIME
20 July 1936

(Entered into force on 9 November 1936)

[League of Nations *Treaty Series,* No. 4015, vol. 173 (1936–37), pp. 213–41]

The 1923 Lausanne convention on the Turkish Straits (Doc. 41) provided for the demilitarization of both shores of the straits, all the islands in the Sea of Marmara, and several islands in the Aegean Sea; for an International Straits Commission, responsible to the League of Nations, to supervise the execution of the convention; and for an international guarantee by the signatories and "in any case by France, Great Britain, Italy and Japan" of the freedom of navigation of the Straits and the security of the demilitarized zones. Irked by the restrictive clauses, Turkey as early as 1933 began to press for a revision of the convention. Italian aggression against Ethiopia in 1935–36, with its implicit threat to the situation in the Mediterranean, brought Britain and Turkey together. Besides these two powers, Australia, Bulgaria, France, Greece, Japan, Rumania, the USSR and Yugoslavia participated in a conference at Montreux (22 June–20 July 1936) which adopted the following instrument. Turkey's demands were met. For under the Montreux arrangements Turkey assumed the functions of the International Commission, while a separate protocol authorized Turkey to remilitarize the straits. Moreover, if Turkey were "threatened with imminent danger of war" or actually engaged in war, articles 20 and 21 laid down that "the passages of warships shall be left entirely to the discretion of the Turkish Government," subject to veto by a two-thirds vote in the League of Nations Council and by a majority of the signatories. All signatories except Japan deposited ratifications on 9 November 1936; the deposit of the Japanese ratification took place on 19 April 1937; Italy adhered to the convention on 2 May 1938. The four annexes and the separate protocol are omitted below. *Survey of International Affairs, 1936,* pp. 584–651; *Actes de la conférence de Montreux concernant le régime des détroits* (proceedings, published in Liége, Belgium, 1936); H. N. Howard, *The Problem of the Turkish Straits,* 1–12; S. Nava, "Il problema del Mediterraneo Orientale," *Oriente Moderno,* 17 (1937), 61–78; M. Beloff, *The Foreign Policy of Soviet Russia,* vol. 2, chap. 3.

ART. 1. The High Contracting Parties recognise and affirm the principle of freedom of transit and navigation by sea in the Straits.

The exercise of this freedom shall henceforth be regulated by the provisions of the present Convention.

SECTION I. MERCHANT VESSELS

ART. 2. In time of peace, merchant vessels shall enjoy complete freedom of transit and navigation in the Straits, by day and by night, under any flag and with any kind of cargo, without any formalities, except as provided in Article 3 below. No taxes or charges other than those authorised by Annex I to the present Convention shall be levied by the Turkish authorities on these vessels when passing in transit without calling at a port in the Straits.

In order to facilitate the collection of these taxes or charges merchant vessels passing through the Straits shall communicate to the officials at the stations referred to in Article 3 their name, nationality, tonnage, destination and last port of call (provenance).

Pilotage and towage remain optional.

ART. 3. All ships entering the Straits by the Ægean Sea or by the Black Sea shall stop at a sanitary station near the entrance to the Straits for the purposes of the sanitary control prescribed by Turkish law within the framework of international sanitary regulations. This control, in the case of ships possessing a clean bill of health or presenting a declaration of health testifying that they do not fall within the scope of the provisions of the second paragraph of the present Article, shall be carried out by day and by night with all possible speed, and the vessels in question shall not be required to make any other stop during their passage through the Straits.

Vessels which have on board cases of plague, cholera, yellow fever, exanthematic typhus or smallpox, or which have had such cases on board during the previous seven days, and vessels which have left an infected port within less than five times twenty-four hours shall stop at the sanitary stations indicated in the preceding paragraph in order to embark such sanitary guards as the Turkish authorities may direct. No tax or charge shall be levied in respect of these sanitary guards and they shall be disembarked at a sanitary station on departure from the Straits.

ART. 4. In time of war, Turkey not being belligerent, merchant vessels, under any flag or with any kind of cargo, shall enjoy freedom of transit and navigation in the Straits subject to the provisions of Articles 2 and 3.

Pilotage and towage remain optional.

ART. 5. In time of war, Turkey being belligerent, merchant vessels not belonging to a country at war with Turkey shall enjoy freedom of transit and navigation in the Straits on condition that they do not in any way assist the enemy.

Such vessels shall enter the Straits by day and their transit shall be effected by the route which shall in each case be indicated by the Turkish authorities.

ART. 6. Should Turkey consider herself to be threatened with imminent danger of war, the provisions of Article 2 shall nevertheless continue to be applied except that vessels must enter the Straits by day and that their transit must be effected by the route which shall, in each case, be indicated by the Turkish authorities.

Pilotage may, in this case, be made obligatory, but no charge shall be levied.

ART. 7. The term "merchant vessels" applies to all vessels which are not covered by Section II of the present Convention.

SECTION II. VESSELS OF WAR

ART. 8. For the purposes of the present Convention, the definitions of vessels of war and of their specification together with those relating to the calculation of tonnage shall be as set forth in Annex II to the present Convention.

ART. 9. Naval auxiliary vessels specifically designed for the carriage of fuel, liquid or non-liquid, shall not be subject to the provisions of Article 13 regarding notification, nor shall they be counted for the purpose of calculating the tonnage which is subject to limitation under Articles 14 and 18, on condition that they shall pass through the Straits singly. They shall, however, continue to be on the same footing as vessels of war for the purpose of the remaining provisions governing transit.

The auxiliary vessels specified in the preceding paragraph shall only be entitled to benefit by the exceptional status therein contemplated if their armament does not include: for use against floating targets, more than two guns of a maximum calibre of 105 millimetres; for use against aerial targets, more than two guns of a maximum calibre of 75 millimetres.

ART. 10. In time of peace, light surface vessels, minor war vessels and auxiliary vessels, whether belonging to Black Sea or non-Black Sea Powers, and whatever their flag, shall enjoy freedom of transit through the Straits without any taxes or charges whatever, provided that such transit is begun during daylight and subject to the conditions laid down in Article 13 and the Articles following thereafter.

Vessels of war other than those which fall within the categories specified in the preceding paragraph shall only enjoy a right of transit under the special conditions provided by Articles 11 and 12.

ART. 11. Black Sea Powers may send through the Straits capital ships of a tonnage greater than that laid down in the first paragraph of Article 14, on condition that these vessels pass through the Straits singly, escorted by not more than two destroyers.

ART. 12. Black Sea Powers shall have the right to send through the Straits, for the purpose of rejoining their base, submarines constructed or purchased outside the Black Sea, provided that adequate notice of the laying down or purchase of such submarines shall have been given to Turkey.

Submarines belonging to the said Powers shall also be entitled to pass through the Straits to be repaired in dockyards outside the Black Sea on condition that detailed information on the matter is given to Turkey.

In either case, the said submarines must travel by day and on the surface, and must pass through the Straits singly.

ART. 13. The transit of vessels of war through the Straits shall be preceded by a notification given to the Turkish Government through the diplomatic channel. The normal period of notice shall be eight days; but it is desirable that in the case of non-Black Sea Powers this period should be increased to fifteen days. The notification shall specify the destination, name, type and number of the vessels, as also the date of entry for the outward passage and, if necessary, for the return journey. Any change of date shall be subject to three days' notice.

Entry into the Straits for the outward passage shall take place within a period of five days from the date given in the original notification. After the expiry of this period, a new notification shall be given under the same conditions as for the original notification.

When effecting transit, the commander of the naval force shall, without being under any obligation to stop, communicate to a signal station at the entrance to the Dardanelles or the Bosphorus the exact composition of the force under his orders.

ART. 14. The maximum aggregate tonnage of all foreign naval forces which may be in course of transit through the Straits shall not exceed 15,000 tons, except in the cases provided for in Article 11 and in Annex III to the present Convention.

The forces specified in the preceding paragraph shall not, however, comprise more than nine vessels.

Vessels, whether belonging to Black Sea or non-Black Sea Powers, paying visits to a port in the Straits, in accordance with the provisions of Article 17, shall not be included in this tonnage.

Neither shall vessels of war which have suffered damage during their passage through the Straits be included in this tonnage; such vessels, while undergoing repair, shall be subject to any special provisions relating to security laid down by Turkey.

ART. 15. Vessels of war in transit through the Straits shall in no circumstances make use of any aircraft which they may be carrying.

ART. 16. Vessels of war in transit through the Straits shall not, except in the event of damage or peril of the sea, remain therein longer than is necessary for them to effect the passage.

ART. 17. Nothing in the provisions of the preceding Articles shall prevent a naval force of any tonnage or composition from paying a courtesy visit of limited duration to a port in the Straits, at the invitation of the Turkish Government. Any such force must leave the Straits by the same route as that by which it entered, unless it fulfils the conditions required for passage in transit through the Straits as laid down by Articles 10, 14 and 18.

ART. 18. (1) The aggregate tonnage which non-Black Sea Powers may have in that sea in time of peace shall be limited as follows:

(*a*) Except as provided in paragraph (*b*) below, the aggregate tonnage of the said Powers shall not exceed 30,000 tons;

(*b*) If at any time the tonnage of the strongest fleet in the Black Sea shall exceed by at least 10,000 tons the tonnage of the strongest fleet in that sea at the date of the signature of the present Convention, the aggregate tonnage of 30,000 tons mentioned in paragraph (*a*) shall be increased by the same amount, up to a maximum of 45,000 tons. For this purpose, each Black Sea Power shall, in conformity with Annex IV to the present Convention, inform the Turkish Government, on the 1st January and the 1st July of each year, of the total tonnage of its fleet in the Black Sea; and the Turkish Government shall transmit this information to the other High Contracting Parties and to the Secretary-General of the League of Nations;

(*c*) The tonnage which any one non-Back Sea Power may have in the Black Sea shall be limited to two-thirds of the aggregate tonnage provided for in paragraphs (*a*) and (*b*) above;

(*d*) In the event, however, of one or more non-Black Sea Powers desiring to send naval forces into the Black Sea, for a humanitarian purpose, the said forces, which shall in no case exceed 8,000 tons altogether, shall be allowed to enter the Black Sea without having to give the notification provided for in Article 13 of the present Convention, provided an authorisation is obtained from the Turkish Government in the following circumstances: if the figure of the aggregate tonnage specified in paragraphs (*a*) and (*b*) above has not been reached and will not be exceeded by the despatch of the forces which it is desired to send, the Turkish Government shall grant the said authorisation within the shortest possible time after receiving the request which has been addressed to it; if the said figure has already been reached or if the despatch of the forces which it is desired to send will cause it to be exceeded, the Turkish Government will immediately inform the other Black Sea Powers of the request for authorisation, and if the said Powers make no objection within twenty-four hours of having received this information, the Turkish Government shall, within forty-eight hours at the latest, inform the interested Powers of the reply which it has decided to make to their request.

Any further entry into the Black Sea of naval forces of non-Black Sea Powers shall only be effected within the available limits of the aggregate tonnage provided for in paragraphs (*a*) and (*b*) above.

(2) Vessels of war belonging to non-Black Sea Powers shall not remain in the Black Sea more than twenty-one days, whatever be the object of their presence there.

ART. 19. In time of war, Turkey not being belligerent, warships shall enjoy complete freedom of transit and navigation through the Straits under the same conditions as those laid down in Articles 10 to 18.

Vessels of war belonging to belligerent Powers shall not, however, pass through the Straits except in cases arising out of the application of Article 25 of the present Convention, and in cases of assistance rendered to a State victim of aggression in virtue of a treaty of mutual assistance binding Turkey, concluded within the framework of the Covenant of the League of Nations, and registered and published in accordance with the provisions of Article 18 of the Covenant.

In the exceptional cases provided for in the preceding paragraph, the limitations laid down in Articles 10 to 18 of the present Convention shall not be applicable.

Notwithstanding the prohibition of passage laid down in paragraph 2 above, vessels of war belonging to belligerent Powers, whether they are Black Sea Powers or not, which have become separated from their bases, may return thereto.

Vessels of war belonging to belligerent Powers shall not make any capture, exercise the right of visit and search, or carry out any hostile act in the Straits.

ART. 20. In time of war, Turkey being belligerent, the provisions of Articles 10 to 18 shall not be applicable; the passage of warships shall be left entirely to the discretion of the Turkish Government.

ART. 21. Should Turkey consider herself to be threatened with imminent danger of war she shall have the right to apply the provisions of Article 20 of the present Convention.

Vessels which have passed through the Straits before Turkey has made use of the powers conferred upon her by the preceding paragraph, and which thus find themselves separated from their bases, may return thereto. It is, however, understood that Turkey may deny this right to vessels of war belonging to the State whose attitude has given rise to the application of the present Article.

Should the Turkish Government make use of the powers conferred by the first paragraph of the present Article, a notification to that effect shall be addressed to the High Contracting Parties and to the Secretary-General of the League of Nations.

If the Council of the League of Nations decide by a majority of two-thirds that the measures thus taken by Turkey are not justified, and if such should also be the opinion of the majority of the High Contracting Parties signatories to the present Convention, the Turkish Government undertakes to discontinue the measures in question as also any measures which may have been taken under Article 6 of the present Convention.

ART. 22. Vessels of war which have on board cases of plague, cholera, yellow fever, exanthematic typhus or smallpox or which have had such cases on board within the last seven days and vessels of war which have left an infected port within less than five times twenty-four hours must pass through the Straits in quarantine and apply by the means on board such prophylactic measures as are necessary in order to prevent any possibility of the Straits being infected.

SECTION III. AIRCRAFT

ART. 23. In order to assure the passage of civil aircraft between the Mediterranean and the Black Sea, the Turkish Government will indicate the air routes available for this purpose, outside the forbidden zones which may be established in the Straits. Civil aircraft may use these routes provided that they give the Turkish Government, as regards occasional flights, a notification of three days, and as regards flights on regular services, a general notification of the dates of passage.

The Turkish Government moreover undertake, notwithstanding any remilitarisation of the Straits, to furnish the necessary facilities for the safe passage of civil aircraft authorised under the air regulations in force in Turkey to fly across Turkish territory between Europe and Asia. The route which is to be followed in the Straits zone by aircraft which have obtained an authorisation shall be indicated from time to time.

SECTION IV. GENERAL PROVISIONS

ART. 24. The functions of the International Commission set up under the Convention relating to the régime of the Straits of the 24th July, 1923, are hereby transferred to the Turkish Government.

The Turkish Government undertake to collect statistics and to furnish information concerning the application of Articles 11, 12, 14 and 18 of the present Convention.

They will supervise the execution of all the provisions of the present Convention relating to the passage of vessels of war through the Straits.

As soon as they have been notified of the intended passage through the Straits of a foreign naval force the Turkish Government shall inform the representatives at Angora of the High Contracting Parties of the composition of that force, its tonnage, the date fixed for its entry into the Straits, and, if necessary, the probable date of its return.

The Turkish Government shall address to the Secretary-General of the League of Nations and to the High Contracting Parties an annual report giving details regarding the movements of foreign vessels of war through the Straits and furnishing all information which may be of service to commerce and navigation, both by sea and by air, for which provision is made in the present Convention.

ART. 25. Nothing in the present Convention shall prejudice the rights and obligations of Turkey, or of any of the other High Contracting Parties members of the League of Nations, arising out of the Covenant of the League of Nations.

SECTION V. FINAL PROVISIONS

ART. 26. The present Convention shall be ratified as soon as possible.

The ratifications shall be deposited in the archives of the Government of the French Republic in Paris.

The Japanese Government shall be entitled to inform the Government of the French Republic through their diplomatic representative in Paris that the ratification has been given, and in that case they shall transmit the instrument of ratification as soon as possible.

A *procès-verbal* of the deposit of ratifications shall be drawn up as soon as six instruments of ratification, including that of Turkey, shall have been deposited. For this purpose the notification provided for in the preceding paragraph shall be taken as the equivalent of the deposit of an instrument of ratification.

The present Convention shall come into force on the date of the said *procès-verbal.*

The French Government will transmit to all the High Contracting Parties an authentic copy of the *procès-verbal* provided for in the preceding paragraph and of the *procès-verbaux* of the deposit of any subsequent ratifications.

ART. 27. The present Convention shall, as from the date of its entry into force, be open to accession by any Power signatory to the Treaty of Peace at Lausanne signed on the 24th July, 1923.

Each accession shall be notified, through the diplomatic channel, to the Government of the French Republic, and by the latter to all the High Contracting Parties.

Accessions shall come into force as from the date of notification to the French Government.

ART. 28. The present Convention shall remain in force for twenty years from the date of its entry into force.

The principle of freedom of transit and navigation affirmed in Article 1 of the present Convention shall however continue without limit of time.

If, two years prior to the expiry of the said period of twenty years, no High Contracting Party shall have given notice of denunciation to the French Government the present Convention shall continue in force until two years after such notice shall have been given. Any such notice shall be communicated by the French Government to the High Contracting Parties.

In the event of the present Convention being denounced in accordance with the provisions of the present Article, the High Contracting Parties agree to be represented at a conference for the purpose of concluding a new Convention.

ART. 29. At the expiry of each period of five years from the date of the entry into force of the present Convention each of the High Contracting Parties shall be entitled to initiate a proposal for amending one or more of the provisions of the present Convention.

To be valid, any request for revision formulated by one of the High Contracting Parties must be supported, in the case of modifications to Articles 14 or 18, by one other High Contracting Party, and, in the case of modifications to any other Article, by two other High Contracting Parties.

Any request for revision thus supported must be notified to all the High Contracting Parties three months prior to the expiry of the current period of five years. This notification shall contain details of the proposed amendments and the reasons which have given rise to them.

Should it be found impossible to reach an agreement on these proposals through the diplomatic channel, the High Contracting Parties agree to be represented at a conference to be summoned for this purpose.

Such a conference may only take decisions by a unanimous vote, except as regards cases of revision involving Articles 14 and 18, for which a majority of three-quarters of the High Contracting Parties shall be sufficient.

The said majority shall include three-quarters of the High Contracting Parties which are Black Sea Powers, including Turkey.

61. TREATY OF PREFERENTIAL ALLIANCE: BRITAIN AND EGYPT
26 August 1936

(Ratifications exchanged, Cairo, 22 December 1936; denounced by Egypt, 15 October 1951; superseded on 19 October 1954 by an agreement on the Suez Canal base)

[Great Britain, *Parliamentary Papers, 1937,* Treaty Series No. 6, Cmd. 5360]

Anglo-Egyptian treaty negotiations, which appeared on the verge of success in the spring of 1930, broke down on 8 May over the question of the Sudan (Doc. 43). Parleys were resumed only after the Italian invasion of Ethiopia, for the resulting international tensions made Egypt and England less inflexible. Conversations between British High Commissioner Sir Miles Lampson and an all-party delegation led by Mustafa Pasha al-Nahhas (Zaghlul's successor as head of the Wafd) opened in Cairo on 2 March 1936. Some of the articles of the stillborn draft of May 1930 (text in *Parliamentary Papers, 1930,* Cmd. 3575, pp. 35–38) were incorporated without change into the more elaborate instrument signed in London on 26 August 1936. In accompanying notes (not reproduced), Nahhas Pasha gave assurances that "British Ambassadors will be considered senior to the other diplomatic representatives accredited to the Court of His Majesty the King of Egypt" and placed on record mutual guarantees comparable to those in paragraphs 5–7 of the annexure to the 1930 Anglo-Iraqi treaty (Doc. 56). The immunities and privileges of British armed forces in Egypt were regulated in a separate convention (not reproduced, text in Cmd. 5360, pp. 23–29). Egypt became a member of the League of Nations on 26 May 1937. The action contemplated in article 13 of the 1936 treaty was taken on 8 May 1937, when all the powers enjoying capitulatory privileges in Egypt adopted a convention in Montreux (text in *U.S. Treaty Series,* No. 939), providing for the immediate termination of the capitulatory regime in Egypt, apart from the mixed courts which were to continue in operation until 1949. *Survey of International Affairs, 1930,* pp. 188–222, *1936,* pp. 662–701, *1937,* vol. 1, pp. 581–607; J. C. Hurewitz, *Middle East Dilemmas,* chap. 3; M. Colombe, *L'Évolution de l'Égypte 1924–1950,* chap. 2; J. Marlowe, *History of Modern Egypt,* chap. 13; on the background of the mixed courts, J. Y. Brinton, *The Mixed Courts of Egypt;* G. Dykmans, *Le Statut contemporain des étrangers en Égypte.*

ART. 1. The military occupation of Egypt by the forces of His Majesty The King and Emperor is terminated.

ART. 2. His Majesty The King and Emperor will henceforth be represented at the Court of His Majesty the King of Egypt and His Majesty the King of Egypt will be represented at the Court of St. James's by Ambassadors duly accredited.

ART. 3. Egypt intends to apply for membership to the League of Nations. His Majesty's Government in the United Kingdom, recognising Egypt as a sovereign independent State, will support any request for admission which the Egyptian Government may present in the conditions prescribed by Article 1 of the Covenant.

ART. 4. An alliance is established between the High Contracting Parties with a view to consolidating their friendship, their cordial understanding and their good relations.

ART. 5. Each of the High Contracting Parties undertakes not to adopt in relation to foreign countries an attitude which is inconsistent with the alliance, nor to conclude political treaties inconsistent with the provisions of the present treaty.

ART. 6. Should any dispute with a third State produce a situation which involves a risk of a rupture with that State, the High Contracting Parties will consult each other with a view to the settlement of the said dispute by peaceful means, in accordance with the provisions of the Covenant of the League of Nations and of any other international obligations which may be applicable to the case.

ART. 7. Should, notwithstanding the provisions of Article 6 above, either of the High Contracting Parties become engaged in war, the other High Contracting Party will, subject always to the provisions of Article 10 below, immediately come to his aid in the capacity of an ally.

The aid of His Majesty the King of Egypt in the event of war, imminent menace of war or apprehended international emergency will consist in furnishing to His Majesty The King and Emperor on Egyptian territory, in accordance with the Egyptian system of administration and legislation, all the facilities and assistance in his power, including the use of his ports, aerodromes and means of communication. It will accordingly be for the Egyptian Government to take all the administrative and legislative measures, including the establishment of martial law and an effective censorship, necessary to render these facilities and assistance effective.

ART. 8. In view of the fact that the Suez Canal, whilst being an integral part of Egypt, is a universal means of communication as also an essential means of communication between the different parts of the British Empire, His Majesty the King of Egypt, until such time as the High Contracting Parties agree that the Egyptian Army is in a position to ensure by its own resources the liberty and entire security of navigation of the Canal, authorises His Majesty The King and Emperor to station forces in Egyptian territory in the vicinity of the Canal, in the zone specified in the Annex to this Article, with a view to ensuring in co-operation with the Egyptian forces the defence of the Canal. The detailed arrangements for the carrying into effect of this Article are contained in the Annex hereto. The presence of these forces shall not constitute in any manner an occupation and will in no way prejudice the sovereign rights of Egypt.

It is understood that at the end of the period of twenty years specified in Article 16 the question whether the presence of British forces is no longer necessary owing to the fact that the Egyptian Army is in a position to ensure by its own resources the liberty and entire security of navigation of the Canal may, if the High Contracting Parties do not agree thereon, be submitted to the Council of the League of Nations for decision in accordance with the provisions of the Covenant in force at the time of signature of the present treaty or to such other person or body of persons for decision in accordance with such other procedure as the High Contracting Parties may agree.

Annex to Article 8

1. Without prejudice to the provisions of Article 7, the numbers of the forces of His Majesty The King and Emperor to be maintained in the vicinity of the Canal shall not exceed, of the land forces, 10,000, and of the air forces, 400 pilots, together with the necessary ancillary personnel for administrative and technical duties. These numbers do not include civilian personnel, *e.g.*, clerks, artisans and labourers.

2. The British forces to be maintained in the vicinity of the Canal will be distributed (*a*) as regards the land forces, in Moascar and the Geneifa area on the south-west side of the Great Bitter Lake, and (*b*) as regards the air forces, within 5 miles of the Port Said–Suez railway from Kantara in the north, to the junction of the railway Suez–Cairo and Suez–Ismailia in the south, together with an extension along the Ismailia–Cairo railway to include the Royal Air Force Station at Abu Sueir and its satellite landing grounds; together with areas suitable for air firing and bombing ranges, which may have to be placed east of the Canal.

3. In the localities specified above there shall be provided for the British land and air forces of the numbers specified in paragraph 1 above, including 4,000 civilian personnel (but less 2,000 of the land forces, 700 of the air forces and 450 civilian personnel for whom accommodation already exists), the necessary lands and durable barrack and technical accommodation, including an emergency water supply. The lands, accommodation and water supply shall be suitable according to modern standards. In addition, amenities such as are reasonable, having regard to the character of these localities, will be provided by the planting of trees and the provision of gardens, playing fields, &c., for the troops, and a site for the erection of a convalescent camp on the Mediterranean coast.

4. The Egyptian Government will make available the lands and construct the accommodation, water supplies, amenities and convalescent camp, referred to in the preceding paragraph as being necessary over and above the accommodation already existing in these localities, at its own expense, but His Majesty's Government in the United Kingdom will contribute (1) the actual sum spent by the Egyptian Government before 1914 on the construction of new barracks as alternative accommodation to the Kasr-el-Nil Barracks in Cairo, and (2) the cost of one-fourth of the barrack and technical accommodation for the land forces. The first of these sums shall be paid at the time specified in paragraph 8 below for the withdrawal of the British forces from Cairo and the second at the time for the withdrawal of the British forces from Alexandria under paragraph 18 below. The Egyptian Government may charge a fair rental for the residential accommodation provided for the civilian personnel. The amount of the rent will be agreed between His Majesty's Government in the United Kingdom and the Egyptian Government.

5. The two Governments will each appoint, immediately the present treaty comes into force, two or more persons who shall together form a committee to whom all questions relating to the execution of these works from the time of their commencement to the time of their completion shall be entrusted. Proposals for, or outlines of, plans and specifications put forward by the representatives of His Majesty's Government in the United Kingdom will be accepted, provided they are reasonable and do not fall outside the scope of the obligations of the Egyptian Government under paragraph 4. The plans and specifications of each of the works to be undertaken by the Egyptian Government shall be approved by the representatives of both Governments on this committee before the work is begun. Any member of this committee, as well as the Commanders of the British forces or their representatives, shall have the right to examine the works at all stages of their construction, and the United Kingdom members of the committee may make suggestions as regards the manner in which the work is carried out. The United

Kingdom members shall also have the right to make at any time, while the work is in progress, proposals for modifications or alterations in the plans and specifications. Effect shall be given to suggestions and proposals by the United Kingdom members, subject to the condition that they are reasonable and do not fall outside the scope of the obligations of the Egyptian Government under paragraph 4. In the case of machinery and other stores, where standardization of type is important, it is agreed that stores of the standard type in general use by the British forces will be obtained and installed. It is, of course, understood that His Majesty's Government in the United Kingdom may, when the barracks and accommodation are being used by the British forces, make at their own expense improvements or alterations thereto and construct new buildings in the areas specified in paragraph 2 above.

6. In pursuance of their programme for the development of road and railway communications in Egypt, and in order to bring the means of communications in Egypt up to modern strategic requirements, the Egyptian Government will construct and maintain the following roads, bridges and railways:—

(A)—*Roads*

(i) Ismailia–Alexandria, via Tel-el-Kebir, Zagazig, Zifta, Tanta, Kafr-el-Zayat, Damanhour.

(ii) Ismailia–Cairo, via Tel-el-Kebir and thence continuing along the Sweet Water Canal to Heliopolis.

(iii) Port Said–Ismailia–Suez.

(iv) A link between the south end of the Great Bitter Lake and the Cairo-Suez road about 15 miles west of Suez.

In order to bring them up to the general standard of good-class roads for general traffic, these roads will be 20 feet wide, have bye-passes round villages, &c., and be made of such material as to be permanently utilisable for military purposes, and will be constructed in the above order of importance. They will comply with the technical specifications set out below which are the ordinary specifications for a good-class road for general traffic.

Bridges and roads shall be capable of carrying a double line of continuous columns of either heavy four-wheeled mechanical transport, six-wheeled mechanical transport or medium tanks. With regard to four-wheeled vehicles, the distance between the front axle of one vehicle and the rear axle of the vehicle next ahead shall be calculated at 20 feet, the load on each rear axle to be 14 tons, on each front axle to be 6 tons and the distance between axles 18 feet. With regard to six-wheeled vehicles, the distance between the front axle of one vehicle and the rear axle of that next ahead shall be calculated to be 20 feet, between rear axle and middle axle to be 4 feet and between middle axle and front axle 13 feet; the load on each rear and middle axle to be 8.1 tons and on each front axle to be 4 tons. Tanks shall be calculated for as weighing 19.25 tons, to be 25 feet over all in length and to have a distance of 3 feet between the front of one tank and the rear of the next ahead; the load of 19.25 tons to be carried by tracks which have a bearing of 13 feet upon the road or bridge.

(B)—*Railways*

(i) Railway facilities in the Canal Zone will be increased and improved to meet the needs of the increased garrison in the zone and to provide facilities for rapid entrainment of personnel, guns, vehicles and stores according to the requirements of a modern army. His Majesty's Government in the United Kingdom are hereby authorised to make at their own expense such subsequent additions and modifications to these railway facilities as the future requirements of the British forces may demand. Where such additions or modifications affect railway lines used for general traffic, the permission of the Egyptian Government must be obtained.

(ii) The line between Zagazig and Tanta will be doubled.

(iii) The Alexandria-Mersa Matruh line will be improved and made permanent.

7. In addition to the roads specified in paragraph 6 (A) above, and for the same

purposes, the Egyptian Government will construct and maintain the following roads:

(i) Cairo south along the Nile to Kena and Kus;

(ii) Kus to Kosseir;

(iii) Kena to Hurghada.

These roads and the bridges thereon will be constructed to satisfy the same standards as those specified in pargraph 6 above.

It may not be possible for the construction of the roads referred to in this paragraph to be undertaken at the same time as the roads referred to in paragraph 6, but they will be constructed as soon as possible.

8. When, to the satisfaction of both the High Contracting Parties, the accommodation referred to in paragraph 4 is ready (accommodation for the forces retained temporarily at Alexandria in accordance with paragraph 18 below not being included) and the works referred to in paragraph 6 above (other than the railways referred to in (ii) and (iii) of part (B) of that paragraph) have been completed, then the British forces in parts of Egypt other than the areas in the Canal Zone specified in paragraph 2 above and except for those maintained temporarily at Alexandria, will withdraw and the lands, barracks, aircraft landing grounds, seaplane anchorages and accommodation occupied by them will be vacated and, save in so far as they may belong to private persons, be handed over to the Egyptian Government.

9. Any difference of opinion between the two Governments relating to the execution of paragraphs 3, 4, 5, 6, 7 and 8 above will be submitted to the decision of an Arbitral Board, composed of three members, the two Governments nominating each a member and the third being nominated by the two Governments in common agreement. The decision of the Board shall be final.

10. In order to ensure the proper training of British troops, it is agreed that the area defined below will be available for the training of British forces: (*a*) and (*b*) at all times of the year, and (*c*) during February and March for annual manœuvres:—

(*a*) West of the Canal: From Kantara in the north to the Suez–Cairo railway (inclusive) in the south and as far as longitude 31 degrees 30 minutes east, exclusive of all cultivation;

(*b*) East of the Canal as required;

(*c*) A continuation of (*a*) as far south as latitude 29 degrees 52 minutes north, thence south-east to the junction of latitude 29 degrees 30 minutes north and longitude 31 degrees 44 minutes east and from that point eastwards along latitude 29 degrees 30 minutes north.

The areas of the localities referred to above are included in the map (scale 1: 500,000) which is annexed to the present Treaty.[1]

11. Unless the two Governments agree to the contrary, the Egyptian Government will prohibit the passage of aircraft over the territories situated on either side of the Suez Canal and within 20 kilometres of it, except for the purpose of passage from east to west or *vice versa* by means of a corridor 10 kilometres wide at Kantara. This prohibition will not, however, apply to the forces of the High Contracting Parties or to genuinely Egyptian air organisations or to air organisations genuinely belonging to any part of the British Commonwealth of Nations operating under the authority of the Egyptian Government.

12. The Egyptian Government will provide when necessary reasonable means of communication and access to and from the localities where the British forces are situated and will also accord facilities at Port Said and Suez for the landing and storage of material and supplies for the British forces, including the maintenance of a small detachment of the British forces in these ports to handle and guard this material and these supplies in transit.

13. In view of the fact that the speed and range of modern aircraft necessitate the use of wide areas for the efficient training of air forces, the Egyptian Government will accord permission to the British air forces to fly wherever they consider it necessary for the purpose of training. Reciprocal treatment will be accorded to Egyptian air forces in British territories.

14. In view of the fact that the safety

[1] Not reproduced.

of flying is dependent upon provision of a large number of places where aircraft can alight, the Egyptian Government will secure the maintenance and constant availability of adequate landing grounds and seaplane anchorages in Egyptian territory and waters. The Egyptian Government will accede to any request from the British air forces for such additional landing grounds and seaplane anchorages as experience may show to be necessary to make the number adequate for allied requirements.

15. The Egyptian Government will accord permission for the British air forces to use the said landing grounds and seaplane anchorages, and in the case of certain of them to send stocks of fuel and stores thereto, to be kept in sheds to be erected thereon for this purpose, and in case of urgency to undertake such work as may be necessary for the safety of aircraft.

16. The Egyptian Government will give all necessary facilities for the passage of the personnel of the British forces, aircraft and stores to and from the said landing grounds and seaplane anchorages. Similar facilities will be afforded to the personnel, aircraft and stores of the Egyptian forces at the air bases of the British forces.

17. The British military authorities shall be at liberty to request permission from the Egyptian Government to send parties of officers in civilian clothes to the Western Desert to study the ground and draw up tactical schemes. This permission shall not be unreasonably withheld.

18. His Majesty the King of Egypt authorises His Majesty The King and Emperor to maintain units of his forces at or near Alexandria for a period not exceeding eight years from the date of the coming into force of the present treaty, this being the approximate period considered necessary by the two High Contracting Parties—

(*a*) For the final completion of the barrack accommodation in the Canal zone;

(*b*) For the improvement of the roads—

(i) Cairo–Suez;

(ii) Cairo–Alexandria via Giza and the desert;

(iii) Alexandria–Mersa Matruh;

so as to bring them up to the standard specified in part (A) of paragraph 6;

(c) The improvement of the railway facilities between Ismailia and Alexandria, and Alexandria and Mersa Matruh referred to in (ii) and (iii) of part (B) of paragraph 6.

The Egyptian Government will complete the work specified in (*a*), (*b*) and (*c*) above before the expiry of the period of eight years aforesaid. The roads and railway facilities mentioned above will, of course, be maintained by the Egyptian Government.

19. The British forces in or near Cairo shall, until the time for withdrawal under paragraph 8 above, and the British forces in or near Alexandria until the expiry of the time specified in paragraph 18 above, continue to enjoy the same facilities as at present.

ART. 9. The immunities and privileges in jurisdictional and fiscal matters to be enjoyed by the forces of His Majesty The King and Emperor who are in Egypt in accordance with the provisions of the present treaty will be determined in a separate convention to be concluded between the Egyptian Government and His Majesty's Government in the United Kingdom.

ART. 10. Nothing in the present treaty is intended to or shall in any way prejudice the rights and obligations which devolve, or may devolve, upon either of the High Contracting Parties under the Covenant of the League of Nations or the Treaty for the Renunciation of War signed at Paris on the 27th August, 1928.[2]

ART. 11. 1. While reserving liberty to conclude new conventions in future, modifying the agreements of the 19th January and the 10th July, 1899, the High Contractting Parties agree that the administration of the Sudan shall continue to be that resulting from the said agreements. The Governor-General shall continue to exercise on the joint behalf of the High Contracting

[2] Treaty Series No. 29 (1929) (Cmd. 3410).

Parties the powers conferred upon him by the said agreements.

The High Contracting Parties agree that the primary aim of their administration in the Sudan must be the welfare of the Sudanese.

Nothing in this article prejudices the question of sovereignty over the Sudan.

2. Appointments and promotions of officials in the Sudan will in consequence remain vested in the Governor-General, who, in making new appointments to posts for which qualified Sudanese are not available, will select suitable candidates of British and Egyptian nationality.

3. In addition to Sudanese troops, both British and Egyptian troops shall be placed at the disposal of the Governor-General for the defence of the Sudan.

4. Egyptian immigration into the Sudan shall be unrestricted except for reasons of public order and health.

5. There shall be no discrimination in the Sudan between British subjects and Egyptian nationals in matters of commerce, immigration or the possession of property.

6. The High Contracting Parties are agreed on the provisions set out in the Annex to this Article as regards the method by which international conventions are to be made applicable to the Sudan.

Annex to Article 11

1. Unless and until the High Contracting Parties agree to the contrary in application of paragraph 1 of this Article, the general principle for the future shall be that international conventions shall only become applicable to the Sudan by the joint action of the Governments of the United Kingdom and of Egypt, and that such joint action shall similarly also be required if it is desired to terminate the participation of the Sudan in an international convention which already applies to this territory.

2. Conventions to which it will be desired that the Sudan should be a party will generally be conventions of a technical or humanitarian character. Such conventions almost invariably contain a provision for subsequent accession, and in such cases this method of making the convention applicable to the Sudan will be adopted. Accession will be effected by a joint instrument, signed on behalf of Egypt and the United Kingdom respectively by two persons duly authorised for the purpose. The method of depositing the instruments of accession will be the subject of agreement in each case between the two Governments. In the event of its being desired to apply to the Sudan a convention which does not contain an accession clause, the method by which this should be effected will be the subject of consultation and agreement between the two Governments.

3. If the Sudan is already a party to a convention, and it is desired to terminate the participation of the Sudan therein, the necessary notice of termination will be given jointly by the United Kingdom and by Egypt.

4. It is understood that the participation of the Sudan in a convention and the termination of such participation can only be effected by joint action specifically taken in respect of the Sudan, and does not follow merely from the fact that the United Kingdom and Egypt are both parties to a convention or have both denounced a convention.

5. At international conferences where such conventions are negotiated, the Egyptian and the United Kingdom delegates would naturally keep in touch with a view to any action which they may agree to be desirable in the interests of the Sudan.

ART. 12. His Majesty The King and Emperor recognises that the responsibility for the lives and property of foreigners in Egypt devolves exclusively upon the Egyptian Government, who will ensure the fulfilment of their obligations in this respect.

ART. 13. His Majesty The King and Emperor recognises that the capitulatory régime now existing in Egypt is no longer in accordance with the spirit of the times and with the present state of Egypt.

His Majesty the King of Egypt desires the abolition of this régime without delay.

Both High Contracting Parties are agreed upon the arrangements with regard to this matter as set forth in the Annex to this Article.

Annex to Article 13

1. It is the object of the arrangement set out in this Annex:—

(i) To bring about speedily the abolition of the Capitulations in Egypt with the disappearance of the existing restrictions on Egyptian sovereignty in the matter of the application of Egyptian legislation (including financial legislation) to foreigners as its necessary consequence;

(ii) To institute a transitional régime for a reasonable and not unduly prolonged period to be fixed, during which the Mixed Tribunals will remain and will, in addition to their present judicial jurisdiction, exercise the jurisdiction at present vested in the Consular Courts.

At the end of this transitional period the Egyptian Government will be free to dispense with the Mixed Tribunals.

2. As a first step, the Egyptian Government will approach the Capitulatory Powers as soon as possible with a view to (*a*) the removal of all restrictions on the application of Egyptian legislation to foreigners, and (*b*) the institution of a transitional régime for the Mixed Tribunals as provided in paragraph 1 (ii) above.

3. His Majesty's Government in the United Kingdom, as the Government of a Capitulatory Power and as an ally of Egypt, are in no way opposed to the arrangements referred to in the preceding paragraph and will collaborate actively with the Egyptian Government in giving effect to them by using all their influence with the Powers exercising capitulatory rights in Egypt.

4. It is understood that in the event of its being found impossible to bring into effect the arrangements referred to in paragraph 2, the Egyptian Government retains its full rights unimpaired with regard to the capitulatory régime, including the Mixed Tribunals.

5. It is understood that paragraph 2 (*a*) involves not merely that the assent of the Capitulatory Powers will be no longer necessary for the application of any Egyptian legislation to their nationals, but also that the present legislative functions of the Mixed Tribunals as regards the application of Egyptian legislation to foreigners will terminate. It would follow from this that the Mixed Tribunals in their judicial capacity would no longer have to pronounce upon the validity of the application to foreigners of an Egyptian law or decree which has been applied to foreigners by the Egyptian Parliament or Government, as the case may be.

6. His Majesty the King of Egypt hereby declares that no Egyptian legislation made applicable to foreigners will be inconsistent with the principles generally adopted in modern legislation or, with particular relation to legislation of a fiscal nature, discriminate against foreigners, including foreign corporate bodies.

7. In view of the fact that it is the practice in most countries to apply to foreigners the law of their nationality in matters of "statut personnel," consideration will be given to the desirability of excepting from the transfer of jurisdiction, at any rate in the first place, matters relating to "statut personnel" affecting nationals of those Capitulatory Powers who wish that their Consular authorities should continue to exercise such jurisdiction.

8. The transitional régime for the Mixed Tribunals and the transfer to them of the jurisdiction at present exercised by the Consular Courts (which régime and transfer will, of course, be subject to the provisions of the special convention referred to in Article 9) will necessitate the revision of existing laws relating to the organisation and jurisdiction of the Mixed Tribunals, including the preparation and promulgation of a new Code of Criminal Procedure. It is understood that this revision will include amongst other matters:—

(i) The definition of the word "foreigner" for the purpose of the future jurisdiction of the Mixed Tribunals;

(ii) The increase of the personnel of the Mixed Tribunals and the Mixed Parquet, which will be necessitated by the proposed extension of their jurisdiction;

(iii) The procedure in the case of pardons or remissions of sentences imposed on foreigners and also in connection with the execution of capital sentences passed on foreigners.

ART. 14. The present treaty abrogates any existing agreements or other instruments whose continued existence is inconsistent with its provisions. Should either High Contracting Party so request, a list of the agreements and instruments thus abrogated shall be drawn up in agreement between them within six months of the coming into force of the present treaty.

ART. 15. The High Contracting Parties agree that any difference on the subject of the application or interpretation of the provisions of the present treaty which they are unable to settle by direct negotiation shall be dealt with in accordance with the provisions of the Covenant of the League of Nations.

ART. 16. At any time after the expiration of a period of twenty years from the coming into force of the treaty, the High Contracting Parties will, at the request of either of them, enter into negotiations with a view to such revision of its terms by agreement between them as may be appropriate in the circumstances as they then exist. In case of the High Contracting Parties being unable to agree upon the terms of the revised treaty, the difference will be submitted to the Council of the League of Nations for decision in accordance with the provisions of the Covenant in force at the time of signature of the present treaty or to such other person or body of persons for decision in accordance with such procedure as the High Contracting Parties may agree. It is agreed that any revision of this treaty will provide for the continuation of the Alliance between the High Contracting Parties in accordance with the principles contained in Articles 4, 5, 6 and 7. Nevertheless, with the consent of both High Contracting Parties, negotiations may be entered into at any time after the expiration of a period of ten years after the coming into force of the treaty, with a view to such revision as aforesaid.

62. DRAFT TREATY OF PREFERENTIAL ALLIANCE AND ACCOMPANYING MILITARY CONVENTION: FRANCE AND LEBANON
13 November 1936

[The original text may be found in France, Ministry of Foreign Affairs, *Rapport à la société des nations sur la situation de la Syrie et du Liban (année 1936)*, pp. 229–50; unofficial translation, courtesy of Department of State, Washington, D.C.]

The replacement of the mandate by Britain's preferential alliance with Iraq (Doc. 56) stirred the envy of nationalists in French-mandated Syria. As a result of talks conducted in the spring and fall of 1933 in Damascus between the French High Commissioner and the Syrian government, an instrument was initialed on 16 November [French text in *Rapport à la société des nations sur la situation de la Syrie et du Liban (année 1933)*, pp. 189–95]. The draft treaty, though patterned on the Anglo-Iraqi arrangement, assured France in Syria more comprehensive controls over military and foreign affairs than Britain enjoyed in Iraq. Syrian nationalist discontent with the terms found such vehement articulation in the Chamber of Deputies on 20–21 November that the High Commissioner suspended the legislature's session on the 24th and two days later instructed the Syrian President to strike the draft treaty from the Chamber's agenda. The growing tension in the eastern Mediterranean, sparked by the Italo-Ethiopian war in 1935–36, broke the impasse between France and Syria, as it had that of longer duration between Britain and Egypt (Doc. 61). Following a fifty-day general strike (11 January–1 March 1936) in Syria staged by the nationalists, the French Government agreed to reopen treaty negotiations. The renewed talks, which were launched in Paris on 1 April, moved steadily toward fruitful conclusion after 11 June when the Popular French government of Léon Blum, which had assumed office a week earlier, conceded the principal demands of the Syrian nationalists. The fresh instrument—a facsimile of the 1933 model, modified to conform with Syrian nationalist claims—was initialed on 9 September [French text in *Rapport . . . (année 1936)*, pp. 201–28]. This time nationalists in

Lebanon prodded France for comparable negotiations, which commenced in Bayrut on 20 October and twenty-five days later yielded the following instruments. The draft treaties of 1936 were largely identical in content and phraseology; the Syrian arrangement, however, was not automatically renewable and granted France only limited military privileges. The legislature of Lebanon on 17 November and that of Syria on 27 December 1936 unanimously approved their respective treaties. But the alliance never went into force, because of the failure of France to ratify the instruments. Five protocols and eleven exchanges of notes, attached to the draft treaty, are omitted below. *Survey of International Affairs, 1934*, pp. 284–301, *1936*, pp. 748–67; A. H. Hourani, *Syria and Lebanon*, chaps. 10, 11; G. Antonius, *Arab Awakening*, chap. 16; E. Rabbath, *Unité syrienne et devenir arabe;* G. Henry-Haye and P. Vienot, *Les Relations de la France et de la Syrie.*

ART. 1. There will be perpetual peace and friendship between France and Lebanon.

An alliance is established between the two independent and soveregin states in consecration of their friendship and of the bonds which unite them for the defense of the country and for the safeguarding of their common interests.

ART. 2. In all matters of foreign policy of a nature to affect their common interests, the two governments agree to consult each other fully and without reserve.

Each of the high contracting parties binds itself not to adopt with regard to any third state any attitude incompatible with the alliance, and to abstain from any agreement incompatible with the present treaty.

Each government will accredit to the other a diplomatic representative.

ART. 3. The two high contracting parties will take all necessary measures to assure, on the day of the cessation of the mandate, the transfer to the Lebanese government alone of the rights and obligations resulting from all treaties, conventions or other international acts concluded by the French government so far as these concern the Lebanon or are in its name.

ART. 4. In case a difference between Lebanon and a third State should create a situation of a nature to cause a risk of rupture with that State, the two Governments would consult each other with a view to a settlement of the difference by peaceful means, in conformity with the stipulations of the Covenant of the League of Nations or of any other international convention applicable to such a case.

If in spite of the measures provided in the preceding paragraph, one of the high contracting parties should find itself engaged in a conflict, the other high contracting party will immediately lend it its aid in the capacity of ally. In case of an imminent threat of war, the high contracting parties shall consult each other immediately in order to take the necessary measures of defense. The assistance of the Lebanese government shall consist in furnishing to the French Government on Lebanese territory all facilities and all assistance in its power, including the use of railways, water courses, ports, aerodromes and bodies of water and other means of communication.

ART. 5. Responsibility for the maintenance of order in Lebanon and that for the defense of the territory are incumbent upon the Lebanese government.

The French Government agrees to render military, aerial and naval aid to Lebanon during the duration of the treaty, following the provisions of the annexed convention.

With a view to facilitating the execution by the French government of the obligations which are incumbent upon it by the terms of the preceding article of the present treaty, the Lebanese Government recognizes that the permanent maintenance and the protection under all circumstances of the means of communication of the French Government which pass through Lebanese territory are in the interest of the alliance.

ART. 6. The present treaty is concluded for a duration of 25 years, and is renewable by tacit continuation for an equal duration.

The annexed conventions and accords of application shall have the same duration as the treaty itself, unless a lesser duration be stipulated in the Act, or unless the high contracting parties are in agreement to revise them in order to take into account new situations.

The negotiations for eventual modifications of the treaty shall be opened if, in the course of the 24th year of its application, one of the two governments should demand it.

ART. 7. The present treaty shall be ratified and the exchange of ratifications effected as soon as possible.

It shall be communicated to the League of Nations.

This treaty shall enter into force, at the same time as the conventions and accords annexed, on the day of the admission of Lebanon to the League of Nations.

ART. 8. From the entry into force of the present treaty, the French Government will be freed from the responsibilities and obligations which are incumbent upon it, so far as Lebanon is concerned, whether arising from international decisions or acts of the League of Nations.

These responsibilities and obligations, so far as they may continue to exist, shall be automatically transferred to the Lebanese Government.

ART. 9. The present treaty is drawn up in French and Arabic; the two texts are official, the French text controlling.

In case a dispute should arise on the subject of the interpretation or the application of this treaty, and this dispute should not be definitely settled by means of direct negotiation, the high contracting parties agree to have recourse to the procedure of conciliation and arbitration provided by the Covenant of the League of Nations. . . .

MILITARY CONVENTION

ART. 1. The Lebanese Government substituting itself for the French authorities, takes under its responsibility the constituted military forces composed of Lebanese elements, together with the charges and the obligations connected therewith.

ART. 2. The Lebanese armed forces must include as a minimum one mixed brigade with its auxiliary services.

ART. 3. The French Government obligates itself to accord to the Government of the Lebanese Republic, upon request, the following facilities, the expenses of which will fall on the Lebanese Government:

a) The placing at the disposition of the Lebanese Government of a military mission for its army, its gendarmery, its navy, or its military aviation.

The role, composition and status of the mission shall be determined by agreement between the two governments prior to the entry in force of the treaty of alliance.

Inasmuch as it would be desirable that the training and instruction shall be identical in the armies of the two high contracting parties, the Lebanese Government obligates itself to engage only Frenchmen in the capacity of instructors and specialists.

The instructors or specialists shall be requested from the French Government and, from the point of view of administration and general discipline, shall be under the jurisdiction of the chief of the military mission.

The officers of the French military mission may be called upon to exercise temporarily an actual command in the Lebanese armed forces, upon request addressed to the representative of the French Government and approved by him. In this case, these officers shall be under the authority of the normal command of the unity to which they are attached so far as concerns the exercise of the command which is entrusted to them.

b) The sending to French schools, instruction centers and bodies of French troops and on board French vessels of war of any of the personnel of the Lebanese armed forces whom the Lebanese Government may judge necessary to have instructed outside of the Lebanon.

ART. 4. In order to facilitate the execution of the obligations of the alliance, the Lebanese Government shall adopt for its armed forces armament, materials and, so far as may be necessary, equipment of the same model as those in the French armed forces.

The French Government will grant all facilities to the Labanese Government in order that the latter may be assured in France of the supply to the Lebanese armed forces of arms, ammunitions, ships, aeroplanes, materials and equipment of the most recent model.

ART. 5. In order to comply with the provisions of the second paragraph of Article 5 of the treaty, the French Government obligates itself to maintain on Lebanese territory, until the conclusion of a new agreement between the two high contracting parties, elements of French forces of the land army, of the air force and of the navy stationed in the Levant.

The especial conditions of this assignment and the collaboration between the French and Lebanese forces shall form the object of periodic agreements between the two governments.

It is specified that the stationing of French forces in Lebanese territory does not constitute an occupation and does not infringe upon the sovereign rights of the Lebanese Government.

ART 6. The Lebanese Government shall accord all possible facilities for the maintenance, instruction, movements, transportation and communications of the French forces, whether in the vicinity of the places where they shall be stationed or in transit between these points, as well as for the transportation, the storage of all provisions and equipment necessary for these forces. These facilities include the use of roads, railways, navigable waters, ports, quays, aerodromes and bodies of water, the right of flight over the territory and the use of the telegraph, telephone and radio-telegraph systems.

In no case may there be established a tariff discriminatory against the French government.

The French war ships shall have general permission to enter and to remain in Lebanese waters and to visit Lebanese ports, it being understood that the Lebanese Government shall receive prior notification of visits to Lebanese ports.

The Lebanese government shall place at the disposition of the French government all grounds and places necessary for the needs of the French forces.

The modalities of application of this provision, as well as the different questions related both to real estate belonging to French military authorities and to that of which they have the use, shall form the object of individual agreements.

ART. 7. In execution of Article 5 of the treaty of alliance, and without prejudice to any modifications which the high contracting parties may agree to make hereafter, the Lebanese Government obligates itself to assure to French forces and to individual French soldiers or sailors, as well as to the French civil employees and their families who may be in Lebanese territory by virtue of the alliance, the privileges and immunities which these military, naval and civil officials enjoyed in the Lebanon at the time of the entry into effect of the present convention.

63. TREATY OF NONAGGRESSION (SA'DABAD PACT): AFGHANISTAN, IRAN, IRAQ AND TURKEY
8 July 1937

(Ratifications deposited, Tehran, 25 June 1938)

[League of Nations, *Treaty Series,* No. 4402, vol. 190 (1938), pp. 21–27]

Border disputes arising from the peace settlement or inherited from earlier centuries kept relations between Iran (as Persia became known after 1935), Turkey and Iraq far from friendly for more than a decade following World War I. An agreement reached in Tehran on 23 January 1932 (text in League of Nations, *Official Journal,* February 1935, pp. 237–39) demarcated the Turco-Iranian frontier. But as late as January 1935 the Council of the League considered an Iraqi territorial complaint against Iran. Although the Council took no decision, Iraq nevertheless requested in January and September 1936 and again in May 1937 that the item be stricken from the Council's agenda. One reason for the Iraqi change of heart could be found in the draft treaty, initialed in Geneva on 2 October 1935 by the Afghan, Iranian, Iraqi and Turkish delegates to the League of Nations, encouraged in their action by the Italo-Ethiopian crisis. According to the preamble of the treaty, signed at Sa'dabad Palace—Riza Shah's summer residence in the northern suburbs of Tehran—on 8 July 1937, the four Muslim states were "actuated by the common purpose of ensuring peace and security in the Near East by means of additional guarantees within the framework of the Covenant of the League of Nations." An accompanying protocol (not reproduced) announced that a permanent council would meet at least once annually. The Sa'dabad Pact, automatically renewable every five years, was never formally terminated. But this was without practical significance, for the quadripartite council, whose chief function apparently was to press for rotational membership in the League Council of the signatory states, did not ever convene after the outbreak of World War II. *Survey of International Affairs, 1936,* pp. 793–803; M. Khadduri, *Independent Iraq,* pp. 247–48, 261–63; A. Khalatbary, *L'Iran et le pacte orientale.*

ART. 1. The High Contracting Parties undertake to pursue a policy of complete abstention from any interference in each other's internal affairs.

ART. 2. The High Contracting Parties expressly undertake to respect the inviolability of their common frontiers.

ART. 3. The High Contracting Parties agree to consult together in all international disputes affecting their common interests.

ART. 4. Each of the High Contracting Parties undertakes in no event to resort, whether singly or jointly with one or more third Powers, to any act of aggression directed against any other of the Contracting Parties.

The following shall be deemed to be acts of aggression:

1. Declaration of war;
2. Invasion of the armed forces of one State, with or without a declaration of war, of the territory of another State;
3. An attack by the land, naval or air forces of one State, with or without a declaration of war, on the territory, vessels or aircraft of another State;
4. Directly or indirectly aiding or assisting an aggressor.

The following shall not constitute acts of aggression:

1. The exercise of the right of legitimate self-defence, that is to say, resistance to an act of aggression as defined above;
2. Action under Article 16 of the Covenant of the League of Nations;
3. Action in pursuance of a decision of the Assembly or Council of the League of Nations, or under Article 15, paragraph 7, of the Covenant of the League of Nations, provided always that in the latter case such action is directed against the State which was the first to attack;
4. Action to assist a State subjected to attack, invasion or recourse to war by another of the High Contracting Parties, in violation of the Treaty for Renunciation of War signed in Paris on August 27th, 1928.

ART. 5. Should one of the High Contracting Parties consider that a breach of Article 4 of the present Treaty has been or is about to be committed, he shall at once bring the matter before the Council of the League of Nations.

The foregoing provision shall not affect the right of such High Contracting Party to take any steps which, in the circumstances, he may deem necessary.

ART. 6. Should one of the High Contracting Parties commit an aggression against a third Power, any other High Contracting Party may denounce the present Treaty, without notice, as towards the aggressor.

ART. 7. Each of the High Contracting Parties undertakes to prevent, within his respective frontiers, the formation or activities of armed bands, associations or organisations to subvert the established institutions, or disturb the order or security of any part, whether situated on the frontier or elsewhere, of the territory of another Party, or to change the constitutional system of such other Party.

ART. 8. The High Contracting Parties, having already recognised, in the General Treaty for Renunciation of War August

27th, 1928, that the settlement or solution of all disputes or conflicts, whatever their nature or origin, which may arise among them, shall never be sought by other than pacific means, reaffirm that principle and undertake to rely upon such modes of procedure as have been or shall be established between the High Contracting Parties in that respect.

ART. 9. No Articles of the present Treaty shall be considered as in any way diminishing the obligations assumed by each of the High Contracting Parties under the Covenant of the League of Nations.

ART. 10. The present Treaty, drawn up in the French language and signed in quadruplicate, one copy having, as they severally recognise, been delivered to each of the High Contracting Parties, is concluded for a period of five years.

On the expiry of that period, and failing its denunciation, with six months' notice, by one of the High Contracting Parties, the Treaty shall be deemed to be renewed for successive periods of five years, until its denunciation with six months' notice by one or more of the High Contracting Parties. On its denunciation as towards one of the Parties, the Treaty shall nevertheless remain in force as between the others.

64. AGREEMENT ON MUTUAL INTERESTS IN THE MEDITERRANEAN: THE UNITED KINGDOM AND ITALY
16 April 1938

[Great Britain, *Parliamentary Papers, 1938,* Treaty Series No. 31, Cmd. 5726]

Italy launched an Arabic program to the Near and Middle East from Radio Bari—the first European station to transmit such broadcasts—in September 1935, on the eve of the invasion of Ethiopia. The program, which Italian agents supplemented by subversive activities, traded on prevailing anti-British and anti-French sentiment in the Arab states and continued at full blast even after the conquest of Ethiopia was completed in May 1936. The Mediterranean repercussions of the Spanish civil war after July 1936 and the creation of the Rome-Berlin Axis the following October stirred increasing anxiety in the United Kingdom about its position in the Near and Middle East. By early 1938 Britain became especially restive over the prominence that Radio Bari accorded to the inflamed Palestine question and the accelerated movement of Italian agents in Yemen and vicinity. In the hope of settling the consequent issues, the United Kingdom concluded with Italy on 16 April 1938 a comprehensive agreement, in which the signatories exchanged guarantees mutually to recognize and respect each other's sphere of influence. Reproduced below are the annexes on the Arabian Peninsula, propaganda and the Suez Canal. As regards Italy's propaganda on the Arab-Zionist dispute, Foreign Minister Count Ciano gave oral assurances that his government "would abstain from creating difficulties and embarrassment to His Majesty's Government in the administration of Palestine" (Great Britain, *Parliamentary Debates, Commons,* 5th ser., vol. 335, col. 538). Italy did in fact suspend hostile radio propaganda for a time, only to have its place taken with even greater effectiveness by Nazi Germany. E. Monroe, *The Mediterranean in Politics,* chaps. 4, 7; *Survey of International Affairs, 1938,* vol. 1, pp. 137–43; J. C. Hurewitz, *The Struggle for Palestine,* chap. 6; S. Arsenian, "Wartime Propaganda in the Middle East," *The Middle East Journal,* 2 (October 1948), 417–29; N. Barbour, "Broadcasting to the Arab World," *ibid.,* 5 (Winter 1951), 57–69.

ANNEX 3. ANGLO-ITALIAN AGREEMENT ON CERTAIN AREAS IN THE MIDDLE EAST

The Government of the United Kingdom of Great Britain and Northern Ireland and the Italian Government,

being desirous of ensuring that there shall be no conflict between their respective policies in regard to the areas in the Middle East referred to in the present agreement,

being desirous, moreover, that the same friendly spirit which has attended the signing of to-day's Protocol, and of the documents annexed thereto, should also animate their relations in regard to those areas,

have agreed as follows:—

ART. 1. Neither Party will conclude any agreement or take any action which might in any way impair the independence or integrity of Saudi Arabia or of the Yemen.

ART. 2. Neither Party will obtain or seek to obtain a privileged position of a political character in any territory which at present belongs to Saudi Arabia or to the Yemen or in any territory which either of those States may hereafter acquire.

ART. 3. The two Parties recognise that, in addition to the obligations incumbent on each of them in virtue of Articles 1 and 2 hereof, it is in the common interest of both of them that no other Power should acquire or seek to acquire sovereignty or any privileged position of a political character in any territory which at present belongs to Saudi Arabia or to the Yemen or which either of those States may hereafter acquire, including any islands in the Red Sea belonging to either of those States, or in any other islands in the Red Sea to which Turkey renounced her rights by Article 16 of the Treaty of Peace signed at Lausanne on the 24th July, 1923. In particular they regard it as an essential interest of each of them that no other Power should acquire sovereignty or any privileged position on any part of the coast of the Red Sea which at present belongs to Saudi Arabia or to the Yemen or in any of the aforesaid islands.

ART. 4. (1) As regards those islands in the Red Sea to which Turkey renounced her rights by Article 16 of the Treaty of Peace signed at Lausanne on the 24th July, 1923, and which are not comprised in the territory of Saudi Arabia or of the Yemen, neither Party will, in or in regard to any such island:—

(*a*) establish its sovereignty, or

(*b*) erect fortifications or defences.

(2) It is agreed that neither Party will object to:—

(*a*) the presence of British officials at Kamaran for the purpose of securing the sanitary service of the pilgrimage to Mecca in accordance with the provisions of the Agreement concluded at Paris on the 19th June, 1926, between the Governments of Great Britain and Northern Ireland and of India on the one part, and the Government of the Netherlands, on the other part; it is also understood that the Italian Government may appoint an Italian Medical Officer to be stationed there on the same conditions as the Netherlands Medical Officer under the said Agreement;

(*b*) the presence of Italian officials at Great Hanish, Little Hanish and Jebel Zukur for the purpose of protecting the fishermen who resort to those islands;

(*c*) the presence at Abu Ail, Centre Peak and Jebel Teir of such persons as are required for the maintenance of the lights on those islands.

ART. 5. (1) The two Parties agree that it is in the common interest of both of them that there shall be peace between Saudi Arabia and the Yemen and within the territories of those States. But, while they will at all times exert their good offices in the cause of peace, they will not intervene in any conflict which, despite their good offices, may break out between or within those States.

(2) The two Parties also recognise that it is in the common interest of both of them that no other Power should intervene in any such conflict.

ART. 6. As regards the zone of Arabia lying to the east and south of the present boundaries of Saudi Arabia and of the Yemen or of any future boundaries which may be established by agreement between the Government of the United Kingdom, on the one hand, and the Governments of Saudi Arabia or of the Yemen, on the other:

(1) The Government of the United Kingdom declare that in the territories of the Arab rulers under their protection within this zone:

(*a*) no action shall be taken by the Government of the United Kingdom, which shall be such as to prejudice in any way the independence or integrity of Saudi Arabia or of the Yemen (which both Parties have undertaken to respect in Article 1 hereof), within any territory at present belonging to those States or within any additional territory which may be recognised by the Government of the United Kingdom as belonging to either of those States as a result of any agreement which may hereafter be concluded between the Government of the United Kingdom and the Government of either of them;

(*b*) the Government of the United Kingdom will not undertake, or cause to be undertaken, any military preparations or works other than military preparations or works of a purely defensive character for the defence of the said territories or of the communications between different parts of the British Empire. Furthermore, the Government of the United Kingdom will not enrol the inhabitants of any of these territories, or cause them to be enrolled, in any military forces other than forces designed and suited solely for the preservation of order and for local defence;

(*c*) while the Government of the United Kingdom reserve the liberty to take in these territories such steps as may be necessary for the preservation of order and the development of the country, they intend to maintain the autonomy of the Arab rulers under their protection.

(2) The Italian Government declare that they will not seek to acquire any political influence in this zone.

ART. 7. The Government of the United Kingdom declare that within the limits of the Aden Protectorate as defined in the Aden Protectorate Order, 1937, Italian citizens and subjects (including Italian companies) shall have liberty to come, with their ships and goods, to all places and ports, and they shall have freedom of entry, travel and residence and the right to exercise there any description of business, profession, occupation or industry, so long as they satisfy and observe the conditons and regulations from time to time applicable in the Protectorate to the citizens and subjects and ships of any country not being a territory under the sovereignty, suzerainty, protection or mandate of His Majesty The King of Great Britain, Ireland and the British Dominions beyond the Seas, Emperor of India.

ART. 8. (1) Should either Party at any time give notice to the other that they consider that a change has taken place in the circumstances obtaining at the time of the entry into force of the present Agreement. such as to necessitate a modification of the provisions of the Agreement, the two Parties will enter into negotiations with a view to the revision or amendment of any of the provisions of the Agreement.

(2) At any time after the expiration of a period of ten years from the entry into force of this Agreement either party may notify the other of its intention to determine the Agreement. Any such notification shall take effect three months after the date on which it is made.

ANNEX 4. DECLARATION ON PROPAGANDA

The two Governments welcome the opportunity afforded by the present occasion to place on record their agreement that any attempt by either of them to employ the methods of publicity or propaganda at its disposal in order to injure the interests of the other would be inconsistent with the good relations which it is the object of the present Agreement to establish and maintain between the two Governments and the peoples of their respective countries.

ANNEX 8. DECLARATION ON THE SUEZ CANAL

The Government of the United Kingdom and the Italian Government hereby reaffirm their intention always to respect and abide by the provisions of the Convention signed at Constantinople on the 29th October, 1888, which guarantees at all times and for all Powers the free use of the Suez Canal.

65. BRITISH POLICY ON PALESTINE
17 May 1939

[Great Britain, *Parliamentary Papers, 1939,* Cmd. 6019]

The situation in Palestine grew progressively more tense in the late 1930's. The Jews of central Europe, uprooted by the spread of Nazism and seeking avenues of escape, pressed for immigration visas to Palestine, as did also the even larger number of Jews in eastern

Europe, who feared that they might soon be overtaken by the holocaust. The Arab nationalists in Palestine, encouraged by the success of the nationalists in Egypt, Syria and Lebanon in winning concessions from Britain and France, organized guerrilla warfare against the British and the Jews. This unrest the Germans and Italians exploited to the full in their accelerated campaigns of propaganda and subversion in the Arab East. Caught in the trap and anxious to line up Arab backing in a region so vital to British imperial defense, the Chamberlain Cabinet followed the line of least resistance in Palestine as in Czechoslovakia. In February–March 1939 a pretense was made in London of conducting round-table discussions, to which were invited the Jewish Agency (representing non-Zionists as well as Zionists), spokesmen of the Palestine Arabs and delegates from the independent Arab states and Transjordan. But the Arabs refused to sit with the Jews. The British put forward proposals totally unacceptable to the Jews, because they were predicated on the desiccation of the Zionist movement, and to an overwhelming majority of the Arabs, because they did not meet the Arab demands in full. The policy statement of 17 May 1939 incorporated with minor change the British proposals of two months earlier. In June the Permanent Mandates Commission of the League of Nations unanimously concluded "that the policy set out in the White Paper was not in accordance with the interpretation which, in agreement with the mandatory Power and the Council, the Commission had placed upon the Palestine mandate" (Permanent Mandates Commission, *Minutes of the Thirty-sixth Session,* p. 275). The Council of the League never reviewed the Commission's opinion, which was only advisory, owing to the virtual suspension of the League's operations in September 1939. Consequently the legality of the White Paper was never clarified, and the policy itself, while not entirely executed, later contributed to the disintegration of the mandate and its chaotic demise. J. C. Hurewitz, *Struggle for Palestine,* chap. 7; P. L. Hanna, *British Policy in Palestine,* chap. 7; *Survey of International Affairs, 1938,* vol. 1, pp. 414–79; N. Barbour, *Palestine Star or Crescent,* chap. 14; M. F. Abcarius, *Palestine through the Fog of Propaganda,* chap. 11.

In the Statement on Palestine, issued on 9th November, 1938, His Majesty's Government announced their intention to invite representatives of the Arabs of Palestine, of certain neighbouring countries and of the Jewish Agency to confer with them in London regarding future policy. It was their sincere hope that, as a result of full, free and frank discussion, some understanding might be reached. Conferences recently took place with Arab and Jewish delegations, lasting for a period of several weeks, and served the purpose of a complete exchange of views between British Ministers and the Arab and Jewish representatives. In the light of the discussions as well as of the situation in Palestine and of the Reports of the Royal Commission and the Partition Commission, certain proposals were formulated by His Majesty's Government and were laid before the Arab and Jewish delegations as the basis of an agreed settlement. Neither the Arab nor the Jewish delegations felt able to accept these proposals, and the conferences therefore did not result in an agreement. Accordingly His Majesty's Government are free to formulate their own policy, and after careful consideration they have decided to adhere generally to the proposals which were finally submitted to, and discussed with, the Arab and Jewish delegations.

2. The Mandate for Palestine, the terms of which were confirmed by the Council of the League of Nations in 1922, has governed the policy of successive British Governments for nearly 20 years. It embodies the Balfour Declaration and imposes on the Mandatory four main obligations. These obligations are set out in Articles 2, 6 and 13 of the Mandate. There is no dispute regarding the interpretation of one of these obligations, that touching the protection of and access to the Holy Places and religious buildings or sites. The other three main obligations are generally as follows:—

(i) To place the country under such political, administrative and economic conditions as will secure the establishment in Palestine of a national home for the Jewish people, to facilitate Jewish immigration under suitable conditions, and to encourage, in co-operation with the Jewish Agency, close settlement by Jews on the land.

(ii) To safeguard the civil and religious

rights of all the inhabitants of Palestine irrespective of race and religion, and, whilst facilitating Jewish immigration and settlement, to ensure that the rights and position of other sections of the population are not prejudiced.

(iii) To place the country under such political, administrative and economic conditions as will secure the development of self-governing institutions.

3. The Royal Commission and previous Commissions of Enquiry have drawn attention to the ambiguity of certain expressions in the Madate, such as the expression "a national home for the Jewish people," and they have found in this ambiguity and the resulting uncertainty as to the objectives of policy a fundamental cause of unrest and hostility between Arabs and Jews. His Majesty's Government are convinced that in the interests of the peace and well-being of the whole people of Palestine a clear definition of policy and objectives is essential. The proposal of partition recommended by the Royal Commission would have afforded such clarity, but the establishment of self-supporting independent Arab and Jewish States within Palestine has been found to be impracticable. It has therefore been necessary for His Majesty's Government to devise an alternative policy which will, consistently with their obligations to Arabs and Jews, meet the needs of the situation in Palestine. Their views and proposals are set forth below under the three heads, (I) The Constitution, (II) Immigration, and (III) Land.

I.—THE CONSTITUTION

4. It has been urged that the expression "a national home for the Jewish people" offered a prospect that Palestine might in due course become a Jewish State or Commonwealth. His Majesty's Government do not wish to contest the view, which was expressed by the Royal Commission, that the Zionist leaders at the time of the issue of the Balfour Declaration recognised that an ultimate Jewish State was not precluded by the terms of the Declaration. But, with the Royal Commission, His Majesty's Government believe that the framers of the Mandate in which the Balfour Declaration was embodied could not have intended that Palestine should be converted into a Jewish State against the will of the Arab population of the country. That Palestine was not to be converted into a Jewish State might be held to be implied in the passage from the Command Paper of 1922 which reads as follows:—

"Unauthorized statements have been made to the effect that the purpose in view is to create a wholly Jewish Palestine. Phrases have been used such as that 'Palestine is to become as Jewish as England is English'. His Majesty's Government regard any such expectation as impracticable and have no such aim in view. Nor have they at any time contemplated . . . . . the disappearance or the subordination of the Arabic population, language or culture in Palestine. They would draw attention to the fact that the terms of the (Balfour) Declaration referred to do not contemplate that Palestine as a whole should be converted into a Jewish National Home, but that such a Home should be founded *in Palestine*."

But this statement has not removed doubts, and His Majesty's Government therefore now declare unequivocally that it is not part of their policy that Palestine should become a Jewish State. They would indeed regard it as contrary to their obligations to the Arabs under the Mandate, as well as to the assurances which have been given to the Arab people in the past, that the Arab population of Palestine should be made the subjects of a Jewish State against their will.

5. The nature of the Jewish National Home in Palestine was further described in the Command Paper of 1922 as follows:

"During the last two or three generations the Jews have recreated in Palestine a community, now numbering 80,000, of whom about one-fourth are farmers or workers upon the land. This community has its own political organs; an elected assembly for the direction of its domestic concerns; elected councils in the towns; and an organisation for the control of its schools. It has its elected Chief Rabbinate and Rabbinical Council for the direction of its religious affairs. Its business is conducted in Hebrew as a vernacular language, and a Hebrew press serves its needs. It has its distinctive intellectual life and displays considerable economic activity. This community, then, with its town and country population, its political, religious and social organisations, its own language, its own customs, its own life, has in fact 'national' characteristics. When it is asked what is meant by the development of the Jewish National Home in Palestine, it may be answered that it is not the imposition of a Jewish nationality upon the inhabitants of Palestine as a whole, but the further development of the existing Jewish community, with the assistance of Jews in other parts of the world, in order that it may become a centre in which the Jewish people as a whole may take, on grounds of religion and race, an interest and a pride. But in order that this community should have the best prospect of free development and provide a full opportunity for the Jewish people to display its capacities, it is essential that it should know that it is in Palestine as of right and not on sufferance. That is the reason why it is necessary that the existence of a Jewish National Home in Palestine should be internationally guaranteed, and that it should be formally recognised to rest upon ancient historic connection."

6. His Majesty's Government adhere to this interpretation of the Declaration of 1917 and regard it as an authoritative and comprehensive description of the character of the Jewish National Home in Palestine. It envisaged the further development of the existing Jewish community with the assistance of Jews in other parts of the world. Evidence that His Majesty's Government have been carrying out their obligation in this respect is to be found in the facts that, since the statement of 1922 was published, more than 300,000 Jews have immigrated to Palestine, and that the population of the National Home has risen to some 450,000, or approaching a third of the entire population of the country. Nor has the Jewish community failed to take full advantage of the opportunities given to it. The growth of the Jewish National Home and its achievements in many fields are a remarkable constructive effort which must command the admiration of the world and must be, in particular, a source of pride to the Jewish people.

7. In the recent discussions the Arab delegations have repeated the contention that Palestine was included within the area in which Sir Henry McMahon, on behalf of the British Government, in October, 1915, undertook to recognise and support Arab independence. The validity of this claim, based on the terms of the correspondence which passed between Sir Henry McMahon and the Sharif of Mecca, was thoroughly and carefully investigated by British and Arab representatives during the recent conferences in London. Their Report, which has been published, states that both the Arab and the British representatives endeavoured to understand the point of view of the other party but that they were unable to reach agreement upon an interpretation of the correspondence. There is no need to summarize here the arguments presented by each side. His Majesty's Government regret the misunderstandings which have arisen as regards some of the phrases used. For their part they can only adhere, for the reasons given by their representatives in the Report, to the view that the whole of Palestine west of Jordan was excluded from Sir Henry McMahon's pledge, and they therefore cannot agree that the McMahon correspondence forms a just basis for the claim that Palestine should be converted into an Arab State.

8. His Majesty's Government are charged as the Mandatory authority "to secure the development of self-governing institutions" in Palestine. Apart from this specific obligation, they would regard it as contrary to the whole spirit of the Mandate system that the population of Palestine should remain for ever under Mandatory tutelage. It is proper that the people of the country should as early as possible enjoy the rights of self-government which are exercised by the people of neighbouring countries. His Majesty's Government are unable at present to foresee the exact con-

stitutional forms which government in Palestine will eventually take, but their objective is self-government, and they desire to see established ultimately an independent Palestine State. It should be a State in which the two peoples in Palestine, Arabs and Jews, share authority in government in such a way that the essential interests of each are secured.

9. The establishment of an independent State and the complete relinquishment of Mandatory control in Palestine would require such relations between the Arabs and the Jews as would make good government possible. Moreover, the growth of self-governing institutions in Palestine, as in other countries, must be an evolutionary process. A transitional period will be required before independence is achieved, throughout which ultimate responsibility for the Government of the country will be retained by His Majesty's Government as the Mandatory authority, while the people of the country are taking an increasing share in the Government, and understanding and co-operation amongst them are growing. It will be the constant endeavour of His Majesty's Government to promote good relations between the Arabs and the Jews.

10. In the light of these considerations His Majesty's Government make the following declaration of their intentions regarding the future government of Palestine:—

(1) The objective of His Majesty's Government is the establishment within ten years of an independent Palestine State in such treaty relations with the United Kingdom as will provide satisfactorily for the commercial and strategic requirements of both countries in the future. This proposal for the establishment of the independent State would involve consultation with the Council of the League of Nations with a view to the termination of the Mandate.

(2) The independent State should be one in which Arabs and Jews share in government in such a way as to ensure that the essential interests of each community are safeguarded.

(3) The establishment of the independent State will be preceded by a transitional period throughout which His Majesty's Government will retain responsibility for the government of the country. During the transitional period the people of Palestine will be given an increasing part in the government of their country. Both sections of the population will have an opportunity to participate in the machinery of government, and the process will be carried on whether or not they both avail themselves of it.

(4) As soon as peace and order have been sufficiently restored in Palestine steps will be taken to carry out this policy of giving the people of Palestine an increasing part in the government of their country, the objective being to place Palestinians in charge of all the Departments of Government, with the assistance of British advisers and subject to the control of the High Commissioner. With this object in view His Majesty's Government will be prepared immediately to arrange that Palestinians shall be placed in charge of certain Departments, with British advisers. The Palestinian heads of Departments will sit on the Executive Council, which advises the High Commissioner. Arab and Jewish representatives will be invited to serve as heads of Departments approximately in proportion to their respective populations. The number of Palestinians in charge of Departments will be increased as circumstances permit until all heads of Departments are Palestinians, exercising the administrative and advisory functions which are at present performed by British officials. When that stage is reached consideration will be given to the question of converting the Executive Council into a Council of Ministers with a consequential change in the status and functions of the Palestinian heads of Departments.

(5) His Majesty's Government make no proposals at this stage regarding the establishment of an elective legislature. Nevertheless they would regard this as an appropriate constitutional development, and, should public opinion in Palestine hereafter show itself in favour of such a development, they will be prepared, provided that local conditions permit, to establish the necessary machinery.

(6) At the end of five years from the restoration of peace and order, an appropriate body representative of the people of Palestine and of His Majesty's Government will be set up to review the working of the constitutional arrangements during the transitional period and to consider and make recommendations regarding the constitution of the independent Palestine State.

(7) His Majesty's Government will require to be satisfied that in the treaty contemplated by sub-paragraph (1) or in the constitution contemplated by sub-paragraph (6) adequate provision has been made for:—

(*a*) the security of, and freedom of access to, the Holy Places, and the protection of the interests and property of the various religious bodies.

(*b*) the protection of the different communities in Palestine in accordance with the obligations of His Majesty's Government to both Arabs and Jews and for the special position in Palestine of the Jewish National Home.

(*c*) such requirements to meet the strategic situation as may be regarded as necessary by His Majesty's Government in the light of the circumstances then existing.

His Majesty's Government will also require to be satisfied that the interests of certain foreign countries in Palestine, for the preservation of which they are at present responsible, are adequately safeguarded.

(8) His Majesty's Government will do everything in their power to create conditions which will enable the independent Palestine State to come into being within ten years. If, at the end of ten years, it appears to His Majesty's Government that, contrary to their hope, circumstances require the postponement of the establishment of the independent State, they will consult with representatives of the people of Palestine, the Council of the League of Nations and the neighbouring Arab States before deciding on such a postponement. If His Majesty's Government come to the conclusion that postponement is unavoidable, they will invite the co-operation of these parties in framing plans for the future with a view to achieving the desired objective at the earliest possible date.

11. During the transitional period steps will be taken to increase the powers and responsibilities of municipal corporations and local councils.

II.—IMMIGRATION

12. Under Article 6 of the Mandate, the Administration of Palestine, "while ensuring that the rights and position of other sections of the population are not prejudiced," is required to "facilitate Jewish immigration under suitable conditions." Beyond this, the extent to which Jewish immigration into Palestine is to be permitted is nowhere defined in the Mandate. But in the Command Paper of 1922 it was laid down that for the fulfilment of the policy of establishing a Jewish National Home

"it is necessary that the Jewish community in Palestine should be able to increase its numbers by immigration. This immigration cannot be so great in volume as to exceed whatever may be the economic capacity of the country at the time to absorb new arrivals. It is essential to ensure that the immigrants should not be a burden upon the people of Palestine as a whole, and that they should not deprive any section of the present population of their employment."

In practice, from that date onwards until recent times, the economic absorptive capacity of the country has been treated as the sole limiting factor, and in the letter which Mr. Ramsay MacDonald, as Prime Minister, sent to Dr. Weizmann in February 1931 it was laid down as a matter of policy that economic absorptive capacity was the sole criterion. This interpretation has been supported by resolutions of the Permanent Mandates Commission. But His Majesty's Government do not read either the Statement of Policy of 1922 or the letter of 1931 as implying that the Mandate requires them, for all time and in all circumstances, to facilitate the immigration of Jews into Palestine subject only to consideration of the country's economic absorptive capacity. Nor do they find anything in the Mandate or in subsequent Statements of Policy to support the view that the establishment of a Jewish National Home in Palestine cannot be effected unless immigration is allowed to continue indefinitely. If immigration has an adverse effect on the economic position in the country, it should clearly be restricted; and equally, if it has a seriously damaging effect on the political position in the country, that is a factor that should not be ignored. Although it is not difficult to contend that the large number of Jewish immigrants who have been admitted so far have been absorbed economically, the fear of the Arabs that this influx will continue indefinitely until the Jewish population is in a position to dominate them has produced consequences which are extremely grave for Jews and Arabs alike and for the peace and prosperity of Palestine. The lamentable disturbances of the past three years are only the latest and most sustained manifestation of this intense Arab apprehension. The methods employed by Arab terrorists against fellow-Arabs and Jews alike must receive unqualified condemnation. But it cannot be denied that fear of indefinite Jewish immigration is widespread amongst the Arab population and that this fear has made possible disturbances which have given a serious setback to economic progress, depleted the Palestine exchequer, rendered life and property insecure, and produced a bitterness between the Arab and Jewish populations which is deplorable between citizens of the same country. If in these circumstances immigration is continued up to the economic absorptive capacity of the country, regardless of all other considerations, a fatal enmity between the two peoples will be perpetuated, and the situation in Palestine may become a permanent source of friction amongst all peoples in the Near and Middle East. His Majesty's Government cannot take the view that either their obligations under the Mandate, or considerations of common sense and justice, require that they should ignore these circumstances in framing immigration policy.

13. In the view of the Royal Commission, the association of the policy of the Balfour Declaration with the Mandate system implied the belief that Arab hostility to the former would sooner or later be overcome. It has been the hope of British Governments ever since the Balfour Declaration was issued that in time the Arab population, recognizing the advantages to be derived from Jewish settlement and development in Palestine, would become reconciled to the further growth of the Jewish National Home. This hope has not been fulfilled. The alternatives before His Majesty's Government are either (i) to seek to expand the Jewish National Home indefinitely by immigration, against the strongly expressed will of the Arab people of the country; or (ii) to permit further expansion of the Jewish National Home by immigration only if the Arabs are prepared to acquiesce in it. The former policy means rule by force. Apart from other considerations, such a policy seems to His Majesty's Government to be contrary to the whole spirit of Article 22 of the Covenant of the League of Nations, as well as to their specific obligations to the Arabs in the Palestine Mandate. Moreover, the relations between the Arabs and the Jews in Palestine must be based sooner or later on mutual tolerance and goodwill; the peace, security and progress of the Jewish National Home itself require this. Therefore His Majesty's Government, after earnest consideration, and taking into account the extent to which the growth of the Jewish National Home has been facilitated over the last twenty years, have decided that the time has come to adopt in principle the second of the alternatives referred to above.

14. It has been urged that all further Jewish immigration into Palestine should be stopped forthwith. His Majesty's Government cannot accept such a proposal. It would damage the whole of the financial and economic system of Palestine and thus affect adversely the interests of Arabs and Jews alike. Moreover, in the view of His Majesty's Government, abruptly to stop further immigration would be unjust to the Jewish National Home. But, above all, His

Majesty's Government are conscious of the present unhappy plight of large numbers of Jews who seek a refuge from certain European countries, and they believe that Palestine can and should make a further contribution to the solution of this pressing world problem. In all these circumstances, they believe that they will be acting consistently with their Mandatory obligations to both Arabs and Jews, and in the manner best calculated to serve the interests of the whole people of Palestine, by adopting the following proposals regarding immigration:—

(1) Jewish immigration during the next five years will be at a rate which, if economic absorptive capacity permits, will bring the Jewish population up to approximately one-third of the total population of the country. Taking into account the expected natural increase of the Arab and Jewish populations, and the number of illegal Jewish immigrants now in the country, this would allow of the admission, as from the beginning of April this year, of some 75,000 immigrants over the next five years. These immigrants would, subject to the criterion of economic absorptive capacity, be admitted as follows:—

(*a*) For each of the next five years a quota of 10,000 Jewish immigrants will be allowed, on the understanding that a shortage in any one year may be added to the quotas for subsequent years, within the five-year period, if economic absorptive capacity permits.

(*b*) In addition, as a contribution towards the solution of the Jewish refugee problem, 25,000 refugees will be admitted as soon as the High Commissioner is satisfied that adequate provision for their maintenance is ensured, special consideration being given to refugee children and dependants.

(2) The existing machinery for ascertaining economic absorptive capacity will be retained, and the High Commissioner will have the ultimate responsibility for deciding the limits of economic capacity. Before each periodic decision is taken, Jewish and Arab representatives will be consulted.

(3) After the period of five years no further Jewish immigration will be permitted unless the Arabs of Palestine are prepared to acquiesce in it.

(4) His Majesty's Government are determined to check illegal immigration, and further preventive measures are being adopted. The numbers of any Jewish illegal immigrants who, despite these measures, may succeed in coming into the country and cannot be deported will be deducted from the yearly quotas.

15. His Majesty's Government are satisfied that, when the immigration over five years which is now contemplated has taken place, they will not be justified in facilitating, nor will they be under any obligation to facilitate, the further development of the Jewish National Home by immigration regardless of the wishes of the Arab population.

III.—LAND

16. The Administration of Palestine is required, under Article 6 of the Mandate, "while ensuring that the rights and position of other sections of the population are not prejudiced," to encourage "close settlement by Jews on the land," and no restriction has been imposed hitherto on the transfer of land from Arabs to Jews. The Reports of several expert Commissions have indicated that, owing to the natural growth of the Arab population and the steady sale in recent years of Arab land to Jews, there is now in certain areas no room for further transfers of Arab land, whilst in some other areas such transfers of land must be restricted if Arab cultivators are to maintain their existing standard of life and a considerable landless Arab population is not soon to be created. In these circumstances, the High Commissioner will be given general powers to prohibit and regulate transfers of land. These powers will date from the publication of this statement of policy and the High Commissioner will retain them throughout the transitional period.

17. The policy of the Government will be directed towards the development of the

land and the improvement, where possible, of methods of cultivation. In the light of such development it will be open to the High Commissioner, should he be satisfied that the "rights and position" of the Arab population will be duly preserved, to review and modify any orders passed relating to the prohibition or restriction of the transfer of land.

18. In framing these proposals His Majesty's Government have sincerely endeavoured to act in strict accordance with their obligations under the Mandate to both the Arabs and the Jews. The vagueness of the phrases employed in some instances to describe these obligations has led to controversy and has made the taks of interpretation difficult. His Majesty's Government cannot hope to satisfy the partisans of one party or the other in such controversy as the Mandate has aroused. Their purpose is to be just as between the two peoples in Palestine whose destines in that country have been affected by the great events of recent years, and who, since they live side by side, must learn to practise mutual tolerance, goodwill and co-operation. In looking to the future, His Majesty's Government are not blind to the fact that some events of the past make the task of creating these relations difficult; but they are encouraged by the knowledge that at many times and in many places in Palestine during recent years the Arab and Jewish inhabitants have lived in friendship together. Each community has much to contribute to the welfare of their common land, and each must earnestly desire peace in which to assist in increasing the well-being of the whole people of the country. The responsibility which falls on them, no less than upon His Majesty's Government, to cooperate together to ensure peace is all the more solemn because their country is revered by many millions of Moslems, Jews and Christians throughout the world who pray for peace in Palestine and for the happiness of her people.

66. TREATY OF MUTUAL ASSISTANCE: BRITAIN, FRANCE AND TURKEY
19 October 1939

(Ratifications deposited in Ankara, 16 November 1939)

[League of Nations, *Treaty Series,* No. 4689, vol. 200 (1940–41), pp. 167–89]

The 1936 Montreux Straits convention (Doc. 60) together with France's progressive cession to Turkey between 1936 and 1939 of the *sanjaq* (provincial district) of Alexandretta—which contained a substantial Turkish population, but not a majority, and which Ankara agreed in 1921 (Doc. 35) and 1926 might remain part of the French mandate on condition that the district was placed under a special regime—erased the young republic's major surviving grievances against Britain and France. The rapprochement found tangible expression in the following fifteen-year tripartite treaty of "mutual assistance in resistance to aggression." Article 7 stipulated that the terms of the pact were "equally binding as bilateral obligations" between Turkey and each of the other signatories. Attached to the treaty were several financial instruments (not reproduced) which provided for an Anglo-French credit to Turkey of £25 million (three-fifths from France) for the purchase of military equipment and further loans totaling £18.5 million. The two sets of obligations were to be amortized over a twenty-year period, the first at 4 per cent and the second at 3 per cent interest. The military convention, which formed an essential element of the tripartite arrangements, was not published with the other instruments. Despite the treaty engagements, Turkey remained neutral throughout most of World War II. J. C. Hurewitz, *Middle East Dilemmas,* chap. 5; W. L. Langer and S. E. Gleason, *The Challenge to Isolation,* pp. 312–18; C. Açikalin, "Turkey's International Relations," *International Affairs,* 23 (October 1947), 477–91; N. E. Kocaeli, "The Development of the Anglo-Turkish Alliance," *Asiatic Review,* (new series) 42 (October 1946), 347–51; Sir H. Knatchbull-Hugessen, *Diplomat in Peace and War,* chap. 12; M. Weygand, *Recalled to Service,* chaps. 1, 3.

ART. 1. In the event of Turkey being involved in hostilities with a European Power in consequence of aggression by that Power against Turkey, France and the United Kingdom will co-operate effectively with Turkey and will lend her all aid and assistance in their power.

ART. 2. (1) In the event of an act of aggression by a European Power leading to war in the Mediterranean area in which France and the United Kingdom are involved, Turkey will collaborate effectively with France and the United Kingdom and will lend them all aid and assistance in her power.

(2) In the event of an act of aggression by a European Power leading to war in the Mediterranean area in which Turkey is involved, France and the United Kingdom will collaborate effectively with Turkey and will lend her all aid and assistance in their power.

ART. 3. So long as the guarantees given by France and the United Kingdom to Greece and Roumania by their respective Declarations of the 13th April, 1939, remain in force, Turkey will co-operate effectively with France and the United Kingdom and will lend them all aid and assistance in her power, in the event of France and the United Kingdom being engaged in hostilities in virtue of either of the said guarantees.

ART. 4. In the event of France and the United Kingdom being involved in hostilities with a European Power in consequence of aggression committed by that Power against either of those States without the provisions of Articles 2 or 3 being applicable, the High Contracting Parties will immediately consult together.

It is nevertheless agreed that in such an eventuality Turkey will observe at least a benevolent neutrality towards France and the United Kingdom.

ART. 5. Without prejudice to the provisions of Article 3 above, in the event of either:

(1) Aggression by a European Power against another European State which the Government of one of the High Contracting Parties had, with the approval of that State, undertaken to assist in maintaining its independence or neutrality against such aggression, or

(2) Aggression by a European Power which while directed against another European State, constituted, in the opinion of the Government of one of the High Contracting Parties, a menace to its own security,

the High Contracting Parties will immediately consult together with a view to such common action as might be considered effective.

ART. 6. The present Treaty is not directed against any country, but is designed to assure France, the United Kingdom and Turkey of mutual aid and assistance in resistance to aggression should the necessity arise.

ART. 7. The provisions of the present Treaty are equally binding as bilateral obligations between Turkey and each of the two other High Contracting Parties.

ART. 8. If the High Contracting Parties are engaged in hostilities in consequence of the operation of the present Treaty, they will not conclude an armistice or peace except by common agreement.

ART. 9. The present Treaty shall be ratified and the instruments of ratification shall be deposited simultaneously at Angora as soon as possible. It shall enter into force on the date of this deposit.

The present Treaty is concluded for a period of fifteen years. If none of the High Contracting Parties has notified the two others of its intention to terminate it six months before the expiration of the said period, the Treaty will be renewed by tacit consent for a further period of five years, and so on.

PROTOCOL NO. 1.

The undersigned Plenipotentiaries state that their respective Governments agree that the Treaty of to-day's date shall be put into force from the moment of its signature.

The present Protocol shall be considered

as an integral part of the Treaty concluded to-day between France, the United Kingdom and Turkey.

PROTOCOL NO. 2.

At the moment of signature of the Treaty between France, the United Kingdom and Turkey, the undersigned Plenipotentiaries, duly authorised to this effect, have agreed as follows:

The obligations undertaken by Turkey in virtue of the above-mentioned Treaty cannot compel that country to take action having as its effect, or involving as its consequence, entry into armed conflict with the Soviet Union.

67. RUSSO-GERMAN NEGOTIATIONS FOR A PROJECTED SOVIET SPHERE OF INFLUENCE IN THE NEAR AND MIDDLE EAST
November 1940

[R. J. Sontag and J. S. Beddie, eds., *Nazi-Soviet Relations 1939–1941*, U.S. Department of State Publication No. 3023 (Washington, 1948), pp. 255–59]

Germany, Italy and Japan concluded a three-power pact for mutual aid on 27 September 1940. At that time the signatory states felt confident that Britain would lose the war and, as a precautionary measure against possible future hostilities among themselves, endeavored to define in advance their respective spheres of influence. In the hope of broadening the understanding to include Russia, the German Foreign Minister, Joachim von Ribbentrop, on 13 October wrote to Stalin in Hitler's name, inviting the Soviet Union to join the three powers in adopting "a long-range policy" and directing "the future development of their peoples into the right channels by delimitation of their interests on a world-wide scale" (full text of letter in Sontag and Beddie, *op. cit.*, pp. 207–13). The Soviet Commissar for Foreign Affairs, Vyacheslav M. Molotov explored the German proposal in detail with Ribbentrop and Hitler in Berlin on 12–13 November. Molotov insisted that his government viewed Russian control of the Turkish Straits as indispensable to Soviet security and believed that "she could reach an agreement with Turkey in regard thereto" (*ibid.*, p. 245). As a result of the conversations, the German Foreign Office drew up the draft of a four-power agreement and two secret protocols. On 25 November Molotov handed the German Ambassador in Moscow, Count Friedrich Werner von der Schulenburg, a written statement elaborating upon specific Soviet demands. The parallel between the Soviet demands of November 1940 and those of 1945–46 in relation to Turkey and Iran aroused in the United States and Britain profound suspicion of the USSR's motives in the Near and Middle East. W. L. Langer and S. E. Gleason, *The Challenge to Isolation 1937–1940*, pp. 312–18, and *The Undeclared War 1940–1941*, pp. 136–46; P. Schmidt, *Statist auf diplomatischer Bühne*, chap. 21; G. Kirk, *The Middle East in the War*, pp. 443–66; C. Açikalin, "Turkey's International Relations," *International Affairs*, 23 (October 1947), pp. 477–91; H. N. Howard, "Germany, the Soviet Union and Turkey during World War II," *Department of State Bulletin*, 19 (18 July 1948), pp. 63–78; J. C. Hurewitz, *Middle East Dilemmas*, chap. 5.

1. DRAFT. AGREEMENT BETWEEN THE STATES OF THE THREE-POWER PACT (GERMANY, ITALY AND JAPAN) AND THE USSR [1]

The Governments of the states of the Three Power Pact, Germany, Italy and Japan, on the one side, and the Government of the U. S. S. R. on the other side, motivated by the desire to establish in their natural spheres of influence in Europe, Asia, and Africa a new order serving the welfare of all peoples concerned and to create a firm and enduring foundation for their common labors toward this goal, have agreed upon the following:

ART. I. In the Three Power Pact of Berlin, of September 27, 1940, Germany, Italy, and Japan agreed to oppose the extension of the war into a world conflict with all possible means and to collaborate toward an early restoration of world peace. They expressed their willingness to extend

[1] The text, discovered among the classified files of the German Embassy in Moscow, was undated but presumably constituted the basis for Schulenburg's talk with Molotov reported on 26 November 1940.

their collaboration to nations in other parts of the world which are inclined to direct their efforts along the same course as theirs. The Soviet Union declares that it concurs in these aims of the Three Power Pact and is on its part determined to cooperate politically in this course with the Three Powers.

ART. II. Germany, Italy, Japan, and the Soviet Union undertake to respect each other's natural spheres of influence. In so far as these spheres of interest come into contact with each other, they will constantly consult each other in an amicable way with regard to the problems arising therefrom.

Germany, Italy, and Japan declare on their part that they recognize the present extent of the possessions of the Soviet Union and will respect it.

ART. III. Germany, Italy, Japan, and the Soviet Union undertake to join no combination of powers and to support no combination of powers which is directed against one of the Four Powers.

The Four Powers will assist each other in economic matters in every way and will supplement and extend the agreements existing among themselves.

ART. IV. This agreement shall take effect upon signature and shall continue for a period of ten years. The Governments of the Four Powers shall consult each other in due time, before the expiration of that period, regarding the extension of the agreement.

Draft. Secret Protocol No. 1

Upon the signing today of the Agreement concluded among them, the Representatives of Germany, Italy, Japan and the Soviet Union declare as follows:

1) Germany declares that, apart from the territorial revisions in Europe to be carried out at the conclusion of peace, her territorial aspirations center in the territories of Central Africa.

2) Italy declares that, apart from the territorial revisions in Europe to be carried out at the conclusion of peace, her territorial aspirations center in the territories of Northern and Northeastern Africa.

3) Japan declares that her territorial aspirations center in the area of Eastern Asia to the south of the Island Empire of Japan.

4) The Soviet Union declares that its territorial aspirations center south of the national territory of the Soviet Union in the direction of the Indian Ocean.

The Four Powers declare that, reserving the settlement of specific questions, they will mutually respect these territorial aspirations and will not oppose their achievement.

Draft. Secret Protocol No. 2 To Be Concluded Among Germany, Italy, and the Soviet Union

On the occasion of the signing today of the Agreement among Germany, Italy, Japan, and the Soviet Union, the Representatives of Germany, Italy and the Soviet Union declare as follows:

1) Germany, Italy, and the Soviet Union agree in the view that it is in their common interest to detach Turkey from her existing international commitments and progressively to win her over to political collaboration with themselves. They declare that they will pursue this aim in close consultation, with a common line of action which is still to be determined.

2) Germany, Italy, and the Soviet Union declare their agreement to conclude, at a given time, a joint agreement with Turkey, wherein the Three Powers would recognize the extent of Turkey's possessions.

3) Germany, Italy, and the Soviet Union will work in common toward the replacement of the Montreux Straits Convention now in force by another convention. By this convention the Soviet Union would be granted the right of unrestricted passage of its navy through the Straits at any time, whereas all other Powers except the other Black Sea countries, but including Germany and Italy, would in principle renounce the right of passage through the Straits for their naval vessels. The passage of commercial vessels through the Straits would, of course, have to remain free in principle.

2. SCHULENBURG TO THE GERMAN FOREIGN OFFICE, 26 NOVEMBER 1940

For the Reich Minister in person.

Molotov asked me to call on him this evening [25 November 1940] and in the presence of Dekanosov stated the following:

The Soviet Government has studied the contents of the statements of the Reich Foreign Minister in the concluding conversation on November 13 and takes the following stand:

"The Soviet Government is prepared to accept the draft of the Four Power Pact which the Reich Foreign Minister outlined in the conversation of November 13, regarding political collaboration and reciprocal economic [support] subject to the following conditions:

"1) Provided that the German troops are immediately withdrawn from Finland, which, under the compact of 1939, belongs to the Soviet Union's sphere of influence. At the same time the Soviet Union undertakes to ensure peaceful relations with Finland and to protect German economic interests in Finland (export of lumber and nickel).

"2) Provided that within the next few months the security of the Soviet Union in the Straits is assured by the conclusion of a mutual assistance pact between the Soviet Union and Bulgaria, which geographically is situated inside the security zone of the Black Sea boundaries of the Soviet Union, and by the establishment of a base for land and naval forces of the U.S.S.R. within range of the Bosphorus and the Dardanelles by means of a long-term lease.

"3) Provided that the area south of Batum and Baku in the general direction of the Persian Gulf is recognized as the center of the aspirations of the Soviet Union.

"4) Provided that Japan [renounces] her rights to concessions for coal and oil in Northern Sakhalin.

"In accordance with the foregoing, the draft of the protocol concerning the delimitation of the spheres of influence as outlined be the Reich Foreign Minister would have to be amended so as to stipulate the focal point of the aspirations of the Soviet Union south of Batum and Baku in the general direction of the Persian Gulf.

"Likewise, the draft of the potocol or agreement between Germany, Italy, and the Soviet Union with respect to Turkey should be amended so as to guarantee a base for light naval and land forces of the U.S.S.R. on [*am*] the Bosporus and the Dardanelles by means of a long-term lease, including—in case Turkey declares herself willing to join the Four Power Pact—a guarantee of the independence and of the territory of Turkey by the three countries named.

"This protocol should provide that in case Turkey refuses to join the Four Powers, Germany, Italy, and the Soviet Union agree to work out and to carry through the required military and diplomatic measures, and a separate agreement to this effect should be concluded.

"Furthermore there should be agreement upon:

"*a*) a third secret protocol between Germany and the Soviet Union concerning Finland (see Point 1 above).

"*b*) a fourth secret protocol between Japan and the Soviet Union concerning the renunciation by Japan of the oil and coal concession in Northern Sakhalin (in return for an adequate compensation).

"*c*) a fifth secret protocol between Germany, the Soviet Union, and Italy, recognizing that Bulgaria is geographically located inside the security zone of the Black Sea boundaries of the Soviet Union and that it is therefore a political necessity that a mutual assistance pact be concluded between the Soviet Union and Bulgaria, which in no way shall affect the internal regime of Bulgaria, her sovereignty or independence."

In conclusion Molotov stated that the Soviet proposal provided for five protocols instead of the two envisaged by the Reich Foreign minister.

68. TREATY OF NONAGGRESSION: GERMANY AND TURKEY
18 June 1941

(Ratifications exchanged, Berlin, 5 July 1941)

[Unofficial translation from the Turkish text in Turkey, *Resmi Gazette,* No. 4849 (2 July 1941), courtesy of the Department of State, Washington, D.C.]

As the date approached for the Nazi offensive against the USSR, Berlin brought increasing pressure to bear upon Ankara. Germany sought advance assurances of Turkish neutrality. Attempts were also made to cajole Turkey into repudiating its alliance of October 1939 with Britain (Doc. 66) and granting transit rights for military assistance—in troops and equipment—to Iraq at the time of the short-lived Rashid 'Ali rebellion in May 1941. But the Turkish government moved slowly, turning a deaf ear to Nazi arguments for breaking with England. By the close of May, moreover, the Rashid 'Ali uprising was quelled. The Germans, in the end, had to satisfy themselves with no more than a treaty of friendship and nonaggression, which stipulated in the preamble that it was "subject to the already existing engagements of each party," thus reserving Turkey's position under its 1935 understanding with the USSR (Doc. 45) and its 1939 arrangement with the United Kingdom. Much to the annoyance of the Wilhelmstrasse the British Ambassador at Ankara throughout the Turco-German conversations was kept fully informed by the Turkish Foreign Minister, with the knowledge and reluctant assent of Nazi Ambassador Franz von Papen. W. L. Langer and S. E. Gleason, *The Undeclared War 1940–1941,* pp. 510–14; F. von Papen, *Memoirs,* chap. 26; Sir H. Knatchbull-Hugessen, *Diplomat in Peace and War,* chap. 13; J. C. Hurewitz, *Middle East Dilemmas,* chap. 5.

The Turkish Republic and the German Reich, desirous of establishing their relations on a basis of mutual confidence and sincere friendship have decided, subject to the already existing engagements of each party, to conclude a treaty. . . .

Art. 1. The Turkish Republic and the German Reich undertake to respect mutually the inviolability and integrity of their territories, and to abstain from all action aimed directly or indirectly against one another.

Art. 2. The Turkish Republic and the German Reich undertake to enter into friendly contact in the future in regard to all matters involving their mutual interests with a view to reaching an agreement for their solution.

Art. 3. The present Treaty which shall enter into force on the date of its signature shall be valid for a period of ten years. The High Contracting Parties shall in due time reach an agreement on the matter of its prolongation.

The present Treaty shall be ratified and the ratifications shall be exchanged in Berlin as soon as possible.

Done in duplicate in the Turkish and German languages both texts being equally binding.

69. AGREEMENT (DE GAULLE-LYTTLETON) ON SYRIA AND LEBANON: BRITAIN AND FRANCE
7 August 1941

[Lyttleton to de Gaulle, Great Britain, *Parliamentary Papers, 1945,* Syria No. 1, Cmd. 6600; de Gaulle to Lyttleton, translated from French text, *idem.*]

Following the capitulation of France to Germany in June 1940, the mandatory regimes in Syria and Lebanon fell under a Vichy administration. An Italian armistice commission arrived before the year was out and provided a convenient guise for the infiltration of Axis agents. During the Iraqi revolt in May 1941, Axis aid to the rebels—including aircraft—was channeled through the French mandated lands. Once the situation in Iraq was brought under control, the British, in concert with the Free French, immediately turned attention to the expulsion of the Vichy forces and Axis agents from Syria and Lebanon. On 8 June, the day military operations began, the Free French and the British issued declarations promising complete independence to the Syrians and the Lebanese (texts in Cmd. 6600). What the United Kingdom and the Free French contemplated was clarified in the exchange of letters, reproduced below, between Oliver Lyttleton, the British Minister of State Resident in the Middle East, and General Charles de Gaulle. But Free French efforts to conclude preferential treaties with the two countries, comparable to those of 1936 that had never been ratified (Doc. 62), proved entirely fruitless and merely precipitated crises—in Lebanon in November 1943 and Syria in May–June 1945—that hardened Syrian and Lebanese hostility toward France. In the end France was compelled, by the force of events, to withdraw its troops from the two countries without benefit of any special treaty relations. A. H. Hourani, *Syria and Lebanon,* chaps. 12, 13; G. Kirk, *The Middle East in the War,* pp. 78–129; G. Catroux, *Dans la Bataille de Méditerranée,* chaps. 5–25, 37, 44–45.

1. LYTTLETON TO DE GAULLE

At the conclusion of our talk to-day I am happy to repeat to you the assurance that Great Britain has no interest in Syria or the Lebanon except to win the war. We have no desire to encroach in any way upon the position of France. Both Free France and Great Britain are pledged to the independence of Syria and the Lebanon. When this essential step has been taken, and without prejudice to it, we freely admit that France should have the predominant position in Syria and the Lebanon over any other European Power. It is in this spirit that we have always acted. You will have seen the recent utterances of the Prime Minister in this sense. I am glad to reaffirm them now to our friends and allies, who have our full sympathy and support.

On our side, I am happy again to receive your assurances of the determination of Free France, as the friend and ally of Great Britain and in accordance with the agreements and declarations which you have already made, to pursue relentlessly to the finish the war against the common enemy. I am happy that we should thus reaffirm our complete understanding and agreement.

2. DE GAULLE TO LYTTLETON

I have received the letter that you were kind enough to write me at the conclusion of our conference of today. I am pleased to take note of the assurances that you have given me anew on the disinterestedness of Great Britain in Syria and Lebanon and on the fact that Great Britain recognizes in advance the pre-eminent and privileged position of France in these states when they achieve their independence in accordance with the undertaking that France has accepted on their behalf.

I take this opportunity to repeat to you that Free France, that is, France, is resolved to pursue the war at the side of Great Britain, its friend and ally, until complete victory against our common enemies.

70. TREATY OF ALLIANCE: BRITAIN AND THE USSR AND IRAN
29 January 1942

[Great Britain, *Parliamentary Papers, 1942,* Persia No. 1, Cmd. 6335]

British and Soviet troops occupied Iran in August–September 1941 after Riza Shah's refusal to expel several hundred Germans from the country. Riza Shah on 16 September abdicated in favor of his son, Muhammad Riza, who proved more cooperative. Aside from eliminating Axis agents, Britain wished to safeguard its oil fields and, as Churchill informed Stalin on 29 August, "to get another through route to you which cannot be cut" [W. S. Churchill, *The Second World War,* vol. 3 (Br. ed.), p. 404]. The occupation, however, aroused in Iranian minds memories of the Anglo–Russian convention of 1907 (I, Doc. 105), for in both instances the Russian zone was in the north and the British in the south, and in their hearts fears of irretrievable loss of their independence. To dispel the anxieties and place the occupation on a legal footing, Britain and Russia concluded the following treaty of alliance with Iran. The occupying powers pledged "jointly and severally . . . to respect the territorial integrity, the sovereignty and political independence of Iran" (article 1) and to withdraw their forces from its territory "not later than six months" after the end of all hostilities (article 5). The treaty required no ratification. Three annexes, appended to the instrument, are omitted below. G. Lenczowski, *Russia and the West in Iran,* chap. 7; G. Kirk, *The Middle East in the War,* pp. 129–41; Churchill, *op. cit.,* chap. 26; Sir R. Bullard, *Britain and the Middle East,* pp. 132–35.

ART. 1. His Majesty The King of Great Britain, Ireland and the British Dominions beyond the Seas, Emperor of India, and the Union of Soviet Socialist Republics (hereinafter referred to as the Allied Powers) jointly and severally undertake to respect the territorial integrity, sovereignty and political independence of Iran.

ART. 2. An alliance is established between the Allied Powers on the one hand and His Imperial Majesty The Shahinshah of Iran on the other.

ART. 3. (i) The Allied Powers jointly and severally undertake to defend Iran by all means at their command from all aggression on the part of Germany or any other Power.

(ii) His Imperial Majesty The Shahinshah undertakes—

(*a*) to co-operate with the Allied Powers with all the means at his command and in every way possible, in order that they may be able to fulfil the above undertaking. The assistance of the Iranian forces shall, however, be limited to the maintenance of internal security on Iranian terriory;

(*b*) to secure to the Allied Powers, for the passage of troops or supplies from one Allied Power to the other or for other similar purposes, the unrestricted right to use, maintain, guard and, in case of military necessity, control in any way that they may require all means of communication throughout Iran, including railways, roads, rivers, aerodromes, ports, pipelines and telephone, telegraph and wireless installations;

(*c*) to furnish all possible assistance and facilities in obtaining material and recruiting labour for the purpose of the maintenance and improvement of the means of communication referred to in paragraph (*b*);

(*d*) to establish and maintain, in collaboration with the Allied Powers, such measures of censorship control as they may require for all the means of communication referred to in paragraph (*b*).

(iii) It is clearly understood that in the application of paragraph (ii) (*b*) (*c*) and (*d*) of the present article the Allied Powers will give full consideration to the essential needs of Iran.

ART. 4. (i) The Allied Powers may maintain in Iranian territory land, sea and air forces in such number as they consider necessary. The location of such forces shall be decided in agreement with the Iranian Government so long as the strategic situation allows. All questions concerning the relations between the forces of the Allied Powers and the Iranian authorities shall be settled so far as possible in co-operation with the Iranian authorities in such a way as to safeguard the security of the said forces. It is understood that the presence of these forces on Iranian territory does not constitute a military occupation and will disturb as little as possible the administration and the security forces of Iran, the economic life of the country, the normal movements of the population and the application of Iranian laws and regulations.

(ii) A separate agreement or agreements shall be concluded as soon as possible after the entry into force of the present Treaty regarding any financial obligations to be borne by the Allied Powers under the provisions of the present article and of paragraphs (ii) (*b*), (*c*) and (*d*) of Article 3 above in such matters as local purchases, the hiring of buildings and plant, the employment of labour, transport charges, &c. A special agreement shall be concluded between the Allied Government and the Iranian Government defining the conditions for any transfers to the Iranian Government after the war of buildings and other improvements effected by the Allied Powers on Iranian territory. These agreements shall also settle the immunities to be enjoyed by the forces of the Allied Powers in Iran.

ART. 5. The forces of the Allied Powers

shall be withdrawn from Iranian territory not later than six months after all hostilities between the Allied Powers and Germany and her associates have been suspended by the conclusion of an armistice or armistices, or on the conclusion of peace between them, whichever date is the earlier. The expression "associates" of Germany means all other Powers which have engaged or may in the future engage in hostilities against either of the Allied Powers.

ART. 6 (i) The Allied Powers undertake in their relations with foreign countries not to adopt an attitude which is prejudicial to the territorial integrity, sovereignty or political independence of Iran, nor to conclude treaties inconsistent with the provisions of the present Treaty. They undertake to consult the Government of His Imperial Majesty the Shahinshah in all matters affecting the direct interests of Iran.

(ii) His Imperial Majesty The Shahinshah undertakes not to adopt in his relations with foreign countries an attitude which is inconsistent with the alliance, nor to conclude treaties inconsistent with the provisions of the present Treaty.

ART. 7. The Allied Powers jointly undertake to use their best endeavours to safeguard the economic existence of the Iranian people against the privations and difficulties arising as a result of the present war. On the entry into force of the present Treaty, discussions shall be opened between the Government of Iran and the Governments of the Allied Powers as to the best possible methods of carrying out the above undertaking.

ART. 8. The provisions of the present Treaty are equally binding as bilateral obligations between His Imperial Majesty The Shahinshah and each of the two other High Contracting Parties.

ART. 9. The present Treaty shall come into force on signature and shall remain in force until the date fixed for the withdrawal of the forces of the Allied Powers from Iranian territory in accordance with Article 5.

71. THE ZIONIST (BILTMORE) PROGRAM
11 May 1942

[The Jewish Agency for Palestine, *Book of Documents submitted to the General Assembly of the United Nations,* pp. 226–27]

The British government promulgated on 28 February 1940 land transfer regulations (text in Great Britain, *Parliamentary Papers, 1940,* Misc. No. 2, Cmd. 6180) to control the sale of land in Palestine by Arabs to Jews in accordance with the 1939 White Paper (Doc. 65). The mandatory's repressive policy toward the Jewish National Home—particularly the rigid application of the immigration and land-sales restrictions—combined in the first half of World War II with the Nazi policy of exterminating the Jews in Europe to persuade the Zionist leaders that the only postwar program to which they could subscribe would be the early development of the Jewish National Home into an independent state. This objective was embodied in a resolution adopted on 11 May 1942 by an extraordinary conference at the Biltmore Hotel in New York City under the sponsorship of American Zionists but with the participation of representatives from Europe and Palestine, including members of the Jewish Agency Executive. Endorsed in Jerusalem the following November by the Inner General Council (the supreme wartime policy-making body of the Zionist movement), the Biltmore Program, as it came to be known, constituted the basis of Zionist demands in later efforts to settle the Palestine problem, first by the mandatory power and then by the United Nations. J. C. Hurewitz, *Struggle for Palestine,* chaps. 10, 12; D. Trevor, *Under the White Paper;* C. Weizmann, "Palestine's Role in the Solution of the Jewish Problem," *Foreign Affairs,* 20 (January 1942), 324–38.

1. American Zionists assembled in this Extraordinary Conference reaffirm their unequivocal devotion to the cause of democratic freedom and international justice to which the people of the United States, allied with the other United Nations, have dedicated themselves, and give expression

to their faith in the ultimate victory of humanity and justice over lawlessless and brute force.

2. This Conference offers a message of hope and encouragement to their fellow Jews in the Ghettos and concentration camps of Hitler-dominated Europe and prays that their hour of liberation may not be far distant.

3. The Conference sends its warmest greetings to the Jewish Agency Executive in Jerusalem, to the Va'ad Leumi, and to the whole Yishuv in Palestine, and expresses its profound admiration for their steadfastness and achievements in the face of peril and great difficulties. The Jewish men and women in field and factory, and the thousands of Jewish soldiers of Palestine in the Near East who have acquitted themselves with honor and distinction in Greece, Ethiopia, Syria, Libya and on other battlefields, have shown themselves worthy of their people and ready to assume the rights and responsibilities of nationhood.

4. In our generation, and in particular in the course of the past twenty years, the Jewish people have awakened and transformed their ancient homeland; from 50,000 at the end of the last war their numbers have increased to more than 500,000. They have made the waste places to bear fruit and the desert to blossom. Their pioneering achievements in agriculture and in industry, embodying new patterns of cooperative endeavor, have written a notable page in the history of colonization.

5. In the new values thus created, their Arab neighbors in Palestine have shared. The Jewish people in its own work of national redemption welcomes the economic, agricultural and national development of the Arab peoples and states. The Conference reaffirms the stand previously adopted at Congresses of the World Zionist Organization, expressing the readiness and the desire of the Jewish people for full cooperation with their Arab neighbors.

6. The Conference calls for the fulfilment of the original purpose of the Balfour Declaration and the Mandate which *"recognizing the historical connection of the Jewish people with Palestine"* was to afford them the opportunity, as stated by President Wilson, to found there a Jewish Commonwealth.

The Conference affirms its unalterable rejection of the White Paper of May 1939 and denies its moral or legal validity. The White Paper seeks to limit, and in fact to nullify Jewish rights to immigration and settlement in Palestine, and, as stated by Mr. Winston Churchill in the House of Commons in May 1939, constitutes "a breach and repudiation of the Balfour Declaration." The policy of the White Paper is cruel and indefensible in its denial of sanctuary to Jews fleeing from Nazi persecution; and at a time when Palestine has become a focal point in the war front of the United Nations, and Palestine Jewry must provide all available manpower for farm and factory and camp, it is in direct conflict with the interests of the allied war effort.

7. In the struggle against the forces of aggression and tyranny, of which Jews were the earliest victims, and which now menace the Jewish National Home, recognition must be given to the right of the Jews of Palestine to play their full part in the war effort and in the defense of their country, through a Jewish military force fighting under its own flag and under the high command of the United Nations.

8. The Conference declares that the new world order that will follow victory cannot be established on foundations of peace, justice and equality, unless the problem of Jewish homelessness is finally solved.

The Conference urges that the gates of Palestine be opened; that the Jewish Agency be vested with control of immigration into Palestine and with the necessary authority for upbuilding the country, including the development of its unoccupied and uncultivated lands; and that Palestine be established as a Jewish Commonwealth integrated in the structure of the new democratic world.

Then and only then will the age-old wrong to the Jewish people be righted.

72. GENERAL NURI AL-SA'ID'S FERTILE CRESCENT SCHEME
December 1942

[General Nuri al-Sa'id, *Arab Independence and Unity* (Baghdad, 1943), pp. 11–12]

Proponents of Arab unity existed from the very birth of Arab nationalism as a political movement on the eve of World War I. Their efforts in the next two decades however had little practical significance, owing to the fragmentation of southwest Asia in the peace settlement of 1919–23 and the consequent growth of state nationalism and rise of local politicians with vested interests who resisted close cooperation. After April 1936, hostility to Zionism and the Jewish National Home in Palestine and to British and French political controls—sentiments sedulously cultivated by the Axis powers—furnished tangible, if negative, foci of Arab unity. Britain accorded recognition to this unity on 9 November 1938 when the Colonial Office invited the independent Arab states to participate in the projected London conferences on Palestine and on 29 May 1941 when Foreign Secretary Anthony Eden declared in his Mansion House address that England "will give . . . full support to any [Arab unity] scheme that commands general approval" (*The Times* [London], 30 May 1941). But as long as the Axis Powers were in the ascendant, Britain's overtures elicited little response. Not until after the turn in the war's tide at the end of 1942, when Britain reestablished its supremacy in the Near and Middle East and an ultimate allied victory in the war was no longer questioned, did Arab spokesmen become more receptive to British suggestions. The first practical proposal came from Nuri Pasha al-Sa'id, then Prime Minister of Iraq, who submitted a memorandum to Richard G. Casey, the British Minister of State Resident in the Middle East, recommending the unification of Syria, Lebanon, Palestine, and Transjordan into a Greater Syria and the latter's merger with Iraq as the first steps in the formation of a League of Arab States. Reproduced below is Nuri Pasha's conclusion. M. Khadduri, "The Scheme of Fertile Crescent Unity, a Study in Inter-Arab Relations," *The Near East and the Great Powers,* ed. by R. N. Frye, pp. 137–77; C. A. Hourani, "The Arab League in Perspective," *The Middle East Journal,* 1 (April 1947), 125–36; G. Kirk, *The Middle East in the War,* pp. 333–44.

In my view the only fair solution, and indeed the only hope of securing permanent peace, contentment and progress in these Arab areas is for the United Nations to declare *now:*—

(1) That Syria, Lebanon, Palestine and Trans-Jordan shall be reunited into one State.

(2) That the form of government of this State, whether monarchical or republican whether unitary or federal, shall be decided by the peoples of this State themselves.

(3) That there shall be created an Arab League to which Iraq and Syria will adhere at once and which can be joined by the other Arab States at will.

(4) That this Arab League shall have a permanent Council nominated by the member States, and presided over by one of the rulers of the States who shall be chosen in a manner acceptable to the States concerned.

(5) The Arab League Council shall be responsible for the following:—

(*a*) Defence.
(*b*) Foreign Affairs.
(*c*) Currency.
(*d*) Communications.
(*e*) Customs.
(*f*) Protection of Minority rights.

(6) The Jews in Palestine shall be given semi-autonomy. They shall have the right to their own rural and urban district administration including schools, health institutes, and police subject to general supervision by the Syrian State.

(7) Jerusalem shall be a city to which members of all religions shall have free access for pilgrimage and worship. A special commission composed of representatives of the three theocratic religions shall be set up to ensure this.

(8) That if they demand it, the Maronites in the Lebanon shall be granted a privileged régime such as they possessed during the last years of the Ottoman Em-

pire. This special régime like those to be set up in paragraphs 6 and 7 above shall rest on an International Guarantee.

If it is possible in the manner suggested above to create a Confederation of Arab States including Iraq, Syria, Palestine and Trans-Jordan at the beginning, to which other Arab States may later adhere, then a great many of the difficulties which have faced Great Britain and France in the Near East during the past two decades will disappear. The Arabs of Palestine at present fear that they will become a minority in a Jewish State, and therefore bitterly oppose the grant of special rights to the Jews, but this hostility would be allayed if Palestine became part of a large strong Arab State. The Jews could establish their National Home in those parts of Palestine, where they are now the majority with a greater feeling of security, because there would be more goodwill on the part of their Arab neighbours, and as a semi-autonomous community in a much larger State their economic opportunities would increase.

The British Empire is not founded on negations but on positive ideals. Free institutions and free co-operation give it a living force of tremendous strength. Upon this foundation of free co-operation a true union of many diverse peoples and countries has been formed, depending less upon stipulations and statistics and more upon the nobler and more permanent principles which are written on the heart and conscience of man. If an opportunity is given to the Arab peoples to establish such a free cooperation among themselves they will be prepared to deal generously with all the Jews living in their midst whether in Palestine or elsewhere. Conditions and guarantees there must be, but let them not constitute a dead hand lest they become a dead letter, as so many minority provisions in European constitutions became during the past twenty years.

If my proposals meet with favour they will require careful examination, so that the appropriate steps are taken at the right time and in the right order. Obviously, the union of the various parts of historic Syria must come first. It may at first take the form of a federation of Syria, Lebanon, Palestine and Trans-Jordan, each state continuing its own local administration, leaving defence, foreign relations, currency and customs to the Central Government. On the other hand it may be found possible to unite Syria at once, making provision for the Jewish enclaves and the Jerusalem régime at the same time. Steps should be taken at once to define these enclaves and for this purpose it would be necessary to prepare an accurate ethnographical map of Palestine showing the number of Arabs and Jews in each Nahya and town, also, a map on the same scale showing the land under cultivation and the land which can be cultivated intensely in the future. An inquiry should also be made as to the number of Jews who have settled in Palestine since the outbreak of the war in September, 1939.

To secure Arab union sacrifices of sovereignty and vested interests may have to be made. Similar sacrifices have been made in the British Dominions and can be equally demanded from Arab leaders.

I have throughout assumed that as France before the war declared that she was prepared to grant independence to Syria and the Lebanon she will not be allowed by the United Nations to repudiate her offers, nor to obstruct any federation of Arab States by insisting on old privileges or antiquated rights.

73. THE TEHRAN DECLARATION
1 December 1943

[*The Department of State Bulletin,* 9 (11 December 1943), 409–10]

The Persian Gulf Service Command (labeled Persian Gulf Command after December 1943), as the United States railroad and motor maintenance and transport units in Iran were called, comprised at its height close to 30,000 troops. Between November 1942, when the PGSC commenced operations in Iran, and the end of the war American forces transshipped some 3.5 million long tons of Soviet-bound lend-lease supplies from American vessels in Iranian ports to Tehran, where the Russians assumed responsibility for the traffic. Indeed, the Iranian corridor became the second most important of five American lend-lease supply routes to Russia in World War II. To clarify the status of American troops, who originally came to Iran on British invitation to assist the Soviet ally, the Iranian government urged the United States to adhere to the tripartite treaty of January 1942 (Doc. 70). "Not considering it feasible to become a party to a treaty of alliance with Iran," observed former Secretary of State Cordell Hull, "we proposed to the Iranians a separate agreement to cover the presence of our troops on their territory" (C. Hull, *Memoirs,* vol. 2, p. 1505). Iran, however, sought wider assurances than the United States was willing to give, so that no agreement of the class requested was ever reached. Still, at the time of the first meeting between Churchill, Roosevelt and Stalin at Tehran in the fall of 1943, the American Legation in the Iranian capital drafted the following declaration, which the three war leaders signed and under which the United States associated itself with the pledge of its two allies to maintain "the independence, sovereignty and territorial integrity of Iran." T. H. V. Motter, *The Persian Corridor and Aid to Russia,* pp. 435–60; Hull, *op. cit.,* pp. 1500–10; J. C. Hurewitz, *Middle East Dilemmas,* chap. 2.

The President of the United States of America, the Premier of the Union of Soviet Socialist Republics, and the Prime Minister of the United Kingdom, having consulted with each other and with the Prime Minister of Iran, desire to declare the mutual agreement of their three Governments regarding their relations with Iran.

The Governments of the United States of America, the Union of Soviet Socialist Republics and the United Kingdom recognize the assistance which Iran has given in the prosecution of the war against the common enemy, particularly by facilitating transportation of supplies from overseas to the Soviet Union. The three Governments realize that the war has caused special economic difficulties for Iran and they are agreed that they will continue to make available to the Government of Iran such economic assistance as may be possible, having regard to the heavy demands made upon them by their world-wide military operations and to the world-wide shortage of transport, raw materials and supplies for civilian consumption.

With respect to the post-war period, the Governments of the United States of America, the Union of Soviet Socialist Republics and the United Kingdom are in accord with the Government of Iran that any economic problem confronting Iran at the close of hostilities should receive full consideration along with those of the other members of the United Nations by conferences or international agencies held or created to deal with international economic matters.

The Governments of the United States of America, the Union of Soviet Socialist Republics and the United Kingdom are at one with the Government of Iran in their desire for the maintenance of the independence, sovereignty and territorial integrity of Iran. They count upon the participation of Iran together with all other peace-loving nations in the establishment of international peace, security and prosperity after the war in accordance with the principles of the Atlantic Charter, to which all four governments have continued to subscribe.

74. UNITED STATES GOVERNMENT PROPOSAL FOR CONSTRUCTING A TRANS-ARABIAN PETROLEUM PIPELINE SYSTEM
5 February 1944

[*The New York Times,* 6 February 1944]

American oil firms acquired by 1939 a 23.75 per cent interest in the Iraq Petroleum Company (Docs. 44, 54), half ownership of a concession in Kuwayt (1934) and exclusive concessions in Bahrayn (1929) and Saudi Arabia (1933, 1939). Saudi Arabia and Kuwayt possessed the largest proved reserves. But the California Arabian Standard Oil Company (CASOC), owned jointly by Standard of California and Texas, began commercial operations in Saudi Arabia on a small scale in October 1938, while the Kuwayt Oil Company, owned jointly by Gulf and Anglo-Iranian, was not to launch operations until 1946. In April 1941 CASOC—or Aramco (Arabian American Oil Company), as it became known after 31 January 1944—proposed to President Roosevelt that the United States government provide ibn Saʿud with an annual grant of 6 million dollars, the amount the king requested from the company, in return for petroleum products at greatly reduced prices, including discount of the king's royalties. "It has now come to a point where it is impossible for the company to continue the growing burden and responsibility of financing an independent country, particularly under present abnormal conditions," the company's memorandum to President Roosevelt observed. "However, the King is desperate. He has told us that unless necessary financial assistance is immediately forthcoming, he has grave fears for the stability of his country" [text in U. S., 80th Cong., 2nd sess., Sen. Rep. No. 440, part 5, *Navy Purchases of Middle East Oil* (Washington, 1948), pp. 4–5]. The suggestion was turned down, because, as Secretary Hull noted in conjunction with a simultaneous request from the United Kingdom to extend lend-lease aid to the Arabian monarch, "the President . . . felt that there was more reason for the British, with their greater strategic and political interests in the Near East, to attend to Ibn Saud's financial needs" (C. Hull, *Memoirs,* vol. 2, p. 1512). Yet less than three years later Secretary of the Interior Harold L. Ickes, president of the recently created, government-owned Petroleum Reserves Corporation, issued the following statement announcing that an agreement in principle had been reached with Aramco and Gulf for the government's erection of a trunk pipeline system, at a cost of 130-165 million dollars, for transporting crude oil from the Persian Gulf to the Mediterranean. The companies for their part undertook to provide a one-billion-barrel reserve for the United States armed forces. The government-sponsored scheme, which stirred a hornet's nest in the American oil industry and aroused the wrath of the United Kingdom, was swiftly jettisoned. But the episode demonstrated the mercurial quality of American policy on the Near and Middle East in the period and, of even greater importance, the belief in United States official circles that the region's oil was vital to the national defense. *Navy Purchases of Middle East Oil;* H. Feis, *Seen from E.A.*, pp. 93–190; Hull, *op. cit.*, pp. 1511–27; *International Petroleum Cartel,* chap. 5; B. Shwadran, *The Middle East, Oil and the Great Powers,* chaps. 12–13.

The directors of Petroleum Reserves Corporation, with the approval of the President of the United States and of the State Department, and acting upon the recommendation of the War Department and Navy Department, joint Chiefs of Staff and the Army-Navy Petroleum Board, have authorized me to enter into an agreement in principle with the Arabian American Oil Company, operating in the Kingdom of Saudi Arabia, and the Gulf Exploration Company, operating in the Sheikdom of Kuwait.

The agreement is conditioned, of course, upon obtaining the sanction of the rulers of Saudi Arabia and Kuwait.

The Petroleum Reserves Corporation does not propose to compete with the private oil industry of this country. On the contrary, its purpose is to promote the private oil industry of this nation, and to further the interests of the people of the United States. In addition to assisting these private American companies in the development of their oil interests in the areas covered by this agreement, the project will promote the interests of the governments and of the peoples of such areas.

The purpose of this agreement is to make provision for a pipeline which will be constructed from the Persian Gulf area to a point on the Eastern Mediterranean, and to provide a reserve of 1,000,000,000 barrels of oil for the naval and military forces of the United States. The terms of the agreement guarantee to the government complete repayment of its investment and costs.

The principles agreed to, which are subject to the working out of a definitive contract, provide that the Petroleum Reserves Corporation will construct, own and maintain a trunk pipeline system to transport crude petroleum from the Persian Gulf area to the Mediterranean.

The government will determine the most feasible plan for operation of the facilities, and will retain supervision thereof. The entire cost of construction plus interest will be returned to the government within a period of twenty-five years, together with such net profit to the government as may be agreed upon in the definitive contract. This is guaranteed by the companies. In other words, the pipeline will eventually cost the Government of the United States nothing. It is estimated that the cost will be between $130,000,000 and $165,000,000, depending on the details of plans to be worked out.

The companies agree to perform at actual cost any work or services which the government may request in connection with this project.

The pipeline facilities will be made available to other oil producers and shippers, in addition to the companies which are now parties to the agrement. Provision is made for other companies to utilize the facilities, provided that they fulfill certain stipulated obligations.

The agreement of the companies to maintain a crude-oil petroleum reserve for the account of the United States, of one billion barrels, or 20 per cent of the total crude reserves if they are less than five billion barrels, will greatly help to assure an adequate supply of petroleum for the military and naval needs of the United States in view of the obligations which this country must assume for the maintenance of collective security in the post-war world.

It will make the oil in this reserve available for Government purchase at any time for military or naval use at 25 per cent below the market price in the Persian Gulf region, or of similar crude oil in the United States, whichever price is lower. The Government is not obligated to take this oil or any part of it, but it has the right to do so at any time, for a period of fifty years. In addition, in times of war or other national emergency, the Government has the option to purchase all of the crude petroleum produced by the companies and all products thereof, to be paid for at such prices as may be agreed upon at the time of taking.

The agreement, in principle, further provides that the companies will not sell petroleum or products to any government or the nationals of any government when, in the opinion of the Department of State, such sales would be unwise in the light of United States foreign policy and the requirements of collective security. The companies also agree that before they negotiate with the governments of any foreign countries with respect to the sale of petroleum and petroleum products from their concessions in Saudi Arabia and Kuwait they will give notice to the Department of State and the Petroleum Reserves Corporation.

In order that the public may be fully informed concerning this agreement in principle, copies are being made available for inspection.

The action which we have taken in cooperation with the American oil companies which have rights to oil in Saudi Arabia and Kuwait is designed to offset, in measure, the dwindling oil reserves in the United States. The known reserves in this country are estimated to be adequate for this nation's needs for only a relatively few years. It is true that there may be inventions or improvements in technology which will result in the discovery of new reserves, or, indeed, in the development of new sources of energy. But it would be imprudent to gamble the future of the nation in such a speculation. The construction of the pipeline will assure that huge quantities of oil in the Persian Gulf region will be available to this country when and if needed. And the setting aside of one billion barrels of oil for military and naval use assures to our armed forces, on very favorable terms, a supply of oil which amounts to several years' requirements at their present unprecedented rate of consumption.

I hope that the announcement and publication of this agreement in principle will eliminate once and for all the apprehensions which have been caused by the organization and activities of Petroleum Reserves Corporation. We are making this announcement of our plans and program as soon as possible in view of the complicated negotiations affecting many agencies of our own and other nations. Premature publicity in this situation might well have made it impossible to conclude the arrangements.

The policy of the Petroleum Reserves Corporation is to aid the private oil business of this country by seeing to it that so far as the foreign-oil situation is concerned the interests of the United States and its military forces are protected, and to do what can be done consistently with the foreign policy of this Government, as administered by the Department of State, to aid the private oil industry of this country to secure against future contingencies an adequate supply of foreign oil.

The pipeline which will be built pursuant to this agreement will serve an essential military purpose and it will also be of lasting benefit to the people of this nation.

75. IRANIAN LAW PROHIBITING THE GRANT OF OIL CONCESSIONS TO FOREIGNERS AND ITS EFFECT
2 December 1944–15 January 1945

[Majlis law translated from the Persian text in Iran, *Majmu'ah-i-Qawanin,* 14, pp. 4–5; Soviet note from *Foreign Relations of the United States: The Conferences at Malta and Yalta 1945* (Washington, D.C., 1955), pp. 334–36; American memorandum, *ibid.,* pp. 342–43; Churchill note, *ibid.,* pp. 336–37]

Late in 1943 the Royal Dutch-Shell, followed early in 1944 by the (American) Socony-Vacuum and Sinclair, companies opened exploratory talks with Iran for oil concessions in the southeastern provinces. The Iranian government in April 1944 employed as petroleum consultants an American firm to frame a concessionary formula that might be used in the projected contracts with the oil companies. The competition for oil contracts was further sharpened by the appearance in Tehran on 15 September—before any agreements had yet been consummated—of a Soviet mission, headed by Assistant Commissar for Foreign Affairs Sergei I. Kavtaradze. The Soviet diplomat proceeded to demand an exclusive five-year exploratory concession embracing the five northern provinces then under Russian occupation. But Kavtaradze's pressure diplomacy merely caused Iranian Prime Minister Muhammad Sa'id Maraghai and his cabinet to bridle. The Iranian government thereupon suspended oil discussions with all foreign representatives for the duration of the war. The *Majlis* (legislature), moreover, adopted the bill reproduced below (item 1), which the USSR chose to regard as an American and British maneuver to prevent the Soviet Union from obtaining any oil concession. The USSR immediately launched a propaganda campaign in Iran of villifying the Western allies, a program that continued with increasing intensity throughout the last year of the war. The Soviet statement (item 2), sent in reply to an American note of 1 November 1944, elaborated upon the official position of the USSR. The American view was outlined in a memorandum (item 3) forming part of a U. S. *Briefing Book* paper for the Yalta conference. Prime Minister Churchill developed the British attitude in a top secret telegram (item 4) to President Roosevelt; paragraph 7 of the last entry, calling attention to a Soviet note to the Foreign Office substantially identical with item 2, has been omitted below. G. Kirk, *The Middle East in the War,* pp. 466–87; G. Lenczowski, *Russia and the West in Iran,* pp. 216–23; H. Feis, *Seen from E.A.,* pp. 173–78; C. Hull, *Memoirs,* vol. 2, pp. 1508–10; A. C. Millspaugh, *Americans in Persia,* pp. 187–90, 233–34; *Foreign Relations of the United States: The Conferences at Malta and Yalta 1945,* pp. 329–45, 738–40 (records).

1. LAW ADOPTED BY THE *Majlis,* 2 DECEMBER 1944

1. No Prime Minister or Minister or Acting Minister or Undersecretary of State may undertake any official discussion or discussions having a legal character, or sign any agreement, regarding a petroleum concession with the official or unofficial representatives of neighboring or distant countries or with the representatives of oil companies or with any other person.

2. The Prime Minister and the Ministers

may however undertake negotiations regarding the sale of petroleum and the manner in which the Iranian Government is to exploit and administer its oil wells. The *Majlis* must, however, be informed of the progress of the negotiations.

3. Any person or persons violating the provisions of the first article shall be sentenced to a term of solitary imprisonment from three to eight years and shall be permanently debarred from Government service.

2. SOVIET NOTE TO THE UNITED STATES, 28 DECEMBER 1944

In September the Soviet Government dispatched to Iran an official commission headed by the Deputy People's Commissar for Foreign Affairs, S. I. Kavtaradze, for negotiating with the Government of Iran regarding the granting of an oil concession for the Soviet Union in the northern regions of Iran. The conditions of a possible agreement, which the Soviet Government had in view to conclude on that subject with the Government of Iran, were very profitable and advantageous for Iran, and, of course were in no degree infringing its sovereignty or independence. It was intended also to consider any suggestions of the part of Iran, and to start practical discussion of the conditions of the agreement in the spirit of the friendly and allied relations existing between the two countries.

In the beginning of the negotiations the head of the Government of Iran, Mr. Saed, declared that his attitude was favorable to the Soviet proposals. On this basis the Soviet Commission started the preliminary work connected with the coming negotiations. However, a month later, the attitude of the Government of Mr. Saed changed, under hidden influences and Mr. Saed declared suddenly to the Soviet Commission his refusal to grant the concession. The Government of Mr. Saed did not even make an attempt to familiarize itself with the Soviet conditions of the concession, which as deemed by the Soviet Government, should have been passed on by the representatives of both sides on the basis of free negotiations and with allowance for mutual interests.

Thus the Government of Mr. Saed was obviously disloyal, with respect to the Soviet side, in the conduct of the negotiations. This disloyal attitude of Mr. Saed toward the proposals of the Soviet Government, which was sincerely looking for ways for a practical achievement of an important economic agreement with Iran, that would be to the advantage of both countries and would lend to Iran considerable economic assistance, as well as other facts, manifesting the hostile attitude of Mr. Saed on a series of questions of Soviet-Iran collaboration, could not but evoke a corresponding negative reaction in the Soviet public opinion and press.

As can be seen from the events which followed in Iran, the hostile attitude taken toward the U. S. S. R. by the former Prime Minister, Mr. Saed, met with disapproval of many Iranian political leaders and wide circles of Iranian public opinion.

Such are the circumstances of the case concerning the Soviet proposals pertaining to the oil concession in Iran. The Soviet Government considers it its duty to mention these circumstances, so that the Government of the United States of America may have correct information on this question.

At the same time the Soviet Government cannot overlook the unsympathetic attitude taken by America with regard to Soviet-Iran negotiations regarding the oil concession. As appears from the information set forth above, any statements about interference on the part of the Soviet in the internal affairs of Iran have no foundation whatever.

The Soviet Government cannot agree with arguments that the granting of an oil concession to the Soviet Union can in any degree affect the sovereignty of Iran. If these arguments were recognized as sound, they would in the first place affect Great Britain which, as is known, has for a long time had an important oil concession in Iran.

In the opinion of the Soviet Government, there are not sufficient reasons to assert either that the question of the granting of an oil concession to the Soviet Union cannot be settled at the present time, and that this question must be postponed until the post-war period.

The former Government of Saed was not able to offer any convincing argument to that effect. The Soviet proposals concerning the oil concessions are in no measure in contradiction with the declaration concerning Iran made on December 1, 1943 by the three Powers. On the contrary, they are in complete accord with this declaration, which contemplates the necessity of lending economic assistance to Iran by the Allies. It is obvious that a positive solution of the question of an oil concession to the Soviet Union would contribute to a further development of good Soviet-Iran relations, and at the same time would become one of the means of lending important economic assistance to Iran. In this respect the Soviet proposals concerning the concession agree entirely with the obligations assumed by the Allies according to the declaration of the three Powers concerning Iran.

The above might be supplemented by the following.

Early in December, concealed from public opinion and in violation of the Iranian Constitution, the former Prime Minister Mr. Saed in concert with a certain Seyid Zia-ed-din succeeded in having passed by the Majlis a resolution forbidding the members of the Iranian Government from entering into negotiations with anyone concerning oil concessions.

In connection with this, the Deputy People's Commissar, S. I. Kavtaradze, paid a visit to the new Prime Minister of Iran and by direction of the Soviet Government made a statement containing the remark, that in the opinion of the Soviet Government the above-mentioned resolution concerning oil concessions must be revised, because it was adopted under the influence of intriguing by hostile elements of the kind of Saed, Seyid Zia-ed-din, and others.

Apart from that, this resolution contradicts the fact of the existence on the territory of Iran of an important oil concession belonging to a foreign country. After having made this statement, S. I. Kavtaradze left for Moscow.

Informing the Government of the United States of America of the above, the Soviet Government considers it necessary to remark that on the question concerning the oil concession in Iran it continues to maintain the attitude expressed in this note, in particular in the statement of the Deputy People's Commissar for Foreign Affairs, S. I. Kavtaradze, cited, made by him to the Prime Minister of Iran mentioned.

3. MEMORANDUM FORMING PART OF A *Briefing Book* PAPER FOR THE YALTA CONFERENCE, 6 JANUARY 1945

Soviet displeasure at the action of the Iranian Government in suspending, until after the war, all negotiations for oil concessions is an ominous development which should be carefully followed.

A brief summary of the immediate background of this matter follows. American and British oil companies began negotiations with the Iranian Government in early 1944 for a petroleum concession in *southern* Iran. The American and British Embassies in Iran were aware of these negotiations but regarded them as private commercial ventures and in no way participated in the negotiations. The negotiations seemed about to terminate successfully in September when a large Soviet delegation, headed by Vice Commissar Kavtaradze, appeared in Tehran and demanded that a concession be granted to the Soviet Government for the five *northern* provinces of Iran. The Iranian Government, alarmed by the sweeping Soviet demands, disturbed by Soviet refusal to discuss terms or conditions, and fearful that Iranian sovereignty would be jeopardized if a foreign government should obtain such wide and lasting control in the country, announced that all petroleum negotiations were suspended until the end of the war.

The United States Government promptly informed the Iranian Government that, while American companies were disappointed, we recognized the sovereign right of Iran to grant or withhold concessions within its territory. We asked that, when negotiations are resumed, American companies be informed and be placed in no less favorable position than granted to any foreign company or government. The British followed a similar policy although they made no formal statement to the Iranian Government, as far as we are aware. The Russians showed great annoyance, taking the Iranian action as an affront. The Soviet press began a strong and concerted attack on Iranian Prime Minister Saed and his Government, accusing Iranian officials of being "disloyal" and Fascist-minded. These attacks and the strong statements of displeasure by Vice Commissar Kavtaradze in Tehran brought about the resignation of the Saed Government.

The American Embassy in Moscow informed the Soviet Government on November 1, 1944, of the attitude we had taken and stated that our action had been based on the Declaration on Iran signed at Tehran by President Roosevelt, Prime Minister Churchill and Marshal Stalin on December 1, 1943. The Soviet Government, in a reply addressed to us on December 28, 1944 strongly supported the action taken by Vice Commissar Kavtaradze, again accused the Iranian Government of unfriendly and "disloyal" action, denied that the granting of an oil concession to the Soviet Government would affect Iranian sovereignty, and declared that the concession would in no way be in contradiction to the Declaration on Iran. The note described the American attitude toward this Soviet-Iranian dispute as "unsympathetic" to the Soviet Government.

The British Government, for its part, subsequently called the attention of the Soviet Government to the harmful effects of Soviet action in Iran and has asked the Russians to state frankly their designs and intentions in this matter. The British have asked us to make similar representations in Moscow but we have taken no action other than our original note of November 1.

The situation is potentially dangerous, not only as regards Iranian sovereignty but in the more important bearing it may have on allied relations. The British, however willing they may be to make concessions to the Russians in Eastern Europe, will probably refuse to consider concessions in the Middle East, which is so vitally important to Empire communications. The consequences of this dispute, if it is allowed to continue, may be serious.

The American Government should continue to maintain the reasonable and tenable position we have taken; that we recognize the sovereign right of Iran to grant or withhold concessions within its territory. We should stress to the Russians, at the highest possible level and in the most friendly and constructive manner, the harmful effects of their action in Iran. While British opposition to the Soviet action may be based primarily on strategic grounds, our chief concern is that the assurances of the great powers of respect for Iranian sovereignty be not violated. The confidence of the world in the Dumbarton Oaks proposals could be seriously affected by action to force Iran to grant an oil concession.

4. TOP SECRET TELEGRAM FROM PRIME MINISTER CHURCHILL TO PRESIDENT ROOSEVELT, 15 JANUARY 1945

1. One of the questions which I think should be discussed at our meeting with Stalin, or between the Foreign Secretaries, is that of Persia.

2. In the declaration about Persia which we and Stalin signed at Teheran in December 1943, it is stated that "The Governments of the United States of America, the USSR and the United Kingdom are at one with the Government of Iran in their desire for the maintenance of the independence, sovereignty and territorial integrity of Iran."

3. You will have seen reports of the recent attitude of the Russians in Persia. We here feel that the various forms of pressure which they have been exerting constitute a departure from the statement quoted above. They have refused to accept the Persian decision to grant no concessions until after the war: and they have brought about the fall of a Persian Prime Minister who, believing that there could be no free or fair negotiations so long as Russian (or

other foreign) troops were in Persia, refused the immediate grant of their oil demands. The new Persian Prime Minister, supported by the Parliament, has maintained his predecessor's attitude on this question. But the Russians have indicated that they do not intend to drop their demands.

4. This may be something of a test case. Persia is a country where we, yourselves and the Russians are all involved: and we have given a joint undertaking to treat the Persians decently. If the Russians are now able not only to save their face by securing the fall of the Persian Prime Minister who opposed them, but also to secure what they want by their use of the big stick, Persia is not the only place where the bad effect will be felt.

5. Please let me know whether you agree that this should be taken up with the Russians: and if so, whether you feel that it should be handled by ourselves with Stalin (as signatories of the Teheran declaration) or by the Foreign Secretaries. I think it should be our object to induce the Russians to admit that the Persians are within their rights in withholding a concession if they wish to do so. We could agree, if necessary, that the oil question should be further reviewed after the withdrawal of foreign troops from Persia.

6. We do not wish the Russian Government to represent that they were not warned in time of the strength of our feelings on this matter. If, therefore, you agree generally with my suggestion, I propose that we should separately or jointly let Stalin know now that we think Persia should be discussed at our next meeting (or by the Foreign Secretaries).

76. THE PACT OF THE ARAB LEAGUE
22 March 1945

[Text printed and distributed by the Arab Office, Washington, D.C., n.d. but probably 1946]

Nuri Pasha's Arab unity plan (Doc. 72) served merely as the first of a series of Arab wartime steps which led to the formation of the Arab League. Foreign Secretary Anthony Eden reaffirmed in Parliament on 24 February 1943 Britain's support of the Arab unity movement but stated that "clearly the initiative . . . would have to come from the Arabs themselves" (Great Britain, *Parliamentary Debates, Commons,* 5th ser., vol. 387, col. 139). Between July 1943 and February 1944 Mustafa Pasha al-Nahhas, then Prime Minister of Egypt, conducted with delegates from Iraq, Transjordan, Saudi Arabia, Syria, Lebanon and Yemen exploratory talks which eventuated in a general conference on Arab unity at Alexandria, Egypt (25 September–7 October 1944). The conference adopted a protocol [text in Arab Information Center (New York), *Basic Documents of the League of Arab States* (New York, 1955), pp. 5–8] which announced that its signatories had decided to create a "League . . . of the independent Arab States" for the purpose, in part, of coordinating "their political plans so as to insure their cooperation" and protecting "their independence and sovereignty against every aggression by suitable means." Between 24 February–1 March 1945 Egypt, Syria, Lebanon and Saudi Arabia—on the invitation of Britain and the United States—declared war against the Axis Powers (Iraq had already done so in January 1943), and thus became eligible for participation in the projected conference on international organization, which was later held in San Francisco (25 April–26 June 1945). In anticipation of this conference and of obtaining international recognition for the Arab bloc as a regional arrangement, six of the participating Arab states signed on 22 March 1945 the pact of the Arab League, which formally brought the regional organization into existence. Announcement of Yemen's ratification of the instrument was made on 11 May 1945; Libya became the eighth member on 28 March 1953; and the Sudan, the ninth on 19 January 1956. M. Khadduri, "The Arab League as a Regional Arrangement," *American Journal of International Law,* 40 (October 1946), 756–77; B. Y. Boutros-Ghali, "The Arab League 1945-1955," *International Conciliation,* May 1955, pp. 386–448; G. Kirk, *The Middle East in the War,* pp. 333–44; M. Laissy, *Du Panarabisme à la ligue arabe.*

ART. 1. The League of the Arab States is composed of the independent Arab States which have signed this pact.

Any independent Arab State has the right to become a member of the League. If it desires to do so, it shall submit a request which will be deposited with the permanent Secretariat-General and submitted to the Council at the first meeting held after submission of the request.

ART. 2. The League has as its purpose the strengthening of the relations between the member states; the coordination of their policies in order to achieve cooperation between them and to safeguard their independence and sovereignty; and a general concern with the affairs and interests of the Arab countries. It has also as its purpose the close cooperation of the member states, with due regard to the organization and circumstances of each state, on the following matters:

A. Economic and financial affairs, including commercial relations, customs, currency, and questions of agriculture and industry.

B. Communications: this includes railroads, roads, aviation, navigation, telegraphs, and posts.

C. Cultural affairs.

D. Nationality, passports, visas, execution of judgments, and extradition of criminals.

E. Social affairs.

F. Health problems.

ART. 3. The League shall possess a Council composed of the representatives of the member state of the League; each state shall have a single vote, irrespective of the number of its representatives.

It shall be the task of the Council to achieve the realization of the objectives of the League and to supervise the execution of agreements which the member states have concluded on the questions enumerated in the preceding article, or on any other questions.

It likewise shall be the Council's task to decide upon the means by which the League is to cooperate with the international bodies to be created in the future in order to guarantee security and peace and regulate economic and social relations.

ART. 4. For each of the questions listed in Article 2 there shall be set up a special committee in which the member states of the League shall be represented. These committees shall be charged with the task of laying down the principles and extent of cooperation. Such principles shall be formulated as draft agreements, to be presented to the Council for examination preparatory to their submission to the aforesaid states.

Representatives of the other Arab countries may take part in the work of the aforesaid committees. The Council shall determine the conditions under which these representatives may be permitted to participate and the rules governing such representation.

ART. 5. Any resort to force in order to resolve disputes arising between two or more member states of the League is prohibited. If there should arise among them a difference which does not concern a state's independence, sovereignty, or territorial integrity, and if the parties to the dispute have recourse to the Council for the settlement of the difference, the decision of the Council shall then be enforceable and obligatory.

In such a case, the states between whom the difference has arisen shall not participate in the deliberations and decisions of the Council.

The Council may lend its good offices for the settlement of all differences which threaten to lead to war between two member states, or a member state and a third state, with a view to bringing about their reconciliation.

Decisions of arbitration and mediation shall be taken by majority vote.

ART. 6. In case of aggression or threat of aggression by one state against a member state, the state which has been attacked or threatened with aggression may demand the immediate convocation of the Council.

The Council shall by unanimous decision determine the measures necessary to repulse the aggression. If the aggressor is a member state, his vote shall not be counted in determining unanimity.

If, as a result of the attack, the government of the state attacked finds itself unable to communicate with the Council, that state's representative in the Council shall have the right to request the convocation of the Council for the purpose indicated in the foregoing paragraph. In the event that this representative is unable to communicate with the Council, any member state of the League shall have the right to request the convocation of the Council.

ART. 7. Unanimous decisions of the Council shall be binding upon all member states of the League; majority decisions shall be binding only upon those states which have accepted them.

In either case the decisions of the Council shall be enforced in each member state according to its respective fundamental laws.

ART. 8. Each member state shall respect the systems of government established in the other member states and regard them as exclusive concerns of those states. Each shall pledge to abstain from any action calculated to change established systems of government.

ART. 9. States of the League which desire to establish closer cooperation and stronger bonds than are provided by this Pact may conclude agreements to that end.

Treaties and agreements already concluded or to be concluded in the future between a member state and another State shall not be binding or restrictive upon other members.

ART. 10. The permanent seat of the League of Arab States is established in Cairo. The Council may, however, assemble at any other place it may designate.

ART. 11. The Council of the League shall convene in ordinary session twice a year, in March and in October. It shall convene in extraordinary session upon the request of two member states of the League whenever the need arises.

ART. 12. The League shall have a permanent Secretariat-General which shall consist of a Secretary-General, Assistant Secretaries, and an appropriate number of officials.

The Council of the League shall appoint the Secretary-General by a majority of two-thirds of the states of the League. The Secretary-General, with the approval of the Council, shall appoint the Assistant Secretaries and the principal officials of the League.

The Council of the League shall establish an administrative regulation for the functions of the Secretariat-General and matters relating to the staff.

The Secretary-General shall have the rank of Ambassador and the Assistant Secretaries that of Ministers Plenipotentiary.

The first Secretary-General of the League is named in an Annex to this Pact.

ART. 13. The Secretary-General shall prepare the draft budget of the League and shall submit it to the Council for approval before the beginning of each fiscal year.

The Council shall fix the share of the expenses to be borne by each state of the League. This share may be reconsidered if necessary.

ART. 14. The members of the Council of the League as well as the members of the committees and the officials who are to be designated in the administrative regulation shall enjoy diplomatic privileges and immunity when engaged in the exercise of their functions.

The buildings occupied by the organs of the League shall be inviolable.

ART. 15. The first meeting of the Council shall be convened at the invitation of the Head of the Egyptian Government. Thereafter it shall be convened at the invitation of the Secretary-General.

The representatives of the member States of the League shall alternatively assume the Presidency of the Council at each of its ordinary sessions.

ART. 16. Except in cases specifically indicated in this Pact, a majority vote of the Council shall be sufficient to make enforceable decisions on the following matters:

A. Matters relating to personnel.

B. Adoption of the budget of the League.

C. Establishment of the administrative

regulations for the Council, the committees, and the Secretariat-General.

D. Decisions to adjourn the sessions.

ART. 17. Each member State of the League shall deposit with the Secretariat-General one copy of every treaty or agreement concluded or to be concluded in the future between itself and another member state of the League or a third state.

ART. 18. If a member state contemplates withdrawal from the League, it shall inform the Council of its intention one year before such withdrawal is to go into effect.

The Council of the League may consider any state which fails to fulfill its obligations under this Pact as having become separated from the League, this to go into effect upon a unanimous decision of the States, not counting the state concerned.

ART. 19. This Pact may be amended with the consent of two-thirds of the states belonging to the League, especially in order to make firmer and stronger the ties between the member states, to create an Arab Tribunal of Arbitration, and to regulate the relations of the League with any international bodies to be created in the future to guarantee security and peace.

Final action on an amendment cannot be taken prior to the session following the session in which the motion was initiated.

If a state does not accept such an amendment it may withdraw at such time as the amendment goes into effect, without being bound by the provisions of the preceding article.

ART. 20. This Pact and its Annexes shall be ratified according to the basic laws in force among the High Contracting Parties.

The instruments of ratification shall be deposited with the Secretariat-General of the Council and the Pact shall become operative as regards each ratifying state fifteen days after the Secretariat-General has received the instruments of ratification from four states.

This Pact has been drawn up in Cairo in the Arabic language on this 8th day of Rabi' II, thirteen hundred and sixty-four (22 March 1945), in one copy which shall be deposited in the safe keeping of the Secretariat-General.

An identical copy shall be delivered to each state of the League.

(1) Annex Regarding Palestine. Since the termination of the last great war the rule of the Ottoman Empire over the Arab countries, among them Palestine, which had become detached from that Empire, has come to an end. She has come to be independent in herself, not subordinate to any other state.

The Treaty of Lausanne proclaimed that her future was to be settled by the parties concerned.

However, even though she was as yet unable to control her own affairs, the Covenant of the League (of Nations) in 1919 made provision for a regime based upon recognition of her independence.

Her international existence and independence in the legal sense cannot, therefore, be questioned, any more than could the independence of the other Arab countries.

Although the outward manifestations of this independence have remained obscured for reasons beyond her control, this should not be allowed to interfere with her participation in the work of the Council of the League.

The States signatory to the Pact of the Arab League are therefore of the opinion that, considering the special circumstances of Palestine, and until that country can effectively exercise its independence, the Council of the League should take charge of the selection of an Arab representative from Palestine to take part in its work.

(2) Annex Regarding Cooperation With Countries Which Are Not Members of the Council of the League. Whereas the member states of the League will have to deal in the Council as well as in the committees with matters which will benefit and affect the Arab world at large:

And Whereas the Council has to take into account the aspirations of the Arab countries which are not members of the Council and has to work toward their realization;

Now therefore, it particularly behooves the states signatory to the Pact of the Arab League to enjoin the Council of the League, when considering the admission of those countries to participation in the committees referred to in the Pact, that it should do its utmost to cooperate with them, and furthermore, that it should spare no effort to learn their needs and understand their aspirations and hopes; and that it should work thenceforth for their best interests and the safeguarding of their future with all the political means at its disposal.

(3) Annex Regarding the Appointment of a Secretary-General of the League. The states signatory to this Pact have agreed to appoint His Excellency Abd-ul-Rahman 'Azzam Bey, to be Secretary-General of the League of Arab States.

This appointment is made for two years. The Council of the League shall hereafter determine the new regulations for the Secretariat-General.

77. PRELIMINARY REPORT (HARRISON) TO PRESIDENT TRUMAN ON DISPLACED PERSONS IN GERMANY AND AUSTRIA
August 1945

[*Department of State Bulletin,* 13 (30 September 1945), 456–63]

President Truman on 22 June 1945 instructed Earl G. Harrison, the American representative on the Intergovernmental Committee on Refugees, to investigate "(1) the conditions under which displaced persons and particularly those who may be stateless or non-repatriable are at present living, especially in Germany and Austria, (2) the needs of such persons, (3) how those needs are being met at present by the military authorities, the governments of residence and international and private relief bodies, and (4) the views of the possibly non-repatriable persons as to their future destinations." Harrison was further directed "to give particular attention to the problems, needs and views of the Jewish refugees among the displaced people, especially in Germany and Austria" [*Department of State Bulletin,* 13 (30 September 1945), 456]. Primarily concerned with the uprooted Jews, the preliminary report, reproduced below, focused attention in the United States on the plight of the Jewish escapers of the Nazi policy of extermination and on their overwhelming desire for rehabilitation in Palestine. The Harrison findings and recommendations, which received President Truman's prompt endorsement, contributed substantially to molding early postwar American public opinion in favor of Zionism. H. S. Truman, *Memoirs,* vol. 2, chap. 10; for further references, see Doc. 81.

I. GERMANY AND AUSTRIA

Conditions

(1) Generally speaking, three months after V–E Day and even longer after the liberation of individual groups, many Jewish displaced persons and other possibly non-repatriables are living under guard behind barbed-wire fences, in camps of several descriptions, (built by the Germans for slave-laborers and Jews) including some of the most notorious of the concentration camps, amidst crowded, frequently unsanitary and generally grim conditions, in complete idleness, with no opportunity, except surreptitiously, to communicate with the outside world, waiting, hoping for some word of encouragement and action in their behalf.

(2) While there has been marked improvement in the health of survivors of the Nazi starvation and persecution program, there are many pathetic malnutrition cases both among the hospitalized and in the general populations of the camps. The death rate has been high since liberation, as was to be expected. One Army Chaplain, a Rabbi, personally attended, since liberation, 23,000 burials (90% Jews) at Bergen Belsen alone, one of the largest and most vicious of the concentration camps, where, incidentally, despite persistent reports to the contrary, fourteen thousand displaced persons are still living, including over seven thousand Jews. At many of the camps and centers, including those where serious starvation cases are, there is a marked and serious lack of needed medical supplies.

(3) Although some Camp Commandants have managed, in spite of the many obvious difficulties, to find clothing of one kind or

another for their charges, many of the Jewish displaced persons, late in July, had no clothing other than their concentration camp garb—a rather hideous striped pajama effect—while others, to their chagrin, were obliged to wear German S.S. uniforms. It is questionable which clothing they hate the more.

(4) With a few notable exceptions, nothing in the way of a program of activity or organized effort toward rehabilitation has been inaugurated and the internees, for they are literally such, have little to do except to dwell upon their plight, the uncertainty of their future and, what is more unfortunate, to draw comparisons between their treatment "under the Germans" and "in liberation." Beyond knowing that they are no longer in danger of the gas chambers, torture, and other forms of violent death, they see—and there is—little change. The morale of those who are either stateless or who do not wish to return to their countries of nationality is very low. They have witnessed great activity and efficiency in returning people to their homes but they hear or see nothing in the way of plans for them and consequently they wonder and frequently ask what "liberation" means. This situation is considerably accentuated where, as in so many cases, they are able to look from their crowded and bare quarters and see the German civilian population, particularly in the rural areas, to all appearances living normal lives in their own homes.

(5) The most absorbing worry of these Nazi and war victims concerns relatives—wives, husbands, parents, children. Most of them have been separated for three, four or five years and they cannot understand why the liberators should not have undertaken immediately the organized effort to re-unite family groups. Most of the very little which has been done in this direction has been informal action by the displaced persons themselves with the aid of devoted Army Chaplains, frequently Rabbis, and the American Joint Distribution Committee. Broadcasts of names and locations by the Psychological Warfare Division at Luxembourg have been helpful, although the lack of receiving sets has handicapped the effectiveness of the program. Even where, as has been happening, information has been received as to relatives living in other camps in Germany, it depends on the personal attitude and disposition of the Camp Commandant whether permission can be obtained or assistance received to follow up on the information. Some Camp Commandants are quite rigid in this particular, while others lend every effort to join family groups.

(6) It is difficult to evaluate the food situation fairly because one must be mindful of the fact that quite generally food is scarce and is likely to be more so during the winter ahead. On the other hand, in presenting the factual situation, one must raise the question as to how much longer many of these people, particularly those who have over such a long period felt persecution and near starvation, can survive on a diet composed principally of bread and coffee, irrespective of the caloric content. In many camps, the 2,000 calories included 1,250 calories of a black, wet and extremely unappetizing bread. I received the distinct impression and considerable substantiating information that large numbers of the German population—again principally in the rural areas—have a more varied and palatable diet than is the case with the displaced persons. The Camp Commandants put in their requisitions with the German burgomeister and many seemed to accept whatever he turned over as being the best that was available.

(7) Many of the buildings in which displaced persons are housed are clearly unfit for winter use and everywhere there is great concern about the prospect of a complete lack of fuel. There is every likelihood that close to a million dispaced persons will be in Germany and Austria when winter sets in. The outlook in many areas so far as shelter, food and fuel are concerned is anything but bright.

II. NEEDS OF THE JEWS

While it is impossible to state accurately the number of Jews now in that part of Germany not under Russian occupation, all indications point to the fact that the number is small, with one hundred thousand probably the top figure; some informed persons contend the number is considerably smaller. The principal nationality groups are Poles, Hungarians, Rumanians, Germans and Austrians.

The first and plainest need of these people is a recognition of their actual status and by this I mean their status as Jews. Most of them have spent years in the worst of the concentration camps. In many cases, although the full extent is not yet known, they are the sole survivors of their families and many have been through the agony of witnessing the destruction of their loved ones. Understandably, therefore, their present condition, physical and mental, is far worse than that of other groups.

While SHAEF (now combined Displaced Persons Executive) policy directives have recognized formerly persecuted persons, including enemy and ex-enemy nationals, as one of the special categories of displaced persons, the general practice thus far has been to follow only nationality lines. While admittedly it is not normally desirable to set aside particular racial or religious groups from their nationality categories, the plain truth is that this was done for so long by the Nazis that a group has been created which has special needs. Jews as Jews (not as members of their nationality groups) have been more severely victimized than the non-Jewish members of the same or other nationalities.

When they are now considered only as members of nationality groups, the result is that special attention cannot be given to their admittedly greater needs because, it is contended, doing so would constitute preferential treatment and lead to trouble with the non-Jewish portion of the particular nationality group.

Thus there is a distinctly unrealistic approach to the problem. Refusal to recognize the Jews as such has the effect, in this situation, of closing one's eyes to their former and more barbaric persecution, which has already made them a separate group with greater needs.

Their second great need can be presented only by discussing what I found to be their

Wishes as to Future Destinations

(1) For reasons that are obvious and need not be labored, most Jews want to leave Germany and Austria as soon as possible. That is their first and great expressed wish and while this report necessarily deals with other needs present in the situation, many of the people themselves fear other suggestions or plans for their benefit because of the possibility that attention might thereby be diverted from the all-important matter of evacuation from Germany. Their desire to leave Germany is an urgent one. The life which they have led for the past ten years, a life of fear and wandering and physical torture, has made them impatient of delay. They want to be evacuated to Palestine now, just as other national groups are being repatriated to their homes. They do not look kindly on the idea of waiting around in idleness and in discomfort in a German camp for many months until a leisurely solution is found for them.

(2) Some wish to return to their countries of nationality but as to this there is considerable nationality variation. Very few Polish or Baltic Jews wish to return to their countries; higher percentages of the Hungarian and Rumanian groups want to return although some hasten to add that it may be only temporarily in order to look for relatives. Some of the German Jews, especially those who have intermarried, prefer to stay in Germany.

(3) With respect to possible places of resettlement for those who may be stateless or who do not wish to return to their homes, Palestine is definitely and preeminently the first choice. Many now have relatives there, while others, having experienced intolerance and persecution in their homelands for years, feel that only in Palestine will they be welcomed and find peace and quiet and be given an opportunity to live and work. In the case of the Polish and the Baltic Jews, the desire to go to Palestine is based in a great majority of the cases on a love for the country and devotion to the Zionist ideal. It is also true,

however, that there are many who wish to go to Palestine because they realize that their opportunity to be admitted into the United States or into other countries in the Western hemisphere is limited, if not impossible. Whatever the motive which causes them to turn to Palestine, it is undoubtedly true that the great majority of the Jews now in Germany do not wish to return to those countries from which they came.

(4) Palestine, while clearly the choice of most, is not the only named place of possible emigration. Some, but the number is not large, wish to emigrate to the United States where they have relatives, others to England, the British Dominions, or to South America.

Thus the second great need is the prompt development of a plan to get out of Germany and Austria as many as possible of those who wish it.

Otherwise the needs and wishes of the Jewish groups among the displaced persons can be simply stated: among their physical needs are clothing and shoes (most sorely needed), more varied and palatable diet, medicines, beds and mattresses, reading materials. The clothing for the camps too is requisitioned from the German population, and whether there is not sufficient quantity to be had or the German population has not been willing or has not been compelled to give up sufficient quantity, the internees feel particularly bitter about the state of their clothing when they see how well the German population is still dressed. The German population today is still the best dressed population in all of Europe.

III. MANNER IN WHICH NEEDS ARE BEING MET

Aside from having brought relief from the fear of extermination, hospitalization for the serious starvation cases and some general improvement in conditions under which the remaining displaced persons are compelled to live, relatively little beyond the planning stage has been done, during the period of mass repatriation, to meet the special needs of the formerly persecuted groups.

UNRRA, being neither sufficiently organized or equipped nor authorized to operate displaced persons camps or centers on any large scale, has not been in position to make any substantial contribution to the situation. Regrettably there has been a disinclination on the part of many Camp Commandants to utilize UNRRA personnel even to the extent available, though it must be admitted that in many situations this resulted from unfortunate experiences Army officers had with UNRRA personnel who were unqualified and inadequate for the responsibility involved. Then, too, in the American and British zones, it too frequently occurred that UNRRA personnel did not include English-speaking members and this hampered proper working relationships.

Under these circumstances, UNRRA, to which has been assigned the responsibility for co-ordinating activities of private social welfare agencies, has been in awkward position when it came to considering and acting upon proposals of one kind or another submitted by well qualified agencies which would aid and supplement military and UNRRA responsibilities. The result has been that, up to this point, very few private social agencies are working with displaced persons, including the Jews, although the situation cries out for their services in many different ways.

It must be said, too, that because of their preoccupation with mass repatriation and because of housing, personnel and transport difficulties, the military authorities have shown considerable resistance to the entrance of voluntary agency representatives, no matter how qualified they might be to help meet existing needs of displaced persons.

IV. CONCLUSIONS AND RECOMMENDATIONS

1. Now that the worst of the pressure of mass repatriation is over, it is not unreasonable to suggest that in the next and perhaps more difficult period those who have suffered most and longest be given first and not last attention.

Specifically, in the days immediately ahead, the Jews in Germany and Austria should have the first claim upon the conscience of the people of the United States and Great Britain and the military and other personnel who represent them in work being done in Germany and Austria.

2. Evacuation from Germany should be the emphasized theme, policy and practice.

(a) Recognizing that repatriation is most desirable from the standpoint of all concerned, the Jews who wish to return to their own countries should be aided to do so without further delay. Whatever special action is needed to accomplish this with respect to countries of reception or consent of military or other authorities should be undertaken with energy and determination. Unless this and other action, about to be suggested, is taken, substantial unofficial and unauthorized movements of people must be expected, and these will require considerable force to prevent, for the patience of many of the persons involved is, and in my opinion with justification, nearing the breaking point. It cannot be overemphasized that many of these people are now desperate, that they have become accustomed under German rule to employ every possible means to reach their end, and that the fear of death does not restrain them.

(b) With respect to those who do not, for good reason, wish to return to their homes, prompt planning should likewise be undertaken. In this connection, the issue of Palestine must be faced. Now that such large numbers are no longer involved and if there is any genuine sympathy for what these survivors have endured, some reasonable extension or modification of the British White Paper of 1939 ought to be possible without too serious repercussions. For some of the European Jews, there is no acceptable or even decent solution for their future other than Palestine. This is said on a purely humanitarian basis with no reference to ideological or political considerations so far as Palestine is concerned.

It is my understanding, based upon reliable information, that certificates for immigration to Palestine will be practically exhausted by the end of the current month (August 1945). What is the future to be? To anyone who has visited the concentration camps and who has talked with the despairing survivors, it is nothing short of calamitous to contemplate that the gates of Palestine should be soon closed.

The Jewish Agency of Palestine has submitted to the British Government a petition that one hundred thousand additional immigration certificates be made available. A memorandum accompanying the petition makes a persuasive showing with respect to the immediate absorptive capacity of Palestine and the current, actual man-power shortages there.

While there may be room for difference of opinion as to the precise number of such certificates which might under the circumstances be considered reasonable, there is no question but that the request thus made would, if granted, contribute much to the sound solution for the future of Jews still in Germany and Austria and even other displaced Jews, who do not wish either to remain there or to return to their countries of nationality.

No other single matter is, therefore, so important from the viewpoint of Jews in Germany and Austria and those elsewhere who have known the horrors of the concentration camps as is the disposition of the Palestine question.

Dr. Hugh Dalton, a prominent member of the new British Government, is reported as having said at the Labour Party Conference in May 1945:

"This Party has laid it down and repeated it so recently as last April . . . that this time, having regard to the unspeakable horrors that have been perpetrated upon the Jews of Germany and other occupied countries in Europe, it is morally wrong and politically indefensible to impose obstacles to the entry into Palestine now of any Jews who desire to go there. . . .

"We also have stated clearly that this is not a matter which should be regarded as one for which the British Government alone should take responsibility; but as it comes, as do many others, in the international field, it is indispensable that there should be close agreement and cooperation among the British, American and Soviet Governments, particularly if we are going to get a sure settlement in Palestine and the surrounding countries. . . ."

If this can be said to represent the viewpoint of the new Government in Great Britain, it certainly would not be inappropriate for the United States Government to express its interest in and support of some equitable solution of the question which would make it possible for some reasonable number of Europe's persecuted Jews, now homeless under any fair view, to resettle in Palestine. That is their wish and it is rendered desirable by the generally-accepted policy of permitting family groups to unite or reunite.

(c) The United States should, under existing immigration laws, permit reasonable numbers of such persons to come here, again particularly those who have family ties in this country. As indicated earlier, the number who desire emigration to the United States is not large.

If Great Britain and the United States were to take the actions recited, it might the more readily be that other countries would likewise be willing to keep their doors reasonably open for such humanitarian considerations and to demonstrate in a practical manner their disapproval of Nazi policy which unfortunately has poisoned so much of Europe.

3. To the extent that such emigration from Germany and Austria is delayed, some immediate temporary solution must be found. In any event there will be a substantial number of the persecuted persons who are not physically fit or otherwise presently prepared for emigration.

Here I feel strongly that greater and more extensive efforts should be made to get them out of camps for they are sick of living in camps. In the first place, there is real need for such specialized places as (a) tuberculosis sanitaria and (b) rest homes for those who are mentally ill or who need a period of readjustment before living again in the world at large—anywhere. Some will require at least short periods of training or retraining before they can be really useful citizens.

But speaking more broadly, there is an opportunity here to give some real meaning to the policy agreed upon at Potsdam. If it be true, as seems to be widely conceded, that the German people at large do not have any sense of guilt with respect to the war and its causes and results, and if the policy is to be "To convince the German people that they have suffered a total military defeat and that they cannot escape responsibility for what they have brought upon themselves," then it is difficult to understand why so many displaced persons, particularly those who have so long been persecuted and whose repatriation or resettlement is likely to be delayed, should be compelled to live in crude, over-crowded camps while the German people, in rural areas, continue undisturbed in their homes.

As matters now stand, we appear to be treating the Jews as the Nazis treated them except that we do not exterminate them. They are in concentration camps in large numbers under our military guard instead of S.S. troops. One is led to wonder whether the German people, seeing this, are not supposing that we are following or at least condoning Nazi policy.

It seems much more equitable and as it should be to witness the very few places where fearless and uncompromising military officers have either requisitioned an entire village for the benefit of displaced persons, compelling the German population to find housing where they can, or have required the local population to billet a reasonable number of them. Thus the displaced persons, including the persecuted, live more like normal people and less like prisoners or criminals or herded sheep. They are in Germany, most of them and certainly the Jews, through no fault or wish of their own. This fact is in this fashion being brought home to the German people but it is being done on too small a scale.

At many places, however, the military government officers manifest the utmost reluctance or indisposition, if not timidity, about inconveniencing the German population. They even say that their job is to get communities working properly and soundly again, that they must "live with the Germans while the dps (displaced persons) are a more temporary problem." Thus (and I am ready to cite the example) if a group of Jews are ordered to vacate their temporary quarters, needed for military purposes, and there are two possible sites, one a block of flats (modest apartments) with conveniences and the other a series of shabby buildings with outside toilet and washing facilities, the burgomeister readily succeeds in persuading the Town Major to allot the latter to the displaced persons and to save the former for returning German civilians.

This tendency reflects itself in other ways, namely, in the employment of German civilians in the offices of military government officers when equally qualified personnel could easily be found among the displaced persons whose repatriation is not imminent. Actually there have been situations where displaced persons, especially Jews, have found it difficult to obtain audiences with military government authorities because ironically they have been obliged to go through German employees who have not facilitated matters.

Quite generally, insufficient use is made of the services of displaced persons. Many of them are able and eager to work but apparently they are not considered in this regard. While appreciating that language difficulties are sometimes involved, I am convinced that, both within and outside camps, greater use could be made of the personal services of those displaced persons who in all likelihood will be on hand for some time. Happily in some camps every effort is made to utilize the services of the displaced persons and these are apt to be the best camps in all respects.

4. To the extent that (a) evacuation from Germany and Austria is not immediately possible and (b) the formerly persecuted groups cannot be housed in villages or billeted with the German population, I recommend urgently that separate camps be set up for Jews or at least for those who wish, in the absence of a better solution, to be in such camps. There are several reasons for this: (1) a great majority want it; (2) it is the only way in which administratively their special needs and problems can be met without charges of preferential treatment or (oddly enough) charges of "discrimination" with respect to Jewish agencies now prepared and ready to give them assistance.

In this connection, I wish to emphasize that it is not a case of singling out a particular group for special privileges. It is a matter of raising to a more normal level the position of a group which has been depressed to the lowest depths conceivable by years of organized and inhuman oppression. The measures necessary for their restitution do not come within any reasonable interpretation of privileged treatment and are required by considerations of justice and humanity.

There has been some tendency at spots in the direction of separate camps for those who might be found to be stateless or nonrepatriable or whose repatriation is likely to be deferred some time. Actually, too, this was announced some time ago as SHAEF policy but in practice it has not been taken to mean much for there is (understandably if not carried too far) a refusal to contemplate possible statelessness and an insistence, in the interests of the large repatriation program, to consider all as repatriable. This results in a resistance to anything in the way of special planning for the "hard core," although all admit it is there and will inevitably appear. While speaking of camps, this should be pointed out: While it may be that conditions in Germany and Austria are still such that certain control measures are required, there seems little justification for the continuance of barbed-wire fences, armed guards, and prohibition against leaving the camp except by passes, which at some places are illiberally granted. Prevention of looting is given as the reason for these stern measures but it is interesting that in portions of the Seventh Army area where greater liberty of movement in and out of camps is given there is actually much less plundering than in other areas where people, wishing to leave camp temporarily, must do so by stealth.

5. As quickly as possible, the actual operation of such camps should be turned over to a civilian agency—UNRRA. That organ-

ization is aware of weaknesses in its present structure and is pressing to remedy them. In that connection, it is believed that greater assistance could be given by the military authorities, upon whom any civilian agency in Germany and Austria today is necessarily dependent so far as housing, transport and other items are concerned. While it is true the military have been urging UNRRA to get ready to assume responsibility, it is also the fact that insufficient cooperation of an active nature has been given to accomplish the desired end.

6. Since, in any event, the military authorities must necessarily continue to participate in the program for all displaced persons, especially with respect to housing, transport, security, and certain supplies, it is recommended that there be a review of the military personnel selected for Camp Commandant positions. Some serving at present, while perhaps adequate for the mass repatriation job, are manifestly unsuited for the longer-term job of working in a camp composed of people whose repatriation or resettlement is likely to be delayed. Officers who have had some background or experience in social welfare work are to be preferred and it is believed there are some who are available. It is most important that the officers selected be sympathetic with the program and that they be temperamentally able to work and to cooperate with UNRRA and other relief and welfare agencies.

7. Pending the assumption of responsibility for operations by UNRRA, it would be desirable if a more extensive plan of field visitation by appropriate Army Group Headquarters be instituted. It is believed that many of the conditions now existing in the camps would not be tolerated if more intimately known by supervisory officers through inspection tours.

8. It is urgently recommended that plans for tracing services, now under consideration, be accelerated to the fullest extent possible and that, in this same direction, communication services, if on open postal cards only, be made available to displaced persons within Germany and Austria as soon as possible. The difficulties are appreciated but it is believed that if the anxiety of the people, so long abused and harassed, were fully understood, ways and means could be found within the near future to make such communication and tracing of relatives possible. I believe also that some of the private agencies could be helpful in this direction if given an opportunity to function.

V. OTHER COMMENTS

While I was instructed to report conditions as I found them, the following should be added to make the picture complete:

(1) A gigantic task confronted the occupying armies in Germany and Austria in getting back to their homes as many as possible of the more than six million displaced persons found in those countries. Less than three months after V–E Day, more than four million of such persons have been repatriated—a phenomenal performance. One's first impression, in surveying the situation, is that of complete admiration for what has been accomplished by the military authorities in so materially reducing the time as predicted to be required for this stupendous task. Praise of the highest order is due all military units with respect to this phase of the post-fighting job. In directing attention to existing conditions which unquestionably require remedying, there is no intention or wish to detract one particle from the preceding statements.

(2) While I did not actually see conditions as they existed immediately after liberation I had them described in detail sufficient to make entirely clear that there has been, during the intervening period, some improvement in the conditions under which most of the remaining displaced persons are living. Reports which have come out of Germany informally from refugees themselves and from persons interested in refugee groups indicate something of a tendency not to take into account the full scope of the overwhelming task and responsibilities facing the military authorities. While it is understandable that those who have been persecuted and otherwise mistreated over such a long period should be impatient at what appears to them to be

undue delay in meeting their special needs, fairness dictates that, in evaluating the progress made, the entire problem and all of its ramifications be kept in mind. My effort has been, therefore, to weigh quite carefully the many complaints made to me in the course of my survey, both by displaced persons themselves and in their behalf, in the light of the many responsibilities which confronted the military authorities.

(3) While for the sake of brevity this report necessarily consisted largely of general statements, it should be recognized that exceptions exist with respect to practically all of such generalizations. One high ranking military authority predicted, in advance of my trip through Germany and Austria, that I would find, with respect to camps containing displaced persons, "some that are quite good, some that are very bad, with the average something under satisfactory." My subsequent trip confirmed that prediction in all respects.

In order to file this report promptly so that possibly some remedial steps might be considered at as early a date as possible, I have not taken time to analyze all of the notes made in the course of the trip or to comment on the situation in France, Belgium, Holland or Switzerland, also visited. Accordingly, I respectfully request that this report be considered as partial in nature. The problems present in Germany and Austria are much more serious and difficult than in any of the other countries named and this fact, too, seemed to make desirable the filing of a partial report immediately upon completion of the mission.

In conclusion, I wish to repeat that the main solution, in many ways the only real solution, of the problem lies in the quick evacuation of all non-repatriable Jews in Germany and Austria, who wish it, to Palestine. In order to be effective, this plan must not be long delayed. The urgency of the situation should be recognized. It is inhuman to ask people to continue to live for any length of time under their present conditions. The evacuation of the Jews of Germany and Austria to Palestine will solve the problem of the individuals involved and will also remove a problem from the military authorities who have had to deal with it. The army's ability to move millions of people quickly and efficiently has been amply demonstrated. The evacuation of a relatively small number of Jews from Germany and Austria will present no great problem to the military. With the end of the Japanese war, the shipping situation should also become sufficiently improved to make such a move feasible. The civilized world owes it to this handful of survivors to provide them with a home where they can again settle down and begin to live as human beings.

78. ANGLO-FRENCH AGREEMENT AND SYRO-LEBANESE COMPLAINT TO THE UN SECURITY COUNCIL 13 December 1945–4 February 1946

[Anglo-French agreement from *The Times* (London), 22 December 1945; Syro-Lebanese complaint from UN, Security Council, *Official Records,* 1st year, 1st ser., suppl. No. 1, pp. 82–83]

When British and Free French troops ousted the Vichy regime from Syria and Lebanon in June–July 1941 (Doc. 69), the United Kingdom retained ultimate security responsibility in the two mandated lands for the war's duration, while the Free French assumed ultimate political responsibility. The presence of British forces, essential in the prosecution of the war, nevertheless added one more irritant to the situation and thus compounded the political confusion. As the Free French blundered from crisis to crisis in attempts to wring preferential alliances from Lebanon and Syria, the British had to intervene in the fall of 1943 and spring of 1945 to prevent matters from getting out of hand The Anglo-French agreement of 13 December 1945, reproduced below, temporarily restored harmonious relations between the two European powers but provoked violent opposition in the two Arab countries.

As members of the UN, Syria and Lebanon presented their complaint—the second of the following documents—to the Security Council, which however took no decision. For the USSR vetoed an American draft resolution recommending that the four parties resume direct negotiations for the withdrawal of "foreign troops . . . as soon as practicable." The Soviet action was traceable to Moscow's desire, in view of Iran's complaint against the USSR (Doc. 80), to embarrass the Western powers. England and France nevertheless immediately opened talks with Syria and Lebanon on the basis of the United States proposal, and full accord was reached for the evacuation of British and French troops from Syria by the end of April and from Lebanon by the end of December 1946 (pertinent documentation in UN, General Assembly, *Official Records,* 1st sess., 2nd part, suppl. No. 1, pp. 107–13). G. Kirk, *The Middle East 1945–1950,* pp. 106–15; E. A. Speiser, *The United States and the Near East,* pp. 99–107; R. Montagne, "France, England and the Arab States," *International Affairs,* 25 (July 1949), 286–94; C. A. Julien, "French Difficulties in the Middle East," *Foreign Affairs,* 24 (January 1946), 327–36.

1. ANGLO-FRENCH AGREEMENT ON MIDDLE EAST POLICY, 13 DECEMBER 1945

British and French military experts will meet at Beirut on December 21, 1945, to draw up the details of a programme for evacuation by stages, with a corresponding regrouping of forces. One of the objects of this discussion will be to fix a very early date on which the withdrawal will begin.

It is understood that the evacuation of Syria shall be carried out *pari passu,* in such a way as to be completed at the same time by the British and French forces. The programme of evacuation will be drawn up in such a way that it will ensure the maintenance in the Levant of sufficient forces to guarantee security, until such time as the United Nations Organization has decided on the organization of collective security in this zone. Until these arrangements have been carried out the French Government will retain forces regrouped in the Lebanon.

His Majesty's Government in the United Kingdom and the French Government will inform the Lebanese and Syrian Governments of the details of the evacuation, and will invite those Governments to appoint as soon as possible representatives empowered to discuss the dispositions to be jointly agreed upon as a result of these decisions. The discussions will also deal with the measures to be taken in order to enable the Lebanese and Syrian Governments to discharge their duty of maintaining order.

The Provisional Government of the French Republic and his Majesty's Government in the United Kingdom, having examined the situation in the Middle East, declare that they are animated by the same intention to do what is required of them to ensure that the independence which has been promised to the countries in question shall be assured and respected.

The two Governments are agreed that it is in their mutual interest to promote, in collaboration with other Governments, the economic well-being of the peoples of this region in conditions of peace and security. They will exchange information as may be required regarding the best means by which this object may be attained. It is their desire that by such exchanges of information they will be able to avoid divergences of policy which might impair their mutual interests. Each Government affirms its intention of doing nothing to supplant the interests or responsibilities of the other in the Middle East, having full regard to the political status of the countries in question.

It is in this spirit that they will examine any proposals submitted to the United Nations Organization on the subject of collective security.

2. SYRO-LEBANESE COMPLAINT TO THE UN SECURITY COUNCIL, 4 FEBRUARY 1946

French and British troops are still being maintained in Syria and Lebanon, although hostilities were ended many months ago.

The presence of these troops, which constitutes a grave infringement of the sovereignty of two States Members of the United Nations, may give rise to serious disputes. The past has shown that some of these troops have been a constant menace to peace and security in this region.

The Governments of Syria and Lebanon expected that these foreign troops would be withdrawn immediately upon the cessation of hostilities with Germany and Japan, and as a result of the representations these Governments have made unceasingly to that end. But on 13 December 1945, they were notified of a Franco-British agreement. . . . [here follow the last two sentences of the second paragraph of the agreement.]

This agreement, accordingly, makes the withdrawal of foreign troops subject to conditions which are inconsistent with the spirit and letter of the United Nations Charter.

Therefore, since the two contracting Powers have themselves referred, in the aforesaid agreement, to the United Nations, the Syrian and Lebanese delegations, acting on the instructions of their Governments, have the honour, in accordance with Article 34 of the Charter, to bring this dispute to the attention of the Security Council and to request it to adopt a decision recommending the total and simultaneous evacuation of the foreign troops from the territories of Syria and Lebanon.

They are ready to assist the Security Council by supplying it with all relevant information for the purpose.

79. EGYPTIAN AND BRITISH VIEWS ON REVISION OF THE 1936 TREATY

20 December 1945–26 January 1946

[*The Times* (London), 31 January 1946]

The original ambiguities of the British occupation of Egypt in 1882 (I, Doc. 90), never subsequently clarified, lived on to plague the relationship between the two countries into the mid-twentieth century. The United Kingdom remained sufficiently powerful, at the close of World War I, to withstand the determined opposition of an increasingly emphatic nationalism and to retain a position of dominance in Egypt. British superiority was ultimately enshrined in the 1936 treaty (Doc. 61). The preferential alliance proved indispensable to the allied military effort in the Middle East in World War II. But the unprecedented drain of its manpower and resources so thoroughly weakened the relative—and indeed effective—power of the United Kingdom, that it was clearly only a matter of time before the British-Egyptian relationship would have to be altered to conform with the emergent realities. In any event, the diplomatic slugging match dragged on for nearly nine years before the parties could agree on the terms of a settlement. Following is the opening exchange of notes that defined the respective positions of the two governments. H. A. R. Gibb, "Anglo-Egyptian Relations: a Revaluation," *International Affairs*, 27 (October 1951), 440–50; J. C. Hurewitz, *Middle East Dilemmas*, chap. 3; Royal Institute of International Affairs, *Great Britain and Egypt 1914–1951*, chaps. 5–8; M. Colombe, *L'Évolution de l'Égypte 1924–1950*, chaps. 3–4, 8.

1. EGYPTIAN PRIME MINISTER TO BRITISH FOREIGN SECRETARY, 20 DECEMBER 1945

The Egyptian Government, certain that they are interpreting a unanimous national sentiment, consider that the manifest interests of Anglo-Egyptian friendship and alliance demand that the two parties should revise, in the light of recent events and of their experience, the arrangements which govern their mutual relations at the present time. It is certain that the treaty of 1936 was concluded in the midst of an international crisis, at a moment when the spectre of war was already appearing, and it is to these circumstances that it clearly owes its present form.

Further, Egypt only accepted it under the pressure of necessity and as a testimony to the loyalty and sincere desire for collaboration which inspire her towards her ally. The treaty thus appeared as a link in the chain of measures taken, and of agreements concluded, to prevent the war which was menacing the world, or to repel aggression if war could not be avoided. If Egypt accepted the treaty with all that it implied in the way of restrictions on her independence, it was because she knew that they were of a transitory character and were destined to disappear at the same time as the circumstances and events by reason of which they had been agreed to.

In fact, the war has exhausted the principal objectives of the treaty and opened the way for the adoption of a new system which would take the place of arrangements established as much under the influence of a mistrust which had not yet entirely disappeared in 1936 as under the inspiration of military conditions which recent events have essentially modified. The international events which have upset the world, the allied victory which has brought the last war to an end, the agreements destined to maintain the peace and security of the world, render several of the provisions of the treaty superfluous and without justification. Moreover, it is not the letter of the text of agreements which decides their efficacity, but rather the good will of the peoples in consenting to them and the spirit governing their application.

Nothing proves better the loyalty with which Egypt honours her obligations than her assistance to her ally during the whole of the war, in the course of which she gave the most concrete evidence of her fidelity to her alliances and of her sincerity in her friendships. The British Government, at the time of trial, obtained from their agreement with Egypt more than the text stipulated, and much more than the most optimistic British negotiators had certainly been able to contemplate. Therefore, now that the circumstances which determined the particular character of the treaty of 1936 have changed, it has become necessary to revise it in order to bring it into harmony with the new international situation; its clauses which detract from the independence and the dignity of Egypt no longer correspond to present conditions.

The presence of foreign forces on our soil in peace-time even if stationed in distant areas, is still wounding to national dignity, and can only be interpreted by Egyptian public opinion as the tangible sign of a mistrust which the British Government themselves, we believe, must regard as unjustified. It would be better for the two countries that their relations should be founded on mutual understanding and confidence. Egypt, conscious of the needs imposed on her by the defence of her territory and of the responsibilities which her participation in the organization of the United Nations entails for her, will moreover shrink from no sacrifice in order, in the immediate future, to place her military potential in a state enabling her to repel aggression pending the arrival of the reinforcements of her allies and of the United Nations.

For this reason, and in view of the unanimous urge of the Egyptian people and their ardent desire to see their relations with Great Britain established on the basis of an alliance and a friendship which will no longer be inspired by past prejudices or out-of-date doctrines, the Egyptian Government express their confidence that these views will be shared by their ally, and that the British Government will take steps to fix an early date for an Egyptian delegation to proceed to London to negotiate with them the revision of the treaty of 1936. It goes without saying that the negotiations will include the question of the Sudan and will be inspired by the interests and aspirations of the Sudanese.

2. BRITISH FOREIGN SECRETARY TO EGYPTIAN PRIME MINISTER, 26 JANUARY 1946

I have the honour to acknowledge receipt of the Note of December 20, 1945, by which the Egyptian Government request his Majesty's Government in the United Kingdom to fix an early date for negotiations for the revision of the Anglo-Egyptian treaty of alliance of August 26, 1936.

His Majesty's Government have been well aware of the desire which has been manifested in Egypt for discussions with them on this subject, and if they have not hitherto responded formally to these expressions of opinion by their allies, the reason has lain first in the continuous pressure of events arising out of the termination of hostilities, and secondly in the necessity of examining the provisions of the Anglo-Egyptian treaty in the light of the Charter of the United Nations and also of the lessons taught by these hostilities.

And in this connexion his Majesty's Government, without wishing at the present stage to examine in detail the contentions in the Egyptian Government's Note, take leave to observe that one of these lessons was the essential soundness of the fundamental principles on which the Anglo-Egyptian treaty of 1936 was based.

It is the policy of his Majesty's Government to consolidate in a spirit of frankness and cordiality the close cooperation achieved by Egypt and the British Commonwealth and Empire during the war, to which your Excellency's Note bears testimony, and to place it on a footing of full and free partnership, as between equals, in the defence of their mutual interests and with full respect for the independence and sovereignty of Egypt. Therefore, notwithstanding the provisions of Article 16 of the treaty of 1936, his Majesty's Government in the United Kingdom declare themselves willing to undertake, with the Government of Egypt, a review of the treaty arrangements between them in the light of their mutual experience and with due regard to the provisions of the Charter of the United Nations for ensuring international peace and security. Instructions will shortly be sent to his Majesty's Ambassador in Cairo to hold preliminary conversations with the Egyptian Government to that end. His Majesty's Government in the United Kingdom take note that the Egyptian Government desire that the forthcoming discussions should include the question of the Sudan.

80. IRANIAN-SOVIET DISPUTE BEFORE THE UN SECURITY COUNCIL AND THE PROPOSED OIL AGREEMENT
2–4 April 1946

[Iranian and Soviet notes from United Nations, General Assembly, *Official Records,* 1st sess., 2nd part, suppl. No. 1, pp. 102–04; draft oil agreement from *Soviet News* (London), 13 September 1947]

Soviet encouragement in the fall of 1945 of separatist movements in northwestern Iran, which formed part of the Russian occupied zone, aroused deep suspicions in Washington and London over Moscow's motives. The suspicions were compounded when the USSR turned a deaf ear to an American suggestion of 24 November 1945 "that arrangements be made immediately for the complete withdrawal of all foreign troops from Iran by January 1, 1946," the date by which the United States had undertaken to evacuate its forces [texts of American and Soviet notes in *The Department of State Bulletin,* 13 (2 and 9 December 1945), 884, 899, 934–35]. The Iranian delegation to the United Nations submitted to the Security Council on 19 January 1946—only two days after that organ was first convened and before it had adopted even provisional rules of procedure—a complaint against "interference of the Soviet Union, through the medium of their officials and armed forces, in the internal affairs of Iran" (Security Council, *Official Records,* 1st year, 1st ser., suppl. No. 1, pp. 16–17). The main issues in dispute were perhaps best elucidated in a letter of 2 April from the Iranian delegate to the UN Secretary-General and one of 3 April from the Soviet delegate, both reproduced below. Since Soviet troops were still in Iran at the time, in violation of the 1942 tripartite treaty of alliance (Doc. 70), Prime Minister Ahmad Qavam on 4 April signed under duress the draft oil agreement—the third of the following documents in the form of a letter from Qavam to the Soviet Ambassador in Tehran. The USSR in the end realized none of its immediate objectives, for Iran reabsorbed the district of Azarbayjan unconditionally by December 1946, while the *Majlis* (legislature) rejected the proposed oil agreement on 22 October 1947 (Doc. 87). G. Lenczowski, *Russia and the West in Iran,* chap. 11; J. C. Hurewitz, *Middle East Dilemmas,* chap. 2; G. Kirk; *The Middle East 1945–1950,* pp. 56–89; J. C. Campbell, *The United States in World Affairs 1945–1947,* chap. 4; H. S. Truman, *Memoirs,* vol. 2, chap. 7; R. Rossow, Jr., "The Battle of Azerbaijan, 1946," *The Middle East Journal,* 10 (Winter 1956), 17–32; A. Roosevelt, Jr., "The Kurdish Republic of Mahabad," *ibid.,* 1 (July 1947), 247–69.

1. LETTER FROM IRANIAN DELEGATE TO UN SECRETARY-GENERAL, 2 APRIL 1946

As stated in my letter of acknowledgment to you of 30 March 1946, I did not fail to cable to my Government on the evening of 29 March the complete text of your communication of the same day, and I requested that an early answer be sent to the two questions suggested by Secretary of State Byrnes and endorsed by the Security Council.

I am now instructed to convey to you, for communication to the Security Council at its meeting of Wednesday, 3 April, the following reply to the two questions:

1. You first ask as to "the existing status of negotiations between the two Governments."

With respect to the interference in the internal affairs of Iran, the subject matter of the first dispute, negotiations have taken place pursuant to the resolution of the Security Council of 30 January 1946. As to these negotiations, I submitted a report to the Council at its meeting on 27 March 1946. The negotiations pursuant to the resolution of 30 January 1946, have achieved no positive results and Soviet agents, officials and armed forces are continuing to interfere in the internal affairs of Iran. They are still preventing the Government of Iran from exercising any authority in the province of Azerbaijan.

Regarding the withdrawal of Soviet troops from Iran, there has been and there can be no negotiation.

2. Your second question is "whether or not the reported withdrawal of troops is conditioned upon the conclusion of agreements between the two Governments on other subjects."

The best way to answer is to give you a simple and exact account of the conversations that have taken place in Teheran since the arrival there of the new Ambassador of the Soviet Union.

On 24 March, the day before the opening meeting of the Security Council in New York, the USSR Ambassador called on the Prime Minister of Iran and handed him three memoranda. One was an announcement that the evacuation of the Red Army from Iran would begin on 24 March and would last from five to six weeks. In this memorandum there was no mention of any condition being attached to the withdrawal of the troops. The second memorandum related to the formation of a joint Iranian-Soviet Corporation for the extraction of oil. The third memorandum dealt with Azerbaijan and suggested a form of autonomous government.

Within a few hours after delivering the three memoranda, the Ambassador of the Soviet Union again called on the Prime Minister and, on the basis of a telegram he had received from Moscow, orally confirmed the promise to evacuate Iran but on the condition that no unforeseen circumstances should occur. When the Iranian Premier objected to this proviso and asked for explanations, the USSR Ambassador did not give a convincing reply. Three days later the Iranian Prime Minister again referred to this proviso and said that the evacuation of the Soviet troops must be unconditional and that he could not agree to the Soviet proposals on the subjects of oil and Azerbaijan. To this the USSR Ambassador replied that if agreement could be reached on these other two subjects, there would be no further cause for anxiety and no unforeseen circumstances would take place. This statement has not been further clarified.

With respect to the other two memoranda, the Prime Minister has outlined his views to the USSR Ambassador. His position is:

(*a*) That as the status of the province of Azerbaijan, like that of all the other provinces in Iran, is regulated by the Iranian Constitution and the law on provincial councils, it is an internal matter with which the Iranian Government will deal;

(*b*) That the formation of a stock company with joint participation by Iran and the Soviet Union is a matter to be submitted for approval to the next Parliament after the Soviet troops have been withdrawn from Iran and elections can be held lawfully for the organization of the fifteenth Legislature.

This is the present state of the discussions on the subject of oil and the future status of Azerbaijan. According to the latest information from my Government dispatched to me on 1 April, no understanding had been arrived at and no agreement had been made.

The Prime Minister of Iran emphatically states that he has not accepted and cannot accept any condition whatsoever being attached to the complete withdrawal of the Red Army from the whole of Iran. These forces should have been unconditionally withdrawn from Iran on or before 2 March last. It is our position, as explained by me at the meeting of the Security Council on Friday last, that the evacuation of the whole of Iran by Soviet forces cannot properly be made dependent upon any conditions, foreseen or unforeseen.

In closing permit me to repeat that, in referring these disputes to the Council, the Iranian Government is animated by no feeling of hostility toward the Soviet Union. It is our hope that the Council will find a just solution which will promote friendly relations in the future.

2. LETTER FROM SOVIET DELEGATE TO UN SECRETARY-GENERAL, 3 APRIL 1946

In reply to your letter of 29 March, in which you, under instructions from the President of the Security Council, request information concerning the state of the negotiations between the Soviet Union and Iranian Governments and, in particular, whether the withdrawal of Soviet troops from Iran is conditional upon the conclusion of an agreement on other matters between the two Governments, I have the honour, on behalf of my Government, to inform you as follows:

These negotiations have already led to an understanding regarding the withdrawal of Soviet troops from Iran; this withdrawal was renewed on 24 March last and will be completed within one and a half months, as I informed the Security Council officially at the meeting of 26 March last.

Thus, the question regarding the evacuation of the Soviet troops which was brought before the Security Council on 18 March by the Iranian Government was settled by the understanding reached between the Soviet Union and Iranian Governments.

As regards the other questions, they are not connected with the question of the withdrawal of Soviet troops.

It is well known that the question of an oil concession or of a mixed joint stock company arose in 1944 independently of the question of the evacuation of the Soviet troops.

3. SOVIET-IRANIAN DRAFT OIL AGREEMENT, 4 APRIL 1946

In supplementing the oral agreement between us, I have the honour to tell you that the Government of His Majesty the Shah-in-Shah of Iran is agreed that the Governments of Iran and the Soviet Union should form a joint Soviet-Iranian company for the development and exploitation of oil resources in Northern Iran, and on the following basic conditions:

1. In the course of the first 25 years of the activity of the company 49 per cent. of the shares will belong to the Iranian side, and 51 per cent. to the Soviet side. In the course of the second 25 years, 50 per cent. of the shares will belong to the Iranian side and 50 per cent. of the shares to the Soviet side.

2. The profits made by the company will be divided in accordance with the ratio of the shares of each side.

3. The borders of the original territory of the company allocated for production and prospecting work will be those drawn on the map which you handed to me during our talk on March 24 of this year, excluding the part of the territory of Western Azerbaijan situated to the west of a line running from the point of intersection of the borders of the U.S.S.R., Turkey and Iran and further to the south on the eastern shore of Lake Rizaiyeh (late Urmia) right up to the town of Miyanduab, as was noted additionally on the above-mentioned map on April 4, 1946.

At the same time the Iranian Government pledges itself not to grant concessions to foreign companies or to Iranian companies in partnership with foreigners or utilising foreign capital, on the territory to the west of the above-mentioned line.

4. The capital of the Iranian side will consist of the oil-bearing lands mentioned in Article 3 which, after the carrying out of the technical work, will possess oil wells the production of which will be utilised by the company. The capital of the Soviet side will consist of all kinds of expenditure on equipment and wages of specialists and workers necessary for the production and refining of the oil.

5. The period of the activity of the company is 50 years.

6. When the period of the activity of the company expires, the Iranian Government will have the right to buy out the shares of the Soviet side or to continue the period of activity of the company.

The security of the districts in which the prospecting work is to take place, of the oil-wells and all the enterprises of the company, will be effected exclusively by the security bodies of Iran.

The treaty on the organisation of the above-mentioned Soviet-Iranian oil company, which will be concluded subsequently in accordance with the content of the present letter, will be presented for endorsement as soon as the newly-elected Mejlis of Iran starts its legislative activity, and in any case not later than seven months from March 24 of this year.

81. RECOMMENDATIONS OF THE ANGLO-AMERICAN COMMITTEE ON PALESTINE AND RELATED PROBLEMS
20 April 1946

[Anglo-American Committee of Inquiry, *Report to the United States Government and His Majesty's Government in the United Kingdom* (Washington, 1946), Dept. of State Publication No. 2536, pp. 1–12]

The Palestine problem by 1945 had long passed the stage of reasonable and peaceful settlement. In the British election campaign (May–July 1945), the Labor Party reaffirmed its postwar international policy statement of April 1944 (text in *The Manchester Guardian,* 24 April 1944), which, as regards Palestine, favored the scrapping of the 1939 White Paper (Doc. 65) and, in effect, the conversion of Palestine into a Jewish state. Soon after the party came to power on 27 July 1945, however, the Labor government reversed its position and tried to persuade the United States to become an equal partner in any settlement demanding the use of force. The United States for its part announced its readiness to furnish financial aid and its inalterable refusal to assume military obligations. The Anglo-American Committee of Inquiry, whose terms of reference were released on 13 November 1945 (*U. S. Executive Agreement Series,* No. 491), was intended to forge a common policy on Palestine by bridging the gap between the Attlee government's sensitiveness to Arab demands and the Truman Administration's sensitiveness to Zionist demands. The joint committee, after hearings in Washington and London (4 January–4 February 1946), conducted a whirlwind investigation of the situation in Palestine and the near-by Arab lands and in the Jewish displaced persons camps in Europe (5 February–24 March). But Foreign Secretary Ernest Bevin's insistence upon transforming the mandate into a UN trusteeship had to be squared with President Truman's insistence on the immediate admission of 100,000 displaced European Jews to Palestine. The committee was thus reduced to recommending the progressive development of the country into a unitary, binational (Arab-Jewish) state, a settlement which, in existing circumstances, had absolutely no prospect of realization. Following are the committee's recommendations, without the commentary, which formed part of a 91-page report. J. C. Hurewitz, *Struggle for Palestine,* chaps. 16–19; E. A. Speiser, *The United States and the Near East,* chap. 9; R. Crossman, *Palestine Mission;* B. C. Crum, *Behind the Silken Curtain;* M. F. Abcarius, *Palestine through the Fog of Propaganda,* chaps. 11–12; D. Horowitz, *State in the Making,* chaps. 1–16; H. S. Truman, *Memoirs,* vol. 2, chaps. 10–11.

Recommendation No. 1. We have to report that such information as we received about countries other than Palestine gave no hope of substantial assistance in finding homes for Jews wishing or impelled to leave Europe.

But Palestine alone cannot meet the emigration needs of the Jewish victims of Nazi and Fascist persecution; the whole world shares responsibility for them and indeed for the resettlement of all "displaced persons."

We therefore recommend that our Governments together, and in association with other countries, should endeavor immediately to find new homes for all such "displaced persons," irrespective of creed or nationality, whose ties with their former communities have been irreparably broken.

Though emigration will solve the problems of some victims of persecution, the overwhelming majority, including a considerable number of Jews, will continue to live in Europe. We recommend therefore that our Governments endeavor to secure that immediate effect is given to the provision of the United Nations Charter calling for "universal respect for, and observance of, human rights and fundamental freedoms for all without distinction as to race, sex, language, or religion" . . . .

Recommendation No. 2. We recommend (*a*) that 100,000 certificates be authorized immediately for the admission into Palestine of Jews who have been the victims of Nazi and Fascist persecution; (*b*) that these certificates be awarded as far as possible in 1946 and that actual immigration be pushed forward as rapidly as conditions will permit. . . .

Recommendation No. 3. In order to dispose, once and for all, of the exclusive claims of Jews and Arabs to Palestine, we regard it as essential that a clear statement of the following principles should be made:

I. That Jew shall not dominate Arab and Arab shall not dominate Jew in Palestine. II. That Palestine shall be neither a Jewish state nor an Arab state. III. That the form of government ultimately to be established, shall, under international guarantees, fully protect and preserve the interests in the Holy Land of Christendom and of the Moslem and Jewish faiths.

Thus Palestine must ultimately become a state which guards the rights and interests of Moslems, Jews and Christians alike; and accords to the inhabitants, as a whole, the fullest measure of self-government, consistent with the three paramount principles set forth above. . . .

Recommendation No. 4. We have reached the conclusion that the hostility between Jews and Arabs and, in particular, the determination of each to achieve domination, if necessary by violence, make it almost certain that, now and for some time to come, any attempt to establish either an independent Palestinian State or independent Palestinian States would result in civil strife such as might threaten the peace of the world.

We therefore recommend that, until this hostility disappears, the Government of Palestine be continued as at present under mandate pending the execution of a trusteeship agreement under the United Nations. . . .

Recommendation No. 5. Looking towards a form of ultimate self-government, consistent with the three principles laid down in Recommendation No. 3, we recommend that the mandatory or trustee should proclaim the principle that Arab economic, educational and political advancement in Palestine is of equal importance with that of the Jews; and should at once prepare measures designed to bridge the gap which now exists and raise the Arab standard of living to that of the Jews; and so bring the two peoples to a full appreciation of their common interest and common destiny in the land where both belong. . . .

Recommendation No. 6. We recommend that, pending the early reference to the United Nations and the execution of a trusteeship agreement, the mandatory should administer Palestine according to the mandate which declares with regard to immigration that "The administration of Palestine, while ensuring that the rights and position of other sections of the population are not prejudiced, shall facilitate Jewish immigration under suitable conditions". . . .

Recommendation No. 7. (*a*) We recommend that the Land Transfers Regulations of 1940 be rescinded and replaced by regulations based on a policy of freedom in the sale, lease or use of land, irrespective of race, community or creed, and providing adequate protection for the interests of small owners and tenant cultivators; (*b*) We further recommend that steps be taken to render nugatory and to prohibit provisions in conveyances, leases and agreements relating to land which stipulate that only members of one race, community or creed may be employed on or about or in connection therewith; (*c*) We recommend that the Government should exercise such close supervision over the Holy Places and localities such as the Sea of Galilee and its vicinity as will protect them from desecration and from uses which offend the conscience of religious people, and that such laws as are required for this purpose be enacted forthwith. . . .

Recommendation No. 8. Various plans for large-scale agricultural and industrial development in Palestine have been presented for our consideration; these projects, if successfully carried into effect, could not only greatly enlarge the capacity of the country to support an increasing population but also raise the living standards of Jew and Arab alike.

We are not in a position to assess the soundness of these specific plans; but we cannot state too strongly that, however technically feasible they may be, they will fail unless there is peace in Palestine. Moreover their full success requires the willing cooperation of adjacent Arab states, since they are not merely Palestinian projects. We recommend therefore that the examination, discussion and execution of these plans be conducted, from the start and throughout, in full consultation and cooperation not only with the Jewish Agency but also with the governments of the neighboring Arab States directly affected. . . .

Recommendation No. 9. We recommend that, in the interests of the conciliation of the two peoples and of general improvement of the Arab standard of living, the educational system of both Jews and Arabs be reformed, including the introduction of compulsory education within a reasonable time. . . .

Recommendation No. 10. We recommend that, if this Report is adopted, it should be made clear beyond all doubt to both Jews and Arabs that any attempt from either side, by threats of violence, by terrorism, or by the organization or use of illegal armies to prevent its execution, will be resolutely suppressed.

Furthermore, we express the view that the Jewish Agency should at once resume active cooperation with the Mandatory in the suppression of terrorism and of illegal immigration, and in the maintenance of that law and order throughout Palestine which is essential for the good of all, including the new immigrants.

82. AGREEMENT OF FRIENDSHIP AND COMMERCE: THE UNITED STATES AND YEMEN

4 May 1946

(Entered into force on 4 May 1946)

[U.S., *Treaties and Other International Acts Series,* No. 1535]

An American diplomatic mission reached San'a, the highland capital of the isolated Arabian land, in mid-April 1946 in response to an invitation of a year earlier from Yahya b. Muhammad Mansur b. Yahya Hamid-al-Din, the Zaydi Imam of Yemen (1904–48), for formal recognition of his kingdom and for the conclusion of a simple agreement of friendship and commerce. The diplomatic conversations moved in circles for three weeks (14 April–4 May) before the plenipotentiaries placed their signatures on the following instrument, essentially identical with the original draft prepared in Washington. The first sentence of article 3 provided the excuse for protracting the parleys. But the real cause of the delay was Sayf-al-Islam Husayn, the Imam's refractory third son, who apparently had assumed ultimate responsibility for the talks without his father's knowledge. Just as the

American group was about to abandon its efforts as useless, the octogenarian Imam dramatically appeared in the negotiating chamber and saved the day. The agreement took the form of an exchange of identical letters, calling attention in the preamble, omitted below, to the United States recognition on 4 March 1946 of "the complete and absolute independence of the Kingdom of the Yemen" and expressing a mutual desire of the parties "to maintain the most-favored-nation principle in its unconditional and unlimited form as the basis of their commercial relations." R. H. Sanger, *The Arabian Peninsula,* chaps. 17–19.

ART. I. The United States of America and the Kingdom of the Yemen will exchange diplomatic representatives and consular officers at a date which shall be fixed by mutual agrement between the two Governments.

ART. II. The diplomatic representatives of each Party accredited to the Government of the other Party shall enjoy in the territories of such other Party the rights, privileges, exemptions and immunities accorded under generally recognized principles of international law. The consular officers of each Party who are assigned to the Government of the other Party, and are duly provided with exequaturs, shall be permitted to reside in the territories of such other Party at the places where consular officers are permitted by the applicable laws to reside; they shall enjoy the honorary privileges and the immunities accorded to officers of their rank by general international usage; and they shall not, in any event, be treated in a manner less favorable than similar officers of any third country.

ART. III. Subjects of His Majesty the King of the Yemen in the United States of America and nationals of the United States of America in the Kingdom of the Yemen shall be received and treated in accordance with the requirements and practices of generally recognized international law. In respect of their persons, possessions and rights, such subjects or nationals shall enjoy the fullest protection of the laws and authorities of the country, and shall not be treated in any manner less favorable than the nationals of any third country. Subjects of His Majesty in the United States of America and nationals of the United States of America in the Kingdom of the Yemen shall be subject to the local laws and regulations, and shall enjoy the rights and privileges accorded in this third Article.

ART. IV. In all matters relating to customs duties and charges of any kind imposed on or in connection with importation or exportation or otherwise affecting commerce and navigation, to the method of levying such duties and charges, to all rules and formalities in connection with importation or exportation, and to transit, warehousing and other facilities, each Party shall accord unconditional and unrestricted most-favored-nation treatment to articles the growth, produce or manufacture of the other Party, from whatever place arriving, or to articles destined for exportation to the territories of such other Party, by whatever route. Any advantage, favor, privilege or immunity with respect to any duty, charge or regulation affecting commerce or navigation now or hereafter accorded by the United States of America or by the Kingdom of the Yemen to any third country will be accorded immediately and unconditionally to the commerce and navigation of the Kingdom of the Yemen and of the United States of America, respectively. The advantages relating to customs duties now or hereafter accorded by the United States of America to the Republic of Cuba shall be excepted from the provisions of this agreement.

ART. V. There shall be excepted from the provisions of Article IV of this Agreement advantages now or hereafter accorded: by virtue of a customs union of which either Party may become a member; to adjacent countries in order to facilitate frontier traffic; and by the United States of America or its territories or possessions to one another or to the Panama Canal Zone.

The last clause shall continue to apply in respect of any advantages now or hereafter accorded by the United States of America or its territories or possessions to one another irrespective of any change in the political status of any such territories or possessions. Nothing in this Agreement shall prevent the adoption or enforcement by either Party within the area of its jurisdiction: of measures relating to the importation or exportation of gold or silver or the traffic in arms, ammunition, and implements of war, and, in exceptional circumstances, all other military supplies; of measures necessary in pursuance of obligations for the maintenance of international peace and security or necessary for the protection of the essential interests of such Party in time of national emergency; or of statues in relation to immigration and travel. Subject to the requirement that, under like circumstances and conditions, there shall be no arbitrary discrimination by either Party against the subjects, nationals, commerce or navigation of the other Party in favor of the subjects, nationals, commerce or navigation of any third country, the provisions of this Agreement shall not extend to prohibitions or restrictions: imposed on moral or humanitarian grounds; designed to protect human, animal, or plant life or health; relating to prison-made goods; or relating to the enforcement of police or revenue law.

ART. VI. The provisions of this Agreement shall apply to all territory under the sovereignty or authority of either of the parties, except the Panama Canal Zone.

ART. VII. This Agreement shall continue in force until superseded by a more comprehensive commercial agreement, or until thirty days from the date of a written notice of termination given by either party to the other Party, whichever is the earlier. Moreover, either Party may terminate Articles I, II, III, or IV on thirty days written notice.

83. EXCHANGE OF NOTES ON THE TURKISH STRAITS: THE UNITED STATES AND THE USSR
7–19 August 1946

[*The Department of State Bulletin,* 15 (1 September 1946), 420–22]

"Churchill challenged the right of the Russians to consider the matter of the Black Sea straits as one in which no one had a voice except themselves and Turkey," reported former President Truman (*Memoirs,* vol. 1, p. 375) in his summary of the Potsdam conference (17 July–2 August 1945). "Molotov replied that similar treaties had existed between Russia and Turkey in the past, and he cited the treaties of 1805 and 1833" (I, Docs. 29, 40). Indeed, ever since the inconclusive exchanges with Nazi Germany in November 1940 (Doc 67), the USSR had sought to modify the 1936 Montreux convention (Doc. 60) to provide for joint Russo-Turkish defense of the straits. The Big Three, at Soviet request, later explored the question at Tehran in November 1943, as did Churchill and Stalin at Moscow in October 1944. The decision was taken at Yalta in February 1945 that the USSR would submit proposals to the next meeting of the three foreign ministers at London. Moscow, instead, brought unilateral pressure to bear upon Turkey, in March 1945, by denouncing the 1935 Russo-Turkish treaty of neutrality and nonaggression (Doc. 45) and, in June 1945, by demanding the cession to Soviet Armenia and Georgia of the adjacent Turkish provinces of Kars and Ardahan. Against this background the conferees at Potsdam agreed that the 1936 straits convention "should be revised as failing to meet present-day conditions" and that the process should be initiated by "direct conversations between each of the three Governments and the Turkish Government" (article 16 of the Potsdam protocol, text in *A Decade of American Foreign Policy,* U.S., 81st Cong., 1st sess., Senate, Doc. 123, pp. 34–48). Alarmed by the implications of the continuity of Tsarist and Soviet policies, so dramatically reaffirmed by the Nazi-Soviet talks of 1940, as revealed in captured German documents, and by Molotov's references to Russo-Ottoman alliances of the early nineteenth century, the Western powers supported Turkey's inflexible opposition to Soviet demands. The respective formal positions of the USSR and of Turkey and the Western powers are most succinctly stated in the following notes. J. C. Hurewitz, *Middle East Dilemmas,* chap. 5; G. Kirk, *The Middle East in the War,* pp. 443–66 and *The Middle East 1945–1950,* pp. 21–37; N. Sadak, "Turkey Faces the Soviets," *Foreign Affairs,* 27 (April

1949), 449–61; A. S. Esmer, "The Straits, Crux of World Politics," *ibid.*, 25 (January 1947), 290–302; H. N. Howard, *The Problem of the Turkish Straits;* N. J. Padelford, "Solutions to the Problem of the Turkish Straits, a Brief Appraisal," *The Middle East Journal,* 2 (April 1948), 175–90; Truman, *op. cit.*, pp. 375–77, 385–86, 408 and vol. 2, chap. 7; J. Byrnes, *Speaking Frankly,* pp. 77–78, 300–03, and passim.

1. SOVIET CHARGÉ D'AFFAIRES (WASHINGTON) TO ACTING SECRETARY OF STATE, 7 AUGUST 1946

By direction of the Soviet Government I have the honor to communicate to you the following:

As is known, the Berlin Conference of the Three Powers on the question of the Montreux Convention adopted a resolution, whereby the three governments declared that the said convention should be revised, since it does not correspond to present conditions. At the same time the three governments agreed that this question was to be the subject of direct negotiations between each of the Three Powers and the Turkish Government. In accordance with this, the Soviet Government on August 7 of this year addressed to the Turkish Government a note which is transcribed below:

"The Ministry of Foreign Affairs of the USSR has the honor to inform the Turkish Government of the following:

"Events which occurred during the past war clearly indicated that the regime of the Black Sea Straits, established by the Straits Convention, signed in 1936 at Montreux, does not meet the interests of the safety of the Black Sea Powers and does not insure conditions under which the use of these Straits for purposes inimical to the Black Sea Powers would be prevented.

"It will suffice to mention a series of incidents during this war, when the Axis Powers directed their warships and auxiliary craft through the Straits into the Black Sea and out of the Black Sea, which in turn gave rise to the corresponding steps and protests registered by the Soviet Government with the Turkish Government.

"On July 9, 1941, the German command sent the German patrol boat 'Seefalke' through the Straits into the Black Sea, which was a gross violation of the Straits Convention and called forth a protest to the Turkish Government on the part of the Soviet Government.

"In August 1941, Turkish authorities gave the Italian auxiliary war vessel 'Tarvizio' permission to pass through the Straits into the Black Sea, which likewise called forth a representation on the part of the Soviet Government, calling to the attention of the Turkish Government the fact that the passage of the Italian auxiliary vessel into the Black Sea would appear to be a violation of the Straits Convention.

"On November 4, 1942, the Soviet Government again called to the attention of the Turkish Government the fact that Germany planned to send to the Black Sea through the Straits auxiliary war ships under the guise of merchant vessels with a total displacement of 140,000 tons. These vessels were intended for the transfer of military forces and war materials of the Axis countries into the Black Sea. In its representation, the Soviet Government emphasized the fact that 'the admission of the aforementioned vessels through the Straits into the Black Sea would be an obvious violation of the Convention regarding the regime of the Straits concluded in Montreux, inasmuch as these vessels are left at the disposal of the German Government and are in reality auxiliary warships.'

"In June 1944, the Soviet Government registered a protest against the fact that toward the end of May and early in June of 1944 there took place a series of passages through the Straits from the Black Sea into the Aegean Sea of German warships and auxiliary warships of varying tonnage of the 'Ems' (8 vessels) and 'Kriegtransport' (5 vessels) types, which had taken part in the naval operations in the Black Sea.

"It is obvious from the aforementioned facts that at the time of the past war with Germany and her allies, the Straits Convention did not prevent the enemy powers from using the Straits for military purposes against the U. S. S. R. and other allied powers, with the Turkish Government not being able to escape the responsibility for this situation.

"In view of this, the Soviet Government suggested to the Berlin Conference of the Three Powers—Great Britain, the United States of America and the Soviet Union, which took place in July and August 1945, to discuss the question that the regime of the Straits, established by the Montreux Convention, does not conform to present conditions and that it is necessary to establish a new regime of the Straits. As is known, the Berlin Conference of the Three Powers adopted a resolution consisting of the following:

"*a*) The three governments declared that the Convention regarding the Straits, concluded in Montreux, should be revised, as it does not meet the conditions of the present time;

"*b*) The three governments agreed that as the proper course the said question would be the subject of direct negotiations between each of the three powers and the Turkish Government.

"The Soviet Government is also acquainted with the contents of the note of November 2, 1945 of the Government of the United States of America and with the note of the British Government of November 21, 1945 addressed to the Government of Turkey on this question.

"For its own part, the Soviet Government proposes to establish for the Straits a new regime, proceeding from the following principles:

"1) The Straits should be always open to the passage of merchant ships of all countries.

"2) The Straits should be always open to the passage of warships of the Black Sea Powers.

"3) Passage through the Straits for warships not belonging to the Black Sea Powers shall not be permitted except in cases specially provided for.

"4) The establishment of a regime of the Straits, as the sole sea passage, leading from the Black Sea and to the Black Sea, should come under the competence of Turkey and other Black Sea Powers.

"5) Turkey and the Soviet Union, as the powers most interested and capable of guaranteeing freedom to commercial navigation and security in the Straits, shall organize joint means of defense of the Straits, for the prevention of the utilization of the Straits by other countries for aims hostile to the Black Sea Powers.

"The Soviet Government is informing the governments of the United States of America and Great Britain regarding the present declaration."

The Soviet Union has directed me to bring this to the knowledge of the Government of the United States of America.

2. ACTING SECRETARY OF STATE TO SOVIET CHARGÉ D'AFFAIRES (WASHINGTON), 19 AUGUST 1946

I acknowledge receipt of your note of August 7, 1946, which sets forth the text of the note addressed on the same day by the Government of the Union of Soviet Socialist Republics to the Government of the Republic of Turkey and express the appreciation of this Government for the courtesy of the Soviet Government in making this information available.

It will be recalled that the American Embassy in Moscow made available to the Soviet Government in November 1945 a copy of the note which the American Embassy in Ankara delivered to the Turkish Government on November 2, 1945.

This Government has given careful study to the views expressed by the Soviet Government in its note to the Turkish Government. It would appear from a comparison of this Government's note of November 2, 1945, with the Soviet note to the Turkish Government of August 7, 1946, that the views of the Governments of the United States and of the Soviet Union, while not in entire accord, are in general agreement with regard to the three following proposals set forth in the Soviet note:

"1. The Straits should be always open to the passage of merchant ships of all countries.

"2. The Straits should be always open to the passage of warships of the Black Sea powers.

"3. Passage through the Straits for warships not belonging to the Black Sea powers shall not be permitted except in cases specially provided for."

The fourth proposal set forth in the Soviet note does not appear to envisage a revision of the Montreux Convention, as suggested in our note to the Turkish Government of November 2, 1945, but rather the establishment of a new régime which would be confined to Turkey and the other Black Sea powers. It is the view of this Government that the régime of the Straits is a matter of concern not only to the Black Sea powers but also to other powers, including the United States. This Government cannot, therefore, agree with the Soviet view that the establishment of the régime of the Straits should come under the competence of the Black Sea powers to the exclusion of other powers.

The fifth proposal set forth in the note of the Soviet Government was that Turkey and the Soviet Union should organize joint means of defense of the Straits. It is the firm opinion of this Government that Turkey should continue to be primarily responsible for the defense of the Straits. Should the Straits become the object of attack or threat of attack by an aggressor, the resulting situation would constitute a threat to international security and would clearly be a matter for action on the part of the Security Council of the United Nations.

It is observed that the note of the Soviet Government contains no reference to the United Nations. The position of the Government of the United States is that the régime of the Straits should be brought into appropriate relationship with the United Nations and should function in a manner entirely consistent with the principles and aims of the United Nations.

The Government of the United States reaffirms its willingness to participate in a conference called to revise the Montreux Convention.

84. DRAFT ANGLO-EGYPTIAN TREATY AND ACCOMPANYING PROTOCOLS
25 October 1946

[Great Britain, *Parliamentary Papers, 1947,* Egypt No. 2, Cmd. 7179]

Anglo-Egyptian talks on revision of the 1936 treaty (Docs. 61, 79) opened in Cairo on 23 April 1946. Prime Minister Isma'il Pasha Sidqi headed the Egyptian delegation, which the Wafd Party boycotted because it could not play a commanding role. The exploratory phase of the negotiations passed without hitch, and in the early fall Sidqi proceeded to London, where he and Foreign Secretary Bevin initialed *ad referendum* on 25 October the draft treaty and two protocols, reproduced below, one stipulating the conditions for British troop withdrawal and the other pertaining to the Sudan. But the draft instruments were never signed, for the Sudan protocol was so worded as to convey conflicting meanings to the signatories, and the negotiations broke down in January 1947 (see text of Bevin's statement, 27 January 1947, Cmd. 7179, pp. 5–7). Although the British evacuated their forces from Alexandria and Cairo by 31 March, these measures could be interpreted as having been taken under the 1936 treaty. British garrisons were confined thereafter to the Suez Canal Zone. Egypt referred the question to the UN Security Council on 11 July 1947. But that organ, incapable of arriving at any decision, suspended discussion of the dispute on 10 September. Although nerves were equally frayed in London and Cairo over the inconclusive diplomacy, the issue was temporarily thrust aside after September 1947 as Britain and Egypt became increasingly distracted by the exploding Palestine problem. See references to Doc. 79; also J. Marlowe, *A History of Modern Egypt and Anglo-Egyptian Relations 1800–1953,* chaps. 16, 17; J. Kimche, *Seven Fallen Pillars,* chap. 20.

ART. 1. The Treaty of Alliance signed in London on 26th August, 1936, together with the Agreed Minute, notes and the Convention of 26th August, 1936, concerning immunities and privileges which accompanied the said Treaty, shall cease to have effect upon the entry into force of the present Treaty.

ART. 2. The High Contracting Parties agree that in the event of Egypt becoming the object of armed aggression or in the event of the United Kingdom becoming involved in war as the result of armed aggression against countries adjacent to Egypt, they shall take, in close co-operation and as a result of consultation, such action as may be recognised as necessary until the Security Council has taken the necessary measures for the re-establishment of peace.

ART. 3. In order to ensure the mutual co-operation and assistance of the High Contracting Parties, and in order to permit of the effective co-ordination of the measures to be taken for their mutual defence, the High Contracting Parties agree to establish a joint Board of Defence composed of the competent military authorities of the two Governments, assisted by such other representatives as the two Governments shall appoint.

The Board is an advisory body whose functions are to study, with a view to proposing to the two Governments the measures to be taken, problems concerning the mutual defence of the High Contracting Parties by land, sea and air, including questions of material and personnel connected therewith and, in particular, the technical requirements of their co-operation and the steps to be taken to enable the armed forces of the High Contracting Parties to be in a position effectively to resist aggression.

The Board shall meet as often as may be necessary in order to carry out these functions. If need arises, the Board shall also examine, on the invitation of, and on the information supplied by, the two Governments, the military repercussions of the international situation, and, in particular, of all events which may threaten the security of the Middle East, and shall make in this respect suitable recommendations to the two Governments, who, in the case of events threatening the security of any one of the neighbouring countries of Egypt, will consult together in order to take in agreement such measures as may be recognised as necessary.

ART. 4. The High Contracting Parties undertake not to conclude any alliance and not to take part in any coalition directed against one of them.

ART. 5. Nothing in the present Treaty can in any way prejudice the rights and obligations which devolve, or may devolve, upon one or other of the High Contracting Parties under the Charter of the United Nations.

ART. 6. The High Contracting Parties agree that any difference on the subject of the application or interpretation of the provisions of the present Treaty, which they are unable to settle by direct negotiation, shall be determined in accordance with the provisions of the Charter of the United Nations, having due regard to the declarations made by both High Contracting Parties under Article 36 (2) of the Statute of the International Court.

ART. 7. The present Treaty is subject to ratification. Ratifications shall be exchanged in Cairo as soon as possible. The Treaty shall come into force on the date of the exchange of ratifications. The present Treaty shall remain in force for a period of twenty years from the date of its coming into force and thereafter it shall remain in force until the expiry of one year after a notice of termination has been given by one High Contracting Party to the other through the diplomatic channel.

DRAFT SUDAN PROTOCOL

The policy which the High Contracting Parties undertake to follow in the Sudan within the framework of the unity between the Sudan and Egypt under the common Crown of Egypt will have for its essential objectives to assure the well-being of the Sudanese, the development of their interests and their active preparation for self-government and consequently the exercise of the right to choose the future status of the Sudan. Until the High Contracting Parties can in full common agreement realise this latter objective after consultation with the Sudanese, the Agreement of 1899 will continue and Article 11 of the Treaty of 1936, together with its Annex and paragraphs 14 to 16 of the Agreed Minute annexed to the same Treaty, will remain in force notwithstanding the first Article of the present Treaty.

DRAFT EVACUATION PROTOCOL

The High Contracting Parties agree that the complete evacuation of Egyptian territory (Egypt) by the British Forces shall be completed by 1st September, 1949.

The towns of Cairo and Alexandria and the Delta shall be evacuated by 31st March, 1947. The evacuation of the remainder of the country shall proceed continuously during the period ending at the date specified in the first paragraph above.

The provisions of the Convention of 26th August, 1936, concerning immunities and privileges will continue provisionally to be applied to the British Forces during the period of their withdrawal from Egypt. Such amendment of the agreement as may be necessary in view of the fact that British troops will after 31st March, 1947, be withdrawn from the Delta and the two cities shall be settled by a subsequent agreement between the two Governments to be negotiated before this date.

85. THE TRUMAN DOCTRINE
12 March 1947

[*The Department of State Bulletin,* 16 (23 March 1947), 534–37]

The United States Policy of containing the Soviet Union, when first announced in March 1947, aimed—as its immediate objectives—at frustrating Russian designs on Greece and Turkey. Nor was it surprising that the Near and Middle East—strategically, an extension of the eastern Mediterranean—should have been singled out. Of all the regions on the Russian periphery this was one of the most exposed. Until the beginning of 1947 the Near and Middle East constituted a zone for whose defense Britain claimed primary responsibility. But World War II left the United Kingdom in a nearly prostrate financial condition. As elsewhere in Asia, Britain was contracting its commitments. Yet the demands of imperial and commonwealth defense and dependence on Near and Middle East oil and markets did not lessen the region's importance to the United Kingdom. American financial and military aid to Turkey (and Greece) was predicated on the assumption that the United States would shore up and supplement Britain's Near and Middle East defense arrangements. But the problems of defense in that region were tightly interlocked with other problems—notably, depressed economic and social conditions, general political instability, the legacy of hostility toward European controls, and intraregional rivalries and conflicts—which did not respond readily to global policy generalizations. Omitted below is the section on Greece. J. C. Hurewitz, *Middle East Dilemmas,* chaps. 1, 5–7; H. L. Hoskins, *The Middle East, Problem Area in World Politics,* chaps. 13–14; Brookings Institution, *The Security of the Middle East, A Problem Paper;* H. S. Truman, *Memoirs,* vol. 2, chaps. 7, 16.

The gravity of the situation which confronts the world today necessitates my appearance before a joint session of the Congress.

The foreign policy and the national security of this country are involved.

One aspect of the present situation, which I wish to present to you at this time for your consideration and decision, concerns Greece and Turkey. . . . [Section on Greece omitted.]

Greece's neighbor, Turkey, also deserves our attention.

The future of Turkey as an independent and economically sound state is clearly no less important to the freedom-loving peoples of the world than the future of Greece. The circumstances in which Turkey finds itself today are considerably different from those of Greece. Turkey has been spared the disasters that have beset Greece. And during the war the United States and Great Britain furnished Turkey with material aid.

Nevertheless, Turkey now needs our support.

Since the war Turkey has sought additional financial assistance from Great Britain and the United States for the purpose of effecting that modernization necessary for the maintenance of its national integrity.

That integrity is essential to the preservation of order in the Middle East.

The British Government has informed us that, owing to its own difficulties, it can no longer extend financial or economic aid to Turkey.

As in the case of Greece, if Turkey is to have the assistance it needs, the United States must supply it. We are the only country able to provide that help.

I am fully aware of the broad implications involved if the United States extends assistance to Greece and Turkey, and I shall discuss these implications with you at this time.

One of the primary objectives of the foreign policy of the United States is the creation of conditions in which we and other nations will be able to work out a way of life free from coercion. This was a fundamental issue in the war with Germany and Japan. Our victory was won over countries which sought to impose their will, and their way of life, upon other nations.

To insure the peaceful development of nations, free from coercion, the United States has taken a leading part in establishing the United Nations. The United Nations is designed to make possible lasting freedom and independence for all its members. We shall not realize our objectives, however, unless we are willing to help free peoples to maintain their free institutions and their national integrity against aggressive movements that seek to impose upon them totalitarian regimes. This is no more than a frank recognition that totalitarian regimes imposed upon free peoples, by direct or indirect aggression, undermine the foundations of international peace and hence the security of the United States.

The peoples of a number of countries of the world have recently had totalitarian regimes forced upon them against their will. The Government of the United States has made frequent protests against coercion and intimidation, in violation of the Yalta agreement, in Poland, Rumania, and Bulgaria. I must also state that in a number of other countries there have been similar developments.

At the present moment in world history nearly every nation must choose between alternative ways of life. The choice is too often not a free one.

One way of life is based upon the will of the majority, and is distinguished by free institutions, representative government, free elections, guaranties, of individual liberty, freedom of speech and religion, and freedom from political oppression.

The second way of life is based upon the will of a minority forcibly imposed upon the majority. It relies upon terror and oppression, a controlled press and radio, fixed elections, and the suppression of personal freedoms.

I believe that it must be the policy of the United States to support free peoples who are resisting attempted subjugation by armed minorities or by outside pressures.

I believe that we must assist free peoples to work out their own destinies in their own way.

I believe that our help should be primarily through economic and financial aid which is essential to economic stability and orderly political processes.

The world is not static, and the *status quo* is not sacred. But we cannot allow changes in the *status quo* in violation of the Charter of the United Nations by such methods as coercion, or by such subterfuges as political infiltration. In helping free and independent nations to maintain their freedom, the United States will be giving effect to the principles of the Charter of the United Nations.

It is necessary only to glance at a map to realize that the survival and integrity of the Greek nation are of grave importance in a much wider situation. If Greece should fall under the control of an armed minority, the effect upon its neighbor, Turkey, would be immediate and serious. Confusion and disorder might well spread throughout the entire Middle East.

Moreover, the disappearance of Greece as an independent state would have a profound effect upon those countries in Europe whose peoples are struggling against great difficulties to maintain their freedoms and their independence while they repair the damages of war.

It would be an unspeakable tragedy if these countries, which have struggled so long against overwhelming odds, should lose that victory for which they sacrificed so much. Collapse of free institutions and loss of independence would be disastrous not only for them but for the world. Discouragement and possibly failure would quickly be the lot of neighboring peoples striving to maintain their freedom and independence.

Should we fail to aid Greece and Turkey in this fateful hour, the effect will be far-reaching to the West as well as to the East.

We must take immediate and resolute action.

I therefore ask the Congress to provide authority for assistance to Greece and Turkey in the amount of $400,000,000 for the period ending June 30, 1948. In requesting these funds, I have taken into consideration the maximum amount of relief assistance which would be furnished to Greece out of the $350,000,000 which I recently requested that the Congress authorize for the prevention of starvation and suffering in countries devastated by the war.

In addition to funds, I ask the Congress to authorize the detail of American civilian and military personnel to Greece and Turkey, at the request of those countries, to assist in the tasks of reconstruction, and for the purpose of supervising the use of such financial and material assistance as may be furnished. I recommend that authority also be provided for the instruction and training of selected Greek and Turkish personnel.

Finally, I ask that the Congress provide authority which will permit the speediest and most effective use, in terms of needed commodities, supplies, and equipment, of such funds as may be authorized.

If further funds, or further authority, should be needed for purposes indicated in this message, I shall not hesitate to bring the situation before the Congress. On this subject the Executive and Legislative branches of the Government must work together.

This is a serious course upon which we embark.

I would not recommend it except that the alternative is much more serious.

The United States contributed $341,000,000,000 toward winning World War II. This is an investment in world freedom and world peace.

The assistance that I am recommending for Greece and Turkey amounts to little more than one-tenth of one percent of this investment. It is only common sense that we should safeguard this investment and make sure that it was not in vain.

The seeds of totalitarian regimes are nurtured by misery and want. They spread and grow in the evil soil of poverty and strife. They reach their full growth when the hope of a people for a better life has died.

We must keep that hope alive.

The free peoples of the world look to us for support in maintaining their freedoms.

If we falter in our leadership, we may endanger the peace of the world—and we shall surely endanger the welfare of our own Nation.

Great responsibilities have been placed upon us by the swift movement of events.

I am confident that the Congress will face these responsibilities squarely.

86. MILITARY MISSION AGREEMENT: THE UNITED STATES AND IRAN
6 October 1947

[U.S., *Treaties and Other International Acts Series,* No. 1666]

The United States, on invitation from Iran, sent advisory missions to the Iranian army and gendarmerie late in 1942. Neither mission at any time during the war exceeded in size twenty-five officers and enlisted men. The two governments formalized the status of the advisory groups by signing at Tehran in November 1943 agreements (U.S., *Executive Agreement Series No. 361*) whose terms the *Majlis* (legislature) had explicitly sanctioned on 21 October 1943. Despite several attempts by the United States War Department in 1944–45 to abolish the missions, they nevertheless survived into the postwar period, for the thinly veiled aggression of the USSR created such uneasy conditions in Iran that the shah's government appealed to the Department of State for the continued services of American military technicians. The following agreement, concluded on the eve of Iran's repudiation of the projected oil contract with the USSR (Doc. 87), extended for approximately a year and a half the life of the military mission. The arrangements were later renewed periodically, supplemented after May 1950 by American military grant aid. T. H. V. Motter, *The Persian Corridor and Aid to Russia,* chap. 21; J. C. Hurewitz, *Middle East Dilemmas,* chap. 2; G. Lenczowski, *Russia and the West in Iran,* chaps. 10–11.

TITLE I—PURPOSE AND DURATION

ART. 1. The purpose of this Mission is to cooperate with the Ministry of War of Iran and with the personnel of the Iranian Army with the view to enhancing the efficiency of the Iranian Army.

ART. 2. This agreement shall be effective from the date of signing of the agreement by the accredited representatives of the Government of the United States of America and the Government of Iran and shall continue in force until March 20, 1949, unless sooner terminated or extended as hereinafter provided.

ART. 3. If the Government of Iran should desire that the services of the Mission be extended beyond the stipulated period, it shall make a written proposal to that effect prior to September 21, 1948. The Government of the United States of America agrees to act upon such proposal prior to December 21, 1948.

ART. 4. This agreement may be terminated prior to March 20, 1949, in the following manner:

A) By either government subject to three months notice in writing to the other government;

B) By either government at any time, upon written notice, if that government considers it necessary due to domestic disturbances or foreign hostilities;

C) By the Government of the United States of America at any time upon written notice that the present statutory authority under which this arrangement is concluded has terminated and that Congress has provided no other authority for the continuation of the Mission;

D) By the recall of the entire personnel of the Mission by the Government of the United States of America in the public interest of the United States of America, without necessity of compliance with provision (A) of the article.

E) The termination of this agreement, however, shall not effect or modify the several obligations of the Government of Iran to the members of the Mission or to their families as set out in Title IV hereof.

TITLE II—COMPOSITION AND PERSONNEL

ART. 5. Initially the Mission shall consist of such numbers of personnel of the United States Army as may be agreed upon by the Minister of War of Iran through his authorized representative in Washington and by the War Department of the United States of America. The individuals to be assigned shall be those agreed upon by the Minister of War of Iran or his authorized representative and by the War Department of the United States of America or its authorized representative.

TITLE III—DUTIES, RANK, AND PRECEDENCE

ART. 6. Members of the Mission shall be assigned to the Department of the Ministry of War designated the Advisory Department. The Advisory Department shall be organized under a table of organization prepared with the agreement of the Chief of Mission and approved by the Minister of War of Iran. Members of the Mission shall be assigned to position vacancies shown on this table, and their assignment shall be published in Iranian Army General Orders.

ART. 7. The senior officer of the Mission shall be appointed Chief of the Mission. Other members of the Mission shall be assigned duties by the Chief of Mission as indicated by the table of organization and approved by the Minister of War of Iran, or such other duties as may be agreed upon between the Minister of War of Iran and the Chief of the Mission.

ART. 8. The duties of the Mission shall be to advise and assist the Ministry of War of Iran and its several departments as well as subordinate sections of the General Staff with respect to plans, problems concerning organization, administrative principles and training methods. These duties involve the principles of work of the General Staff and all departments of the Ministry of War in Tehran and their field agencies except tactical and strategical plans or operations against a foreign enemy, which are not related to the duties of the Mission.

ART. 9. Members of the Mission will assume neither command nor staff responsibility in the Iranian Army. They may, however, make such official inspections and investigations as may be necessary and are approved by the Minister of War of Iran and directed by the Chief of the Mission.

ART. 10. Each member of the Mission shall serve in the Mission with the rank he holds in the United States Army but shall have precedence over all Iranian Army officers of the same rank. Each member of the Mission shall be entitled to all benefits and privileges which the regulations of the Iranian Army provide for officers of corresponding rank of the Iranian Army. Members of the Mission shall wear the United States Army uniform with a shoulder sleeve insignia indicating service with the Iranian Army.

ART. 11. Members of the Mission in case of violation of the laws and regulations of the Iranian Government, may be separated from the service of the Iranian Army and in such case will have only the right to draw travel expenses back to America.

ART. 12. In the normal execution of their duties as defined in Article 8 and 9, the Chief of the Mission, and other members when so directed by him, are authorized to visit and inspect any part of the Iranian military establishment, and officers in authority shall facilitate such inspections and make available plans, records, reports, and correspondence as required. Members of the Mission will not concern themselves with secret matters except when it is essential to their duties and then only with the approval of the Ministry of War. Each member of the Mission has the obligation not to divulge or in any way disclose to any foreign government or any person whatsoever any secret or confidential matter of which he may have become cognizant in his capacity as a member of the Mission. This obligation shall continue in force after the termination of the services of the member or the mission and after the expiration or cancellation of this agreement.

TITLE IV—COMPENSATION AND PERQUISITIES

ART. 13. Members of the Mission shall receive from the Government of Iran such fixed annual compensation and emoluments, payable in American currency or dollar draft or check, allowances as may be agreed upon between the Government of the United States of America and the Government of Iran for each member. Such compensation and emoluments shall be paid in twelve (12) equal monthly installments, each due and payable on the last day of the month. The compensation and emoluments shall not be subject to any tax, now or hereafter in effect, of the Government of Iran or of any of its political or administrative subdivisions. Should there, however, at present or while this agreement is in effect, be any taxes that might affect such compensation and emoluments, such taxes shall be borne by the Ministry of War of Iran, in order to comply with the provisions of this Article that the compensation agreed upon shall be net.

ART. 14. The compensation and emoluments indicated in the preceding article shall commence for each member of the Mission upon arrival in Iran and, except as otherwise expressly provided in this agreement, shall continue, following the termination of duty with the Mission, or following the termination of the Mission under Article 4 of this agreement, likewise for the return trip to the United States of America and thereafter for the period of any accumulated leave which may be due the member.

ART. 15. The additional compensation and emoluments due for the period of the return trip and accumulated leave shall be paid to each member of the Mission before his departure from Iran and such compensation and emoluments shall be computed for travel by the shortest route usually travelled to the port of entry in the United States of America, regardless of the route and method of travel used by the member of the Mission.

ART. 16. During the period of the present national emergency in the United States of America, expense of transportation of each member of the Mission and his household effects, baggage and automobile from and to the United States of America shall be paid by the Government of the United States of America. If the period of this agreement extends beyond the date on which the national emergency in the United States of America is terminated, notification of the termination of the national emergency having been communicated to the Government of Iran in writing by the Government of the United States of America, expenses (except in case a member is replaced with less than two years service in the Mission for the convenience of the Government of the United States of America) for transportation of each member of the Mission and his household effects, baggage and automobile shall be paid by the Government of Iran. First-class accommodations for travel will be furnished the members of the Mission via the shortest usually traveled route between the port of embarkation in the United States of America and their official residence in Iran, both for the outward and return journey.

ART. 17. At any time during the period of this agreement, as may be elected by each member, the family of each member of the Mission shall be furnished by the Government of Iran with first-class accommodations for travel, via the shortest usually traveled route between the port of embarkation in the United States of America and the official residence of the member in Iran, both for the outward and for the return journey. Throughout this agreement the term "Family" is limited to mean wife and dependent children.

ART. 18. Compensation for transportation and travel expenses on official business of the Government of Iran shall be provided by the Government of Iran in accordance with the travel regulations of the Iranian Army.

ART. 19. In addition to the United States Government transportation available to the Mission, the Government of Iran shall place other means of transportation (vehicle and aircraft) at the disposal of the Mission, when deemed necessary for the performance of official duties and will provide one third of the gasoline and oils required for the United States Government vehicles at the disposal of the Mission, as determined by the Chief of the Mission. The number and type of United States Government vehicles shall be determined by the War Department of the United States of America and authority is granted for the entry and exit from Iran, in accordance with the existing law, of one United States Army aircraft with crew as considered necessary by the Chief of the Mission, in the performance of official duties, provided that the Chief of the Mission previously informs the Iranian authorities concerned of the matter according to existing rules and regulations of Iran. All the United States Government vehicles placed at the disposal of the Mission for operation within Iran will be subject to the laws of Iran.

ART. 20. The Government of Iran shall provide for members of the Mission suitable office space and facilities such as office equipment, stenographic and clerical help, civilian interpreters and orderlies, as indicated on the table of organizaton of the Advisory Department, and shall give necessary assistance for the smooth operation and improvement of the work of the Mission.

ART. 21. If any member of the Mission, or any of his family, should die in Iran, the Government of Iran shall have the body transported to such place in the United States of America as the surviving members of the family may decide, but the cost to the Government of Iran shall not exceed the cost of transporting the remains from the place of decease to New York City. Should the deceased be a member of the Mission, his services with the Mission shall be considered to have terminated fifteen (15) days after his death. Return transportation to New York City for the family of the deceased member and for their baggage, household effects, and automobile shall be provided as prescribed in Article 17. All allowances due the deceased member, including salary for fifteen (15) days subsequent to his death, and reimbursement for expenses and transportation due the deceased member for travel performed on official business of the Government of Iran, shall be paid to the widow of the deceased member or to any other person who may have been designated in writing by the deceased while serving under the terms of this agreement; but such widow or other person shall not be compensated for accrued leave due and not taken by the deceased. All compensation due the widow, or other person designated by the deceased, under the provisions of this article, shall be paid within fifteen (15) days of the decease of said member.

ART. 22. If a member of the Mission becomes ill or suffers injury, he shall, at the discretion of the Chief of the Mission, be placed in such hospital as the Chief of the Mission deems suitable, after consultation with the Ministry of War of Iran, and all expenses incurred as the result of such illness or injury while the patient is a member of the Mission and remains in Iran shall be paid by the Government of Iran. If the hospitalized member is a commissioned officer, he shall pay his cost of subsistence. Families will enjoy the same privileges agreed upon in this article for members of the Mission, except that a member of the Mission shall in all cases pay the cost of subsistence incident to hospitalization of a member of his family. Any member of the Mission unable to perform his duties with the Mission by reason of long continued physical disability shall be replaced.

TITLE V—STIPULATIONS AND CONDITIONS

ART. 23. Each member of the Mission shall be entitled to one months annual leave with pay, or to a proportional part thereof with pay for any fractional part of the year. Unused portions of said leave shall be cumulative from year to year during service as a member of the Mission. This leave may be spent in Iran, in the United States of America, or in other countries, but the expense of travel and transportation not otherwise provided for in this agreement shall be borne by the member of the Mission taking such leave. All travel time on leave shall count as leave. The Government of Iran agrees to grant the leave therein specified according to the written application approved by the Chief of Mission with due consideration for the convenience of the Government of Iran.

ART. 24. So long as this agreement, or any extension thereof, is in effect, the Government of Iran shall not engage the services of any personnel of any other foreign government for duties of any nature connected with the Iranian Army, except by mutual agreement between the Government of the United States of America and the Government of Iran.

ART. 25. The Government of Iran shall grant exemption from custom duties or other imports on articles imported into Iran by members of the Mission for their personal use or the use of their families, provided that their request for free entry has received the approval of the Ambassador of the United States of America or the Charge d'Affairs, ad interim, and from all export duties on articles purchased in Iran for their personal use or the use of their families. The Government of Iran shall grant free and unrestricted passage of mail to and from members of the Mission from and to the United States when transportation of such mail is furnished by the Government of the United States of America. The Chief of the Mission is responsible that no contraband is sent or received by members of the Mission or their families.

87. IRANIAN LAW REJECTING THE DRAFT OIL AGREEMENT WITH THE USSR
22 October 1947

[Translated from the Persian text in Iran, Majlis, *Majmu'ah-i-Qawanin*, vol. 15, pp. 431–32]

The draft oil concession, which the USSR pressured Prime Minister Qavam into signing on 4 April 1946 (Doc. 80) required parliamentary ratification both under the constitution (article 24, fundamental laws of 30 December 1906) and under express legislation of the *Majlis* itself (Doc. 75). But the statutory term of the 14th *Majlis* expired in mid-March 1946, and a law that it enacted forbade the holding of new elections while foreign troops remained on Iranian soil. The legal technicalities enabled Qavam to delay the election for the 15th *Majlis* until after the end of the year, by which time the Iranian government had reasserted its sovereignty over the rebellious Azarbayjan province. The election itself consumed more than a half-year longer. With its territorial integrity and political sovereignty fully restored and with the moral encouragement of the United States Ambassador, the Iranian government guided through the new legislature the following bill, approved by a vote of 102 to 2. G. Kirk, *The Middle East 1945–1950,* pp. 56–89; G. Lenczowski, *Russia and the West in Iran,* chap. 11; J. C. Hurewitz, *Middle East Dilemmas*, chap. 2; L. V. Thomas and R. N. Frye, *The United States and Turkey in Iran,* pp. 229–44.

1. Where as the Prime Minister, in good faith and in accordance with his interpretation of article 2 of the Law of 2 December 1944, entered into conversations and proceeded to the drafting of the Agreement of 4 April 1946 regarding the establishment of a joint Irano-Soviet Oil Company and whereas the *Majlis* does not consider these actions to be in conformity with the actual intent of the above-mentioned Law, therefore the *Majlis* considers the above-mentioned conversations and agreement to be null and void. Article 3 of the Proclamation of 5 April 1946 is also declared null and void by the Majlis.

2. The Government is directed to provide scientific and technical means of exploration for the purpose of discovering oil deposits and to prepare, within a period of five years, complete and comprehensive scientific and technical plans and charts of the oil-bearing regions of Iran so that the *Majlis,* thus informed on the existence of oil in adequate quantities, will be able to take measures for the commercial exploitation of this national wealth by enacting appropriate legislation.

3. The grant of any concession to foreigners for the purpose of extracting petroleum or any derivative as well as the establishment for this purpose of any company in which foreigners have any interest whatsoever are absolutely forbidden.

4. If, following the technical exploration mentioned in paragraph 2 above, it should become established with certainty that petroleum exists in the northern regions of Iran in quantities suitable for commercial exploitation, the Government is authorized to enter into negotiations with the Government of the USSR with a view to selling such petroleum, [and] the results of such negotiations shall be reported to the *Majlis.*

5. In all instances wherein the rights of the Iranian people in the economic wealth of the country have been infringed—whether in the matter of subsoil resources, or otherwise, and especially with regard to the southern oil concession—the Government is directed to enter into negotiations and to take appropriate action toward the reestablishment of these rights, informing the *Majlis* of the results obtained.

88. UN GENERAL ASSEMBLY'S RESOLUTION ON THE PARTITION OF PALESTINE
29 November 1947

[Resolution 181(II)]

Following the collapse in February 1947 of Britain's formal negotiations with the Arabs and informal talks with the Zionists, the Labor government decided to refer the Palestine question to the UN General Assembly. At England's request the Assembly was convened in special session (28 April–15 May 1947) "for the purpose of constituting and instructing a special committee to prepare for the consideration, at the [next] regular session of the Assembly, of the [Palestine] question" (UN Doc. A/286). The Assembly on 15 May created the UN Special Committee on Palestine, or UNSCOP as it was commonly known, consisting of the representatives of eleven smaller states, chosen on the principle of geographic distribution, so as to insure neutrality. UNSCOP was given "the widest powers to ascertain and record facts, and to investigate all questions and issues relevant to the problem of Palestine," and was instructed to "prepare a report . . . and . . . submit such proposals as it may consider appropriate . . . not later than 1 September 1947" [resolution 106 (S-1)]. UNSCOP's majority presented to the second regular session of the Assembly (16 September–29 November 1947) a proposal for dividing Palestine into Arab and Jewish states which were to remain in economic union and the establishment of a special international regime for the City of Jerusalem and its immediate environs. The Assembly adopted the proposal, with some modification, on 29 November 1947. The Palestine Arabs with the united backing of the Arab states refused to accept the Assembly's recommendations and attempted forcibly to prevent implementation. But the Palestine Jews—with the cooperation until April 1948 of the UN Palestine Commission, a subsidiary organ created by the Assembly to supervise the execution of the resolution—went ahead with their plans for forming a provisional council of government. Thus on the eve of the mandate's expiry on 14 May, the Palestine Jews proclaimed their independence, and the Jewish provisional council of government became the Provisional government of Israel. The parties later reversed their attitudes toward the 1947 Assembly resolution. By the mid-1950's the Arab states were demanding a literal application of its provisions, while Israel took a flexible stand. J. C. Hurewitz, *Struggle for Palestine,* chaps. 22–23, epilogue; J. García-Granados, *The Birth of Israel;* M. Zafrulla Khan, *Palestine in the U.N.O.;* K. Roosevelt, "The Partition of Palestine, A Lesson in Pressure Politics," *The Middle East Journal,* 2 (January 1948), 1–16; D. Horowitz, *State in the Making,* chaps. 24–51; H. S. Truman, *Memoirs,* vol. 2, chaps. 11–12.

A

The General Assembly,

Having met in special session at the request of the mandatory Power to constitute and instruct a special committee to prepare for the consideration of the question of the future government of Palestine at the second regular session;

Having constituted a Special Committee and instructed it to investigate all questions and issues relevant to the problem of Palestine, and to prepare proposals for the solution of the problem, and

Having received and examined the report of the Special Committee (document A/364) including a number of unanimous recommendations and a plan of partition with economic union approved by the majority of the Special Committee,

Considers that the present situation in Palestine is one which is likely to impair the general welfare and friendly relations among nations;

Takes note of the declaration by the mandatory Power that it plans to complete its evacuation of Palestine by 1 August 1948;

Recommends to the United Kingdom, as the mandatory Power for Palestine, and to all other Members of the United Nations the adoption and implementation, with regard to the future government of Palestine, of the Plan of Partition with Economic Union set out below;

Requests that

(*a*) The Security Council take the necessary measures as provided for in the plan for its implementation;

(*b*) The Security Council consider if circumstances during the transitional period require such consideration, whether the situation in Palestine constitutes a threat to the peace. If it decides that such a threat exists, and in order to maintain international peace and security, the Security Council should supplement the authorization of the General Assembly by taking measures, under Articles 39 and 41 of the Charter, to empower the United Nations Commission, as provided in this resolution, to exercise in Palestine the functions which are assigned to it by this resolution;

(*c*) The Security Council determine as a threat to the peace, breach of the peace or act of aggression, in accordance with Article 39 of the Charter, any attempt to alter by force the settlement envisaged by this resolution;

(*d*) The Trusteeship Council be informed of the responsibilities envisaged for it in this plan;

Calls upon the inhabitants of Palestine to take such steps as may be necessary on their part to put this plan into effect;

Appeals to all Governments and all peoples to refrain from taking any action which might hamper or delay the carrying out of these recommendations. . . .

PLAN OF PARTITION WITH ECONOMIC UNION

PART I. FUTURE CONSTITUTION AND GOVERNMENT OF PALESTINE

A. TERMINATION OF MANDATE, PARTITION AND INDEPENDENCE

1. The Mandate for Palestine shall terminate as soon as possible but in any case not later than 1 August 1948.

2. The armed forces of the mandatory Power shall be progressively withdrawn from Palestine, the withdrawal to be completed as soon as possible but in any case not later than 1 August 1948.

The mandatory Power shall advise the Commission, as far in advance as possible, of its intention to terminate the Mandate and to evacuate each area.

The mandatory Power shall use its best endeavours to ensure that an area situated in the territory of the Jewish State, including a seaport and hinterland adequate to provide facilities for a substantial immigration, shall be evacuated at the earliest possible date and in any event not later than 1 February 1948.

3. Independent Arab and Jewish States and the Special International Regime for the City of Jerusalem, set forth in part III of this plan, shall come into existence in Palestine two months after the evacuation of the armed forces of the mandatory Power has been completed but in any case not later than 1 October 1948. The boundaries of the Arab State, the Jewish State, and the City of Jerusalem shall be as described in parts II and III below.

4. The period between the adoption by the General Assembly of its recommendation on the question of Palestine and the establishment of the independence of the Arab and Jewish States shall be a transitional period.

B. STEPS PREPARATORY TO INDEPENDENCE

1. A Commission shall be set up consisting of one representative of each of five Member States. The Members represented on the Commission shall be elected by the General Assembly on as broad a basis, geographically and otherwise, as possible.

2. The administration of Palestine shall, as the mandatory Power withdraws its armed forces, be progressively turned over to the Commission, which shall act in conformity with the recommendations of the General Assembly, under the guidance of the Security Council. The mandatory Power shall to the fullest possible extent coordinate its plans for withdrawal with the plans of the Commission to take over and administer areas which have been evacuated.

In the discharge of this administrative responsibility the Commission shall have authority to issue necessary regulations and take other measures as required.

The mandatory Power shall not take any action to prevent, obstruct or delay the implementation by the Commission of the measures recommended by the General Assembly.

3. On its arrival in Palestine the Commission shall proceed to carry out measures for the establishment of the frontiers of the Arab and Jewish States and the City of Jerusalem in accordance with the general lines of the recommendations of the General Assembly on the partition of Palestine. Nevertheless, the boundaries as described in part II of this plan are to be modified in such a way that village areas as a rule will not be divided by state boundaries unless pressing reasons make that necessary.

4. The Commission, after consultation with the democratic parties and other public organizations of the Arab and Jewish States, shall select and establish in each State as rapidly as possible a Provisional Council of Government. The activities of both the Arab and Jewish Provisional Councils of Government shall be carried out under the general direction of the Commission.

If by 1 April 1948 a Provisional Council of Government cannot be selected for either of the States, or, if selected, cannot carry out its functions, the Commission shall communicate that fact to the Security Council for such action with respect to that State as the Security Council may deem proper, and to the Secretary-General for communication to the Members of the United Nations.

5. Subject to the provisions of these recommendations, during the transitional period the Provisional Councils of Government, acting under the Commission, shall have full authority in the areas under their control, including authority over matters of immigration and land regulation.

6. The Provisional Council of Government of each State, acting under the Commission, shall progressively receive from the Commission full responsibility for the administration of that State in the period between the termination of the Mandate and the establishment of the State's independence.

7. The Commission shall instruct the Provisional Councils of Government of both the Arab and Jewish States, after their formation, to proceed to the establishment of administrative organs of government, central and local.

8. The Provisional Council of Government of each State shall, within the shortest time possible, recruit an armed militia from the residents of that State, sufficient in number to maintain internal order and to prevent frontier clashes.

This armed militia in each State shall, for operational purposes, be under the command of Jewish or Arab officers resident in that State, but general political and military control, including the choice of the militia's High Command, shall be exercised by the Commission.

9. The Provisional Council of Government of each State shall, not later than two months after the withdrawal of the armed forces of the mandatory Power, hold elections to the Constituent Assembly which shall be conducted on democratic lines.

The election regulations in each State shall be drawn up by the Provisional Council of Government and approved by the Commission. Qualified voters for each State for this election shall be persons over eighteen years of age who are: (*a*) Palestinian citizens residing in that State and (*b*) Arabs and Jews residing in the State, although not Palestinian citizens, who, before voting, have signed a notice of intention to become citizens of such State.

Arabs and Jews residing in the City of Jerusalem who have signed a notice of intention to become citizens, the Arabs of the Arab State and the Jews of the Jewish State, shall be entitled to vote in the Arab and Jewish States respectively.

Women may vote and be elected to the Constituent Assemblies.

During the transitional period no Jew shall be permitted to establish residence in the area of the proposed Arab State, and no Arab shall be permitted to establish residence in the area of the proposed Jewish State, except by special leave of the Commission.

10. The Constituent Assembly of each State shall draft a democratic constitution for its State and choose a provisional gov-

ernment to succeed the Provisional Council of Government appointed by the Commission. The constitutions of the States shall embody chapters 1 and 2 of the Declaration provided for in section C below and include *inter alia* provisions for:

(*a*) Establishing in each State a legislative body elected by universal suffrage and by secret ballot on the basis of proportional representation, and an executive body responsible to the legislature;

(*b*) Settling all international disputes in which the State may be involved by peaceful means in such a manner that international peace and security, and justice, are not endangered;

(*c*) Accepting the obligation of the State to refrain in its international relations from the threat or use of force against the territorial integrity or political independence of any State, or in any other manner inconsistent with the purposes of the United Nations;

(*d*) Guaranteeing to all persons equal and non-discriminatory rights in civil, political, economic and religious matters and the enjoyment of human rights and fundamental freedoms, including freedom of religion, language, speech and publication, education, assembly and association;

(*e*) Preserving freedom of transit and visit for all residents and citizens of the other State in Palestine and the City of Jerusalem, subject to considerations of national security, provided that each State shall control residence within its borders.

11. The Commission shall appoint a preparatory economic commission of three members to make whatever arrangements are possible for economic co-operation, with a view to establishing, as soon as practicable, the Economic Union and the Joint Economic Board, as provided in section D below.

12. During the period between the adoption of the recommendations on the question of Palestine by the General Assembly and the termination of the Mandate, the mandatory Power in Palestine shall maintain full responsibility for administration in areas from which it has not withdrawn its armed forces. The Commission shall assist the mandatory Power in the carrying out of these functions. Similarly the mandatory Power shall co-operate with the Commission in the execution of its functions.

13. With a view to ensuring that there shall be continuity in the functioning of administrative services and that, on the withdrawal of the armed forces of the mandatory Power, the whole administration shall be in the charge of the Provisional Councils and the Joint Economic Board, respectively, acting under the Commission; there shall be a progressive transfer, from the mandatory Power to the Commission, of responsibility for all the functions of government, including that of maintaining law and order in the areas from which the forces of the mandatory Power have been withdrawn.

14. The Commission shall be guided in its activities by the recommendations of the General Assembly and by such instructions as the Security Council may consider necessary to issue.

The measures taken by the Commission, within the recommendations of the General Assembly, shall become immediately effective unless the Commission has previously received contrary instructions from the Security Council.

The Commission shall render periodic monthly progress reports, or more frequently if desirable, to the Security Council.

15. The Commission shall make its final report to the next regular session of the General Assembly and to the Security Council simultaneously.

C. DECLARATION

A declaration shall be made to the United Nations by the provisional government of each proposed State before independence. It shall contain *inter alia* the following clauses:

General provision

The stipulations contained in the declaration are recognized as fundamental laws of the State and no law, regulation or official action shall conflict or interfere with these stipulations, nor shall any law, regulation or official action prevail over them.

Chapter 1

Holy Places, religious buildings and sites

1. Existing rights in respect of Holy Places and religious buildings or sites shall not be denied or impaired.

2. In so far as Holy Places are concerned, the liberty of access, visit and transit shall be guaranteed, in conformity with existing rights, to all residents and citizens of the other State and of the City of Jerusalem, as well as to aliens, without distinction as to nationality, subject to requirements of national security, public order and decorum.

Similarly, freedom of worship shall be guaranteed in conformity with existing rights, subject to the maintenance of public order and decorum.

3. Holy Places and religious buildings or sites shall be preserved. No act shall be permitted which may in any way impair their sacred character. If at any time it appears to the Government that any particular Holy Place, religious building or site is in need of urgent repair, the Government may call upon the community or communities concerned to carry out such repair. The Government may carry it out itself at the expense of the community or communities concerned if no action is taken within a reasonable time.

4. No taxation shall be levied in respect of any Holy Place, religious building or site which was exempt from taxation on the date of the creation of the State.

No change in the incidence of such taxation shall be made which would either discriminate between the owners or occupiers of Holy Places, religious buildings or sites, or would place such owners or occupiers in a position less favourable in relation to the general incidence of taxation than existed at the time of the adoption of the Assembly's recommendations.

5. The Governor of the City of Jerusalem shall have the right to determine whether the provisions of the Constitution of the State in relation to Holy Places, religious buildings and sites within the borders of the State and the religious rights appertaining thereto, are being properly applied and respected, and to make decisions on the basis of existing rights in cases of disputes which may arise between the different religious communities or the rites of a religious community with respect to such places, buildings and sites. He shall receive full co-operation and such privileges and immunities as are necessary for the exercise of his functions in the State.

Chapter 2

Religious and minority rights

1. Freedom of conscience and the free exercise of all forms of worship, subject only to the maintenance of public order and morals, shall be ensured to all.

2. No discrimination of any kind shall be made between the inhabitants on the ground of race, religion, language or sex.

3. All persons within the jurisdiction of the State shall be entitled to equal protection of the laws.

4. The family law and personal status of the various minorities and their religious interests, including endowments, shall be respected.

5. Except as may be required for the maintenance of public order and good government, no measure shall be taken to obstruct or interfere with the enterprise of religious or charitable bodies of all faiths or to discriminate against any representative or member of these bodies on the ground of his religion or nationality.

6. The State shall ensure adequate primary and secondary education for the Arab and Jewish minority respectively, in its own language and its cultural traditions.

The right of each community to maintain its own schools for the education of its own members in its own language, while conforming to such educational requirements of a general nature as the State may impose, shall not be denied or impaired. Foreign educational establishments shall continue their activity on the basis of their existing rights.

7. No restriction shall be imposed on the

free use by any citizen of the State of any language in private intercourse, in commerce, in religion, in the Press or in publications of any kind, or at public meetings.[1]

8. No expropriation of land owned by an Arab in the Jewish State (by a Jew in the Arab State) [2] shall be allowed except for public purposes. In all cases of expropriation full compensation as fixed by the Supreme Court shall be paid previous to dispossession.

Chapter 3

Citizenship, international conventions and financial obligations

1. *Citizenship.* Palestinian citizens residing in Palestine outside the City of Jerusalem, as well as Arabs and Jews who, not holding Palestinian citizenship, reside in Palestine outside the City of Jerusalem shall, upon the recognition of independence, become citizens of the State in which they are resident and enjoy full civil and political rights. Persons over the age of eighteen years may opt within one year from the date of recognition of independence of the State in which they reside for citizenship of the other State, providing that no Arab residing in the area of the proposed Arab State shall have the right to opt for citizenship in the proposed Jewish State and no Jew residing in the proposed Jewish State shall have the right to opt for citizenship in the proposed Arab State. The exercise of this right of option will be taken to include the wives and children under eighteen years of age of persons so opting.

Arabs residing in the area of the proposed Jewish State and Jews residing in the area of the proposed Arab State who have signed a notice of intention to opt for citizenship of the other State shall be eligible to vote in the elections to the Constituent Assembly of that State, but not in the elections to the Constituent Assembly of the State in which they reside.

2. *International conventions.* (*a*) The State shall be bound by all the international agreements and conventions, both general and special, to which Palestine has become a party. Subject to any right of denunciation provided for therein, such agreements and conventions shall be respected by the State throughout the period for which they were concluded.

(*b*) Any dispute about the applicability and continued validity of international conventions or treaties signed or adhered to by the mandatory Power on behalf of Palestine shall be referred to the International Court of Justice in accordance with the provisions of the Statute of the Court.

3. *Financial obligations.* (*a*) The State shall respect and fulfil all financial obligations of whatever nature assumed on behalf of Palestine by the mandatory Power during the exercise of the Mandate and recognized by the State. This provision includes the right of public servants to pensions, compensation or gratuities.

(*b*) These obligations shall be fulfilled through participation in the Joint Economic Board in respect of those obligations applicable to Palestine as a whole, and individually in respect of those applicable to, and fairly apportionable between, the States.

(*c*) A Court of Claims, affiliated with the Joint Economic Board, and composed of one member appointed by the United Nations, one representative of the United Kingdom and one representative of the State concerned, should be established. Any dispute between the United Kingdom and the State respecting claims not recognized by the latter should be referred to that Court.

(*d*) Commercial concessions granted in respect of any part of Palestine prior to the adoption of the resolution by the General Assembly shall continue to be valid according to their terms, unless modified by agree-

[1] The following stipulation shall be added to the declaration concerning the Jewish State: "In the Jewish State adequate facilities shall be given to Arabic-speaking citizens for the use of their language, either orally or in writing, in the legislature, before the Courts and in the administration."

[2] In the declaration concerning the Arab State, the words "by an Arab in the Jewish State" should be replaced by the words "by a Jew in the Arab State."

ment between the concession-holder and the State.

Chapter 4

Miscellaneous provisions

1. The provisions of chapters 1 and 2 of the declaration shall be under the guarantee of the United Nations, and no modifications shall be made in them without the assent of the General Assembly of the United Nations. Any Member of the United Nations shall have the right to bring to the attention of the General Assembly any infraction or danger of infraction of any of these stipulations, and the General Assembly may thereupon make such recommendations as it may deem proper in the circumstances.

2. Any dispute relating to the application or the interpretation of this declaration shall be referred, at the request of either party, to the International Court of Justice, unless the parties agree to another mode of settlement.

D. ECONOMIC UNION AND TRANSIT

1. The Provisional Council of Government of each State shall enter into an undertaking with respect to Economic Union and Transit. This undertaking shall be drafted by the Commission provided for in section B, paragraph 1, utilizing to the greatest possible extent the advice and co-operation of representative organizations and bodies from each of the proposed States. It shall contain provisions to establish the Economic Union of Palestine and provide for other matters of common interest. If by 1 April 1948 the Provisional Councils of Government have not entered into the undertaking, the undertaking shall be put into force by the Commission.

The Economic Union of Palestine

2. The objectives of the Economic Union of Palestine shall be:

(*a*) A customs union;

(*b*) A joint currency system providing for a single foreign exchange rate;

(*c*) Operation in the common interest on a non-discriminatory basis of railways; inter-State highways; postal, telephone and telegraphic services, and ports and airports involved in international trade and commerce;

(*d*) Joint economic development, especially in respect of irrigation, land reclamation and soil conservation;

(*e*) Access for both States and for the City of Jerusalem on a non-discriminatory basis to water and power facilities.

3. There shall be established a Joint Economic Board, which shall consist of three representatives of each of the two States and three foreign members appointed by the Economic and Social Council of the United Nations. The foreign members shall be appointed in the first instance for a term of three years; they shall serve as individuals and not as representatives of States.

4. The functions of the Joint Economic Board shall be to implement either directly or by delegation the measures necessary to realize the objectives of the Economic Union. It shall have all powers of organization and administration necessary to fulfil its functions.

5. The States shall bind themselves to put into effect the decisions of the Joint Economic Board. The Board's decisions shall be taken by a majority vote.

6. In the event of failure of a State to take the necessary action the Board may, by a vote of six members, decide to withhold an appropriate portion of that part of the customs revenue to which the State in question is entitled under the Economic Union. Should the State persist in its failure to co-operate, the Board may decide by a simple majority vote upon such further sanctions, including disposition of funds which it has withheld, as it may deem appropriate.

7. In relation to economic development, the functions of the Board shall be the planning, investigation and encouragement of joint development projects, but it shall not undertake such projects except with the assent of both States and the City of Jerusalem, in the event that Jerusalem is directly involved in the development project.

8. In regard to the joint currency system the currencies circulating in the two States and the City of Jerusalem shall be

issued under the authority of the Joint Economic Board, which shall be the sole issuing authority and which shall determine the reserves to be held against such currencies.

9. So far as is consistent with paragraph 2 (*b*) above, each State may operate its own central bank, control its own fiscal and credit policy, its foreign exchange receipts and expenditures, the grant of import licenses, and may conduct international financial operations on its own faith and credit. During the first two years after the termination of the Mandate, the Joint Economic Board shall have the authority to take such measures as may be necessary to ensure that—to the extent that the total foreign exchange revenues of the two States from the export of goods and services permit, and provided that each State takes appropriate measures to conserve its own foreign exchange resources—each State shall have available, in any twelve months' period, foreign exchange sufficient to assure the supply of quantities of imported goods and services for consumption in its territory equivalent to the quantities of such goods and services consumed in that territory in the twelve months' period ending 31 December 1947.

10. All economic authority not specifically vested in the Joint Economic Board is reserved to each State.

11. There shall be a common customs tariff with complete freedom of trade between the States, and between the States and the City of Jerusalem.

12. The tariff schedules shall be drawn up by a Tariff Commission, consisting of representatives of each of the States in equal numbers, and shall be submitted to the Joint Economic Board for approval by a majority vote. In case of disagreement in the Tariff Commission, the Joint Economic Board shall arbitrate the points of difference. In the event that the Tariff Commission fails to draw up any schedule by a date to be fixed, the Joint Economic Board shall determine the tariff schedule.

13. The following items shall be a first charge on the customs and other common revenue of the Joint Economic Board:

(*a*) The expenses of the customs service and of the operation of the joint services;

(*b*) The administrative expenses of the Joint Economic Board;

(*c*) The financial obligations of the Administration of Palestine consisting of:

(i) The service of the outstanding public debt;

(ii) The cost of superannuation benefits, now being paid or falling due in the future, in accordance with the rules and to the extent established by paragraph 3 of chapter 3 above.

14. After these obligations have been met in full, the surplus revenue from the customs and other common services shall be divided in the following manner: not less than 5 per cent and not more than 10 per cent to the City of Jerusalem; the residue shall be allocated to each State by the Joint Economic Board equitably, with the objective of maintaining a sufficient and suitable level of government and social services in each State, except that the share of either State shall not exceed the amount of that State's contribution to the revenues of the Economic Union by more than approximately four million pounds in any year. The amount granted may be adjusted by the Board according to the price level in relation to the prices prevailing at the time of the establishment of the Union. After five years, the principles of the distribution of the joint revenues may be revised by the Joint Economic Board on a basis of equity.

15. All international conventions and treaties affecting customs tariff rates, and those communications services under the jurisdiction of the Joint Economic Board, shall be entered into by both States. In these matters, the two States shall be bound to act in accordance with the majority vote of the Joint Economic Board.

16. The Joint Economic Board shall endeavour to secure for Palestine's exports fair and equal access to world markets.

17. All enterprises operated by the Joint Economic Board shall pay fair wages on a uniform basis.

Freedom of transit and visit

18. The undertaking shall contain provisions preserving freedom of transit and visit for all residents or citizens of both States and of the City of Jerusalem, subject to security considerations; provided that each State and the city shall control residence within its borders.

Termination, modification and interpretation of the undertaking

19. The undertaking and any treaty issuing therefrom shall remain in force for a period of ten years. It shall continue in force until notice of termination, to take effect two years thereafter, is given by either of the parties.

20. During the initial ten-year period, the undertaking and any treaty issuing therefrom may not be modified except by consent of both parties and with the approval of the General Assembly.

21. Any dispute relating to the application or the interpretation of the undertaking and any treaty issuing therefrom shall be referred, at the request of either party, to the International Court of Justice, unless the parties agree to another mode of settlement.

E. ASSETS

1. The movable assets of the Administration of Palestine shall be allocated to the Arab and Jewish States and the City of Jerusalem on an equitable basis. Allocations should be made by the United Nations Commission referred to in section B, paragraph 1, above. Immovable assets shall become the property of the government of the territory in which they are situated.

2. During the period between the appointment of the United Nations Commission and the termination of the Mandate, the mandatory Power shall, except in respect of ordinary operations, consult with the Commission on any measure which it may contemplate involving the liquidation, disposal or encumbering of the assets of the Palestine Government, such as the accumulated treasury surplus, the proceeds of Government bond issues, State lands or any other asset.

F. ADMISSION TO MEMBERSHIP IN THE UNITED NATIONS

When the independence of either the Arab or the Jewish State as envisaged in this plan has become effective and the declaration and undertaking, as envisaged in this plan, have been signed by either of them, sympathetic consideration should be given to its application for admission to membership in the United Nations in accordance with Article 4 of the Charter of the United Nations.

PART II. BOUNDARIES [1]

A. THE ARAB STATE

The area of the Arab State in Western Galilee is bounded on the west by the Mediterranean and on the north by the frontier of the Lebanon from Ras en Naqura to a point north of Saliha. From there the boundary proceeds southwards, leaving the built-up area of Saliha in the Arab State, to join the southernmost point of this village. Thence it follows the western boundary line of the villages of 'Alma, Rihaniya and Teitaba, thence following the northern boundary line of Meirun village to join the Acre-Safad sub-district boundary line. It follows this line to a point west of Es Sammu'i village and joins it again at the northernmost point of Farradiya. Thence it follows the sub-district boundary line to the Acre-Safad main road. From here it follows the western boundary of Kafr I'nan village until it reaches the Tiberias-Acre sub-district boundary line, passing to the west of the junction of the Acre-Safad and Lubiya-Kafr I'nan roads. From the south-west corner of Kafr I'nan village the boundary line follows the western boundary of the Tiberias sub-district to a point close to the boundary line between the villages of Maghar and Eilabun, thence bulging out to the west to include as much of the eastern part of the plain of Battuf as is necessary for the reservoir proposed by the Jewish

[1] The boundary lines described in part II are indicated in Annex A. The base map used in marking and describing this boundary is "Palestine 1:250,000" published by the Survey of Palestine, 1946. [Map omitted.]

Agency for the irrigation of lands to the south and east.

The boundary rejoins the Tiberias sub-district boundary at a point on the Nazareth-Tiberias road southeast of the built-up area of Tur'an; thence it runs southwards, at first following the sub-district boundary and then passing between the Kadoorie Agricultural School and Mount Tabor, to a point due south at the base of Mount Tabor. From here it runs due west, parallel to the horizontal grid line 230, to the north-east corner of the village lands of Tel Adashim. It then runs to the north-west corner of these lands, whence it turns south and west so as to include in the Arab State the sources of the Nazareth water supply in Yafa village. On reaching Ginneiger it follows the eastern, northern and western boundaries of the lands of this village to their south-west corner, whence it proceeds in a straight line to a point on the Haifa-Afula railway on the boundary between the villages of Sarid and El Mujeidil. This is the point of intersection.

The south-western boundary of the area of the Arab State in Galilee takes a line from this point, passing northwards along the eastern boundaries of Sarid and Gevat to the north-eastern corner of Nahalal, proceeding thence across the land of Kefar ha Horesh to a central point on the southern boundary of the village of 'Ilut, thence westwards along that village boundary to the eastern boundary of Beit Lahm, thence northwards and north-eastwards along its western boundary to the north-eastern corner of Waldheim and thence north-westwards across the village lands of Shafa 'Amr to the south-eastern corner of Ramat Yohanan. From here it runs due north-north-east to a point on the Shafa 'Amr-Haifa road, west of its junction with the road to I'Billin. From there it proceeds north-east to a point on the southern boundary of I'Billin situated to the west of the I'Billin-Birwa road. Thence along that boundary to its westernmost point, whence it turns to the north, follows across the village land of Tamra to the north-westernmost corner and along the western boundary of Julis until it reaches the Acre-Safad road. It then runs westwards along the southern side of the Safad-Acre road to the Galilee-Haifa District boundary, from which point it follows that boundary to the sea.

The boundary of the hill country of Samaria and Judea starts on the Jordan River at the Wadi Malih southeast of Beisan and runs due west to meet the Beisan-Jericho road and then follows the western side of that road in a north-westerly direction to the junction of the boundaries of the sub-districts of Beisan, Nablus, and Jenin. From that point it follows the Nablus-Jenin sub-district boundary westwards for a distance of about three kilometres and then turns north-westwards, passing to the east of the built-up areas of the villages of Jalbun and Faqqu'a, to the boundary of the sub-districts of Jenin and Beisan at a point north-east of Nuris. Thence it proceeds first northwestwards to a point due north of the built-up area of Zir'in and then westwards to the Afula-Jenin railway, thence northwestwards along the district boundary line to the point of intersection on the Hejaz railway. From here the boundary runs south-westwards, including the built-up area and some of the land of the village of Kh.Lid in the Arab State to cross the Haifa-Jenin road at a point on the district boundary between Haifa and Samaria west of El Mansi. It follows this boundary to the southernmost point of the village of El Buteimat. From here it follows the northern and eastern boundaries of the village of Ar'ara, rejoining the Haifa-Samaria district boundary at Wadi'Ara, and thence proceeding south-south-westwards in an approximately straight line joining up with the western boundary of Qaqun to a point east of the railway line on the eastern boundary of Qaqun village. From here it runs along the railway line some distance to the east of it to a point just east of the Tulkarm railway station. Thence the boundary follows a line half-way between the railway and the Tulkarm-Qalqiliya-Jaljuliya and Ras el Ein road to a point just east of Ras el Ein station, whence it proceeds along the railway some distance to the east of it to the point on the railway line south of the junction of the Haifa-Lydda and Beit Nabala lines, whence it proceeds along the southern border of Lydda airport to its south-west corner, thence in a south-westerly direction to a point just west of the built-up area of Sarafand el 'Amar, whence it turns south, passing just to the west of the built-up area of Abu el Fadil to the northeast corner of the lands of Beer Ya'Aqov. (The boundary line should be so demarcated as to allow direct access from the Arab State to the airport.) Thence the boundary line follows the western and southern boundaries of Ramle village, to the north-east corner of El Na'ana village, thence in a straight line to the southernmost point of El Barriya, along the eastern boundary of that village and the southern boundary of 'Innaba village. Thence it turns north to follow the southern side of the Jaffa-Jerusalem road until El Qubab, whence it follows the road to the boundary of Abu Shusha. It runs along the eastern boundaries of Abu Shusha, Seidun, Hulda to the southernmost point of Hulda, thence westwards in a straight line to the north-eastern corner of Umm Kalkha, thence following the northern boundaries of Umm Kalkha, Qazaza and the northern and western boundaries of Mukhezin to the Gaza district boundary and thence runs across the village lands of El Mismiya, El Kabira, and Yasur to the southern point of intersection, which is midway between the built-up areas of Yasur and Batani Sharqi.

From the southern point of intersection the boundary lines run north-westwards between the villages of Gan Yavne and Barqa to the sea at a point half way between Nabi Yunis and Minat el Qila, and south-eastwards to a point west of Qastina, whence it turns in a south-westerly direction, passing to the east of the built-up areas of Es Sawafir, Esh Sharqiya and Ibdis. From the south-east corner of the Ibdis village it runs to a point south-west of the built-up area of Beit 'Affa, crossing the Hebron-El Majdal road just to the west of the built-up area of Iraq Suweidan. Thence it proceeds southwards along the western village boundary of El Faluja to the Beersheba sub-district boundary. It then runs across the tribal lands of 'Arab el Jubarat to a point on the boundary between the sub-districts of Beersheba and Hebron north of Kh. Khuweilifa, whence it proceeds in a south-westerly direction to a point on the Beersheba-Gaza main road two kilometres to the north-west of the town. It then turns south-eastwards to reach Wadi Sab' at a point situated one kilometre to the west of it. From here it turns north-eastwards and proceeds along Wadi Sab' and along the Beersheba-Hebron road for a distance of one kilometre, whence it turns eastwards and runs in a straight line to Kh. Kuseifa to join the Beersheba-Hebron sub-district boundary. It then follows the Beersheba-Hebron boundary eastwards to a point north of Ras Ez Zuweira, only departing from it so as to cut across the base of the indentation between vertical grid lines 150 and 160.

About five kilometres north-east of Ras ez Zuweira it turns north, excluding from the Arab State a strip along the coast of the Dead Sea not more than seven kilometres in depth, as far as Ein Geddi, whence it turns due east to join the Transjordan frontier in the Dead Sea.

The northern boundary of the Arab section of the coastal plain runs from a point between Minat el Qila and Nabi Yunis, passing between the built-up areas of Gan Yavne and Barqa to the point of intersection. From here it turns south-westwards, running across the lands of Batani Sharqi, along the eastern boundary of the lands of Beit Daras and across the lands of Julis, leaving the built-up areas of Batani Sharqi and Julis to the westwards, as far as the north-west corner of the lands of Beit Tima. Thence it runs east of El Jiya across the village lands of El Barbara along the eastern boundaries of the villages of Beit Jirja, Deir Suneid and Dimra. From the south-east corner of Dimra the boundary passes across the lands of Beit Hanun, leaving the Jewish lands of Nir-Am to the eastwards. From the southeast corner of Beit Hanun the line runs south-west to a point south of the parallel grid line 100, then turns north-west for two kilometres, turning again in a south-westerly direction and continuing in an almost straight line to the north-west corner of the village lands of Kirbet Ikhza'a. From there it follows the boundary line of this village to its southernmost point. It then runs in a southerly direction along the vertical grid line 90 to its junction with the horizontal grid line 70. It then turns south-eastwards to Kh. el Ruheiba and then proceeds in a southerly direction to a point known as El Baha, beyond which it crosses the Beersheba-El 'Auja main road to the west of Kh. el Mushrifa. From there it joins Wadi El Zaiyatin just to the west of El Subeita. From there it turns to the north-east and then to the south-east following this wadi and passes to the east of 'Abda to join Wadi Nafkh. It then bulges to the south-west along Wadi Nafkh, Wadi Ajrim and Wadi Lassan to the point where Wadi Lassan crosses the Egyptian frontier.

The area of the Arab enclave of Jaffa consists of that part of the town-planning area of Jaffa which lies to the west of the Jewish quarters lying south of Tel-Aviv, to the west of the continuation of Herzl street up to its junction with the Jaffa-Jerusalem road, to the south-west of the section of the Jaffa-Jerusalem road lying south-east of that junction, to the west of Miqve Yisrael lands, to the north-west of Holon local council, to the north of the line linking up the north-west corner of Holon with the north-east corner of Bat Yam local council area and to the north of Bat Yam local council area. The question of Karton quarter will be decided by the Boundary Commission, bearing in mind among other considerations the desirability of including the smallest possible number of its Arab inhabitants and the largest possible number of its Jewish inhabitants in the Jewish State.

B. THE JEWISH STATE

The north-eastern sector of the Jewish State (Eastern Galilee) is bounded on the north and west by the Lebanese frontier and on the east by the frontiers of Syria and Transjordan. It includes the whole of the Hula Basin, Lake Tiberias, the whole of the Beisan sub-district, the boundary line being extended to the crest of the Gilboa mountains and the Wadi Malih. From there the Jewish State extends north-west, following the boundary described in respect of the Arab State.

The Jewish section of the coastal plain extends from a point between Minat et Qila and Nabi Yunis in the Gaza sub-district and includes the towns of Haifa and Tel-Aviv, leaving Jaffa as an enclave of the Arab State. The eastern frontier of the Jewish State follows the boundary described in respect of the Arab State.

The Beersheba area comprises the whole of the Beersheba sub-district, including the Negeb and the eastern part of the Gaza sub-district, but excluding the town of Beersheba and those areas described in respect of the Arab State. It includes also a strip of land along the Dead Sea stretching from the Beersheba-Hebron sub-district boundary line to Ein Geddi, as described in respect of the Arab State.

C. THE CITY OF JERUSALEM

The boundaries of the City of Jerusalem are as defined in the recommendations on the City of Jerusalem. (See Part III, Section B, below).

PART III. CITY OF JERUSALEM

A. SPECIAL REGIME

The City of Jerusalem shall be established as a *corpus separatum* under a special international regime and shall be administered by the United Nations. The Trusteeship Council shall be designated to discharge the responsibilities of the Administering Authority on behalf of the United Nations.

B. BOUNDARIES OF THE CITY

The City of Jerusalem shall include the present municipality of Jerusalem plus the surrounding villages and towns, the most eastern of which shall be Abu Dis; the most southern, Bethelehem; the most western, Ein Karim (including also the built-up area of Motsa); and the most northern Shu'fat, as indicated on the attached sketch-map (annex B).

C. STATUTE OF THE CITY

The Trusteeship Council shall, within five months of the approval of the present plan, elaborate and approve a detailed Statute of the City which shall contain *inter alia* the substance of the following provisions:

1. *Government machinery; special objectives.* The Administering Authority in discharging its administrative obligations shall pursue the following special objectives:

(*a*) To protect and to preserve the unique spiritual and religious interests located in the city of the three great monotheistic faiths throughout the world, Christian, Jewish and Moslem; to this end to ensure that order and peace, and especially religious peace, reign in Jerusalem.

(*b*) To foster co-operation among all the inhabitants of the city in their own interests as well as in order to encourage and support the peaceful development of the mutual relations between the two Palestinian peoples throughout the Holy Land; to promote the security, well-being and any constructive measures of development of the residents, having regard to the special circumstances and customs of the various peoples and communities.

2. *Governor and administrative staff.* A Governor of the City of Jerusalem shall be appointed by the Trusteeship Council and shall be responsible to it. He shall be selected on the basis of special qualifications and without regard to nationality. He shall not, however, be a citizen of either State in Palestine.

The Governor shall represent the United Nations in the City and shall exercise on their behalf all powers of administration, including the conduct of external affairs. He shall be assisted by an administrative staff classed as international officers in the meaning of Article 100 of the Charter and chosen whenever practicable from the residents of the city and of the rest of Palestine on a non-discriminatory basis. A detailed plan for the organization of the administration of the city shall be submitted by the Governor to the Trusteeship Council and duly approved by it.

3. *Local autonomy.* (*a*) The existing local autonomous units in the territory of the city (villages, townships and municipalities) shall enjoy wide powers of local government and administration.

(*b*) The Governor shall study and submit for the consideration and decision of the Trusteeship Council a plan for the establishment of special town units consisting, respectively, of the Jewish and Arab sections of new Jerusalem. The new town units shall continue to form part of the present municipality of Jerusalem.

4. *Security measures.* (*a*) The City of Jerusalem shall be demilitarized; its neutrality shall be declared and preserved, and no para-military formations, exercises or activities shall be permitted within its borders.

(*b*) Should the administration of the City of Jerusalem be seriously obstructed or prevented by the non-co-operation or interference of one or more sections of the population, the Governor shall have authority to take such measures as may be necessary to restore the effective functioning of the administration.

(*c*) To assist in the maintenance of internal law and order and especially for the protection of the Holy Places and religious buildings and sites in the city, the Governor shall organize a special police force of adequate strength, the members of which shall be recruited outside of Palestine. The Governor shall be empowered to direct such budgetary provision as may be necessary for the maintenance of this force.

5. *Legislative organization.* A Legislative Council, elected by adult residents of the city irrespective of nationality on the basis of universal and secret suffrage and proportional representation, shall have powers of legislation and taxation. No legislative measures shall, however, conflict or interfere with the provisions which will be set forth in the Statute of the City, nor shall any law, regulation, or official action prevail over them. The Statute shall grant to the Governor a right of vetoing bills inconsistent with the provisions referred to in

the preceding sentence. It shall also empower him to promulgate temporary ordinances in case the Council fails to adopt in time a bill deemed essential to the normal functioning of the administration.

6. *Administration of justice.* The Statute shall provide for the establishment of an independent judiciary system, including a court of appeal. All the inhabitants of the City shall be subject to it.

7. *Economic union and economic regime.* The City of Jerusalem shall be included in the Economic Union of Palestine and be bound by all stipulations of the undertaking and of any treaties issued therefrom, as well as by the decisions of the Joint Economic Board. The headquarters of the Economic Board shall be established in the territory of the City.

The Statute shall provide for the regulation of economic matters not falling within the regime of the Economic Union, on the basis of equal treatment and non-discrimination for all Members of the United Nations and their nationals.

8. *Freedom of transit and visit; control of residents.* Subject to considerations of security, and of economic welfare as determined by the Governor under the directions of the Trusteeship Council, freedom of entry into, and residence within, the borders of the City shall be guaranteed for the residents or citizens of the Arab and Jewish States. Immigration into, and residence within, the borders of the city for nationals of other States shall be controlled by the Governor under the directions of the Trusteeship Council.

9. *Relations with the Arab and Jewish States.* Representatives of the Arab and Jewish States shall be accredited to the Governor of the City and charged with the protection of the interests of their States and nationals in connexion with the international administration of the City.

10. *Official languages.* Arabic and Hebrew shall be the official languages of the city. This will not preclude the adoption of one or more additional working languages, as may be required.

11. *Citizenship.* All the residents shall become *ipso facto* citizens of the City of Jerusalem unless they opt for citizenship of the State of which they have been citizens or, if Arabs or Jews, have filed notice of intention to become citizens of the Arab or Jewish State respectively, according to part I, section B, paragraph 9, of this plan.

The Trusteeship Council shall make arrangements for consular protection of the citizens of the City outside its territory.

12. *Freedoms of citizens.* (*a*) Subject only to the requirements of public order and morals, the inhabitants of the City shall be ensured the enjoyment of human rights and fundamental freedoms, including freedom of conscience, religion and worship, language, education, speech and Press, assembly and association, and petition.

(*b*) No discrimination of any kind shall be made between the inhabitants on the grounds of race, religion, language or sex.

(*c*) All persons within the City shall be entitled to equal protection of the laws.

(*d*) The family law and personal status of the various persons and communities and their religious interests, including endowments, shall be respected.

(*e*) Except as may be required for the maintenance of public order and good government, no measures shall be taken to obstruct or interfere with the enterprise of religious or charitable bodies of all faiths or to discriminate against any representative or member of these bodies on the ground of his religion or nationality.

(*f*) The City shall ensure adequate primary and secondary education for the Arab and Jewish communities respectively, in their own languages and in accordance with their cultural traditions.

The right of each community to maintain its own schools for the education of its own members in its own language, while conforming to such educational requirements of a general nature as the City may impose, shall not be denied or impaired. Foreign educational establishments shall continue their activity on the basis of their existing rights.

(*g*) No restriction shall be imposed on the free use by any inhabitant of the City of any language in private intercourse, in commerce, in religion, in the Press or in publications of any kind, or at public meetings.

13. *Holy Places.* (*a*) Existing rights in respect of Holy Places and religious buildings or sites shall not be denied or impaired.

(*b*) Free access to the Holy Places and religious buildings or sites and the free exercise of worship shall be secured in conformity with existing rights and subject to the requirements of public order and decorum.

(*c*) Holy Places and religious buildings or sites shall be preserved. No act shall be permitted which may in any way impair their sacred character. If at any time it appears to the Governor that any particular Holy Place, religious building or site is in need of urgent repair, the Governor may call upon the community or communities concerned to carry out such repairs. The Governor may carry it out himself at the expense of the community or communities concerned if no action is taken within a reasonable time.

(*d*) No taxation shall be levied in respect of any Holy Place, religious building or site which was exempt from taxation on the date of the creation of the City. No change in the incidence of such taxation shall be made which would either discriminate between the owners or occupiers of Holy Places, religious buildings or sites, or would place such owners or occupiers in a position less favourable in relation to the general incidence of taxation than existed at the time of the adoption of the Assembly's recommendations.

14. *Special powers of the Governor in respect of the Holy Places, religious buildings and sites in the City and in any part of Palestine.* (*a*) The protection of the Holy Places, religious buildings and sites located in the City of Jerusalem shall be a special concern of the Governor.

(*b*) With relation to such places, buildings and sites in Palestine outside the city, the Governor shall determine on the ground of powers granted to him by the Constitutions of both States whether the provisions of the Constitutions of the Arab and Jewish States in Palestine dealing therewith and the religious rights appertaining thereto are being properly applied and respected.

(*c*) The Governor shall also be empowered to make decisions on the basis of existing rights in cases of disputes which may arise between the different religious communities or the rights of a religious community in respect of the Holy Places, religious buildings and sites in any part of Palestine.

In this task he may be assisted by a consultative council of representatives of different denominations acting in an advisory capacity.

D. DURATION OF THE SPECIAL REGIME

The Statute elaborated by the Trusteeship Council on the aforementioned principles shall come into force not later than 1 October 1948. It shall remain in force in the first instance for a period of ten years, unless the Trusteeship Council finds it necessary to undertake a re-examination of these provisions at an earlier date. After the expiration of this period the whole scheme shall be subject to re-examination by the Trusteeship Council in the light of the experience acquired with its functioning. The residents of the City shall be then free to express by means of a referendum their wishes as to possible modifications of the regime of the City.

PART IV. CAPITULATIONS

States whose nationals have in the past enjoyed in Palestine the privileges and immunities of foreigners, including the benefits of consular jurisdiction and protection, as formerly enjoyed by capitulation or usage in the Ottoman Empire, are invited to renounce any right pertaining to them to the reestablishment of such privileges and immunities in the proposed Arab and Jewish States and the City of Jerusalem.

89. TREATY OF ALLIANCE: BRITAIN AND TRANSJORDAN
15 March 1948

(Ratifications exchanged, London, 30 April 1948)

[Great Britain, *Parliamentary Papers, 1948,* Treaty Series No. 26, Cmd. 7404]

The Labor government in London, soon after embarking on its career in July 1945, recognized that the British defense system in the Near and Middle East required adjustment to postwar realities. The scope and quality of accommodation that the Attlee Cabinet sought were disclosed, in part, in the abortive treaties of alliance with Egypt (Doc. 84) and Iraq (text in *Parliamentary Papers, 1948,* Iraq No. 1, Cmd. 7309). Iraq repudiated the second instrument, signed at Portsmouth on 15 January 1948, before the month was out because of vehement nationalist demonstrations. Under the stillborn instruments Britain would have surrendered its permanent bases. In time of peace, joint Anglo-Egyptian and Anglo-Iraqi defense boards would have been charged with coordinating the military planning of the signatory states, and, in time of war or threat of war, England would have enjoyed the use of bases in the two Arab lands. Meanwhile, on the eve of the termination of the mandate in Transjordan in 1946, England obtained from Amir 'Abdallah a 25-year preferential alliance (text in *Parliamentary Papers, 1946,* Treaty Series No. 32, Cmd. 6916) on the pattern of the prewar models in the Arab East. However, owing to the cool reception in the Arab League states of the 1946 treaty, the United Kingdom agreed to bring the terms of the alliance into line with the arrangements it was seeking in Egypt and Iraq. The Anglo-Transjordan treaty of 1948, signed in 'Amman, was, with the necessary changes, identical in phraseology with the rejected Anglo-Iraqi instrument. Omitted below are the exchanges of notes. E. Wright, "Abdallah's Jordan: 1947–1951," *The Middle East Journal,* 5 (Autumn 1951), 439–60; Royal Institute of International Affairs, *The Middle East, A Political and Economic Survey,* chap. 7; M. Khadduri, *Independent Iraq,* chap. 12; S. H. Longrigg, *Iraq 1900 to 1950,* chap. 10.

ART. 1. There shall be perpetual peace and friendship between His Britannic Majesty and His Majesty the King of the Hashimite Kingdom of Transjordan.

A close alliance shall continue between the High Contracting Parties in consecration of their friendship, their cordial understanding and their good relations.

Each of the High Contracting Parties undertakes not to adopt in regard to foreign countries an attitude, which is inconsistent with the Alliance or might create difficulties for the other party thereto.

ART. 2. Should any dispute between either High Contracting Party and a third State produce a situation which would involve the risk of a rupture with that State, the High Contracting Parties will concert together with a view to the settlement of the said dispute by peaceful means in accordance with the provisions of the Charter of the United Nations and of any other international obligations which may be applicable to the case.

ART. 3. Should either High Contracting Party notwithstanding the provisions of Article 2 become engaged in war, the other High Contracting Party will, subject always to the provisions of Article 4 immediately come to his aid as a measure of collective defence.

In the event of an imminent menace of hostilities the High Contracting Parties will immediately concert together the necessary measures of defence.

ART. 4. Nothing in the present Treaty is intended to, or shall in any way prejudice the rights and obligations which devolve, or may devolve, upon either of the High Contracting Parties under the Charter of the United Nations or under any other existing international agreements, conventions or treaties.

ART. 5. The present Treaty of which the Annex is an integral part shall replace the Treaty of Alliance signed in London on 22nd March, 1946, of the Christian Era, together with its Annex and all Letters and Notes, interpreting or otherwise exchanged in 1946 in connexion therewith, provided however that Article 9 of the said Treaty shall remain in force in accordance with and as modified by the notes exchanged on this day on this subject.

ART. 6. Should any difference arise relative to the application or interpretation of the present Treaty and should the High Contracting Parties fail to settle such difference by direct negotiations, it shall be referred to the International Court of Justice unless the parties agree to another mode of settlement.

ART. 7. The present Treaty shall be ratified and shall come into force upon the exchange of instruments of ratification which shall take place in London as soon as possible. It shall remain in force for a period of 20 years from the date of its coming into force. At any time after 15 years from the date of the coming into force of the present Treaty, the High Contracting Parties will at the request of either of them, negotiate a revised Treaty which shall provide for the continued co-operation of the High Contracting Parties in the defence of their common interests. The period of 15 years shall be reduced if a complete system of security agreements under Article 43 of the Charter of the United Nations is concluded before the expiry of this period. At the end of 20 years, if the present Treaty has not been revised, it shall remain in force until the expiry of one year after notice of termination has been given by either High Contracting Party to the other through the diplomatic channel.

ANNEX

ART. 1. (*a*) The High Contracting Parties recognise that, in the common interests of both, each of them must be in a position to discharge his obligations under Article 3 of the Treaty.

(*b*) In the event of either High Contracting Party becoming engaged in war, or of a menace of hostilities, each High Contracting Party will invite the other to bring to his territory or territory controlled by him the necessary forces of all arms. Each will furnish to the other all the facilities and assistance in his power, including the use of all means and lines of communication, and on financial terms to be agreed upon.

(*c*) His Majesty the King of the Hashimite Kingdom of Transjordan will safeguard, maintain and develop as necessary the airfields, ports, roads and other means and lines of communication in and across the Hashimite Kingdom of Transjordan as may be required for the purposes of the present Treaty and its annex and will call upon His Britannic Majesty's assistance as may be required for this purpose.

(*d*) Until such time as the High Contracting Parties agree that the state of world security renders such measures unnecessary, His Majesty the King of the Hashimite Kingdom of Transjordan invites His Britannic Majesty to maintain units of the Royal Air Force at Amman and Mafrak airfields. His Majesty the King of the Hashimite Kingdom of Transjordan will provide all the necessary facilities for the accommodation and maintenance of the units mentioned in this paragraph, including facilities for the storage of their ammunition and supplies and the lease of any land required.

ART. 2. In the common defence interests of the High Contracting Parties a permanent joint advisory body will be set up immediately on the coming into force of the present Treaty to co-ordinate defence matters between the Governments of the High Contracting Parties within the scope of the present Treaty.

This body, which will be known as the Anglo-Transjordan Joint Defence Board, will be composed of competent military representatives of the Governments of the High Contracting Parties in equal numbers, and its functions will include:—

(*a*) The formulation of agreed plans in the strategic interests common to both countries.

(*b*) Immediate consultation in the event of any threat of war.

(*c*) The co-ordination of measures to enable the forces of either High Contracting Party to fulfil their obligations under Article 3 of the present Treaty and in particular measures for the safeguarding, maintenance and development of the airfields, ports and lines of communication referred to in Article 1 (*c*) of this Annex.

(*d*) Consultation regarding training and the provision of equipment. The Joint Defence Board shall submit annual reports thereon and recommendations to the Governments of the two High Contracting Parties.

(*e*) Arrangements regarding the joint training operations referred to in Article 6 of this Annex.

(*f*) The consideration of and if necessary recommendation for the location of His Britannic Majesty's forces at places in Transjordan other than those provided for in Article 1 (*d*) of this Annex.

ART. 3. His Britannic Majesty will reimburse to His Majesty the King of the Hashimite Kingdom of Transjordan all expenditure which the Government of the Hashimite Kingdom of Transjordan may incur in connexion with the provision of facilities under Article 1 (*c*) and (*d*) of the present Annex and will repair or pay compensation for any damage due to the actions of members of His Britannic Majesty's armed forces, other than damage caused in military operations undertaken in accordance with Article 3 of the present Treaty.

ART. 4. His Majesty the King of the Hashimite Kingdom of Transjordan agrees to afford on request all necessary facilities for the movement of units of His Britannic Majesty's forces in transit across the Hashimite Kingdom of Transjordan, with their supplies and equipment, on the same financial terms as those applicable to the forces of His Majesty the King of the Hashimite Kingdom of Transjordan.

ART. 5. Pending the conclusion of an agreement between the High Contracting Parties defining in detail the jurisdictional and fiscal immunities of members of the forces of His Britannic Majesty in the Hashimite Kingdom of Transjordan, they will continue to enjoy the immunities which are accorded to them at present, including the provision that, in accordance with the established principles of international law governing the immunities of Sovereigns and sovereign States, no demand will be made for the payment by His Britannic Majesty of any Transjordan taxation in respect of immovable property leased or owned by His Britannic Majesty or in respect of his movable property, including customs duty on goods imported or exported by or on behalf of His Britannic Majesty. The privileges and immunities to be extended to the units and personnel of the armed forces of His Majesty the King of the Hashimite Kingdom of Transjordan visiting or present in British territory shall be defined in similar agreements on a reciprocal basis.

ART. 6. In order that the armed forces of the High Contracting Parties should attain the necessary efficiency in co-operation with each other and in view of the desirability of establishing identity between the training and methods employed by the Transjordan and British forces respectively:—

(1) His Britannic Majesty offers appropriate facilities in the United Kingdom and in any British colony or protectorate administered by the Government of the United Kingdom for the training of the armed forces of His Majesty the King of the Hashimite Kingdom of Transjordan.

(2) His Britannic Majesty will make available operational units of his armed forces to engage in joint training operations with the armed forces of His Majesty the King of the Hashimite Kingdom of Transjordan for a sufficient period in each year.

(3) His Majesty the King of the Hashimite Kingdom of Transjordan agrees to make available facilities in the Hashimite Kingdom of Transjordan for the purposes of this joint training.

(4) His Britannic Majesty will provide on request any British service personnel whose services are required to ensure the efficiency of the military units of the forces of the King of the Hashimite Kingdom of Transjordan.

(5) His Britannic Majesty will (*a*) afford all possible facilities to His Majesty the King of the Hashimite Kingdom of Transjordan for the military instruction of

Transjordan officers at schools of instruction maintained for His Britannic Majesty's forces, and (*b*) provide arms, ammunition, equipment and aircraft and other war material for the forces of His Majesty the King of the Hashimite Kingdom of Transjordan.

(6) His Majesty the King of the Hashimite Kingdom of Transjordan will (*a*) meet the cost of instruction and equipment referred to in paragraph 5 (*a*) and (*b*) above, (*b*) ensure that the armament and essential equipment of his forces shall not differ in type from those of the forces of His Britannic Majesty, (*c*) send any personnel of his forces, that may be sent abroad for training, to military schools, colleges and training centres maintained for His Britannic Majesty's forces.

ART. 7. His Majesty the King of the Hashimite Kingdom of Transjordan gives permission for ships of His Britannic Majesty's Navy to visit the ports of the Hashimite Kingdom of Transjordan at any time upon giving notification to the Government of the Hashimite Kingdom of Transjordan.

90. EGYPTIAN-ISRAEL ARMISTICE AGREEMENT
24 February 1949

[United Nations, Security Council, *Official Records,* 4th year, spec. suppl. No. 3]

"The recent disturbances in Palestine . . . constitute a serious and direct threat to peace and security within the territories of the Arab states themselves," the Arab League Secretary-General, ʻAbd-al-Rahman Pasha ʻAzzam, notified the UN Secretary-General on 15 May 1948 when the Arab League states sent units of their regular armed forces into Palestine. "For these reasons, and considering that the security of Palestine is a sacred trust for them, and out of anxiousness to check the further deterioration of the prevailing conditions and to prevent the spread of disorder and lawlessness into the neighbouring Arab lands, and in order to fill the vacuum created by the termination of the Mandate and the failure to replace it by any legally constituted authority, the Arab Governments find themselves compelled to intervene for the sole purpose of restoring peace and security and establishing law and order in Palestine" (UN Doc. S/745). But the Arab military effort, which from the outset suffered from lack of coordination and common planning, became entirely disjointed by January 1949. Israel for its part consolidated its position in areas allocated to it by the General Assembly's partition resolution (Doc. 88) and occupied substantial fragments of zones originally assigned to the Arabs. When Britain threatened in the circumstances to go to Egypt's aid by invoking the 1936 treaty (Doc. 61), Egypt preferred as the lesser of two evils to conclude an armistice agreement with Israel, negotiated and signed on the island of Rhodes (12 January–24 February 1949) under the auspices of UN Acting Mediator Ralph J. Bunche. Once the Arab ice was broken, Lebanon followed on 23 March, Transjordan (known thereafter as Jordan) on 3 April and Syria on 20 July (texts in UN, Security Council, *Official Records,* 4th year, spec. suppls. Nos. 4, 1, 2, respectively). Iraq had already signified its acceptance of the armistice conditions agreeable to Palestine's immediate neighbors, while Saʻudi Arabia (which had only sent token troops) declared that it would be guided in its decision by the Arab League. The Arab-Israel armistice system thus came into being under the supervision of four separate mixed armistice commissions, whose chairman in each case was the UN Chief of Staff of the Truce Supervision Organization or one of his senior aides. The Chief of Staff, in turn, was responsible to the Security Council, so that ultimately that organ still concerned itself with the execution of the armistice conditions. Omitted below are three annexes. S. Rosenne, *Israel's Armistice Agreements with the Arab States;* J. C. Hurewitz, "The Israel-Syrian Crisis in the Light of the Arab-Israel Armistice System," *International Organization,* 5 (August 1951), pp. 459–79; P. Mohn, "Problems of Truce Supervision," *International Conciliation,* February 1952; M. Alami, "The Lesson of Palestine," *The Middle East Journal,* 3 (October 1949), 373–405; J. B. Glubb, "Violence on the Jordan-Israel Border, a Jordanian View," *Foreign Affairs,* 32 (July 1954), 552–62; M. Dayan, "Israel's Border and Security Problems," *ibid.,* 33 (January 1955), 250–67.

PREAMBLE

The Parties to the present Agreement, responding to the Security Council resolution of 16 November 1948 calling upon them, as a further provisional measure under Article 40 of the Charter of the United Nations and in order to facilitate the transition from the present truce to permanent peace in Palestine, to negotiate an Armistice; having decided to enter into negotiations under United Nations Chairmanship concerning the implementation of the Security Council resolutions of 4 and 16 November 1948; and having appointed representatives empowered to negotiate and conclude an Armistice Agreement;

The undersigned representatives, in the full authority entrusted to them by their respective Governments, have agreed upon the following provisions:

ART. I. With a view to promoting the return to permanent peace in Palestine and in recognition of the importance in this regard of mutual assurances concerning the future military operations of the Parties, the following principles, which shall be fully observed by both Parties during the Armistice, are hereby affirmed:

1. The injunction of the Security Council against resort to military force in the settlement of the Palestine question shall henceforth be scrupulously respected by both Parties.

2. No aggressive action by the armed forces—land, sea, or air—of either Party shall be undertaken, planned, or threatened against the people or the armed forces of the other; it being understood that the use of the term "planned" in this context has no bearing on normal staff planning as generally practiced in military organizations.

3. The right of each Party to its security and freedom from fear of attack by the armed forces of the other shall be fully respected.

4. The establishment of an armistice between the armed forces of the two Parties is accepted as an indispensable step toward the liquidation of armed conflict and the restoration of peace in Palestine.

ART. II. 1. In pursuance of the foregoing principles and of the resolutions of the Security Council of 4 and 16 November 1948, a general armistice between the armed forces of the two Parties—land, sea and air—is hereby established.

2. No element of the land, sea or air military or para-military forces of either Party, including non-regular forces, shall commit any warlike or hostile act against the military or para-military forces of the other Party, or against civilians in territory under the control of that Party; or shall advance beyond or pass over for any purpose whatsoever the Armistice Demarcation Line set forth in Article VI of this Agreement except as provided in Article III of this Agreement; and elsewhere shall not violate the international frontier; or enter into or pass through the air space of the other Party or through the waters within three miles of the coastline of the other Party.

ART. III. 1. In pursuance of the Security Council's resolution of 4 November 1948, and with a view to the implementation of the Security Council's resolution of 16 November 1948, the Egyptian Military Forces in the AL FALUJA area shall be withdrawn.

2. This withdrawal shall begin on the day after that which follows the signing of this Agreement, at 0500 hours GMT, and shall be beyond the Egypt-Palestine frontier.

3. The withdrawal shall be under the supervision of the United Nations and in accordance with the Plan of Withdrawal set forth in Annex I to this Agreement.

ART. IV. With specific reference to the implementation of the resolutions of the Security Council of 4 and 16 November 1948, the following principles and purposes are affirmed:

1. The principle that no military or political advantage should be gained under the truce ordered by the Security Council is recognized.

2. It is also recognized that the basic purposes and spirit of the Armistice would not be served by the restoration of previously held military positions, changes from those now held other than as specifi-

cally provided for in this Agreement, or by the advance of the military forces of either side beyond positions held at the time this Armistice Agreement is signed.

3. It is further recognized that rights, claims or interests of a non-military character in the area of Palestine covered by this Agreement may be asserted by either Party, and that these, by mutual agreement being excluded from the Armistice negotiations, shall be, at the discretion of the Parties, the subject of later settlement. It is emphasized that it is not the purpose of this Agreement to establish, to recognize, to strengthen, or to weaken or nullify, in any way, any territorial, custodial or other rights, claims or interests which may be asserted by either Party in the area of Palestine or any part or locality thereof covered by this Agreement, whether such asserted rights, claims or interests derive from Security Council resolutions, including the resolution of 4 November 1948 and the Memorandum of 13 November 1948 for its implementation, or from any other source. The provisions of this Agreement are dictated exclusively by military considerations and are valid only for the period of the Armistice.

ART. V. 1. The line described in Article VI of this Agreement shall be designated as the Armistice Demarcation Line and is delineated in pursuance of the purpose and intent of the resolutions of the Security Council of 4 and 16 November 1948.

2. The Armistice Demarcation Line is not to be construed in any sense as a political or territorial boundary, and is delineated without prejudice to rights, claims and positions of either Party to the Armistice as regards ultimate settlement of the Palestine question.

3. The basic purpose of the Armistice Demarcation Line is to delineate the line beyond which the armed forces of the respective Parties shall not move except as provided in Article III of this Agreement.

4. Rules and regulations of the armed forces of the Parties, which prohibit civilians from crossing the fighting lines or entering the area between the lines, shall remain in effect after the signing of this Agreement with application to the Armistice Demarcation Line defined in Article VI.

ART. VI. 1. In the GAZA-RAFAH area the Armistice Demarcation Line shall be as delineated in paragraph 2.B (i) of the Memorandum of 13 November 1948 on the implementation of the Security Council resolution of 4 November 1948, namely by a line from the coast at the mouth of the Wadi Hasi in an easterly direction through Deir Suneid and across the Gaza-Al Majdal Highway to a point 3 kilometres east of the Highway, then in a southerly direction parallel to the Gaza-Al Madjal Highway, and continuing thus to the Egyptian frontier.

2. Within this line Egyptian forces shall nowhere advance beyond their present positions, and this shall include Beit Hanun and its surrounding area from which Israeli forces shall be withdrawn to north of the Armistice Demarcation Line, and any other positions within the line delineated in paragraph 1 shall be evacuated by Israeli forces as set forth in paragraph 3.

3. Israeli outposts, each limited to platoon strength, may be maintained in this area at the following points: Deir Suneid, on the north side of the Wadi (MR 10751090); 700 SW of Sa'ad (MR 10500982); Sulphur Quarries (MR 09870924); Tall-Jamma (MR 09720887); and KH AL Ma'in (MR 09320821). The Israeli outpost maintained at the Cemetery (MR 08160723) shall be evacuated on the day after that which follows the signing of this Agreement. The Israeli outpost at Hill 79 (MR 10451017) shall be evacuated not later than four weeks following the day on which this Agreement is signed. Following the evacuation of the above outposts, new Israeli outpost may be established at MR 08360700, and at a point due east of Hill 79 east of the Armistice Demarcation Line.

4. In the BETHLEHEM-HEBRON area, wherever positions are held by Egyptian forces, the provisions of this Agreement shall apply to the forces of both Parties in each locality, except that the demarcation of the Armistice Line and reciprocal arrangements for withdrawal and reduction of

forces shall be undertaken in such manner as may be decided by the Parties, at such time as an Armistice Agreement may be concluded covering military forces in that area other than those of the Parties to this Agreement, or sooner at the will of the Parties.

ART. VII. 1. It is recognized by the Parties to this Agreement that in certain sectors of the total area involved, the proximity of the forces of a third party not covered by this Agreement makes impractical the full application of all provisions of the Agreement to such sectors. For this reason alone, therefore, and pending the conclusion of an Armistice Agreement in place of the existing truce with that third party, the provisions of this Agreement relating to reciprocal reduction and withdrawal of forces shall apply only to the western front and not to the eastern front.

2. The areas comprising the western and eastern fronts shall be as defined by the United Nations Chief of Staff of the Truce Supervision Organization, on the basis of the deployment of forces against each other and past military activity or the future possibility thereof in the area. This definition of the western and eastern fronts is set forth in Annex II of this Agreement.

3. In the area of the western front under Egyptian control, Egyptian defensive forces only may be maintained. All other Egyptian forces shall be withdrawn from this area to a point or points no further east than El Arish-Abou Aoueigila.

4. In the area of the western front under Israeli control, Israeli defensive forces only, which shall be based on the settlements, may be maintained. All other Israeli forces shall be withdrawn from this area to a point or points north of the line delineated in paragraph 2.A of the Memorandum of 13 November 1948 on the implementation of the resolution of the Security Council of 4 November 1948.

5. The defensive forces referred to in paragraphs 3 and 4 above shall be as defined in Annex III to this Agreement.

ART. VIII. 1. The area comprising the village of El Auja and vicinity, as defined in paragraph 2 of this Article, shall be demilitarized, and both Egyptian and Israeli armed forces shall be totally excluded therefrom. The Chairman of the Mixed Armistice Commission established in Article X of this Agreement and United Nations Observers attached to the Commission shall be responsible for ensuring the full implementation of this provision.

2. The area thus demilitarized shall be as follows: From a point on the Egypt-Palestine frontier five (5) kilometres north-west of the intersection of the Rafah-El Auja road and the frontier (MR 08750468), south-east to Khashm El Mamdud (MR 09650414), thence south-east to Hill 405 (MR 10780285), thence south-west to a point on the Egypt-Palestine frontier five (5) kilometres south-east of the intersection of the old railway tracks and the frontier (MR 09950145), thence returning north-west along the Egypt-Palestine frontier to the point of origin.

3. On the Egyptian side of the frontier, facing the El Auja area, no Egyptian defensive positions shall be closer to El Auja than El Qouseima and Abou Aoueigila.

4. The road Taba-Qouseima-Auja shall not be employed by any military forces whatsoever for the purpose of entering Palestine.

5. The movement of armed forces of either Party to this Agreement into any part of the area defined in paragraph 2 of this Article, for any purpose, or failure by either Party to respect or fulfil any of the other provisions of this Article, when confirmed by the United Nations representatives, shall constitute a flagrant violation of this Agreement.

ART. IX. All prisoners of war detained by either Party to this Agreement and belonging to the armed forces, regular or irregular, of the other Party shall be exchanged as follows:

1. The exchange of prisoners of war shall be under United Nations supervision and control throughout. The exchange shall begin within ten days after the signing of this Agreement and shall be completed not later than twenty-one days following. Upon the signing of this Agreement, the Chairman of the Mixed Armistice Commission estab-

lished in Article X of this Agreement, in consultation with the appropriate military authorities of the Parties, shall formulate a plan for the exchange of prisoners of war within the above period, defining the date and places of exchange and all other relevant details.

2. Prisoners of war against whom a penal prosecution may be pending, as well as those sentenced for crime or other offence, shall be included in this exchange of prisoners.

3. All articles of personal use, valuables, letters, documents, identification marks, and other personal affects of whatever nature, belonging to prisoners of war who are being exchanged, shall be returned to them, or, if they have escaped or died, to the Party to whose armed forces they belonged.

4. All matters not specifically regulated in this Agreement shall be decided in accordance with the principles laid down in the International Convention relating to the Treatment of Prisoners of War, signed at Geneva on 27 July 1929.

5. The Mixed Armistice Commission established in Article X of this Agreement shall assume responsibility for locating missing persons, whether military or civilian, within the areas controlled by each Party, to facilitate their expeditious exchange. Each Party undertakes to extend to the Commission full co-operation and assistance in the discharge of this function.

ART. X. 1. The execution of the provisions of this Agreement shall be supervised by a Mixed Armistice Commission composed of seven members, of whom each Party to this Agreement shall designate three, and whose Chairman shall be the United Nations Chief of Staff of the Truce Supervision Organization or a senior officer from the Observer personnel of that Organization designed by him following consultation with both Parties to this Agreement.

2. The Mixed Armistice Commission shall maintain its headquarters at El Auja, and shall hold its meetings at such places and at such times as it may deem necessary for the effective conduct of its work.

3. The Mixed Armistice Commission shall be convened in its first meeting by the United Nations Chief of Staff of the Truce Supervision Organization not later than one week following the signing of this Agreement.

4. Decisions of the Mixed Armistice Commission, to the extent possible, shall be based on the principle of unanimity. In the absence of unanimity, decisions shall be taken by a majority vote of the members of the Commission present and voting. On questions of principle, appeal shall lie to a Special Committee, composed of the United Nations Chief of Staff of the Truce Supervision Organization and one member each of the Egyptian and Israeli Delegations to the Armistice Conference at Rhodes or some other senior officer, whose decisions on all such questions shall be final. If no appeal against a decision of the Commission is filed within one week from the date of said decision, that decision shall be taken as final. Appeals to the Special Committee shall be presented to the United Nations Chief of Staff of the Truce Supervision Organization, who shall convene the Committee at the earliest possible date.

5. The Mixed Armistice Commission shall formulate its own rules of procedure. Meetings shall be held only after due notice to the members by the Chairman. The quorum for its meetings shall be a majority of its members.

6. The Commission shall be empowered to employ Observers, who may be from among the military organizations of the Parties or from the military personnel of the United Nations Truce Supervision Organization, or from both, in such numbers as may be considered essential to the performance of its functions. In the event United Nations Observers should be so employed, they shall remain under the command of the United Nations Chief of Staff of the Truce Supervision Organization. Assignments of a general or special nature given to United Nations Observers attached to the Mixed Armistice Commission shall be subject to approval by the United Nations Chief of Staff or his designated representative on the Commission, whichever is serving as Chairman.

7. Claims or complaints presented by either Party relating to the application of this Agreement shall be referred immediately to the Mixed Armistice Commission through its Chairman. The Commission shall take such action on all such claims or complaints by means of its observation and investigation machinery as it may deem appropriate, with a view to equitable and mutually satisfactory settlement.

8. Where interpretation of the meaning of a particular provision of this Agreement is at issue, the Commission's interpretation shall prevail, subject to the right of appeal as provided in paragraph 4. The Commission, in its discretion and as the need arises, may from time to time recommend to the Parties modifications in the provisions of this Agreement.

9. The Mixed Armistice Commission shall submit to both Parties reports on its activities as frequently as it may consider necessary. A copy of each such report shall be presented to the Secretary-General of the United Nations for transmission to the appropriate organ or agency of the United Nations.

10. Members of the Commission and its Observers shall be accorded such freedom of movement and access in the areas covered by this Agreement as the Commission may determine to be necessary, provided that when such decisions of the Commission are reached by a majority vote United Nations Observers only shall be employed.

11. The expenses of the Commission, other than those relating to United Nations Observers, shall be apportioned in equal shares between the two Parties to this Agreement.

ART. XI. No provision of this Agreement shall in any way prejudice the rights, claims and positions of either Party hereto in the ultimate peaceful settlement of the Palestine question.

ART. XII. The present Agreement is not subject to ratification and shall come into force immediately upon being signed.

2. This Agreement, having been negotiated and concluded in pursuance of the resolution of the Security Council of 16 November 1948 calling for the establishment of an armistice in order to eliminate the threat to the peace in Palestine and to facilitate the transition from the present truce to permanent peace in Palestine, shall remain in force until a peaceful settlement between the Parties is achieved, except as provided in paragraph 3 of this Article.

3. The Parties to this Agreement may, by mutual consent, revise this Agreement or any of its provisions, or may suspend its application, other than Articles I and II, at any time. In the absence of mutual agreement and after this Agreement has been in effect for one year from the date of its signing, either of the Parties may call upon the Secretary-General of the United Nations to convoke a conference of representatives of the two Parties for the purpose of reviewing, revising or suspending any of the provisions of this Agreement other than Articles I and II. Participation in such conference shall be obligatory upon the Parties.

4. If the conference provided for in paragraph 3 of this Article does not result in an agreed solution of a point in dispute, either Party may bring the matter before the Security Council of the United Nations for the relief sought on the grounds that this Agreement has been concluded in pursuance of Security Council action toward the end of achieving peace in Palestine.

5. This Agreement supersedes the Egyptian-Israeli General Cease-Fire Agreement entered into by the Parties on 24 January 1949.

6. This Agreement is signed in quintuplicate, of which one copy shall be retained by each Party, two copies communicated to the Secretary-General of the United Nations for transmission to the Security Council and to the United Nations Conciliation Commission on Palestine, and one copy to the Acting Mediator on Palestine.

91. SUPPLEMENTAL AGREEMENT: IRAN AND THE ANGLO-IRANIAN OIL COMPANY
17 July 1949

[Great Britain, *Parliamentary Papers, 1951,* Persia No. 1, Cmd. 8425, pp. 19–22]

Iran's revenue from the Anglo-Iranian Oil Company (AIOC) rose sharply in the decade following 1939, particularly after 1944, as a result of the rapid expansion of the company's production. Iran nevertheless became disgruntled in the early postwar years with the financial arrangements, since the royalty and tax rates which foreign companies paid the governments in Latin America, especially Venezuela, were considerably higher. Paragraph 5 of the 1947 law rejecting the draft oil agreement with the USSR (Doc. 87) also instructed the government to enter into negotiations with AIOC for an upward revision of the company's payments to Iran. After more than six months of negotiation the following supplemental agreement, retroactive to 1 January 1948, was initialed by the company representative and the Iranian Finance Minister. Under the supplemental instrument, which consisted of a complicated series of amendments of the agreement of 29 April 1933 (Doc. 58), the government's income was to be augmented by some 50 per cent. The company also guaranteed an annual minimal payment to the government of £4 million, except for periods when a *force majeure* might interfere with production. The fresh terms encountered growing opposition in the *Majlis,* which ultimately rejected the supplemental agreement, canceled the 1933 concession and enacted a law nationalizing the oil industry (Doc. 95). G. Kirk, *The Middle East 1945–1950,* pp. 90–105; J. C. Hurewitz, *Middle East Dilemmas,* chap. 2; W. J. Levy, "Iranian Royalty Question Serious Problem," *Oil Forum,* 5 (February 1951), 44–46, 60; A. W. Ford, *The Anglo-Iranian Oil Dispute of 1951–1952,* pp. 48–51; B. Shwadran, *The Middle East, Oil and the Great Powers,* chap. 5; L. P. Ewell-Sutton, *Persian Oil,* chaps. 12–15.

Whereas on 29th April, 1933, an Agreement (herein called "the Principal Agreement") was entered into between the Imperial Government of Persia (now known as "the Imperial Iranian Government") of the one part and the Anglo-Persian Oil Company, Limited (now known as the "Anglo-Iranian Oil Company, Limited") of the other part which established a Concession for the regulation of the relations between the two parties above mentioned

And whereas the Government and the Company have after full and friendly discussion agreed that in view of the changes in economic conditions brought about by the World War of 1939–1945 the financial benefits accruing to the Government under the Principal Agreement should be increased to the extent and in the manner hereinafter appearing

And whereas for this purpose the parties have agreed to enter into a Supplemental Agreement:—

Now it is hereby agreed between the Imperial Iranian Government and the Anglo-Iranian Oil Company, Limited, as follows:—

1. This Agreement is supplemental to and shall be read with the Principal Agreement.

2. Any of the terms used herein which have been defined in the Principal Agreement shall have the same meaning as in the Principal Agreement, save that, for the purposes of this Agreement, all references in the Principal Agreement to Persia, Persian, the Imperial Government of Persia and the Anglo-Persian Oil Company, Limited, shall be read as references to Iran, Iranian, the Imperial Iranian Government and the Anglo-Iranian Oil Company, Limited, respectively and the references to the Permanent Court of International Justice shall be read as references to the International Court of Justice established by the United Nations.

3.—(*a*) In respect of the calendar year ended 31st December, 1948, and thereafter, the rate of the annual royalty payable to the Government under sub-clause (I) (*a*) of Article 10 of the Principal Agreement shall be increased from four shillings to six shillings per ton of petroleum sold for consumption in Iran or exported from Iran.

(*b*) The Company shall within a period of thirty days from the date of coming into force of this Agreement, pay to the Government the sum of three million three hundred and sixty-four thousand four hundred and fifty-nine pounds sterling £3,364,-459), as a retrospective application to cover the calendar year ended 31st December, 1948, of the modification introduced by sub-clause (*a*) of this Clause 3, taking into account the provisions of sub-clause (V) (*a*) of Article 10 of the Principal Agreement.

4.—(*a*) In order that the Government may receive a greater and more certain and more immediate benefit in respect of amounts placed to the General Reserve of the Anglo-Iranian Oil Company, Limited, than that provided by sub-clause (I) (*b*) and sub-clause (III) (*a*) of Article 10 of the Principal Agreement, the Company shall pay to the Government in respect of each amount placed to the General Reserve of the Anglo-Iranian Oil Company, Limited, in respect of each financial period for which the accounts of that company are made up (starting with the financial period ended 31st December, 1948) a sum equal to twenty per cent (20%) of a figure to be arrived at by increasing the amount placed to General Reserve (as shown by the published accounts for the financial period in question) in the same proportion as twenty shillings sterling (s.20/-) bear the difference between twenty shillings sterling (s.20/-) and the Standard Rate of British Income Tax in force at the relevant date.

The relevant date shall be the date of the final distribution to the Ordinary Stockholders in respect of the financial period in question, or, in the event of there being no such final distribution, a date one calendar month after the date of the Annual General Meeting at which the accounts in question were presented.

Examples of the implementation of the principle set out in this sub-clause (*a*) have been agreed between the parties hereto and are set out in the Schedule to this Agreement.

(*b*) If in respect of any financial period for which the accounts of the Anglo-Iranian Oil Company, Limited, are made up (starting with the financial period ended 31st December, 1948) the total amount payable by the Company to the Government under sub-clause (*a*) of this Clause 4 and sub-clause (I) (*b*) of Article 10 of the Principal Agreement shall be less than four million pounds sterling (£4,000,000) the Company shall pay to the Government the difference between the said total amount and four million pounds sterling (£4,000,-000). Provided, however, that if during any such financial period the Company shall have ceased, owing to events outside its control, to export petroleum from Iran, the amount payable by the Company in respect of such period in accordance with the foregoing provisions of this sub-clause (*b*) shall be reduced by a sum which bears the same proportion to such amount as the period of such cessation bears to such financial period.

(*c*) Any sum due to the Government in respect of any financial period under sub-clause (*a*) or sub-clause (*b*) of this Clause 4 shall be paid on the relevant date appropriate to that financial period.

(*d*) The provisions of Clause (V) of Article 10 of the Principal Agreement shall not apply to any payments made by the Company to the Government in accordance with sub-clause (*a*) or sub-clause (*b*) of this Clause 4.

5.—(*a*) In respect of the sum of fourteen million pounds sterling (£14,000,000) shown in the Balance Sheet of the Anglo-Iranian Oil Company, Limited, dated 31st December, 1947, as constituting the General Reserve of that company, the Company shall, within a period of thirty days from the date of coming into force of this Agreement, pay to the Government the sum of five million and ninety thousand nine hundred and nine pounds sterling (£5,090,-909).

(*b*) The provisions of Clause (V) of Article 10 of the Principal Agreement shall not apply to the payment to be made by the Company in accordance with sub-clause (*a*) of this Clause 5.

6. The payments to be made by the Company under Clauses 4 and 5 of this

Agreement shall be in lieu of and in substitution for—

(i) any payments to the Government under sub-clause (I) (*b*) of Article 10 of the Principal Agreement in respect of any distribution relating to the General Reserve of the Company, and

(ii) any payment which might become payable by the Company to the Government in respect of the General Reserve under sub-clause (III) (*a*) of Article 10 of the Principal Agreement on the expiration of the Concession or in the case of surrender by the Company under Article 25 of the Principal Agreement.

7.—(*a*) In respect of the calendar year ended 31st December, 1948, and thereafter, the rate of payment to be made by the Company to the Government in accordance with sub-clause (I) (*c*) of Article 11 of the Principal Agreement which relates to the payment to be made in respect of the excess over 6,000,000 tons shall be increased from ninepence to one shilling.

(*b*) The Company shall, within a period of thirty days from the date of coming into force of this Agreement, pay to the Government the sum of three hundred and twelve thousand nine hundred pounds sterling (£312,900), as a retrospective application to cover the calendar year ended 31st December, 1948, of the modification introduced by sub-clause (*a*) of this Clause 7, taking into account the provisions of sub-clause (V) of Article 10 of the Principal Agreement.

8.—(*a*) At the end of sub-clause (*a*) of Article 19 of the Principal Agreement there shall be added a paragraph in the following terms: "If at any time either party shall consider that either Roumanian prices or Gulf of Mexico prices no longer provide suitable standards for fixing 'basic prices,' then the 'basic prices' shall be determined by mutual agreement of the parties, or in default of such agreement by arbitration under the provisions of Article 22. The 'basic prices' so determined shall become binding on both parties by an agreement effected by exchange of letters between the Government (which shall have full capacity to enter into such an agreement) and the Company."

(*b*) As from 1st June, 1949, the prices at which the Company shall sell motor spirit, kerosene and fuel oil, produced from Iranian petroleum to consumers other than the Government for internal consumption in Iran, shall be the basic prices with a deduction of twenty-five per cent. (25%), instead of a deduction of ten per cent (10%)

Examples of the Implementation of the Principle set out in Sub-clause (a) *of Clause 4 of the Within Written Agreement on the Assumption that £1,000,000 is Placed to General Reserve*

	Example I	*Example II*	*Example III*
1. Standard Rate of British Income Tax ...	10*s*. in the £1	9*s*. in the £1	5*s*. in the £1
2. Amount placed to General Reserve as shown by the published accounts for the financial period in question	£1,000,000	£1,000,000	£1,000,000
3. The above amount is increased as follows:—			

A "*Twenty Shillings sterling*"	*Standard Rate of British Income Tax*	*B* *Difference*	*Proportionate Increase* *A*	*B*	*Example I*	*Example II*	*Example III*
20*s*.	10*s*.	10*s*.	20	10	£2,000,000		
20*s*.	9*s*.	11*s*.	20	11	...	£1,818,182	
20*s*.	5*s*.	15*s*.	20	15	...	...	£1,333,333

	Example I	*Example II*	*Example III*
4. The "sum equal to 20%" which is therefore payable to the Iranian Government is	£400,000	£363,636	£266,667

as provided in sub-clause (*b*) of Article 19 of the Principal Agreement.

9. In consideration of the payment of the above sums by the Company the Government and the Company agree that all their obligations one to another accrued up to 31st December, 1948, in respect of sub-clause 1 (*a*) and sub-clause 1 (*b*) of Article 10 and in respect of Article 11 of the Principal Agreement and also in respect of the General Reserve have been fully discharged.

10. Subject to the provisions of this Agreement, the provisions of the Principal Agreement shall remain in full force and effect.

11. This Agreement shall come into force after ratification by the Majlis and on the date of its promulgation by Decree of His Imperial Majesty the Shah. The Government undertakes to submit this Agreement, as soon as possible, for ratification by the Majlis.

92. TRIPARTITE (BRITAIN, FRANCE AND THE UNITED STATES) DECLARATION ON SECURITY IN THE ARAB-ISRAEL ZONE 25 May–21 June 1950

[Tripartite declaration from *Department of State Bulletin*, 22 (5 June 1950), 886; Israel reply translated from the Hebrew text in Israel, 1st Kneset, 2nd sess., *Divrei ha-Kneset*, vol. 5, pp. 1571–72; Arab League Council reply translated from the Arabic text in *Revue égyptienne de droit international* (Arabic section), vol. 6 (1950), pp. 151–52]

The conclusion of the Arab-Israel armistice in 1949 (Doc. 92) did not soon lead, as some optimistically had hoped, to formal peace. Britain's resumption of arms shipments to Egypt, Iraq and Jordan, in accordance with treaty obligations, was accompanied by widespread talk in the Arab East of a "second round" against Israel. For its part Israel continued to maintain a state of viligance, purchasing military equipment wherever available and stepping up its production of small arms. A miniature arms race thus developed. Meanwhile, the cleavage within the Arab League between the Hashimi bloc (Jordan and Iraq) and the others was widened, and Jordan threatened with expulsion. The immediate cause of friction arose from the enlargement of Jordan's domain. On the eve of the signature of the Israel-Jordan armistice agreement, Iraqi troops withdrew from the interior of central Palestine, leaving the sector entirely to the military administration of King 'Abdallah's Arab Legion. Jordan progressively absorbed the district in the ensuing year. Palestine Arabs were encouraged to participate on 11 April 1950 in the Jordan election, and the new legislature formalized the annexation on 24 April by adopting a resolution giving its blessing to the merger. Three days later Britain granted *de jure* recognition to 'Abdallah's enlarged kingdom. The tripartite statement was intended to stress to the governments concerned that the Western powers would not tolerate any renewal of the Arab-Israel war or any punitive action against Jordan. Apart from the three-power declaration, the formal replies of Israel and the Arab states are reproduced below. J. C. Hurewitz, *Middle East Dilemmas*, chap. 4; G. Kirk, *The Middle East 1945–1950*, pp. 294–319.

1. TRIPARTITE DECLARATION, 25 MAY 1950

The Governments of the United Kingdom, France, and the United States, having had occasion during the recent Foreign Ministers meeting in London to review certain questions affecting the peace and stability of the Arab states and of Israel, and particularly that of the supply of arms and war material to these states, have resolved to make the following statements:

1. The three Governments recognize that the Arab states and Israel all need to maintain a certain level of armed forces for the purposes of assuring their internal security and their legitimate self-defense and to permit them to play their part in the defense of the area as a whole. All applications for arms or war material for these countries will be considered in the light of these principles. In this connection the

three Governments wish to recall and reaffirm the terms of the statements made by their representatives on the Security Council on August 4, 1949, in which they declared their opposition to the development of an arms race between the Arab states and Israel.

2. The three Governments declare that assurances have been received from all the states in question, to which they permit arms to be supplied from their countries, that the purchasing state does not intend to undertake any act of aggression against any other state. Similar assurances will be requested from any other state in the area to which they permit arms to be supplied in the future.

3. The three Governments take this opportunity of declaring their deep interest in and their desire to promote the establishment and maintenance of peace and stability in the area and their unalterable opposition to the use of force or threat of force between any of the states in that area. The three Governments, should they find that any of these states was preparing to violate frontiers or armistice lines, would, consistently with their obligations as members of the United Nations, immediately take action, both within and outside the United Nations, to prevent such violation.

2. STATEMENT BY THE ISRAEL PRIME MINISTER BEFORE THE KNESET, 31 MAY 1950

The publication a week ago of the declaration by the three great powers—the United States, Britain and France—on arms and security in the Arab states and Israel did not escape notice in our country, although the exaggerated sensitivity toward political declarations by foreign powers, so natural when our land was under foreign rule, is now a matter of history. The young state that emerged from a defensive war, when [Israel] fought alone against six Arab states that invaded the country in violation of the United Nations charter, views its existence, security and future as dependent primarily on its own efforts to conquer the desert, absorb immigrants and mobilize the spiritual and material resources of the nation. But it does not ignore for one moment the inescapable fact that the world in which we live is based upon mutual cooperation between the large nations and the small, and that even a great power cannot any longer live in isolated security, to say nothing of such a small and weak state as that of Israel. We ardently desire friendly relations with all nations, near and far, and the strengthening of security and peace in the world.

The *Kneset* has surely noted that the three-power declaration is a unilateral instrument, issued to define the policy of the above powers toward the state of Israel and the Arab states on the question of arms and security. It is not necessary to stress here that the policy of the state of Israel is formulated only by the government of Israel in accordance with the sovereign will of the people and the consent of the *Kneset*. The declaration was transmitted to the government of Israel by the ambassadors of the three powers for information only.

Insofar as the declaration is designed to strengthen security and peace, even if only in the restricted Arab-Israel zone, it will receive the faithful support of the government of Israel. In the view of the government of Israel, the bolstering of peace in one corner of the world will contribute, directly and indirectly, to bolstering peace throughout the world.

The government of Israel welcomes the statement of the three powers against an arms race between the Arab states and Israel.

This statement, as it is noted in the declaration, was made by the three powers in the Security Council as early as 4 August 1949. But the government of Israel must call attention, with astonishment and concern, to the fact that from that time to the present, as before the above date, the furnishing of arms has continued to one side only—the Arab states, which have not ceased to threaten a new war against Israel and up to the present have refused to discuss peace with us. At the same time there is constant refusal to furnish arms and war material to Israel. This discrimination undermines the security of the state of Israel and endangers the peace in the Near East.

The three powers now inform us that they have received assurances from the states to which arms have been supplied that they harbor no aggressive designs on any other state. But these assurances by the Arab states have not been accompanied by any practical guarantee. Moreover, [they] patently contradict the ceaseless preparations for war against the state of Israel.

Whoever knows the truth of the situation in the [Arab] lands will understand without hesitation that the arms sent to these states, if used at all, will be used against Israel, and perhaps against Israel alone.

The government of Israel expresses satisfaction that the three powers now recognize that Israel has no less a need than the Arab states to maintain armed forces of a certain level.

Israel has never had, and never will have, aggressive intentions against anyone. Israel's hand is extended in peace to all the Arab states, severally and jointly. But Israel has the right and the duty to look after its own security, and the three powers have recognized this. The government of Israel hopes that this recognition will be translated into action, and that the discrimination against Israel in the supply of arms will be stopped completely by the governments that have signed the declaration.

The government of Israel received with particular satisfaction the public announcement by the three powers of their deep interest in and their desire to promote peace and stability in the Arab states and Israel, and of their unalterable opposition to the use of force or threat of the use of force by any state in this part of the world.

The three powers have pledged to take action against every violation of the frontiers or armistice lines, in accordance with their obligations as members of the United Nations. This pledge applies equally to the frontiers of the Arab states and to the domain of Israel, as fixed in armistice agreements with Egypt, Transjordan, Syria and Lebanon.

As a government directly concerned and as a member of the United Nations, the government of Israel feels obliged to state that it is not sufficient merely to prevent hostilities among neighbors. There is also a need to support and accelerate the negotiations for an enduring peace among all nations, among them Israel and the Arab states, and for this purpose it is essential to employ the full authority and resources of the United Nations.

The government of Israel will lend its hand faithfully to any endeavor designed to strengthen peace among all nations, and to raise the power and authority of the United Nations.

3. STATEMENT BY THE ARAB LEAGUE COUNCIL, 21 JUNE 1950

The governments of the Arab states, severally and jointly, have studied the joint declaration issued by the United Kingdom, France and the United States on 25 May 1950. The exchange of views on this declaration was one of the most important reasons that prompted the Arab states to expedite the meeting of the Arab League Council on 12 June 1950 and was one of the most important items on the agenda of the meeting.

The Arab states have agreed to issue the following statement:

1. No one is more anxious than the Arab states about the preservation of peace and stability in the Middle East. The [Arab lands stand] by nature at the head of the peace-loving countries. Successive events have proved the degree of their respect for the United Nations Charter.

2. If the Arab states shave shown, and continue to show, an interest in meeting their military needs, this has been due to their deep sense of responsibility for safeguarding the internal security of their countries, insuring the legitimate defense of their neutrality and fulfilling the obligation of safeguarding international security in this region. This is primarily the obligation of [the Arab states] and of the Arab League as a regional organization under article 52 of the United Nations Charter.

3. Even before the three powers ever

thought of issuing their declaration, the Arab governments on their own initiative had decided to express the peaceful intentions of the Arabs and to refute the allegations that Israel has persisted in circulating [to the effect] that the Arab states are requesting arms for aggressive purposes. [The Arab states] hereby reiterate their peaceful intentions and declare that the arms that have been, or may be, ordered from the three powers or from others will be used solely for defensive purposes.

4. It goes without saying that the level of armed forces maintained by every state for defense purposes and for participation in the maintenance of international security is a matter that can only be estimated by the state concerned. It is also subject to various factors, chiefly the size of the population, the area of the country and the length and diversity of its frontiers.

5. The Arab states take note of the assurances that they have received to the effect that the three powers did not intend by their declaration to favor Israel, or to exert pressure on the Arab states to enter into negotiations with Israel, or to affect the final settlement of the Palestine problem or to preserve the *status quo;* but that they did intend to express their opposition to the use of force or to the violation of the armistice lines.

6. The Arab states declare that the most preferable and reliable measures for maintaining peace and stability in the Middle East would consist in solving its problems on the basis of right and justice, re-establishing the conditions of understanding and harmony that once prevailed and hastening the execution of the United Nations resolution on the return of the Palestine refugees to their homes and on compensation for their material losses.

7. The Arab states also take note of assurances given them that the three-power declaration, both in its manner of presentation and in its provision for prior guarantees from the states purchasing arms, neither signifies the division of this region into zones of influence nor in any way infringes on the independence and sovereignty of the Arab states.

8. It is self-evident that the doubts, which the assurances mentioned in the preceding paragraph were designed to dispel, were raised by paragraph 3 of the three-power declaration, which laid down that, if the three powers should find that any state of this region was preparing to violate the frontiers or the armistice lines of another state, they would immediately take action, within or outside the United Nations, to prevent such violation.

There is no doubt that action alone will dispel these doubts, if it demonstrates that the three powers are in fact concerned with maintaining peace in the Middle East impartially and on the basis of right and justice and respect for the sovereignty of the states and without subjecting them to domination or influence.

9. In conclusion the Arab states can only affirm once again that, despite their anxiety for peace, they cannot approve any action that would harm their sovereignty and their independence.

93. TREATY OF JOINT DEFENSE AND ECONOMIC COOPERATION: THE STATES OF THE ARAB LEAGUE
17 June 1950

(Entered into force, 23 August 1952)

[The Arab Information Center, *Basic Documents of the League of Arab States* (New York, 1955), pp. 21–25]

Defeat in the Palestine war, among other consequences, served to underline the political disunity and military weakness of the Arab League states. Overwhelmed by a sense of shame and indignity, which hurt even more than the material losses, politicians in the several participating Arab countries—especially Egypt and Iraq—took to quarreling among themselves and accusing one another for the debacle. A few Arab spokesmen, however, in soul-searching analysis, placed a large measure of the blame for the disastrous military performance of the Arab armies on the Arabs themselves. In perhaps the most eloquent statement of this class, Musa al-'Alami, a Palestine Arab, fearlessly called attention to the fact that "our [the Arab states'] forces were disunited in the face of the enemy, our fronts independent of each other, our war local. Our armies had no unified command. It is true that they agreed upon a [combined] high command, but it remained nominal" ["The Lesson of Palestine," *Middle East Journal*, 3 (October 1949), 382, as translated from the Arabic by C. Hourani]. To correct the military deficiencies and strengthen the economic ties among the Arab League lands, the following treaty was framed at Cairo in April 1950. Egypt, Lebanon, Syria, Sa'udi Arabia and Yemen signed the instrument on 17 June 1950. Iraq and Jordan did not append their signatures until 2 February 1951 and 16 February 1952, respectively. B. Y. Boutros-Ghali, "The Arab League 1945–1955." *International Conciliation*, May 1955; *Survey of International Affairs, 1951*, pp. 255–60.

The Governments of:

The Hashimite Kingdom of Jordan
The Syrian Republic
The Kingdom of Iraq
The Kingdom of Saudi Arabia
The Lebanese Republic
The Kingdom of Egypt
The Motawakilite Kingdom of Yemen

In view of the desire of the above-mentioned Governments to consolidate relations between the States of the Arab League; to maintain their independence and their mutual heritage; in accordance with the desire of their peoples, to cooperate for the realization of mutual defense and the maintenance of security and peace according to the principles of both the Arab League Pact and the United Nations Charter, together with the aims of the said Pacts; and to consolidate stability and security and provide means of welfare and development in the countries.

The following government delegates of . . . , having been duly accredited and fully authorized by their respecive governments, approve the following:

ART. 1. The Contracting States, in an effort to maintain and stabilize peace and security, hereby confirm their desire to settle their international disputes by peaceful means, whether such disputes concern relations among themselves or with other Powers.

ART. 2. The Contracting States consider any [act of] armed aggression made against any one or more of them or their armed forces, to be directed against them all. Therefore, in accordance with the right of self-defense, individually and collectively, they undertake to go without delay to the aid of the State or States against which such an act of aggression is made, and immediately to take, individually and collectively, all steps available, including the use of armed force, to repel the aggression and restore security and peace. In conformity with Article 6 of the Arab League Pact and Article 51 of the United Nations Charter, the Arab League Council and U.N. Security Council shall be notified of such act of aggression and the means and procedure taken to check it.

ART. 3. At the invitation of any one of the signatories of this Treaty the Contracting States shall hold consultations whenever there are reasonable grounds for the belief that the territorial integrity, independence, or security of any one of the parties is threatened. In the event of the threat of war or the existence of an international emergency, the Contracting States shall immediately proceed to unify their plans and defensive measures, as the situation may demand.

ART. 4. The Contracting States, desiring to implement fully the above obligations and effectively carry them out, shall cooperate in consolidating and coordinating their armed forces, and shall participate according to their resources and needs in preparing individual and collective means of defense to repulse the said armed aggression.

ART. 5. A Permanent Military Commission composed of representatives of the General Staffs of the armies of the Contracting States shall be formed to draw up plans of joint defense and their implementation. The duties of the Permanent Military Commission which are set forth in an Annex attached to this Treaty, include the drafting of necessary reports on the method of cooperation and participation mentioned in Article 4. The Permanent Military Commission shall submit to the Joint Defense Council, provided hereunder in Article 6, reports dealing with questions within its province.

ART. 6. A Joint Defense Council under the supervision of the Arab League Council shall be formed to deal with all matters concerning the implementation of the provisions of Articles 2, 3, 4, and 5 of this Treaty. It shall be assisted in the performance of its task by the Permanent Military Commission referred to in Article 5. The Joint Defense Council shall consist of the Foreign Ministers and the Defense Ministers of the Contracting States or their representatives. Decisions taken by a two-thirds majority shall be binding on all the Contracting States.

ART. 7. The Contracting States, in order to fulfill the aims of this Treaty, and to bring about security and prosperity in the Arab countries, and in an effort to raise the standard of living in them, undertake to cooperate in the development of their economies and the exploitation of their natural resources; to facilitate the exchange of their respective agricultural and industrial products; and generally to organize and coordinate their economic activities and to conclude the necessary inter-Arab agreements to realize such aims.

ART. 8. An Economic Council consisting of the Ministers in charge of economic affairs, or their representatives if necessary, shall be formed by the Contracting States to submit recommendations for the realization of all such aims as are set forth in the previous article. The Council may, in the performance of its duties, seek the cooperation of the Committee for Financial and Economic Affairs referred to in Article 4 of the Arab League Pact.

ART. 9. The Annex to this Treaty shall be considered an integral and indivisible part of it.

ART. 10. The Contracting States undertake to conclude no international agreements which may be contradictory to the provisions of this Treaty, nor to act, in their international relations, in a way which may be contrary to the aims of this Treaty.

ART. 11. No provision of this Treaty shall in any way affect, or is intended to affect, any of the rights or obligations devolving upon the Contracting States from the United Nations Charter or the responsibilities borne by the United Nations Security Council for the maintenance of international peace and security.

ART. 12. After a lapse of 10 years from the date of the ratification of this Treaty, any one of the Contracting States may withdraw from it, providing 12 months' notice is previously given to the Secretariat-General of the Arab League. The Secretariat-General of the League shall inform the other Contracting States of such notice.

ART. 13. This Treaty shall be ratified by each Contracting State according to the constitutional procedure of its own government. The Treaty shall come into force for the ratifying State 15 days after the receipt by the Secretariat-General of the instruments of ratification from at least four States. This Treaty is drafted in Arabic in Cairo on April 13, 1950. One signed copy shall be deposited with the Secretariat-General of the Arab League; equally authentic copies shall be transmitted to each of the Contracting States.

MILITARY ANNEX

1. The Permanent Military Commission provided for in Article 5 of the Joint Defense and Economic Cooperation Treaty between the States of the Arab League, shall undertake the following:

(a) in cooperation with the Joint Defense Council, to prepare plans to deal with all anticipated dangers or armed aggression that may be launched against one or more of the Contracting States or their armed forces, such plans to be based on the principles determined by the Joint Defense Council;

(b) to submit proposals for the organization of the forces of the Contracting States, stipulating the minimum force for each in accordance with military exigencies and the potentialities of each State;

(c) to submit proposals for increasing the effectiveness of the forces of the Contracting States in so far as their equipment, organization, and training are concerned; so that they may keep pace with modern military methods and development; and for the unification and coordination of all such forces;

(d) to submit proposals for the exploitation of natural, agricultural, industrial, and other resources of all Contracting States in favor of the inter-Arab military effort and joint defense;

(e) to organize the exchange of training missions between the Contracting States for the preparation of plans, participation in military exercises and maneuvers and the study of their results, recommendations for the improvement of methods to ensure close cooperation in the field, and for the general improvement of the forces of all the Contracting States;

(f) to prepare the necessary data on the resources and military potentialities of each of the Contracting States and the part to be played by the forces of each in the joint military effort;

(g) to discuss the facilities and various contributions which each of the Contracting States, in conformity with the provisions of this Treaty, might be asked to provide, during a state of war, on behalf of the armies of such other Contracting States as might be operating on its territory.

2. The Permanent Military Commission may form temporary or permanent subcommittees from among its own members to deal with any of the matters falling within its jurisdiction. It may also seek the advice of any experts whose views on certain questions are deemed necessary.

3. The Permanent Military Commission shall submit detailed reports on the results of its activities and studies to the Joint Defense Council provided for in Article 6 of this Treaty, as well as an annual report giving full particulars of its work and studies during the year.

4. The Permanent Military Commission shall establish its headquarters in Cairo but may hold meetings in any other place the Commission may specify. The Commission shall elect its Chairman for two years; he may be reelected. Candidates for the Chairmanship shall hold at least the rank of a high commanding officer. Each member of the Commission must have as his original nationality that of the Contracting State he represents.

5. In the event of war, the supreme command of the joint forces shall be entrusted to the Contracting State possessing the largest military force taking actual part in field operations, unless, by unanimous agreement, the Commander-in-Chief is selected otherwise. The Commander-in-Chief shall be assisted in directing military operations by a Joint Staff.

94. AGREEMENT (JIDDAH) FOR EQUAL SHARING OF THE PROFITS: THE SA'UDI ARAB GOVERNMENT AND ARAMCO
30 December 1950

[Translated from the Arabic texts in *Umm al-Qura,* 4 November and 27 December 1950 and 20 July 1951]

The Sa'udi Arab government, as late as 1945, received less than 5 million dollars in annual revenues from Aramco, the American-owned oil company that was exploiting an exclusive concession in the desert realm. The king's oil royalties multiplied by 1948 to a figure in excess of 30 million dollars and by the following year to one larger than 65 million dollars (including 9.5 million dollars from the Pacific Western Oil Corporation, another American firm, as a bonus payment for an exclusive concession in the Sa'udi half of the neutral zone adjoining Kuwayt). In 1949, with oil revenues pouring into ibn Sa'ud's coffers at an unprecedented rate, the government nevertheless began to press the company for an even larger percentage of the returns, especially after the Anglo-Iranian Oil Company undertook, in a supplemental agreement with Iran of 17 July (Doc. 91), to make more generous payments to its host government. Informal talks between the Sa'udi Arab government and Aramco, however, jogged along until after the government on 20 August 1950 demanded modification in the terms of the original concession of 29 May 1933, thus compelling the company to initiate concrete negotiations. Before the year was out the parties concluded the following agreement, which introduced into the Near and Middle East the principle of equal sharing of the profits by government and company, on the pattern of the arrangement adopted by Venezuela two years earlier. Comparable contractual adjustments were made in Kuwayt on 1 December 1951, in Iraq on 18 February 1952 and ultimately in Iran on 19–20 September 1954 (Doc. 104). L. M. Fanning, *Foreign Oil and the Free World,* chaps. 7–11; UN, Dept. of Economic Affairs, *Summary of Recent Economic Developments in the Middle East, 1950–51,* chap. 2, *1952–53,* chap. 2 and *Review of Economic Conditions in the Middle East, 1951–52,* chap. 3.

Agreement concluded on 30 December 1950 between the government of the Sa'udi Arab Kingdom, hereinafter called "the Government," represented by His Excellency al-Shaykh 'Abdallah al-Sulayman al-Hamdan, Minister of Finance, and The Arabian American Oil Company, hereinafter called "Aramco," represented by F. A. Davies, its Executive Vice-President and Senior Resident Officer in the Sa'udi Arab Kingdom.

Whereas, the Government for a period of many months has been seeking additional revenue from Aramco, has held views different from those of Aramco on many long-standing interpretations of Aramco's concession and other agreements, and has made many claims and exactions which Aramco has contested as contrary to Aramco's concessionary rights and immunities; and

Whereas, the Government by letter of 20 August 1950 demanded amendment of certain conditions of Aramco's concession and other outstanding agreements and on 5 September 1950 submitted some thirteen points for discussion; and

Whereas, the Government on 4 November 1950 and on 27 December 1950 promulgated income tax decrees providing, among other things, for the taxation of business profits within the Sa'udi Arab Kingdom; and

Whereas, both the Government and Aramco recognize the necessity for resolving all matters in dispute so that Aramco may proceed with the development of oil resources in areas of Aramco's concession in full agreement with and having full cooperation from the Government;

Now, therefore, it is hereby agreed as follows:

1. Anything in article 21 in Aramco's concessionary agreement [of 29 May 1933] notwithstanding, Aramco submits to the income taxes provided in royal decrees No. 17/2/28/3321 and No. 17/2/28/7634 hereto attached for reference, it being understood that:

a. In no case shall the total of such taxes and all other taxes, royalties, rentals and exactions of the Government for any year exceed fifty per cent (50%) of the gross income of Aramco, after such gross income has been reduced by Aramco's cost of operation, including losses and depreciation, and by income taxes, if any, payable to any foreign country but not reduced by any taxes, royalties, rentals, or other exactions of the Government for such year; and

b. In all other respects Aramco's exemptions and immunities set forth in article 21 of the concession agreement shall continue in full force and effect.

2. It is further understood that:

a. Aramco shall have the option to pay the taxes imposed by said decrees No. 17/2/28/3321 and No. 17/2/28/7634 in the currencies of the Sa'udi Arab Kingdom or in other currencies in the proportions in which Aramco receives such currencies from its sales.

b. The term "exactions of the Government" as herein used shall include, among other things, the amount of all fees and charges for services rendered to Aramco in excess of the cost of such services and all duties on imports by Aramco for Aramco, for its service organizations and for the use and benefit of Aramco employees and of such organizations, except duties on food and items imported by Aramco for sale in its canteens.

3. The Government recognizes the continuing nature of the provisions of articles 1 and 2 of this agreement, and agrees that the new arrangement described therein constitutes a complete satisfaction of all outstanding claims and demands of the Government with respect both to the past and to the future; the Government agrees that Aramco may continue to conduct its operations in accordance with the Aramco concessionary agreements in the same manner as in the past.

4. The following are examples of the effect of article 3:

a. The demands of the Government's letter of 20 August 1950, and the Government's points for discussion of 5 September 1950, are fully satisfied.

b. Aramco's practices of using the English ton of 2,240 pounds in computation of royalties, selecting the locations for royalty gauging, taking natural salt for use in Aramco's operations, and using crude oil, gas, and petroleum products free of royalty in Aramco's operations and facilities in Sa'udi Arabia, are in accordance with the terms of the concessionary agreement.

c. The Government agrees that Aramco may gauge and deliver oil to the Trans-Arabian Pipe Line Company at al-Qaysumah.

d. The Jiddah radio agreement of 6 March 1949 is in full force and effect.

These articles in no way limit the all-inclusive generality of article 3.

5. The Government agrees that:

a. The agreement concluded in the month of March 1948 to the contrary notwithstanding, all monetary and currency exchanges between Aramco and the Government, including gold equivalents payable by Aramco to the Government, shall be at official rates recognized by the International Monetary Fund or by any other internationally accepted authority in case the International Monetary Fund is discontinued or no longer quotes exchange rates.

b. The Government will make available to Aramco Sa'udi Arab currencies, including gold, silver, and base metal coins at the same rates as they are made available to the public. Aramco shall have the right to purchase Sa'udi Arab currencies in the open market at current rates. If the Sa'udi Arab riyal rate should rise above the cost of minting new riyals plus transportation and insurance charges, the Government undertakes to supply Aramco's riyal requirements at cost plus said charges.

6. The free gasoline and kerosene that shall be offered the Government pursuant to article 8 of the Supplemental Agreement dated 31 May 1939 is hereby increased commencing 1 January 1951 to two million six hundred and fifty thousand (2,650,000) American gallons of gasoline per annum and to two hundred thousand (200,000) American gallons of kerosene per annum, all in bulk at Ras-al-Tannurah. Aramco agrees further to offer the Government commencing 1 January 1951 seven thousand five hundred (7,500) tons per annum of road asphalt at Ras-al-Tannurah, the said asphalt to be supplied in drums, provided that drums are available at reasonable cost. No royalty shall be payable on crude oil required for the manufacture of gasoline, kerosene and asphalt offered free by Aramco and taken by the Government. The costs of producing the said crude oil and of manufacturing the said free gasoline, kerosene, and asphalt shall be regarded as an expense of operations and not as an exaction within the meaning of article 2(b) of this agreement. It is understood that all the said free gasoline, kerosene and asphalt is for the ordinary requirements of the Government and not for sale outside or inside of Sa'udi Arabia.

7. Aramco agrees, commencing 1 January 1951, to pay the Government seven

hundred thousand dollars ($700,000.00) per annum toward the expenses, support and maintenance of representatives of the Government concerned with the admnistration of Aramco operations. The said amount of seven hundred thousand dollars ($700,000.00) shall be paid in equal installments in January, April, July and October of each year and shall be viewed as an expense of operations and not as an exaction within the meaning of article 2(b) of this agreement. The Government accepts Aramco's undertaking to pay the said amount of seven hundred thousand dollars ($700,000.00) per annum as full satisfaction of all claims and demands for expenses, support and maintenance of representatives of the Government concerned with the administration of Aramco's operations, including all such representatives of the national, provincial and municipal governments, police, guards, guides, soldiers and officials of the customs, immigration and quarantine services. It is understood that the said payment without limiting the generality of the foregoing shall be in lieu of all claims for salaries, wages, expense, transport, free services, residence and construction of every description, and all payments and services otherwise accruing after 1 January 1951 pursuant to article 20 of Aramco's concessionary agreement.

8. Aramco confirms its policy of conducting its operations in accordance with first-class oil field practice and its accounting in accordance with generally recognized standards. The Government for its part confirms the Government's confidence in the management of Aramco in conducting Aramco's operations.

9. This agreement shall become effective on the date hereof and shall remain in full force and effect for the duration of the concessionary agreement.

ROYAL DECREE NO. 17/2/28/3321, SIGNED ON 2 NOVEMBER AND PROMULGATED ON 4 NOVEMBER 1950

With the help of God Almighty we 'Abd-al-'Aziz bin 'Abd-al-Rahman al-Faysal, King of the Sa'udi Arab Kingdom, in consideration of what has been submitted to us by our Minister of Finance regarding the necessity of increasing the income of the Government to enable it to carry the burden of general reforms, and to promote the general welfare of the country and to improve the standards of living, have agreed to the institution of an income tax in accordance with the ordinance, the text of which follows and which we have approved and for execution of which we have issued our order:

ART. 1. This ordinance prescribes a tax on personal income of individuals and on the income or profits derived from the investments of capital.

The word "income," wherever it occurs in this ordinance, means all personal income earned or deriving from the investment of capital within the Sa'udi Arab Kingdom and where it has joint rights in the two Neutral Zones between it and Iraq or Kuwayt.

ART. 2. Personal income in this ordinance shall mean all kinds and descriptions of compensation for personal services that an individual receives as wages from the person or the company employing him, or from anyone acting on their behalf. This ordinance also applies to the salaries of the employees of the Sa'udi Arab Government.

Everything paid in cash and also the amount of the value, according to a reasonable estimate, of chattels or other things given in lieu of any salary or the amounts deducted from salary or wages to settle debts shall be considered as personal income.

ART. 3. Taxable personal income is that which exceeds annually twenty thousand Sa'udi Arab riyals.

ART. 4. The tax rate applicable to personal income is five per cent (5%) of the taxable income as defined in this ordinance; and the amount shall be collected by the means specified in instructions that shall be issued by the Minister of Finance.

ART. 5. Anyone employing a person or persons liable to personal income tax shall deduct the amount of the tax from the wages and salaries of such persons and shall pay the deducted amounts to the authorities designated by the Ministry of Finance, on or before the fifteenth day of the month following the month for which the deduction was made. He shall also record this on the required form under the supervision of the official delegated by the Ministry of Finance.

If he should delay or fail to pay the tax on behalf of the person or persons whom he employs, he will become responsible for payment of such amount, and the Ministry of Finance shall have the right to collect it from him by such means as it may decide.

Anyone employing another person or persons shall give notice of the amount of tax deducted from wages or salaries, and he shall record it on the proper form.

Companies that are registered in accordance with the Law for the Registration of Companies, approved by royal decree No. 144, shall have the right to deduct the amounts of the taxes due from the wages of their workmen and the salaries of their employees and pay the taxes at one time for a period not exceeding three months, on or before the fifteenth day of the month following the period for which the taxes were deducted.

If any employer of another person or persons should delay paying the taxes due within five days from the legal date for payment, he shall be fined an additional amount of ten per cent (10%) of the original amount due; and if the period of delay should exceed fifteen days, the fine shall be twenty-five per cent (25%).

ART. 6. Income from capital, according to this ordinance, shall mean all income or profit, including the profits deriving from any enterprise or transaction in which capital is used, such as the purchase and sale of different kinds and descriptions of goods, the products from lands, the exchange of any kind of money and the hiring and letting of any properties whether movable or immovable. Capital shall include animals, trucks, ships, other means of transportation, machinery and equipment. Capital shall not include the requisite tools which an individual laborer owns and uses in performing his work or trade.

ART. 7. The net profit deriving from the investment of capital, subject to income tax under this ordinance, shall be considered to be all income, receipts, and profits, meaning thereby the gross proceeds of commercial transactions completed during the year. (Gross proceeds shall include all sums of money received in addition to properties and acquisitions which may be acquired without payment of money). Deductions will include the cost of goods sold, the ordinary and necessary operating expenses of the enterprise, and a reasonable amount for depreciation, but not the personal expenses of the owner of the enterprise.

The net profit deriving from the investment of capital shall be estimated at fifteen per cent (15%) of the gross proceeds, unless the taxpayer is able to persuade the responsible officials to the contrary by force of adequate documents and accurate records.

ART. 8. The income tax on the net profit deriving from investment of capital shall be collected at the rate of ten per cent (10%) after deduction of the sum of the twenty thousand riyals exempted as stipulated in article 3 and in paragraph (e) of article 17 of this ordinance.

ART. 9. Every person liable to the tax on net profits deriving from the investment of capital shall file a declaration thereof and pay the tax therein indicated to the official whom the Ministry of Finance shall delegate for the collection of the amount.

The declaration shall be written on the form which the said Ministry shall prescribe. The declaration shall be filed and the tax indicated in the declaration shall be paid on or before the fifteenth day of the month following its due date.

If the person subject to the tax should delay or fail to pay what is due within five days from the legally prescribed date, he shall be fined an additional amount of ten per cent (10%) of the sum due. If the delay exceeds fifteen days, the fine shall be twenty-five per cent (25%).

ART. 10. The word "company" in this

ordinance shall mean any company that is registered or that is required to be registered, in accordance with the Law for the Registration of Companies, approved by royal decree No. 144. This expression shall include also all companies engaged in any kind of business in the Sa'udi Arab Kingdom and where the Sa'udi Arab Kingdom has joint rights in the two Neutral Zones between it and Iraq or Kuwayt.

ART. 11. The rate of tax on companies shall be twenty per cent (20%) of their net profit, as that profit is defined in this ordinance. The tax shall be collected annually.

ART. 12. The net profit of companies subject to the tax shall be the total gross income, as defined therein, after deduction of the amounts which this ordinance prescribes.

ART. 13. The gross income subject to the tax in accordance with this ordinance shall comprise all income, profits, and earnings of whatever kind and in whatever form paid, deriving from all kinds of industry and commerce such as buying and selling and financial or commercial transactions, from dealing with and developing oil or other mineral resources, and from movable or immovable properties, including all income from commissions or from profits on shares or securities or any profits or earnings from any commercial transactions the object of which is profit, and earnings from any source whatsoever. Gross income for any company incorporated under the laws of any country other than Sa'udi Arabia, and conducting its operations at the same time both outside and inside the Sa'udi Arab Kingdom, shall comprise all the income which that company receives locally from any source whatsoever within the kingdom. That part of the income which the company receives from the conduct of operations both inside and outside the country and is derived from local sources shall be added thereto. The Sa'udi Arab Kingdom, whenever and wherever it occurs in this ordinance, shall embrace its joint rights in the two Neutral Zones between it and Iraq or Kuwayt.

ART. 14. Amounts that are deductible for the determination of the net profits of companies in accordance with this ordinance are as follows:

(a) All the ordinary and necessary expenses that the business or the enterprise requires and the expenditure of which takes place during the year, including therein a reasonable amount for the salaries of employees and for compensation granted for any personal services.

(b) Travel expenses that are connected with the business or the enterprise.

(c) Payments for properties rented in connection with the business or the enterprise.

(d) Any losses incurred by the business or the enterprise and not otherwise compensated.

(e) A reasonable amount for depreciation of properties used or employed in the operations.

ART. 15. Every company subject to this ordinance must file a declaration on the official form and pay the amount shown thereon to the official designated by the Ministry of Finance for the purpose. The said declaration must be filed and the required amount paid on or before the fifteenth day of the third month following the end of the year for which the declaration was made.

In case of failure to file the declaration and to pay the amount within five days from the fixed time, a fine amounting to ten per cent (10%) of the tax shall be added to the sum due. If the delay exceeds a period of fifteen days, the fine shall become twenty-five per cent (25%).

ART. 16. The taxpayer shall enter in the records of his accounts all the gross income that he receives in the year and shall do the same with the amounts deducted (except for depreciation and depletion). When the taxpayer proves that his records are correct and that they reflect truly his gross income and the deductions, he may submit the declaration on the basis of those records. If an auditor who is legally and internationally recognized certifies to the accuracy of the records for any year in which the tax is due, the declarations on the basis of the said records shall be considered correct.

If the taxpayer declares that he keeps records in a clear manner on the basis of a financial year different from the calendar year, he may request the Ministry of Finance that it permit him to make his declarations in accordance with the financial year that he follows. In that case he shall submit declarations and pay the tax on the fifteenth day of the third month after the end of the financial year that he follows. Penalties for delay in submitting the declarations and in paying the tax shall be as mentioned in article 15 of this ordinance.

ART. 17. [The following] shall be exempt from the provisions of this ordinance:

(a) The royal family.

(b) Officers and men of the armed forces, police and coast guard.

(c) Persons officially appointed to religious posts in mosques.

(d) Foreign ambassadors, ministers plenipotentiary and other diplomatic representatives, consuls and foreign consular representatives, on condition of reciprocal treatment and within the limits of this treatment.

(e) Persons whose income does not exceed annually twenty thousand Sa'udi Arab riyals.

(f) Animals and plants on which the alms tax [*al-zakah*] is paid.

(g) Contributions and aids paid to the Government, charitable organizations and social welfare institutions that are recognized by the Sa'udi Arab Government.

ART. 18. (a) The Minister of Finance shall enforce the income tax laws, and a special department for taxes shall be formed in the Ministry of Finance.

(b) To facilitate the enforcement of this ordinance the Kingdom shall be divided administratively into not more than six districts, in accordance with what the Minister of Finance deems necessary for the administration and enforcement of this ordinance. In each district a director shall be appointed and shall have therein an office where the inhabitants of the district shall submit their declarations and pay the taxes due. The said director shall receive the taxes due and shall pay them monthly to the Ministry of Finance.

(c) A committee composed of three qualified and expert persons shall be [appointed] in each district to check the declarations and to decide whether the amount should be increased. The committee shall have the right to request that the taxpayer present himself personally, or that he delegate someone to appear before it on his behalf. It shall have the right also to request the taxpayer or his agent to submit records and books for checking; the records and books shall be returned to their owner upon his request after the committee has checked them.

(d) When the committee discovers a tax due and not mentioned in the declaration, or any tax on which declaration was not made, it shall have the right to collect the tax due and a fine amounting to twenty-five per cent (25%) from the properties of the taxpayer, in accordance with instructions which the district director may issue.

(e) When the district director pays to the Ministry of Finance the taxes collected in any month of the year, he shall send an accompanying list of the names and addresses of the persons who paid the taxes and the amount paid by each.

(f) Companies incorporated outside Sa'udi Arabia and under laws of the country in which they are incorporated, but conducting operations both inside and outside of the Sa'udi Arab Kingdom, shall submit their declarations to the tax department in Jiddah. The head of the department shall appoint a special committee composed of three qualified and expert persons to review and check their declarations. Those companies shall have the right to delegate any of their employees to appear on their behalf before the said committee, if such is requested. Such companies shall have the right to defend the accuracy of the taxes about which investigation is in progress. The committee shall have the right to check the records and accounts of those companies at any time it deems fit but not to hold the records and accounts for such a period as to hamper the operations of the companies.

(g) The committee shall have no right to impose on the companies the additional taxes which it estimates except after obtaining the approval of the Minister of Finance or whoever may be acting on his behalf.

ART. 19. The Minister of Finance is accorded full authority to take all measures necessary for the enforcement of this ordinance and the collection of the taxes prescribed thereunder. This includes without limitation the employment and training of the necessary employees, the issuance of necessary official forms, instructions and orders, notification to taxpayers concerning payment of the taxes and whatever may be connected therewith, and obliging individuals and companies to keep records which will facilitate the collection of the taxes.

ART. 20. The tax prescribed by this ordinance shall be effective for the first time on 13 October 1950.

ROYAL DECREE NO. 17/2/28/7634, SIGNED ON 26 DECEMBER AND PROMULGATED ON 27 DECEMBER 1950

With the help of God Almighty we, 'Abd-al-'Aziz bin 'Abd-al-Rahman al-Faysal, King of the Sa'udi Arab Kingdom, in consideration of what has been submitted to us by our Minister of Finance and having reviewed the royal decree No. 17/2/28/3321 of 2 November 1950, have agreed to the institution of an additional income tax on companies engaged in the production of petroleum or other hydrocarbons in accordance with the ordinance of which the text follows and for the execution of which we have issued our order:

ART. 1. On every company registered or required to be registered in accordance with the Decree for the Registration of Companies, approved by royal decree No. 144, and engaged in the production of petroleum or other hydrocarbons in the Sa'udi Arab Kingdom an income tax of fifty per cent (50%) of the net operating income shall be imposed for each taxable year ending after the date of this decree. From such tax the amount provided in article 3 of this decree shall be deducted. The tax before the deduction is designated in this decree as "the provisional income tax" (and [the tax] after the deduction, "the additional income tax").

ART. 2. Net operating income under article 1 of this decree means gross income described in article 13 of royal decree No. 17/2/28/3321, after the deduction of the following:

(a) The amounts that are allowable as deductions under article 14 of the said royal decree, exclusive of amounts paid or payable to the Sa'udi Arab Government, and

(b) Income taxes, if any, to the extent that such taxes have actually been paid by the company or are payable by it to any foreign country after the company has provided for the income taxes imposed by the Sa'udi Arab Government.

ART. 3. The amount to be deducted under article 1 of this decree shall be the total of all taxes (except the income tax imposed by this decree), royalties, rentals, duties and all other sums paid or payable to the Sa'udi Arab Government. If the total of the foregoing exceeds the provisional income tax, the excess shall be deducted from the income tax that would otherwise be payable for the same taxable year under royal decree No. 17/2/28/3321.

ART. 4. The taxable year shall be the annual accounting period regularly followed in keeping the records of the company. Net operating income, gross income, deductions and all other items relating to the taxable year and entering into the determination of income taxes shall be computed on the accrual method of accounting, if such method is regularly followed in keeping the records of the company.

ART. 5. Articles 15, 16, 17, 18 and 19, of royal decree No. 17/2/28/3321 shall be applicable to the additional income tax, unless differently provided for in this decree. Such additional income tax and the income tax imposed by royal decree No. 17/2/28/3321 shall be paid in equal installments once every three months commencing with the date the declaration on the official form is due. The Minister of

Finance may grant reasonable extensions for filing the declarations and paying the income taxes imposed both by this decree and by royal decree No. 17/2/28/3321.

95. NATIONALIZATION OF THE OIL INDUSTRY IN IRAN
1 May 1951

[Great Britain, *Parliamentary Papers, 1951,* Persia No. 1, Cmd. 8425, pp. 29–31]

The supplemental agreement that the Anglo-Iranian Oil Company and the Iranian government initialed in July 1949 (Doc. 91) was placed without delay before the *Majlis* (the lower chamber of the legislature, after 1949) for ratification. But in the ten days remaining before the statutory expiry of the 15th *Majlis,* the chairman of its oil committee, Dr. Muhammad Musaddiq, who had spearheaded the drive since 1944 against the grant of concessions to foreigners, easily prevented action by filibustering tactics. In the general election that followed, the National Front, a small group of deputies led by Musaddiq, campaigned on a platform calling for the nationalization of the oil resources and industry in the country. In the 16th *Majlis,* which convened in June 1950, the National Front found support from Ayatullah Sayyid Abu-al-Qasim Kashani, who had been exiled sixteen months earlier because of implication in a plot to murder the shah and who had just returned to take his seat as deputy to which he had been elected *in absentia.* Kashani, as spokesman for religious reaction, saw in the popular incitement against foreignism an opportunity to regain for his class the political influence that it had lost under Riza Shah. The government withdrew the supplemental agreement from the legislature on 26 December 1950, after it had become manifest that the instrument could not possibly receive the requisite support. The announcement early in January 1951 of Aramco's fresh arrangement with Sa'udi Arabia (Doc. 94) played into the hand of the proponents of nationalization. General 'Ali Razmara, the prime minister, who had opposed their efforts on the ground that Iran did not have sufficient technicians to run the oil industry, was murdered by a religious fanatic on 7 March 1951. The *Majlis* oil committee within twenty-four hours passed a resolution recommending nationalization, which was endorsed by the lower chamber a week later and by the newly created Senate on 20 March. By 30 April, two days after Musaddiq became prime minister, both houses adopted the following law—promulgated by the shah on 1 May—stipulating the conditions for the nationalization of the oil industry. O. J. Lissitzyn, "Iranian Oil, Foreign Investments and the Law," *Foreign Affairs Reports* [Delhi], 2 (February-March 1953), 17–39; J. C. Hurewitz, *Middle East Dilemmas,* chap. 2; B. Shwadran, *The Middle East, Oil and the Great Powers,* chap. 5; *Survey of International Affairs, 1951,* pp. 292–337; A. W. Ford, *The Anglo-Iranian Oil Dispute of 1951–1952;* L. P. Elwell-Sutton, *Persian Oil,* chaps. 16–21.

ART. 1. With a view to arranging the enforcement of the law of 24th and 29th Esfand, 1329 (15th and 20th March, 1951), concerning the nationalisation of the oil industry throughout Persia, a mixed board composed of five Senators and five Deputies elected by either of the two Houses and of the Minister of Finance or his Deputy shall be formed.

ART. 2. The Government is bound to dispossess at once the former Anglo-Iranian Oil Company under the supervision of the mixed board. If the Company refuses to hand over at once on the grounds of existing claims on the Government, the Government can, by mutual agreement, deposit in the Bank Milli Iran or in any other bank up to 25 per cent. of current revenue from the oil after deduction of exploitation expenses in order to meet the probable claims of the Company.

ART. 3. The Government is bound to examine the rightful claims of the Government as well as the rightful claims of the Company under the supervision of the mixed board and to submit its suggestions to the two Houses of Parliament in order that the same may be implemented after approval by the two Houses.

ART. 4. Inasmuch as the nationalisation of the oil industry was also approved by the Senate on 29th Esfand (20th March,

1951) and inasmuch as all income from oil and oil products are the established property of the Persian nation the Government is bound to audit the Company's accounts under the supervision of the mixed board which must also closely supervise exploitation as from the date of the implementation of this law until the appointment of an executive body.

ART. 5. The mixed board must draw up, as soon as possible, the statute of the National Oil Company in which provision is to be made for the setting up of an executive body and a supervisory body of experts, and must submit the same to the two Houses for approval.

ART. 6. For the gradual replacement of foreign experts by Persian experts the mixed board is bound to draw up regulations for sending, after competitive examinations, a number of students each year to foreign countries to undertake study in the various branches of required knowledge and gain experience in oil industries, the said regulations to be carried out by the Ministry of Education after the approval of the Council of Ministers. The expenses connected with the study of such students shall be met out of oil revenues.

ART. 7. All purchasers of products derived from the wells taken back from the former Anglo-Iranian Oil Company can in future buy annually the same quantity of oil they used to buy annually from the Company from the beginning of the Christian year 1948 up to 29th Esfand, 1329 (20th March, 1951), at a reasonable international price. For any surplus quantity they shall have priority in the event of equal terms of purchase being offered.

ART. 8. All proposals formulated by the mixed board for the approval of the Majlis and submission to the Majlis must be sent to the Oil Commission.

ART. 9. The mixed board must finish its work within three months as from the date of approval of this law and must submit the report of its activities to the Majlis in accordance with Article 8. In the event of requiring an extension it must apply, giving valid reasons, for such extension. Whilst, however, the extension is before the two Houses for approval the mixed board can continue its functions.

96. AIR BASE (DHAHRAN) AGREEMENT: SA'UDI ARABIA AND THE UNITED STATES
18 June 1951

[U.S., *Treaties and Other International Acts Series,* No. 2290]

Late in World War II the United States decided with King ibn Sa'ud's blessing to erect "for use in the redeployment of [American] troops to and from the Far East" at Dhahran [al-Zahran] on the Persian Gulf coast, less than five miles from one of Aramco's principal settlements, a military air base "that could accommodate the largest type of aircraft." Since Washington still viewed the security of the Near and Middle East primarily as a British responsibility, the United Kingdom was informed of American plans. But the feeling prevailed in Whitehall "that no military necessity for the airfield existed" (U.S., 80th Cong., 2nd sess., Sen. Rep. No. 440, part 5, p. 17), so that months rolled by before British opposition dissolved. Construction, which actually commenced on the morrow of V-J Day (14 August 1945), was completed in March 1946, too late for redeployment service. By the time the three-year period for American operation of the base passed in 1949, however, the United States was saddled with leadership in the Western alliance for containing Soviet aggression, and the Dhahran base, so close to an exposed frontier of the USSR, assumed fresh strategic significance. American efforts to prolong the air-base rights met with a cool reception in Sa'udi Arabia, still smarting from the Palestine war. King ibn Sa'ud on 23 June 1949 consented to a six-month extension, renewed with difficulty for comparable brief periods until early in 1951, when the United States finally began to press in earnest for the following agreement, which took the form of an exchange of notes. Success could be attributed, among other reasons, to the profit-sharing arrangement with Aramco of December 1950 (Doc. 94), which promised the Sa'udi realm the greatest revenues in its history, and to a mutual defense assistance agreement of 18 June 1951 (U. S., *Treaties and Other International Acts Series,* No. 2289), declaring the Arabian kingdom eligible for reimbursable United States military aid. Reproduced below is the Sa'udi Foreign Minister's letter to the American Ambassador. H. L. Hoskins, *The Middle East, Problem Area in World Politics,* chap. 13; J. C. Hurewitz, *Middle East Dilemmas,* chap. 4; *Survey of International Affairs, 1951,* pp. 21–28.

I have the honor to inform Your Excellency that as of this date the Agreement between the Government of the Kingdom of Saudi Arabia and the Government of the United States of America concerning Dhahran Airfield, concluded on June 23, 1949, as extended, will be terminated. In view of the desire of the Government of Saudi Arabia to offer to the Government of the United States of America certain facilities after that date, I have the honor to transmit to Your Excellency herein below the provisions upon which agreement was reached for the continuation of the use of facilities and services at Dhahran Airfield by the transient and supporting aircraft of the Government of the United States, in accordance with the conditions mentioned in this letter. It is my hope that you will inform me in your reply of the approval thereof by the Government of the United States in order to consider this note and Your Excellency's reply an agreement committing the two parties.

1. The term Dhahran Airfield as used in this Agreement means the area of land in the so-called Dammam tracts measuring five statute miles on each side of a square with the center located at the terminal building of the existing airdrome.

2. (a). In accordance with the request of the Saudi Arabian Government, the Government of the United States agrees to send, at its expense, to Dhahran Airfield a Mission to be employed for training Saudi nationals and for organizing the operations of the Dhahran Airport technical administration.

(b). The number of the members of the Mission will be determined by request of the head of the Mission and approval thereof by the Saudi Arabian Minister of Defense. Such specification in numbers of personnel will be reviewed from time to time in the light of developing circumstances and requirements.

(c). The Mission referred to in paragraph (a) above is permitted to employ an additional number of civilians on the Airfield on condition that such civilians shall be the subjects of the Kingdom of Saudi Arabia or the subjects of the United States or the subjects of a third state friendly to both, and that the number of non-Saudi personnel will be determined by request of the Mission and approval of the Saudi Arabian Minister of Defense. Such specification in numbers of personnel will be reviewed from time to time in the light of developing circumstances and requirements.

(d). It is provided that there must not be among members of the Mission or among the other employees any individual who is objectionable to the Saudi Arabian Government, and that the Government of the United States will submit a detailed list of the names and identity of these personnel and employees.

(e). If the Saudi Arabian Government requests the Mission to send out or replace any of its personnel or employees whom the Saudi Arabian Government does not desire to remain in the country, the Mission will carry out such request promptly.

3. (a). United States aircraft are permitted to use the Saudi Arabian Government Airport at Dhahran to land and take off for refueling and other technical services such as maintenance and repair.

(b). United States aircraft are permitted to fly over those air routes of Saudi Arabia of which the Saudi Arabian Government permits the use.

(c). United States aircraft are permitted to perform air rescue operations for aircraft which are in need of aid, upon notice to the Saudi Arabian Government. In performing such air rescue, vehicles and crash boats may be used to the extent necessary for air rescue operations.

(d). The number of aircraft which will be permitted to be based at Dhahran Airfield and which will be used for air rescue and other authorized operations will be determined by request of the United States Mission and approval of the Saudi Arabian Minister of Defense. Such specification in the number of aircraft will be reviewed from time to time in the light of developing circumstances and requirements.

4. In accordance with paragraph 23 of the existing Dhahran Airfield Agreement which states that all fixed installations and other property used in operation and maintenance of the Airfield will be returned to the Saudi Arabian Government upon termination of the Agreement, and in view of the fact that the said Agreement is being terminated and that such installations and properties thereby revert to the Saudi Arabian Government, and, due to the desire of the Saudi Arabian Government to facilitate the errand of the Mission, it agrees to place at the disposition of the Mission at Dhahran Airfield, rent free, certain existing buildings and installations as specified in the list agreed upon by the appropriate authorities of the two Governments and approved by the Saudi Arabian Minister of Defense. This list will be reviewed from time to time in the light of developing circumstances and requirements.

5. (a). The United States Mission at Dhahran Airfield will perform the necessary technical operations, and such operations will be determined and agreed upon between the members of the Mission and the appropriate officials of the Saudi Arabian Government, and, after obtaining the approval of the Saudi Arabian Minister of Defense, the Mission will perform its duties on the Base, provided that such duties will be reviewed from time to time subject to the technical developments and circumstances.

(b). The United States Mission is permitted to administer, at Dhahran Airfield only, and in addition to what is mentioned in paragraph (a), matters connected with United States military aircraft, the military personnel and the civilian employees of the Mission. The Mission at Dhahran Airfield will not act in any other matters except when specifically authorized by the Saudi Arabian Government.

(c). Civil aviation operations and all other aviation operations at Dhahran Airfield, with the exception of those mentioned in paragraphs 5 (a) and (b) will be administered by the Saudi Arabian Government under its responsibility. The Saudi Arabian Government will take the necessary action to prevent interference with the operations of United States aircraft as authorized under this Agreement. All regulations and instructions of the Saudi Arabian Government will be applied to civilian aircraft which are permitted by the Saudi Arabian Government to use Dhahran Airfield, including compliance by such aircraft with the international provisions which are accepted by the Saudi Arabian Government. The Saudi Arabian Government will also perform customs procedures, collection of fees, inspections, passport control and similar matters.

6. (a). To assure efficient operation and the furnishing of technical services at Dhahran Airfield to the best possible extent the United States Mission will be permitted to improve, alter, modify and replace buildings and facilities for improvement purposes or, after notifying the Saudi Arabian Government, and obtaining its approval, to construct such buildings and facilities at Dhahran Airfield (including runways, taxiways, parking aprons, weather services, radio communications and navigational aids) as may be deemed necessary for the purpose of this Agreement. The Saudi Arabian Government will issue instructions to the appropriate authorities to prohibit the construction of buildings or obstacles for a distance of five kilometers in the plain west of the present Airfield, and it will also issue instructions to prevent the construction of obstacles in the approaches to the runways.

(b). Such installations and constructions will become, as soon as they are established, the property of the Saudi Arabian Government. All fixed properties will also be considered as belonging to the Saudi Arabian Government as soon as they are established. The Saudi Arabian Government will permit such new installations and fixed items to remain at the disposition of the United States Mission during the period of this Agreement.

(c). It is agreed that the United States Mission will not remove any of the property and installations which have been installed and have become the property of the Saudi Arabian Government. In case the Mission replaces any installations or property which has become the property of the Saudi Arabian Government, then such replacements will become the property of the Saudi Arabian Government and the items which were removed will become the property of the United States Government.

(d). Neither the Mission nor the United States Government has the right to sell, lease, donate or pledge to a third party anything granted to it in this Agreement or which has been put at its disposition at Dhahran Airfield under this Agreement.

7. The Mission is permitted to employ radio codes.

8. The Mission may construct at the expense of the United States Government a railway spur to connect Dhahran Airfield with the railway which passes through the city of Dhahran. This spur will be considered as soon as constructed the property of the Saudi Arabian Government. The use of such spur during the period of this Agreement will be subject to a special agreement.

9. (a). The Saudi Arabian Government will accord exemption from customs duties, taxes and all Government charges on materials, equipment and supplies necessary for the construction, maintenance, supply and operation of the Airfield, provided that the Mission will submit to the appropriate authorities of the Saudi Arabian Government the official bills of lading and manifests on the material, equipment and supplies imported for the operation and maintenance of Dhahran Airfield.

(b). The Saudi Arabian Government accords the military personnel of the Mission personal exemption from customs duties and Government charges for themselves or their personal effects which may be brought in for their personal use provided that such effects will be subject to submission of official bills of lading and manifest and provided that quantities of such effects will be within reasonable limits and that no such articles will be sold unless the appropriate authorities of the Saudi Arabian Government are informed in order that the applicable taxes may be collected. Civilians of United States nationality who are attached to the Mission will also be accorded exemption from customs duties, taxes and Government charges for themselves or on their personal effects which may be brought in for their personal use provided that such effects will also be subject to submission of official bills of lading and manifest and provided that the quantities of such effects will be within reasonable limits and that no such articles will be sold unless the appropriate authorities of the Saudi Arabian Government are informed in order that the applicable taxes may be collected.

(c). It is understood that the Mission will inform the appropriate authorities of the Saudi Arabian Government of anything the Mission may intend to sell in order that the applicable taxes may be collected.

(d). Subject to the provisions of paragraph 6 (b) the Mission may withdraw from Saudi Arabia any of those items which have been brought in after notifying the Saudi Arabian Government; if the United States has no special interest in using such items in some other place outside Saudi Arabia, these items will be offered for sale to the Saudi Arabian Government at a fair price. In case the Saudi Arabian Government does not wish to buy these items they may then be exported free of any export charges.

10. The Mission is permitted to receive its military mail and to send it to and from Dhahran Airfield exempt from customs duties provided that parcel post will be in accordance with the terms of paragraph 9 (a).

11. The members of the Mission, its personnel and employees may carry on any social activities on condition that they will take into account the local customs and laws in effect in Saudi Arabia.

12. (a). The complete authority and

sovereignty inside and outside of Dhahran Airfield is the absolute right of the Saudi Arabian Government and it will make arrangements for guarding and maintaining the safety of the Airport.

(b). The United States Mission will assign special guards for the installations which are used by the Mission and such guards will be responsible for such installations under their guard inside the Airfield.

(c). The Mission shall comply with the request of the Director of the Dhahran Airport in appointing certain responsible persons from the Mission to accompany the Saudi patrol guards to identify members of the Mission and to cooperate during patrol duty.

13. (a). All United States military personnel, members of the Mission, and all civilian employees of the Mission who are United States nationals or the nationals of other friendly states and their dependents at Dhahran Airfield shall obey all applicable laws and regulations of the Kingdom of Saudi Arabia.

(b). Any offense committed by any of the individuals referred to in (a) with the exception of American military personnel will be subject to the local jurisdiction of the Kingdom of Saudi Arabia.

(c). Depending on international authority, the Saudi Arabian Government agrees that:

(i) If any member of the armed forces of the United States commits an offense inside Dhahran Airfield he will be subject to United States military jurisdiction.

(ii) In the case of any offense committed by a member of the armed forces of the United States outside Dhahran Airfield at Al Khobar, Dammam, Dhahran, Ras Tanura, the beaches south of Al Khobar to Half Moon Bay, and the roads leading to these places, the Saudi Arabian authorities will arrest the offender and after promptly completing the preliminary investigation will turn such person over to the Mission at Dhahran Airfield for trial and punishment under American military jurisdiction.

(iii) Any offense committed by a member of the armed forces of the United States outside the places mentioned in (i) and (ii) will be subject to the local jurisdiction of the Kingdom of Saudi Arabia.

(d). Claims for compensation for damages arising out of acts of members of the armed forces of the United States will be settled by agreement between the appropriate Saudi Arabian authorities and the Head of the Mission. In case no agreement is reached, settlement will be made through diplomatic channels.

14. Members, personnel and employees of the Mission who are United States nationals will be in possession of valid passports or identification papers to be presented to the appropriate authorities upon arrival at Dhahran Airfield. All of them must obtain Saudi visas from the point of departure, and if, for unavoidable reasons, it is impossible to obtain such visas, the Saudi Arabian Government will honor competent United States Government travel orders on condition that such persons are not undesirable. If anyone arrives without having followed the said arrangements, he will be subject to the laws and regulations of the Saudi Arabian Government.

15. The United States Government agrees to provide the Saudi Arabian Government the following services:

(a). A military training program, the details of which will be agreed upon in a separate agreement and whereby an American military mission will be sent to Saudi Arabia.

(b). Training in the maintenance and operation of airfields to a maximum at one time of one hundred Saudi Arabian students selected by the Saudi Arabian Government. The Saudi Arabian Government will select from these students, in consultation with the Mission twenty Saudi Arabian students to pursue at United States Air Force schools in the United States advanced technical training in airfield operation and maintenance, under conditions embodied in the attached annex.

Saudi Arab students of the Training Mission who have completed a course of technical training in United States schools and who have been found fully qualified in their technical specialty will, to the maximum degree possible, be given consideration and priority for employment at Dhahran Airfield. Every opportunity will be taken to increase the training and experience of these advanced graduates to the degree where they will be capable of administering and operating the international airports of Saudi Arabia. Rates of pay will be on the same scale as others of equal qualifications.

(c). In cases of emergency the United States will provide Saudi Arabia for its state-owned aircraft at delivery cost price, aircraft parts, including engines, when such parts can be made available from stock at Dhahran Airfield. In the event that such parts cannot be made available at Dhahran Airfield, the United States will assist Saudi Arabia in procuring them from commercial sources.

(d). The Mission will make available, within the capabilities of its facilities in operation at Dhahran Airfield, its weather services, radio communications, air rescue and aircraft operation services for the use of civilian aircraft which are authorized by the Saudi Arabian Government to use Dhahran Airfield.

(e). The United States Mission will provide the best of its ability and within its capabilities at Dhahran Airfield medical treatment and dispensary services for Saudi Arabian nationals who are employees of the United States Mission for Saudi members and students of the United States Training Mission.

In the event of epidemic or infectious diseases the United States Mission will assist the Saudi Arabian Government to the extent possible to combat the situation.

16. Upon the termination of this Agreement, the Mission will return to the Saudi Arabian Government in sound operating condition all fixed installations, properties and equipment of which it makes use in the operation and maintenance of Dhahran Airfield.

17. (a). The Mission is permitted to construct wells, water reservoirs or dams to insure an ample supply of water for Dhahran Airfield.

(b). The Mission will undertake, in cooperation with the appropriate Saudi authorities, to take such steps as may be mutually agreed upon to improve health and sanitation in areas contiguous to Dhahran Airfield.

18. The Mission is permitted to contract for any construction work at Dhahran Airfield authorized by this Agreement without restriction as to choice of contractor provided that the contracting firm or the people working with it will not be unacceptable to the Saudi Arabian Government. So far as may be practicable, Saudi nationals will be given preference in employment and contracts.

19. Nothing in this Agreement shall be interpreted or construed to infringe or detract in any way from the complete and absolute sovereignty of the Saudi Arabian Government over Dhahran Airfield, nor does it include any authorization whatsoever which would for any reason permit flying over, landing or conducting any aviation operations over or near the Holy Places or over any prohibited areas.

20. This Agreement shall come into force as of this date, shall continue in force for a period of five years, and shall remain in force for an additional period of five years thereafter unless, six months prior to the termination of the first five year period, either party to the Agreement gives to the other notice of intention to modify or terminate the Agreement.

ANNEX

The following are the conditions covering the training of Saudi Arabian students in the United States as specified in paragraph 15 (b).:

1. Transportation from Dhahran to the United States and return will be furnished by the United States Air Force via military aircraft at no cost to the Saudi Arabian Government. Travel within the United States will be at the expense of the Saudi Arabian Government although the United States Air Force will render all advice and assistance to trainees.

2. Saudi students will mess at their own expense on a cost basis at Officers' Messes at the established local rates.

3. Where quarters are available, they will be furnished on a scale equivalent to that authorized officers of the United States Air Force. No reimbursement will be made to the United States for this service. Where quarters are not available, the officer trainee or the Saudi Arabian Government will make their own arrangements at no cost to the United States Government.

4. All training will be without cost to the Saudi Arabian Government except as herein provided. Special clothing and equipment required for the prescribed training courses will be furnished for use during the training course upon a temporary loan basis at no cost to the Saudi Arabian Government.

5. Commissary, post exchange and similar privileges which are ordinarily available to officers of the United States Air Force will be extended to these trainees.

6. Medical care will be furnished when available on the same basis as furnished United States Air Force personnel, at no cost to the Saudi Arabian Government other than for subsistence.

97. FOUR-POWER (BRITAIN, FRANCE, TURKEY AND THE UNITED STATES) PROPOSALS FOR A MIDDLE EAST COMMAND 13 October–10 November 1951

[*The Department of State Bulletin,* 25 (22 October 1951), 647–48, (19 November 1951), 817–18]

The Western search for ways to develop a "situation of strength" in the Near and Middle East gathered momentum after the outbreak of the Korean war in June 1950. The British defense system in that region, which had proved so invaluable to the allied cause in two world wars, was contracting steadily. The overriding Western strategic problem at the time was to keep the Suez Canal base within the allied orbit. Anglo-Egyptian talks (June 1950–July 1951) turned out to be less exploratory than explosive, so that the breach between the two positions widened appreciably. At this juncture the United States took the initiative in persuading Britain, France and Turkey to become with itself co-sponsors of an Allied Middle East Command with which Egypt would be invited to associate itself as a founder member. The projected scheme, it was hoped, by substituting a joint allied for an exclusive British base in the canal zone, would meet at once Egyptian demands for the elimination of British hegemony and allied needs for the continued maintenance of the vital canal base in a condition for immediate emergency use. Inasmuch as Egyptian territory was slated under the scheme to serve as an allied base, the failure to consult the Egyptian government in formulating the plans wounded nationalist sensitivities. But this merely added another emotional irritant to an already highly charged situation, for, in the final analysis, the Western powers and Egypt were at cross purposes. The allies were anxious to bolster their defense against the USSR; Egypt, to rid itself of foreign controls. Egyptian rejection of the four-power proposal was accordingly a foregone conclusion. Following the Egyptian Parliament's enactment on 15 October 1951 of decree laws repudiating the 1899 Anglo-Egyptian condominium agreements on the Sudan (I, Doc. 99) and the 1936 treaty (Doc. 61), the four allies issued on 10 November a fresh set of principles under which any Near and Middle East state might voluntarily join the proposed allied-sponsored organization. J. C. Hurewitz, *Middle East Dilemmas,* chap. 3; *Survey of International Affairs, 1951,* pp. 255–92; H. L. Hoskins, *Middle East, Problem Area,* chaps. 13–14; R. P. Stebbins, *The United States in World Affairs,* pp. 281–93.

1. INVITATION TO EGYPT TO PARTICIPATE IN A NEW MIDDLE EAST COMMAND, 13 OCTOBER 1951

Document A

POINT I. Egypt belongs to the free world and in consequence her defense and that of the Middle East in general is equally vital to other democratic nations.

POINT II. The defense of Egypt and of other countries in the Middle East against aggression from without can only be secured by the cooperation of all interested powers.

POINT III. The defense of Egypt can only be assured through the effective defense of the Middle East area and the coordination of this defense with that of adjacent areas.

POINT IV. It therefore seems desirable to establish an Allied Middle East Command in which the countries able and willing to contribute to the defense of the area should participate. France, Turkey, the United Kingdom and the United States are prepared to participate with other interested countries in establishing such a Command. Invitations to participate in the Command have been addressed to Australia, New Zealand, the Union of South Africa, who have indicated their interest in the defense of the area and who have agreed in principle.

POINT V. Egypt is invited to participate as a founder member of the Middle East Command on a basis of equality and partnership with other founder members.

POINT VI. If Egypt is prepared to cooperate fully in the Allied Command Organization in accordance with the provisions of the attached annex, His Majesty's Government for their part would be willing to agree to supersession of the 1936 Treaty and would also be willing to agree to withdraw from Egypt such British forces as are not allocated to the Allied Middle East Command by agreement between the Egyptian Government and the Governments of other countries also participating as founder members.

POINT VII. As regards armed forces to be placed at the disposal of the Allied Middle East Command and the provision to that Command of the necessary strategic defense facilities, such as military and air bases, communications, ports, etc., Egypt will be expected to make her contribution on the same footing as other participating powers.

POINT VIII. In keeping with the spirit of these arrangements Egypt would be invited to accept a position of high authority and responsibility with the Allied Middle East Command and to designate Egyptian officers for integration in the Allied Middle East Command Headquarters staff.

POINT IX. Facilities to train and equip her forces will be given to Egypt by those participating members of the Allied Command in a position to do so.

POINT X. The detailed organization of the Allied Middle East Defense Organization and its exact relationship with the N.A.T.O. have yet to be worked out in consultation between all the powers concerned. For this purpose it is proposed that all founding members of the Allied Middle East Command should send military representatives to a meeting to be held in the near future with the object of preparing detailed proposals for submission to the governments concerned.

Document B. Technical Annex

[1] In common with other participating powers who are making similar contributions to the defense of the area.

(a) Egypt will agree to furnish to proposed Allied Middle East Command Organization such strategic defense and other facilities on her soil as are indispensable for the organization in peacetime of the defense of the Middle East.

(b) that she will undertake to grant forces of the Allied Middle East Command all necessary facilities and assistance in the event of war, imminent menace of war, or apprehended international emergency including the use of Egyptian ports, airfields and means of communication.

[2] We should also hope that Egypt would agree to the Allied Supreme Commander's Headquarters being located in her territory.

[3] In keeping with the spirit of these arrangements, it would be understood

(a) that the present British base in Egypt would be formally handed over to the Egyptians on the understanding that it would simultaneously become an Allied base within the Allied Middle East Command with full Egyptian participation in the running of this base in peace and war

(b) that the strength of the Allied force of participating nations to be stationed in Egypt in peacetime would be determined between the participating nations including Egypt from time to time as progress is made in building up the force of the Allied Middle East Command.

[4] It also would be understood that an air defense organization including both the Egyptian and Allied forces would be set up under the command of an officer with joint responsibility to the Egyptian Government and to the Allied Middle East Command for the protection of Egypt and Allied bases.

2. FOUR-POWER STATEMENT ON THE MIDDLE EAST COMMAND, 10 NOVEMBER 1951

In proceeding with their announced intention to establish the Middle East Command, the Governments of the United States, United Kingdom, France, and Turkey state that they are guided by the following principles:

1. The United Nations is a world response to the principle that peace is indivisible and that the security of all states is jeopardized by breaches of the peace anywhere; at the same time it is incumbent upon the states of any area to be willing and able to undertake the initial defense of their area.

2. The defense of the Middle East is vital to the free world and its defense against outside aggression can be secured only by the cooperation of all interested states.

3. The Middle East Command is intended to be the center of cooperative efforts for the defense of the area as a whole; the achievement of peace and security in the area through the Middle East Command will bring with it social and economic advancement.

4. A function of the Middle East Command will be to assist and support the states willing to join in the defense of the Middle East and to develop the capacity of each to play its proper role in the defense of the area as a whole against outside aggression. It will not interfere in problems and disputes arising within the area. The establishment of the Middle East Command in no way affects existing arrangements relating to such matters, notably the armistice agreements and the United States-United Kingdom-French Tripartite Declaration of May 1950.

5. The task of the Middle East Command at the outset will be primarily one of planning and providing the Middle East States on their request with assistance in the form of advice and training. Requests for arms and equipment made by states in the area willing to join in its defense to sponsoring states in a position to assist in this connection will be filled by them to the extent possible following the coordination of such requests through the Middle East Command.

6. The Supreme Allied Commander Middle East will command forces placed at his disposal and will develop plans for the operations of all forces within the area (or to be introduced into the area) in time of war or international emergency. However, the placing of forces under the command of the Supreme Allied Commander Middle East in peacetime is not a prerequisite for joining in the common effort for the defense of the Middle East. Movement of those troops placed under the command of the Supreme Allied Commander Middle East to or within the territories or states joining in the defense of the Middle East will be made only with the agreement of the state or states concerned and in full accord with their national independence and sovereignty.

7. While details have yet to be formulated, the sponsoring states intend that the Middle East Command should be an integrated allied command, not a national command. The responsibility of the Supreme Allied Commander Middle East will be to insure the effectiveness of the corporate defense enterprise represented by the command. All states joining in this enterprise will be individually associated with the command on the basis of equality through a Middle East Defense Liaison Organization which will be located at Middle East Command Headquarters and will be the link between the command and the countries ready to join in the defense of this area.

8. Any facilities granted to the Middle East Command by states joining in the defense of the Middle East will be the subject of specific agreements.

9. The broad mission of the Middle East Command and its cooperative character make it necessary that all States, whether territorially or not part of the area, act in the best interests of the cooperative defense of the area; the Middle East Command naturally will not further the national interest of any particular state.

10. A continuing objective of the Middle East Command is to reduce such deficiencies as exist at present in the organization and capacity for defense in a vitally important area so that the peacetime role of the states of the area in Middle East defense will progressively increase, thus permitting the peacetime role of states not territorially part of the Middle East to be decreased proportionately.

11. The sponsoring states of the Middle East Command do not regard the initial form in which the Middle East Command will be organized as unchangeable; they believe that the Middle East Command through mutual understanding should evolve in the manner which will enable it most effectively to provide for the defense of the Middle East area as a whole.

98. SOVIET-AMERICAN EXCHANGE OF NOTES ON THE PROPOSED MIDDLE EAST COMMAND
24 November–18 December 1951

[*The Department of State Bulletin*, 25 (31 December 1951), 1054–56]

Although the Middle East Command proposal was destined to remain a command on paper only, the very announcement of the scheme aroused profound hostility in the Kremlin. Soviet sensitivity to Western controls in the Near and Middle East derived chiefly from that region's location adjacent to an exposed district of the USSR, where are concentrated principal Russian industries and petroleum resources. Postwar Soviet policy toward the Near and Middle East thus aimed, as its immediate strategic objective, to eliminate British and French preferential rights and military bases and to prevent the United States from filling the resultant power vacuum. The Kremlin manifestly saw in the plan for a Middle East Command a serious threat to Soviet strategy. By the same token, the United States and its allies were determined to seal the Near and Middle East against Russian penetration. The nature of the Soviet-West diplomatic contest in the region in this period is brought into sharp focus in the following exchange of notes. For references, see Doc. 97.

1. SOVIET NOTE, 24 NOVEMBER 1951

In connection with the message of the Governments of the United States of America, England, France, and Turkey to the Governments of Egypt, Syria, Lebanon, Iraq, Saudi Arabia, Yemen, Israel, and Transjordan regarding the creation of the so-called united Middle Eastern Command, the Soviet Government considers it necessary to state the following to the Government of the United States of America:

As seen from the proposals contained in the mentioned message and equally in the declaration published November 10 by the four Governments on this question and transmitted to the Governments of the stated countries in the Near and Middle East, the Governments of the United States of America, England, France, and Turkey foresee: The subordination of the armed forces of the countries of the Near and Middle East to the so-called unified command; the disposition of foreign armed forces in the territories of the Near and Middle East countries; putting at the disposal of the mentioned command by the Near and Middle East countries of military bases, communications, ports, and other constructions; the establishment of a connection between this command and the Atlantic bloc organization.

The proposals and declaration by the four Governments give evidence that plans of the organization of a so-called Middle East Command represent nothing other than an attempt to draw the countries of the Near and Middle East into military undertakings being realized by the aggressive Atlantic bloc. In this connection certain of the four Government initiators of the creation of the Middle East Command who maintain their troops and military bases in the Near Eastern countries already are strengthening their military forces presently there.

Thus attempting to draw the countries of the Near and Middle East into aggressive military undertakings of the Atlantic bloc, the Government of the United States of America equally as other initiators of the creation of the Middle East Command aim to transform the countries of the Near and Middle East into a *place d'armes* for the armed forces of the Atlantic bloc. The demand of the four countries can only be assessed as directed toward assuring the presence of foreign armed forces in the mentioned countries and the extension of the network of military bases of foreign governments contrary to the will of the people in these countries. It is not difficult to see that the realization of these undertakings, which actually mean the occupation of the Near and Middle East countries by the troops of foreign governments, is calculated to assure to these governments the possibility of continuous interference in the internal affairs of the Near and Middle East countries and the deprivation of their national independence.

The Government of the United States of America as also the Governments of England, France, and Turkey are attempting to justify the organization of the Middle East Command by referring to some sort of threat allegedly existing for these countries and the necessity for the defense of Near and Middle East regions. However, such references are absolutely groundless and cannot be assessed other than an attempt to deceive public opinion and attract its attention from the actual aggressive plans of the Four Powers.

If speaking of the threat to the independence and sovereignty of these countries, then such a threat arises exactly from the countries initiators of the organization plan for the creation of the Middle East Command who continue unwilling to reconcile themselves with the idea that the peoples of the Near and Middle East, as all other sovereign peoples, have inalienable rights to conduct their own independent national policy free from any kind of external pressure.

The Government of the U.S.S.R. considers it necessary to direct the attention of the Government of the United States of America to the fact that it cannot pass by these new aggressive plans expressed in the creation of the Middle East Command in an area situated not far from the borders of the Soviet Union. The Soviet Government considers it necessary also to state that the responsibility for the situation which can arise as a result of this will rest with the Government of the United States of America and other initiators of the creation of the mentioned command.

2. U.S. REPLY, 18 DECEMBER 1951

The Government of the United States has given careful consideration to the note of the Government of the U.S.S.R. of November 24 concerning the proposed establishment of the Middle East Command.

It is apparent that the Soviet Union has placed a completely erroneous interpretation upon the Middle East Command and has chosen to ignore the clearly-stated purposes and principles upon which the Middle East Command will be founded.

The allegation of the Soviet Union that the Middle East Command is aggressive in intent is utterly without foundation. On the contrary, the statement of principles published by the United Kingdom, France, Turkey, and the United States on November 10 make it abundantly clear that the Middle East Command is designed (1) to create a voluntary cooperative defense organization to provide for the security of the Middle East area as a whole in the event that that area should become a target of outside aggression, and (2) to assist the states in the area to preserve and strengthen their independence and freedom so that their economic well-being and social institutions can develop in an atmosphere unclouded by fear for their security.

The Middle East Command proposals and principles are based upon the inherent right of self-defense set forth in article 51 of the Charter of the United Nations. Such self-defense is facilitated by cooperative measures like the Middle East Command. The need for these cooperative measures arises from the concern over present tensions in the world situation which have been created by the Soviet Union's aggressive actions. Soviet efforts externally and internally at subversion against the states of the Middle East do not contribute to lessening these tensions.

The United States notes with surprise the assertion by the U.S.S.R. that the idea that any threat exists to the Middle East states is "absolutely groundless." The United States Government reminds the Soviet Government that on November 25, 1940, a proposal of U.S.S.R. People's Commissar for Foreign Affairs Molotov to German Ambassador Schulenberg to reach agreement with the Nazi Government of Germany on the delimitation of the spheres of influence between the Axis Powers and the U.S.S.R. provided, among other things, that the U.S.S.R. be enabled to establish "a base for land and naval forces" within range of the Turkish Straits and that "the area south of Batum and of Baku in the general direction of the Persian Gulf is recognized as the center of the aspirations of the Soviet Union." In light of the Soviet attitude toward the Middle East area since the end of World War II, the United States Government can only assume that the aims set forth by Mr. Molotov in 1940 remain the policy of the Soviet Government.

With respect to the Soviet Allegation that the sponsors of the Middle East Command intend to convert the Middle East into a *place d'armes,* with a view to occupying the states in the area and interfering with their internal affairs, the principles submitted to the Middle East states on November 10 make it clear that (a) the Middle East Command will not interfere in matters arising within the area; (b) that movement of Middle East Command forces to or within the territories of the Middle East states will be made only with the agreement of the state or states concerned in full accord with their national independence and sovereignty; and (c) that facilities granted to the Middle East Command will likewise be the subject of specific agreements.

The United States and other members of the NATO have frequently been exposed to the purely propagandistic charge from the U.S.S.R. that the NATO is aggressive. That this charge is a complete distortion of the facts is made clear by the terms of the Treaty, by the steps taken under it, and by the foreign policies of the members. Being devoted to the cause of peace, the members believe that they can best serve this cause by their just determination to defend themselves against aggression. The United States wishes to make quite clear to the Soviet Union that neither the NATO nor the Middle East Command is aggressive in intent. As is well known to the Soviet Union and to the Governments satellite to it, there has been no aggression whatsoever originating from the countries who are members of these organizations. Furthermore, there will not be any. Therefore, the Soviet reference to "the aggressive Atlantic Bloc" is once again rejected as being without any foundation whatsoever.

The Middle East Command proposals and principles, based on the concept that those states choosing to participate in the Command will do so voluntarily as equal members, have been placed before the governments of the sovereign and independent Middle East states for their study and evaluation in the light of their own national interests. The decision as to whether they will elect to participate in the Command and freely accept the benefits and responsibilities of such participation belongs to these states alone and not to the Soviet Government. The recent Soviet threats to these states warning against their participation in the Middle East Command constitute interference in the affairs of these countries. The United States Government believes, as the Soviet Government professes to do, that the peoples of the Middle East have the right to conduct their national policies "free from any kind of external pressure." The Government of the U.S.S.R. bears the responsibility for the present situation, not those states which, either individually or collectively under the Charter of the United Nations, take legitimate measures of self-defense in the interest of their own security and of international peace.

99. AGREEMENT ON SELF-GOVERNMENT AND SELF-DETERMINATION FOR THE SUDAN: BRITAIN AND EGYPT
12 February 1953

[Great Britain, *Parliamentary Papers, 1953,* Treaty Series No. 47, Cmd. 8904]

At the time that the four-power plan for a Middle East Command was presented to Egypt on 13 October 1951 (Doc. 98), the United Kingdom simultaneously put forward its separate suggestions for a settlement in the Sudan (text in *Parliamentary Papers, 1951,* Egypt No. 2, Cmd. 8419, pp. 45–46). But the Egyptian government brushed aside the Sudan scheme together with the Middle East Command proposals. There Anglo-Egyptian negotiations stalled for a full year. On 22 October 1952 Britain, which had in 1943 introduced without Egyptian approval a measure of autonomy in the Sudan's northern provinces and five years later broadened the base to include the entire country, endorsed—subject to the rights reserved to the co-domini—a draft self-government statute that had been framed by a Sudanese constitutional commission under a British chairman. The British move roused to action the military government in Egypt, which only three months earlier had brought an end to the twenty-nine-year-old constitutional regime and to the Hilmi dynasty, founded at the start of the nineteenth century by Mehmed 'Ali. An Egyptian of Sudanese birth and rearing, Prime Minister Muhammad Nagib, the junta's "front" man, in talks at Cairo reached an informal understanding on 29 October with the pro-British as well as the pro-Egyptian Sudanese factions. Egypt withdrew its objection to the draft self-government statute in return for Sudanese endorsement of the Egyptian demand for the creation of two international commissions, one to advise the British Governor-General on implementation of the statute and the other to supervise the first general elections. The Egyptian-Sudanese rapprochement rendered feasible a resumption of Anglo-Egyptian negotiations, which, with the friendly assistance of the United States, culminated in the following agreement. The annexes, agreed minutes, exchanges of notes and the self-government statute have been omitted below. M. Abbas, *The Sudan Question* (background); M. Neguib, *Egypt's Destiny,* chap. 7; Sir H. MacMichael, *The Sudan,* pp. 181–242; Great Britain, *Parliamentary Papers, 1953,* Egypt No. 2, Cmd. 8767 (documents); P. B. Broadbent, "Sudanese Self-Government," *International Affairs,* 30 (July 1954), 320–30.

Art. 1. In order to enable the Sudanese people to exercise Self-Determination in a free and neutral atmosphere, a transitional period providing full self-government for the Sudanese shall begin on the day specified in Article 9 below.

Art. 2. The transitional period, being a preparation for the effective termination of the dual Administration, shall be considered as a liquidation of that Administration. During the transitional period the sovereignty of the Sudan shall be kept in reserve for the Sudanese until Self-Determination is achieved.

Art. 3. The Governor-General shall, during the transitional period, be the supreme constitutional authority within the Sudan. He shall exercise his powers as set out in the Self-Government Statute with the aid of a five-member Commission, to be called the Governor-General's Commission, whose powers are laid down in the terms of reference in Annex I to the present Agreement.

Art. 4. This Commission shall consist of two Sudanese proposed by the two contracting Governments in agreement, one Egyptian citizen, one citizen of the United Kingdom and one Pakistani citizen, each to be proposed by his respective Government. The appointment of the two Sudanese members shall be subject to the subsequent approval of the Sudanese Parliament when it is elected, and the Parliament shall be entitled to nominate alternative candidates in case of disapproval. The Commission hereby set up will be formally appointed by Egyptian Government decree.

ART. 5. The two contracting Governments agree that, it being a fundamental principle of their common policy to maintain the unity of the Sudan as a single territory, the special powers which are vested in the Governor-General by Article 100 of the Self-Government Statute shall not be exercised in any manner which is in conflict with that policy.

ART. 6. The Governor-General shall remain directly responsible to the two contracting Governments as regards:

(*a*) external affairs;

(*b*) any change requested by the Sudanese Parliament under Article 101 (1) of the Statute for Self-Government as regards any part of the Statute;

(*c*) any resolution passed by the Commission which he regards as inconsistent with his responsibilities. In this case he will inform the two contracting Governments, each of which must give an answer within one month of the date of formal notice. The Commission's resolutions shall stand unless the two Governments agree to the contrary.

ART. 7. There shall be constituted a Mixed Electoral Commission of seven members. These shall be three Sudanese appointed by the Governor-General with the approval of his Commission, one Egyptian citizen, one citizen of the United Kingdom, one citizen of the United States of America, and one Indian citizen. The non-Sudanese members shall be nominated by their respective Governments. The Indian member shall be Chairman of the Commission. The Commission shall be appointed by the Governor-General on the instructions of the two contracting Governments. The terms of reference of this Commission are contained in Annex II to this Agreement.

ART. 8. To provide the free and neutral atmosphere requisite for Self-Determination there shall be established a Sudanisation Committee consisting of:

(*a*) an Egyptian citizen and a citizen of the United Kingdom to be nominated by their respective Governments and subsequently appointed by the Governor-General, together with three Sudanese members to be selected from a list of five names submitted to him by the Prime Minister of the Sudan. The selection and appointment of these Sudanese members shall have the prior approval of the Governor-General's Commission;

(*b*) one or more members of the Sudan Public Service Commission who will act in a purely advisory capacity without the right to vote;

(*c*) the function and terms of reference of this Committee are contained in Annex III to this Agreement.

ART. 9. The transitional period shall begin on the day designated as "the appointed day" in Article 2 of the Self-Government Statute. Subject to the completion of the Sudanisation as outlined in Annex III to this Agreement, the two contracting Governments undertake to bring the transitional period to an end as soon as possible. In any case this period shall not exceed three years. It shall be brought to an end in the following manner. The Sudanese Parliament shall pass a resolution expressing their desire that arrangements for Self-Determination shall be put in motion and the Governor-General shall notify the two contracting Governments of this resolution.

ART. 10. When the two contracting Governments have been formally notified of this resolution, the Sudanese Government, then existing, shall draw up a draft law for the election of the Constituent Assembly which it shall submit to Parliament for approval. The Governor-General shall give his consent to the law with the agreement of his Commission. Detailed preparations for the process of Self-Determination, including safeguards assuring the impartiality of the elections and any other arrangements designed to secure a free and neutral atmosphere, shall be subject to international supervision. The two contracting Governments will accept the recommendations of any international body which may be set up to this end.

ART. 11. Egyptian and British military forces shall withdraw from the Sudan immediately upon the Sudanese Parliament adopting a resolution expressing its desire that arrangements for Self-Determination be put in motion. The two contracting Governments undertake to complete the withdrawal of their forces from the Sudan within a period not exceeding three months.

ART. 12. The Constituent Assembly shall have two duties to discharge. The first will be to decide the future of the Sudan as one integral whole. The second will be to draw up a constitution for the Sudan compatible with the decision which shall have been taken in this respect, as well as an electoral law for a permanent Sudanese Parliament. The future of the Sudan shall be decided either:

(*a*) by the Constituent Assembly choosing to link the Sudan with Egypt in any form, or

(*b*) by the Constituent Assembly choosing complete independence.

ART. 13. The two contracting Governments undertake to respect the decision of the Constituent Assembly concerning the future status of the Sudan and each Government will take all the measures which may be necessary to give effect to its decision.

ART. 14. The two contracting Governments agree that the draft Self-Government Statute shall be amended in accordance with Annex IV to this Agreement.

ART. 15. This Agreement and its attachments shall come into force upon signature.

100. REPORT ON THE NEAR AND MIDDLE EAST BY SECRETARY OF STATE JOHN FOSTER DULLES
1 June 1953

[*The Department of State Bulletin,* 28 (15 June 1953), 831–35]

Less than four months after entering office, Secretary of State John Foster Dulles, accompanied by Mutual Security Director Harold E. Stassen, spent two and one-half weeks (11–28 May 1953) in visiting most of the Near and Middle East lands. The unprecedented trip dramatically underscored the substantial development of United States interest and responsibility in that strategic region in the postwar period. In the following report delivered over national radio and television networks, Secretary Dulles demonstrated that the Republican Administration would not recoil from obligations in the Near and Middle East accepted its Democratic predecessor. Indeed, he suggested that the United States would offer to the area even greater economic and military assistance than in the past. Among notable changes in emphasis from that of the outgoing administration, Secretary Dulles proposed to inaugurate an "impartial" policy in the Arab-Israel zone and to abandon as sterile in the immediate future efforts to create a region-wide collective security system (Doc. 97) in favor of one that would embrace "the northern tier of nations," where, he felt, because of proximity to the USSR there was an "awareness of the [Soviet and communist] danger." R. P. Stebbins, *The United States in World Affairs 1953,* chap. 5; J. W. Spain, "Middle East Defense: a New Approach," *The Middle East Journal,* 8 (Summer 1954), pp. 251–66; H. L. Hoskins, *Middle East, Problem Area,* chaps. 12–14.

About 3 weeks ago, the Director for Mutual Security, Mr. Harold Stassen, and I and our associates set out, at President Eisenhower's request, on a trip to 12 countries which lie in between the Mediterranean in Europe and China in Asia. I shall give you our country-by-country impressions and then our general conclusions.

First, let me say that everywhere we were well received. This was encouraging, for several of the countries feel that the United States policies have, in recent years, been harmful and even antagonistic to them. The Communists have vigorously exploited this feeling. They staged some hostile demonstrations. But these were inconsequential. The governments received us with warm hospitality, and as we drove through the streets, the people usually greeted us with friendly smiles and applause. The political leaders talked intimately with us, and we gained new friendships and new understanding which will stand us in good stead for the future. Also in each capital I spoke to all of the United States Foreign Service personnel. They are a fine body of men and women of whom we can be proud.

It is high time that the United States Government paid more attention to the Near East and South Asia, which, until our trip, no United States Secretary of State has ever visited. Our postward attention has been primarily given to Western Europe. That area was and is very important, but not all-important.

It came as a surprising shock when the 450 million Chinese people, whom we had counted as friends, fell under Communist domination. There could be equally dangerous developments in the Near East and South Asia. The situation calls for urgent concern.

The area we visited contains about one-fourth of the world's population. It represents about one-half of the people of the world who are still free of Communist domination.

The Near East possesses great strategic importance as the bridge between Europe, Asia, and Africa. The present masters of the Kremlin, following the lead of past military conquerors, covet this position. In 1940 Soviet leaders specified, in secret negotiations with the Nazis, that Soviet "territorial aspirations center . . . in the direction of the Indian Ocean and . . . the Persian Gulf."

This area contains important resources vital to our welfare—oil, manganese, chrome, mica, and other minerals. About 60 percent of the proven oil reserves of the world are in the Near East.

Most important of all, the Near East is the source of three great religions—the Jewish, the Christian, and the Moslem—which have for centuries exerted an immense influence throughout the world. Surely we cannot ignore the fate of the peoples who have first received and then passed on to us the great spiritual truths from which our own society derives its inner strength.

EGYPT AND THE SUEZ BASE

Our first stop was in Egypt. There we had 3 days in which to get acquainted with General Naguib, who heads the Government. He is a popular hero, and I could readily see why. He and his associates are determined to provide Egypt with a vigorous government which will truly serve the people. Also, they seek to end the stationing of British troops and exercise of British authority at the Suez base.

Before we arrived in Egypt, a very tense situation had developed between the British and the Egyptian Governments. Conversations looking to an orderly withdrawal of British troops had been suspended, and there was danger that hostilities would break out.

We discussed the situation with General Naguib. The heart of the trouble is not so much the presence of British troops, for both sides agreed that they should be withdrawn, but the subsequent authority over and management of this gigantic base, its airstrips, and its depots of supplies. Experienced administrative and technical personnel is needed to keep the base in operating efficiency and the provision of this personnel causes difficult. The matter has an importance which goes beyond Egypt, for the base serves all Near Eastern and indeed Western security.

I am convinced that there is nothing irreconcilable between this international concern and Egyptian sovereignty. We asked, with some success, that there be further time to find a peaceful solution. The United States is prepared to assist in any desired way.

Egypt stands at the threshold of what can be a great new future. If this Suez problem can be satisfactorily solved, I am confident that Egypt can find the means to develop its land and lift up its people and add a new bright chapter to a glorious past.

ISRAEL, JERUSALEM, AND REFUGEES

Next we went to Israel. We were impressed by the vision and supporting energy with which the people are building their new nation. Inspired by a great faith, they are now doing an impressive work of creation. They face hard internal problems, which I believe they can solve. Furthermore, the Prime Minister, Ben Gurion, and other Israeli officials asserted convincingly their desire to live at peace with their Arab neighbors.

Jerusalem is divided into armed camps split between Israel and the Arab nation of Jordan. The atmosphere is heavy with hate. As I gazed on the Mount of Olives, I felt anew that Jerusalem is, above all, the holy place of the Christian, Moslem, and Jewish faiths. This has been repeatedly emphasized by the United Nations. This does not necessarily exclude some political status in Jerusalem for Israel and Jordan. But the world religious community has claims in Jerusalem which take precedence over the political claims of any particular nation.

Closely huddled around Israel are most of the over 800,000 Arab refugees, who fled from Palestine as the Israeli took over. They mostly exist in makeshift camps, with few facilities either for health, work, or recreation. Within these camps the inmates rot away, spiritually and physically. Even the Grim Reaper offers no solution, for as the older die, infants are born to inherit their parents' bitter fate.

Some of these refugees could be settled in the area presently controlled by Israel. Most, however, could more readily be integrated into the lives of the neighboring Arab countries. This, however, awaits on irrigation projects, which will permit more soil to be cultivated.

Throughout the area the cry is for water for irrigation. United Nations contributions and other funds are available to help refugees, and Mr. Stassen and I came back with the impression that they can well be spent in large part on a coordinated use of the rivers which run through the Arab countries and Israel.

JORDAN

Irrigation needs became most vivid as we motored from Jerusalem to Amman, the capital of Jordan. The road goes through the Dead Sea area, a scene of desolation with no sign of life other than the tens of thousands of refugees who survive precariously on the parched land largely by aid of United Nations doles. Later on, as we flew north, we observed the waters of the Yarmak River, which could perhaps be diverted so as to return some of this vast desert valley into fertile land.

At Amman we dined with the charming and able new King Husein and his Government. They are preoccupied with the problem of refugees and of relations with Israel. The inflow of refugees has almost doubled the population, and the long armistice line with Israel gives rise to frequent and dangerous shooting episodes.

SYRIA, LEBANON, IRAQ, AND SAUDI ARABIA

From Jordan we went to Syria. There we were impressed by General Shishakli. He is eager to develop the resources of his country, which are substantial. Thus, the living standards of the Syrian people could be raised. This would, in turn, enable them to receive more refugees into a land which relatively is sparsely populated.

From Damascus, the capital of Syria, we motored to Beirut, the capital of Lebanon. The road took us over a mountain range, with refreshing snow in sharp contrast to the heat of the desert plains.

You will recall that Beirut is the home of the American University, which has educated many of the Arab leaders of today. President Chamoun of Lebanon talked to us of his high hopes for his country and pointed to the role it might play, representing uniquely a meeting of East and West.

Leaving Lebanon for Iraq, we flew over the Tigris and Euphrates Valleys. This was the site of the Garden of Eden. Under its new ruler, King Faisal—who visited the United States last summer—the Government of Iraq is beginning to develop these valleys and restore their former productivity. The revenues from the oil production are being largely directed to this and other construction purposes. Iraq can be, and desires to be, the granary for much of this part of the world.

In Saudi Arabia we were received by King Ibn Saud, one of the great Near Eastern figures of this century, conspicuous in his dignity and singleness of purpose. He is a good friend of the United States, as he has shown by deeds. Our policy will be to reciprocate this friendship. In Saudi Arabia

Americans and Arabs are working together in good fellowship in the vast oil fields of the country. It is a good relationship.

INDIA AND PAKISTAN

We left the Arab area to go first to India and then to Pakistan. These two nations, although independent for less than 6 years, already play an influential part in world affairs.

In India I met again with Mr. Nehru, one of the great leaders of our time. We had long conversations together in the intimacy of his home. His calm demeanor and lofty idealism impressed me. We reviewed together the international problems which concern both our countries, including the problem of a Korean armistice and the threat to Southeast Asia. We did not always agree, but we did clear up some misunderstandings and, I felt, gained respect for the integrity of our respective purposes. India is now supporting the armistice position of the United Nations Command in Korea.

Mr. Stassen and I also obtained a clearer view of the Government of India's 5-year program to improve the welfare of the Indian people.

India is the world's largest self-governing nation. It has about 2,000 miles of common boundary with Communist China. There is occurring between these two countries a competition as to whether ways of freedom or police-state methods can achieve better social progress. This competition affects directly 800 million people in these 2 countries. In the long run, the outcome will affect all of humanity, including ourselves. Our interest fully justifies continuing, on a modest scale, some technical assistance and external resources to permit India to go on with its 5-year plan.

Pakistan is the largest of the Moslem nations and occupies a high position in the Moslem world. The strong spiritual faith and martial spirit of the people make them a dependable bulwark against communism.

The new Prime Minister, Mohammed Ali, whom we recently knew as Ambassador to Washington, energetically leads the new Government. We met with a feeling of warm friendship on the part of the people of Pakistan toward the United States.

A grave and immediate problem is the shortage of wheat. Without large imports, widespread famine conditions will ensue. Last year we helped India in a similar emergency. I believe that prompt United States wheat assistance to Pakistan is essential.

It is not possible to think about United States aid without also thinking that these countries cannot afford to waste their efforts in quarreling with each other and diverting their strength for possible use against each other.

That thought applies to the dispute between India and Pakistan about Kashmir. It is my impression from my conversations with the Prime Ministers of India and Pakistan that this controversy can be settled. Surely it needs to be settled. We tried, tactfully but firmly, to make clear that the United States, as a friend of both countries, hopes for an accord which would make more fruitful such economic aid as we render.

IRAN

It was not practical to include Iran in our schedule. However, we arranged that our Ambassador to Iran should meet us in Pakistan. Iran is now preoccupied with its oil dispute with Great Britain. But still the people and the Government do not want this quarrel to expose them to Communist subversion. They have not forgotten the Soviet occupation of 1941–1946.

The United States will avoid any unwanted interference in the oil dispute. But we can usefully continue technical aid and assistance to this agricultural nation of Iran and in that way perhaps help prevent an economic collapse which would play into the hands of predatory forces.

TURKEY, GREECE, AND LIBYA

After Pakistan, we went to Turkey and Greece. These two countries have clearly demonstrated their intent to stand steadfast against Communist aggression and subversion. Despite their heavy commitments to NATO, both countries have contributed valiantly to the United Nations efforts in Korea.

We, in turn, plan to continue to help Greece and Turkey to grow stronger. They are valiant in spirit and hold a strategic position in Europe and Asia which enables them to help us. While in Greece I dined with the King and Queen and passed on to this charming couple President Eisenhower's invitation that they visit us this fall.

Our last stop before returning to the United States was Libya, the newest member of the family of nations. This country is located at a key spot on the North African coast on the Mediterranean. It has recently become an independent nation by action of the United Nations. Libya is cooperating with the United States and the United Kingdom in strengthening its own defenses and those of the Mediterranean area.

Let me turn now to conclusions.

1. *Colonialism.* Most of the peoples of the Near East and South Asia are deeply concerned about political independence for themselves and others. They are suspicious of the colonial powers. The United States too is suspect because, it is reasoned, our NATO alliance with France and Britain requires us to try to preserve or restore the old colonial interests of our allies.

I am convinced that United States policy has become unnecessarily ambiguous in this matter. The leaders of the countries I visited fully recognize that it would be a disaster if there were any break between the United States and Great Britain and France. They don't want this to happen. However, without breaking from the framework of Western unity, we can pursue our traditional dedication to political liberty. In reality, the Western powers can gain, rather than lose, from an orderly development of self government.

I emphasize, however, the word "orderly." Let none forget that the Kremlin uses extreme nationalism to bait the trap by which it seeks to capture the dependent peoples.

2. *Living Standards.* The peoples of the Near East and Asia demand better standards of living, and the day is past when their aspirations can be ignored. The task is one primarily for the governments and the peoples themselves. In some cases they can use their available resources, such as oil revenues, to better advantage. There are, however, ways in which the United States can usefully help, not with masses of money but by contributing advanced technical knowledge about transport, communication, fertilization, and use of water for irrigation. Mr. Stassen and I feel that money wisely spent for this area under the mutual security program will give the American people a good return in terms of better understanding and cooperation.

3. *Arab Good Will.* The United States should seek to allay the deep resentment against it that has resulted from the creation of Israel. In the past we had good relations with the Arab peoples. American educational institutions had built up a feeling of good will, and also American businessmen had won a good reputation in this area. There was mutual confidence to mutual advantage.

Today the Arab peoples are afraid that the United States will back the new State of Israel in aggressive expansion. They are more fearful of Zionism than of communism, and they fear lest the United States become the backer of expansionist Zionism.

On the other hand, the Israeli fear that ultimately the Arabs may try to push them into the sea.

In an effort to calm these contradictory fears the United States joined with Britain and France in a Declaration of May 25, 1950, which stated that "the three Governments, should they find that any of these states (of the Near East) was preparing to violate frontiers or armistice lines, would, consistently with their obligations as members of the United Nations, immediately take action, both within and outside the United Nations, to prevent such violation." That Declaration when made did not reassure the Arabs. It must be made clear that the present U.S. administration stands fully behind that Declaration. We cannot afford to be distrusted by millions who could be sturdy friends of freedom. They must not further swell the ranks of Communist dictators.

The leaders in Israel themselves agreed with us that United States policies should be impartial so as to win not only the respect and regard of the Israeli but also of the Arab peoples. We shall seek such policies.

4. *Peace Between Israel and the Arab Nations.* There is need for peace in the Near East. Today there is an uneasy military armistice between Israel and the Arab States, while economic warfare is being conducted by the Arab States, in retaliation for alleged Israeli encroachments. The area is enfeebled by fear and by wasteful measures which are inspired by fear and hate.

Israel should become part of the Near East community and cease to look upon itself, or be looked upon by others, as alien to this community. This is possible. To achieve it will require concessions on the part of both sides. But the gains to both will far outweigh the concessions required to win those gains.

The parties concerned have the primary responsibility of bringing peace to the area. But the United States will not hestitate by every appropriate means to use its influence to promote a step-by-step reduction of tension in the area and the conclusion of ultimate peace.

5. *Middle East Defense Organization.* A Middle East Defense Organization is a future rather than an immediate possibility. Many of the Arab League countries are so engrossed with their quarrels with Israel or with Great Britain or France that they pay little heed to the menace of Soviet communism. However, there is more concern where the Soviet Union is near. In general, the northern tier of nations shows awareness of the danger.

There is a vague desire to have a collective security system. But no such system can be imposed from without. It should be designed and grow from within out of a sense of common destiny and common danger.

While awaiting the formal creation of a security association, the United States can usefully help strengthen the interrelated defense of those countries which want strength, not as against each other or the West, but to resist the common threat to all free peoples.

6. *Friendly Understanding.* In conclusion, let me recall that the primary purpose of our trip was to show friendliness and to develop understanding. These peoples we visited are proud peoples who have a great tradition and, I believe, a great future. We in the United States are better off if we respect and honor them, and learn the thoughts and aspirations which move them. It profits nothing merely to be critical of others.

President Eisenhower's administration plans to make friendship—not faultfinding—the basis of its foreign policy. President Eisenhower brought with him from Europe an unprecedented measure of understanding and personal friendships. Before he was inaugurated, he went to Korea. Twice since inauguration, Mr. Stassen and I have been to Europe. Now we have been to the Near East and South Asia. Later this month, the President's brother, Dr. Milton Eisenhower, and Assistant Secretary of State Cabot will go to South America.

Thus your Government is establishing the world-wide relationships and gathering the information which will enable us better to serve you, the American people.

101. SOVIET-TURKISH EXCHANGES OF NOTES ON VISITS BY AMERICAN AND BRITISH FLEETS TO TURKISH PORTS IN THE STRAITS
20–31 July 1953

[Reproduced with permission from *The Current Digest of the Soviet Press* (New York), 5 (15 August 1953), p. 14 and (12 September 1953), pp. 16–17, as translated from *Pravda* and *Izvestia,* 21 July and 1 August 1953]

The steady decline after 1946 of Western controls, matched—if not surpassed—by the heavy-handed diplomacy of the USSR, was stimulating in many Near and Middle East lands—particularly in the Arab states and in Musaddiq's Iran—the growth of a desire to avoid entanglements with any great power. Following the death of Stalin early in March 1953, the successor regime began to alter its tactics. Reflective of the new spirit in Moscow were an unsolicited statement by Foreign Minister Vyacheslav M. Molotov on 30 May renouncing the 1945 territorial claims against Turkey and suggesting that the straits question might be settled by negotiation [texts of exchange of notes in *The Current Digest of the Soviet Press,* 5 (29 August 1953), 21–22]; the resumption in mid-July of Soviet diplomatic relations with Israel after a six-month hiatus [texts *ibid.* (15 August 1953), 13–14]; and Premier Georgi M. Malenkov's foreign policy address before the Supreme Soviet on 8 August, a statement weighted with mellifluous comments on Russia's immediate Near and Middle East neighbors [text *ibid.* (5 September 1953), 8–12] In this twilight period of transition from Stalinist to post-Stalinist diplomacy, the following Soviet-Turkish diplomatic exchanges served notice to the outside world that the new Russian leadership was no less concerned than its predecessor about Western access to Near and Middle East bases. The altered tactics of the United States (Doc. 100) and of the USSR in the Near and Middle East could hardly fail to upset the earlier postwar pattern of international politics in that region. But what shape the new pattern might take could not yet be determined even vaguely. R. P. Stebbins, *The United States in World Affairs 1953,* chaps. 2, 5.

1. SOVIET FOREIGN MINISTRY TO TURKISH AMBASSADOR IN MOSCOW, 20 JULY 1953

The U.S.S.R. Ministry of Foreign Affairs has the honor of giving the following message to the Embassy of the Turkish Republic.

The Turkish Ministry of Foreign Affairs has reported to the Soviet Embassy in Ankara that from July 22 to 27 a formation of U.S. naval vessels composed of 10 ships, including two cruisers, three destroyers, four mine sweepers and one landing ship, will be in the port of Istanbul. After this, from July 27 to Aug. 3, a formation of British naval vessels composed of 22 ships, including three cruisers, four destroyers, six mine sweepers and four landing ships, will be in the port of Istanbul.

In connection with this report by the Turkish Foreign Ministry, it is impossible not to note the fact that recently the touching of foreign naval formations, including large naval vessels, in ports of the Black Sea straits has become more frequent and the above-mentioned visits to the port of Istanbul by 10 American and 22 British naval vessels may be viewed as a kind of military demonstration.

In view of the circumstances, the Soviet government hopes for further information from the Turkish government.

2. TURKISH FOREIGN MINISTRY TO SOVIET AMBASSADOR IN ANKARA, 24 JULY 1953

On July 20, 1953, his Excellency Mr. Zorin, Deputy Foreign Minister of the U.S.S.R., gave the Turkish Ambassador in Moscow a verbal note, the text of which was immediately published by the Soviet government, in which the Foreign Ministry, making a pretext of calls at Istanbul to be made in the immediate future by the American fleet and later by the British fleet, states that it cannot refrain from calling attention to the fact that recently visits to the straits ports by foreign naval formations, including large vessels, are becoming more frequent, that the two visits under discussion can be viewed as a kind of military demonstration and expresses hope of additional information from the Turkish government.

In answer to this note the Foreign Ministry of the Turkish Republic has the honor of requesting the U.S.S.R. embassy to be so kind as to report the following to its government:

The government of the U.S.S.R., being regularly informed under Art. 24 of the Montreux Convention on the straits regime, cannot but know that the visits referred to in the above-mentioned note are courtesy visits.

Since Arts. 14 (paragraph three) and 17 of the Montreux Convention grant naval forces on courtesy visits to the straits complete freedom as to tonnage and since the visits under discussion are being made in full conformity with these articles, their frequent repetition cannot be interpreted other than as happy evidence of the friendly ties uniting Turkey with the countries to which the invited fleets belong.

In view of what is set forth above and taking into account that all data and information concerning the two visits, to which the Soviet government deemed it necessary to call special attention, were reported to it in the necessary manner and in due form, the Turkish government cannot conceal its surprise at the fact that the Soviet government deemed it necessary to demand additional information, which could be viewed as a kind of intervention on a question which is left by international custom to the discretion of the countries concerned.

3. SOVIET FOREIGN MINISTRY TO TURKISH AMBASSADOR IN MOSCOW, 31 JULY 1953

In connection with the Turkish Foreign Ministry's note of July 24, the U.S.S.R. Foreign Ministry has the honor of making the following statement to the embassy of the Turkish Republic:

In its note of July 20 the U.S.S.R. Foreign Ministry, referring to a report by the Turkish Foreign Ministry on a visit to the port of Istanbul this July by U.S. naval units comprising 10 ships and of British naval units comprising 22 ships, called attention to the fact that recent calls at ports on the Black Sea straits by foreign naval formations including large vessels, have become more frequent. The Ministry also stated that the visits by 10 American and 22 British naval vessels, mentioned in the note, to the port of Istanbul may be viewed as a kind of military demonstration.

Having studied the Turkish Foreign Ministry's answer to this note July 24, the U.S.S.R. Foreign Ministry deems it necessary to add that in recent years the number of visits to the Black Sea straits by large foreign naval vessels has increased considerably. The following official data prove this:

The Black Sea straits have been visited by:

In 1950—33 foreign naval vessels with a displacement of 197,800 tons.

In 1951—49 foreign naval vessels with a displacement of 378,800 tons.

In 1952—69 foreign naval vessels with a displacement of 587,727 tons.

In seven months of 1953—60 foreign naval vessels with a displacement of more than 300,000 tons.

In view of this, when visits to the Black Sea straits by foreign naval vessels have reached the above-mentioned large dimensions, the request by the U.S.S.R. Foreign Ministry for additional information from the Turkish Foreign Ministry concerning the increasing frequency of visits to the Black Sea straits by large foreign naval formations could not come as a surprise.

Yet the Turkish Foreign Ministry, in its answering note of July 24, deemed it possible to reduce this whole question to its narrowly formal aspect which, in the given instance, has no real significance. As for the Soviet side's above-mentioned request for additional information on a matter of importance to the Soviet Union and quite natural in normal relations between two neighboring states, the Turkish Foreign Ministry found it possible to view this request as a kind of intervention in a question within Turkey's competence, although there was no foundation at all for such a conclusion.

The U.S.S.R. Foreign Ministry is sending this reply to the Turkish Foreign Ministry's note of July 24 to confirm the importance of the question raised in the Ministry's note of July 20, 1953.

102. AGREEMENT OF FRIENDLY COOPERATION: PAKISTAN AND TURKEY
2 April 1954

(Ratifications exchanged, Ankara, 12 June 1954)
[Pakistan, *Treaty Series (1954),* No. 4]

The practical significance of Secretary Dulles' "northern tier" concept began to clarify early in 1954. On 2 April Turkey and Pakistan, with United States encouragement, concluded in Karachi the present agreement. This was followed on 19 May by a mutual assistance agreement between Pakistan and the United States [Pakistan, *Treaty Series (1954),* No. 9], under which Pakistan became eligible for American military grant aid. The Pakistan-Turkish agreement, although intended to serve as the nucleus of the projected "northern tier" collective security arrangement, was for all practical purposes superseded by the Turco-Iraqi agreement of 24 February 1955 (Doc. 107). Omitted below is the amendment of 19 August 1954, effected by an exchange of notes between the Pakistan Chargé d'Affaires in Ankara and the Turkish Foreign Minister, which altered article 4 (b) to read "production and supply of arms and ammunition." J. W. Spain, "Military Assistance for Pakistan," *The American Political Science Review,* 48 (September 1954), 738–51.

Pakistan and Turkey

Reaffirming their faith in the Purposes and Principles of the Charter of the United Nations and their determination always to endeavour to apply and give effect to these Purposes and Principles,

Desirous of promoting the benefits of greater mutual cooperation deriving from the sincere friendship happily existing between them,

Recognising the need for consultation and cooperation between them in every field for the purpose of promoting the well-being and security of their peoples,

Being convinced that such cooperation would be to the interest of all peace-loving nations and in particular also to the interest of nations in the region of the Contracting Parties, and would consequently serve to ensure peace and security which are both indivisible,

Have therefore decided to conclude this Agreement for friendly Cooperation. . . .

ART. 1. The Contracting Parties undertake to refrain from intervening in any way in the internal affairs of each other and from participating in any alliance or activities directed against the other.

ART. 2. The Contracting Parties will consult on international matters of mutual interest and, taking into account international requirements and conditions, cooperate between them to the maximum extent.

ART. 3. The Contracting Parties will develop the cooperation, already established between them in the cultural field under a separate Agreement, in the economic and technical fields also by concluding, if necessary, other agreements.

ART. 4. The consultation and cooperation between the Contracting Parties in the field of defence shall cover the following points:

a. exchange of information for the purpose of deriving benefit jointly from technical experience and progress,

b. endeavours to meet, as far as possible, the requirements of the Parties in the production of arms and ammunition,

c. studies and determination of the ways and extent of cooperation which might be effected between them in accordance with Article 51 of the Charter of the United Nations, should an unprovoked attack occur against them from outside.

ART. 5. Each Contracting Party declares that none of the international engagements now in force between it and any third State is in conflict with the provisions of this Agreement and that this Agreement shall not affect, nor can it be interpreted so as to affect, the aforesaid engagements, and undertakes not to enter into any international engagement in conflict with this Agreement.

ART. 6. Any State, whose participation is considered by the Contracting Parties useful for achieving the purposes of the present Agreement, may accede to the present Agreement under the same conditions and with the same obligations as the Contracting Parties.

Any accession shall have legal effect, after the instrument of accession is duly deposited with the Government of Turkey from the date of an official notification by the Government of Turkey to the Government of Pakistan.

ART. 7. This Agreement, of which the English text is authentic, shall be ratified by the Contracting Parties in accordance with their respective constitutional processes, and shall enter into force on the date of the exchange of the instruments of ratification in Ankara.

In case no formal notice of denunciation is given by one of the Contracting Parties to the other, one year before the termination of a period of five years from the date of its entry into force, the present Agreement shall automatically continue in force for a further period of five years, and the same procedure will apply for subsequent periods thereafter.

103. MILITARY ASSISTANCE AGREEMENT: THE UNITED STATES AND IRAQ
21 April 1954

[U.S., *Treaties and Other International Acts Series,* No. 3108]

When the United States first assumed defense obligations in the postwar Near and Middle East, it adhered to the principle of severely limiting military assistance commitments in the Arab-Israel zone. The policy of caution was premised on the assumption that the individual states concerned were too preoccupied with their immediate rivalries and disputes seriously to sense any danger from the Soviet colossus and therefore to make common cause with the West; and that the movement of American arms into the area would upset the tricky military equilibrium. Under the "northern tier" dispensation the original caution gave way to the bold experiment of entering with Iraq into the following cooperative military arrangement, effected by an exchange of notes of which the one from the American Ambassador to the Iraqi Acting Foreign Minister appears below. Iraq pledged to employ the grant aid "solely to maintain its internal security and its legitimate self defense" and solemnly declared "that it will not undertake any act of aggression against any other state" (article 1). These assurances, however, failed to persuade Israel of Iraq's pacific intentions. J. W. Spain, "Middle East Defense: a New Approach," *The Middle East Journal,* 8 (Summer 1954), 251–66.

I have the honor to refer to the Foreign Office Memorandum of March 1953 requesting the United States Government to provide arms assistance to Iraq, and the Embassy's interim reply of June 1953, stating that the United States Government was giving this request careful consideration. I am now pleased to inform you that the United States Government has acted favorably on this request and is prepared to grant military assistance to the Government of Iraq. Such assistance will be provided subject to the provisions of applicable legislative authority and will be related in character, timing and amount to international developments in the area. In addition, it is proposed that any such assistance be provided in accordance with the following terms and such additional arrangements as may from time to time be agreed upon.

1. It is the understanding of my government that the Government of Iraq will use such equipment, materials or services as may be provided solely to maintain its internal security and its legitimate self defense, and that it will not undertake any

act of aggression against any other state.

2. My government also understands that the Government of Iraq agrees that it will:

(a) join in promoting international understanding and good will, and maintaining world peace;

(b) take such action as may be mutually agreed upon to eliminate causes of international tension;

(c) make, consistent with its political and economic stability, the full contribution permitted by its manpower, resources, facilities and general economic condition to the development and maintenance of its own defensive strength and the defensive strength of the free world;

(d) take all reasonable measures which may be needed to develop its defense capacities; and

(e) take appropriate steps to insure the effective utilization of the economic and military assistance provided by the United States.

3. (a) The Government of Iraq will, consistent with the Charter of the United Nations, furnish to the Government of the United States, or to such other governments as may be agreed upon, such equipment, materials, services in excess of Iraq's own requirements, or other assistance as may be agreed upon in order to increase their capacity for individual and collective self defense and to facilitate their effective participation in the United Nations system for collective security.

(b) The Government of Iraq further understands that the Government of the United States may request the Government of Iraq to facilitate the production and export to the United States, under terms and conditions to be agreed, of raw and semi-processed materials required by the United States as a result of deficiencies or potential deficiencies in its own resources, and which may be available in Iraq. Arrangements for such transfers shall give due regard to reasonable requirements for domestic use and commercial export of Iraq.

4. It is further understood that your Government will not without the prior consent of the Government of the United States, transfer title to or possession of any equipment, materials, information or services furnished, that your Government will protect the security of any items, information or services furnished and that your Government will, upon request, negotiate appropriate arrangements for the protection of patent rights relating to the defense effort.

5. In the mutual interest of both Governments to insure maximum possible realization of the objectives of this agreement, the following arrangements are also proposed:

(a) The Government of Iraq will establish procedures which will protect from attachment, seizure or other legal or administrative process any funds allocated to or derived from any program of assistance undertaken by the Government of the United States.

(b) In accordance with the prevailing laws of Iraq, the Iraq Government will pay all customs duties and dues and local taxes and dues (if any) on equipment and materials imported into Iraq pursuant to Paragraph 1 of this note.

(c) The Government of Iraq will offer for return to the Government of the United States, in accordance with mutually satisfactory procedures, any equipment or materials furnished under this agreement which are no longer required or used exclusively for the purposes stated in Paragraph 1.

(d) The Government of Iraq will receive the personnel of the Government of the United States who will discharge in Iraqi territory the responsibilities of the Government of the United States under this agreement and who will be accorded facilities and authority to observe the progress of the assistance furnished pursuant to this agreement. The number of personnel assigned under this paragraph will be governed by mutual understanding between the two governments as the program develops. Personnel so assigned will be granted the same status, privileges and immunities as are enjoyed by personnel of United States Technical Missions presently operating in Iraq in accordance with existing agreements.

(e) The Government of Iraq agrees to extend to personnel assigned to Iraq under the terms of the agreement, the same privileges with respect to the import of personal property for their personal use as are accorded personnel assigned to Iraq under the terms of the Technical Co-operation Agreement of April 10, 1951, between the United States and Iraq.

(f) The Government of Iraq will, in accordance with the arrangements used to provide facilities and other assistance for experts of United States missions presently operating in Iraq under existing agreements, make possible Iraqi dinars for use in covering the expenses of such personnel incurred in Iraq in the course of carrying out the purpose of this agreement.

(g) Each Government will take appropriate measures, consistent with security, to keep the public informed of operations under this agreement.

I have the honor to propose that, if these understandings are acceptable to the Government of Iraq, this note and your note in reply constitute an understanding between our two Governments, effective on the date of your reply, to remain in force until one year after the receipt by either party of written notice of the intention of the other party to terminate it, except that the provisions of Paragraphs 1, 4 and 5 (c) shall remain in force until otherwise agreed by the two Governments.

104. THE IRAN-CONSORTIUM AGREEMENT
19–20 September 1954

(Entered into force on 29 October 1954)

[U.S., 84th Cong., House of Representatives, Committee on the Judiciary, *Hearings before Antitrust Subcommittee* (Subcommittee No. 5), part 2, pp. 1563–1651]

The Anglo-Iranian dispute after May 1951 focused on the nationalization of the oil industry in Iran (Doc. 95), which entailed the cancellation of the Anglo-Iranian Oil Company's concession (whose expiry date was 1993) and the Iranian government's seizure within its domains of the company's vast properties. During the long premiership (28 April 1951–20 August 1953) of Muhammad Musaddiq, the father of nationalization, United States mediatory efforts appeared totally wasted. But even after the suppression of Musaddiq and the restoration of the shah's authority under the premiership (20 August 1953–17 April 1955) of Major-General Fazallah Zahidi, more than a year passed between the first appearance at Tehran on 17 October 1953 of Herbert Hoover, Jr., the American mediator, and the ratification of the eventual agreement, reproduced below. Full accommodation was achieved through complex negotiations simultaneously conducted on various levels—intercompany, company-governmental and intergovernmental—and in widely scattered places—chiefly Washington, London and Tehran. The final arrangement reflected the entangling issues involved. Iran's irreducible demands were met, for the principle of nationalization was embodied in the fresh contract, as was that of Iran's refusal to permit the return of the AIOC as exclusive foreign petroleum concessionaire in the southern part of the country. Similarly, AIOC and the British government received satisfaction in their minimal claims to fair compensation and to a principal role in the operational functions of the revived industry. Reaffirmation of the area-wide principle of equal profit-sharing between company and government, first introduced into the Near and Middle East in December 1950 by Aramco in Sa'udi Arabia (Doc. 94), also pleased all the oil companies in the region. The devices by which these seemingly contradictory purposes were reconciled attested to the ingenuity of the legal mind. A consortium was created comprising the major petroleum firms operating in the Near and Middle East: AIOC (renamed British Petroleum Company in December 1954) holding a 40 per cent interest, Royal Dutch-Shell 14 per cent, the California Standard, Gulf, New Jersey Standard, Socony-Vacuum (renamed Socony Mobil on 29 April 1955) and Texas companies 8 per cent each (reduced in April 1955 to 7 per cent by the sale of the difference to American independent oil firms), and the Compagnie Française des Pétroles 6 per cent. AIOC transferred its rights in Iran to the consortium, reputedly for 1 billon dollars, payable in part with the proceeds from operations in Iran of the consortium participants' subsidiaries. Thus relieved of the major burden, Iran undertook, as its total share of compensation, to pay AIOC £25 million in ten annual equal installments. The National Iranian Oil Company, an agency of the Iranian government, entrusted production and processing operations of the oil industry within virtually the same area of the former AIOC concession to an Exploration and Producing Company and a Refining Company, which the consortium incorporated in the Netherlands and registered in Iran; and the marketing operations to such trading companies as the consortium participants severally might select for the purpose. All these provisions were incorporated in the following agreement, which (English text) was signed in Tehran and The Hague on 19 September and in London and New York on the following day and which was ratified by the Iranian *Majlis* (lower house) on 21 October 1954 and by the Senate precisely a week later and was promulgated by the shah on 29 October. The consortium agreement, valid for twenty-five years, was conditionally renewable for three five-year periods. The remaining instruments, including the intercompany agreement setting up the consortium, were not yet released as of the time of writing. The net effect of the settlement in Iran was to preserve intact the essential structure of company-government relations in the neighboring oil-producing countries. W. J. Levy, "Economic Problems Facing a Settlement of the Iranian Oil Controversy," *Middle East Journal,* 8 (Winter 1954), 91–95; L. P. Elwell-Sutton, *Persian Oil;* B. Shwadran, *The Middle East Oil and the Great Powers,* chaps. 5–6; UN, Department of Economic and Social Affairs, *Economic Developments in the Middle East, 1945 to 1954,* chap. 3.

This Agreement, made in two Parts, as to Part I by and between Iran, acting through the Imperial Government of Iran, and the National Iranian Oil Company (a corporation organized and existing under the laws of Iran), as First Parties; and Gulf Oil Corporation (a corporation organized and existing under the laws of Pennsylvania, U. S. A.), Socony-Vacuum Oil Company Incorporated (a corporation organized and existing under the laws of New York, U. S. A.), Standard Oil Company (a corporation organized and existing under the laws of New Jersey, U. S. A.), Standard Oil Company of California (a corporation organized and existing under the laws of Delaware, U. S. A.), The Texas Company (a corporation organized and existing under the laws of Delaware, U. S. A.), Anglo-Iranian Oil Company, Limited (a corporation organized and existing under the laws of the United Kingdom), N. V. De Bataafsche Petroleum Maatschappij (a corporation organized and existing under the laws of the Netherlands) and Compagnie Francaise des Petroles (a corporation organized and existing under the laws of France), as Second Parties and as to Part II by and between First Parties; and Anglo-Iranian Oil Company, Limited (a corporation organized and existing under the laws of the United Kingdom) as Third Party;

As to Part I Witnesseth:

PART I

Whereas, both the Government of Iran and the National Iranian Oil Company desire to increase the production and sale of Iranian oil, and thereby to increase the benefits flowing to the Iranian nation from said oil, but additional capital, experienced management, and technical skills are required in order to produce, refine, transport and market such oil in quantities sufficient to effect this increase in a substantial amount; and

Whereas, the international oil companies named above as Second Parties to this Agreement are in a position and are willing to supply such capital, management and skills; and

Whereas, said companies and their affiliated companies have interests in transportation, refining and marketing facilities established throughout the world over many years at great expense, and are in a position to market substantial quantities of Iranian oil and the products derived therefrom throughout a large part of the world over a considerable period of time, to the mutual benefit of the Iranian nation and themselves; and

Whereas, in order to insure that sufficient oil and products are available for such purposes over said period of time, the Parties are agreed that said companies should undertake the operation and management of certain of the oil properties (but not all of them) of the Government of Iran and the National Iranian Oil Company, including the Abadan Refinery, as hereinafter set forth; and

Whereas, both the Government of Iran and the National Iranian Oil Company, on the one hand, and said companies, on the other hand, are also agreed upon an equitable sharing of the profits resulting from the production and refining and sale of Iranian oil as hereinafter set forth; and

Whereas, each of the Parties has willingly entered into the negotiations leading up to this Agreement and such negotiations have been amicably carried out with the object of assuring to the Government of Iran and the National Iranian Oil Company, on the one hand, a substantial export market for Iranian oil and a means of increasing the material benefits to and prosperity of the Iranian people, and to the companies, on the other hand, the degree of security and the prospect of reasonable rewards necessary to justify the commitment of their resources and facilities to the reactivation of the Iranian oil industry; and

Whereas, the Parties intend that to these ends the provisions of this Agreement shall be carried out in a spirit of good faith and good will

Now therefore, it is hereby agreed by and between the First Parties and Second Parties:

ART. 1. Unless the context otherwise requires, the following definitions of certain terms hereinafter used in this Part I shall apply for the purposes of such Part

A. "This Agreement" means Part I of this Agreement and Schedule 1 attached hereto.

B. "NIOC" means the National Iranian Oil Company and "IOC" means the Iran Oil Company.

C. "Consortium members" means the Second Parties and any person to whom a sale, assignment or transfer is made in accordance with Article 39 of this Agreement.

D. "Exploration and Producing Company" means the Iraanse Aardolie Exploratie en Productie Maatschappij (Iranian Oil Exploration and Producing Company) N.V.

E. "Refining Company" means the Iraanse Aardolie Raffinage Maatschappij (Iranian Oil Refining Company) N.V.

F. "Operating Companies" means the Exploration and Producing Company and the Refining Company.

G. "Trading Companies" shall have the meaning set forth in Article 18 of this Agreement.

H. "Area" means the area from time to time covered and affected by this Agreement, as determined in accordance with the provisions of Articles 2 and 49 of this Agreement.

I. "Crude oil" means crude petroleum, asphalt (except asphalt from deposits being worked by persons other than NIOC on or before the Effective Date) and all liquid hydrocarbons in their natural state or obtained by condensation or extraction from natural gas. When crude oil is processed otherwise than at refinery and a part thereof is put back into the crude oil stream, "crude oil" shall include the part so put back.

J. "Petroleum product" means any finished or semi-finished product derived from crude oil by condensation, refining, chemical treatment or any other method of process, whether now known or not.

K. "Natural gas" means wet gas, dry gas, all other gaseous hydrocarbons produced through oil or gas wells and the residue gas remaining after the extraction of liquid hydrocarbons from such wet gas.

L. "Refinery" means the Abadan refinery, and any other refinery or refineries which may be built by the Refining Company within the Area, together with all facilities, equipment and appurtenances.

M. "Internal consumption in Iran" means the consumption in Iran of the product or substances concerned, in contrast to its export from Iran, but for the purpose of this definition shall not include consumption in Iran by the Operating Companies.

N. "Posted price" of Iranian crude oil means

(1) in the case of crude oil loaded on board tankship for export from Iran the price f.o.b. tankship at seaboard terminal, being the price at which crude oil of equivalent quality and gravity is offered for sale by a Trading Company or its affiliated company to buyers generally for delivery under similar conditions and at the same seaboard terminal, and

(2) in the case of crude oil delivered to refinery the price of crude oil of equivalent quality and gravity offered for sale as above f.o.b. tankship at refinery port less such an amount (not exceeding 8d. per cubic meter) as may fairly and reasonably be attributed to the loading charge of crude oil at such refinery port.

O. "Applicable posted price" means, in relation to any Iranian crude oil, the individual posted price of the particular Trading Company or its affiliated company for such crude oil as of the date of export or delivery to refinery, as the case may be.

P. "Subsidiary company" or "subsidiary," in relation to a Consortium member, means any corporation all the voting shares of which are owned by either the Consortium member, or a Parent company of the Consortium member, or either of them together with one or more additional persons each of which is a Consortium member or Parent company.

Q. "Affiliated company" or "affiliate," in relation to a Consortium member or Trading Company nominated by such Consortium member, means any corporation

(1) which owns 50% or more of the voting shares of that Consortium member, or

(2) 50% or more of the voting shares of which are owned by either the Consortium member, or a Parent company of the Consortium member, or either of them together with one or more additional persons each of which is a Consortium member or Parent company.

R. "Parent company," as used in the preceding two definitions, means a corporation or corporations which own all the voting shares of a Consortium member; and "own," as used in this and the preceding two definitions, means beneficially own directly or through one or more other corporations.

S. "Person" means natural or juridical person, and includes partnership, firm, company, unincorporated association and corporation.

T. "Term of this Agreement" and "remaining life of this Agreement" shall have the meanings set forth in Article 49 of this Agreement.

U. "Cubic meter" means one cubic meter at sixty degrees Fahrenheit and at normal atmospheric pressure.

V. "Effective Date" means the date on which this Agreement comes into force under Article 51 hereof.

W. Periods of time referred to in this Agreement shall be reckoned on the basis of the solar calendar. "Year" means a calendar year beginning January 1, and "quarter" means a period of three months beginning January 1, April 1, July 1, or October 1, each in accordance with the Gregorian calendar.

ART. 2. A. The Area covered and affected by this Agreement, subject to the provisions of Article 49 of this Agreement, is all that set out in Schedule 1 attached hereto.

B. "Mile" as used in said Schedule 1 shall mean an English statute mile of 5280 feet.

C. The respective rights of NIOC and IOC in the above-mentioned Area shall be, and are hereby, adjusted so as to conform with the provisions of this Agreement.

ART. 3. A. With the object of implementing this Agreement, and for the purpose of having the functions of exploration, producing, refining, transportation and the other functions specified in Article 4 of this Agreement carried out, the Consortium members have caused the Operating Companies to be incorporated under the laws of the Netherlands and undertake to cause the said Operating Companies to sign this Agreement. Upon signing this Agreement said Operating Companies shall be deemed to be parties to this Agreement, and the Consortium members hereby jointly and severally guarantee the due performance by the Operating Companies of their respective obligations under this Agreement.

B. It is agreed that the constitution and internal management, rights, powers and obligations of the Operating Companies shall be as provided in this Agreement.

C. The constitution and internal management of the Operating Companies shall be regulated by the Articles of Association (Statuten) of those Companies. In accordance with Iranian law, the Operating Companies have been duly registered in Iran, and in connection therewith certified copies of their Articles of Association (Statuten) as at the date of such registration have been duly filed with the Companies Registration Section of the Registration Department of Tehran. Those Articles of Association (Statuten) have been read and the relevant parts thereof have been approved by the representatives of Iran.

D. The Board of Directors of each Company shall consist of seven directors, and no increase shall be made in the number of directors in either Board without the consent of Iran. The Consortium members undertake with Iran that two of the members of the Board of each Company shall be persons nominated by NIOC.

E. The remuneration of the directors of each Operating Company relating to their duties in connection with participating in Board Meetings shall be such as may be agreed from time to time between NIOC and that Operating Company, and shall be included in its operating costs.

ART. 4. The Operating Company shall have for the term of this Agreement all rights and powers to carry out, within the Area and on behalf of Iran and NIOC as hereinafter in this Article set forth, the following functions:—

(1) The Exploration and Producing Company shall have the rights and powers to carry out the following functions namely to explore for (by geological, geophysical or other methods including drilling for the purpose of determining sub-surface geological conditions) to drill for and to produce, extract and take crude oil and natural gas, to operate field topping plants and sulphur plants and otherwise process oil and gas produced by it to the extent necessary for its operations, to store such oil and gas and derivatives and products therefrom and to transport and deliver the same by any means, including loading on board ship.

(2) The Refining Company shall have the rights and powers to carry out the following functions namely to refine and to process crude oil and natural gas produced by the Exploration and Producing Company, to refine and manufacture derivatives and products therefrom alone or with other substances and to store, pack, transport and deliver by any means, including loading on board ship, such crude oil, natural gas, derivatives and products.

B. Each of the Operating Companies shall have the rights and powers in connection with the carrying out of its functions to dig, sink, bore, drive, build, construct, erect, lay, provide, operate, maintain and administer pits, shafts, wells, trenches, excavations, dams, drains, watercourses, plants, tanks, reservoirs and other storage facilities, refineries, topping plants, casinghead gasoline plants, sulphur plants and other facilities for producing, refining and processing crude oil and natural gas, pipelines, pumping stations, power houses, power stations, power lines, telegraph, telephone, radio and other communications facilities, factories, warehouses, offices, houses, buildings, ports, docks, harbors, piers, jetties, dredgers, breakwaters, submarine loading lines and terminal facilities, vessels, conveyances, railways, roads, bridges, ferries, airways, airports and other transport facilities, garages, hangars, workshops, foundries, and repair shops and all ancillary services in its opinion required for the purposes of or in connection with its operations and all such further or other rights and powers as are or may become necessary or reasonably incidental to the carrying out of any of its functions, it being understood that the creation of any railway lines, ports, telephone, telegraph and wireless services and aviation facilities in Iran shall require the previous consent in writing of Iran, which consent shall not be unreasonably withheld or delayed.

C. The Operating Companies shall also have the rights and powers in connection with their functions to carry out such operations outside the Area as are provided for by Articles 7, 8, 9 and 36 of this Agreement.

D. Without prejudice to the provisions of Section C of Article 41 of this Agreement, the respective rights and powers of the Operating Companies under this Agreement shall not be revoked or modified at any time during the term of this Agreement.

E. The Operating Companies shall exercise their respective rights and powers set out in the preceding Sections of this Article on behalf of Iran and NIOC in the manner and within the limits herein provided, namely:—

(1) they shall be subject to obligations to Iran and NIOC in respect of the exercise of such rights and powers to the extent set out in Section F of this Article; and

(2) they shall be subject to supervision by Iran and NIOC in the exercise of such rights and powers to the extent set out in Section G of this Article.

F. The obligations of the Operating Companies to Iran and NIOC shall be the following:—

(1) to conform with good oil industry practice and sound engineering principles applicable and appropriate to operations under similar conditions in conserving the deposits of hydrocarbons, in operating the oilfields and refinery and in conducting development operations, all within the Area;

(2) to carry out such exploration operations as are economically justifiable with a view to providing sufficient reserves to support the rate of production of oil within the Area;

(3) to maintain full records of all technical operations and to keep accounts in such a manner as to present a fair, clear and accurate record of all the activities of the Operating Companies, and for this purpose in consultation with NIOC to devise a suitable accounting system and to revise the same from time to time in the light of future developments;

(4) to minimize the employment of foreign personnel by ensuring, so far as reasonably practicable, that foreign personnel are engaged only to occupy positions for which the Operating Companies do not find available Iranians having the requisite qualifications and experience;

(5) to prepare in consultation with NIOC plans and programs for industrial and technical training and education and to cooperate in their execution with a view to training Iranians to replace foreign personnel as soon as reasonably practicable and to affording Iranians every possible opportunity for occupying responsible positions in the operations of the Operating Companies;

(6) to be always mindful, in the conduct of their operations, of the rights and interests of Iran.

G. In order to enable Iran and NIOC to maintain the necessary degree of supervision over the operations of the Operating Companies to satisfy themselves that the Operating Companies are carrying out their obligations set out in Section F of this Article, the Operating Companies shall afford to Iran and NIOC all facilities:—

(1) if Iran and NIOC do not wish to accept the regular external audit of the accounts of the Operating Companies, to have the same specially audited by an independent international firm of accountants or by independent qualified accountants experienced in accountancy pertaining to oil producing and refining, acting on behalf of Iran and NIOC and at their expense. In that event, NIOC shall give notice in writing to the relevant Operating Company within six months after the end of the year to which such regular external audit relates of its desire to have a special audit and shall procure that such special audit is carried out with reasonable despatch so as not to delay unduly the final settlement by the Operating Company of any matters arising out of the audit of its accounts.

(2) to have supplied to NIOC upon its request and within a reasonable time by and at the expense of the Operating Com-

panies all such information as NIOC may require in the form of accurate copies of such of the Operating Companies' plans, maps, sections and reports as shall be in final form and relate to topographical, geological, geophysical, drilling, producing, refining and other similar relevant matters within the Area;

(3) to have communicated to NIOC, upon its request and within a reasonable time, by the Operating Companies all important scientific and technical data resulting from their operations under this Agreement;

(4) to enable NIOC to inspect at all reasonable times by technical experts chosen by NIOC the technical activities of the Operating Companies, and to have placed at the disposal of such experts all of the Operating Companies' records and information relating to scientific and technical data and all measuring apparatus and means of measurement and testing.

Any expenses incurred by the Operating Companies in affording to Iran and NIOC the facilities set out above shall be included in their operating costs.

H. The supervision provided for by Section G of this Article shall be exercised subject to the following conditions, namely:—

(1) the said supervision shall not be exercised in such a manner as to hinder, impede or affect adversely the operations of the Operating Companies;

(2) except as otherwise agreed in writing between NIOC and the Operating Companies, any plans, maps, sections, reports, records, scientific and technical data, and any other similar information relating to the technical operations of the Operating Companies under this Agreement shall be treated by Iran and NIOC and the Operating Companies as confidential in the sense that their contents or effect shall not be disclosed by Iran or NIOC without the consent of the Operating Companies or by an Operating Company without the consent of NIOC, such consents not to be unreasonably withheld or delayed.

I. Subject to the provisions of Sections F and G of this Article, the Operating Companies shall determine and have full and effective management and control of all their operations.

J. The nature and extent of the foregoing rights, powers and obligations of the Operating Companies as well as the nature and extent of the supervision to be exercised by Iran and NIOC shall be strictly limited to what is clearly stated in this Article.

ART. 5. A. Iran and NIOC undertake that neither of them, and no person other than the Operating Companies, shall at any time during the term of this Agreement carry out within the Area any of the functions specified in Paragraphs (1) and (2) of Section A of Article 4 of this Agreement.

B. Notwithstanding the provisions of Section A of this Article and subject to the provisions of Section C of this Article, NIOC may

(1) explore for, drill for and produce crude oil and natural gas to meet its requirements of petroleum products for internal consumption in Iran, in areas agreed by the Exploration and Producing Company to be such that their exploration and development can not be economically justified for export purposes but which in the opinion of NIOC justify exploration and development to provide crude oil and natural gas to meet NIOC's requirements of petroleum products for internal consumption in Iran; and

(2) install within the Area, elsewhere than at then existing installations operated by either of the Operating Companies, additional facilities for refining, processing, storing, packing and transporting by pipe line crude oil, natural gas, and derivatives and products therefrom, and use such additional facilities for these purposes but such additional facilities may be installed and used in respect of crude oil or natural gas produced by the Exploration and Producing Company or by NIOC within the Area pursuant to Paragraph (1) of this Section, only to the extent necessary to meet NIOC's requirements of petroleum products for internal consumption in Iran; provided always that no additional facilities shall be installed or used in such manner as unrea-

sonably to hinder or interfere with the carrying out by the Operating Companies of any of their respective functions.

C. For the implementation of the provisions of Section B of this Article, NIOC may consult with the appropriate Operating Company with a view to reaching a mutually acceptable agreement whereby that Operating Company would be willing to carry out for and at the expense of NIOC any of the activities mentioned in Paragraph (1) of Section B of this Article and, insofar as they relate to oil produced within the Area, any of the activities mentioned in Paragraph (2) of Section B of this Article.

ART. 6. A. The Operating Companies shall have for so long as they may require them during the term of this Agreement, the unrestricted right, in their operations, to use and move within the Area all the fixed assets relating to the exploration for and the production, transportation, refining and loading of crude oil, natural gas and petroleum products, which are located within the Area on the Effective Date. Any transfer of any of the said fixed assets from one Operating Company to the other shall require the prior consent in writing of NIOC which shall not be unreasonably withheld or delayed.

B. If the Operating Companies consider that any new, additional or substitute fixed assets are necessary or desirable in their operations, they shall erect or install them. Such new, additional or substitute fixed assets shall be the property of NIOC, but the Operating Company which erected or installed such assets shall have for so long as it may require them during the term of this Agreement, the unrestricted right, in its operations, to use and move within the Area all such assets.

C. (1) On the Effective Date NIOC shall deliver over to the Operating Companies all the following items, relating to the operations contemplated by this Agreement, which are located within the Area on such date, namely, all stocks of stores and materials, all movable plant and equipment, all mechanical transport and all drilling plant and tools; excepting therefrom only such items as are for use in internal distribution or are located at internal distribution depots, and such items as NIOC and the Operating Companies may agree should be retained by NIOC for its operations.

(2) The Operating Companies shall provide, as they consider necessary, new or additional stores and materials, movable plant and equipment, mechanical transport and drilling plant and tools.

D. In view of obligations which the Consortium members have assumed and which benefit Iran, Iran and NIOC shall permit the Operating Companies to use the assets referred to in Section A of this Article and to receive delivery from NIOC of the items referred to in Paragraph (1) of Section C of this Article without any cost or charge of any kind to the Operating Companies by Iran or NIOC, and the Operating Companies shall be entitled to include in their operating costs the amounts provided for in Paragraphs (1) and (2) of this Section:

(1) During the first ten years of operations hereunder, in each year a fixed assets charge in respect of the assets referred to in Section A of this Article of £2,600,000, in the case of the Exploration and Producing Company, and £4,100,000, in the case of the Refining Company, shall be included in their respective operating costs. The proceeds of such fixed assets charges shall be disposed of by the Operating Companies as they see fit.

(2) (a) As the stores and materials referred to in Paragraph (1) of Section C of this Article are used, the Operating Company using them shall include the book value thereof (as at the time they were originally put in stock), either in its operating or other costs or in capital expenditure, depending on the use made by the Operating Company of the particular items. The original cost of each item of movable plant and equipment, mechanical transport and drilling plant and tools (reduced by depreciation for periods prior to the Effective Date at a rate based on its estimated useful life ascertained in accordance with good accounting and engineering practice) shall be depreciated at a rate based on the portion of its estimated useful life remaining after the Effective Date (ascertained as

aforesaid) and the Operating Company using such items shall include such depreciation either in its operating or other costs or in capital expenditure, as appropriate. If, however, any of such stocks of stores and materials, movable plant and equipment or mechanical transport are used in the non-basic operations (as defined in Article 17 of this Agreement) carried on by NIOC, the Operating Company in question may deduct the said book value of any stores and materials so used or the appropriate part of depreciation of movable plant and equipment and mechanical transport, computed on the basis provided above, from any payment due from such Operating Company to NIOC in respect of expenditure for non-basic operations. Any sums included, as aforesaid, by an Operating Company in its capital expenditure shall be treated in all respects under Section E of this Article as if they were costs of new, additional or substitute fixed assets. The proceeds of any charges made under this Paragraph to operating or other costs or to capital expenditure shall be disposed of by the Operating Companies as they see fit.

(b) The cost of any new or additional stores and materials shall be treated in the same way as provided in sub-paragraph (a) of this Paragraph for the book value of stores and materials and any new or additional movable plant and equipment, mechanical transport and drilling plant and tools shall be depreciated in the manner provided for such items in said sub-paragraph (a).

E. (1) The Operating Companies shall finance, free of interest, the cost of the erection or installation of the new, additional or substitute assets referred to in Section B of this Article and NIOC shall owe the amount of the cost of each such asset to the Operating Company which erected or installed such asset. Each debt so incurred shall be repayable in equal annual installments over the ten-year period following the commencement of use of the asset with respect to which such debt was incurred or over such lesser period as NIOC may agree. The Operating Company which erected or installed such asset shall credit NIOC, for each year during such ten-year period or such lesser period (as the case may be) with a fixed assets charge in respect of such asset in each year of such period equal, in the case of the ten-year period, to one-tenth of the cost of such asset or, in the case of a lesser period, to that proportion of the cost of such asset which one year bears to the total number of years in such lesser period, thereby extinguishing the debt at the end of the period in question.

(2) In consideration of the amount credited to NIOC under Paragraph (1) of this Section, Iran and NIOC shall permit the Operating Companies to use such new, additional or substitute assets during the term of this Agreement or for so long as the Operating Companies may require such assets without any cost or charge of any kind to the Operating Companies by Iran or NIOC after the end of the period during which such amount is to be credited. The Operating Companies shall be entitled to include in their operating costs the fixed assets charge provided for under said Paragraph (1).

ART. 7. A. The Operating Companies shall have the right within the Area to the exclusive use without charge of:—

(1) all lands which NIOC or IOC at present use or have the right to use for their operations other than internal distribution, except the right of way for the pipe line from the Naft-i-Shah field to the Kermanshah refinery and the lands on which the pumping stations and the terminal in connection with such pipe line are located; and

(2) any lands belonging to Iran which they may reasonably require for their use for or in connection with their operations under this Agreement, provided that the use of such land shall require the previous consent in writing of Iran which shall be applied for through NIOC and shall not be unreasonably withheld or delayed. In the case of land not then in use by Iran or others Iran's consent shall be given gratuitously, but in the case of land then in use by Iran or others, a rent therefor shall be payable by the relevant Operating Com-

pany to NIOC as if the land had been leased by NIOC under Section B of this Article, all the relevant provisions of which shall apply accordingly.

B. (1) If any further lands within the Area are reasonably required by the Operating Companies for their use in connection with their operations under this Agreement such lands shall, upon request made by the Operating Companies or either of them to NIOC, without unreasonable delay be purchased or leased, whichever may in the circumstances be considered more economical by the relevant Operating Company, by NIOC in its own name but for the use of the relevant Operating Company. The purchase price or rent shall be reasonable, based only on the existing use of the land, and not in excess of the market price or rent for similar land in the same district.

(2) If the lands are purchased or leased in consideration of a lump sum payment the amount of the lump sum payment shall be paid by the relevant Operating Company to NIOC and shall constitute a debt due from NIOC to the relevant Operating Company, repayable in equal installments over the twenty years following the acquisition of the land, or over the remaining life of this Agreement, which ever is the lesser. The Operating Company shall credit to NIOC for each year during such twenty-year period or lesser period (as the case may be) a land assets charge equal, in the case of the twenty-year period to one twentieth of the amount of the lump sum payment or, in the case of a lesser period, to that proportion of the lump sum payment which one year bears to the total number of years in the lesser period, thereby extinguishing the debt at the end of the period in question.

(3) If the lands are leased in consideration of the payment of a periodic rent, the relevant Operating Company shall for the remainder of the term of this Agreement or of the lease, whichever is the shorter, pay to NIOC for payment to the lessor the periodic rent as and when it falls due.

(4) In consideration of the crediting of the said land assets charge or the payment of the said rent, as the case may be, the relevant Operating Company shall be entitled to the exclusive use for the remainder of the term of this Agreement of the lands acquired under this Section free of any further cost to them. The said land assets charge or rent shall be included in the operating costs of the relevant Operating Company.

C. If the Operating Companies or either of them reasonably require for their operations under this Agreement any rights in or over land whether inside or outside the Area less than a right to the exclusive use of land, including but not limited to such rights as easements, rights of way, wayleaves and rights to lay or pass on, over or under land any roads, railways, pipes, pipe lines, sewers, drains, wires, cables, lines or similar objects, they shall give NIOC notice in writing to this effect. NIOC shall forthwith acquire such rights in its own name but for use by the relevant Operating Company for the remainder of the term of this Agreement at a price or a rent which shall be reasonable having regard to the character of the land and the nature of the right required. If the rights are acquired in consideration of a lump sum payment, the provisions of Paragraph (2) of Section B of this Article shall apply, and if the rights are acquired in consideration of a periodic rent the provisions of Paragraph (3) of Section B of this Article shall apply. In either case, the land assets charge or periodic rent shall be included in the operating costs of the relevant Operating Company and no further charge shall be payable by the relevant Operating Company in respect of the possession or exercise of the said right.

D. Any reduction in the Area made pursuant to Article 49 of this Agreement shall not affect the rights of the Operating Companies to exercise, in or over the lands so relinquished, without any further payment to NIOC (except for payment over by NIOC to the owner or lessor as the case may be), any rights of the character referred to in Section C of this Article.

ART. 8. A. The Operating Companies may use free of charge for the purposes of their operations under this Agreement, but subject to any then existing rights of persons not parties to this Agreement and also subject to payment where such payment is customary, any water which they may find upon, or under, or passing through:

(1) the lands which they use;

(2) lands belonging to Iran which are not then in use by Iran or others, subject to the consent of Iran which shall not be unreasonably withheld or delayed.

B. (1) If any further water rights, whether inside or outside the Area, are reasonably required by the Operating Companies for their operations under this Agreement, such rights shall, upon request made by the Operating Companies or either of them to NIOC, without unreasonable delay be purchased or leased, whichever may in the circumstances be considered more economical by the relevant Operating Company, by NIOC in its own name but for the benefit for the remainder of the term of this Agreement of the relevant Operating Company. NIOC need not comply with the said request if to do so would seriously prejudice irrigation or navigation, or would deprive any cultivated lands, houses or watering places for livestock of a reasonable supply of water. The purchase price or rent of rights so acquired shall be reasonable, and not in excess of the market price or rent for similar rights in the same district.

(2) If the rights are acquired in consideration of a lump sum payment, the provisions of Paragraph (2) of Section B of Article 7 of this Agreement shall apply, and if the rights are acquired in consideration of a periodic rent the provisions of Paragraph (3) of the said Section shall apply. In either case, the land assets charge or periodic rent shall be included in the operating costs of the relevant Operating Company and no further charge shall be payable by the relevant Operating Company in respect of the possession or exercise of the said rights for the term of this Agreement.

ART. 9. For the purposes of their operations under this Agreement, the Operating Companies or either of them may take, subject to any then existing rights of persons not parties to this Agreement, from the lands which they use and from lands belonging to Iran within the Area which are not then in use by Iran or others and which the Operating Companies are not then using, and may utilize, without any charge to them, any kinds of soil, sand, lime, stone, gypsum and other building materials, subject to the payment of reasonable compensation to third parties who may suffer injury as a result of the said taking or utilization. Any payment of compensation for such injury shall be included in the operating costs of the relevant Operating Company.

ART. 10. A. The Exploration and Producing Company shall have the right to use in its operations crude oil produced by it and any petroleum products manufactured by it or by the Refining Company.

B. The Refining Company shall have the right to use in its operations any petroleum products manufactured by it or by the Exploration and Producing Company.

C. The Exploration and Producing Company shall pay the Refining Company for any petroleum products manufactured by the latter and used by the former pursuant to Section A of this Article, the weighted average of the posted prices of the crude oil delivered to refinery and used in their manufacture, plus the Refining Company's cost of refining in respect of such products.

The Refining Company shall pay the Exploration and Producing Company for any substance other than crude oil or natural gas produced or manufactured by the latter and used by the former a price to be agreed between them and approved in writing by NIOC, which approval shall not be unreasonably withheld or delayed.

D. Payments made by either Operating Company to the other pursuant to the foregoing provisions of this Article shall be included in its operating costs by the Company making the payments and shall be credited to operating costs by the Company receiving the payments.

E. The use by the Exploration and Producing Company of crude oil and the use by either Operating Company of petroleum products, pursuant to the provisions of this Article, shall be free of any obligation on the part of that Operating Company to make any payment to Iran or NIOC in respect of any such crude oil or petroleum products.

ART. 11. A. To the extent that natural gas produced by the Exploration and Producing Company is required for the purposes of its operations, such Company may take and use such gas free of any payment to NIOC.

B. (1) The Exploration and Producing Company may deliver to the Refining Company at the refinery such natural gas as the Refining Company requires as fuel for the purposes of its operations.

(2) In respect of gas supplied to it under this Section, the Refining Company shall pay NIOC for each thousand cubic meters of gas so supplied 5% of the weighted average of the posted prices (as at the date of delivery of the gas) for one cubic meter of 37°-37.9° API crude oil of Agha Jari quality f.o.b. Bandar Mashur, and, in addition, shall pay to the Exploration and Producing Company:

(a) in the case of natural gas produced as an incident to the production of crude oil, the cost of delivering such gas from the field gas/oil separator to the refinery;

(b) in the case of natural gas produced from a field which is primarily a producer of natural gas, the cost of production and delivery to the refinery of such natural gas.

C. If in any year the Refining Company has taken natural gas under Section B of this Article, and export sales of natural gas have been made in the Persian Gulf area in that year in comparable quantities, then, if the overall revenue which would have resulted to Iran and NIOC from such export sales had they been effected by the Trading Companies is at a higher rate per thousand cubic meters than the rate of the payment to NIOC provided for by the said Section B, NIOC may by notice to the Refining Company request it to increase its payments to NIOC for natural gas delivered to the refinery during that year so that they will be at such higher rate. If the Refining Company is unwilling to comply with the request, it shall not be bound to do so, but in that event the Refining Company shall cease to use for the purposes of its operations natural gas produced by the Exploration and Producing Company until it is able to agree with NIOC as to the payments to be made to NIOC for such natural gas.

D. Payments by the Refining Company to NIOC under Section B of this Article shall be made as follows:

(1) Within 15 days after the end of each quarter in any year, the Refining Company shall estimate on the basis of the latest available information the payment to be made to NIOC under the said Section in respect of natural gas supplied during that year up to the end of that quarter and shall pay to NIOC the amount so estimated, less any payments made in respect of previous quarters in that year.

(2) Within three months after the end of each year the Refining Company shall calculate the total amount payable to NIOC under the said Section in respect of natural gas supplied during the year. If as a result of such calculation any further amount shall be found due from the Refining Company to NIOC, the Refining Company shall forthwith pay it. If as a result of such calculation any amount shall be found due from NIOC to the Refining Company it shall be carried forward and treated as a payment on account of the sums payable by the Refining Company to NIOC under the said Section for the then current year; but if no sums become so payable for the then current year the said amount shall be paid by NIOC to the Refining Company.

E. Payments made by the Refining Company under Section B of this Article shall be included in its operating costs.

ART. 12. The Exploration and Producing Company shall have the right, on such terms and conditions as may be agreed in writing between NIOC and the Consortium members, to recycle to the reservoir distillate or residue or both from field topping plants to such extent as the Refining Company may from time to time request.

ART. 13. A. The Operating Companies shall be entitled to the following fees:—

(1) Exploration and Producing Company —One shilling per cubic meter of crude oil delivered hereunder

(2) Refining Company—One shilling per cubic meter of crude oil refined hereunder.

B. Costs incurred by an Operating Company and payable to it under the terms of this Agreement shall be computed on the basis of generally accepted principles of accounting, consistently applied, and shall include all relevant costs of that Company including but without in any way limiting the generality of the foregoing a proper allocation of administrative, overhead and establishment expenses, any relevant fixed assets charge, land assets charge, rent, nonbasic assets charge, and depreciation of movable plant and equipment, mechanical transport and drilling plant and tools.

C. Each Trading Company shall pay each Operating Company its fee with respect to crude oil delivered or refined for the account of such Trading Company. The Trading Companies shall reimburse each Operating Company the appropriate part of its operating costs and expenses. The portion of such costs and expenses to be reimbursed by each Trading Company shall be determined by agreement among the Trading Companies.

D. The Trading Companies shall provide each Operating Company from time to time, free of interest, such funds as such Operating Company may require for working capital and for the financing of assets and facilities to be used in its operations and as are not otherwise provided for in this Agreement. The portion of such funds to be thus provided by each Trading Company shall be determined by agreement among the Trading Companies.

ART. 14. A. The Exploration and Producing Company shall deliver to NIOC such petroleum products and derivatives normally manufactured by the Exploration and Producing Company as NIOC may require for internal consumption in Iran and as are not required by the Operating Companies for their operations. The Exploration and Producing Company shall also deliver to refinery, for the account of NIOC, such crude oil as the Refining Company may from time to time request in order to meet NIOC's requirements of petroleum products and derivatives for internal consumption in Iran. The quantity of crude oil to be thus delivered to refinery for the account of NIOC shall be sufficient to cover the crude oil and petroleum products which will be used, consumed and lost by the refinery in manufacturing products for the account of NIOC.

B. The Refining Company shall refine such crude oil as is delivered to it under Section A of this Article and shall deliver to NIOC such quantities of the types and grades of petroleum products and derivatives as are normally manufactured in the refinery and as NIOC may require for internal consumption in Iran.

C. NIOC shall notify the Operating Companies, within fifteen days after the Effective Date as to its estimated requirements quarter by quarter for each petroleum product up to the end of 1955. In 1955 and in each succeeding year during the term of this Agreement, NIOC shall on or before July 1, notify the Operating Companies of its requirements quarter by quarter for each petroleum product during the following year.

D. The quantity of crude oil delivered in any period for the account of NIOC pursuant to the foregoing provisions of this Article shall be ascertained in accordance with methods to be agreed in writing from time to time between NIOC and the Operating Companies.

E. In respect of the quantity of crude oil ascertained under Section D of this Article NIOC shall pay

(1) to the Exploration and Producing Company its fee as provided for in Article 13 of this Agreement and a proper allocation of the total operating costs of the Exploration and Producing Company; and

(2) to the Refining Company, its fee as provided for in the said Article 13 and a proper allocation of the total operating costs of the Refining Company.

ART. 15. A. The Exploration and Producing Company shall deliver to NIOC natural gas produced by the Exploration and Producing Company and required by NIOC for internal consumption in Iran (including any requirements for manufacture in Iran of derivatives whether for internal consumption in Iran or for export), to the extent to which the Exploration and Producing Company has natural gas available for supply to NIOC after meeting:

(1) the requirements of the Operating Companies as provided for in Article 11 of this Agreement;

(2) the requirements of the Trading Companies for the purpose of fulfilling commitments entered into by them or any of them after consultation with NIOC and the Operating Companies as to whether or not natural gas for meeting such commitments is available.

In the case of natural gas produced in association with crude oil, such delivery shall be made at the field gas/oil separator, and in other cases such delivery shall be made at such place in or adjacent to the gas field as the Exploration and Producing Company may determine.

B. Where natural gas supplied or to be supplied to NIOC under this Article is produced as an incident to the production of crude oil, the following provisions shall apply:

(1) If additional facilities are required for the purpose of enabling NIOC to take delivery of the gas, the capital for such facilities shall be provided by NIOC. Such additional facilities, together with all facilities for production and delivery to NIOC of natural gas, shall be operated by the Exploration and Producing Company.

(2) NIOC shall pay to the Exploration and Producing Company its costs of delivering the gas to NIOC, including the costs of operating all facilities used for that purpose.

C. Where natural gas supplied or to be supplied to NIOC under this Article is produced from a field which is primarily a producer of natural gas, the following provisions shall apply:

(1) If the gas produced from the field is solely for delivery to NIOC:

(a) NIOC shall provide the capital for any additional facilities required for development, production and delivery after the field has come into production. Such additional facilities, together with all facilities for production and delivery to NIOC of natural gas, shall be operated by the Exploration and Producing Company.

(b) NIOC shall pay to the Exploration and Producing Company its costs of producing the gas and delivering it to NIOC, including the costs of operating all facilities used for such production and delivery.

(2) If the Trading Companies or the Operating Companies or any of them also take natural gas from the field, NIOC shall not be obligated to provide any of the capital required, but the entire operating costs shall be borne by those taking the gas in proportion to their takings.

ART. 16. NIOC shall pay to the Operating Companies, the estimated amounts due to them, respectively, under Articles 14 and 15 of this Agreement in respect of that quarter, as billed by them, based on their estimate of operating costs, and such payments shall be made within fifteen days from the date of presentation of the bills. Within three months after the end of each year each Operating Company shall adjust its billings for such year in accordance with a final determination of its operating costs and NIOC shall thereupon be debited or credited with any difference, as the case may be.

ART. 17. A. (1) NIOC will, subject to the provisions of this Agreement, continue to perform and carry out its operations. Accordingly NIOC undertakes (subject to any special arrangements between itself and the relevant Operating Company) to perform and carry out non-basic operations as hereinafter defined.

(2) NIOC shall retain, for the purpose of carrying out non-basic operations, all the assets within the Area which are used or available for operations of that kind on the Effective Date and undertakes that all such assets shall during the period of their useful life be used or made available exclusively for the purpose of non-basic operations.

(3) NIOC shall perform and carry out non-basic operations with due regard to economy and efficiency and in such a manner as to meet the reasonable requirements of the Operating Companies.

B. In this Agreement, the term "non-basic operations" means the provision, maintenance and administration of the following ancillary services, insofar as such services are required by the Operating Companies in support of their operations:

Housing estates
Maintenance of roads used by the public
Medical and health services
Operation of food supply system, of canteens, restaurants, and clothing stores
Industrial and technical training and education
Guarding of property
Welfare facilities
Public transport
Communal water and electricity supplies
Other public services
Such further services as may be agreed upon between NIOC and the relevant Operating Company

and includes also the provision, maintenance and administration of warehouse and other auxiliary services, insofar as such auxiliary services are required in connection with the services above mentioned.

C. In respect of each year, unless otherwise agreed between NIOC and the relevant Operating Company, NIOC shall prepare, in consultation with that Operating Company, on or before November 1 of the preceding year, a budget of capital expenditure and operating expenses for NIOC's non-basic operations for that Company, and the capital expenditure and operating expenses included in the budget with the agreement of both parties are hereinafter referred to as "approved capital expenditure" or "approved operating expenses," as the case may be.

D. (1) The capital required to meet approved capital expenditure shall be provided in equal parts by NIOC and the relevant Operating Company. The part provided by the Operating Company shall constitute a debt due from NIOC to the Operating Company, which shall be repayable in equal annual installments over the ten-year period following the commencement of use of the asset with respect to which the debt was incurred, or over the then remaining life of this Agreement, whichever is the lesser. The Operating Company shall credit to NIOC for each year during such ten-year or lesser period a non-basic assets charge in respect of such asset equal, in the case of the ten-year period to one-tenth of the amount of the debt, or in the case of a lesser period, to that proportion of the debt which one year bears to the total number of years in the lesser period, thereby extinguishing the debt at the end of the period in question.

(2) The relevant Operating Company shall loan to NIOC free of interest the sums required by NIOC, during the first two years after the Effective Date, for the purpose of providing NIOC's share of approved capital expenditure. The provisions relating to debts contained in Paragraph (1) of this Section shall apply in relation to any debt so incurred by NIOC and any debt so incurred shall be extinguished by the crediting of non-basic assets charges in the manner provided by that Paragraph.

(3) In respect of NIOC's one half share of approved capital expenditure for which no loan has been made by the relevant Operating Company under Paragraph (2) of this Section, NIOC shall in each year charge to the relevant Operating Company in Iranian currency as part of NIOC's operating costs a non-basic assets charge equivalent to the non-basic assets charge credited to NIOC for that year by the relevant Operating Company in respect of the same assets.

(4) In consideration of the credits and charges in respect of any asset provided for by this Section, NIOC agrees that for so long as such asset is capable of use it shall be used or held available for non-basic operations.

E. (1) NIOC shall in the first instance bear the operating costs of its non-basic operations, but the relevant Operating Company shall refund such costs to NIOC to such extent as is reasonable having regard to the costs actually incurred and to the approved operating expenses.

(2) Provisional payments in respect of the sums due from an Operating Company under this Section shall be made by the Company on the basis of monthly state-

ments presented by NIOC to the Company. Such statements shall be prepared on the basis of the best estimates which can then be made of the costs incurred, and in respect of each year a final adjustment shall be made, by payment or repayment as the case may require, on the basis of a statement which shall be presented to the Operating Company by NIOC within three months from the end of the year in question.

(3) An Operating Company shall be entitled to set off against any sums payable by it to NIOC under the preceding Paragraphs of this Section the cost of any supplies or services provided by it in connection with the non-basic operations carried on for the benefit of the Operating Company by NIOC.

F. Any non-basic assets charges credited to or charged by NIOC, and any costs incurred by NIOC and refunded under Section E of this Article, shall be included in the operating costs of the relevant Operating Company.

G. NIOC shall keep the accounts of its non-basic operations in such a manner as to present a fair, clear and accurate record of the cost of such operations to NIOC and shall make such accounts available to the Operating Companies on request. For the foregoing purposes NIOC shall, in consultation with the Operating Companies, devise a suitable accounting system and revise the same from time to time in the light of future developments.

H. Where capital expenditure or operating costs are attributable partly to NIOC's non-basic operations and partly to other operations of NIOC, they shall be apportioned equitably on the basis of generally accepted principles of accounting, consistently applied, and the responsibilities of the Operating Companies under this Article shall extend only to such part of the expenditure or costs as is properly attributable to non-basic operations.

ART. 18. A. The Consortium members shall purchase crude oil and may purchase natural gas from NIOC and shall resell in Iran for export from Iran

(1) the crude oil and natural gas so purchased, except so much thereof as is delivered to refinery hereunder, and

(2) the petroleum products derived in Iran from the crude oil so delivered.

Any such purchase or resale shall be made upon the terms and subject to the conditions set forth in this Agreement.

B. Any Consortium member may from time to time assign to one or more subsidiaries nominated by it to act as Trading Companies hereunder a part or all of that Consortium member's rights and obligations pertaining to the purchases and resales referred to in Section A of this Article, and Iran and NIOC hereby consent to any such assignment; provided, however, that no such assignment shall relieve any Consortium member of its obligations under this Agreement. Any Trading Company to which such an Assignment is made shall be deemed to become a party to this Agreement. Any Consortium member which makes the purchases and resales referred to in Section A of this Article either itself or through a branch office in Iran shall be included in the term "Trading Company" as used in this Agreement.

C. Each Trading Company shall be registered in Iran and shall have the same nationality as that of the Consortium member by which it is nominated unless such Consortium member considers that tax or foreign exchange requirements outside Iran make another nationality desirable, in which case the Consortium member may choose such other nationality for the Trading Company in question.

D. (1) Trading Companies referred to in Section B of this Article shall purchase from NIOC all crude oil produced by the Exploration and Producing Company other than crude oil used or consumed in the latter Company's operations and crude oil required to meet NIOC's requirements for petroleum products for internal consumption in Iran under Article 14 of this Agreement.

(2) The Trading Companies may purchase from NIOC any natural gas produced by the Exploration and Producing Company to the extent to which such gas is not required by the Operating Companies for

their operations or by NIOC for internal consumption in Iran, it being understood that before any long-term commitment is made for the use or sale of natural gas by a Trading Company it will consult with the Operating Companies and with NIOC as to whether or not natural gas for meeting such commitment is available.

(3) Title to crude oil and natural gas sold to the Trading Companies by NIOC shall pass at wellhead.

E. The Exploration and Producing Company shall deliver crude oil to refinery or f.o.b. tankship or to any other point of export from Iran as desired by the Trading Company purchasing the same and shall deliver natural gas to any point in Iran from which the natural gas can be exported as such or processed, as desired by the Trading Company purchasing the same.

ART. 19. The total quantity of crude oil to be produced by the Exploration and Producing Company shall be, in addition to the quantity required for petroleum products and as crude oil for use exclusively in the operations of the Exploration and Producing Company and to cover its operational losses, the sum of

(1) the quantity required to meet NIOC's requirements for petroleum products and derivatives for internal consumption in Iran;

(2) the quantity (if any) required to provide NIOC with crude oil in kind pursuant to Article 23 of this Agreement; and

(3) the quantity required by the Trading Companies as determined by them.

ART. 20. A. The Consortium members guarantee

(1) that if the Effective Date is on or before October 1, 1954, the aggregate of

(a) the quantity of crude oil exported from Iran by the Trading Companies and their customers, and

(b) the quantity of crude oil delivered to refinery for the account of the Trading Companies, and

(c) the quantity of crude oil, if any, delivered to NIOC under Article 23 hereof shall be not less than the following quantities, namely:—

In the year 1955...17,500,000 cubic meters
In the year 1956...27,500,000 cubic meters
In the year 1957...35,000,000 cubic meters

(2) that if the Effective Date is after October 1, 1954, the quantities so guaranteed shall apply (in the above order) to the first three annual periods commencing three months after the Effective Date.

B. Following the above annual period in which the guaranteed quantity of 35 million cubic meters shall have been attained, it would be the policy of the Consortium members, assuming favorable operating and economic conditions in Iran, to adjust the quantity so attained in such manner as would reasonably reflect the trend of supply and demand for Middle East crude oil.

ART. 21. A. If the Effective Date is on or before October 1, 1954, the Consortium members will strive for, without guaranteeing, the following refinery export program:

In the year 1955—
7,500,000 cubic meters of crude oil
In the year 1956—
12,000,000 cubic meters of crude oil
In the year 1957—
15,000,000 cubic meters of crude oil

B. If the Effective Date is after October 1, 1954, the Consortium members will strive for, without guaranteeing, the quantities above referred to (in the above order) in the first three annual periods commencing three months after the Effective Date.

ART. 22. A. Each Trading Company shall pay NIOC for the quantities of crude oil set out in Section B below a stated payment at the rate of 12½% of the applicable posted price of such crude oil.

B. The said quantities shall be the aggregate of the following, namely:

(1) the quantity of crude oil purchased and sold in Iran by that Trading Company, and

(2) the quantity of crude oil purchased and delivered to refinery for the account of that Trading Company, and

(3) the quantity of crude oil, if any, delivered to NIOC under Article 23 of this Agreement for the account of that Trading Company,

but if any crude oil is acquired by that Trading Company from another Trading Company, the two Trading Companies shall, as between themselves and NIOC, together be liable for the stated payment for such crude oil.

C. Each Trading Company shall pay NIOC for natural gas purchased by that Trading Company a stated payment for each 1,000 cubic meters of such gas equal to 5% of that Trading Company's posted price for 1 cubic meter of 37°-37.9° API crude oil of Agha Jari quality f.o.b. Bandar Mashur as at the date of delivery of such gas.

D. Payments to NIOC under this Article shall be made as follows:

(1) Within fifteen days after the end of each quarter the Exploration and Producing Company shall estimate the stated payment to be made by each Trading Company in respect of that quarter under the provisions of Sections A and C above and the Trading Company concerned shall pay the amount so estimated, after deducting the value at the applicable posted price of any crude oil taken in kind in accordance with Article 23 of this Agreement. Such estimate shall be based on the latest available information as to quantities and prices and shall be cumulative for the year in question so that in estimating the amount payable in respect of each quarter there shall be deducted the total amount of any payments for any previous quarter or quarters of such year.

(2) Within three months after the end of each year the Exploration and Producing Company shall calculate the total stated payment for that year for each Trading Company. If as a result of such calculation and after taking into account the value of any crude oil taken in kind as aforesaid, any further amount shall be found due to NIOC, the Trading Company shall forthwith pay it. If as a result of such calculation any amount shall be found due from NIOC to that Trading Company it shall be carried forward and treated as a payment on account of the stated payment for the then current year.

ART. 23. A. Subject to the provisions of this Article, NIOC shall be entitled to elect to take crude oil (valued at the applicable posted price thereof) in lieu of all or part of the stated payments for crude oil referred to in Article 22 of this Agreement.

B. On or before March 31 in each year the Trading Companies, through the Exploration and Producing Company, shall notify NIOC in writing of the estimated quantity of crude oil (in this Article called the "programmed quantity") to be sold in Iran by or delivered to refinery for the account of the Trading Companies in each quarter of the next following year (in this Article called "the year of delivery").

C. NIOC may, by notice in writing to the Exploration and Producing Company given not later than June 30 in each year, elect to take in kind in each quarter of the year of delivery such quantity of crude oil (not exceeding 12½% of the programmed quantity for each such quarter) as NIOC shall specify in such notice.

D. The crude oil so specified shall be delivered f.o.b. tankship at any existing or future crude oil loading port in Iran free of any payment by NIOC. Liftings shall be spread as nearly as may be practicable evenly over each quarter, and at each loading port shall be as nearly as may be proportionately of the same quantity, quality and gravity as the crude oil delivered f.o.b. tankship at that loading port for the Trading Companies during such quarter.

E. The value at the applicable posted price of the crude oil delivered in kind in any quarter to NIOC for the account of the Trading Companies shall be deducted in arriving at the sums payable in respect of that quarter under Article 22 of this Agreement and shall be taken into account in making the calculations in accordance with Section D of that Article.

F. All matters required for the implementation of this Article and not hereinbefore specifically provided for shall be determined in such manner as NIOC and the Exploration and Producing Company may in writing agree.

ART. 24. A. On, or as soon as practicable after, the Effective Date, an inventory shall be taken of the quantities and grades of crude oil and of petroleum products in storage tanks at loading ports within the Area and reasonably available for shipment. The inventory shall be taken by NIOC and a representative of each of the Operating Companies and shall be in writing.

B. After the inventory has been taken:

(1) NIOC shall be entitled to have delivered to it, free of any charge to it except delivery costs, such of the petroleum products at the Abadan refinery included in the inventory (or their equivalent) as NIOC may require for internal consumption in Iran. Except for Paragraph C thereof, Article 14 of this Agreement shall not apply to any petroleum products so taken.

(2) The Trading Companies may sell for export any crude oil included in the inventory or they may have any such crude oil refined by the Refining Company. Each Trading Company shall pay NIOC the stated payment referred to in Article 22 of this Agreement on all such crude oil taken by it.

C. At the end of the term of this Agreement there shall be left in storage the same quantities and same grades of crude oil as are shown to have been in storage by the inventory referred to in Section A of this Article or such other grades and quantities as NIOC, at or before the end of the term of this Agreement, may in writing agree are the equivalent; and any petroleum products of marketable quality left in storage tanks at the Abadan Refinery and reasonably available for shipment may be sold for export by the Trading Companies, free of any payment to NIOC, except delivery costs, during the three months following the end of the term of this Agreement.

ART. 25. A. (1) Each Trading Company shall publish or cause to be published and notified to NIOC posted prices for each point of export from Iran and for each quality and gravity of its crude oil.

(2) Iran shall be entitled, at any time, to call upon any Trading Company to establish that its applicable posted prices apply to Iranian crude oil available to buyers generally.

B. Each Trading Company shall sell crude oil and petroleum products in Iran at such prices that its total gross receipts in each year from such sales are not less than the following:

(1) a sum equal to the value at the applicable posted price of all crude oil (including any crude oil taken in kind by NIOC under Article 23 of this Agreement for the account of that Trading Company) exported from Iran in that year by that Trading Company and its customers

plus

(2) the aggregate of the following:

(a) a sum equal to the value at the applicable posted price of all crude oil delivered to refinery in that year for the account of that Trading Company, and

(b) a sum equal to the aggregate of the Refining Company's fee for refining the crude oil so delivered and the amount of its operating costs in respect thereof, and

(c) a sum which, when added to such fee as aforesaid gives a result equal to the value at the applicable posted price of 5% of the crude oil so delivered

minus

(3) a sum equal to such total discounts as may be applicable, under such rates and formulas as Iran may approve in accordance with Section D below, to all crude oil referred to in Paragraphs (1) and (2) of this Section.

C. Notwithstanding the provisions of Section B above, any Trading Company may sell crude oil and petroleum products in Iran to any other Trading Company which is subject to Iranian income tax (whether or not its affiliated company) at any price. In that event the minimum obligation of the first-mentioned Trading Company under said Section B shall be adjusted accordingly but the second-mentioned Trading Company shall sell its crude oil and petroleum products (including crude oil and petroleum products acquired from the first-mentioned Trading Company), at such prices that its total gross receipts from such sales are not less than those specified in said Section B.

D. Iran, acting through NIOC or any

other agency of Iran's choosing, shall from time to time consult with the Trading Companies with a view to determining discounts from the Trading Companies' posted prices of crude oil and may approve rates and formulas for discounts to be applied for such periods as it may prescribe in determining the minimum obligations of the Trading Companies under said Section B.

ART. 26. A. The following provisions shall apply to the bunkering at Iranian ports of vessels owned or chartered by or subject to bunkering contracts with a Consortium member or any nominee of a Consortium member:—

(1) At Abadan, any such vessel shall be bunkered by the Refining Company for the account of any person or persons specified by that Consortium member, and such person or persons shall pay to the Refining Company a fee of 5/– per ton on the bunker fuel supplied.

(2) At Bandar Mashur and any future crude oil loading port in Iran, any such vessel shall be bunkered by the Exploration and Producing Company for the account of any person or persons specified by that Consortium member, and such person or persons shall pay to the Exploration and Producing Company a fee of 5/– per ton on the bunker fuel supplied together with the costs of moving such fuel from Abadan.

(3) At other ports in Iran, any such vessel shall be bunkered by NIOC for the account of any person or persons specified by that Consortium member, and such person or persons shall pay to NIOC in respect of such bunkering the costs and expenses thereof together with a fee at the rate of 10/– per ton on the bunker fuel supplied.

B. (1) Except as provided in Section A of this Article the following provisions shall apply to the bunkering at Iranian ports of Iranian flag vessels and vessels engaged in Iranian coastwise trade:

(a) At Abadan, Bandar Mashur and any future crude oil loading port in Iran, such vessels shall be bunkered by the relevant Operating Company for the account of NIOC.

(b) At other ports in Iran, such vessels shall be bunkered by NIOC.

(2) All bunker fuel required for the bunkering of vessels under this Section (but no other fuel required for the bunkering of vessels) shall for all purposes of this Agreement be treated as part of NIOC's requirements for internal consumption in Iran.

C. The bunkering of all other vessels at Iranian ports shall be carried out in accordance with separate arrangements to be agreed upon between NIOC and the Consortium members or any of them.

D. This Article applies only to bunkers produced from crude oil produced within the Area.

ART. 27. A. Crude oil delivered for export shall be measured at loading tanks and crude oil delivered to refinery shall be measured at refinery storage tanks, unless, in either case NIOC and the relevant Operating Company shall otherwise agree in writing.

B. Natural gas shall be measured by meter at the point of delivery or by any other means which NIOC and the relevant Operating Company may agree in writing.

ART. 28. A. Iran undertakes that throughout the term of this Agreement the provisions of law and the rates of income tax governing the Iranian income tax liability of the Trading Companies and the Operating Companies shall be not less favorable to them than the provisions and rates in the law existing on August 1, 1954, with the amendments set forth in Schedule 2 attached to this Agreement.

B. It is agreed that the following are in conformity with the meaning of the Iranian Income Tax Act as amended in accordance with said Schedule 2:—

(1) All "stated payments" with respect to crude oil and natural gas provided for in this Agreement shall be recognized as "stated payments" within the meaning of Article 35 of the Income Tax Act as so amended or any provision which may be enacted in substitution thereof.

(2) All operating costs of the Operating Companies (including payments by the Operating Companies to affiliated companies

or others for services actually rendered outside Iran) in connection with the operations in Iran of the Operating Companies shall be allowed as deductions under said Article 35, without prejudice to any adjustment which may be required consequent upon any matters arising out of an audit requested by Iran and NIOC under Paragraph (1) of Section G of Article 4 of this Agreement.

(3) Deductible expenses of each Trading Company shall be as follows:—

(a) Payments to the Operating Companies of their fees and reimbursement for their operating costs and expenses; and

(b) Payments to another Trading Company for crude oil and petroleum products purchased under Article 25 of this Agreement; and

(c) Office and other expenses (not described in sub-paragraphs (a) and (b) of this Section) of the Trading Company in Iran (including but not limited to salaries, wages, rents, office supplies and services, and accounting and auditing fees), the fair and reasonable expenses of sale, including fees for brokerage and selling services performed outside Iran; it being agreed that the amount of office and other expenses and expenses of sale described in this subparagraph shall in no event in total exceed a sum calculated by deducting from the amount arrived at under (I) following the amount arrived at under (II) following:—

(I) 2.3% of 87½% of the following:—

(i) the value (computed at the applicable posted price) of all crude oil purchased and sold by it, except to another Trading Company,

plus

(ii) the value (computed at the applicable posted price) of all crude oil purchased by it and delivered to refinery and used in the manufacture of products sold by it, except to another Trading Company,

plus

(iii) the value (computed at the applicable posted price) of crude oil delivered for its account to NIOC in lieu of the 12½% stated payment as provided in Article 23 of this Agreement.

(II) 2.3% of the amount of such discounts as may be applicable under Article 25 thereof.

The expenses of the Trading Company described in this subparagraph (c) shall be subject to audit and verification, but such expenses actually paid to affiliated companies or others shall be allowed as fair and reasonable to the extent that the expenses so described do not exceed the 2.3% limitation set forth above.

C. If the income and receipts actually realized by the Trading Companies and the Operating Companies from their sales, operating and functions under this Agreement are in accordance with the provisions of this Agreement, the Trading Companies and the Operating Companies shall not for Iranian income tax purposes be deemed to have any further income or receipts from their sales, operations and functions under this Agreement.

D. Except for the following:—

(1) Income taxes payable by the Trading Companies and the Operating Companies, as limited in accordance with this Agreement, on all of their net income in Iran derived from oil operations as well as any other net income earned in Iran;

(2) The payments and credits agreed to be made hereunder by the Trading Companies and the Operating Companies;

(3) Customs duties as limited in accordance with this Agreement;

(4) Payment to Iran of taxes required to be withheld from payments of salaries and wages to directors and employees (which taxes shall be computed by applying the scale of rates set forth in the income tax law to the amount of salary or wages for each month without regard to salary or wages for other months) and from payments to contractors for work carried out in Iran;

(5) Charges and fees for services rendered by governmental authorities on request or to the public generally, such as tolls, water rates, sanitary and sewage charges, provided such charges and fees are reasonable and non-discriminatory;

(6) Taxes and fees of general application, such as documentary stamp taxes,

civil and commercial registry fees, and patent and copyright fees, provided they are at rates no higher than those generally applicable in Iran;

the Consortium members, the Trading Companies, their respective affiliates, the customers of any of them, and any transportation companies (insofar as purchases, sales, exports or transportation of Iranian crude oil, natural gas or products from either of them or income derived from such purchases, sales, exports or transportation, is concerned), and the Operating Companies (in respect of their operations and functions under this Agreement) shall be free of all taxation by any governmental authority in Iran (whether central or local) and free of any requirement to make any payment or credit of any nature whatever to any such authority; and no taxes shall be imposed with respect to dividends paid by any of them out of income derived from purchases, sales exports or transportation of Iranian crude oil, natural gas or products from either of them or out of income derived from the operations and functions of the Operating Companies under this Agreement.

ART. 29. Any dispute between Iran and any of the Trading Companies or either of the Operating Companies relating to taxes on income derived from purchases, sales, exports or transportation of Iranian crude oil, natural gas or products, or from operations and functions under this Agreement, shall be a dispute to be decided by arbitration in the manner provided in Article 44 of this Agreement.

ART. 30. A. All stated payments due to NIOC under Article 22 of this Agreement and all payments of income tax to Iran by the Operating Companies and the Trading Companies shall be made in sterling

Provided, however, that if at any time—

(1) the sterling thus received by Iran or NIOC shall not be freely convertible into U. S. dollars, and

(2) the British Government shall have discontinued the arrangements negotiated concurrently with this Agreement (or any modification of, or substitute for, those arrangements that may be agreed with Iran) relative to the convertibility into U. S. dollars of the sterling thus received,

the matter shall be the subject of consultation between Iran and the Consortium members, with the object of agreeing alternative provisions regarding the currency of payment.

B. Failing agreement the Consortium members would consider, at the request of Iran and NIOC, and in the light of the circumstances prevailing at the time, part of the payments to Iran and NIOC being made in hard currencies other than sterling on the basis that the proportion of the total payments which would be made in each of such hard currencies would be equal to the proportion in which the Trading Companies have realized f.o.b. Iran from their customers that hard currency from the sale of crude oil, petroleum products and natural gas produced by the Operating Companies.

C. Any payments due to Iran or NIOC under this Agreement other than those referred to in Section A of this Article and all payments due from NIOC to the Operating Companies shall be made in Iranian currency. For this purpose operating and other costs expressed in sterling shall be converted into Iranian currency at the weighted average monthly rate of exchange at which Iranian currency was purchased for sterling by the relevant Operating Company during such month.

ART. 31. A. (1) Iran shall take the necessary steps to insure that the Consortium members, the Trading Companies, the affiliates of any of them and the Operating Companies shall be able to buy Iranian currency with sterling at the commercial bank rate of exchange and without discrimination against them, the full value of any exchange certificate, fee or any similar device being reckoned as an integral part of the rate of exchange.

(2) The "commercial bank rate of exchange" means the bank rate of exchange used or available on the day in question for purchasing Iranian currency with any non-Iranian currency being the proceeds or

any part of the proceeds of exporting any goods which constitute main items of export (in order of value) from Iran other than crude oil produced in the Area and products derived therefrom. If at any time there is more than one bank rate applicable to such goods, the "commercial bank rate of exchange" shall mean the best of such rates.

(3) (a) If any dispute arises under this Section, any party to such dispute may submit the same to arbitration by a sole arbitrator to be appointed at the request of the said party by the Managing Director of the International Monetary Fund. The provisions of Sections D through K of Article 44 of this Agreement shall apply in any such arbitration.

(b) If for any reason such an appointment cannot be made or if no appointment as aforesaid is made within two months of the date of the said request, either party may submit the dispute to arbitration under said Article 44.

(c) For the purposes of sub-Paragraphs (a) and (b) of this Paragraph a Trading Company shall be represented by the Consortium member which nominated it.

B. For the purpose of this Agreement and of ascertaining gross income earned in Iran for Iranian income tax purposes posted prices quoted in currency other than sterling shall be converted into sterling on the basis of the par values for the time being established under the Articles of Agreement of the International Monetary Fund. Failing values so established Iran and the Consortium members shall seek agreement as to an acceptable basis for such conversion. In default of such agreement the conversion shall be made on the basis of the mean of the London buying and selling rates of exchange as between sterling and the currency in question as certified by the Chase National Bank, London, as at the close of business on the day in question.

C. In the case of any day when no London buying and selling rates are quoted, the rate to be used instead of the mean of the London buying and selling rates of exchange for the purposes of Section B of this Article shall be the mean of the last previous London quotations for the foreign currency in question as certified by the Chase National Bank, London. Where the foreign currency in question is not quoted in London, the rate to be used for the purposes aforesaid, instead of the mean of the London buying and selling rates of exchange, shall be such rate as the Chase National Bank, London, considers to be appropriate having regard to transactions in that foreign currency.

ART. 32. A. (1) The Consortium members, the Trading Companies, the affiliates of any of them and the Operating Companies shall not be obliged to convert into Iranian currency any part of their funds; provided, however, that the Operating Companies shall convert into Iranian currency through the Bank Melli Iran such funds as they consider necessary for meeting the costs of their operations in Iran. None of such members, Companies or affiliates shall be restrained from freely retaining or disposing of any funds or assets outside Iran, including such funds or assets as may result from their activities in Iran, or restrained from maintaining foreign exchange accounts in Iran with the Bank Melli Iran and freely retaining or disposing of, including exporting, any funds standing to the credit thereof.

(2) At the end of the term of this Agreement the Consortium members, the Trading Companies, the affiliates of any of them and the Operating Companies shall be free to convert into sterling any funds in Iranian currency which are surplus to their requirements in Iran, insofar as such funds have been the proceeds of the conversion of foreign currency into Iranian currency, and shall be free to dispose of, including export, any sterling so obtained.

B. (1) Non-Iranian directors and employees of any of the Trading Companies or Operating Companies and the families of such directors and employees shall not be restrained from freely retaining or disposing of any of their funds or assets outside Iran and shall be free to import such foreign funds into Iran as are required for their own needs and not for speculation in Iran. Such persons shall not be allowed to effect in Iran exchange transactions of any kind through channels other than the Bank Melli Iran or such other channels as Iran shall approve.

(2) Any director or employee of any of the Trading Companies or Operating Companies shall, upon the termination of his service in Iran and departure from Iran, be entitled freely to export from Iran, in sterling, or in the case of a U. S. national, in U. S. dollars, an amount not exceeding 50% of his last 24 months' salary from the Company or Companies concerned.

C. In this Article the term "the Bank Melli Iran" shall include any successor to or substitute for the Bank Melli Iran.

ART. 33. A. (1) The principal books and accounts of the Operating Companies and of the Trading Companies in Iran shall be kept in sterling and records shall be kept in Iranian currency for those transactions made in Iranian currency.

(2) Any sums reimbursed or provided by the Trading Companies to the Operating Companies pursuant to Section C or Section D of Article 13 of this Agreement shall be reimbursed or provided in sterling. The cost of erection, installation or acquisition of assets in accordance with Articles 6, 7 and 8 and capital provided by the Operating Companies in accordance with Article 17 of this Agreement shall be expressed in sterling.

B. For all the purposes of this Agreement and for the purposes of ascertaining net income in Iran for Iranian income tax purposes all expenditures and receipts of the Operating Companies and the Trading Companies shall be expressed in sterling. For the purposes of converting into sterling all expenditures and receipts in Iranian currency of the Operating Companies and the Trading Companies such conversion shall be made at the weighted average monthly rate of exchange at which Iranian currency was purchased for sterling by the relevant Company during such month. At the end of each year any exchange differences (expressed in sterling) on the books of such Company due to variations in the exchange rate as between Iranian currency and sterling shall be deducted from or added to, as the case may be, the operating costs or expenses of the Company in question.

C. Any expenditures of the Trading Companies which may be incurred in any currency other than sterling or Iranian currency shall be converted into sterling at the arithmetic average of the mean of the daily London buying and selling rates of exchange as between sterling and that currency for the month in question.

ART. 34. A. All machinery, equipment, craft, apparatus, tools, instruments, spare parts, materials, timber, chemicals, blending materials and additives, automative equipment and other vehicles, aircraft, building materials of all descriptions, steelwork, office fittings, equipment and furniture, ships' stores, provisions, protective clothing and equipment, instructional equipment, petroleum products not available from their operations in Iran and all other articles required exclusively for the efficient and economical conduct and performance of the operations and functions of NIOC or of the Operating Companies under this Agreement shall be imported without any license and exempt from import and other customs duties, charges and other taxes and payments. The foregoing articles shall include medical, surgical and hospital supplies, medical products and drugs and equipment, furniture and instruments required for the installation and operation of hospitals and dispensaries.

B. Such articles as may be considered appropriate for the use or consumption of the directors, employees (and their respective dependents) of NIOC or the Operating Companies shall be imported without necessity of any license and free of regulation by any Government monopoly but upon the payment of any import and customs duties and other taxes generally applicable at the time of importation; but such articles shall not be resold except to the said directors, employees and dependents, exclusively for their use or consumption.

C. Without limiting the generality of their foregoing rights, the Operating Companies in the acquisition of equipment and supplies for their own use or consumption shall give preference to articles made or produced in Iran provided the said articles, as compared to similar articles of foreign origin, can be acquired on equally advantageous conditions with due regard to their quality, their price, their availability at the time and in the quantities required, and their suitability for the purposes for which they are intended. In comparing the price of imported articles with articles made or produced in Iran account shall be taken of freight and of any customs duty payable under this Agreement on the imported articles.

D. The Operating Companies shall have the right as and when they require to re-export any of the articles imported pursuant to Sections A and B above, when no longer required for use in Iran by them, except for such of the articles as may, under this Agreement, have become the property of Iran or NIOC, without any license and exempt from export duties or other taxes or payments. The Operating Companies shall also have the right, subject to approval by NIOC, which approval will not be unreasonably withheld or delayed, to sell such articles in Iran, it being understood that in any such case it will be the responsibility of the buyer to pay any applicable duties and to comply with any formalities prescribed by the then current regulations, and to furnish the Operating Companies with the necessary clearance documents.

E. All imports and exports under this Agreement shall be subject to customs documentation and formalities (but not to any payments from which they are exempt under the relevant provisions of this Agreement) not more onerous than those generally applicable. Such documentation and formalities will be handled simply and expeditiously and to this end necessary arrangements may from time to time be made between the Operating Companies, the Trading Companies or any of them and the Iranian Customs authorities.

ART. 35. A. Subject only to the obligation to give precedence to the requirements of Iran for its internal consumption in Iran, the Consortium members, the Trading Companies, the affiliates of any of them and their respective customers shall be free to sell or otherwise dispose of the crude oil and natural gas purchased from NIOC under this Agreement and products manufactured by the Operating Companies therefrom, for export and consumption outside Iran, to such persons and at such prices as the said members, Companies, affiliates or customers individually may freely determine, and to carry away the same from Iran by any means and under any conditions they may deem advisable.

B. The export of said substances shall be exempt from customs duties and export taxes, and shall not be subject to other taxes, charges or payments to any governmental authority in Iran (whether central or local). The said substances may be freely exported from Iran by the Consortium members, the Trading Companies, the affiliates of any of them and their respective customers without the necessity of a license or other special formalities, save only such documentation and formalities as are in accordance with Section E of Article 34 of this Agreement, or arrangements made thereunder.

C. Insofar as any exports referred to in this Article and any imports and re-exports referred to in Article 34 are concerned, the exporter or importer may freely decide whether and with whom and the extent to which the vessels, crews, cargoes and freight shall be insured.

ART. 36. The Operating Companies, the Trading Companies and their personnel and the families of such personnel shall enjoy complete freedom of movement for persons, belongings, equipment and all goods, and shall enjoy freedom and security of communication both within the Area and between the Area and other places in Iran where those Companies carry on business. The manner in which facilities shall be granted by Iran for the purpose of ensuring such freedom of movement and freedom and security of communication shall be determined after consultation between Iran and the Operating Companies.

ART. 37. A. The Ministry of Finance

shall have full and complete power and authority to execute and administer this Agreement on behalf of Iran. The said Ministry may take any action or give any consent on behalf of Iran which may be necessary or convenient under or in connection with this Agreement or for its better implementation and any action so taken or consent so given shall be binding upon Iran. Any party hereto requiring or desiring any such consent or action shall apply therefor to the said Ministry. All Iranian authorities shall implement all such instructions as the Ministry of Finance shall give them in connection with the execution and administration of this Agreement and such authorities shall have full power and authority to do so. If the Ministry of Finance should for any reason no longer exercise its powers and authority under this Section, such powers and authority shall be exercised by such other Ministry or agency as the Council of Ministers shall designate.

B. NIOC shall have all rights and powers which it may at any time require in order to enter into any arrangements which may be necessary or desirable in connection with the activities and operations contemplated in this Agreement.

ART. 38. A. Iran hereby guarantees the due performance by NIOC of its obligations under this Agreement.

B. If the functions of NIOC are transferred to another person under the control of or responsible to Iran, such person shall assume all the obligations of NIOC under this Agreement and Iran shall continue as guarantor of the performance of those obligations.

C. If NIOC ceases to exist and its functions are not transferred to another person under the control of or responsible to Iran, all the obligations of NIOC under this Agreement shall be the direct obligations of Iran.

ART. 39. Every Consortium member shall have the right, at any time during the term of this Agreement, to sell, assign or transfer to another person all or any part of such Consortium member's right, title and interest in, to and under this Agreement upon the condition that such person if not already a party to this Agreement thereby becomes a party to this Agreement and assumes all the obligations of a Consortium member hereunder; provided, however, that no such sale, assignment or transfer shall be effective until Iran has given its written consent thereto, which consent shall not be unreasonably withheld or delayed; and, provided, further, that such written consent shall not be required in any case where the person so acquiring an interest is an affiliated company of the Consortium member so selling, assigning or transferring, it being expressly understood, however, that no such sale, assignment or transfer to an affiliated company shall relieve such Consortium member from its obligations under this Agreement.

ART. 40. A. Iran and NIOC hereby release each of the Consortium members and such of their affiliates as are or shall become parties to this Agreement from all claims and demands of Iran and NIOC or either of them in respect of any matter prior to the Effective Date.

B. Iran and NIOC and each of them hereby agree to indemnify each of the Consortium members and such of their affiliates as are or shall become parties to this Agreement in respect of any claims and demands which may be made against them or any of them by any person

(1) arising out of the oil operations in Iran of the Anglo-Iranian Oil Company, Limited prior to the events of 1951, or

(2) arising directly or indirectly from the events of 1951, or arising out of or connected with any arrangements entered into by Iran or NIOC before the Effective Date, provided, however, that the indemnity granted under this paragraph (2) to Anglo-Iranian Oil Company, Limited and its affiliates shall not include:

(a) any claims arising by reason of Anglo-Iranian Oil Company, Limited having brought to the notice of intending purchasers and others the dispute which had arisen in regard to the title to Iranian oil and having otherwise sought to defend their legal rights, or, any damages which may have been or may be awarded against Anglo-Iranian Oil Company, Limited by foreign courts as a result of litigation commenced before the Effective Date in relation to any transaction entered into between NIOC and foreign purchasers of Iranian oil, or

(b) any claims which may be made against Anglo-Iranian Oil Company, Limited by third parties in regard to any failure of Anglo-Iranian Oil Company, Limited to supply oil as a result of the events of 1951.

ART. 41. A. The parties undertake to carry out the terms and provisions of this Agreement in accordance with the principles of mutual good will and good faith and to respect the spirit as well as the letter of the said terms and provisions.

B. No general or special legislative or administrative measures or any other act whatsoever of or emanating from Iran or any governmental authority in Iran (whether central or local) shall annul this Agreement, amend or modify its provisions or prevent or hinder the due and effective performance of its terms. Such annulment, amendment or modification shall not take place except by agreement of the parties to this Agreement.

C. Unless the parties otherwise agree, this Agreement shall not be terminated or dissolved prior to the expiration of its term except by a decision, made by an Arbitration Board or sole arbitrator appointed in accordance with Article 44 of this Agreement, that it has been terminated by breach or dissolved by total impossibility of performance.

ART. 42. A. If in the opinion of any party to this Agreement any other party is in default in the performance of any obligation hereunder, the first party shall first give the other party written notice specifying the respects in which a default is believed to exist and calling upon such other party to remedy the default. Unless the matter is disposed of by agreement within thirty days after the receipt of such notice or such longer period as may be agreed to by the parties, then the complaint may be referred to a Conciliation Committee under Article 43 of this Agreement. Any complaint which either party does not wish to refer to a Conciliation Committee, or which is not determined by a binding ruling of a Conciliation Committee, may then be submitted by the first party to arbitration under Article 31 or 44 of this Agreement as the case may be.

B. For the purposes of this Article and of the said Articles 43 and 44, a Trading Company shall be represented by the Consortium member which nominated it.

ART. 43. The parties to any complaint arising under Article 42 of this Agreement may agree that the matter shall be referred to a mixed Conciliation Committee composed of four members, two nominated by each party, whose duty shall be to seek a friendly solution of the complaint. The Conciliation Committee, after having heard the representatives of the parties, shall give a ruling within three months from the date on which the complaint was referred to it. The ruling, in order to be binding, must be unanimous.

ART. 44. A. (1) Except as provided in Article 31 of this Agreement, Arbitration in accordance with the provisions of this Article shall be the sole method of determining any dispute between the parties to this Agreement arising out of, or relating to, the execution or interpretation of this Agreement, the determination of the rights and obligations of the parties hereunder, or the operation of this Article, and which is neither resolved under Article 42 nor determined under Article 43.

(2) Arbitration proceedings shall be instituted by a notice in writing given by the complainant to the respondent.

B. (1) If the dispute relates to technical or accounting questions it may by agreement between the parties be referred either to a single expert or to a body of three experts, of whom two shall be appointed by the parties (one by each) and the third shall be appointed by mutual consent. If the parties cannot agree upon the single or the third expert either party may request the Director of the Eidgenössische Technische Hochschule of Zurich when the question is a technical one, or the President of the Schweizerische Kammer für Revisionswesen of Zurich when the question relates to accountancy, to appoint the single expert or the third expert. If within one month from the institution of the proceedings the parties are not in agreement that the dispute shall be referred to an expert or experts as specified above the arbitration procedure stipulated in Section C and the following Sections of this Article shall apply.

(2) The appointment of an expert or experts by the parties shall be effected within one month from the institution of the proceedings. The appointment of the third expert shall be made within a further period of one month in case of agreement between the parties, or of two months in cases where he is appointed after the failure of the parties to agree. The appointment of a single expert shall be made within three months of the institution of proceedings in cases where he is appointed after the failure of the parties to agree.

(3) The technical or accounting questions to be decided shall be clearly and precisely defined by the parties in the terms of reference. The decision of the single expert or of the three experts shall be given within six months of the appointment of the single expert or the third expert, as the case may be. If the dispute is referred to three experts the decision may be given by a majority. The expert or experts shall give their decision on technical or accounting questions only and the decision so given shall be final and binding on the parties.

(4) If during any proceedings before an expert or experts acting under Paragraphs (1), (2) and (3) of this Section, there arises in the opinion of the expert or experts or of either of the parties, a question of law (which expression shall include any question as to the interpretation of this Agreement) the determination of which is necessary to a decision upon the technical or accounting question in issue, the question of law shall, if not determined by agreement between the parties, be submitted to arbitration under Section C and the following Sections of this Article by the parties or either of them, either upon their own initiative or at the request of the expert or experts.

(5) For the purpose in this connection of determining time limits under the following Sections of this Article, the notification by either party to the other of its intention to submit a question of law to arbitration as aforesaid, together with a statement of the said question, shall be treated as the institution of proceedings in respect thereof by the party giving the notice.

(6) The proceedings before the expert or experts need not be suspended when a question of law arising in the course thereof is submitted to arbitration under Paragraphs (4) and (5) of this Section, unless in the opinion of the expert or experts the question of law is of such a nature that the proceedings cannot usefully be continued until it has been determined. If the proceedings are suspended pending the determination of a question of law, the parties shall bring the determination, as soon as it has been effected, to the knowledge of the expert or experts in order that he or they shall resume the proceedings and reach a final decision as soon as possible on the technical or accountancy question which is the subject of the dispute.

C. (1) If the parties do not agree that a dispute shall be referred to an expert or experts under Section B of this Article, or if they do so agree but the appointments provided for are not made or a decision is not given within the time limited for the purpose, or if in the circumstances set out in Paragraph (4) of Section B of this Article either of the parties seeks the determination of a question of law, each of the parties shall appoint an arbitrator, and the two arbitrators before proceeding to arbitration shall appoint an umpire who shall be the President of the Arbitration Board. If the two arbitrators cannot within four months of the institution of proceedings agree on the person of the umpire, the latter shall, if the parties do not otherwise agree, be appointed at the request of either party, by the President of the International Court of Justice.

(2) If one of the parties does not appoint its arbitrator or does not advise the other party of the appointment made by it within two months of the institution of proceedings, the other party shall have the

right to apply to the President of the International Court of Justice to appoint a sole arbitrator.

(3) If the President of the International Court of Justice is a national of Iran or of any of the nations in which the other parties to this Agreement are incorporated, he shall not make the appointments referred to in Paragraphs (1) and (2) of this Section. If for this or any other reason whatsoever the appointment of a sole arbitrator or an umpire is not made in accordance with Paragraphs (1) and (2) of this Section then, unless the parties shall have otherwise agreed in writing, the said appointment shall be made at the request of either party by the Vice-President of the International Court of Justice (provided that he is not a national of Iran or of any of the nations in which the other parties to this Agreement are incorporated) or, failing him, by the President of the Swiss Federal Tribunal or, failing him, by the President or equivalent judge of the highest court of any of the following nations in the order stated: Denmark, Sweden, Brazil.

(4) The appointment of an umpire or sole arbitrator under Paragraphs (1), (2) or (3) of this Section shall be within the complete discretion of the person authorized to make it, and the exercise of his discretion may not be questioned by either party. The person so appointed should not be closely connected with, nor have been in the public service of, nor be a national of, Iran, the nations in which the other parties to this Agreement are incorporated, any member of the British Commonwealth of Nations, or a Protectorate, Colony or country administered or occupied by any of the above nations.

(5) If the arbitration is referred to an Arbitration Board the award may be given by a majority. The parties shall comply in good faith with the award of a sole arbitrator or of an Arbitration Board.

D. The place and procedure of arbitration shall be determined by the parties. In case of failure to reach agreement, such place and procedure shall be determined by the experts, the third expert, the umpire or the sole arbitrator (as the case may be).

E. The parties shall extend to the expert or experts or the Arbitration Board or the sole arbitrator all facilities (including access to the Area) for obtaining any information required for the proper determination of the dispute. The absence or default of any party to an arbitration shall not be permitted to prevent or hinder the arbitration procedure in any or all of its stages.

F. Pending the issue of a decision or award, the operations or activities which have given rise to the arbitration need not be discontinued. In case the decision or award recognizes that the complaint was justified, provision may be made therein for such reparation as may appropriately be made in favor of the complainant.

G. The costs of an arbitration shall be awarded at the entire discretion of the expert or experts or the Arbitration Board or the sole arbitrator (as the case may be).

H. If for any reason an expert, member of an Arbitration Board or sole arbitrator after having accepted the functions placed upon him is unable or unwilling to enter upon or to complete the determination of a dispute, then, unless the parties otherwise agree, either party may request the President of the International Court of Justice to decide whether the original appointment is to be treated as at an end. If he so decides, he shall request the person or persons who made the original appointment to appoint a substitute within such time as he shall specify, and if within the time so specified no substitute has been appointed, or if the original appointment was made by him, he shall himself appoint a substitute. If the President of the International Court of Justice is a national of Iran or of any of the nations in which the other parties to this Agreement are incorporated, or if for this or any other reason his functions under this Paragraph are not performed by him, they shall devolve on one of the other persons referred to in Paragraph (3) of Section C of this Article in the order therein provided.

I. Should the International Court of Justice be replaced by or its functions substantially devolve upon or be transferred to any new international tribunal of similar type and competence, the functions of the President of the International Court of Justice exercisable under this Article shall be exercisable by the President of the new international tribunal without further agreement between the parties hereto.

J. Wherever appropriate, decisions and awards hereunder shall specify a time for compliance therewith.

K. Either party may, within fifteen days of the date of the communication of the decision or award to the parties, request the expert or experts or the Arbitration Board or the sole arbitrator (as the case may be) who gave the original decision or award, to interpret the same. Such a request shall not affect the validity of the decision or award. Any such interpretation shall be given within one month of the date on which it was requested and the execution of the decision or award shall be suspended until the interpretation is given or the expiry of the said month, whichever first occurs.

ART. 45. A. If any final decision or award given under Article 44 of this Agreement contains no order other than that a defined sum of money specified in the decision or award shall be paid to Iran or NIOC by any other party, and if that sum shall not have been paid within the time limited by such decision or award or, if no time is therein limited, within three months thereof, Iran shall have the right to prohibit all exports of crude oil and petroleum products from Iran by the party in default until such sum is paid.

B. If the party liable to execute a final award given in accordance with Article 44 of this Agreement, fails to comply therewith within the time specified in such award for compliance or, if no time is therein specified, within six months after the communication thereof to the parties, the party in favor of which the award has been given shall be entitled to seek the termination of this Agreement by a decision of an Arbitration Board or sole arbitrator made in accordance with Section C of this Article. Any such decision shall be without prejudice to any accrued or accruing rights and liabilities arising out of the operation of this Agreement prior to its termination hereunder, including such other rights, sums or damages as may have been awarded by the Arbitration Board or sole arbitrator.

C. The power to make the decision provided for by Section B of this Article shall only be exercisable subject to the conditions following, namely:—

(1) the decision shall be made only by the Arbitration Board or sole arbitrator who made the final award concerned;

(2) if the Arbitration Board or sole arbitrator who made such award is for any reason unable or unwilling to act, the question of termination for non-compliance with an award shall be referred to arbitration in accordance with Article 44 of this Agreement in the manner provided for determination of disputes;

(3) no decision terminating this Agreement shall be made unless the Arbitration Board or sole arbitrator shall first have prescribed a further period (not being less than 90 days) for compliance with the award and after the expiration of such further period shall have found that the award has not then been complied with.

ART. 46. In view of the diverse nationalities of the parties to this Agreement, it shall be governed by and interpreted and applied in accordance with principles of law common to Iran and the several nations in which the other parties to this Agreement are incorporated, and in the absence of such common principles, then by and in accordance with principles of law recognized by civilized nations in general, including such of those principles as may have been applied by international tribunals.

ART. 47. A. Where any event such as (but not limited to) war, insurrection, civil commotion, strike, storm, tidal wave, flood, epidemic, explosion, fire, lightning or earthquake is beyond the reasonable control of any party bound by an obligation hereunder and renders impossible or hinders or delays the performance of such obligation, the failure or omission of such party to perform such obligation shall not be treated as a failure or omission to comply with this Agreement.

B. Subject and without prejudice to the provisions of Section B of Article 41 of this Agreement, where any such party as aforesaid fails or omits to perform an obligation hereunder in obedience to any Governmental act, order, regulation or decree, provided it is proved that such failure or omission is the necessary consequence of such act, order, regulation or decree, such failure or omission shall not be treated as a failure or omission to comply with this Agreement.

C. Nothing contained in this Article shall prevent any party to this Agreement from referring to arbitration under Article 44 of this Agreement the question of whether or not this Agreement should be dissolved by total impossibility of performance.

ART. 48. A. The Persian and the English texts of this Agreement are both valid. In case of dispute which is referred to arbitration, both texts shall be laid before the Arbitration Board or the sole arbitrator (as the case may be) who shall interpret the intention of the parties from both texts. If there is any divergence between the texts as to the rights and duties hereunder of the parties, the English text shall prevail.

B. The English and Persian texts may be signed under hand or seal by any of the parties hereto on the same or on different dates. The signing of this Agreement shall be considered complete when any single copy of either of such texts is so signed by all of such parties.

ART. 49. A. The term of this Agreement shall be twenty-five years from the Effective Date plus any additional periods during which the Agreement is continued in effect in the manner herein provided.

B. If at or before the expiration of the twenty-third year after the Effective Date the Exploration and Producing Company acting for the Consortium members shall give to Iran and NIOC written notice of the desire of the Consortium members to continue this Agreement in effect beyond the initial twenty-five year period, this Agreement shall thereby be continued in effect for an additional five years, provided

(1) that none of the Consortium members shall at the date of the giving of such notice be in default under the provisions of Section B of Article 45 of this Agreement;

(2) that the Exploration and Producing Company shall, during the five years prior to the year in which the said notice is given, have spent on exploration for or development of oil pools in Iran which had not been discovered by the Effective Date an amount not less than the aggregate of the fees earned by it during such five year period under Article 13 of this Agreement after deduction of Iranian income tax; and

(3) that the Exploration and Producing Company submits with the said notice a map outlining a reduced area in which operations shall take place during the additional period, which reduced area must in no case exceed 80% of the area described in Article 2 of this Agreement. The area excluded to arrive at such reduced area shall, except as to islands, comprise blocks of not less than 2,000 square miles each with an average length of not more than six times their average width.

C. The Consortium members, acting through the Exploration and Producing Company, shall be entitled to give up to two further similar written notices, in each case at or before the expiration of the third year of the then current additional five year period, and in each such case this Agreement shall by such notice be continued in effect for an additional five years after the expiration of the then current additional five year period, subject in each case to the same provisos as apply to the notice under Section B hereof, save only that the reduced area shall not exceed 80% of the area outlined on the map submitted with the notice which continued the Agreement in effect for the then current period.

D. Any notice given under Section B or C hereof shall constitute an undertaking:—

(1) by the Consortium members and Operating Companies to continue to comply with their respective obligations under this Agreement during the remaining life of this Agreement; and

(2) by the Exploration and Producing Company to continue to spend, on the average, on its operations during the remaining life of this Agreement an amount not less than the aggregate of the fees to be earned by it during the remaining life of this Agreement under Article 13 of this Agreement, after deduction of Iranian income tax.

E. In this Agreement the expression "term of this Agreement" shall mean the term defined in Section A of this Article, and the expression "remaining life of this Agreement" shall mean in relation to any particular time the period (if any) then remaining of the initial twenty-five year period and of any additional period or periods in respect of which a notice under Section B or C of this Article has then been given.

ART. 50. Any notice required or authorized to be given under this Agreement to any party shall be deemed to have been duly given when given in writing and delivered:

(1) In the case of a notice to Iran, addressed to the Ministry of Finance or to such other Ministry as may be designated by the Council of Ministers under the provisions of Article 37 of this Agreement at the principal office of the Ministry in question.

(2) In the case of a notice to NIOC, at NIOC's head office.

(3) In the case of a notice to any of the Second Parties, at its address hereinafter mentioned, or at such other address as it may from time to time by written notice to Iran and NIOC designate for the purpose:

Gulf Oil Corporation,
Gulf Building,
Post Office Box No. 1166,
Pittsburgh, Pennsylvania, U. S. A.

Socony-Vacuum Oil Company, Incorporated,
26 Broadway,
New York, 4,
New York, U. S. A.

Standard Oil Company (New Jersey),
30, Rockefeller Plaza,
New York, 20,
New York, U. S. A.

Standard Oil Company of California,
225, Bush Street,
San Francisco, 4,
California, U. S. A.

The Texas Company,
135, East 42nd Street,
New York, 17,
New York, U. S. A.

Anglo-Iranian Oil Company, Limited,
Britannic House,
Finsbury Circus,
London, E. C. 2, England.

N. V. De Bataafsche Petroleum Maatschappij,
Carel van Bylandtlaan, 30,
The Hague, The Netherlands.

Compagnie Francaise des Petroles,
11, Rue du Docteur Lancereaux,
Paris, France.

(4) In the case of a notice to an Operating Company or a Trading Company, at the registered office of such Company in Iran.

(5) In the case of a notice to any person who becomes a Consortium member by substitution or assignment under the terms of this Agreement, at the head office of such person.

ART. 51. A. This Agreement shall come into force as soon as all of the following events shall have occurred, namely:

(1) Part I of this Agreement has been signed under hand or seal by the First and Second Parties and Part II of this Agreement has been signed under hand or seal by the First and Third Parties;

(2) Iran has duly enacted the amendments to the Iranian Income Tax Act which are set forth in Schedule 2 attached to this Agreement, and such amendments have become effective;

(3) Part I and Part II of this Agreement

have been ratified and duly enacted as part of the law of Iran by act of the Majlis and Senate and assent of H. I. M. the Shah; provided, however, that if within a reasonable time after the signing of this Agreement by the Second Parties the other events named in this Section shall not all have occurred, this Agreement shall be null and void.

B. The statute embodying the provisions of Part I and Part II of this Agreement as part of the law of Iran shall take effect on the day on which it receives the assent of H. I. M. the Shah.

C. Nothing in this document shall, or shall be construed to, have any effect or bind any of the parties to this Agreement prior to, or in respect of any period before, the coming into force of this Agreement. . . .

And as to Part II Witnesseth:

PART II

Whereas, the conclusion of the arrangements embodied in Part I of this Agreement necessitated an agreement on the question of compensation; and

Whereas, Iran and Anglo-Iranian Oil Company, Limited have given careful consideration to the financial matters outstanding between them and have made a meticulous examination of all their respective claims and counterclaims; and

Whereas, in making such examination they have had regard to the arrangements made in Part I of this Agreement, including provisions therein contained in respect of the use of the Southern assets, and in consideration of such arrangements Anglo-Iranian Oil Company, Limited has agreed to relinquish all claims in respect of the said assets; and

Whereas, in making such examination they have also taken into account the value of the internal distribution assets, the Kermanshah Refinery, and the Naft-i-Shah oilfield, and the disruption of the enterprise of Anglo-Iranian Oil Company, Limited, on the one hand, and the disruption of Iran's economy arising out of the failure of the two parties to reach a settlement following upon the passing of the Nationalization Laws relating to the Iranian oil industry in 1951 on the other hand; and

Whereas, they have also taken into account Iran's view that in equity Iran should receive upon the coming into force of this Agreement additional sums which would have accrued to Iran under the Supplemental Agreement of 1949 if it had come into force (hereinafter referred to as "the additional sums")

Now therefore, it is hereby agreed by and between the First Parties and the Third Party:

ART. 1. A. Anglo-Iranian Oil Company, Limited shall pay to Iran the additional sums and it is agreed that the additional sums totalling £51 million will in turn be set off against the amount payable by Iran to Anglo-Iranian Oil Company, Limited representing the balance struck after the examination of the other claims and counter-claims above referred to, and it is accordingly agreed between Iran and Anglo-Iranian Oil Company, Limited that, in the result, a net amount of £25 million, free of interest, is due and payable by Iran to Anglo-Iranian Oil Company, Limited.

B. Accordingly, in settlement of the amounts due from each party to the other as set out in Section A of this Article Iran hereby agrees to pay to Anglo-Iranian Oil Company, Limited the sum of £25 million by the installments and at the times set out in Section C of this Article.

C. The said sum shall be paid in ten equal annual installments of £2,500,000, the first of such annual installments being due and payable in London on January 1, 1957, and the remaining nine installments being due and payable in London on January 1, in each succeeding year.

D. At the request of Iran, it has been agreed that the method of payment of any installment provided for in Section C of this Article shall be by payment of such installment as it falls due to Anglo-Iranian Oil Company, Limited by a Trading Company nominated by Anglo-Iranian Oil Company, Limited under the provisions of Part I of this Agreement; and the payment of any such sum evidenced by the written receipt of Anglo-Iranian Oil Company,

Limited, which shall be accepted as proof of payment, shall discharge pro tanto any liability of that Trading Company for payment of Iranian income tax whether then due or thereafter becoming due and be treated in all respects as a payment of Iranian income tax. To the extent to which, for any reason, payment of the said installments or any part thereof shall not be made to Anglo-Iranian Oil Company, Limited in the manner provided by the foregoing provisions of this Section, Iran shall remain liable for payment.

ART. 2. The payment by Iran in manner provided by Article 1 of this Part of this Agreement of the sum of £25 million is agreed by Iran to be made and is accepted by Anglo-Iranian Oil Company, Limited, in full and final settlement of all claims and counterclaims by Iran and NIOC on the one hand and by Anglo-Iranian Oil Company, Limited on the other, in respect of any matter prior to the Effective Date. Accordingly:—

A. Anglo-Iranian Oil Company, Limited hereby releases Iran and NIOC and each of them from all claims and demands in respect of any matter prior to the Effective Date;

B. Iran and NIOC and each of them hereby release Anglo-Iranian Oil Company, Limited from all claims and demands of them or either of them in respect of any matter prior to the Effective Date; and

C. Iran and NIOC and each of them hereby agree to indemnify Anglo-Iranian Oil Company, Limited in respect of any claims and demands which may be made against Anglo-Iranian Oil Company, Limited by any person in respect of any matter arising out of the oil operations in Iran of Anglo-Iranian Oil Company, Limited.

ART. 3. The following Articles of Part I of this Agreement shall apply to this Part of this Agreement, namely, Articles 1, 28, 32, 37, 38, 41 (Sections A and B), 42 (Section B), 44, 46, 48 and 50.

ART. 4. A. Anglo-Iranian Oil Company, Limited shall have the right at any time to sell, assign or transfer to another person its rights under Article 1 of this Part of this Agreement and that person shall upon such sale, assignment or transfer becoming effective succeed for all the purposes of Articles 1 and 3 of this Part of this Agreement to the rights and powers of Anglo-Iranian Oil Company, Limited.

B. The expression "Anglo-Iranian Oil Company, Limited" where it occurs in Sections A, B and C of Article 2 of this Part of this Agreement shall include its affiliates.

ART. 5. This Part of this Agreement shall come into force on the Effective Date. . . .

SCHEDULE 1. AREA

All the area bounded by a line starting from *Point 1* where the meridian of longitude of 46° East of Greenwich intersects the present Iran/Iraq international frontier line at latitude approximately 33°30′, thence on a straight line to

Point 2 at longitude 45°55′ latitude 34° 8′, thence on a straight line to

Point 3 at longitude 45°40′ latitude 34° 30′, thence due east to

Point 4 at longitude 46°0′ latitude 34° 30′, thence on a straight line to

Point 5 at longitude 48°0′ latitude 33° 30′, thence on a straight line to

Point 6 at longitude 49°0′ latitude 33° 20′, thence due south to

Point 7 at longitude 49°0′ latitude 32° 45′, thence due east to

Point 8 at longitude 49°30′ latitude 32° 45′, thence on a straight line to

Point 9 at longitude 50°0′ latitude 32° 25′, thence due south to

Point 10 at longitude 50°0′ latitude 31° 35′, thence on a straight line to

Point 11 at longitude 51°0′ latitude 30° 45′, thence due east to

Point 12 at longitude 51°30′ latitude 30° 45′, thence on a straight line to

Point 13 at longitude 52°0′ latitude 30° 30′, thence due south to

Point 14 at longitude 52°0′ latitude 30° 0′, thence on a straight line to

Point 15 at longitude 54°0′ latitude 29° 10′, thence due south to

Point 16 at longitude 54°0′ latitude 28° 50′, thence on a straight line to

Point 17 at longitude 55°0′ latitude 28° 30′, thence on a straight line to

Point 18 at longitude 57°20′ latitude 27° 30′, thence due south to

Point 19 at longitude 57°20′ latitude 26° 20′, thence due west to a point three miles west of the lowest tide line of the mainland,

thence following a line lying three miles offshore from the lowest tide line of the mainland (including as mainland Abadan Island and any other land area bounded in whole or part by any river, creek, inlet, canal or other inland water) to the point where this line intersects the present international Iran/Iraq frontier near the mouth of the Shatt-al-Arab,

thence following such international frontier to *Point 1* defined above.

In addition, the Area shall include the islands of Kharg, Khargu, Shu Aib, Hindurabi, Qais, Qishm, Hengam and Hormuz and the area lying within a line three miles offshore from the lowest tide line of each of such islands.

SCHEDULE 2. INCOME TAX AMENDMENTS

The Income Tax Act of 1949 shall be amended by the addition of the following Article after Article 34:

"*Article 35:*—In the case of companies whose net income (profit) is derived from the sale of petroleum or other hydrocarbons produced in or exported from Iran or the sale of rights and interests in or over such petroleum or other hydrocarbons, or from conducting operations for production or refining of petroleum or other hydrocarbons, for the purposes of collection there shall be deducted from the amount of tax to be paid on their net income as provided by Article 7 an amount equal to any stated payment or any other payments of a similar nature paid to the Government, NIOC, or any other agency of the Government in respect of such petroleum or hydrocarbons. No amount equal to such stated payment or other payment of a similar nature shall be allowed as such a deduction more than once, and such companies shall not be entitled to the rates lower than the maximum rate under Article 4 nor to the exemption provided for in part (a) of Article 3 of the legal instrument dated 20th Azar 1331.

"Net income of such a company for any period represents the difference between its gross income earned in Iran and the expenses related to the earning of such income. Net income shall be computed in accordance with consistent and generally accepted accounting practice.

"In the computation of net income of such a company the following items wheresoever incurred shall, regardless of the provisions of Article 7, be deductible:—

(a) The cost to the company of goods sold or services rendered by the company in connection with the carrying on of its operations in Iran;

(b) Expenses which are incurred by the company (other than stated payment or any other payment of a similar nature for which a reduction is allowed under the foregoing provisions of this Article) in connection with the carrying on of its operations in Iran including, without in any way limiting the generality of the foregoing, administrative, overhead and establishment expenses; contributions; and rents or other charges for the use of any property; all such deductions to be supported by documents or records;

(c) A reasonable amount in each year for depreciation, obsolescence, exhaustion and depletion for the amortization of capital expenditure made by the company in connection with its operations in Iran; and

(d) Losses sustained in connection with the carrying on of the operations in Iran of the company and not compensated for by insurance or otherwise, including without in any way limiting the generality of the foregoing, bad debts, losses arising out of claims for damages against the company and losses resulting from damage to or the destruction or loss of stock in trade or any property used in connection with the said operations in Iran.

"Such companies shall not be subject to the provisions of Article 12 with respect to payments made to them in connection with the operations specified in the first paragraph of this Article 35, nor to the provisions of Article 20, nor to any other income tax rate or surcharge in addition to the tax provided in Article 7 and this Article 35; the regulations under Article 25 shall not restrict the deductions provided for in this Article 35; no income shall be taxed more than once under Article 27; and the information in the accounts of such a company as certified by chartered accountants shall be accepted by the Ministry of Finance as correct for the purposes of determining net income subject to income tax."

105. AGREEMENT ON THE SUEZ CANAL BASE: BRITAIN AND EGYPT
19 October 1954

(Ratifications exchanged, Cairo, 6 December 1954)
[Great Britain, *Parliamentary Papers, 1954,* Egypt No. 2, Cmd. 9298]

Agreement on the Sudan in February 1953 (Doc. 99) enabled the United Kingdom and Egypt to concentrate on settling their differences over the Suez Canal base. Yet more than nineteen months elapsed before the details of a settlement were drafted. The negotiations were conducted in three stages. The first, labeled "informal" on Egyptian insistence, consisted of inconclusive exchanges at Cairo (27 April–6 May, 30 July–21 October 1953) on the basis of a British statement of terms. The informal talks broke down on two points. Egypt wished to make a British return to and reactivation of the canal base conditional upon an armed attack on any country party to the Arab League mutual security pact (Doc. 93), while the United Kingdom sought to broaden the sphere by including non-Arab Muslim states in the Near and Middle East. Similarly, the British demanded that their technicians who were to remain at the base for the duration of the proposed agreement should be uniformed soldiers; the Egyptians, that the British technical personnel should be wholly civilianized. The differences were eliminated by compromise in the second stage (11–27 July 1954), which produced a mutually acceptable instrument called "heads of agreement" (*Parliamentary Papers, 1954,* Egypt. No. 1, Cmd. 9230), defining the principles for an Anglo-Egyptian accord on the canal base. The final or technical stage, devoted to filling in the details, proved hardly less time-consuming than the earlier phases of the negotiations. Even so simple a matter as reference to the 1936 treaty (Doc. 61), which was being superseded, gave rise to acrimonious debate. The Egyptian delegation maintained that Egypt's unilateral abrogation of the treaty on 15 October 1951 was irrevocable, the British delegation that the unilateral act was inadmissible. The innocuous, if somewhat unusual, formula of article 2 in the final agreement represented a compromise, for attention was not called to Egypt's earlier denunciation and Britain alone declared the termination of the 1936 treaty. In the Suez negotiations, as in those on the Sudan, American Ambassador Jefferson Caffery's good offices contributed substantially to the ultimate product. Omitted below are the annexes, the exchanges of notes and an agreed minute, including an exchange of notes on reserves of petroleum products [Treaty Series No. 24 (1955), Cmd. 9390] and an exchange of notes of 3 May 1955 [Egypt No. 1 (1955), Cmd. 9466]. A. Hourani, "The Anglo-Egyptian Agreement," *The Middle East Journal,* 9 (Summer 1955), 239–55; "Middle East Defence," *Round Table,* 178 (March 1955), 130–37; Sir B. Horrocks, "Middle East Defense—British View," *Middle Eastern Affairs,* 6 (February 1955), 33–41; G. Abdul Nasser, *Egypt's Liberation.*

ART. 1. Her Majesty's Forces shall be completely withdrawn from Egyptian territory in accordance with the Schedule set forth in Part A of Annex I within a period of twenty months from the date of signature of the present Agreement.

ART. 2. The Government of the United Kingdom declare that the Treaty of Alliance signed in London on the 26th of August, 1936, with the Agreed Minute, Exchanged Notes, Convention concerning the immunities and privileges enjoyed by the British Forces in Egypt and all other subsidiary agreements, is terminated.

ART. 3. Parts of the present Suez Canal Base, which are listed in Appendix A to Annex II, shall be kept in efficient working order and capable of immediate use in accordance with the provisions of Article 4 of the present Agreement. To this end they shall be organised in accordance with the provisions of Annex II.

ART. 4. In the event of an armed attack by an outside Power on any country which at the date of signature of the present Agreement is a party to the Treaty of Joint Defence between Arab League States, signed in Cario on the 13th of April, 1950, or on Turkey, Egypt shall afford to the United Kingdom such facilities as may be necessary in order to place the Base on a war footing and to operate it effectively. These facilities shall include the use of Egyptian ports within the limits of what is strictly indispensable for the above-mentioned purposes.

ART. 5. In the event of the return of British Forces to the Suez Canal Base area in accordance with the provisions of Article 4, these forces shall withdraw immediately upon the cessation of the hostilities referred to in that Article.

ART. 6. In the event of a threat of an armed attack by an outside Power on any country which at the date of signature of the present Agreement is a party to the Treaty of Joint Defence between Arab League States or on Turkey, there shall be immediate consultation between Egypt and the United Kingdom.

ART. 7. The Government of the Republic of Egypt shall afford over-flying, landing and servicing facilities for notified flights of aircraft under Royal Air Force control. For the clearance of any flights of such aircraft, the Government of the Republic of Egypt shall accord treatment no less favourable than that accorded to the aircraft of any other foreign country with the exception of States parties to the Treaty of Joint Defence between Arab League States. The landing and servicing facilities mentioned above shall be afforded at Egyptian Airfields in the Suez Canal Base area.

ART. 8. The two Contracting Governments recognise that the Suez Maritime Canal, which is an integral part of Egypt, is a waterway economically, commercially and strategically of international importance, and express the determination to uphold the Convention guaranteeing the freedom of navigation of the Canal signed at Constantinople on the 29th of October, 1888.

ART. 9. (*a*) The United Kingdom is accorded the right to move any British equipment into or out of the Base at its discretion.

(*b*) There shall be no increase above the level of supplies as agreed upon in Part C of Annex II without the consent of the Government of the Republic of Egypt.

ART. 10. The present Agreement does not affect and shall not be interpreted as affecting in any way the rights and obligations of the parties under the Charter of the United Nations.

ART. 11. The Annexes and Appendices to the present Agreement shall be considered as an integral part of it.

ART. 12. (*a*) The present Agreement shall remain in force for the period of seven years from the date of its signature.

(*b*) During the last twelve months of that period the two Contracting Governments shall consult together to decide on such arrangements as may be necessary upon the termination of the Agreement.

(*c*) Unless both the Contracting Governments agree upon any extension of the Agreement it shall terminate seven years after the date of signature and the Government of the United Kingdom shall take away or dispose of their property then remaining in the Base.

ART. 13. The present Agreement shall have effect as though it had come into force on the date of signature. Instruments of ratification shall be exchanged in Cario as soon as possible.

106. CONVENTION TO SETTLE FRONTIER AND FINANCIAL QUESTIONS: IRAN AND THE USSR
2 December 1954

(Ratifications exchanged, Moscow, 20 May 1955)

[Unofficial translation from the Persian, courtesy of the Department of State, Washington, D.C.]

The new departure in post-Stalinist Russian diplomacy (Doc. 101) toward Iran was revealed on 8 August 1953, when Premier Georgi M. Malenkov announced in his foreign policy statement to the Supreme Soviet that "on the initiative of the Soviet Union, talks are being held [with Iran] concerning a settlement of a number of frontier problems and mutual financial claims" (from text in *New York Times*, 10 August 1953). At stake were 8 million dollars and 11 tons of gold that accrued to Iran's credit in Moscow in World War II under a financial agreement of 10 March 1943. Frontier disputes arising from imprecise demarcation by mixed boundary commissions, west of the Caspian Sea as early as 1828–29 (I, Doc. 38) and east of it between 1886 and 1894, further strained relations between the two neighbors. The boundary controversy involved relatively minor rectification. Yet, ever since the 1921 Soviet-Iranian treaty (Doc. 33), repeated efforts to reach an amicable adjustment proved fruitless. The timing of the latest Soviet move was calculated to bring the greatest political returns to the Kremlin, for the financial fortunes of the two-year-old Musaddiq government had sunk to their nadir by the midsummer of 1953. But less than a fortnight after Malenkov's disclosure in Moscow, the Musaddiq regime was overthrown. Negotiatons with the pro-West Zahidi government moved so slowly that more than a year elapsed before the following agreed instrument was framed. In an accompanying exchange of notes, not reproduced, the USSR undertook to "pay Iran the sum of ten million (10,000,000) rials within a period of one year from the effective date of the Convention . . . through delivery of commodities valued at average world prices. . . . [and at the rate of] eighty-two (82) rials to one American dollar." Two other exchanges of notes of 2 December 1954 and 29 January 1955, relating to boundary rectification, are also omitted below, as are the sketch and boundary maps annexed to the original instruments.

ART. 1. The High Contracting Parties, earnestly desiring to resolve the differences relating to the question of the course in certain regions of the state boundary line between Iran and the Union of Soviet Socialist Republics and thus to resolve the boundary question as a whole on the basis of respect for mutual interests, are agreed that a new state boundary line shall be established in the regions of Moghan, Dyman, Yedi Evlar, Sarakhs, and also in the Atrek region from the hill of Senger Tepe (Saghir Tepe) along the border to the Caspian Sea. The course of the new boundary line in the areas mentioned above is defined in Article 2 of the present Convention.

The High Contracting Parties confirm that the boundary between Iran and the Union of Soviet Socialist Republics along the entire remaining line is unchanged; however, the boundary region located on the right bank of the Aras River across from the former fortress of Abbasabad, as well as the village of Hisar with its portion of land, remain within the territory of Iran, and the village of Firuzeh and its surrounding lands remain within the territory of the Union of Soviet Socialist Republics.

In view of the foregoing provisions, the High Contracting Parties declare that hereafter all questions relating to the entire course of the state boundary line between Iran and the Union of Soviet Socialist Republics are resolved and that the High Contracting Parties have no territorial claims against each other.

ART. 2. In conformity with Article 1 of the present Convention, the state boundary line between Iran and the Union of Soviet Socialist Republics shall be as follows:

a) The Trans-Caucasian (Western) Frontier. The state boundary line between Iran and the Union of Soviet Socialist Republics, from where the state boundaries of Iran, the Union of Soviet Socialist Republics, and the Republic of Turkey meet at the junction of the Aras River and the Lower Kara Su, runs to a point in the middle of the channel of the Aras River northwest of the Iranian village of Tazakend, located approximately 5.2 kilometers east southeast of the center of the Soviet village of Ashaqa-Qara Guvandli and 3.6 kilometers north northeast of the center of the Iranian village of Qemishli, following the channel of the Aras River in the manner described in the document defining the Irano-Russian border signed at Bahramlu by the Commissioners of the two Governments on January 18, 1829, with the exception that the portion of boundary land on the right bank of the Aras River across from the former fortress of Abbasabad remains within Iranian territory and that the boundary line passes in front of the said fortress along the channel of the Aras River.

The boundary line from the said point in the Aras River inclines east and, coinciding with the present boundary line, extends to a point located approximately 4.5 kilometers northeast of the center of the Iranian village of Qemishli and 4 kilometers southeast of the southern outskirts of the Soviet village of Haji Babali.

From this point the boundary line leaves the present boundary line and extends in a straight line approximately 4 kilometers east southeast to a point located approximately 7 kilometers east northeast of the center of the Iranian village of Qemishli, 3.6 kilometers southeast of the center of a nameless Soviet village and 2 kilometers northeast of the trigonometrical point bearing landmark 27/2.

From here the boundary line runs in a straight line southeast to a point located approximately 5.2 kilometers southeast of Tepe Shahriar, 1.1 kilometers south of the trigonometrical point bearing landmark 68/8 and 4.4 kilometers north northwest of the cemetery of the Iranian village of Belyasuvar (Talesh-Mikailu).

The boundary line then runs in a straight line southeast to a point on the present boundary line in the northeastern outskirts of the Iranian village of Belyasuvar (Talesh-Mikailu), located approximately 1.1 kilometers east northeast of the cemetery of the Iranian village of Belyasuvar (Talesh-Mikailu) and 5.5 kilometers east of the trigonometrical point bearing landmark 68/8.

From here the boundary line inclines south and, coinciding with the present boundary line, extends to a point in the middle of the Bolgar Chai (Belharud) in such a manner as to leave the Soviet village of Belyasuvar within the territory of the Union of Soviet Socialist Republics and the Iranian village of Belyasuvar within the territory of Iran.

From the point in the middle of the Bolgar Chai to Siqnaq Rock, which is located approximately 1 kilometer southwest of the summit of Jogeyr (Jogeyra) Mountain and 5.5 kilometers north northwest of the center of the Soviet village of Dyman, the boundary line runs in the manner described in the document defining the Irano-Russian frontier signed at Bahramlu by the Commissioners of the two Governments on January 18, 1829.

The new boundary line begins from Siqnaq Rock, extending in almost a straight line to the summit of the elevation bearing landmark 1619/2, which is located approximately 600 meters southeast of the mountain of Qarvoldash (Qaravoltash) and 1.1 kilometers north of the center of the Iranian village of Qanibolagh.

From the summit of the elevation bearing landmark 1619/2 to the Caspian Sea the boundary line runs in the manner described in the document defining the Irano-Russian frontier signed at Bahramlu by the Commissioners of the two Governments on January 18, 1829, with the exception that the portion of Soviet territory called Yedi Evlar is ceded to Iran and that the boundary line in this area coincides with the present channel of the Astara Chai.

b) The Trans-Caspian (Eastern) Frontier Area. The boundary line between Iran and the Union of Soviet Socialist Republics, from where the state boundaries of Iran, the Union of Soviet Socialist Republics and Afghanistan meet to a point in the center of the western branch of the Tedzhen River (Harirud) located approximately 2.7 kilometers northeast of Masjed-e-Uli Baba and 5.8 kilometers north northwest of the center of the Soviet village of Sarakhs, runs in the middle of the deepest channel of the Tedzhen River in the manner described in Protocol No. 3 of June 19, 1894, relating to the demarcation of the Irano-Russian border in the region from Zolfaqar to Khemli Tepe and as traced on the map attached to the said Protocol.

From the above-mentioned point the new boundary line on the Tedzhen River begins, extending along the middle of the deepest channel of the Tedzhen River to a point in the middle of the Tedzhen River located approximately 3.4 kilometers east of Khomli Tepe (Tepe Khomli) and 4.1 kilometers north northeast of Tepe Qesi.

From here the boundary inclines west, running in a straight line for approximately 3.4 kilometers to the summit of Khomli Tepe (Tepe Khomli), where the new boundary line ends.

From Khomli Tepe (Tepe Khomli) to Boundary Marker No. 1, which is located between the ruins of Qal'eh Baba Durmaz and Gasan Kuli Bayand is situated on the mountain of Ziraku (Zireh Kah?) approximately 2.3 kilometers southwest of Baba Durmaz Spring as specified in the Protocol relating to the Irano-Russian border east of the Caspian Sea signed at Ashkhabad on January 30, 1886, the boundary line to Baba Durmaz runs in the manner described in Protocol No. 5, signed at Ashkhabad on November 8, 1894, relating to the demarcation of the Irano-Russian border in the region of Khomli Tepe (Tepe Khomli) and in the manner in which this boundary is traced on the map attached to the said Protocol, leaving Qal'eh Hisar and its portion of land within Iranian territory.

Thereafter, from the afore-mentioned Boundary Marker No. 1 to Boundary Marker No. 31 in the vicinity of Gaduk-e-Bir, which is situated as specified in the Protocol of January 30, 1886, the boundary line of this region runs in the manner described in the Protocol of January 30, 1886, relating to the Irano-Russian border east of the Caspian Sea for the distance from the ruins of Qal'eh Baba Durmaz to Gasan Kuli Bay; and this boundary line in this area is as traced on the map attached to the said Protocol.

From Boundary Marker No. 31 in the vicinity of Gaduk-e-Bir to Boundary Marker No. 41 situated on the summit of Kuh-e-Kenareh (Kenara) as specified in the Protocol of January 30, 1886, the boundary line, leaving the village of Firuzeh and the surrounding lands within the territory of the Union of Soviet Socialist Republics, runs in the manner described in Protocol No. 6 of November 9, 1894, relating to the demarcation of the Irano-Russian frontier from Gaduk-e-Bir to Kuh-e-Kenareh; and this boundary runs as traced on the map attached to the said Protocol.

From Boundary Marker No. 41 situated on the summit of Kuh-e-Kenareh to Gudri Pass on the Atrek River, the boundary line of this area runs in the manner described in the Protocol of January 30, 1886, relating to the Irano-Russian border and in the manner this boundary line in this region is traced on the map attached to the said Protocol.

From Gudri Pass to a point on the present boundary line located approximately 300 meters west of the trigonometrical point bearing landmark 6/2 on the hill of Senger Tepe (Saghir Tepe), the boundary line runs in the manner described in the Protocol of March 6, 1886, relating to the boundary line between Iran and the Trans-Caspian Province from Gudri Pass to the Caspian Sea, and in the manner in which the said boundary from Gudri Pass to the hill of Senger Tepe (Saghir Tepe) is traced on the map attached to the said Protocol.

Here the new boundary line begins, from a point on the present boundary line located approximately 300 meters west of the trigonometrical point bearing landmark 6/2 located on the hill of Senger Tepe (Saghir Tepe), and runs in a straight line to a point located approximately 2.2 kilometers south of Soviet Fishing Post No. 1, 22.6 kilometers northwest of the Iranian lagoon of

Naftlijeh, and 22 kilometers west southwest of the center of the Soviet village of Hajiab, i.e. to the point where the present boundary line reaches the coast of the Caspian Sea.

ART. 3. The High Contracting Parties are agreed that there shall be a demarcation and redemarcation of the boundaries between Iran and the Union of the Soviet Socialist Republics. To this end, within a time limit not to exceed three months from the effective date of the present Convention, an Irano-Soviet Mixed Commission shall be formed to undertake the task of demarcation and redemarcation. In the course of demarcating the border in the regions of Moghan, Dyman, Yedi Evlar, Atrek and Sarakhs as newly determined, and in the course of redemarcating all of the remaining border between Iran and the Union of Soviet Socialist Republics, the work of the Irano-Soviet Mixed Commission shall be governed by the present Convention.

The Irano-Soviet Mixed Commission shall complete the demarcation and redemarcation of the entire Irano-Soviet boundary within a period of one and one-half years from the date of its formation.

ART. 4. The High Contracting Parties are agreed that all financial claims and counterclaims relating to World War II, including claims arising out of the Agreement concerning payments of March 18, 1943, between Iran and the Union of Soviet Socialist Republics, shall be definitively settled as follows:

a) Within two weeks from the effective date of the present Convention, the State Bank of the Union of the Soviet Socialist Republics shall deliver in two installments to the Bank Melli Iran, at the frontier railway station at the Iranian village of Julfa, eleven million one hundred ninety-six thousand seventy grams and three-tenths gram (11,196,070.3) gold for the discharge of claims on the part of Iran arising out of the Agreement of March 18, 1943, referred to in the present Article.

b) Within one year from the effective date of the present Convention, the Union of the Soviet Socialist Republics shall discharge the sum of eight million six hundred forty-eight thousand six hundred nineteen American dollars and seven cents ($8,648,-619.07) arising out of the above-mentioned Agreement of March 18, 1943, through delivery to Iran of commodities valued at average world prices, within time limits and in accordance with a list of goods to be agreed upon between the Ministry of Foreign Trade of the Union of Soviet Socialist Republics, through the Trade Agency in Iran of the Union of Soviet Socialist Republics, and the Ministry of National Economy of Iran.

c) All financial claims and counter-claims of the two Parties set forth in the negotiations held by the two Parties in the years 1950–1951 are considered as discharged.

The two Parties declare that with the conclusion of the present Convention they have no financial claims against each other of any kind relating to World War II. . . .

PROTOCOL

In conformity with the agreement constituted by the signing of the Convention of December 2, 1954 relating to the Settlement of Frontier and Financial Questions between Iran and the Union of Soviet Socialist Republics, the two Parties are agreed on the following provisions:

1. The boundary line in the Namin area runs as described in the document of January 18, 1829, defining the Irano-Russian boundary. In this connection the present Soviet dirt road remains within the territory of the Union of Soviet Socialist Republics at the five points mentioned hereinbelow and as traced on the sketch attached to the present Protocol.

The said points are as follows:

Point No. 1, of 1100 meters in length, is located south of the mountain of Qeyurdi. The extremities of this point on the present boundary line are located approximately, one within 250 meters south of the summit of the mountain of Qeyurdi, and the other 1300 meters south southwest of the summit of that mountain.

Point No. 2, of 1100 meters in length, is located west of the elevation bearing landmark 2161/7. The extremities of this point on the present boundary line are located approximately, one within 520 meters north of the summit of the elevation bearing landmark 2161/7, and the other 500 meters south southeast of the summit of that elevation.

Point No. 3, of 1000 meters in length, is located southwest of the mountain of Balmadin. The extremities of this point on the present boundary are located approximately, one within 450 meters northwest of the summit of the mountain of Balmadin, and the other 450 meters southeast of the summit of that mountain.

Point No. 4, of 1260 meters in length, is located south of the mountain of Qezelasar (Khazilas). The extremities of this point on the present boundary line are located approximately, one within 720 meters southwest of the summit of the mountain of Qezelasar (Khazilas), and the other 550 meters southeast of the summit of that mountain.

Point No. 5, of 6400 meters in length, is located between the mountains of Mardasiqi and Manarak. The extremities of this point on the present boundary line are located approximately, one 800 meters northwest of the summit of the mountain of Mardasiqi, and the other 100 meters north of the mountain of Manarak.

At the time of redemarcation of the boundary, the Soviet dirt road at Points Nos. 2, 3, 4 and 5 in the Namin area shall be moved upward as far as possible towards the ridge line, taking into consideration the conditions of the terrain. The redemarcation of state boundaries shall be effected in this manner.

The measurements of the lengths of the above-mentioned five points in the Namin area have been taken from the present Soviet dirt road.

2. The cession by the Union of Soviet Socialist Republics to Iran of the Yedi Evlar region, which has become detached as a result of the deviation of the channel of the Astara Chai, is considered to be an exception to the established rules and principles of international law, according to which a change in the channel of a frontier stream does not alter the location of a state boundary (if no special agreement on the matter exists between the two Parties).

3. By the designation of the Protocols mentioned in paragraph b) *The Trans-Caspian (Eastern) Frontier Area* of the present Convention, i.e. the Protocol of January 30, 1886, relating to the Irano-Russian boundary line east of the Caspian Sea in the region from the ruins of Qal'eh Baba Durmaz to Gasan Kuli Bay, and the Protocol of March 6, 1886, relating to the boundary line between Iran and the Trans-Caspian Province from Gudri Pass to the Caspian Sea, is meant the Protocols of demarcation commissions formed pursuant to Article 2 of the Convention of December 9, 1881, between Iran and Russia.

By the designation of Protocol No. 3 of June 19, 1894, relating to the demarcation of the Irano-Russian boundary in the region from Zolfaghar to Khomli Tepe, of Protocol No. 5 of November 8, 1894, relating to the demarcation of the Irano-Russian boundary in the region from Khomli Tepe to Baba Durmaz, and of Protocol No. 6 of November 9, 1894, relating to the demarcation of the Irano-Russian boundary in the region from Gaduk-e-Bir to the mountain of Kenareh, is meant the Protocols of demarcation commissions formed pursuant to Articles 4 and 5 of the Convention of May 27, 1893, between Iran and Russia.

4. The settlement of boundary disputes in the Atrek region has been effected by the two Parties, with due regard to the border as defined in the Protocol of March 6, 1886, relating to the boundary line between Iran and the Trans-Caspian Province from Gudri Pass to the Caspian Sea, and also with due regard to the present boundary line now existing in that region, in such a manner that the new boundary line is determined to run between the hill of Senger Tepe (Saghir Tepe) and the Caspian Sea, the precise course being as mentioned in Article 2 of, and as traced on the map attached to, the present Convention. The settlement of this question has been achieved with due regard to proposals made

by the Soviet Union for the definitive settlement of the frontier question.

The present Protocol is an integral part of the Convention of December 2, 1954.

107. PACT (BAGHDAD) OF MUTUAL COOPERATION: TURKEY AND IRAQ
24 February 1955

(Ratifications exchanged, Ankara, 15 April 1955)
[Great Britain, *Parliamentary Papers, 1955,* Misc. No. 5, Cmd. 9429]

Announcement by Turkey and Iraq in mid-January 1955 of plans to conclude a military alliance in cooperation with the West precipitated a crisis in the Arab League. The Revolutionary Command Council (military government) in Egypt was apparently persuaded that Iraq's contemplated action would destroy Arab solidarity in international politics, would thereby weaken the Arab League security system (Doc. 93) and would accordingly curtail in the West the bargaining influence of Egypt, the League's dominant member. Despite mounting Egyptian pressures, including sponsorship in Cairo of an emergency meeting of the premiers and foreign ministers of the Arab League states (22 January–6 February 1955), Iraq signed the following military alliance, which replaced the Turco-Pakistan agreement of 2 April 1954 (Doc. 102) as the basic instrument of the "northern tier" collective security arrangement. One reason for Iraq's insistence upon a fresh formula may be found in article 5, which lays down that the "pact shall be open for accession to any member of the Arab League or any other State actively concerned with the security and peace in this region and which is fully recognised by both of the High Contracting Parties." The last phrase, it is clear, was designed explicitly to exclude Israel. Britain acceeded to the Baghdad Pact—as the Turco-Iraqi alliance became known—on 5 April, Pakistan on 23 September and Iran on 25 October 1955. Indeed, the shah's government took its action in the face of a Soviet note of protest (Doc. 114).

Whereas the friendly and brotherly relations existing between Iraq and Turkey are in constant progress, and in order to complement the contents of the Treaty of Friendship and Good Neighbourhood concluded between His Majesty the King of Iraq and his Excellency the President of the Turkish Republic signed in Ankara on March 29, 1946, which recognised the fact that peace and security between the two countries is an integral part of the peace and security of all the nations of the world and in particular the nations of the Middle East, and that it is the basis for their foreign policies;

Whereas Article 11 of the Treaty of Joint Defence and Economic Co-operation between the Arab League States provides that no provision of that treaty shall in any way affect, or is designed to affect, any of the rights and obligations accruing to the Contracting Parties from the United Nations Charter;

And having realised the great responsibilities borne by them in their capacity as members of the United Nations concerned with the maintenance of peace and security in the Middle East region which necessitate taking the required measures in accordance with article 51 of the United Nations Charter;

They have been fully convinced of the necessity of concluding a pact fulfilling these aims. . . .

ART. 1. Consistent with article 51 of the United Nations Charter the High Contracting Parties will co-operate for their security and defence. Such measures as they agree to take to give effect to this co-operation may form the subject of special agreements with each other.

ART. 2. In order to ensure the realisation and effect application of the co-operation provided for in article 1 above, the competent authorities of the High Contracting Parties will determine the measures to be taken as soon as the present pact enters into force. These measures will become operative as soon as they have been approved by the Governments of the High Contracting Parties.

ART. 3. The High Contracting Parties

undertake to refrain from any interference whatsoever in each other's internal affairs. They will settle any dispute between themselves in a peaceful way in accordance with the United Nations Charter.

ART. 4. The High Contracting Parties declare that the dispositions of the present pact are not in contradiction with any of the international obligations contracted by either of them with any third State or States. They do not derogate from and cannot be interpreted as derogating from, the said international obligations. The High Contracting Parties undertake not to enter into any international obligation incompatible with the present pact.

ART. 5. This pact shall be open for accession to any member of the Arab League or any other State actively concerned with the security and peace in this region and which is fully recognised by both of the High Contracting Parties. Accession shall come into force from the date on which the instrument of accession of the State concerned is deposited with the Ministry for Foreign Affairs of Iraq.

Any acceding State party to the present pact may conclude special agreements, in accordance with article 1, with one or more States parties to the present pact. The competent authority of any acceding State may determine measures in accordance with article 2. These measures will become operative as soon as they have been approved by the Governments of the parties concerned.

ART. 6. A Permanent Council at ministerial level will be set up to function within the framework of the purposes of this pact when at least four Powers become parties to the pact.

The Council will draw up its own rules of procedure.

ART. 7. This pact remains in force for a period of five years renewable for other five-year periods. Any Contracting Party may withdraw from the pact by notifying the other parties in writing of its desire to do so six months before the expiration of any of the above-mentioned periods, in which case the pact remains valid for the other parties.

ART. 8. This pact shall be ratified by the contracting parties and ratifications shall be exchanged at Ankara as soon as possible. Thereafter it shall come into force from the date of the exchange of ratifications.

In witness whereof, the said plenipotentiaries have signed the present pact in Arabic, Turkish and English, all three texts being equally authentic except in the case of doubt when the English text shall prevail.

108. SPECIAL AGREEMENT: BRITAIN AND IRAQ
4 April 1955

[Great Britain, *Parliamentary Papers, 1955,* Treaty Series No. 50, Cmd. 9544]

Because of the failure to obtain Iraqi ratification of the draft agreement signed at Portsmouth on 15 January 1948 (Doc. 89), the 1930 treaty of alliance (Doc. 56) continued to govern Anglo-Iraqi relations in the decade following World War II. The present special agreement, which automatically came into force upon the United Kingdom's accession to the Baghdad Pact (Doc. 107) on 5 April 1955, ended Britain's preferential alliance with Iraq and established a relationship between the two countries more closely in accord with postwar realities. Reproduced below are the main instrument and two subsidiary agreements in the form of memoranda, defining the conditions of military cooperation. Omitted are exchanges of notes declaring that the terms of the two memoranda should remain valid for the same period as the special agreement and that the United Kingdom would provide pensions, gratuities, vocational training and grants to Iraqi levies and civilian employees of the R.A.F. under the expiring preferential alliance.

ART. 1. The two Contracting Governments shall maintain and develop peace and friendship between their two countries and shall co-operate for their security and defence in accordance with the Pact of Mutual Co-operation.

ART. 2. The Treaty of Alliance between

the United Kingdom and Iraq, signed at Bagdad on June 30, 1930, with annexure and Notes exchanged, shall terminate from the date when the present Agreement comes into force.

ART. 3. The Government of Iraq by the present Agreement undertake no obligations beyond the frontiers of Iraq.

ART. 4. The Government of Iraq assume full responsibility for the defence of Iraq and will command and guard all defence installations in Iraq.

ART. 5. In accordance with Article 1 of the Pact, there shall be close co-operation between the competent authorities of the two Governments for the defence of Iraq. This co-operation shall include planning, combined training and the provision of such facilities as may be agreed upon between the two Contracting Governments for this purpose and with the object of maintaining Iraq's armed forces at all times in a state of efficiency and readiness.

ART. 6. The Government of the United Kingdom shall, at the request of the Government of Iraq, do their best

(*a*) to afford help to Iraq;

(i) in creating and maintaining an effective Iraqi Air Force by means of joint training and exercises in the Middle East;

(ii) in the efficient maintenance and operation of such airfields and other installations as may from time to time be agreed to be necessary;

(*b*) to join with the Government of Iraq in

(i) establishing an efficient system of warning against air attack;

(ii) ensuring that equipment for the defence of Iraq is kept in Iraq in a state of readiness;

(iii) training and equipping Iraqi forces for the defence of their country; and

(*c*) to make available in Iraq technical personnel of the British forces for the purpose of giving effect to the provisions of paragraphs (*a*) and (*b*) of this Article.

ART. 7. Service aircraft of the two countries shall enjoy staging and overflying facilities in each other's territories.

ART. 8. In the event of an armed attack against Iraq or threat of an armed attack which, in the opinion of the two Contracting Governments, endangers the security of Iraq, the Government of the United Kingdom at the request of the Government of Iraq shall make available assistance, including if necessary armed forces to help to defend Iraq. The Government of Iraq shall provide all facilities and assistance to enable such aid to be rapid and effective.

ART. 9. (*a*) The present Agreement shall come into force on the date on which the United Kingdom becomes a party to the Pact.

(*b*) The Agreement shall remain in force so long as both Iraq and the United Kingdom are parties to the Pact.

MEMORANDUM NO. 1

1. (*a*) Command of Habbaniya, Shaiba and Margil shall pass as from the date of signature of the Special Agreement to the Government of Iraq and Iraqi officers of appropriate rank shall be appointed for this purpose on May 2, 1955.

(*b*) All flying units of the Royal Air Force now stationed in Habbaniya and Shaiba shall be withdrawn progressively, and their withdrawal shall be completed within one year after the date of signature of the Special Agreement.

(*c*) As the withdrawal of these flying units proceeds, the Government of the United Kingdom shall also progressively withdraw members of their technical and administrative personnel and personnel of authorised service organisations until only those remain in Iraq who are required for the purpose of the Special Agreement and this Memorandum.

2. (*a*) Under the Special Agreement, British personnel shall be in Iraq to assist the Iraqi Forces with training and with the installation, operation and maintenance of facilities and equipment, and to service aircraft.

(*b*) The command and administration of British personnel and installations shall be the responsibility of the Government of the United Kingdom and for this purpose the Government of the United Kingdom shall make available the necessary British staff to command and administer them under the overall authority of the Iraqi officer in charge of each establishment.

(*c*) The senior British officer appointed in each case shall act in close liaison with the Iraqi officer in command.

3. The provisions of the Agreement regarding the Status of Forces of Parties to the North Atlantic Treaty, signed in London on June 19, 1951 shall apply to the forces of each Government in the territories of the other Government. Detailed arrangements for the application of those provisions shall be made by the two Governments as soon as possible. Until such detailed arrangements have been made in Iraq, the provisions at present applicable to British forces there shall continue to apply.

4. (*a*) In accordance with Article 4 of the Special Agreement, the Government of Iraq shall assume responsibility for the protection of all airfields and installations in Iraq and to this end shall incorporate into the Iraqi Forces those members of the R.A.F. Levies of Iraq, who wish to volunteer. The Government of the United Kingdom shall, for a limited period, make available for loan to the Iraqi forces British personnel, as far as possible from among those now serving with the Royal Air Force Levies, Iraq, to facilitate such transfer and integration.

(*b*) The two Governments shall use their best endeavours to ensure that as many as possible of the civilians at present employed at Habbaniya, Shaiba and Margil shall continue in employment there.

5. The Government of the United Kingdom undertake, in accordance with Article 6 (*a*) and (*c*) of the Special Agreement and in order to facilitate the closest cooperation between the air forces of the two countries, to do their best:

(*a*) to provide expert advice and assistance in operational and technical matters, including the extension of Iraqi airfields, and in the construction of such adidtional airfields and facilities as may be agreed to be necessary;

(*b*) to provide personnel to assist in the training of the Royal Iraqi Air Force and to offer continuous consultations regarding methods and techniques of training at all stages;

(*c*) to arrange that Royal Air Force squadrons and other British aircraft shall make periodic visits to Iraq in accordance with the provisions of the Special Agreement and this Memorandum, in particular for the purpose of joint training at all times;

(*d*) to make available in Iraq British personnel for the servicing, maintenance and repair of British aircraft as well as for such airfield services as it may be agreed that they should provide on airfields jointly used by both parties;

(*e*) to grant facilities, including instructional courses abroad, for training Iraqi personnel if suitable facilities are not available in Iraq;

(*f*) to facilitate as far as possible the supply of necessary aircraft and associated equipment of modern design.

6. The Government of the United Kingdom shall do their best to join with the Government of Iraq in establishing as soon as possible an efficient system for anti-aircraft defence, including radar warning system and a system for aircraft reporting. For these purposes, the Government of the United Kingdom shall make available to the Government of Iraq the co-operation and advice of qualified service and technical personnel.

7. For the purposes of Article 8 of the Special Agreement, the Iraqi land forces shall be so trained as to facilitate closest co-operation with land forces of the United Kingdom and suitably trained and experienced British personnel shall be made available to assist in the training of Iraqi land forces and to attend and advise on field and other exercises. The Government of the United Kingdom shall do their best to facilitate the supply to the Government of Iraq of arms and other appropriate equipment of modern design.

8. The Government of the United Kingdom will co-operate with the Government of Iraq in establishing in advance and maintaining to an agreed standard such maintenance installations, including tank repair facilities, as may be agreed to be

necessary in the event of an armed attack for Iraqi forces and British forces co-operating with them. Expert service advice on their siting and construction, and advice and assistance in their maintenance and manning, shall be made available by the Government of the United Kingdom.

9. (*a*) The Government of the United Kingdom shall make available, as may be agreed between the two Governments, the co-operation and advice of suitably qualified service and technical personnel with a view to the establishment of an organisation for mine watching and mine clearance on the Shatt el Arab.

(*b*) The Government of Iraq shall continue to permit British naval units to visit the Shatt el Arab at any time on previous notification being given.

10. The existing procedures and facilities under which aircraft, under the control of the R.A.F., overfly, land, refuel and are serviced in Iraq, shall be continued. Similar procedures shall apply and similar facilities shall be made available in the United Kingdom and its dependent territories to aircraft under the control of Royal Iraqi Air Force.

11. (*a*) The Government of the United Kingdom shall join with the Government of Iraq in establishing in Iraq stocks of military stores and equipment for use by the armed forces of the two countries for the defence of Iraq in the event of an armed attack against Iraq. These stocks shall be stored at sites in Iraq to be agreed between the competent authorities of the two Governments.

(*b*) The Government of Iraq shall provide the depôts necessary for the safe keeping of those stocks and shall assume full responsibility for their security.

(*c*) For administrative purposes, stocks which are the property of the Government of Iraq shall be stored separately from those which are the property of the Government of the United Kingdom.

(*d*) The stocks shall be kept in a state of readiness at all times. Accordingly, provision shall be made for their maintenance, turn-over, inspection and periodical replacement, and each Government shall provide the personnel necessary for those purposes with respect to the stocks belonging to them.

(*e*) The Government of the United Kingdom may freely dispose of any items of such stocks, the property of the Government of the United Kingdom, which may become surplus to British requirements, subject to the offer of first refusal to the Government of Iraq in the case of any property to be disposed of in Iraq.

12. (*a*) The Government of Iraq shall make available essential services for the use of British personnel and shall, if necessary, allocate suitable accommodation for them and their families.

(*b*) Where new installations are from time to time agreed to be necessary for the purposes of the Special Agreement and this Memorandum, the terms of their provision shall be agreed between the two Governments.

MEMORANDUM NO. 2

(a) All immovable property now in British ownership shall either continue in British ownership or be handed over to the Government of Iraq, or be freely disposed of by the Government of the United Kingdom. Certain installations that will serve the needs of both Governments shall be handed over to the Government of Iraq free of charge. All other immovable property handed over to the Government of Iraq as above shall be paid for at its *in situ* value.

(*b*) Where installations have been handed over free of charge the Government of the United Kingdom shall enjoy full rights of free user. Where the Government of Iraq have paid for immovable property, they shall be entitled to make a reasonable charge, to be settled by agreement, for its subsequent use by the Government of the United Kingdom.

(*c*) Each Government shall be responsible for the operation and maintenance of immovable property in their ownership. The two Governments shall agree on the standards to be observed, and, in appropriate cases, the apportionment of costs, in respect of the operation and maintenance of the installations which serve the needs of both Governments.

(*d*) Movable property required for the operation of any property handed over under paragraph (*a*) above shall be paid for by the Government of Iraq at full cost, if new, and if used, at a fair valuation. The Government of the United Kingdom shall retain all other movable property and shall have the right to dispose of it in Iraq or elsewhere.

(*e*) The Government of Iraq shall bear the cost of their air warning system and of improving their military airfields to standards to be agreed.

(*f*) Each Government shall meet the cost of its own forces and any civilian personnel employed by it, except that the cost to the Government of Iraq of British personnel loaned or seconded to the Iraqi forces shall be mutually agreed.

(*g*) Any other financial questions shall be settled by agreement between the two Governments.

109. PROPOSALS BY SECRETARY OF STATE DULLES FOR A SETTLEMENT IN THE ARAB-ISRAEL ZONE
26 August 1955

[*The Department of State Bulletin,* 33 (5 September 1955), 378-80]

While promoting the organization of the "northern tier" security regime, the United States also quietly sought to narrow the Arab-Israel gap by attempting to negotiate with the governments concerned an agreement for the integrated development of the Jordan River system, under American financial and technical sponsorship. As the summer of 1955 approached its end, some American observers believed that both the defense and the development schemes, each embracing a different segment of the Near and Middle East, might reach early fruition. If these estimates were correct, the time was also approaching for taking bolder measures than any in the past to curb tensions in the Arab-Israel zone, especially on the Egyptian frontier, for Egypt and Israel were the two countries where the altered emphasis in the United States Near and Middle East policy of the two preceding years was producing the most adverse effects. American officals were particularly exercised over word from Cairo that Egypt was about to conclude a deal with Czechoslovakia for heavy arms (Doc. 111). In this context must be viewed the following address before the Council on Foreign Relations in New York, where Secretary Dulles announced that "given a solution of the other related problems, he [President Eisenhower] would recommend that the United States join in formal treaty engagements to prevent or thwart any effort by either side to alter by force the boundaries between Israel and its Arab neighbors." The British Foreign Office endorsed the Dulles proposal on 27 August (text in the *New York Times,* 28 August 1955), reaffirming the United Kingdom's offer of 4 April 1955 "to guarantee by treaty or treaties with the parties concerned any territorial settlement so agreed."

One of the first things I did as Secretary of State was to go to the Middle East. I wanted to see for myself that area so rich in culture and religious tradition, yet now so torn by strife and bitterness. So, in the spring of 1953, I visited Egypt, Israel, Jordan, Syria, Lebanan, Iraq, and Saudi Arabia. Upon my return I spoke of the impressions gathered on that trip and of the hopes which I held as a result of talks with leaders and people there.

Some of those hopes have become realities. At that time the Suez Base was a center of controversy and of potential strife. Now, as a result of patient effort, in a spirit of conciliation, the problem of the Suez Base has been successfully resolved.

Another problem which was then concerning many of the leaders in the Middle East was that of the security of the area. It was clear that effective defense depended upon collective measures and that such measures, to be dependable, needed to be a natural drawing together of those who felt a sense of common destiny in the face of what could be a common danger. Here, too, there has been some encouraging progress.

A third problem which called for attention was the need for water to irrigate land. I mentioned in my report the possibility that the rivers flowing through the Jordan Valley might be used to make this valley a source of livelihood rather than dispute. Since then Ambassador Eric Johnston has held talks with the governments of countries through which the River Jordan runs. They have shown an encouraging willingness to accept the principle of coordinated arrangements for the use of the waters. Plans for the development of the valley are well advanced. Ambassador Johnston is now on his fourth visit to the countries concerned in an effort to eliminate the small margins of difference which still exist.

A beginning has been made, as you see, in doing away with the obstacles that stand in the way of the aspirations of the Middle Eastern peoples. It is my hope—and that is the hope of which I would now speak—that the time has come when it is useful to think in terms of further steps toward stability, tranquillity, and progress in the Middle East.

THE ARAB-ISRAEL PROBLEM

What are the principal remaining problems? They are those which were unresolved by the armistices of 1949 which ended the fighting between Israelis and Arabs. Before taking up these problems specifically, I would first pay high tribute to what the United Nations has done to preserve tranquillity and to serve humanity in the area. Despite these indispensable efforts, three problems remain that conspicuously require to be solved.

The first is the tragic plight of the 900,000 refugees who formerly lived in the territory that is now occupied by Israel.

The second is the pall of fear that hangs over the Arab and Israel people alike. The Arab countries fear that Israel will seek by violent means to expand at their expense. The Israelis fear that the Arabs will gradually marshal superior forces to be used to drive them into the sea, and they suffer from the economic measures now taken against them.

The third is the lack of fixed permanent boundaries between Israel and its Arab neighbors.

There are other important problems. But if these three principal problems could be dealt with, then the way would be paved for the solution of others.

These three problems seem capable of solution, and surely there is need.

Border clashes take an almost weekly toll of human lives and inflame an already dangerous mood of hatred. The sufferings of the Arab refugees are drawn out almost beyond the point of endurance. The fears which are at work, on each side, lead to a heavy burden of armament, which constitutes a serious drag on economic and social progress. Responsible leaders are finding it hard to turn their full attention and energies to the positive task of creating conditions of healthy growth.

Serious as the present situation is, there is a danger that, unless it improves, it will get worse. One ill leads to another, and cause and effect are hard to sort out. The atmosphere, if it worsens, could becloud clear judgments, making appear attractive what would in fact be reckless.

Both sides suffer greatly from the present situation, and both are anxious for what they would regard as a just and equitable solution. But neither has been able to find that way.

This may be a situation where mutual friends could serve the common good. This is particularly true since the area may not, itself, possess all of the ingredients needed for the full and early building of a condition of security and well-being.

The United States, as a friend of both Israelis and Arabs, has given the situation deep and anxious thought and has come to certain conclusions, the expression of which may help men of good will within the area to fresh constructive efforts. I speak in this matter with the authority of President Eisenhower.

PROPOSED LOAN TO ISRAEL

To end the plight of the 900,000 refugees requires that these uprooted people should, through resettlement and—to such an extent as may be feasible—repatriation, be enabled to resume a life of dignity and self-respect. To this end, there is need to create more arable land where refugees can find permanent homes and gain their own livelihood through their own work. Fortunately, there are practical projects for water development which can make this possible.

All this requires money.

Compensation is due from Israel to the refugees. However, it may be that Israel cannot, unaided, now make adequate compensation. If so, there might be an international loan to enable Israel to pay the compensation which is due and which would enable many of the refugees to find for themselves a better way of life.

President Eisenhower would recommend substantial participation by the United States in such a loan for such a purpose. Also he would recommend that the United States contribute to the realization of water development and irrigation projects which would, directly or indirectly, facilitate the resettlement of the refugees.

These projects would, of course, do much more than aid in the resettlement of refugees. They would enable the people throughout the area to enjoy a better life. Furthermore, a solution to the refugee problem would help in eliminating the problem of recurrent incidents which have plagued and embittered the settlements on both sides of the borders.

COLLECTIVE SECURITY MEASURES

The second principal problem which I mentioned is that of fear. The nature of this fear is such that it is hardly within the capacity of the countries of the area, acting alone, to replace the fear with a sense of security. There, as in many other areas, security can be assured only by collective measures which commit decisive power to the deterring of aggression.

President Eisenhower has authorized me to say that, given a solution of the other related problems, he would recommend that the United States join in formal treaty engagements to prevent or thwart any effort by either side to alter by force the boundaries between Israel and its Arab neighbors. I hope that other countries would be willing to join in such a security guaranty, and that it would be sponsored by the United Nations.

By such collective security measures the area could be relieved of the acute fears which both sides now profess. The families located near the boundaries could relax from the strain of feeling that violent death may suddenly strike them; the peoples of the area whose standards of living are already too low would no longer have to carry the burden of what threatens to become an armaments race if indeed it does not become a war; the political leadership of the area could devote itself to constructive tasks.

PROBLEM OF BOUNDARIES

If there is to be a guaranty of borders, it would be normal that there should be prior agreement upon what the borders are. That is the third major problem. The existing lines separating Israel and the Arab States were fixed by the armistice agreements of 1949. They were not designed to be permanent frontiers in every respect; in part, at least, they reflected the status of the fighting at the moment.

The task of drawing permanent boundaries is admittedly one of difficulty. There is no single and sure guide, for each of two conflicting claims may seem to have merit. The difficulty is increased by the fact that even territory which is barren has acquired a sentimental significance. Surely the over-all advantages of the measures here outlined would outweigh vastly any net disadvantages of the adjustments needed to convert armistice lines of danger into boundary lines of safety. In spite of conflicting claims and sentiments, I believe it is possible to find a way of reconciling the vital interests of all the parties. The United States would be willing to help in the search for a solution if the parties to the dispute should desire.

If agreement can be reached on these basic problems of refugees, fear, and boundaries, it should prove possible to find solutions for other questions, largely economic, which presently fan the flames of hostility and resentment.

It should also be possible to reach agreement on the status of Jersusalem. The United States would give its support to a United Nations review of this problem.

I have not attempted to enumerate all the issues on which it would be desirable to have a settlement; nor have I tried to outline in detail the form which a settlement of any of the elements might take. I have tried to show that possibilities exist for an immeasurable improvement and that the possibilities do not require any nation taking action which would be against its interests, whether those interests be measured in terms of material strength or in terms of national prestige and honor. I have also, I trust, made clear that the Government of the United States is disposed to enlarge those possibilities by contributions of its own, if this be desired by those concerned.

Both sides in this strife have a noble past, a heritage of rich contributions to civilization; both have fostered progress in science and the arts. Each side is predominantly representative of one of the world's great religions. Both sides desire to achieve a good life for their people and to share, and contribute to, the advancements of this century.

At a time when a great effort is being made to ease the tension which has long prevailed between the Soviet and Western worlds, can we not hope that a similar spirit should prevail in the Middle East? That is our plea. The spirit of conciliation and of the good neighbor brings rich rewards to the people and to the nations. If doing that involves some burdens, they are burdens which the United States would share, just as we would share the satisfaction which would result to all peoples if happiness, contentment, and good will could drive hatred and misery away from peoples whom we hold in high respect and honor.

110. TRIPARTITE (GREECE, TURKEY AND THE UNITED KINGDOM) COMMUNIQUÉ ON CYPRUS
1 September 1955

[Great Britain, *Parliamentary Papers, 1955,* Miscellaneous No. 18, Cmd. 9594, pp. 26–28]

The United Kingdom originally occupied Cyprus in 1878 (I, Doc. 85) as an eastern Mediterranean outpost to discourage further Russian advances against Ottoman domain in Asia and to safeguard the imperial route through the Suez Canal. But the island's significance in British strategic thinking diminished sharply after the occupation of Egypt in 1882. Upon declaring war against the Ottoman Empire in November 1914, Britain annexed Cyprus, and in the treaty of Lausanne nearly nine years later (Doc. 41) Turkey recognized the annexation retroactively. Whitehall converted Cyprus into a crown colony in 1925. Following disorders in 1931, the experiment with embryonic autonomous institutions was suspended. No serious efforts were made to restore limited self-government until 1947–48. The British offer at that time was rejected by the Greek-speaking population, who represented 80 per cent of the somewhat less than half-million total and who demanded *enosis* or union with Greece, a movement that ultimately elicited official sponsorship from the Greek government. But London refused to entertain *enosis,* partly because of unsettled conditions in Greece and even more because of the increasingly acute Anglo-Egyptian problem. Once the decision was taken to wind up the British base at Suez, Cyprus stock on the British strategic market rose to its original (1878–82) value. The Suez base, it will be recalled, had become in the spring of 1947 the administrative and operational headquarters of the British Middle East defense system, stretching from Malta to the Persian Gulf. Cyprus was selected to replace the Suez base in that role after the signature in October 1954 of the Anglo-Egyptian agreement (Doc. 105). By then, however, the Cyprus issue had expanded into a three-cornered dispute, for Turkey took up the cause of the Turkish-speaking minority on the island, roughly 20 per cent of the total. Agitation by the Greek majority on Cyprus threatened to jeopardize British strategic plans, following the inconclusive debate of the question before the UN General Assembly's ninth session in the fall of 1954. A tripartite conference at London (29 August–7 September 1955) failed to reconcile the conflicting views. The anti-Greek riots at Istanbul and Izmir (6–7 September) over the Cyprus issue symptomized a rekindling of the traditional Greco-Turkish hostility. From the deterioration in Greece's relations with two of its NATO allies only the USSR stood to gain. The following agreed communiqué presents in summary form the respective positions of the three parties. For more detailed statements at the 1955 London conference, see Cmd. 9594.

As previously agreed, the Tripartite Conference on the Eastern Mediterranean and Cyprus this morning heard a statement by the Turkish Foreign Minister. The three Foreign Ministers met again at Lancaster House in the afternoon, when they agreed to issue the following summaries of the points of view of the three Governments as they had been put forward in the three opening statements.

In explaining the point of view of Her Majesty's Government Mr. Macmillan had emphasised that this was a conference between friends and allies whose unity was vital to the free world. The three countries represented had special responsibilities, not only to themselves but to their partners, which overrode all others. It was their duty to explain their points of view in all frankness and then to seek the best means to reconcile their differences.

These differences centred on Cyprus. But they threatened allied harmony and the smooth working of common defence over a much wider area. Consequently the British Government had thought it right that all aspects of our present problems, including the position in Cyprus, should be embraced in a wider consideration of political and defence questions in the Eastern Mediterranean.

History had given each of the three countries special interests in Cyprus. For Great Britain, Cyprus was both a territory, indisputably under British Sovereignty, for whose progress and welfare Her Majesty's Government were responsible; and also the vital defensive position at the hinge of the North Atlantic and Middle Eastern defence systems. British responsibilities included those arising from the British Government's adherence to the Turco-Iraqi Pact, from the Anglo-Iraqi Agreement, from the Anglo-Jordanian Alliance and from the Tripartite Declaration of 1950. To discharge these responsibilities, Britain needed not merely a "base" but the posssession and use of the whole island and its facilities.

Her Majesty's Government were determined to fulfil the first duty of any government in maintaining law and order in Cyprus. They had sought to promote self-government. A serious responsibility lay on those who had caused violence and had obstructed democratic evolution. But for this, elected representatives of the Cypriot Government mght be taking part in the present Conference. Self-government must be the first aim. He believed it could be realised with proper regard for the rights of all, if there were a common effort.

Britain would abandon neither her interests and responsibilities nor those for which she was trustee. But it was the object of Her Majesty's Government to seek through conciliation a settlement which would meet British requirements and the special circumstances of Cyprus. They looked forward to reaching agreement through discussion, and would not be inflexible.

Following Mr. Macmillan, the Greek Foreign Minister, after expressing his thanks to Her Majesty's Government for their initiative in convening the Tripartite Conference, voiced the satisfaction of the Greek Government who had consistently held the opinion that political questions of common concern to friendly and allied States should be solved by direct discussions amongst them.

M. Stephanopoulos then proceeded to a statement of the Greek Government's views on the question of Cyprus and its strategic implications.

He said that Greece recognised the need for Britain's presence for defensive purposes in Cyprus in order to be able to meet British contractual obligations in the Middle East and the Eastern Mediterranean as well as in the interests of Greece's own security. However, the Greek Foreign Minister pointed out that the question of sovereignty did not prejudice nor was it bound up with questions of defence and he quoted the example of N.A.T.O., whose strategic requirements had been successfully met by the establishment of allied bases on various territories without regard to the question of sovereignty.

M. Stephanopoulos repeatedly emphasized that the military and defensive value of the British bases in Cyprus would be enhanced, were the present ill-feeling among the Cypriot population to be changed into a spirit of spontaneous and unqualified co-operation. This result, said M. Stephanopoulos, could only be achieved by granting to the Cypriot population the right of self-determination. This right constituted one of the fundamental principles of the United Nations Charter and could certainly not be denied to a people with the high moral and cultural standards of the Cypriots.

Greece, stated M. Stephanopoulos, had not claimed and did not claim the right to decide by herself on the future destiny of Cyprus. Similarly, she denied that right to any third party, for that was the exclusive prerogative of the population of Cyprus. The Greek Government's sole endeavour had been to secure to the people of Cyprus their right to self-determination within a reasonably short period of time, during which Cyprus would be given self-government.

Greece repudiated all use of violence, which was contrary to her peaceful policy.

Greece, concluded M. Stephanopoulos, was willing to subscribe to any guarantee Her Majesty's Government would wish to have with respect to their military bases in Cyprus as well as any guarantee Turkey would wish to obtain concerning the Turkish minority in Cyprus.

Greece was convinced that, by granting the right of self-determination to the people of Cyprus, the common defence would be strengthened and that Cyprus would thus become a point of further contact and closer union between the three friendly and allied Nations.

M. Zorlu, the Turkish Foreign Minister, in explaining the point of view of the Turkish Government, said that the administration of Cyprus had been transferred to Great Britain in 1878 in return for a commitment on the part of Great Britain to come to the aid of Turkey in case of Russian aggression. According to Article 20 of the Treaty of Lausanne, Turkish sovereignty over Cyprus had lapsed on November 5, 1914, and British sovereignty had been recognised as from that date. The question of the nationality of the inhabitants of the Island had been settled by Article 21, which provided that the inhabitants would acquire British nationality, except for those who opted for Turkish nationality. Hence Cyprus had been exclusively a "matter of concern" for Turkey and Great Britain, and it had been so recognised by all signatories, including Greece, and the fate of Cyprus had been definitely determined by the Treaty of Lausanne.

Consequently, to call for a change in the status of the Island was tantamount to seeking a *modification* of that Treaty. Such a course would upset a whole political settlement in the area based upon the abandonment of an expansionist policy by Greece in return for the acceptance by Turkey of the boundaries of the Treaty of Lausanne, and would create a number of grave questions, which would also enable Turkey to put forward certain demands.

Turkey looked upon the "Cyprus question" as a British domestic issue. Turkey would continue to regard it as such so long as Britain retained sovereignty and the *status quo* was maintained. If there was any question of the Island changing hands, then it should revert to Turkey.

Turkey's interest in Cyprus was based on history, proximity, economy, military strategy, and on the sacred right of all countries to existence and security.

Cyprus was a prolongation of the Anatolian mainland and in all the course of history its fate had followed that of Anatolia. As an integral part of Turkey, the make-up of its population had never been a matter of consideration. Likewise to-day, one could not speak of 100,000 Turks living on the Island without mentioning 300,000 Turkish Cypriots living in Turkey.

Economically too, the Island, which depended for survival on outside aid, was a part of Anatolia, where the food-stuffs it needed were grown in abundance.

Strategically, the vital interests of Turkey and the requirements of defence and logistics made it imperative that the Island should belong either to Turkey or to a country which was as closely interested as Turkey in the fate of Turkey's eastern neighbours.

In case of war, Turkey could only be supplied through her southern ports, and whoever controlled Cyprus was in a position to control those ports.

As a result of the foregoing factors the principle of self-determination could not be applied to Cyprus.

This principle itself, as most international lawyers agreed, was a vague and undefined concept which had often lent itself to exploitation for ulterior motives. It often clashed with the right of sovereignty of States. It could not prevail over realities based on historical, geographical, strategic and security requirements. In itself a noble principle, which Turkey advocated, it must not be allowed to become an element of injustice, insecurity and trouble. Likewise, Turkey was not opposed to self-government, but its undiscerning application must not be allowed to cause trouble.

The two communities now living on the Island had been driven to antagonism. Consequently, what Cyprus needed before self-government was a return to peace and quiet, where clerics refrained from indulging in politics.

Even when the climate became suitable for self-government, the guiding principle should not be a consideration of majorities and minorities but that of granting full equality to the two groups.

The Cyprus question had been responsible for disturbing the co-operation of three allied countries closely concerned with the Eastern Mediterranean. The Turkish position had been clearly stated by Prime Minister Menderes and fully endorsed by the whole Turkish nation including all political parties. Turkey was extremely eager to maintain friendship and co-operation with Greece and hoped and expected that her friends and Allies, acting in the same spirit, would appreciate her position.

111. PRIME MINISTER 'ABD-AL-NASIR'S ANNOUNCEMENT OF THE EGYPTIAN AGREEMENT WITH CZECHOSLOVAKIA FOR THE PURCHASE OF ARMS

27 September 1955

[Unofficial translation, courtesy of the Department of State, Washington, D.C.]

The Revolutionary Command Council (military government) in Egypt by October 1954 had resolved the two major foreign issues inherited from the *ancien régime.* The RCC reached agreements with the United Kingdom for winding up the condominium over the Sudan (Doc. 99) and the British base in the Suez Canal zone (Doc. 105). Neither issue might have been settled satisfactorily or with such relative speed, had it not been for the persistent and tactful mediation of American Ambassador Jefferson Caffery. Still, from this indispensable diplomatic assistance to the RCC the United States proved unable to benefit, partly because of fortuitous circumstances. Caffery's diplomatic utility in Cairo virtually vanished by October 1954, for in RCC eyes he had been identified in the domestic political crisis of the preceding eight months with Muhammad Nagib, who was about to be relieved of the presidency (14 November). Although Caffery soon withdrew into overdue retirement from the foreign service, his successor, Henry A. Byroade, did not reach Cairo —owing to delay by the Senate in approving his nomination—until 27 February 1955. By then Egyptian sensitivities over the Baghdad Pact (Doc. 107)—widely viewed in the Arab East as an American-sponsored effort to destroy the Egyptian-led security system of the

Arab League (Doc. 93)—had injected into the talks emotional complications. Growing tension on the Israel frontier, moreover, immeasurably compounded the difficulties. The RCC, as a military government dedicated to developing a self-reliant army, gave high priority to procuring modern military equipment, which it felt Britain had withhelc deliberately under the 1936 alliance (Doc. 61). The United States was willing to make Egypt eligible for military grant aid, subject to a liberal construction of the usual conditions laid down by Congress—association with the American-led western mutual security program and acceptance of an American military aid mission. When Prime Minister Gamal 'Abd-al-Nasir and the RCC rejected the conditions as likely to arouse Egyptian nationalist suspicions, the United States could fulfill Egyptian wants only through the sale of the requested weapons. But investment in military "hardware" of the kind that the RCC sought proved more expensive than Egypt could afford, for it had few dollars to spare and its chief exportable product—cotton—was not in demand in the cotton-glutted American market. Here the negotiations deadlocked, and as the months rolled by, the stalemate produced friction on which the USSR and its satellites traded. Prague and Cairo in September 1955 entered into an accord providing for the barter, reputedly at nominal cost, of Czech heavy weapons—including tanks, jet planes and submarines—for Egyptian cotton and rice. Thus the United States and its Western allies suddenly faced the prospects of competition with the Soviet orbit in the supply of arms to a notably unstable area. In the following speech, delivered—without a prepared text, it was reported—before an armed forces exhibition in Cairo, 'Abd-al-Nasir presents the RCC version of the factors leading to the arms deal.

My Brothers,

I am glad today to see this exhibition which the armed forces have set up to show the extent of progress and development which the army has made.

I am glad also to speak to you today for I now recall my last talk to the men of the armed forces some months ago. I remember also that I spoke then to thousands of officers. Now I see them amongst us. I see them carrying out their duty on the frontiers of our homeland for the safety of our country and for the glory of our country.

When I speak to you now, my brothers, I speak to all the men of the armed forces; I speak to all the men of the fatherland; I speak to Egypt—Egypt which revolted on July 23, 1952—Egypt which placed its faith in the goals of this Revolution; Egypt which was determined to achieve these goals—Egypt which finally threw off the occupation and threw off slavery. When I speak to you today, I speak to all Egypt.

My brothers, this is my feeling when I look at the battlefield, and I see the men of the armed forces on guard along the frontiers; when I look at the frontiers of Egypt and see the men of the armed forces standing staunch and firm and faithful, exerting every effort for the safety of this country and its sons.

The fifth goal of your Revolution was to set up a strong national army. From the beginning of the Revolution you have all exerted every effort to achieve this goal and we have worked with you with all our might and with every means at our disposal. We have worked with you to achieve this goal because to achieve it means liberty; to achieve it means glory; to achieve it means dignity.

My brothers, we met the greatest obstacles—we met many difficulties in achieving our aim. We did everything we could to set up military factories; we did everything we could to provide the army with the heavy armaments it needed; and we did everything we could so that Egypt's army might be a strong national army.

Yes, my brothers, we did a lot.

But there were the greatest difficulties in our way. We believed that if we wanted to create such an army for Egypt we had to preserve our freedom. We believed that if we wanted to achieve this strong national army for Egypt, we had to become free in our internal and our foreign policies.

My brothers, we will never agree that this army be formed at the expense of this country's freedom, or at the expense of this country's glory, or at the expense of this country's dignity. We have always been determined that the formation of this strong national army should go hand in hand with true liberty and with real glory.

We have proclaimed Egypt's policy on many occasions. We declared that Egypt after the Revolution of July 23 would go forward with its independent policy; it would go forward having rid itself of imperialism; it would go forward having rid itself of domination; and it would go forward having rid itself of foreign influence. These were our hopes and these were your hopes. We did everything we could to preserve these hopes. We did everything we could, my brothers, to preserve these goals—and we were confronted by many obstacles.

You know that heavy weapons are controlled by the big powers. You know that the big powers have never agreed to supply our army with heavy weapons except with conditions and except with stipulations. You know that we refused these conditions and these stipulations because we are jealous of our true freedom and we are jealous of our independent policy. We are anxious that Egypt have a strong independent policy so that we may make of Egypt a new independent personality which will really rid itself of imperialism, will really rid itself of occupation, will really rid itself of foreign domination in all its aspects. We have been making progress along this path.

Today, my brothers, we hear an outcry from London, we hear an outcry from Washington about the arming of Egypt's troops. But I would like to tell you that throughout the last three years we have tried to get heavy weapons for the army by every means, not for aggressive purposes, not to attack, not to make war, but for defense, for security, for peace.

We wanted to strengthen our army so as to provide security for ourselves, to provide security for our nation, to provide security for our "Arabism." We wanted to get weapons for the army so that we could always feel secure, safe, and tranquil. We never intended to strengthen our army for aggressive purposes. We never intended to strengthen the army for wars. But the army which is the defender and protector of our homeland must always stand prepared to defend the borders and the country's honor. Such is our purpose and this is our goal. We have always declared this throughout the last three years. We do not want arms for aggression. We want arms so that we can be tranquil, so that we feel at peace and not threatened.

Today, my brothers, I sense an outcry here and I sense an outcry there. I sense these outcries now that we have been able to obtain for the army the weapons of which it is in need, without conditions and without restrictions, so as to achieve the goal which this Revolution undertook—that Egypt should have a strong national army to defend its true independence and protect its true freedom.

On this occasion I would like to tell you, my brothers, the story of the arming of our troops. When the Revolution took place we went to each of the states, we went to every quarter to get weapons for the army. We went to Britain; we went to France; we went to America; we went to the rest of the states to get weapons for the army in the interest of peace and defense. What did we get? We got only demands. They wanted to arm the troops after we had signed a document or after we had signed a pact. We declared that even though we had wanted and had decided to arm our troops, we would never sign a document. We were arming our troops in the interest of our freedom, of our independent personality, of our Revolution, of the glory of our country, of Egypt's dignity. We declared that we would not arm our troops at the expense of our freedom.

We requested arms but what was the result? The result, my brothers, is a long and bitter story. I remember now, I remember as I talk to you that we sometimes humiliated ourselves but we never abandoned our principles. We humiliated ourselves when we requested arms—we begged for arms—but at the same time we were determined to hold to our principles and we were determined to preserve our high ideals. And what was the result? Never, my brothers, could we achieve our goal, the greatest goal for which this Revolution was undertaken, the creation of a strong national army.

France always bargained with us. She bargained with us over North Africa. She says to us, "We will give you arms on the condition that you should not criticize our position in North Africa, and on condition that you relinquish your 'Arabism,' that you relinquish your humanitarianism and on condition that you should keep silent and close your eyes when you see the massacres in North Africa."

We said to her, "How can we relinquish our 'Arabism'? How can we give up our humanitarianism? We never can."

France's arms offer to us was always like a sword above our necks. We were always being threatened, my brothers, with the cutting off of arms. We were always being threatened, my brothers, with the supply of arms to Israel and the cutting off of arms for Egypt. This is the story of France and now I'll tell you the story of America.

From the time of the Revolution we asked for arms and we were promised arms. And what was the result?

The promise was a promise circumscribed with conditions. We would get arms if we signed a mutual security pact. We would get arms if we would sign some form of alliance. We refused to sign a mutual security pact. We refused to sign any form of alliance. And, my brothers, we could never get a single weapon from America.

What was the story of England. England told us that she was ready to supply us arms. We accepted gratefully. What was the result? England provided us with a quantity of arms which was not sufficient to achieve the goals of this Revolution.

What was the result of all this, my brothers? The army opposing us is obtaining arms from various parts of the world. Israel's army has been able to obtain arms from England, France, Belgium, Canada, Italy and from various other states. It can always find someone to supply it arms, while we read in the foreign press—in the British, American or French newspapers—that Israel's army can defeat all the Arab armies combined. It was only last month, my brothers, that I read many articles in that sense, that the Israeli army could defeat Egypt, that the Israeli army could beat the Arabs, that the Israeli army was superior in armament, that the Israeli army was superior in equipment.

This is what they have said in their press and I said to them, since you feel like this why do you prevent us from obtaining arms? I asked them this, and what was the result? France complained about our feelings towards North Africa, and prevented us from obtaining arms.

When we saw this, when we saw this domination, when we saw this influence which was being used against us, we decided to ask all the states of the world to supply us arms without conditions. I told them these arms would not be used for aggression, that they would be used for defense, that we had no aggressive intent, that our intentions were peaceful, that we wanted to have a strong independent army to defend our country and help it to achieve its free and independent goals, that we want to have a strong army not for aggression but for defense.

I said this, my brothers, in the name of Egypt to America, to England, to France, to Russia, to Czechoslovakia and to the rest of the states and I waited for their answers. I waited, and what was the result? I got answers from some of them that I could get arms with conditions. I refused, for I have already told you that although we are ready to humiliate ourselves by asking for arms, we will never abandon our principles.

We received a reply from Czechoslovakia saying that she was prepared to supply arms in accordance with our needs and those of Egypt's army on a commercial basis, the transaction to be considered like any other commercial transaction. We agreed and last week Egypt signed a commerial agreement with Czechoslovakia to supply us arms. This agreement permits Egypt to pay in Egyptian products such as cotton and rice. This offer we gratefully accepted. In this way, my brothers, we achieve one of the goals of the Revolution, the formation of a strong national army.

Today, my brothers, as I talk to you I sense the outcry raised here and there—an outcry in London, an outcry in Washington. These outcries seek to continue to control us, to continue to influence us.

We will fight to destroy this control. We will fight to destroy this influence. We will fight to achieve the goals of the Revolution and we will fight to create a strong national army able to achieve the greatest goals of the Revolution, able to obtain peace. Yes, my brothers, peace—that peace which we proclaimed at Bandung, the peace which we have proclaimed on many occasions.

This army which we create is for the sake of peace. We create it so that we can be secure in our lot, we create it so that Egypt will not be a state of refugees. We create it against aggression, we create it against any territorial designs against our nation's soil.

When I hear someone say that this opens the way for Russian influence or foreign influence in Egypt or the Middle East, I think of the remote past and I say that this commercial agreement without conditions does not open the way for Russian or foreign influence, but, my brothers, it means the eradication of the foreign influence which so long oppressed and dominated us.

My brothers, when we are able to equip our army with the necessary arms without conditions or restrictions, we destroy foreign control—that control which I have felt and which you have felt in the guise of equipping our army and in the guise of providing it with arms. Those who talk to us about foreign influence know that they themselves have no intention of seeing foreign influence wiped out.

We intend to destroy foreign influence. Egypt—independent Egypt, revolutionary Egypt, strong Egypt—will never allow foreign influence in her land. They know we will never accept their influence, and their control. They know that Egypt after the Revolution of July 23 has determined to destroy forever foreign influence, foreign oppression and foreign control and to go forward as a free independent power with her own foreign policy, motivated by her own interests and not by the interest of any of the foreign camps.

They know this when they talk of influence for they think that it is their influence which has come to an end in this country—that it is their influence which has gone away forever.

Today we are a free and independent nation. We will fight for our liberty and we will fight for our independence and may God be with us all.

112. STATEMENT ON FOREIGN AFFAIRS BY ISRAEL PREMIER AND FOREIGN MINISTER MOSHE SHARETT 18 October 1955

[Israel Office of Information (New York), *Israel Digest,* 26 October 1955, special supplement]

Israel's appeals to Washington for military assistance and for security guarantees more explicit than those in the tripartite declaration of May 1950 (Doc. 92) grew steadily more insistent after the conclusion of the United States military aid agreement with Iraq in April 1954 (Doc. 103). The search for security in Israel could only be appreciated in the context of the land's geopolitical setting. Israel everywhere, the Mediterranean boundary excepted, abutted states whose governments refused to recognize it. Indeed, no locality in Israel was further than ten minutes by slow plane from a hostile frontier, and the peculiar configuration gave the country a relatively larger frontier than the average for a land of that size. The memory of the war for independence, when the nascent state at the most critical juncture had to fend for itself, combined with the exposed location and the undiminished enmity of immediate neighbors to prevent the Israel government and people from relaxing their round-the-clock vigilance. This helped explain Israel's policy of "massive retaliation"—on an Arab-Israel scale—for the daily Arab raids and incidents of infiltration, many the result of crowded refugee conditions in the sandy waste that was the Gaza Strip or of the Jordan armistice line that separated uprooted peasants from their former lands. But many others were committed with the foreknowledge, and at times complicity, of the Arab governments, as part of a larger policy of attrition that included economic boycott and attempted blockade of Israel. The progressive breakdown of the armistice machinery, to which the endless round of incidents and retaliation contributed, added to the restiveness. Given these regional conditions, Israel had developed a policy of maintaining its demonstrated military advantage, as the most reliable defense arrangement. But once the United States began to furnish Iraq with military grant aid, and Czechoslovakia, with Soviet blessings, began to sell heavy military equipment to Egypt at substantial discount, a sense of insecurity spread through Israel. As long as Moscow reaped benefits from courting the Arab states, there was little hope of redress from the Soviet orbit, since Israel had formally aligned itself with the West in 1951. What was left of British power in the Near and Middle East seemed too intimately tied to the Arab zone to sustain Israel's trust in help from the United Kingdom. Nor did the Quai d'Orsay appear more inviting than Whitehall, in view of France's preoccupation with the contagious revolt in French North Africa. Israel directed its pleas, in the circumstances, primarily to the United States. In the following statement to the *Kneset* (Israel legislature), Premier and Foreign Minister Moshe Sharett elaborated upon his government's position.

The *Knesset* yesterday resumed its normal sessions after a recess during which there occurred a number of events of the deepest significance—some of a grave and threatening nature—affecting Israel's security and foreign relations. We have passed through a period of bloody attacks along our borders and within our territory. We cannot know whether that phase has reached its end.

An address by the Secretary of State of the United States, dealing with a number of the basic problems on our political agenda, has required our concentrated study and reaction. The prolonged negotiations, with American mediation, on a regional water plan for us and our neighbors, have passed through a further laborious stage and reached the threshold of decision. And finally and most significantly, there has taken place in the Middle East a development which confronts us with the distressing prospect of the accrual to the strongest state among our adversaries of a far-reaching military advantage which threatens us with dangers the like of which we have not known since our War of Independence.

In my brief remarks to the *Knesset* a week ago I said that these subjects demanded the immediate and earnest attention of the House. Allow me now, before entering upon my report, to express the sincere hope that the discussion in the House will be balanced and responsible, characterized by an earnest desire to reach among us the greatest possible degree of harmony and unity in both word and deed.

RENEWED EGYPTIAN AGGRESSION

The renewal of Egyptian aggressive actions along the Gaza strip jeopardized the security of our settlements in that border area and deeper in the country. The Egyptians resorted to the odious tactic of sending gangs deep into Israel to commit acts of murder and destruction. Vigorous reaction became imperative and the Defense Army of Israel struck against one of the nests of the gangsters. With the cessation, however, of attacks in the south, similar gangs began to operate in the northern sections of the country.

According to information in our possession, these too were organized primarily on the criminal initiative of Egypt, assisted by other Arab factors, particularly Syria. We must once more warn Egypt that it will be considered liable for the continuation of such murderous activities, though this warning in no way absolves from responsibility those other Arab countries bound by the Armistice Agreements to prevent the penetration into Israel from their territory of armed forces.

The Army of Israel and our Border Police stand on watch, and are alert and vigilant. Meanwhile the Egyptian acts of lawlessness in the frontier zone along the Sinai border forced us to create certain physical facts. The situation in that region was restored to normal, though it has apparently again deteriorated.

If Egypt proposes once more to disregard the obligations it has recently undertaken, we reserve to ourselves the freedom to act in accordance with the requirements of the situation.

In relation to all these questions we are anxious to act in full cooperation with the competent organs of the U.N. in accordance with the Armistice Agreements. But we shall insist upon bilateral fidelity to these agreements, and will not agree to their being observed by one side, while the other side feels free to violate them at will.

A most conspicuous violation of the Armistice Agreements is implicit in the recent Egyptian regulations regarding entry into the Gulf of *Eilat* (*Aqaba*) aimed at obstructing the passage of Israel ships to the southern harbor of our country. These regulations are in contravention not only of the Armistice Agreements, but of resolutions of the Security Council and of principles of international law relating to the freedom of shipping in open waters and in straits between seas. Here, too, we reserve for ourselves full freedom of action at the time and in the manner we shall find suitable.

SECRETARY DULLES' ADDRESS

At the very time that Egyptian aggressiveness was renewed, Mr. Dulles addressed the Council for Foreign Relations in New York.

The Government of Israel has studied this address with all the earnestness which its authorship and content commanded. I have had the opportunity to give public expression to our initial reactions, pointing to both the positive and the negative aspects of the address.

In comparison to various earlier definitions of American policy, this statement evidenced a fuller understanding of Israel's unique problems. Primarily, it aimed at achieving an agreed peace settlement between Israel and its neighbors; at setting up barriers to mutual aggression in the region through a system of security pacts; at preventing an arms race and thus liberating national resources for development purposes.

At the same time, the speech contained pronouncements which raised much misgiving, and called for fundamental clarification.

In discussing the question of the Arab refugees, the Secretary of State reverted to the solution, among others, of repatriation in Israel, even though he did not particularly emphasize this demand and indeed stressed the test of its feasibility.

The main solution advocated by Mr. Dulles was resettlement of the refugees in the neighboring countries. On the basis of Israel's standing pledge to pay compensation for abandoned lands, Mr. Dulles announced his Government's readiness to participate in a loan which would enable Israel to carry out its undertaking. However, implicit in Mr. Dulles' remarks was the assumption that the process of paying compensation could be implemented while at the same time the Arab states, which in one way or another would benefit thereby, continued to inflict serious financial losses on Israel by boycott and blockade. Nor did Mr. Dulles' remarks include any reference to the question of the fate in store for the property abandoned in Arab countries by the large numbers of Jews who migrated to Israel.

The section of Mr. Dulles' address which has aroused most opposition on our part is that dealing with boundaries. Earlier in the speech he referred to the territory of Israel as "the territory, that is now occupied by Israel," as if to indicate that the matter was still pending and that Israel's sovereign rights over its territory could still be called in question.

In the passage devoted to boundaries Mr. Dulles referred to conflicting territorial claims, each of which, as he put it, "may seem to have merit." He suggested further that some areas are of no vital importance to their owners, but have merely "acquired a sentimental significance."

Mr. Dulles finally expressed the view that since the existing boundary lines are temporary and have not been finally determined, they cannot properly serve as the basis for a security pledge, and that only when they have been suitably corrected can their stability and protection be guaranteed by treaties.

These statements might well be interpreted as aiming at the contraction of Israel's territory in order to satisfy the expansive ambitions of the Arabs, particularly in the *Negev* including *Eilat*.

TERRITORIAL INTEGRITY

We reasserted in unequivocal terms that Israel was determined to preserve its territorial integrity from *Dan* to *Eilat* and that no unilateral concessions on its part were even conceivable.

Why do I specify "unilateral"? Because in drawing up peace treaties and even in the process of implementing armistice agreements, it is possible to consider such slight border adjustments as might prove acceptable and mutually beneficial to both sides.

We differed from Mr. Dulles, however, on the question as to whether the time was now ripe for an agreement of this kind. Moreover, it seemed to us that there was an implicit contradiction in his thesis regarding the dependence of security treaties on frontier corrections. If, as Mr. Dulles stated, the fears of mutual aggression prevailing in the area call for security treaties, surely they should at the outset guarantee the stability of the existing border lines.

On the other hand, if no guarantee is to be given for the preservation of the existing lines on the ground that these have not been finally determined, then the fear of aggression remains unchanged and any public affirmation of its existence, unaccompanied by a remedy, must of necessity only aggravate the situation.

In discussions with representatives of the United States Government it was explained that there had been no intention on its part to expect from Israel unilateral territorial concessions, whether in the *Negev* or in any other area, nor was there any idea of far-reaching alterations in the existing frontiers, but only that of minor mutual border rectifications aimed at eliminating potential points of friction and trouble.

A similar explanation was also received from the British Government, which, as will be recalled, identified itself with Mr. Dulles' statement. But even these explanations, intended as they were to allay serious fears, did not convince us of the practicability or logic of this request for border rectifications at the present stage, particularly in the context of a plan for security treaties. I have said "request" and not "condition," because in the conversations with United States representatives no confirmation was gleaned of the assumption that in his speech Mr. Dulles intended to set the frontier adjustments as an indispensable condition to a security treaty.

THE REGIONAL WATER PLAN

The Secretary of State set special emphasis on the readiness of the President of the United States—to whom I should like to take this opportunity of wishing on the part of the Government of Israel and of you all a speedy and complete recovery—to recommend allocations for the realization of water development and irrigation projects in the countries of the Middle East.

This is one of the assumptions on which Ambassador Eric Johnston as President Eisenhower's special envoy has for the last two years been pursuing the negotiations on an interstate water settlement between us and the neighboring countries. Mr. Johnston visited us some days ago for the fourth time and on his departure stated—and we have no reason to question his statement—that the gap between Israel and the Arab states on the distribution of the water has been greatly narrowed.

This is an advance which has been achieved by considerable effort, and should by no means be disparaged. Nevertheless, it is apparently a fact that Mr. Johnston has not yet secured an agreement in principle from the Arab governments concerned to enter into a water arrangement to which

Israel is a party, whatever the water distribution plan on which it is ultimately based.

The Government of Israel has been extremely patient in order to give the Special Envoy of the President of the United States every conceivable chance to carry out his task of bringing the parties to an accord on one of the principal elements of their economic development. But the patience of Israel is by no means inexhaustible. As before, we favor an agreed arrangement between countries which fate has brought together as having stakes in the same water sources.

On the other hand, we are not prepared to forgo indefinitely the realization of vital development projects based upon our own rights, until the other side is ready to cooperate, with or without intermediaries.

The Government earnestly hopes that the fate of the plan which has been the subject of these negotiations will finally be decided, for good or ill, by the beginning of the coming work season. In other words, it is our firm hope that whichever way the decision goes, the work in which we are so vitally interested will be renewed in that season, and carried on without interruption.

EGYPT-CZECHOSLOVAK ARMS DEAL

And now, honored members of the *Knesset,* I come to the very serious event which occurred some three weeks ago and which has cast a deep shadow on the entire scene of the State's foreign and defense affairs. I refer to the agreement between the ruler of Egypt and the Czechoslovak Government—which from a political and military standpoint implies the linking up between Egypt and the entire Soviet Bloc—for the supply of heavy and modern arms to Egypt, by all accounts in very considerable quantities.

This departure is liable to bring about a revolutionary and ominous change in Israel's security situation.

Both parties attempted to describe the arrangement as a purely commercial deal—perfectly simple and legitimate. Both parties went on to explain that the arms were merely intended to satisfy the defense needs of a free and sovereign state. Neither of the parties ignored Israel or pretended that the arms were not destined to be used against her.

Both sought to justify this great addition to Egyptian arms with the argument that they were to enable a handicapped Egypt to attain to Israel's level of armament. We heard Colonel Nasser tell wild and fantastic tales about the hoards of arms that Israel had obtained from various sources while in the official organ of the Czechoslovak Government *"Rude Pravo"* we read:

"Nor is it possible to ignore the growing tension on the borders of Israel and its Arab neighbors and the continued arming of Israel with weapons from the United States, Britain and France. This arouses the Arab states' concern for their own security."

The mouthpiece of the Czech regime did not rest satisfied with this warning about the dangers threatening the many and vast Arab states from small and solitary Israel. It took good care to give to the Arab states in general and to Egypt in particular a testimonial of rectitude drawn up in the best style of the World Peace Movement. It runs as follows:

"The peace-loving policy of the Arab states is well known. Egypt in particular is advancing towards the strengthening of its political independence and its economic development, and is pursuing a policy of international cooperation and calm. The Egyptian Government's striving to raise the level of its army must be seen as no more than a legitimate desire to raise a national army appropriate to its weight and standing in the Middle East such as would ensure its sovereignty and security."

At this point Prague and Cairo cease to prophesy in the same style. The Egyptian leader is not afraid to formulate for himself a certificate of good behavior completely different from that bestowed upon him by the paper named "Red Justice" (*"Rude Pravo"*).

EGYPT'S 'DEDICATION TO PEACE'

Here is his pledge of dedication to peace as made in a statement to an Egyptian paper:

"It is utterly inconceivable that Egypt should ever consider peace with Israel or even think of recognizing it."

And in another statement:

"The problem of Palestine will not be solved and there will be no peace between us and the Jews so long as even the slightest right of the Arabs of that country is controlled by the enemy. A man can forget everything except blood, vengeance and honor."

And in another paper:

"The Arabs consider Israel an artificial state which has to be annihilated."

And in one of his speeches:

"Israel is a sword suspended over us, over our freedom and honor. Never will we negotiate with Israel."

And here is his remarkable contribution to international co-operation and calm: the Egyptian press and the Cairo radio have been carrying on a veritable campaign of glorification and hero worship in honor of the murderous Egyptian gangs. The Government's official radio mouthpiece calls out:

"The Arab peoples will cleanse Palestine. Hold your tears in readiness, Israel, for the day of your annihilation: henceforth there are to be no complaints and protests, deliberations and negotiations, but only the army and the use of force."

Yet another clarion call from the same bugle:

"We cannot but be in a state of war with Israel. This impels us to mobilize all Arab resources for its final liquidation. We ask that our production should be military production and meet our war needs. We want all our newspapers and radio stations to proclaim the total mobilization of forces for the liberation of Palestine."

And only a few days ago we heard the ruler of Egypt speak in terms so familiar to us from other sources:

"The Arab states stand as one bloc in the face of World Zionist machinations and Jewish wealth. They would prefer cooperation with the West, but America's subjection to the rule of Zionist organizations has made this cooperation impossible and has compelled Egypt to depend on arms supplies from Czechoslovakia in order to defend herself and to save the Arab world."

SOVIET RESPONSIBILITY

Can the nature of its new partner be unknown to the Soviet Government, which is undoubtedly the source of inspiration for this so-called commercial transaction between Egypt and Czechoslovakia?

Did not its delegates at the present session of the United Nations Assembly listen to the speech of hatred, poison and warmongering delivered by the Egyptian Foreign Minister?

Or is the U.S.S.R. unaware of the patent fact that Israel offers peace, while Egypt seeks war and thirsts for vengeance?

Does it not realize that to supply plentiful and heavy armaments to Egypt means letting loose a war of destruction against Israel?

How does the U.S.S.R. justify the sale of such quantities of *such* weapons to *this* Egypt?

What is all this about a financial transaction, cotton and rice, modest means of self-defense and all the other whitewash of which the statement of the TASS agency is compounded?

This Soviet initiative in the strife-torn Middle East, this so dangerous disturbance of the balance of armed forces, this vehement spur to the arms race, the giving of free rein to fierce, aggressive instincts—what relation does all this bear to the policy of international tension, progressive disarmament and a gradual working towards a stable world peace which the U.S.S.R. at present avows?

But not only does the Soviet Union bear the brunt of Israel's accusations. We must again affirm that regardless of the motives and considerations, national or of world import, which shape the policy of each of the world's powers; for us the decisive point and the one which determines our attitude towards each world power, is the extent to which its policy and actions ensure or imperil, reinforce or undermine, the existence and security of Israel.

In this respect a heavy and primary responsibility rests with the Western Powers. In London and in Washington the myth has been fostered of the new, enlightened regime in Egypt, the strong man who stands at its head and the danger of Egypt's return to chaos should he fall.

In Washington and London a policy has been developed of free and unrequited concessions to this Egyptian regime, of satisfying its claims and according it assistance without, heaven forbid, making them conditional upon peace with Israel or even the removal of the sea blockade, the illegality of which is so flagrantly obvious and which is tantamount to international piracy.

The Western Powers were the first in the Middle East to try to bribe wavering regimes with military assistance and to bolster up the position of every ruling military caste with arms supplies. Some of these trends have since been abandoned but the fact remains that they were initiated.

Is it to be wondered at, if the conclusion has been drawn from all this, that it is possible and worthwhile to speculate on one's inflated values and raise one's price by spurring on competition?

There is no certainty that the deplorable policy of the past will not continue in the future and lead as before, consciously or unconsciously, to the sacrificing of Israel.

ISRAEL'S, ARABS' MILITARY STRENGTH

What is the truth about the relative strength of Israel and the Arab nations which surround her, which maintain a state of war against her and which are constantly vowing to wipe her off the face of the earth?

The truth is that the strength in military manpower of the Arab states—that is to say their regular armies and the reserves—is more than twice greater than our own, and this while taking into account that in an emergency we undertake a full mobilization, while they only raise troops subject to normal military service.

The truth is that the military budgets of Egypt, Syria, the Lebanon, Jordan, Iraq and Saudi Arabia amount to £ 140m. annually together or IL.700m., while Israel's entire budget—ordinary and development, including the defense budget—amounts to IL.631m. The military budget of Egypt alone is almost equal to the entire budget of Israel.

The truth is that Egypt's army alone is superior to the Israel Defense Forces in all categories of heavy weapons for use on land, sea and in the air.

The truth is that there are Arab states which possess heavy arms which we do not have—they are sold to them, but not to us.

Our strength indeed is in quality—in the morale of the Army, its organizational and technical superiority. But quality, even the highest, can never serve as a full substitute for a vast quantitative advantage.

WIDENING GAP

Since the establishment of the State we have been under the threat of the widening gap between the military power of the Arab states and that of our own army—which also is growing, which improves consistently, which progresses in equipment and fighting capacity, but which necessarily lags behind quantitatively as regards both manpower and weapons.

That is why our cry has always been: No arms race! No supply of any weapons whatever to states which maintain war, which plot war, which flatly refuse to make peace. And something in this direction has been achieved.

But faced with an alarming and decisive increase—in the immediate future and the coming few years—in the armed power of Egypt, our first demand is—arms! Arms in quantity, of quality—cheaply! This claim is directed first and foremost towards the Great Powers who undertook publicly to keep the military balance between us and the States who are hostile to us.

The supply of arms, whether by gift or sale, and particularly where heavy and modern equipment is concerned, constitutes a political fact. But above all it is a military and security factor. From this viewpoint what causes us concern in the Egyptian-Czech transaction is the quantity and quality of the armaments which are being transferred, rather than their origin.

The supply of arms by Czechoslovakia to Egypt is dangerous because it flows to an Egypt which is hostile to us. The same applies to the American arms which are at present being supplied to Iraq or to arms of any power which may at any future time be supplied to Syria. These countries are hostile towards us and their arms are liable to be used against us. It is our position that arms must not be given or sold to states which do not seek peace—states whose declared and real policies are war.

Thus it is our stand that there is a duty and an obligation to sell or to grant arms to that state which offers peace—but which is compelled to defend itself as against neighbors who deny it peace and conspire aggression against it.

And because the obtaining of arms is for us an imperative, military and defensive necessity—that is to say a first essential for existence—we will not hesitate to obtain them from every possible source.

SECURITY PACT

However, not only arms are needed by us. The change which has taken place in these weeks and which is pregnant with grave implications has invested with additional urgency Israel's need for a security pact—not for one dependent on a parallel agreement with Egypt, but a defense agreement made with Israel to meet the strengthening of the offensive potential of Egypt.

The defense pact which we need is not directed and cannot be directed at aggression against any other power. It is designed to serve as one of the basic pillars of our defense against aggression. Therefore, such a pact is justified and vital. It can be justified to every power which is in a position to conclude such an agreement, and yet would withhold lest it complicates its position in relation to states. It can be likewise justified to any power that is liable to stigmatize it on the false pretense that it is aimed against her.

Mr. Dulles said in his speech that the security pact which America would sign, should she do so, would be open to the participation of other powers and could come under the auspices of the United Nations. For us a security pact with the United States is especially important—for a long time we have considered ourselves entitled to it—and now all the more.

But just as I have emphasized our need for a security pact in addition to the supply of arms, I must stress even more emphatically that no security pact is a substitute for arms. With all the importance attaching to a security pact with the United States, (and who knows whether it will materialize), not in this alone lies our salvation.

The capacity for defense when war breaks out, the ability to deter the enemy from attack and so to avoid war, depends first and foremost upon the military strength of the one who is the target of aggression. So it has always been everywhere. So it particularly is in the case of Israel at the present stage.

ARMS FOR ISRAEL

What is happening around us does not mean for us a choice between a little less or a little more security. The alternative might be immeasurably graver than that. It is liable to lead us to fairly far-reaching conclusions. It also imposes upon us cool judgment and a firm inner balance.

Above all it enjoins upon our people in Israel alertness, unity and a persevering well-planned effort to enhance our economic consolidation and defensive capacity.

At this hour, from this House, from this our Capital, let the call go out to all Israel citizens, to the Jewish people in its dispersion and to the whole world—arms for Israel!

113. OFFER BY SIR ANTHONY EDEN IN (GUILDHALL) SPEECH TO MEDIATE THE ARAB-ISRAEL DISPUTE
9 November 1955

[Text as transcribed by British Information Services (New York) from the B.B.C. Overseas Service]

The Dulles proposals of August 1955 (Doc. 109) were greeted with qualified approval by Israel and categorical resentment by the Arab states. The untutored eye would detect nothing in the secretary of state's phraseology that was emotional and little that could be characterized as partisan to either contestant, that little being evenly distributed between the two. Explanation for the Arab and Israel reactions had clearly to be sought less in any hidden meaning with which the Dulles statement might have been laden than in the standards by which Israelis and Arabs had come to judge every scheme for "solving" the Arab-Israel problem. Israel insisted that any enduring settlement would have to build on the basis of conditions in the Arab-Israel zone prevailing *after* the 1949 armistice. With equal firmness the Arab states held that they would not consent to any peace that was not based on the execution of "UN resolutions," that is, on conditions prevailing *before* the expiry of the Palestine mandate in May 1948. The UN resolutions which the Arabs had in mind included General Assembly resolution 181(II) or the original partition plan (Doc. 88) with precise boundary recommendations and a scheme—reaffirmed by resolution 303(IV)—for the internationalization of Jerusalem and resolution 194(III/1) or the enabling act of the Conciliation Commission for Palestine stipulating in article 11 "that the [Arab] refugees wishing to return to their homes and live at peace with their neighbours should be permitted to do so at the earliest practicable date." From the Arab standpoint Secretary Dulles committed a cardinal sin by not even mentioning UN resolutions. Prime Minister Sir Anthony Eden sought to redress the balance in the following statement, which paid obeisance to UN resolutions on Palestine and indicated that peace could be reached only by "some compromise between these two [the Arab and the Israel] positions." Sir Anthony's suggestion won the conditional praise of Arab spokesmen and the absolute denunciation of Israel Prime Minister David Ben-Gurion. But of more alarming significance to the West was the loss of political initiative in the Arab-Israel zone to the USSR on terms which it was not in the United States or British interest to rival. Once Egypt had consented to purchase war materials from the Soviet bloc at bargain prices (Doc. 111), other Arab states might follow suit. The USSR was expected to exploit to the full the diplomatic leverage with which the purveyor of modern arms was vested. President Eisenhower, on the very day of Sir Anthony's speech, pointedly observed that the United States does "not intend to contribute to an arms competition in the Near East because we do not think such a race would be in the true interest of any of the participants." At the same time, the President reaffirmed that the 1950 tripartite declaration (Doc. 92) "still remains our policy" (full text of the President's statement in *New York Times,* 10 November 1955). Only that section of Eden's Guildhall speech relating to the Arab-Israel area appears below.

And here, My Lord Mayor, I have to discuss a grave situation with you. Between Israel and Egypt lies an area of dangerous tension. During the past seven years we have been trying to bring about some kind of settlement—successive governments in this country and our allies in that part of the world—and to prevent competition in armaments there. We have not been entirely unsuccessful. Despite frontier incidents from time to time—some more serious than others—there has been no war since 1948. The level of arms has been kept comparatively low, and this applies especially to more modern weapons. There's been some kind of a balance, though naturally each side cries loudly that it is less favored than the other.

My Lord Mayor, I had hopes, real hopes, that many peoples in these lands were beginning to see that a way to peace must somehow be found in all their interests. We have been working for a long time past without publicity to promote such a result. In this connection the reception given to Mr. Dulles' proposals last August was by no means discouraging. It should be followed up, but now—now into this delicate situation the Soviet Government have decided to inject a new element of danger and to deliver weapons of war, tanks, aeroplanes, even submarines, to one side only. It is fantastic to pretend that this deliberate act of policy was an innocent commercial transaction. Of course, my Lord Mayor, it is no such thing. It is a move to gain popularity at the expense of the restraint shown by the West, and by this means it is intended to make it easier for Communism to penetrate the Arab world. Its consequences should be clear for all to see. Many proud states, some of which have not long enjoyed independence and national identity, will be threatened with submergence in the Communist Empire if they fall victims to these tactics. For our part, we find it impossible to reconcile this Soviet action with protestations that they wish to end the cold war in the new spirit of Geneva. The authors of these actions must have known well enough in advance what the effect of the sudden arrival of these large quantities of arms must be. It has brought a sharp increase of tension with very dangerous possibilities, particularly between Egypt and Israel. And yet, when nations face each other in hostility, it's not much use just blaming them for getting arms wherever they can. It is not with the recipients but with the suppliers that the main responsibility must lie.

BRITISH AIMS

Now, my Lord Mayor, what is our immediate task? It is to prevent the outbreak of war. General Burns, United Nations Chief of Staff in Palestine and a distinguished Canadian soldier, has been tireless in his efforts to keep the forces of the two sides apart. He and his staff have shown patience and courage in hazardous work, and we should all be most grateful to them. At this moment, General Burns is urging both sides to withdraw their forces from the El Auja demilitarized zone. We are giving him full diplomatic support for his present proposal in the capitals concerned. But let there be no mistake: were any country to reject counsels of moderation, it would forfeit the sympathy of this, and I believe every other, peace-loving nation; and once lost that sympathy might be hard to regain.

My Lord Mayor, you were kind enough to refer to my experience at the Foreign Office; and I would just in that connection like to say this: I have never known a situation where it was clearer that neither party had anything whatever to hope for in the long term from any military conflict. It is in the interests of both to put the demilitarized zone between them. I saw General Burns when he was in London three days ago, and he knows that if there is any further help we can give him we shall be glad to do so. It will be a great gain if the risk of frontier incidents can be reduced. It will be a greater gain if the tragic problem of the refugees can be dealt with. I much regret that the hard work which Mr. Johnston of the United States has devoted to preparing irrigation schemes has not yet been accepted by those concerned. It should be, for it is in the interests of all, Israeli and Arab alike; and we are ready to help here also, as we have done with the Arab refugees. But, my Lord Mayor, beneath the volcanic crust of these smouldering dangers lies a deeper peril [still]: the hostility between Israel and her Arab neighbors is unreconciled. Here time has proved no healer. There is no progress to report to you since the armistice agreement six years ago. If it were not for these harsh and enduring sentiments, the countries of the Middle East could give all their efforts to their economic and social plans. They could concentrate on building up happy and prosperous societies in their lands. As I have said, we have tried for a long time past to find common ground for some kind of settlement. I think that the time has come now when the acute dangers of the situation command us to try again. We must somehow attempt to deal with the root cause of the trouble, and our country has a special responsibility in all this, for we have a long tradition of friendship with the Middle East. I believe that it should be possible to find common ground between the two positions. There is, after all, one interest which both parties ought to share. Neither Israel nor her Arab neighbors can want to see their differences turned to the advantage of anyone else: and there is somebody else quite ready to receive the advantage.

Now Sir, from that starting point, can we not all look once again at the proposals which the United States Government and we ourselves have advocated? We have only one desire in this—if our Arab and Israeli friends would only believe us—to help to find a means of living which will enable the peoples concerned to dwell side by side in peace.

FRONTIER PROBLEMS

Let us give one instance. If there could be accepted arrangements between them about their boundaries, we, Her Majesty's Government, and, I believe, the United States Government and perhaps other powers also, would be prepared to give a formal guarantee to both sides; and that might bring real confidence and security at last. Our countries would also offer substantial help, financial and other, over this tragic problem of the refugees.

All this we will do. But can we not now move even a little further than this? And I think the Guildhall is the right place to make this suggestion. The position today is that the Arabs on the one side take their stand on the 1947 and other United Nations resolutions. That is where they are. They have said that they would be willing to open discussions with Israel from that basis. The Israelis on the other side, found themselves on the later armistice agreement of 1949, and on the present territories which they occupy. Now, My Lord Mayor, between those two positions there is, of course, a wide [gap. But is it] so wide that no negotiation is possible to bridge it? It is not right, I agree, that United Nations resolutions should be ignored, but equally can it be maintained the United Nations resolutions on Palestine can now be put into operation just as they stand? The stark truth is that if these nations want to win a peace, which is in both their interests and to which we want to help them, they must make some compromise between these two positions.

OFFER OF SERVICES

My Lord Mayor, I have finished. I am convinced that it is possible to work this out. And if we could do so it would bring relief and happiness to millions, and the sooner the better. If we fail to do so, none can tell what the consequences will be. I want to say tonight, My Lord Mayor, that Her Majesty's Government, and I personally, are available to render any service in this cause. If there is anything—anything—that we can do to help we would gladly do it for the sake of peace.

114. SOVIET-IRANIAN EXCHANGE OF NOTES ON THE BAGHDAD PACT
26 November–7 December 1955

[Soviet note reproduced with permission from *The Current Digest of the Soviet Press* (New York), 7 (11 January 1956), pp. 22–23, as translated from *Pravda* and *Izvestia,* 27 November 1955; the Iranian reply translated from the original Persian by the Iranian government and reproduced with the courtesy of the Department of State, Washington, D. C.]

Prime Minister Husayn 'Ala's announcement on 11 October 1955 that Iran would accede to the Baghdad Pact (Doc. 107) drew an immediate protest from the USSR. "The accession of Iran to this military alignment," Moscow charged, "is incompatible with the interests of consolidating peace and security in the region of the Middle and Near East and contradicts the good-neighborly relations between Iran and the Soviet Union and certain treaty obligations of Iran" (text in *New York Times,* 13 October 1955). Tehran denied the Soviet allegations in a memorandum of 17 October and insisted that Iran's accession to the pact, "which is within the framework of the U.N. Charter and which aims only to strengthen the bases of peace and security in the Middle and Near East and throughout the world, is fully natural" [text in *The Current Digest of the Soviet Press,* 7 (11 January 1956), p. 22]. The council of the pact convened in Baghdad on 21–22 November in constituent session, under the chairmanship of Prime Minister Nuri Pasha al-Sa'id and attended by the premiers of Iran, Pakistan and Turkey, the foreign minister of Britain and observers from the United States. The council created a permanent secretariat, with its seat in the Iraqi capital, and an economic and a military committee. The following notes, exchanged soon after the Baghdad meeting, developed the Soviet and Iranian positions in full detail. The USSR, it will be observed, accused Iran of violating the Soviet-Iranian treaty of guarantee and neutrality of 1 October 1927 (Doc. 51).

1. SOVIET NOTE TO IRAN, 26 NOVEMBER 1955

In connection with the Iranian government's Oct. 17 reply to the Soviet government's Oct. 12 statement, the U.S.S.R. government considers it essential to state the following:

(1) The Soviet government regrets that it is forced to state that the Iranian government, despite frequent friendly warnings from the Soviet Union, has joined the Near and Middle Eastern military grouping—the Turkey-Iraq-Pakistan alliance—known as the Baghdad bloc, in which Britain is also a partner.

As a result of this Iran has become a member of a military grouping which is the tool of certain aggressive circles. By joining this group Iran, strange as it may seem, has linked her policy to the interests of forces alien to Iran which hope to maintain and restore the colonial dependence of the countries in this region.

In this connection, the Soviet government believes it essential to confirm the fact that Iran's accession to the Baghdad military grouping is incompatible with the interests of strengthening peace and security in the Near and Middle East and is contrary to Iran's good-neighbor relations with the Soviet Union and to certain of Iran's treaty obligations.

(2) The Iranian government's Oct. 17 reply attempts to justify Iran's accession to the Baghdad bloc by referring to the supposedly defensive purposes of this military alliance. However, references of this kind are contrary to the actual situation.

As is well known, the first article of the Baghdad Pact envisages military collaboration between members of this pact. The measures for carrying out this collaboration are to be determined by special agreements. The results of such collaboration can be seen in the fact that Iraq, a member of the Baghdad Pact, has also concluded a special agreement with another, stronger member of this pact—Britain—which grants Britain the use of Iraq's air borders, airfields and territory for the needs of British armed forces and places Iraq's armed forces under the control of British instructors and advisers.

The nature of the obligations of the Near and Middle Eastern states belonging to the Baghdad bloc is also shown by the contents of a special document, published in the foreign press, which is a supplement to the Baghdad Pact. The document provides that each of the contracting parties be bound, under certain circumstances, to put its territory, airfields and military installations at the disposal of the forces of any other party. It is clear from American, British and Turkish press reports that Turkey's armed forces, which the Western powers plan to entrust with an "offensive" toward the Caucasus, are to enter Iran and occupy Iranian Azerbaidzhan and Kurdistan.

The aggressive nature of the Baghdad military bloc is also indicated by a statement by Turkish Prime Minister Menderes, made recently at the congress of the Turkish Democratic Party, that as a result of Turkey's participation in the North Atlantic bloc and her signing of the Baghdad Pact, which Iran has now joined, "a complete northern front has been established." This is also shown by the statements of U.S. officials, who have frequently stressed that the Baghdad military pact and Iran's accession to it are part of American military plans for setting up a so-called "northern tier" of Middle Eastern states. This is confirmed by statements by the government heads and Ministers of the Baghdad bloc countries made at the first session of the Baghdad Pact Council which just ended (Nov. 21–22) and at which U.S. representatives were present as observers.

One cannot help but point out in this connection that the U.S.A. and Great Britain are sending arms and military equipment to the Baghdad bloc countries in ever increasing quantities, making these deliveries conditional upon certain military and political obligations which further complicate the situation in the Near and Middle East and endanger the security and national independence of the countries in that region. It is therefore no accident that the Arab states and other states in this area which border on the Baghdad bloc countries have taken a negative attitude toward the Baghdad bloc and consider it a direct threat to their vital interests.

At the same time, the construction of air and naval bases is proceeding intensively in Turkey, one of the active members of the Baghdad Pact, and other measures are being carried out under U.S. guidance for turning Turkey into a military and strategic springboard directed against the peace-loving states on her borders.

The true nature of the Baghdad military bloc is also evident in the fact that Turkey and Britain—members of the Baghdad bloc—are also members of the NATO military grouping (North Atlantic bloc), and that Pakistan and Britain are members of another military and political grouping in Southeast Asia named SEATO. NATO is an aggressive military grouping directed against the Soviet Union and other peace-loving countries, and SEATO is a tool of the colonial powers. As is well known, colonialism and all its manifestations were condemned at the Bandung conference of African and Asian countries.

As a connecting link between NATO and SEATO, the Baghdad bloc is a threat to peace not only in the Middle and Near East but also outside this area. In this connection the linking of the Baghdad bloc with the above-mentioned military groupings makes it possible for the Near and Middle Eastern countries to become involved in armed conflicts which may arise in other parts of the world.

In this way, the establishment of the Baghdad bloc and Iran's accession to it are not brought about by defensive needs but serve the purposes of certain powers which are striving to turn the Near and Middle Eastern countries, including Iran, into their military springboards and to ensure in this way the stationing of foreign armed forces and the establishment of their own military bases in these countries. At the same time, it is well known that Iran has never been and is not threatened by anyone, and that the threat to Iran's security and independence comes primarily from those powers which are setting up aggressive blocs directed against other states.

(3) The Iranian government's statement to the effect that its policy is based on the struggle to eradicate colonialism and that this struggle "makes the idea of restoring any kind of colonialism in the world lack substance" is contrary to the facts given above and to the fact that the colonial powers are now trying to maintain and restore colonial enslavement in economically underdeveloped countries. These countries' participation in blocs leads to their loss of independence, to the strengthening of their economic and political dependence on foreign powers.

It is no accident that during the preparations for joining military blocs these countries are flooded with foreign military advisers who infiltrate the military and state apparatus, leading to a gradual loss of prestige for the armies of these countries. These countries are also sent numerous "civil advisers" who by various means gain control of the economy of these countries and help foreign capital to seize their natural resources, primarily their oil resources.

The arms race and the military construction being carried out according to the plans and aims of the above-mentioned groupings are a heavy burden on the budgets and economies of countries belonging to these groupings, forcing them to rely on foreign credit and loans, which increases their dependence upon foreign states and leads to a lower standard of living for their people. All this is happening in the Baghdad bloc countries, including Iran, and cannot help but contradict the national aspirations and interests of the people of these Near and Middle Eastern countries which belong to the Baghdad bloc.

(4) Despite the Iranian government's assertions, the creation of the Baghdad military bloc has nothing in common with the aims of the U.N., and the Iranian government's references to the participation of both the Soviet Union and Iran in the United Nations cannot serve to justify Iran's accession to the bloc, since the aims of the U.N. are to support international peace and security and to develop friendly relations among nations, and the creation of the Baghdad bloc serves the opposite purpose.

(5) The Soviet government notes that the Iranian government's statement about its respect for its international obligations does not accord with the Iranian government's actions, so that, despite the obligations under Art. 3 of the Oct. 1, 1927, Soviet-Iranian treaty of guarantee and neutrality, the decision was made to join the Baghdad bloc, which is directed against the U.S.S.R. Art. 3 of the Soviet-Iranian treaty states: "Each party agrees not to participate either formally or in practice in any political alliance or agreement directed against the other party's security on land or at sea, nor against its integrity, independence or sovereignty."

The Iranian government's references to its sovereign rights in joining the Baghdad bloc cannot justify the violation of Iran's international obligations. The Soviet Union, strictly following the principles of its policy in relations with other states, has always respected Iran's sovereignty and independence and Iran's right to solve independently any questions of domestic and foreign policy. However, it stands to reason on this point that both parties must observe the obligations they assumed voluntarily in the Soviet-Iranian treaties.

The Soviet government notes that Iran's accession to the Baghdad bloc seriously harms Soviet-Iranian relations, at a moment when, through the efforts of the Soviet Union and a number of other states, certain advances have been made in easing international tension and establishing confidence among states and when the Soviet Union has taken a number of steps to strengthen and develop good-neighbor relations with Iran.

The situation created by Iran's accession to the aggressive Baghdad bloc is fraught with danger for the borders of the Soviet Union. In view of this, the Soviet government cannot be impartial regarding Iran's accession to the Baghdad Pact.

In connection with what has been stated above, the U.S.S.R. government cannot accept the Iranian government's reply as satisfactory and reaffirms its Oct. 12 statement. The Iranian government is entirely responsible for any possible consequences ensuing from its decision to join the Baghdad military bloc.

2. IRANIAN NOTE TO THE USSR, 7 DECEMBER 1955

The Imperial Iranian Embassy in reply to the Note No. 126 dated November 26, 1955, from the Ministry of Foreign Affairs of the Union of the Soviet Socialist Republics, relating to the Adherence of Iran to the Baghdad Pact finds it necessary to state as follows:

In view of the fact that the contents of the Note, No. 126 of 26th November, 1955, of the Ministry for Foreign Affairs of the U.S.S.R. were already briefly mentioned in their communication of 12th October last, and that an adequate reply was given in the Iranian Memorandum of October 17th, a further reply seems unnecessary. Nevertheless, as the Government of the U.S.S.R. have reiterated in full the former points raised in their Note, and have attributed their own interpretation to them, the Imperial Government considers it advisable to reply comprehensively and once again to the points raised in the Note in question.

I) The Imperial Iranian Government on repeated occasions both verbally and in writing, have notified the competent authorities of the Soviet Union that the sovereign rights and responsibilities of Iran in the preservation of her boundaries make it incumbent upon them to adopt any and every measure which they deem necessary for securing the interests of the country and the welfare of their people; and that any criticism on the part of any foreign government concerning the line of conduct adopted in this connection will be considered a distinct intervention in her internal affairs and cannot therefore be acceptable.

The accession of Iran to the Defense Pact of Baghdad, based on Article 5 [1] of the Charter of the United Nations, is one of these fundamental steps which the Imperial Government deem essential for the welfare of the Iranian Nation. This Pact has no objective other than the consolidation of the fundamentals of peace and security in the Middle East; it is thus, undoubtedly, an effective contribution to the peace of the world. The Iranian Government therefore consider any other interpretation in connection with their accession to the Pact as an unfriendly gesture. To interpret the Pact as an alignment against anyone, or as an instrument of certain aggressive circles, is entirely incorrect and in no way corresponds with the facts. Furthermore, the assumption that the Imperial Government may link their policy with the interests of foreign powers whose objects in Iran are the establishment of colonial policies is no more than an illusion and a myth. The Iranian Nation, as evidenced in the pages of history, has constantly fought against the colonial policy of the Great Powers, and has spared no effort and sacrifice in the protection of her frontiers and the establishment of her sovereign rights and of her political and economic independence. Iran has, throughout the brilliant annals of her existence, preserved her national traditions and has never allowed any foreign power to interfere or exert influence in her internal affairs and in her foreign policy. This attitude will be strictly maintained and resolutely observed in the future.

In this connection, the Imperial Iranian Government find it necessary to emphasize that the accession of Iran to the Baghdad Pact is not only conducive to peace and security in the Middle East, but it is also an effective instrument in the preservation of tranquility and the development of sincere cooperation; a fact which is bound to redound favourably to all Iran's neighbors.

It is a source of great surprise that the Government of the U.S.S.R. consider the accession of Iran to the Baghdad Pact as incompatible with Iran's Treaty obligations. The Imperial Government, animated by respect for the existing good relations and by their desire for the continuation and consolidation of friendly intercourse, are reluctant to recall the pages of contemporary history and to enumerate the many patent examples of violations of Treaty obligations which the Government of the U.S.S.R. have perpetrated. Here they wish to repeat the Defensive Pact of Baghdad, which has been concluded in accordance with Article 51 of the Charter of the United Nations, is not for an aggressive purpose, nor is it directed against any country; its object is defense against any kind of aggression. Consequently the Defense Pact of Baghdad cannot be incompatible with any Treaty obligations. It is a natural right of defense as well as one of the established international rights of mankind and an inherent right resulting from natural law which no treaty can deprive any country from exercising.

II) The text of the Baghdad Pact, which has been concluded in accordance with Article 51 of the Charter of the United Nations, has been published and is to be registered with the Secretariat of the United Nations, in accordance with Article 102 of the Charter. The signatories to this Pact firmly believe that its conclusion, which implements the provisions of the Charter, has provided an important guarantee in the establishment of peace and security in the Middle East.

Article I of the Pact to which reference has been made in the Soviet Note is so clear that it leaves no doubt for erroneous interpretation. It confirms the fact that the object of the Baghdad Pact is the defense and security of the member countries; and any cooperation that may ensue therefrom by special agreement is solely for the purpose of implementing this joint objective.

There are no special protocols appended to the Baghdad Pact to which the Iranian Government has adhered and press reports to which the Government of the U.S.S.R. have referred in this connection are mere fabrication and sheer falsehood. Also the American, British and Turkish press reports, as referred to in the Note from the Soviet Union, are based on illusions and are categorically denied by the Iranian Government. Consequently, a reply to the points raised in Note No. 126, based on false reports and irresponsible sources, seems superfluous.

It is also necessary to point out that there are no conditions attached to the military and financial assistance which has for long been given and is still being extended to Iran by the United States Government. This help, which cannot possibly harm the security and independence of Iran, rather strengthens the military and financial structure of the country, thereby contributing substantially to the general security and well being of the people.

As to the reference made to the North Atlantic Treaty (NATO) and the South East Asian Treaty (SEATO) and their link with the Baghdad Pact, it should be borne in mind that although the Imperial Iranian Government's obligations are solely within the limits of the Baghdad Pact, nonetheless, considering the provisions of the aforesaid Treaties, the signatories have undertaken according to the provisions of the United Nations Charter, "to settle any international dispute in which they may be involved by peaceful means in such a manner that international peace and security and justice are not endangered, and to refrain from the threat or use of force in any manner inconsistent with the purposes of the United Nations."

It therefore follows that none of the treaties in question, including that of Baghdad could have been concluded against or for the purpose of attack and aggression towards any particular government or governments and that the treaties in question are solely for the purpose of legitimate defence against all and every aggression and for the purpose of securing general peace and security.

III) As regards the conclusions reached by the Soviet Government to the effect that the *modus operandi* of the Great Powers in joining such pacts is to weaken the member countries and establish foreign influence in their military and administrative organisations, it might be stated that in the first place every independent country is free to take any steps it considers in its own interests, and that in the second place the Government of the U.S.S.R. are well aware that the Iranian Government would, under no circumstances, tolerate the slightest action by a foreign government that would be detrimental to the independence and the sovereign rights of Iran.

As to the point raised by the Soviet Government that at the Bandung Conference colonialism was condemned with all its manifestations, reference to the minutes of that conference would reveal that this proposal was tabled by the representative of Iran, in accordance with instructions from the Iranian Government, and its adoption was followed with great enthusiasm, so that in accordance with the definite policy of Iran, colonialism with all its manifestations may be condemned for all time. It would, therefore, appear that the suspicions harboured by the Soviet Government concerning the attitude of the Iranian Government in its condemnation of colonial policy is based on complete disregard of facts.

IV) The Iranian Government once again declares emphatically that contrary to the views of the Soviet Government, the Baghdad Pact is fully in accord with the purposes of the United Nations Organization in the preservation of international peace and security and in the development of friendly relations between nations; furthermore, the Iranian Government does not agree in any way with the contention of the Soviet Government that the Baghdad Pact is a military bloc. The registration of the Pact in the Secretariat of the United Nations Organization is the best proof of this view.

V) The Iranian Government, as evidenced by Iran's long history, have always been loyal to their commitments and have sincerely upheld them. As repeatedly declared, the Baghdad Pact is not in any way directed against the Soviet Government and has been concluded solely for the purpose of defense and to forestall aggression; it is not incompatible with Article III of the Security and Neutrality Pact of Iran and is, moreover, similar to the pacts which the Soviet Government has signed with other countries. The Iranian Government are not aware of any alliance directed against the Government of the U.S.S.R. in the sense that accession to it might provide violation of their pledges.

As already stated, the Iranian Government have always respected their obligations, never broken a promise, and have never attacked or harboured aggressive designs against any country, whereas on the contrary, the U.S.S.R. in deliberate violation of their undertakings, as stipulated in Articles II and III of the Security and Neutrality Pact, in 1320 (1941) invaded Iran with their armed forces, without any justification and attacked certain parts of the territory of this country and its defenseless inhabitants. Even in express violation of their commitments they refused to withdraw their armed forces from Iranian territory at the agreed time after the termination of World War II. Later they spared no effort in trying to disintegrate important sections of Iranian territory, such as the provinces of Azerbaijan and Kurdistan and other northern regions; they encouraged and supported the formation of traitorous and subversive bands; they did not refrain from any action to prevent the dispatch of Iranian Security forces to deal with the rebels.

Today, relying on the same treaty, so often broken by them, they interpret the Iranian Government's adherence, in accordance with its undoubted sovereign rights, to the Baghdad Pact, which has no other object than legitimate self-defense, as a violation of the said treaty.

The Iranian Government does not in any way agree with the contention of the Government of the U.S.S.R. that the accession of Iran to the Baghdad Pact is liable to harm the amicable relations between the two countries. The Iranian Government has great interest in the consolidation of friendship between the two neighbouring peoples. It has spared no effort in the past, and will continue to strive in the future, to strengthen these ties.

The Iranian Government is of the opinion that the Pact of Baghdad, which has cemented the foundation of peace and security in the Middle East, has, equally, contributed effectively to the lessening of international tension which the Soviet Government maintain has been achieved as a result of their efforts in conjunction with those of other Great Powers to establish confidence and good understanding.

The Iranian Government cannot conceive of any valid reason for the anxiety of the Government of the U.S.S.R. in the situation created by the accession of Iran to the Baghdad Pact and in the fear that this may involve certain dangers for the frontiers of the Soviet Union.

In conclusion, the Iranian Government finds it necessary to reaffirm that considering the clarity of the provisions of the Baghdad Pact and of the incontestable fact that it has been concluded on the basis of the Charter of the United Nations, solely for the purpose of legitimate defence as well as for the prevention of aggression, therefore the responsibility for any act detrimental to the relations between the two countries which may ensue as a result of the incorrect interpretation given by the Government of the Soviet Union to Iran's accession to the Baghdad Pact, will devolve entirely upon the Government of the U.S.S.R.

INDEX

Entries are restricted to titles and introductory comments

References are to document numbers, not page numbers.

References are to document numbers, not page numbers.

References are to document numbers, not page numbers.